CRIC

2

FOREWORD

As *Playfair* reaches its landmark 75th edition, it is hard to imagine that we have ever welcomed a new season with quite so many issues dogging the game as now, both on the field and off it. On the field, I write this as England begin a series in the West Indies hoping to turn round a run of form that has seen them lose their last four series, latterly avoiding a 5-0 whitewash in the Ashes thanks only to a last-wicket stand by veteran bowlers James Anderson and Stuart Broad, who held out for a draw in the fourth Test. The decision not to take them to the Caribbean remains, to me, a baffling one. As it is, England go into a series where victory is essential to start the rebuilding process with a frontline bowling line-up that (Ben Stokes apart) has won a solitary cap between them in the West Indies.

The challenges of the last two years, with Covid isolation protocols and team bubbles, have begun to take an increasing toll on our players. Jason Roy recently became the latest to take an indefinite leave of absence from the game, but we are seeing many other top players from around the world taking breaks or retiring from one format or another. Yet still, despite these clear warning signs, we cram the schedule with more and more tours, formats and matches. Money is the driving force, of course, but inevitably the quality of play will eventually suffer as players opt out or play on when their tank is empty.

Some might argue that we have seen this in the performances of England's Test batsmen of late. These things can be cyclical, but one hopes the noises emanating from the ECB that they understand the importance of Test cricket will lead to a domestic framework that gives our red-ball batters more of a chance. As it is, the Test career records on pages 53-63 reveal that just four England players have a Test average of more than 35: Gary Ballance (debut 2013-14), Alastair Cook (retired), Joe Root (debut 2012-13) and Ben Stokes (debut 2013-14) – eight years is a long time to wait for another to announce himself. Of all the Test-playing nations, only Ireland has fewer batters above that benchmark.

But perhaps the most damning events of the close season came with the allegations by Azeem Rafiq about the racism he faced at Yorkshire. The experiences he suffered were bad enough, but the way that the cricketing authorities handled the issue was arguably even worse. Under parliamentary scrutiny, so many of the game's leading figures came across as (at best) desperately out of touch, and too quick to deny that there might just be an issue here. Cricket needs to provide a welcoming environment for everyone and a pathway for all players to progress as far as their abilities and potential will take them, if they want it. The make-up of our county squads suggests that we are missing out on bringing through enough players from more diverse backgrounds, whether it's their race or their schooling that is preventing them from going further.

This year's worthy front cover star is Adil Rashid, who ended the IT20 tour of the West Indies as England's all-time leading wicket-taker in this format (with 81), overtaking Chris Jordan, while the ICC rankings put him third in the world. The Yorkshire star has become a master of his profession, and he now has 300 international wickets for England.

We will be welcoming New Zealand (again) and South Africa for Test series this summer, as well as India, who will play one Test held over from 2021 plus some white-ball matches. I hope they will provide plenty of inspirational cricket in front of packed houses as we look to move on, finally, from the Covid era. As I've often urged in previous years, let us take the opportunity to get out there and support our local county this summer – and don't forget to take your copy of the 75th edition of *Playfair* with you!

Ian Marshall
Eastbourne, 9 March 2022

PLAYFAIR AT 75

Since taking over as the Editor in 2009, following the sad demise of Bill Frindall, I have tried to stay true to the Annual's traditions, while reflecting the changes that continue to take place in the game. My Foreword looks more closely at the current state of the game, but here I want to look back at the origins of *Playfair*, and to compare and contrast between then and now.

The first edition of *Playfair* was published in April 1948, edited by Peter West, with statistics from Roy Webber. Peter gave the first pages to a piece by C.B.Fry, who looked forward with eager anticipation to the Ashes series that summer. Don Bradman's side have since become known as 'The Invincibles', so we can see how that turned out. By the time they began the first Test on 10 June, they had already played 12 games in six weeks – not far off the length of an entire Ashes tour these days. The Test series ended in a 4-0 defeat for England (some things never change!).

Fry, like many cricket lovers, looked back as well as forward, remembering opening the batting for England alongside W.G.Grace. Apparently Grace's 'lambent dark eyes' would have admired the 'versatile, polished technique of our Denis Compton' and the '*multum in parvo* power …of W.J.Edrich'. Fry distinguished between the two by giving the amateur Edrich his initials, while Compton, a professional, was referred to by his first name. Happily, such distinctions have long since vanished. (It is a pleasing coincidence that, in this year's register, the only player I spotted with an antecedent who was active in the game in 1948 is Kent's new recruit, and Denis's grandson, Ben Compton.)

In his Preface, West celebrated that nearly three million fans had gone to watch matches during the 1947 first-class summer 'despite football's encroachment until mid-June' (the winter of 1946-47 was bitterly cold, hence the overrunning football season). By comparison. in the summer of 2019 some 752,000 supporters went to watch the Cricket World Cup alone, so the numbers going to matches have held up better than some might think, thanks in the main to the various shorter formats. As for the encroachment of football, that too remains.

As he looked forward to the Ashes, West lamented the weakness in England's bowling options whereas now it is the batters who appear to be struggling. The biggest threat that concerned him was the Control of Engagement Order, by which the Ministry of Labour could prevent people from leaving certain key industries (such as mining) as the nation rebuilt after the Second World War. This might have meant that some players' winter jobs were deemed too important for them to leave to play for their counties, but the crisis was averted.

The Annual in 1948 ran to just 144 pages, as opposed to this year's 352, and was priced at 3s 6d (17½ pence). It boasted over 150 pictures throughout, nearly all portraits or team line-ups. As *Wisden* continues to do, *Playfair* found space for some schoolboy cricket, focusing on games played at Lord's. When Marlborough beat Malvern in a two-innings match there, it was noted that 'Rugby, Marlborough's traditional opponents in the Schools' week, had to cry off because of illness'. It's a line that seems all too familiar over the last two years. Meanwhile the season ahead ran from 28 April, when the Australians took on Worcestershire, to 19 September when the tourists played Scotland at Aberdeen; the 26-match County Championship took place between 8 May and 30 August. This summer, just seven rounds will take place within that portion of the season, with nine either before or after in spring or autumn.

The Obituaries section of the 1948 Annual perhaps highlights the biggest change we have seen in this period. Norman Harding was Kent's opening bowler and had taken 64 wickets during the summer of 1947 but succumbed to 'infant paralysis', or polio as we would call it, in September. He was just 31. In so many ways, the world has changed during the lifetime of the *Playfair Cricket Annual*, but its importance to cricket fans as a companion to the season remains as strong as ever.

GUIDE TO USING PLAYFAIR

The basic layout of *Playfair* remains the same for this anniversary edition. The Annual is divided into five sections, as follows: Test match cricket, county cricket, international limited-overs cricket (including IT20), other cricket (IPL, Big Bash, The Hundred, Ireland and women's international cricket), and fixtures for the coming season. Each section, where applicable, begins with a preview of forthcoming events, followed by events during the previous year, then come the player records, and finally the records sections.

Within the players' register, there has been some debate with the county scorers over those who are defined as 'Released/Retired', pointing out that some players are drafted in for a game or two, and may re-appear in the current season, despite not having a contract as the book goes to press. What I try to do is to ensure that everyone who appeared in last season's games is included somewhere – this way, at least, if they do play in 2022 their details are available to readers. This issue has become more problematic because of the overlap between The Hundred and the Royal London Cup. Players' Second XI Championship debuts and their England Under-19 Test appearances are given for those under the age of 25. As the final Hundred draft is not concluded until the end of the month, there is no separate register of the squads for The Hundred this year; players' appearances in The Hundred are listed in the county register.

In the county limited-overs records in the Register, those records denoted by '50ov' cover any limited-overs game of 50 or more overs – in the early days, each team could have as many as 65 overs per innings. The '40ov' section refers to games of 40 or 45 overs per innings.

For both men's and women's IT20 records sections, I have taken the decision to limit the records listed to those games that feature at least one side that has appeared in an official LOI. While I welcome the ICC's efforts to broaden the game's profile, there have been some horrible mismatches.

ACKNOWLEDGEMENTS AND THANKS

This book could not have been compiled without the assistance of many people giving so generously of their time and expertise, so I must thank the following for all they have done to help ensure this edition of *Playfair Cricket Annual* could be written:

At the counties, I would like to thank the following for their help over the last year: Derbyshire – Stephen Martin and John Brown; Durham – Sam Blacklock and William Dobson; Essex – George Haberman and Tony Choat; Glamorgan – Andrew Hignell; Gloucestershire – Lizzie Allen and Adrian Bull; Hampshire – Tim Tremlett; Kent – Freddie Young and Lorne Hart; Lancashire – Diana Lloyd and Chris Rimmer; Leicestershire – Dan Nice and Paul Rogers; Middlesex – Steven Fletcher and Don Shelley; Northamptonshire – Tony Kingston; Nottinghamshire – Helen Palmer and Roger Marshall; Somerset – Spencer Bishop and Polly Rhodes; Surrey – Steve Howes and Phil Makepeace; Sussex – Colin Bowley and Graham Irwin; Warwickshire – Keith Cook and Mel Smith; Worcestershire – Carrie Lloyd and Sue Drinkwater; Yorkshire – Cecilia Allen and John Potter.

Thanks to Alan Fordham for the Principal Fixtures, Andy Smith for the Second XI Fixtures, Richard Logan for the National County Fixtures and Chris Kelly for the Professional Umpires' Team. I am hugely grateful as always to Philip Bailey for providing the first-class, List A and T20 career records.

At Headline, my thanks go to Jonathan Taylor for his support and encouragement throughout the year; Louise Rothwell ensures the Annual is printed at great speed (in current circumstances, this is even more difficult that usual); Shadé Owomoyela did an excellent job with the *Playfair* website last summer so it provided all the latest information on newcomers. John Skermer has been diligently checking the proofs since 2008, but has decided that this one must be his last, as he is hanging up his red pencil – enjoy your retirement, and thanks for all your work over the last 15 editions. At Letterpart, the *Playfair* typesetter since 1994, Chris Leggett and Caroline Leggett have developed some exciting new systems that have helped them turn round the proofs quicker than ever.

Finally, as always, thanks to my daughters, Kiri and Sophia, for being so understanding of my hectic final schedule; my wife, Sugra, was as helpful and supportive as ever – and all of them did their best to ensure our household's newest addition, puppy Luna, did not eat any of the Annual or the memory stick on which it is saved. Thank you all.

TOURING TEAMS REGISTER 2022

Neither New Zealand nor South Africa had selected their 2022 touring teams at the time of going to press. The following players, who had represented those teams in Test matches since 3 December 2020, were still available for selection:

NEW ZEALAND

Full Names	*Birthdate*	*Birthplace*	*Team*	*Type F-C*	*Debut*
BLUNDELL, Thomas Ackland	01.09.90	Wellington	Wellington	RHB/WK	2012-13
BOULT, Trent Alexander	22.07.89	Rotorua	Northern D	RHB/LFM	2008-09
CONWAY, Devon Philip	08.07.91	Johannesburg, SA	Wellington	LHB/RM	2008-09
DE GRANDHOMME, Colin	22.07.86	Harare, Zim	Northern D	RHB/RMF	2005-06
HENRY, Matthew James	14.12.91	Christchurch	Canterbury	RHB/RFM	2010-11
JAMIESON, Kyle Alex	30.12.94	Auckland	Auckland	RHB/RFM	2014-15
LATHAM, Thomas William Maxwell	02.04.92	Christchurch	Canterbury	LHB/WK	2010-11
MITCHELL, Daryl Joseph	20.05.91	Hamilton	Canterbury	RHB/RM	2011-12
NICHOLLS, Henry Michael	15.11.91	Christchurch	Canterbury	LHB/OB	2011-12
PATEL, Ajaz Yunus	21.10.88	Bombay, India	Central D	LHB/SLA	2012-13
RAVINDRA, Rachin	18.11.99	Wellington	Wellington	LHB/SLA	2018-19
SANTNER, Mitchell Josef	05.02.92	Hamilton	Northern D	LHB/SLA	2011-12
SOMERVILLE, William Edgar Richard	09.08.84	Wadestown	Auckland	RHB/OB	2004-05
SOUTHEE, Timothy Grant	11.12.88	Whangarei	Northern D	RHB/RMF	2006-07
WAGNER, Neil	13.03.86	Pretoria, SA	Northern D	LHB/LMF	2005-06
WATLING, Bradley-John	09.07.85	Durban, SA	Northern D	RHB/WK	2004-05
WILLIAMSON, Kane Stuart	08.08.90	Tauranga	Northern D	RHB/OB	2007-08
YOUNG, William Alexander	22.11.92	New Plymouth	Central D	RHB/OB	2011-12

SOUTH AFRICA

Full Names	*Birthdate*	*Birthplace*	*Team*	*Type F-C*	*Debut*
BAVUMA, Temba	17.05.90	Cape Town	Lions	RHB/RM	2008-09
ELGAR, Dean	11.06.87	Welkom	Northerns	LHB/SLA	2005-06
ERWEE, Sarel Johannes	10.11.89	Pietermaritzburg	KZN Coastal	LHB/OB	2008-09
HAMZA, Mogammad Zubayr	19.06.95	Cape Town	Western P	RHB/LB	2013-14
JANSEN, Marco	01.05.00	Potchefstroom	Eastern P	RHB/LF	2018-19
LINDE, George Fredrik	04.12.91	Cape Town	Cape Cobras	LHB/SLA	2011-12
MAHARAJ, Keshav Athmanand	07.02.90	Durban	Dolphins	RHB/SLA	2006-07
MARKRAM, Aiden Kyle	04.10.94	Pretoria	Titans	RHB/OB	2014-15
MULDER, Peter Wiaan Adriaan	19.02.98	Johannesburg	Gauteng	RHB/RFM	2016-17
NGIDI, Lungisani True-man	29.03.96	Durban	Titans	RHB/RFM	2015-16
NORTJE, Anrich Arno	16.11.93	Uitenhage	Warriors	RHB/RF	2012-13
OLIVIER, Duanne	09.05.92	Groblersdal	Gauteng	RHB/RF	2010-11
PETERSEN, Keegan Darryl	08.08.93	Paarl	KZN Coastal	RHB/LB	2011-12
RABADA, Kagiso	25.05.95	Johannesburg	Lions	LHB/RF	2013-14
SIPAMLA, Lubabalo Lutho	12.05.98	Port Elizabeth	Gauteng	RHB/RF	2016-17
STUURMAN, Glenton Anric	10.08.92	Oudtshoorn	Eastern P	RHB/RM	2013-14
VAN DER DUSSEN, Hendrik Erasmus	07.02.89	Pretoria	Lions	RHB/LB	2007-08
VERREYNNE, Kyle	12.05.97	Pretoria	Western P	RHB/WK	2014-15

ENGLAND v NEW ZEALAND

SERIES RECORDS
1928 to 2021

HIGHEST INNINGS TOTALS

England	in England	567-8d	Nottingham	1994
	in New Zealand	593-6d	Auckland	1974-75
New Zealand	in England	551-9d	Lord's	1973
	in New Zealand	615-9d	Mt Maunganui	2019-20

LOWEST INNINGS TOTALS

England	in England	122	Birmingham	2021
	in New Zealand	58	Auckland	2017-18
New Zealand	in England	47	Lord's	1958
	in New Zealand	26	Auckland	1954-55
HIGHEST MATCH AGGREGATE		1610 for 40 wickets	Lord's	2015
LOWEST MATCH AGGREGATE		390 for 30 wickets	Lord's	1958

HIGHEST INDIVIDUAL INNINGS

England	in England	310*	J.H.Edrich	Leeds	1965
	in New Zealand	336*	W.R.Hammond	Auckland	1932-33
New Zealand	in England	206	M.P.Donnelly	Lord's	1949
	in New Zealand	222	N.J.Astle	Christchurch	2001-02

HIGHEST AGGREGATE OF RUNS IN A SERIES

England	in England	469	(av 78.16)	L.Hutton	1949
	in New Zealand	563	(av 563.00)	W.R.Hammond	1932-33
New Zealand	in England	462	(av 77.00)	M.P.Donnelly	1949
	in New Zealand	347	(av 69.40)	P.G.Fulton	2012-13

RECORD WICKET PARTNERSHIPS – ENGLAND

1st	231	A.N.Cook (116)/N.R.D.Compton (117)	Dunedin	2012-13
2nd	369	J.H.Edrich (310*)/K.F.Barrington (163)	Leeds	1965
3rd	245	J.Hardstaff jr (114)/W.R.Hammond (140)	Lord's	1937
4th	266	M.H.Denness (181)/K.W.R.Fletcher (216)	Auckland	1974-75
5th	242	W.R.Hammond (227)/L.E.G.Ames (103)	Christchurch	1932-33
6th	281	G.P.Thorpe (200*)/A.Flintoff (137)	Christchurch	2001-02
7th	149	A.P.E.Knott (104)/P.Lever (64)	Auckland	1970-71
8th	246	L.E.G.Ames (137)/G.O.B.Allen (122)	Lord's	1931
9th	163*	M.C.Cowdrey (128*)/A.C.Smith (69*)	Wellington	1962-63
10th	59	A.P.E.Knott (49)/N.Gifford (25*)	Nottingham	1973

RECORD WICKET PARTNERSHIPS – NEW ZEALAND

1st	276	C.S.Dempster (136)/J.E.Mills (117)	Wellington	1929-30
2nd	241	J.G.Wright (116)/A.H.Jones (143)	Wellington	1991-92
3rd	213*	K.S.Williamson (104*)/L.R.P.L.Taylor (105*)	Hamilton	2019-20
4th	174	D.P.Conway (200)/H.M.Nicholls (61)	Lord's	2021
5th	180	M.D.Crowe (142)/S.A.Thomson (69)	Lord's	1994
6th	142	B.J.Watling (85)/C.de Grandhomme (72)	Christchurch	2017-18
7th	261	B.J.Watling (205)/M.J.Santner (126)	Mt Maunganui	2019-20
8th	104	D.A.R.Moloney (64)/A.W.Roberts (66*)	Lord's	1937
9th	118	J.V.Coney (174*)/B.L.Cairns (64)	Wellington	1983-84
10th	118	N.J.Astle (222)/C.L.Cairns (23*)	Christchurch	2001-02

BEST INNINGS BOWLING ANALYSIS

England	in England	7- 32	D.L.Underwood	Lord's	1969
	in New Zealand	7- 47	P.C.R.Tufnell	Christchurch	1991-92
		7- 47	R.J.Sidebottom	Napier	2007-08
New Zealand	in England	7- 74	B.L.Cairns	Leeds	1983
	in New Zealand	7-143	B.L.Cairns	Wellington	1983-84

BEST MATCH BOWLING ANALYSIS

England	in England	12-101	D.L.Underwood	The Oval	1969
	in New Zealand	12- 97	D.L.Underwood	Christchurch	1970-71
New Zealand	in England	11-169	D.J.Nash	Lord's	1994
	in New Zealand	10-100	R.J.Hadlee	Wellington	1977-78

HIGHEST AGGREGATE OF WICKETS IN A SERIES

England	in England	34	(av 7.47)	G.A.R.Lock	1958
	in New Zealand	24	(av 17.08)	R.J.Sidebottom	2007-08
New Zealand	in England	21	(av 26.61)	R.J.Hadlee	1983
	in New Zealand	15	(av 19.53)	R.O.Collinge	1977-78
		15	(av 24.73)	R.J.Hadlee	1977-78
		15	(av 18.33)	T.A.Boult	2017-18

RESULTS SUMMARY – ENGLAND v NEW ZEALAND – IN ENGLAND

		Series			Lord's			The Oval			Manchester			Leeds			Birmingham			Nottingham		
	Tests	*E*	*NZ*	*D*	*E*	*NZ*	*D*	*E*	*NZ*	*D*	*E*	*NZ*	*D*	*E*	*NZ*	*D*	*E*	*NZ*	*D*	*E*	*NZ*	*D*
1931	3	1	–	2	–	–	1	1	–	–	–	–	1	–	–	–	–	–	–	–	–	–
1937	3	1	–	2	–	–	1	–	–	1	1	–	–	–	–	–	–	–	–	–	–	–
1949	4	–	–	4	–	–	1	–	–	1	–	–	1	–	–	1	–	–	–	–	–	–
1958	5	4	–	1	1	–	–	–	–	1	1	–	–	1	–	–	1	–	–	–	–	–
1965	3	3	–	–	1	–	–	–	–	–	–	–	–	1	–	–	1	–	–	–	–	–
1969	3	2	–	1	1	–	–	1	–	–	–	–	–	–	–	–	–	–	–	–	–	1
1973	3	2	–	1	–	–	1	–	–	–	–	–	–	1	–	–	–	–	–	1	–	–
1978	3	3	–	–	1	–	–	1	–	–	–	–	–	–	–	–	–	–	–	1	–	–
1983	4	3	1	–	1	–	–	1	–	–	–	–	–	–	1	–	–	–	–	1	–	–
1986	3	–	1	2	–	–	1	–	–	1	–	–	–	–	–	–	–	–	–	–	1	–
1990	3	1	–	2	–	–	1	–	–	–	–	–	–	–	–	–	1	–	–	–	–	1
1994	3	1	–	2	–	–	1	–	–	–	–	–	1	–	–	–	–	–	–	1	–	–
1999	4	1	2	1	–	1	–	–	1	–	–	–	1	–	–	–	1	–	–	–	–	–
2004	3	3	–	–	1	–	–	–	–	–	–	–	–	1	–	–	–	–	–	1	–	–
2008	3	2	–	1	–	–	1	–	–	–	1	–	–	–	–	–	–	–	–	1	–	–
2013	2	2	–	–	1	–	–	–	–	–	–	–	–	1	–	–	–	–	–	–	–	–
2015	2	1	1	–	1	–	–	–	–	–	–	–	–	–	1	–	–	–	–	–	–	–
2021	2	–	1	1	–	–	1	–	–	–	–	–	–	–	–	–	–	1	–	–	–	–
	56	30	6	20	8	1	9	4	1	4	3	–	4	5	2	1	4	1	–	6	1	2

ENGLAND v NEW ZEALAND – IN NEW ZEALAND

		Series			Christchurch			Wellington			Auckland			Dunedin			Hamilton			Napier			Mt Maunganui		
	Tests	*E*	*NZ*	*D*	*E*	*NZ*	*D*	*E*	*NZ*	*D*	*E*	*NZ*	*D*	*E*	*NZ*	*D*	*E*	*NZ*	*D*	*E*	*NZ*	*D*	*E*	*NZ*	*D*
1929-30	4	1	–	3	1	–	–	–	–	1	–	–	2	–	–	–	–	–	–	–	–	–	–	–	–
1932-33	2	–	–	2	–	–	1	–	–	–	–	–	1	–	–	–	–	–	–	–	–	–	–	–	–
1946-47	1	–	–	1	–	–	1	–	–	–	–	–	–	–	–	–	–	–	–	–	–	–	–	–	–
1950-51	2	1	–	1	–	–	1	1	–	–	–	–	–	–	–	–	–	–	–	–	–	–	–	–	–
1954-55	2	2	–	–	–	–	–	–	–	–	1	–	–	1	–	–	–	–	–	–	–	–	–	–	–
1958-59	2	1	–	1	1	–	–	–	–	–	–	–	1	–	–	–	–	–	–	–	–	–	–	–	–
1962-63	3	3	–	–	1	–	–	1	–	–	1	–	–	–	–	–	–	–	–	–	–	–	–	–	–
1965-66	3	–	–	3	–	–	1	–	–	–	–	–	1	–	–	1	–	–	–	–	–	–	–	–	–
1970-71	2	1	–	1	1	–	–	–	–	–	–	–	1	–	–	–	–	–	–	–	–	–	–	–	–
1974-75	2	1	–	1	–	–	1	–	–	–	1	–	–	–	–	–	–	–	–	–	–	–	–	–	–
1977-78	3	1	1	1	1	–	–	–	1	–	–	–	1	–	–	–	–	–	–	–	–	–	–	–	–
1983-84	3	–	1	2	–	1	–	–	–	1	–	–	1	–	–	–	–	–	–	–	–	–	–	–	–
1987-88	3	–	–	3	–	–	1	–	–	1	–	–	1	–	–	–	–	–	–	–	–	–	–	–	–
1991-92	3	2	–	1	1	–	–	–	–	1	1	–	–	–	–	–	–	–	–	–	–	–	–	–	–
1996-97	3	2	–	1	1	–	–	1	–	–	–	–	1	–	–	–	–	–	–	–	–	–	–	–	–
2001-02	3	1	1	1	1	–	–	–	–	1	–	1	–	–	–	–	–	–	–	–	–	–	–	–	–
2007-08	3	2	1	–	–	–	–	1	–	–	–	–	–	–	–	–	–	1	–	1	–	–	–	–	–
2012-13	3	–	–	3	–	–	–	–	–	1	–	–	1	–	–	1	–	–	–	–	–	–	–	–	–
2017-18	2	–	1	1	–	–	1	–	–	–	–	1	–	–	–	–	–	–	–	–	–	–	–	–	–
2019-20	2	–	1	1	–	–	–	–	–	–	–	–	–	–	–	–	–	–	1	–	–	–	–	1	–
	50	18	6	27	8	1	7	4	1	6	4	2	11	1	–	2	–	1	1	1	–	–	–	1	–
Totals	107	48	12	47																					

ENGLAND v SOUTH AFRICA

SERIES RECORDS

1928 to 2019-20

Key to grounds: Durban – [1]Lord's, [2]Kingsmead; Johannesburg – [1]Old Wanderers, [2]Ellis Park, [3]Wanderers.

HIGHEST INNINGS TOTALS

England	in England	604-9d	The Oval	2003
	in South Africa	654-5	Durban[2]	1938-39
South Africa	in England	682-6d	Lord's	2003
	in South Africa	627-7d	Cape Town	2015-16

LOWEST INNINGS TOTALS

England	in England	76	Leeds	1907
	in South Africa	92	Cape Town	1898-99
South Africa	in England	30	Birmingham	1924
	in South Africa	30	Port Elizabeth	1895-96
HIGHEST MATCH AGGREGATE		1981 for 35 wickets	Durban[2]	1938-39
LOWEST MATCH AGGREGATE		378 for 30 wickets	The Oval	1912

HIGHEST INDIVIDUAL INNINGS

England	in England	219	M.E.Trescothick	The Oval	2003
	in South Africa	258	B.A.Stokes	Cape Town	2015-16
South Africa	in England	311*	H.M.Amla	The Oval	2012
	in South Africa	275	G.Kirsten	Durban[2]	1999-00

HIGHEST AGGREGATE OF RUNS IN A SERIES

England	in England	753	(av 94.12)	D.C.S.Compton	1947
	in South Africa	656	(av 72.88)	A.J.Strauss	2004-05
South Africa	in England	714	(av 79.33)	G.C.Smith	2003
	in South Africa	625	(av 69.44)	J.H.Kallis	2004-05

RECORD WICKET PARTNERSHIPS – ENGLAND

1st	359	L.Hutton (158)/C.Washbrook (195)	Johannesburg[2]	1948-49
2nd	280	P.A.Gibb (120)/W.J.Edrich (219)	Durban[2]	1938-39
3rd	370	W.J.Edrich (189)/D.C.S.Compton (208)	Lord's	1947
4th	286	K.P.Pietersen (152)/I.R.Bell (199)	Lord's	2008
5th	237	D.C.S.Compton (163)/N.W.D.Yardley (99)	Nottingham	1947
6th	399	B.A.Stokes (258)/J.M.Bairstow (150*)	Cape Town	2015-16
7th	152	I.R.Bell (199)/S.C.J.Broad (76)	Lord's	2008
8th	154	C.W.Wright (71)/H.R.Bromley-Davenport (84)	Johannesburg[1]	1895-96
9th	106	G.P.Swann (85)/J.M.Anderson (29)	Centurion	2009-10
10th	92	C.A.G.Russell (111)/A.E.R.Gilligan (39*)	Durban[2]	1922-23

RECORD WICKET PARTNERSHIPS – SOUTH AFRICA

1st	338	G.C.Smith (277)/H.H.Gibbs (179)	Birmingham	2003
2nd	259	G.C.Smith (131)/H.M.Amla (311*)	The Oval	2012
3rd	377*	H.M.Amla (311*)/J.H.Kallis (182*)	The Oval	2012
4th	214	H.W.Taylor (121)/H.G.Deane (93)	The Oval	1929
5th	212	A.G.Prince (149)/A.B.de Villiers (174)	Leeds	2008
6th	171	J.H.B.Waite (113)/P.L.Winslow (108)	Manchester	1955
7th	167	T.Bavuma (102*)/C.H.Morris (69)	Cape Town	2015-16
8th	150	G.Kirsten (130)/M.Zondeki (59)	Leeds	2003
9th	137	E.L.Dalton (117)/A.B.C.Langton (73*)	The Oval	1935
10th	103	H.G.Owen-Smith (129)/A.J.Bell (26*)	Leeds	1929

BEST INNINGS BOWLING ANALYSIS

England	in England	9-57	D.E.Malcolm	The Oval	1994
	in South Africa	9-28	G.A.Lohmann	Johannesburg[1]	1895-96

South Africa	in England	7- 65	S.J.Pegler	Lord's	1912
	in South Africa	9-113	H.J.Tayfield	Johannesburg[3]	1956-57

BEST MATCH BOWLING ANALYSIS

England	in England	15- 99	C.Blythe	Leeds	1907
	in South Africa	17-159	S.F.Barnes	Johannesburg[1]	1913-14
South Africa	in England	10- 87	P.M.Pollock	Nottingham	1965
	in South Africa	13-144	K.Rabada	Centurion	2015-16

HIGHEST AGGREGATE OF WICKETS IN A SERIES

England	in England	34	(av 8.29)	S.F.Barnes	1912
	in South Africa	49	(av 10.93)	S.F.Barnes	1913-14
South Africa	in England	33	(av 19.78)	A.A.Donald	1998
	in South Africa	37	(av 17.18)	H.J.Tayfield	1956-57

RESULTS SUMMARY
ENGLAND v SOUTH AFRICA – IN ENGLAND

		Series			Lord's			Leeds			The Oval			Birmingham			Manchester			Nottingham		
	Tests	E	SA	D	E	SA	D	E	SA	D	E	SA	D	E	SA	D	E	SA	D	E	SA	D
1907	3	1	–	2	–	–	1	1	–	–	–	–	1	–	–	–	–	–	–	–	–	–
1912	3	3	–	–	1	–	–	1	–	–	1	–	–	–	–	–	–	–	–	–	–	–
1924	5	3	–	2	1	–	–	1	–	–	–	–	1	1	–	–	–	–	1	–	–	–
1929	5	2	–	3	–	–	1	1	–	–	–	–	1	–	–	1	1	–	–	–	–	–
1935	5	–	1	4	–	1	–	–	–	1	–	–	1	–	–	–	–	–	1	–	–	1
1947	5	3	–	2	1	–	–	1	–	–	–	–	1	–	–	–	1	–	–	–	–	1
1951	5	3	1	1	1	–	–	–	–	1	1	–	–	–	–	–	1	–	–	–	1	–
1955	5	3	2	–	1	–	–	–	1	–	1	–	–	–	–	–	–	1	–	1	–	–
1960	5	3	–	2	1	–	–	–	–	–	–	–	1	1	–	–	–	–	1	1	–	–
1965	3	–	1	2	–	–	1	–	–	–	–	–	1	–	–	–	–	–	–	–	1	–
1994	3	1	1	1	–	1	–	–	–	1	1	–	–	–	–	–	–	–	–	–	–	–
1998	5	2	1	2	–	1	–	1	–	–	–	–	–	–	–	1	–	–	1	1	–	–
2003	5	2	2	1	–	1	–	–	1	–	1	–	–	–	–	1	–	–	–	1	–	–
2008	4	1	2	1	–	–	1	–	1	–	1	–	–	–	1	–	–	–	–	–	–	–
2012	3	–	2	1	–	1	–	–	–	1	–	1	–	–	–	–	–	–	–	–	–	–
2017	4	3	1	–	1	–	–	–	–	–	1	–	–	–	–	–	1	–	–	–	1	–
	68	30	14	24	7	5	4	6	3	4	7	1	7	2	1	3	4	1	4	4	3	2

ENGLAND v SOUTH AFRICA – IN SOUTH AFRICA

		Series			Port Elizabeth			Cape Town			Johannesburg			Durban			Centurion		
	Tests	E	SA	D	E	SA	D	E	SA	D	E	SA	D	E	SA	D	E	SA	D
1888-89	2	2	–	–	1	–	–	1	–	–	–	–	–	–	–	–	–	–	–
1891-92	1	1	–	–	–	–	–	1	–	–	–	–	–	–	–	–	–	–	–
1895-96	3	3	–	–	1	–	–	1	–	–	1	–	–	–	–	–	–	–	–
1898-99	2	2	–	–	–	–	–	1	–	–	1	–	–	–	–	–	–	–	–
1905-06	5	1	4	–	–	–	–	1	1	–	–	3	–	–	–	–	–	–	–
1909-10	5	2	3	–	–	–	–	1	1	–	1	1	–	–	1	–	–	–	–
1913-14	5	4	–	1	1	–	–	–	–	–	2	–	–	1	–	1	–	–	–
1922-23	5	2	1	2	–	–	–	1	–	–	–	1	1	1	–	1	–	–	–
1927-28	5	2	2	1	–	–	–	1	–	–	1	1	–	–	1	1	–	–	–
1930-31	5	–	1	4	–	–	–	–	–	1	–	1	1	–	–	2	–	–	–
1938-39	5	1	–	4	–	–	–	–	–	1	–	–	2	1	–	1	–	–	–
1948-49	5	2	–	3	1	–	–	–	–	1	–	–	2	1	–	–	–	–	–
1956-57	5	2	2	1	–	1	–	1	–	–	1	1	–	–	–	1	–	–	–
1964-65	5	1	–	4	–	–	1	–	–	1	–	–	2	1	–	–	–	–	–
1995-96	5	–	1	4	–	–	1	–	1	–	–	–	1	–	–	1	–	–	1
1999-00	5	1	2	2	–	–	1	–	1	–	–	1	–	–	–	1	1	–	–
2004-05	5	2	1	2	1	–	–	–	1	–	1	–	–	–	–	1	–	–	1
2009-10	4	1	1	2	–	–	–	–	–	1	–	1	–	1	–	–	–	–	1
2015-16	4	2	1	1	–	–	–	–	–	1	1	–	–	1	–	–	–	1	–
2019-20	4	3	1	–	1	–	–	1	–	–	1	–	–	–	–	–	–	1	–
	85	34	20	31	6	1	3	10	5	6	10	10	9	7	2	10	1	2	3
Totals	153	64	34	55															

STATISTICAL HIGHLIGHTS IN 2021 TESTS

Including Tests from No. 2397 (Australia v India, 3rd Test), No. 2400 (New Zealand v Pakistan, 2nd Test) and No. 2402 (South Africa v Sri Lanka, 2nd Test) to No. 2441 (Australia v England, 3rd Test) and No. 2444 (South Africa v India, 1st Test).
† = National record

TEAM HIGHLIGHTS

HIGHEST INNINGS TOTALS

659-6d†	New Zealand v Pakistan	Christchurch
648-8d	Sri Lanka v Bangladesh (*1st Test*)	Pallekele
578	England v India	Chennai

HIGHEST FOURTH INNINGS TOTAL

395-7	West Indies (set 395) v Bangladesh	Chittagong

LOWEST INNINGS TOTALS

62	New Zealand v India	Mumbai
68	England v Australia	Melbourne
78	India v England	Leeds
81	England v India (*3rd Test*)	Ahmedabad
87	Bangladesh v Pakistan	Mirpur
97	West Indies v South Africa (*1st Test*)	Gros Islet

HIGHEST MATCH AGGREGATE

1328-37	Australia (369 & 294) v India (336 & 329-7)	Brisbane

BATSMEN'S MATCH (Qualification: 1200 runs, average 60 per wicket)

75.82 (1289-17)	Bangladesh (541-7d & 100-2) v Sri Lanka (648-8d)	Pallekele

LOWEST MATCH AGGREGATE

387-30	England (112 & 81) v India (145 & 49-0) (*3rd Test*)	Ahmedabad

This was the shortest Test, in terms of balls bowled (842), since WW2 and the lowest match aggregate since 1958.

LARGE MARGINS OF VICTORY

Inns & 176 runs	New Zealand (659-6d) beat Pakistan (297 & 186)	Christchurch
372 runs	India (325 & 276-7d) beat New Zealand (62 & 167)	Mumbai
316 runs	India (329 & 286) beat England (134 & 164) (*2nd Test*)	Chennai

NARROW MARGINS OF VICTORY

17 runs	West Indies (409 & 117) beat Bangladesh (296 & 213)	Mirpur
1 wkt	West Indies (253 & 168-9) beat Pakistan (217 & 203)	Kingston

60 EXTRAS IN AN INNINGS

	B	*LB*	*W*	*NB*		
64	27	8	17	12	New Zealand (659-6d) v Pakistan	Christchurch

BATTING HIGHLIGHTS

DOUBLE HUNDREDS

Abid Ali	215*	Pakistan v Zimbabwe (*2nd Test*)	Harare
D.P.Conway	200	New Zealand v England	Lord's
Hashmatullah Shahidi	200*	Afghanistan v Zimbabwe (*2nd Test*)	Abu Dhabi
F.D.M.Karunaratne	244	Sri Lanka v Bangladesh (*1st Test*)	Pallekele
K.R.Mayers	210*	West Indies v Bangladesh	Chittagong
J.E.Root (2)	228	England v Sri Lanka (*1st Test*)	Galle
	218	England v India (*1st Test*)	Chennai
K.S.Williamson	238	New Zealand v Pakistan	Christchurch

MOST SIXES IN AN INNINGS

7	K.R.Mayers (210*)	West Indies v Bangladesh	Chittagong
7	Q.de Kock (141*)	South Africa v West Indies (*1st Test*)	Gros Islet

MOST RUNS FROM BOUNDARIES IN AN INNINGS

Runs	*6s*	*4s*			
122	7	20	K.R.Mayers	West Indies v Bangladesh	Chittagong

HUNDRED ON DEBUT

D.P.Conway 200 New Zealand v England Lord's

Seventh to score a double century on debut.

S.S.Iyer 105 India v New Zealand Kanpur

K.R.Mayers 210* West Indies v Bangladesh Chittagong

Sixth to score a double century on debut, and the first to do so in the fourth innings of a Test.

P.N.Silva 103 Sri Lanka v West Indies North Sound

LONG INNINGS (Qualification: 600 mins and/or 400 balls)

Min	*Balls*			
637	407	Abid Ali (215*)	Pakistan v Zimbabwe (*2nd Test*)	Harare
590	443	Hashmatullah Shahidi (200*)	Afghanistan v Zimbabwe (*2nd Test*)	Abu Dhabi
698	437	F.D.M.Karunaratne (244)	Sri Lanka v Bangladesh	Pallekele

FIRST-WICKET PARTNERSHIP OF 100 IN EACH INNINGS

146/151	Abid Ali/Abdullah Shaifq	Pakistan v Bangladesh	Chittagong

OTHER NOTABLE PARTNERSHIPS

Qualifications: 1st-4th wkts: 225 runs; 5th-6th: 200; 7th: 175; 8th: 150; 9th: 125; 10th: 100.

Second Wicket

236	Abid Ali/Azhar Ali	Pakistan v Zimbabwe (*2nd Test*)	Harare

Third Wicket

242†	Nazmul Hossain/Mominul Haque	Bangladesh v Sri Lanka	Pallekele

Fourth Wicket

369†	K.S.Williamson/H.M.Nicholls	New Zealand v Pakistan	Christchurch
345	F.D.M.Karunaratne/D.M.de Silva	Sri Lanka v Bangladesh	Pallekele
307†	Hashmatullah Shahidi/Asghar Afghan	Afghanistan v Zimbabwe (*2nd Test*)	Abu Dhabi

The record partnership for Afghanistan for all wickets.

Fifth Wicket

206	Mushfiqur Rahim/Liton Das	Bangladesh v Pakistan	Chittagong

Eighth Wicket

187†	S.C.Williams/D.T.Tiripano	Zimbabwe v Afghanistan (*2nd Test*)	Abu Dhabi
169	Abid Ali/Nauman Ali	Pakistan v Zimbabwe (*2nd Test*)	Harare

Ninth Wicket

191†	Mahmudullah/Taskin Ahmed	Bangladesh v Zimbabwe	Harare

BOWLING HIGHLIGHTS

EIGHT WICKETS IN AN INNINGS

A.Y.Patel 10-119 New Zealand v India Mumbai

The third best analysis in Test cricket.

Sajid Khan 8- 42 Pakistan v Bangladesh Mirpur

TEN WICKETS IN A MATCH

L.Ambuldeniya	10-210	Sri Lanka v England (*2nd Test*)	Galle
Hasan Ali	10-114	Pakistan v South Africa	Rawalpindi
K.A.Jamieson	11-117	New Zealand v Pakistan	Christchurch
P.A.K.P.Jayawickrama	11-178	Sri Lanka v Bangladesh (*2nd Test*)	Pallekele
A.R.Patel	11- 70	India v England (*3rd Test*)	Ahmedabad
A.Y.Patel	14-225	New Zealand v India	Mumbai
Rashid Khan	11-275	Afghanistan v Zimbabwe (*2nd Test*)	Abu Dhabi

Sajid Khan	12-126	Pakistan v Bangladesh	Mirpur
Shaheen Shah Afridi	10- 94	Pakistan v West Indies (*2nd Test*)	Kingston
R.T.M.Wanigamuni	11-136	Sri Lanka v West Indies (*2nd Test*)	Galle

FIVE WICKETS IN AN INNINGS ON DEBUT

S.M.Boland	6- 7	Australia v England	Melbourne

The joint second-best six-for analysis in Test history.

P.A.K.P.Jayawickrama†	6-92	Sri Lanka v Bangladesh (*2nd Test*)	Pallekele
	5-86	Sri Lanka v Bangladesh (*2nd Test*)	Pallekele
Nauman Ali	5-35	Pakistan v South Africa	Karachi
A.R.Patel	5-60	India v England (*2nd Test*)	Chennai

† *The first Sri Lankan ever to take ten or more wickets on debut; the tenth best analysis by a debutant.*

HAT-TRICK

K.A.Maharaj	South Africa v West Indies (*2nd Test*)	Gros Islet

60 OVERS IN AN INNINGS

Rashid Khan	62.5-17-137-7	Afghanistan v Zimbabwe (*2nd Test*)	Abu Dhabi

MOST RUNS CONCEDED IN AN INNINGS

L.Ambuldeniya	45-4-176-3	Sri Lanka v England (*1st Test*)	Galle

WICKET-KEEPING HIGHLIGHTS

FIVE WICKET-KEEPING DISMISSALS IN AN INNINGS

J.C.Buttler	5ct	England v India	Leeds
A.T.Carey	5ct	Australia v England	Brisbane
Q.de Kock	5ct	South Africa v Sri Lanka	Johannesburg
D.P.D.N.Dickwella	5ct	Sri Lanka v West Indies (*2nd Test*)	North Sound

EIGHT WICKET-KEEPING DISMISSALS IN A MATCH

T.A.Blundell	8ct	New Zealand v England	Birmingham
J.C.Buttler	8ct	England v India	Leeds
A.T.Carey	8ct	Australia v England	Brisbane
J.Da Silva	8ct	West Indies v Pakistan (*1st Test*)	Kingston
Q.de Kock	8ct	South Africa v Sri Lanka	Johannesburg

FIELDING HIGHLIGHTS

FOUR CATCHES IN AN INNINGS IN THE FIELD

M.M.Ali	4ct	England v India	The Oval
D.M.de Silva	4ct	Sri Lanka v West Indies (*2nd Test*)	Galle
H.D.R.L.Thirimanne	5ct	Sri Lanka v England (*2nd Test*)	Galle

First instance in Tests of a fielder taking all five catches off one bowler (L.Ambuldeniya).

SIX CATCHES IN A MATCH IN THE FIELD

M.M.Ali	6ct	England v India	The Oval
S.P.D.Smith	6ct	Australia v England	Adelaide

ALL-ROUND HIGHLIGHTS

HUNDRED AND FIVE WICKETS IN AN INNINGS

R.Ashwin	106	5-43	India v England (*2nd Test*)	Chennai

LEADING TEST AGGREGATES IN 2021

1000 RUNS IN 2021

	M	I	NO	HS	Runs	Avge	100	50
J.E.Root (E)	15	29	1	228	**1708**	61.00	6	4

RECORD CALENDAR YEAR RUNS AGGREGATE

	M	I	NO	HS	Runs	Avge	100	50
M.Yousuf (P) (2006)	11	19	1	202	**1788**	99.33	9	3

RECORD CALENDAR YEAR RUNS AVERAGE

	M	I	NO	HS	Runs	Avge	100	50
G.St A.Sobers (WI) (1958)	7	12	3	365*	1193	**132.55**	5	3

1000 RUNS IN DEBUT CALENDAR YEAR

	M	I	NO	HS	Runs	Avge	100	50
M.A.Taylor (A) (1989)	11	20	1	219	**1219**	64.15	4	5
A.C.Voges (A) (2015)	12	18	6	269*	**1028**	85.66	4	3
A.N.Cook (E) (2006)	13	24	2	127	**1013**	46.04	4	3

50 WICKETS IN 2021

	M	O	R	W	Avge	Best	5wI	10wM
R.Ashwin (I)	9	387.1	899	**54**	16.64	6-61	3	–

RECORD CALENDAR YEAR WICKETS AGGREGATE

	M	O	R	W	Avge	Best	5wI	10wM
M.Muralitharan (SL) (2006)	11	588.4	1521	**90**	16.90	8-70	9	5
S.K.Warne (A) (2005)	14	691.4	2043	**90**	22.70	6-46	6	2

40 WICKET-KEEPING DISMISSALS IN 2021

	M	Dis	Ct	St
J.C.Buttler (E)	9	**42**	41	1

RECORD CALENDAR YEAR DISMISSALS AGGREGATE

	M	Dis	Ct	St
J.M.Bairstow (E) (2016)	17	**70**	66	4

20 CATCHES BY FIELDERS IN 2021

	M	Ct
J.E.Root (E)	15	**21**

RECORD CALENDAR YEAR FIELDER'S AGGREGATE

	M	Ct
G.C.Smith (SA) (2008)	15	**30**

TEST MATCH SCORES
AFGHANISTAN v ZIMBABWE (1st Test)

At Sheikh Zayed Stadium, Abu Dhabi, on 2, 3 March 2021.
Toss: Afghanistan. Result: **ZIMBABWE** won by ten wickets.
Debuts: Afghanistan – Abdul Malik, Abdul Wasi, Munir Ahmad; Zimbabwe – W.N.Madhevere.

AFGHANISTAN

Abdul Malik	b Muzarabani	0	(2)	c Chakabva b Nyauchi	0
Ibrahim Zadran	c Musakanda b Nyauchi	31	(1)	c Chakabva b Tiripano	76
Rahmat Shah	c Chakabva b Muzarabani	6	(4)	lbw b Nyauchi	0
Munir Ahmad	c Sikandar Raza b Nyauchi	12	(3)	lbw b Muzarabani	1
Hashmatullah Shahidi	b Nyauchi	5		c Madhevere b Nyauchi	4
†Afsar Zazai	c Chakabva b Tiripano	37		lbw b Williams	0
*Asghar Stanikzai	c Chakabva b Muzarabani	13		b Muzarabani	14
Abdul Wasi	c Kasuza b Sikandar Raza	3		b Burl	9
Hamza Hotak	not out	16		not out	21
Yamin Ahmadzai	c Tiripano b Williams	1		c Williams b Tiripano	0
Zahir Khan	c Williams b Muzarabani	0		c Nyauchi b Tiripano	0
Extras	(B 4, NB 2, W 1)	7		(B 4, LB 1, W 5)	10
Total	**(47 overs)**	**131**		**(45.3 overs)**	**135**

ZIMBABWE

P.S.Masvaure	lbw b Hotak	15	not out	5
K.T.Kasuza	b Ahmadzai	0	not out	11
T.K.Musakanda	b Hotak	7		
*S.C.Williams	c Shahidi b Hotak	105		
W.N.Madhevere	lbw b Hotak	0		
Sikandar Raza	c Malik b Hotak	43		
R.P.Burl	lbw b Zadran	8		
†R.W.Chakabva	c Malik b Khan	44		
D.T.Tiripano	c Zadran b Khan	6		
B.Muzarabani	not out	12		
V.M.Nyauchi	b Hotak	0		
Extras	(B 2, LB 6, NB 1, W 1)	10	(LB 1)	1
Total	**(72 overs)**	**250**	**(0 wkts; 3.2 overs; 15 mins)**	**17**

ZIMBABWE	*O*	*M*	*R*	*W*		*O*	*M*	*R*	*W*
Muzarabani	12	3	48	4		8	4	14	2
Nyauchi	10	1	34	3		7	1	30	3
Tiripano	12	5	24	1	(4)	9.3	2	23	3
Burl	7	1	9	0	(5)	7	0	13	1
Williams	3	2	4	1	(3)	6	0	28	1
Sikandar Raza	3	0	8	1		4	0	16	0
Madhevere						4	1	6	0
AFGHANISTAN									
Yamin Ahmadzai	17.1	2	48	1	(2)	1.2	0	5	0
Hamza Hotak	25	3	75	6	(1)	2	0	11	0
Zahir Khan	19	0	81	2					
Abdul Wasi	8.5	0	25	0					
Ibrahim Zadran	2	0	13	1					

FALL OF WICKETS

	Afg	Z	Afg	Z
Wkt	*1st*	*1st*	*2nd*	*2nd*
1st	0	5	5	–
2nd	8	22	6	–
3rd	37	38	15	–
4th	52	38	21	–
5th	69	109	21	–
6th	91	137	47	–
7th	109	212	81	–
8th	122	224	129	–
9th	123	250	129	–
10th	131	250	135	–

Umpires: Ahmed Shah Pakteen (*Afghanistan*) (1) and Alim Dar (*Pakistan*) (135).
Referee: R.S.Madugalle (*Sri Lanka*) (196). **Test No. 2413/1 (Afg5/Z111)**

AFGHANISTAN v ZIMBABWE (2nd Test)

At Sheikh Zayed Stadium, Abu Dhabi, on 10, 11, 12, 13, 14 March 2021.
Toss: Afghanistan. Result: **AFGHANISTAN** won by six wickets.
Debuts: Afghanistan – Sayed Shirzad, Shahidullah.

AFGHANISTAN

Ibrahim Zadran	c Sikandar Raza b Burl	72	(2)	c Musakanda b Burl	29
Javed Ahmadi	c Williams b Nyauchi	4	(1)	b Muzarabani	4
Rahmat Shah	run out	23		b Burl	58
Hashmatullah Shahidi	not out	200	(6)	not out	6
*Asghar Stanikzai	lbw b Sikandar Raza	164			
Nasir Ahmadzai	not out	55	(5)	not out	4
†Afsar Zazai					
Hamza Hotak					
Sayed Shirzad					
Rashid Khan					
Shahidullah			(4)	c Kasuza b Muzarabani	0
Extras	(B 16, LB 1, NB 5, W 5)	27		(B 4, NB 2, W 1)	7
Total	**(4 wkts dec; 160.4 overs)**	**545**		**(4 wkts; 26.1 overs)**	**108**

ZIMBABWE

P.S.Masvaure	b Hotak	65	c and b Ahmadi	15
K.T.Kasuza	c Zazai b Khan	41	c Shah b Khan	30
T.K.Musakanda	lbw b Khan	41	lbw b Khan	15
*S.C.Williams	c Hotak b Shirzad	8	not out	151
W.N.Madhevere	c Zazai b Shirzad	0	c Zazai b Shirzad	0
Sikandar Raza	c Shah b Khan	85	c Ahmadzai b Khan	22
R.P.Burl	b Hotak	0	lbw b Khan	0
†R.W.Chakabva	c Zadran b Khan	33	lbw b Khan	0
D.T.Tiripano	c Ahmadzai b Hotak	3	lbw b Khan	95
B.Muzarabani	run out	0	c Zazai b Hotak	17
V.M.Nyauchi	not out	0	lbw b Khan	0
Extras	(B 2, LB 6, NB 1, W 2)	11	(B 12, LB 7, W 1)	20
Total	**(91.3 overs)**	**287**	**(148.5 overs)**	**365**

ZIMBABWE	*O*	*M*	*R*	*W*		*O*	*M*	*R*	*W*
Muzarabani	26	5	62	0		9.1	1	25	2
Nyauchi	24	4	102	1		6	1	28	0
Tiripano	20.4	1	83	0	(4)	4	0	17	0
Sikandar Raza	31	4	79	1					
Williams	30	4	97	0	(3)	3	0	18	0
Burl	20	1	69	1	(5)	4	1	16	2
Madhevere	9	0	36	0					
AFGHANISTAN									
Sayed Shirzad	15	3	48	2		27	7	49	1
Hamza Hotak	32	6	73	3	(3)	34	7	104	1
Rashid Khan	36.3	3	138	4	(2)	62.5	17	137	7
Javed Ahmadi	8	1	20	0		16	5	40	1
Shahidullah						5	1	6	0
Asghar Stankzai						1	0	1	0
Rahmat Shah						3	0	9	0

FALL OF WICKETS

	Afg	Z	Z	Afg
Wkt	*1st*	*1st*	*2nd*	*2nd*
1st	6	91	44	8
2nd	56	133	46	89
3rd	121	145	101	91
4th	428	145	102	101
5th	–	186	140	–
6th	–	189	140	–
7th	–	242	142	–
8th	–	251	329	–
9th	–	287	362	–
10th	–	287	365	–

Umpires: Ahmed Shah Pakteen (*Afghanistan*) (2) and Alim Dar (*Pakistan*) (136).
Referee: R.S.Madugalle (*Sri Lanka*) (197). **Test No. 2414/2 (Afg6/Z112)**

WEST INDIES v SRI LANKA (1st Test)

At Sir Vivian Richards Stadium, North Sound, Antigua, on 21, 22, 23, 24, 25 March 2021.
Toss: West Indies. Result: **MATCH DRAWN**.
Debut: Sri Lanka – P.N.Silva.

SRI LANKA

*F.D.M.Karunaratne	c Campbell b Cornwall	12	(2)	c Campbell b Roach	3
H.D.R.L.Thirimanne	b Holder	70	(1)	b Roach	76
B.O.P.Fernando	run out	4		c Da Silva b Mayers	91
L.D.Chandimal	c Da Silva b Holder	4		c Da Silva b Mayers	4
D.M.de Silva	b Roach	13		b Joseph	50
P.N.Silva	c Holder b Roach	9		c Roach b Cornwall	103
†D.P.D.N.Dickwella	c Cornwall b Holder	32		b Roach	96
R.A.S.Lakmal	c Brathwaite b Holder	3		run out	8
P.V.D.Chameera	b Roach	2		c Mayers b Cornwall	6
L.Ambuldeniya	lbw b Holder	3		c Holder b Cornwall	10
M.V.T.Fernando	not out	1		not out	0
Extras	(B 4, LB 6, NB 1, W 5)	16		(B 13, LB 5, NB 11)	29
Total	**(69.4 overs)**	**169**		**(149.5 overs)**	**476**

WEST INDIES

*K.C.Brathwaite	c de Silva b Lakmal	3	b Ambuldeniya	23
J.D.Campbell	c Dickwella b Chameera	42	c Dickwella b M.V.T.Fernando	11
N.E.Bonner	lbw b Ambuldeniya	31	not out	113
K.R.Mayers	c de Silva b Lakmal	45	c Thirimanne b Ambuldeniya	52
J.Blackwood	b Lakmal	2	b M.V.T.Fernando	4
J.O.Holder	b Lakmal	19	not out	18
†J.Da Silva	c Dickwella b Chameera	46		
A.S.Joseph	c Chandimal b Lakmal	0		
R.R.S.Cornwall	b M.V.T.Fernando	61		
K.A.J.Roach	not out	5		
S.T.Gabriel	lbw b M.V.T.Fernando	0		
Extras	(B 1, LB 6, NB 9, W 1)	17	(B 4, LB 8, NB 3)	15
Total	**(103 overs)**	**271**	**(4 wkts; 100 overs)**	**236**

WEST INDIES	*O*	*M*	*R*	*W*		*O*	*M*	*R*	*W*
Roach	16	2	47	3		27	3	74	3
Gabriel	9	2	22	0		18	2	67	0
Cornwall	14	6	25	1	(5)	42.5	4	137	3
Joseph	11	2	32	0		21	2	83	1
Holder	17.4	6	27	5	(3)	22	4	40	0
Mayers	2	0	6	0	(7)	9	2	24	2
Brathwaite					(6)	9	1	30	0
Blackwood						1	0	3	0
SRI LANKA									
Lakmal	25	9	47	5		25	10	33	0
M.V.T.Fernando	17	6	52	2		19	0	73	2
Chameera	22	1	71	2	(4)	18	3	44	0
Ambuldeniya	28	6	64	1	(3)	28	9	62	2
De Silva	11	2	30	0		10	5	12	0

FALL OF WICKETS

	SL	WI	SL	WI
Wkt	*1st*	*1st*	*2nd*	*2nd*
1st	17	13	8	12
2nd	29	69	170	78
3rd	54	95	178	183
4th	76	120	189	204
5th	92	133	259	–
6th	150	169	438	–
7th	160	171	460	–
8th	163	261	462	–
9th	164	271	476	–
10th	169	271	476	–

Umpires: G.O.Brathwaite (*West Indies*) (1) and J.S.Wilson (*West Indies*) (20).
Referee: Sir R.B.Richardson (*West Indies*) (30). **Test No. 2415/21 (WI553/SL294)**

WEST INDIES v SRI LANKA (2nd Test)

At Sir Vivian Richards Stadium, North Sound, Antigua, on 29, 30, 31 March, 1, 2 April 2021.
Toss: Sri Lanka. Result: **MATCH DRAWN**.
Debuts: None.

WEST INDIES

*K.C.Brathwaite	b Chameera	126		b Chameera	85
J.D.Campbell	c Dickwella b Lakmal	5		c Dickwella b Lakmal	10
N.E.Bonner	b Lakmal	0			
K.R.Mayers	c Dickwella b M.V.T.Fernando	49		lbw b Lakmal	55
J.Blackwood	c Dickwella b Lakmal	18	(3)	c Dickwella b Chameera	18
J.O.Holder	c Thirimanne b De Silva	30	(5)	not out	71
†J.Da Silva	c Dickwella b Chameera	1	(6)	not out	20
A.S.Joseph	lbw b Ambuldeniya	29			
R.R.S.Cornwall	c M.V.T.Fernando b Lakmal	73			
K.A.J.Roach	c Dickwella b Chameera	9			
S.T.Gabriel	not out	1			
Extras	(B 6, NB 7)	13		(B 2, LB 12, NB 6, W 1)	21
Total	**(111.1 overs)**	**354**		**(4 wkts dec; 72.4 overs)**	**280**

SRI LANKA

*F.D.M.Karunaratne	c Bonner b Joseph	1	(2)	lbw b Mayers	75
H.D.R.L.Thirimanne	b Roach	55	(1)	c Cornwall b Joseph	39
B.O.P.Fernando	lbw b Mayers	18		not out	66
L.D.Chandimal	c sub (H.R.Walsh) b Gabriel	44		not out	10
D.M.de Silva	lbw b Blackwood	39			
P.N.Silva	c sub (H.R.Walsh) b Roach	51			
†D.P.D.N.Dickwella	c Da Silva b Holder	20			
R.A.S.Lakmal	c Brathwaite b Joseph	6			
P.V.D.Chameera	c Da Silva b Holder	2			
L.Ambuldeniya	not out	5			
M.V.T.Fernando	c Da Silva b Roach	0			
Extras	(B 4, LB 5, NB 7, W 1)	17		(LB 1, NB 1, W 1)	3
Total	**(107 overs)**	**258**		**(2 wkts; 79 overs)**	**193**

SRI LANKA	*O*	*M*	*R*	*W*		*O*	*M*	*R*	*W*
Lakmal	28	11	94	4		14	3	62	2
M.V.T.Fernando	27	4	71	1		12.4	1	49	0
Ambuldeniya	25	5	88	1					
Chameera	21.1	4	69	3		18	0	74	2
De Silva	10	3	26	1	(3)	28	3	81	0
WEST INDIES									
Roach	18	5	58	3		12	2	33	0
Gabriel	16	3	37	1	(4)	5.2	2	20	0
Joseph	22	4	64	2	(5)	10	2	33	1
Holder	21	3	39	2	(2)	10	3	24	0
Mayers	11	7	10	1	(8)	6	4	5	1
Cornwall	15	5	25	0	(3)	26.4	8	53	0
Blackwood	4	0	16	1	(6)	6	1	17	0
Brathwaite					(7)	3	0	7	0

FALL OF WICKETS

	WI	SL	WI	SL
Wkt	*1st*	*1st*	*2nd*	*2nd*
1st	11	18	14	101
2nd	15	64	58	146
3rd	86	77	140	–
4th	120	152	227	–
5th	171	177	–	–
6th	185	203	–	–
7th	222	214	–	–
8th	325	231	–	–
9th	351	258	–	–
10th	354	258	–	–

Umpires: G.O.Brathwaite (*West Indies*) (2) and J.S.Wilson (*West Indies*) (21).
Referee: Sir R.B.Richardson (*West Indies*) (31). **Test No. 2416/22 (WI554/SL295)**

SRI LANKA v BANGLADESH (1st Test)

At Pallekele Cricket Stadium, on 21, 22, 23, 24, 25 April 2021.
Toss: Bangladesh. Result: **MATCH DRAWN.**
Debuts: None.

BANGLADESH

Tamim Iqbal	c Thirimanne b M.V.T.Fernando	90	not out	74
Saif Hasan	lbw b M.V.T.Fernando	0	c Dickwella b Lakmal	1
Nazmul Hossain	c and b Kumara	163	b Lakmal	0
*Mominul Haque	c Thirimanne b D.M.de Silva	127	not out	23
Mushfiqur Rahim	not out	68		
†Liton Das	c B.O.P.Fernando b M.V.T.Fernando	50		
Mehedi Hasan	c Dickwella b Lakmal	3		
Taijul Islam	c Dickwella b M.V.T.Fernando	2		
Taskin Ahmed	not out	6		
Abu Jayed				
Ebadat Hossain				
Extras	(B 9, LB 6, NB 6, W 11)	32	(NB 2)	2
Total	**(7 wkts dec; 173 overs)**	**541**	**(2 wkts; 33 overs)**	**100**

SRI LANKA

*F.D.M.Karunaratne	c Nazmul b Taskin	244
H.D.R.L.Thirimanne	lbw b Mehedi	58
B.O.P.Fernando	c Liton b Taskin	20
A.D.Mathews	b Taijul	25
D.M.de Silva	b Taskin	166
P.N.Silva	c Liton b Ebadat	12
†D.P.D.N.Dickwella	run out	31
P.W.H.de Silva	b Taijul	43
R.A.S.Lakmal	not out	22
M.V.T.Fernando	not out	0
C.B.R.L.S.Kumara		
Extras	(B 4, LB 10, NB 3, W 10)	27
Total	**(8 wkts dec; 179 overs)**	**648**

SRI LANKA	*O*	*M*	*R*	*W*		*O*	*M*	*R*	*W*
Lakmal	36	14	81	1		8	2	21	2
M.V.T.Fernando	35	9	96	4		5	2	18	0
Kumara	28	4	88	1					
Mathews	7	1	14	0					
D.M.de Silva	30	1	130	1	(3)	11	1	46	0
P.W.H.de Silva	36	2	111	0	(4)	9	0	15	0
Karunaratne	1	0	6	0					
BANGLADESH									
Abu Jayed	19	2	76	0					
Taskin Ahmed	30	6	112	3					
Ebadat Hossain	21	1	99	1					
Mehedi Hasan	58	6	161	1					
Taijul Islam	45	9	163	2					
Mominul Haque	4	0	18	0					
Saif Hasan	2	0	5	0					

FALL OF WICKETS

	B	SL	B
Wkt	*1st*	*1st*	*2nd*
1st	8	114	21
2nd	152	157	27
3rd	394	190	–
4th	424	535	–
5th	511	544	–
6th	515	553	–
7th	524	585	–
8th	–	647	–
9th	–	–	–
10th	–	–	–

Umpires: H.D.P.K.Dharmasena (*Sri Lanka*) (68) and R.S.A.Palliyaguruge (*Sri Lanka*) (6).
Referee: R.S.Madugalle (*Sri Lanka*) (198). **Test No. 2417/21 (SL296/B122)**

SRI LANKA v BANGLADESH (2nd Test)

At Pallekele Cricket Stadium, on 29, 30 April, 1, 2, 3 May 2021.
Toss: Sri Lanka. Result: **SRI LANKA** won by 209 runs.
Debuts: Sri Lanka – P.A.K.P.Jayawickrama; Bangladesh – Shoriful Islam.

SRI LANKA

*F.D.M.Karunaratne	c Liton b Shoriful	118	(2)	c sub (Yasir Ali) b Saif	66
H.D.R.L.Thirimanne	c Liton b Taskin	140	(1)	c Nazmul b Mehedi	2
B.O.P.Fernando	c Liton b Mehedi	81		st Liton b Taijul	1
A.D.Mathews	c Liton b Taskin	5		c sub (Yasir Ali) b Taijul	12
D.M.de Silva	c Nazmul b Taijul	2		c Nazmul b Mehedi	41
P.N.Silva	b Taskin	30		c Shoriful b Taijul	24
†D.P.D.N.Dickwella	not out	77		c Taijul b Taskin	24
R.T.M.Wanigamuni	c Mushfiqur b Taskin	33		c Tamim b Taijul	8
R.A.S.Lakmal				b Taijul	12
M.V.T.Fernando					
P.A.K.P.Jayawickrama			(10)	not out	3
Extras	(B 3, LB 2, NB 1, W 1)	7		(NB 1)	1
Total	**(7 wkts dec; 159.2 overs)**	**493**		**(9 wkts dec; 42.2 overs)**	**194**

BANGLADESH

Tamim Iqbal	c Thirimanne b Jayawickrama	92	c Dickwella b Wanigamuni	24
Saif Hasan	c de Silva b Jayawickrama	25	c Lakmal b Jayawickrama	34
Nazmul Hossain	c Thirimanne b Wanigamuni	0	b Jayawickrama	26
*Mominul Haque	lbw b Wanigamuni	49	b Wanigamuni	32
Mushfiqur Rahim	lbw b Jayawickrama	40	c de Silva b Wanigamuni	40
†Liton Das	c Thirimanne b Jayawickrama	8	lbw b Jayawickrama	17
Mehedi Hasan	lbw b Jayawickrama	16	c P.N.Silva b Jayawickrama	39
Taijul Islam	hit wkt b Lakmal	9	c Dickwella b de Silva	2
Taskin Ahmed	lbw b Jayawickrama	0	c Karunaratne b Wanigamuni	7
Shoriful Islam	b Lakmal	0	not out	0
Abu Jayed	not out	0	lbw b Jayawickrama	0
Extras	(B 2, LB 9, NB 1)	12	(B 3, LB 2, NB 1)	6
Total	**(83 overs)**	**251**	**(71 overs)**	**227**

BANGLADESH	*O*	*M*	*R*	*W*		*O*	*M*	*R*	*W*
Abu Jayed	22	4	69	0					
Taskin Ahmed	34.2	7	127	4	(4)	4	0	26	1
Mehedi Hasan	36	7	118	1	(1)	14	3	66	2
Shoriful Islam	29	6	91	1	(2)	1	0	8	0
Taijul Islam	38	7	83	1	(3)	19.2	2	72	5
Saif Hasan					(5)	4	0	22	1
SRI LANKA									
Lakmal	10	0	30	2		4	2	14	0
M.V.T.Fernando	7	1	19	0					
Mathews	2	0	7	0					
Wanigamuni	31	7	86	2	(2)	28	2	103	4
Jayawickrama	32	7	92	6	(3)	32	10	86	5
De Silva	1	0	6	0	(4)	7	1	19	1

FALL OF WICKETS

	SL	B	SL	B
Wkt	*1st*	*1st*	*2nd*	*2nd*
1st	209	98	14	31
2nd	213	99	15	73
3rd	319	151	39	104
4th	328	214	112	134
5th	382	224	124	171
6th	382	224	162	183
7th	493	241	178	206
8th	–	243	180	227
9th	–	246	194	227
10th	–	251	–	227

Umpires: H.D.P.K.Dharmasena (*Sri Lanka*) (69) and R.S.A.Palliyaguruge (*Sri Lanka*) (7).
Referee: R.S.Madugalle (*Sri Lanka*) (199). **Test No. 2418/22 (SL297/B123)**

ZIMBABWE v PAKISTAN (1st Test)

At Harare Sports Club, on 29, 30 April, 1 May 2021.
Toss: Zimbabwe. Result: **PAKISTAN** won by an innings and 116 runs.
Debuts: Zimbabwe – R.Kaia, R.Ngarava, M.Shumba; Pakistan – Sajid Khan.

ZIMBABWE

P.S.Masvaure	c Butt b Afridi	11		absent hurt	–
K.T.Kasuza	b Hasan	0	(1)	lbw b Hasan	28
T.K.Musakanda	b Nauman	14	(2)	run out	43
*B.R.M.Taylor	c Ashraf b Hasan	5		c Hasan b Nauman	29
M.Shumba	run out	27	(3)	c Rizwan b Nauman	4
R.Kaia	lbw b Hasan	48	(5)	lbw b Ashraf	0
†R.W.Chakabva	c Butt b Hasan	19	(6)	not out	14
D.T.Tiripano	not out	28	(7)	b Hasan	2
T.S.Chisoro	b Afridi	9	(8)	c Butt b Hasan	0
B.Muzarabani	b Afridi	14	(9)	b Hasan	2
R.Ngarava	b Afridi	1	(10)	b Hasan	5
Extras		–		(B 2, LB 5)	7
Total	**(59.1 overs; 249 mins)**	**176**		**(46.2 overs)**	**134**

PAKISTAN

Imran Butt	c Chakabva b Ngarava	91
Abid Ali	c Taylor b Chisoro	60
Azhar Ali	c Musakanda b Tiripano	36
*Babar Azam	c Kaia b Tiripano	0
Fawad Alam	c Chakabva b Muzarabani	140
†Mohammad Rizwan	b Muzarabani	45
Faheem Ashraf	c Chisoro b Tiripano	0
Hasan Ali	c Chakabva b Muzarabani	30
Nauman Ali	c Musakanda b Muzarabani	0
Sajid Khan	c Chakabva b Ngarava	7
Shaheen Shah Afridi	not out	4
Extras	(B 1, LB 3, NB 8, W 1)	13
Total	**(133 overs; 559 mins)**	**426**

PAKISTAN	*O*	*M*	*R*	*W*		*O*	*M*	*R*	*W*
Shaheen Shah Afridi	15.1	5	43	4		11	1	35	0
Hasan Ali	15	2	53	4		12.2	2	36	5
Nauman Ali	11	2	29	1	(4)	9	1	27	2
Faheem Ashraf	7	3	14	0	(3)	10	2	22	1
Sajid Khan	11	1	37	0		4	0	7	0
ZIMBABWE									
Muzarabani	31	8	73	4					
Ngarava	29	4	104	2					
Chisoro	34	7	89	1					
Tiripano	23	6	89	3					
Shumba	9	3	29	0					
Kaia	7	0	38	0					

FALL OF WICKETS

	Z	P	Z
Wkt	*1st*	*1st*	*2nd*
1st	0	115	48
2nd	18	176	68
3rd	30	182	92
4th	30	226	95
5th	89	333	117
6th	124	334	124
7th	127	395	124
8th	141	395	128
9th	164	412	134
10th	176	426	–

Umpires: M.Erasmus (*South Africa*) (65) and L.Rusere (*Zimbabwe*) (1).
Referee: A.J.Pycroft (*Zimbabwe*) (79). **Test No. 2419/18 (Z113/P436)**

ZIMBABWE v PAKISTAN (2nd Test)

At Harare Sports Club, on 7, 8, 9, 10 May 2021.
Toss: Pakistan. Result: **PAKISTAN** won by an innings and 147 runs.
Debuts: Zimbabwe – L.M.Jongwe; Pakistan – Tabish Khan.

PAKISTAN

Imran Butt	c Tiripano b Ngarava	2
Abid Ali	not out	215
Azhar Ali	c Shumba b Muzarabani	126
*Babar Azam	c Kasuza b Muzarabani	2
Fawad Alam	b Muzarabani	5
Sajid Khan	c Chakabva b Tiripano	20
†Mohammad Rizwan	c Ngarava b Chisoro	21
Hasan Ali	c Chakabva b Jongwe	0
Nauman Ali	st Chakabva b Chisoro	97
Tabish Khan		
Shaheen Shah Afridi		
Extras	(B 7, LB 8, NB 2, W 5)	22
Total	**(8 wkts dec; 147.1 overs; 637 mins)**	**510**

ZIMBABWE

K.T.Kasuza	b Hasan	4		b Nauman	22
T.K.Musakanda	lbw b Tabish	0		c Rizwan b Afridi	8
†R.W.Chakabva	c Abid b Hasan	33		c Azam b Nauman	80
*B.R.M.Taylor	c Rizwan b Afridi	9		c Rizwan b Afridi	49
M.Shumba	lbw b Sajid	2		c Butt b Nauman	16
T.S.Chisoro	c Butt b Hasan	1	(9)	b Afridi	8
L.M.Jongwe	b Hasan	19	(6)	c Rizwan b Afridi	37
D.T.Tiripano	c sub (Saud Shakil) b Sajid	23	(7)	lbw b Nauman	0
R.Kaia	c Azhar b Hasan	11	(8)	c Sajid b Nauman	0
R.Ngarava	not out	15		b Afridi	0
B.Muzarabani	run out	7		not out	4
Extras	(B 4, LB 3, W 1)	8		(B 1, LB 5, NB 1)	7
Total	**(60.4 overs; 258 mins)**	**132**		**(68 overs; 299 mins)**	**231**

ZIMBABWE	*O*	*M*	*R*	*W*		*O*	*M*	*R*	*W*
Muzarabani	29	6	82	3					
Ngarava	24	5	58	1					
Jongwe	17	1	68	1					
Tiripano	22	5	83	1					
Chisoro	40.1	7	131	2					
Shumba	15	1	73	0					
PAKISTAN									
Shaheen Shah Afridi	14	4	34	1		20	5	52	5
Tabish Khan	15	8	22	1		11	3	46	0
Hasan Ali	13	4	27	5		10	7	9	0
Nauman Ali	6	3	3	0	(5)	21	3	86	5
Sajid Khan	12.4	6	39	2	(4)	6	1	32	0

FALL OF WICKETS

	P	Z	Z
Wkt	*1st*	*1st*	*2nd*
1st	12	0	13
2nd	248	23	63
3rd	252	40	142
4th	264	47	170
5th	303	53	188
6th	340	68	196
7th	341	77	196
8th	510	108	205
9th	–	110	205
10th	–	132	231

Umpires: M.Erasmus (*South Africa*) (66) and L.Rusere (*Zimbabwe*) (2).
Referee: A.J.Pycroft (*Zimbabwe*) (80). **Test No. 2420/19 (Z114/P437)**

ENGLAND v NEW ZEALAND (1st Test)

At Lord's London, on 2, 3, 4 (*no play*), 5, 6 June 2021.
Toss: New Zealand. Result: **MATCH DRAWN**.
Debuts: England – J.R.Bracey, O.E.Robinson; New Zealand – D.P.Conway.

NEW ZEALAND

T.W.M.Latham	b Robinson	23		lbw b Broad	36
D.P.Conway	run out	200		b Robinson	23
*K.S.Williamson	b Anderson	13		lbw b Robinson	1
L.R.P.L.Taylor	lbw b Robinson	14	(5)	c Bracey b Wood	33
H.M.Nicholls	c Robinson b Wood	61	(6)	c Burns b Root	23
†B.J.Watling	c Sibley b Wood	1	(7)	not out	15
C.de Grandhomme	lbw b Robinson	0	(8)	not out	9
M.J.Santner	c Anderson b Wood	0			
K.A.Jamieson	c Crawley b Robinson	9			
T.G.Southee	c Bracey b Anderson	8			
N.Wagner	not out	25	(4)	c Bracey b Robinson	10
Extras	(B 7, LB 15, NB 2)	24		(B 6, LB 12, NB 1)	19
Total	**(122.4 overs; 578 mins)**	**378**		**(6 wkts dec; 52.3 overs)**	**169**

ENGLAND

R.J.Burns	c Watling b Southee	132	c Southee b Wagner	25
D.P.Sibley	lbw b Jamieson	0	not out	60
Z.Crawley	c Watling b Southee	2	c Nicholls b Southee	2
*J.E.Root	c Taylor b Jamieson	42	lbw b Wagner	40
O.J.D.Pope	lbw b Southee	22	not out	20
D.W.Lawrence	c de Grandhomme b Southee	0		
†J.R.Bracey	b Southee	0		
O.E.Robinson	c Jamieson b Southee	42		
M.A.Wood	c Watling b Jamieson	0		
S.C.J.Broad	b Wagner	10		
J.M.Anderson	not out	8		
Extras	(B 4, LB 4, NB 8, W 1)	17	(B 8, LB 10, NB 5)	23
Total	**(101.1 overs; 477 mins)**	**275**	**(3 wkts; 70 overs; 312 mins)**	**170**

ENGLAND	*O*	*M*	*R*	*W*		*O*	*M*	*R*	*W*
Anderson	28	7	83	2		15.3	3	44	0
Broad	27	5	79	0		12	1	34	1
Robinson	28	6	75	4		14	5	26	3
Wood	27	8	81	3		7	0	31	1
Root	12.4	1	38	0		4	0	16	1
NEW ZEALAND									
Southee	25.1	8	43	6		17	1	37	1
Jamieson	26	8	85	3		15	6	28	0
De Grandhomme	15	5	24	0		7	3	12	0
Wagner	24	3	83	1	(5)	16	7	27	2
Santner	10	4	30	0	(4)	13	3	38	0
Williamson	1	0	2	0		2	0	10	0

FALL OF WICKETS

Wkt	NZ *1st*	E *1st*	NZ *2nd*	E *2nd*
1st	58	4	39	49
2nd	86	18	57	56
3rd	114	111	74	136
4th	288	140	105	–
5th	292	140	133	–
6th	293	140	159	–
7th	294	203	–	–
8th	317	207	–	–
9th	338	223	–	–
10th	378	275	–	–

Umpires: M.A.Gough (*England*) (19) and R.A.Kettleborough (*England*) (69).
Referee: B.C.Broad (*England*) (107). **Test No. 2421/106 (E1035/NZ447)**

ENGLAND v NEW ZEALAND (2nd Test)

At Edgbaston, Birmingham, on 10, 11, 12, 13 June 2021.
Toss: England. Result: **NEW ZEALAND** won by eight wickets.
Debuts: None.

ENGLAND

R.J.Burns	c Latham b Boult	81	c Latham b Henry	0
D.P.Sibley	c Blundell b Henry	35	c Mitchell b Henry	8
Z.Crawley	c Mitchell b Wagner	0	lbw b Henry	17
*J.E.Root	c Blundell b Henry	4	c Blundell b Patel	11
O.J.D.Pope	c Blundell b Patel	19	lbw b Wagner	23
D.W.Lawrence	not out	81	c Blundell b Wagner	0
†J.R.Bracey	c Mitchell b Boult	0	b Patel	8
O.P.Stone	lbw b Patel	20	c Blundell b Boult	15
M.A.Wood	b Henry	41	c Blundell b Wagner	29
S.C.J.Broad	c Blundell b Boult	0	b Boult	1
J.M.Anderson	lbw b Boult	4	not out	0
Extras	(B 5, LB 10, NB 2, W 1)	18	(B 5, LB 4, NB 1)	10
Total	**(101 overs)**	**303**	**(41.1 overs)**	**122**

NEW ZEALAND

*T.W.M.Latham	lbw b Broad	6	not out	23
D.P.Conway	c Crawley b Broad	80	c Bracey b Broad	3
W.A.Young	c Pope b Lawrence	82	b Stone	8
L.R.P.L.Taylor	c Bracey b Stone	80	not out	0
H.M.Nicholls	c Bracey b Root	21		
†T.A.Blundell	c Root b Broad	34		
D.J.Mitchell	c Crawley b Stone	6		
N.Wagner	b Anderson	0		
M.J.Henry	lbw b Wood	12		
A.Y.Patel	lbw b Broad	20		
T.A.Boult	not out	12		
Extras	(B 13, LB 21, NB 1)	35	(B 4, NB 2, W 1)	7
Total	**(119.1 overs)**	**388**	**(2 wkts; 10.5 overs; 52 mins)**	**41**

NEW ZEALAND	*O*	*M*	*R*	*W*		*O*	*M*	*R*	*W*
Boult	29	6	85	4	(2)	10.1	2	34	2
Henry	26	7	78	3	(1)	12	2	36	3
Wagner	21	6	68	1		10	1	18	3
Mitchell	11	2	23	0					
Patel	14	4	34	2	(4)	9	4	25	2
ENGLAND									
Anderson	29	9	68	1		5	1	11	0
Broad	23.1	8	48	4		4	1	13	1
Wood	25	3	85	2	(4)	0.5	0	8	0
Stone	24	5	92	2	(3)	1	0	5	1
Root	15	3	45	0					
Lawrence	3	0	16	1					

FALL OF WICKETS

	E	NZ	E	NZ
Wkt	*1st*	*1st*	*2nd*	*2nd*
1st	72	15	0	6
2nd	73	137	17	33
3rd	85	229	30	–
4th	127	292	58	–
5th	169	312	58	–
6th	175	335	71	–
7th	222	336	76	–
8th	288	353	120	–
9th	289	361	121	–
10th	303	388	122	–

Umpires: R.K.Illingworth (*England*) (54) and R.A.Kettleborough (*England*) (70).
Referee: B.C.Broad (*England*) (108). **Test No. 2422/107 (E1036/NZ448)**

WEST INDIES v SOUTH AFRICA (1st Test)

At Daren Sammy National Cricket Stadium, Gros Islet, St Lucia, on 10, 11, 12 June 2021.
Toss: West Indies. Result: **SOUTH AFRICA** won by an innings and 63 runs.
Debuts: West Indies – J.N.T.Seales; South Africa – K.D.Petersen, K.Verreynne.

WEST INDIES

*K.C.Brathwaite	b Nortje	15		lbw b Rabada	7
S.D.Hope	b Nortje	15	(3)	c Mulder b Nortje	12
N.E.Bonner	c de Kock b Rabada	10			
R.L.Chase	c Markram b Ngidi	8		b Maharaj	62
K.R.Mayers	c van der Dussen b Nortje	1		c Mulder b Nortje	12
J.Blackwood	c Petersen b Nortje	1		c van der Dussen b Rabada	13
J.O.Holder	c Markram b Ngidi	20		b Maharaj	4
†J.Da Silva	c Mulder b Ngidi	0		b Rabada	9
R.R.S.Cornwall	c Markram b Ngidi	13		c van der Dussen b Rabada	0
K.A.J.Roach	c de Kock b Ngidi	1		not out	13
J.N.T.Seales	not out	0		c Mulder b Nortje	3
K.O.A.Powell			(2)	lbw b Rabada	14
Extras	(LB 4, NB 3, W 6)	13		(B 8, LB 2, NB 2, W 1)	13
Total	**(40.5 overs)**	**97**		**(64 overs)**	**162**

SOUTH AFRICA

*D.Elgar	c Blackwood b Roach	0
A.K.Markram	c Da Silva b Seales	60
K.D.Petersen	c Holder b Seales	19
H.E.van der Dussen	c Hope b Holder	46
K.Verreynne	c Da Silva b Seales	6
†Q.de Kock	not out	141
P.W.A.Mulder	c Da Silva b Holder	25
K.A.Maharaj	c Powell b Cornwall	0
K.Rabada	c Holder b Roach	4
A.A.Nortje	c Hope b Holder	7
L.T.Ngidi	c Da Silva b Holder	0
Extras	(B 4, LB 1, NB 6, W 3)	14
Total	**(96.5 overs)**	**322**

SOUTH AFRICA	*O*	*M*	*R*	*W*		*O*	*M*	*R*	*W*
Rabada	10	2	24	1		20	9	34	5
Ngidi	13.5	7	19	5		13	3	31	0
Nortje	11	3	35	4		14	5	46	3
Maharaj	4	3	6	0	(5)	11	5	23	2
Mulder	2	0	9	0	(4)	6	1	18	0
WEST INDIES									
Roach	20	3	64	2					
Holder	20.5	4	75	4					
Seales	21	6	75	3					
Mayers	8	2	28	0					
Cornwall	18	1	61	1					
Chase	9	5	14	0					

FALL OF WICKETS

	WI	SA	WI
Wkt	*1st*	*1st*	*2nd*
1st	24	0	12
2nd	31	34	25
3rd	45	113	37
4th	46	119	51
5th	56	162	97
6th	56	215	125
7th	56	222	140
8th	74	233	141
9th	80	312	146
10th	97	322	162

Umpires: G.O.Brathwaite (*West Indies*) (3) and J.S.Wilson (*West Indies*) (22).
Referee: Sir R.B.Richardson (*West Indies*) (32). **Test No. 2423/29 (WI555/SA444)**
K.O.A.Powell replaced N.E.Bonner at the start of the South Africa innings (concussion substitute).

WEST INDIES v SOUTH AFRICA (2nd Test)

At Daren Sammy National Cricket Stadium, Gros Islet, St Lucia, on 18, 19, 20, 21 June 2021.
Toss: West Indies. Result: **SOUTH AFRICA** won by 158 runs.
Debuts: None.

SOUTH AFRICA

*D.Elgar	b Mayers	77	(2)	c Holder b Roach	10
A.K.Markram	c Chase b Gabriel	0	(1)	c Holder b Roach	4
K.D.Petersen	c Holder b Seales	7		b Mayers	18
H.E.van der Dussen	b Roach	4		not out	75
K.Verreynne	c Da Silva b Gabriel	27		c Da Silva b Mayers	6
†Q.de Kock	c Hope b Mayers	96		c Da Silva b Holder	0
P.W.A.Mulder	c Da Silva b Roach	8		c Hope b Mayers	0
K.A.Maharaj	c Da Silva b Holder	12		c Holder b Seales	6
K.Rabada	not out	21		c sub (D.M.Bravo) b Roach	40
A.A.Nortje	c Seales b Mayers	1		c Da Silva b Roach	3
L.T.Ngidi	c sub (D.M.Bravo) b Roach	1		st Da Silva b Brathwaite	6
Extras	(B 9, LB 20, NB 3, W 12)	44		(B 1, LB 1, W 4)	6
Total	**(112.4 overs)**	**298**		**(53 overs)**	**174**

WEST INDIES

*K.C.Brathwaite	c de Kock b Rabada	0		c Elgar b Rabada	6
K.O.A.Powell	lbw b Ngidi	5		c Nortje b Maharaj	51
S.D.Hope	b Ngidi	43		c Markram b Rabada	2
R.L.Chase	c Verreynne b Nortje	4		absent hurt	
K.R.Mayers	c Markram b Maharaj	12	(4)	c Elgar b Rabada	34
J.Blackwood	c Elgar b Maharaj	49	(5)	c de Kock b Ngidi	25
J.O.Holder	c Petersen b Rabada	10	(6)	c Petersen b Maharaj	0
†J.Da Silva	c de Kock b Mulder	7	(7)	c Mulder b Maharaj	0
K.A.J.Roach	c de Kock b Mulder	1	(8)	c Ngidi b Maharaj	27
J.N.T.Seales	c Verreynne b Mulder	0	(9)	c Nortje b Maharaj	7
S.T.Gabriel	not out	0	(10)	not out	2
Extras	(B 6, LB 3, NB 4, W 5)	18		(B 4, LB 3, NB 2, W 2)	11
Total	**(54 overs)**	**149**		**(58.3 overs)**	**165**

WEST INDIES	*O*	*M*	*R*	*W*		*O*	*M*	*R*	*W*
Roach	21.4	6	45	3		13	1	52	4
Gabriel	16	4	65	2		6	0	28	0
Seales	19	4	44	1		11	3	34	1
Holder	21	5	47	1	(5)	11	2	24	1
Chase	15	4	26	0					
Mayers	15	6	28	3	(4)	9	2	24	3
Brathwaite	5	0	14	0	(6)	3	0	10	1
SOUTH AFRICA									
Rabada	13	6	24	2		16	3	44	3
Ngidi	7	0	27	2		10	2	29	1
Nortje	12	0	41	1	(4)	11	3	35	0
Maharaj	18	2	47	2	(3)	17.3	7	36	5
Mulder	4	3	1	3		4	0	14	0

FALL OF WICKETS

	SA	WI	SA	WI
Wkt	*1st*	*1st*	*2nd*	*2nd*
1st	1	0	4	16
2nd	26	8	33	26
3rd	37	30	44	90
4th	124	54	52	107
5th	203	97	53	107
6th	239	115	54	107
7th	275	143	73	147
8th	275	145	143	158
9th	281	145	152	165
10th	298	149	174	–

Umpires: G.O.Brathwaite (*West Indies*) (4) and J.S.Wilson (*West Indies*) (23).
Referee: Sir R.B.Richardson (*West Indies*) (33). **Test No. 2424/30 (WI556/SA445)**

INDIA v NEW ZEALAND (Only Test – ICC Final)

At The Rose Bowl, Southampton, on 18 (*no play*), 19, 20, 21 (*no play*), 22, 23 June 2021.
Toss: New Zealand. Result: **NEW ZEALAND** won by eight wickets.
Debuts: None.

INDIA

R.G.Sharma	c Southee b Jamieson	34		lbw b Southee	30
S.Gill	c Watling b Wagner	28		lbw b Southee	8
C.A.Pujara	lbw b Boult	8		c Taylor b Jamieson	15
*V.Kohli	lbw b Jamieson	44		c Watling b Jamieson	13
A.M.Rahane	c Latham b Wagner	49		c Watling b Boult	15
†R.R.Pant	c Latham b Jamieson	4		c Nicholls b Boult	41
R.A.Jadeja	c Watling b Boult	15		c Watling b Wagner	16
R.Ashwin	c Latham b Southee	22		c Taylor b Boult	7
I.Sharma	c Taylor b Jamieson	4	(10)	not out	1
J.J.Bumrah	lbw b Jamieson	0	(11)	c Latham b Southee	0
Mohammed Shami	not out	4	(9)	c Latham b Southee	13
Extras	(LB 3, NB 2)	5		(B 1, LB 8, NB 1, W 1)	11
Total	**(92.1 overs)**	**217**		**(73 overs)**	**170**

NEW ZEALAND

T.W.M.Latham	c Kohli b Ashwin	30	st Pant b Ashwin	9
D.P.Conway	c Shami b I.Sharma	54	lbw b Ashwin	19
*K.S.Williamson	c Kohli b I.Sharma	49	not out	52
L.R.P.L.Taylor	c Gill b Shami	11	not out	47
H.M.Nicholls	c R.G.Sharma b I.Sharma	7		
†B.J.Watling	b Shami	1		
C.de Grandhomme	lbw b Shami	13		
K.A.Jamieson	c Bumrah b Shami	21		
T.G.Southee	b Jadeja	30		
N.Wagner	c Rahane b Ashwin	0		
T.A.Boult	not out	7		
Extras	(B 4, LB 16, NB 6)	26	(LB 11, NB 2)	13
Total	**(99.2 overs)**	**249**	**(2 wkts; 45.5 overs)**	**140**

NEW ZEALAND	*O*	*M*	*R*	*W*		*O*	*M*	*R*	*W*
Southee	22	6	64	1		19	4	48	4
Boult	21.1	4	47	2		15	2	39	3
Jamieson	22	12	31	5		24	10	30	2
De Grandhomme	12	6	32	0					
Wagner	15	5	40	2	(4)	15	2	44	1
INDIA									
I.Sharma	25	9	48	3		6.2	2	21	0
Bumrah	26	9	57	0	(3)	10.4	2	35	0
Mohammed Shami	26	8	76	4	(2)	10.5	3	31	0
Ashwin	15	5	28	2		10	5	17	2
Jadeja	7.2	2	20	1		8	1	25	0

FALL OF WICKETS

	I	NZ	I	NZ
Wkt	*1st*	*1st*	*2nd*	*2nd*
1st	62	70	24	33
2nd	63	101	51	44
3rd	88	117	71	–
4th	149	134	72	–
5th	156	135	109	–
6th	182	162	142	–
7th	205	192	156	–
8th	213	221	156	–
9th	213	234	170	–
10th	217	249	170	–

Umpires: M.A.Gough (*England*) (20) and R.K.Illingworth (*England*) (55).
Referee: B.C.Broad (*England*) (109). **Test No. 2425/50 (I551/NZ449)**

ZIMBABWE v BANGLADESH (Only Test)

At Harare Sports Club, on 7, 8, 9, 10, 11 July 2021.
Toss: Bangladesh. Result: **BANGLADESH** won by 220 runs.
Debuts: Zimbabwe – T.Kaitano, D.N.Myers.

BANGLADESH

Saif Hasan	b Muzarabani	0	(2)	c Myers b Ngarava	43
Shadman Islam	c Taylor b Ngarava	23	(1)	not out	115
Nazmul Hossain	c Myers b Muzarabani	2	(3)	not out	117
*Mominul Haque	c Myers b Nyauchi	70			
Mushfiqur Rahim	lbw b Muzarabani	11			
Shakib Al Hasan	c Chakabva b Nyauchi	3			
†Liton Das	c Nyauchi b Tiripano	95			
Mahmudullah	not out	150			
Mehedi Hasan	lbw b Tiripano	0			
Taskin Ahmed	b Shumba	75			
Ebadat Hossain	lbw b Muzarabani	0			
Extras	(B 10, LB 11, NB 16, W 2)	39		(B 1, NB 3, W 5)	9
Total	**(126 overs; 665 mins)**	**468**		**(1 wkt dec; 67.4 overs; 259 mins)**	**284**

ZIMBABWE

M.Shumba	lbw b Shakib	41		c sub (Yasir Ali) b Taskin	11
T.Kaitano	c Liton b Mehedi	87		lbw b Shakib	7
*B.R.M.Taylor	c sub (Yasir Ali) b Mehedi	81		c and b Mehedi	92
D.N.Myers	c Mehedi b Shakib	27		c Shadman b Mehedi	26
T.H.Maruma	lbw b Shakib	0	(6)	lbw b Mehedi	0
R.Kaia	c Liton b Taskin	0	(7)	lbw b Taskin	0
†R.W.Chakabva	not out	31	(8)	b Taskin	1
D.T.Tiripano	lbw b Mehedi	2	(5)	c Liton b Ebadat	52
V.M.Nyauchi	b Mehedi	0		c Shakib b Taskin	10
B.Muzarabani	b Mehedi	2		not out	30
R.Ngarava	c Nazmul b Shakib	0		b Mehedi	10
Extras	(B 3, LB 2)	5		(B 5, LB 11, NB 1)	17
Total	**(111.5 overs; 494 mins)**	**276**		**(94.4 overs; 415 mins)**	**256**

ZIMBABWE	*O*	*M*	*R*	*W*		*O*	*M*	*R*	*W*
Muzarabani	29	4	94	4		12	4	27	0
Ngarava	23	5	83	1		9	0	36	1
Tiripano	23	5	58	2		11	2	33	0
Nyauchi	17	1	92	2		10	1	36	0
Myers	3	1	13	0					
Shumba	21	4	64	1	(5)	12.4	0	67	0
Kaia	10	0	43	0	(6)	13	2	84	0
BANGLADESH									
Taskin Ahmed	24	10	46	1	(3)	24	4	82	4
Ebadat Hossain	21	8	58	0	(4)	11	2	39	1
Shakib Al Hasan	34.5	10	82	4	(1)	25	9	44	1
Mehedi Hasan	31	5	82	5	(2)	30.4	10	66	4
Mominul Haque	1	0	3	0					
Mahmudullah					(5)	4	0	9	0

FALL OF WICKETS

	B	Z	B	Z
Wkt	*1st*	*1st*	*2nd*	*2nd*
1st	4	61	88	15
2nd	8	176	–	110
3rd	68	225	–	132
4th	106	228	–	159
5th	109	229	–	159
6th	132	261	–	160
7th	270	263	–	164
8th	270	263	–	198
9th	461	269	–	239
10th	468	276	–	256

Umpires: M.Erasmus (South Africa) (67) and L.Rusere (Zimbabwe) (3).
Referee: A.J.Pycroft (Zimbabwe) (81). Test No. 2426/18 (Z115/B124)

ENGLAND v INDIA (1st Test)

At Trent Bridge, Nottingham, on 4, 5, 6, 7, 8 (*no play*) August 2021.
Toss: England. Result: **MATCH DRAWN.**
Debuts: None.

ENGLAND

R.J.Burns	lbw b Bumrah	0	c Pant b Siraj	18
D.P.Sibley	c Rahul b Shami	18	c Pant b Bumrah	28
Z.Crawley	c Pant b Siraj	27	c Pant b Bumrah	6
*J.E.Root	lbw b Thakur	64	c Pant b Bumrah	109
J.M.Bairstow	lbw b Shami	29	c Jadeja b Siraj	30
D.W.Lawrence	c Pant b Shami	0	lbw b Thakur	25
†J.C.Buttler	c Pant b Bumrah	0	b Thakur	17
S.M.Curran	not out	27	c Siraj b Bumrah	32
O.E.Robinson	c Shami b Thakur	0	c Rahane b Shami	15
S.C.J.Broad	lbw b Bumrah	4	b Bumrah	0
J.M.Anderson	b Bumrah	1	not out	0
Extras	(B 1, LB 8, NB 4)	13	(B 5, LB 2, NB 10, W 6)	23
Total	**(65.4 overs; 323 mins)**	**183**	**(85.5 overs; 400 mins)**	**303**

INDIA

R.G.Sharma	c Curran b Robinson	36	(2) not out	12
K.L.Rahul	c Buttler b Anderson	84	(1) c Buttler b Broad	26
C.A.Pujara	c Buttler b Anderson	4	not out	12
*V.Kohli	c Buttler b Anderson	0		
A.M.Rahane	run out	5		
†R.R.Pant	c Bairstow b Robinson	25		
R.A.Jadeja	c Broad b Robinson	56		
S.M.Thakur	c Root b Anderson	0		
Mohammed Shami	b Robinson	13		
J.J.Bumrah	c Broad b Robinson	28		
M.Siraj	not out	7		
Extras	(B 7, LB 5, NB 8)	20	(LB 1, NB 1)	2
Total	**(84.5 overs; 456 mins)**	**278**	**(1 wkt; 14 overs; 99 mins)**	**52**

INDIA	*O*	*M*	*R*	*W*		*O*	*M*	*R*	*W*
Bumrah	20.4	4	46	4		19	2	64	5
Mohammed Shami	17	2	28	3	(3)	15.5	1	72	1
Siraj	12	2	48	1	(2)	25	3	84	2
Thakur	13	3	41	2		13	1	37	2
Jadeja	3	0	11	0		13	3	39	0
ENGLAND									
Anderson	23	8	54	4		5	1	12	0
Broad	20	3	70	0		5	1	18	1
Robinson	26.5	6	85	5		4	0	21	0
Curran	15	2	57	0					

FALL OF WICKETS

	E	I	E	I
Wkt	*1st*	*1st*	*2nd*	*2nd*
1st	0	97	37	34
2nd	42	104	46	–
3rd	66	104	135	–
4th	138	112	177	–
5th	138	145	211	–
6th	145	205	237	–
7th	155	205	274	–
8th	155	232	295	–
9th	160	245	295	–
10th	183	278	303	–

Umpires: M.A.Gough (*England*) (21) and R.A.Kettleborough (*England*) (71).
Referee: B.C.Broad (*England*) (110). **Test No. 2427/127 (E1037/I552)**

ENGLAND v INDIA (2nd Test)

At Lord's, London, on 12, 13, 14, 15, 16 August 2021.
Toss: England. Result: **INDIA** won by 151 runs.
Debuts: None.

INDIA

R.G.Sharma	b Anderson	83	(2)	c Ali b Wood	21
K.L.Rahul	c Sibley b Robinson	129	(1)	c Buttler b Wood	5
C.A.Pujara	c Bairstow b Anderson	9		c Root b Wood	45
*V.Kohli	c Root b Robinson	42		c Buttler b Curran	20
A.M.Rahane	c Root b Anderson	1		c Buttler b Ali	61
†R.R.Pant	c Buttler b Wood	37		c Buttler b Robinson	22
R.A.Jadeja	c Anderson b Wood	40		b Ali	3
Mohammed Shami	c Burns b Ali	0	(9)	not out	56
I.Sharma	lbw b Anderson	8	(8)	lbw b Robinson	16
J.J.Bumrah	c Buttler b Anderson	0		not out	34
M.Siraj	not out	0			
Extras	(B 8, LB 5, NB 2)	15		(B 2, LB 12, NB 1)	15
Total	**(126.1 overs)**	**364**		**(8 wkts; 109.3 overs)**	**298**

ENGLAND

R.J.Burns	lbw b Shami	49	c Siraj b Bumrah	0
D.P.Sibley	c Rahul b Siraj	11	c Pant b Shami	0
H.Hameed	b Siraj	0	lbw b I.Sharma	9
*J.E.Root	not out	180	c Kohli b Bumrah	33
J.M.Bairstow	c Kohli b Siraj	57	lbw b I.Sharma	2
†J.C.Buttler	b I.Sharma	23	c Pant b Siraj	25
M.M.Ali	c Kohli b I.Sharma	27	c Kohli b Siraj	13
S.M.Curran	c R.G.Sharma b I.Sharma	0	c Pant b Siraj	0
O.E.Robinson	lbw b Siraj	6	lbw b Bumrah	9
M.A.Wood	run out	5	not out	0
J.M.Anderson	b Shami	0	b Siraj	0
Extras	(B 5, LB 6, NB 17, W 5)	33	(B 17, LB 7, NB 4, W 1)	29
Total	**(128 overs)**	**391**	**(51.5 overs)**	**120**

ENGLAND	*O*	*M*	*R*	*W*		*O*	*M*	*R*	*W*
Anderson	29	7	62	5		25.3	6	53	0
Robinson	33	10	73	2		17	6	45	2
Curran	22	2	72	0	(4)	18	3	42	1
Wood	24.1	2	91	2	(3)	18	4	51	3
Ali	18	1	53	1		26	1	84	2
Root						5	0	9	0
INDIA									
I.Sharma	24	4	69	3	(5)	10	3	13	2
Bumrah	26	6	79	0	(1)	15	3	33	3
Mohammed Shami	26	3	95	2	(2)	10	5	13	1
Siraj	30	7	94	4		10.5	3	32	4
Jadeja	22	1	43	0	(3)	6	3	5	0

FALL OF WICKETS

	I	E	I	E
Wkt	*1st*	*1st*	*2nd*	*2nd*
1st	126	23	18	1
2nd	150	23	27	1
3rd	267	108	55	44
4th	278	229	155	67
5th	282	283	167	67
6th	331	341	175	90
7th	336	341	194	90
8th	362	357	209	120
9th	364	371	–	120
10th	364	391	–	120

Umpires: M.A.Gough (*England*) (22) and R.K.Illingworth (*England*) (56).
Referee: B.C.Broad (*England*) (111). **Test No. 2428/128 (E1038/I553)**

ENGLAND v INDIA (3rd Test)

At Headingley, Leeds, on 25, 26, 27, 28 August 2021.
Toss: India. Result: **ENGLAND** won by an innings and 76 runs.
Debuts: None.

INDIA

R.G.Sharma	c Robinson b Overton	19	lbw b Robinson	59
K.L.Rahul	c Buttler b Anderson	0	c Bairstow b Overton	8
C.A.Pujara	c Buttler b Anderson	1	lbw b Robinson	91
*V.Kohli	c Buttler b Anderson	7	c Root b Robinson	55
A.M.Rahane	c Buttler b Robinson	18	c Buttler b Anderson	10
†R.R.Pant	c Buttler b Robinson	2	c Overton b Robinson	1
R.A.Jadeja	lbw b Curran	4	c Buttler b Overton	30
Mohammed Shami	c Burns b Overton	0	b Ali	6
I.Sharma	not out	8	c Buttler b Robinson	2
J.J.Bumrah	lbw b Curran	0	not out	1
M.Siraj	c Root b Overton	3	c Bairstow b Overton	0
Extras	(LB 11, NB 5)	16	(B 4, LB 4, NB 5, W 2)	15
Total	**(40.4 overs)**	**78**	**(99.3 overs)**	**278**

ENGLAND

R.J.Burns	b Shami	61
H.Hameed	b Jadeja	68
D.J.Malan	c Pant b Siraj	70
*J.E.Root	b Bumrah	121
J.M.Bairstow	c Kohli b Shami	29
†J.C.Buttler	c I.Sharma b Shami	7
M.M.Ali	c sub (A.R.Patel) b Jadeja	8
S.M.Curran	c sub (M.A.Agarwal) b Siraj	15
C.Overton	lbw b Shami	32
O.E.Robinson	b Bumrah	0
J.M.Anderson	not out	0
Extras	(B 8, LB 4, NB 8, W 1)	21
Total	**(132.2 overs)**	**432**

ENGLAND	*O*	*M*	*R*	*W*		*O*	*M*	*R*	*W*
Anderson	8	5	6	3		26	11	63	1
Robinson	10	3	16	2		26	6	65	5
Curran	10	2	27	2	(4)	9	1	40	0
Ali	2	0	4	0	(5)	14	1	40	1
Overton	10.4	5	14	3	(3)	18.3	6	47	3
Root						6	1	15	0
INDIA									
I.Sharma	22	0	92	0					
Bumrah	27.2	10	59	2					
Mohammed Shami	28	8	95	4					
Siraj	23	3	86	2					
Jadeja	32	8	88	2					

FALL OF WICKETS

	I	E	I
Wkt	*1st*	*1st*	*2nd*
1st	1	135	34
2nd	4	159	116
3rd	21	298	215
4th	56	350	237
5th	58	360	239
6th	67	383	239
7th	67	383	254
8th	67	418	257
9th	67	431	278
10th	78	432	278

Umpires: R.A.Kettleborough (*England*) (72) and A.G.Wharf (*England*) (1).
Referee: B.C.Broad (*England*) (112). **Test No. 2429/129 (E1039/I554)**

ENGLAND v INDIA (4th Test)

At The Oval, London, on 2, 3, 4, 5, 6 September 2021.
Toss: England. Result: **INDIA** won by 157 runs.
Debuts: None.

INDIA

R.G.Sharma	c Bairstow b Woakes	11		c Woakes b Robinson	127
K.L.Rahul	lbw b Robinson	17		c Bairstow b Anderson	46
C.A.Pujara	c Bairstow b Anderson	4		c Ali b Robinson	61
*V.Kohli	c Bairstow b Robinson	50		c Overton b Ali	44
R.A.Jadeja	c Root b Woakes	10		lbw b Woakes	17
A.M.Rahane	c Ali b Overton	14		lbw b Woakes	0
†R.R.Pant	c Ali b Woakes	9		c and b Ali	50
S.N.Thakur	lbw b Woakes	57		c Overton b Root	60
U.T.Yadav	c Bairstow b Robinson	10		c Ali b Overton	25
J.J.Bumrah	run out	0		c Ali b Woakes	24
M.Siraj	not out	1		not out	3
Extras	(LB 8)	8		(LB 7, NB 2)	9
Total	**(61.3 overs)**	**191**		**(148.2 overs)**	**466**

ENGLAND

R.J.Burns	b Bumrah	5		c Pant b Thakur	50
H.Hameed	c Pant b Bumrah	0		b Jadeja	63
D.J.Malan	c Sharma b Yadav	31		run out	5
*J.E.Root	b Yadav	21		b Thakur	36
C.Overton	c Kohli b Yadav	1	(9)	b Yadav	10
O.J.D.Pope	b Thakur	81	(5)	b Bumrah	2
†J.M.Bairstow	lbw b Siraj	37	(6)	b Bumrah	0
M.M.Ali	c Sharma b Jadeja	35	(7)	c sub (S.A.Yadav) b Jadeja	0
C.R.Woakes	run out	50	(8)	c Rahul b Yadav	18
O.E.Robinson	b Jadeja	5		not out	10
J.M.Anderson	not out	1		c Pant b Yadav	2
Extras	(B 1, LB 14, NB 8)	23		(B 2, LB 5, NB 7)	14
Total	**(84 overs)**	**290**		**(92.2 overs)**	**210**

ENGLAND	*O*	*M*	*R*	*W*		*O*	*M*	*R*	*W*
Anderson	14	3	41	1		33	10	79	1
Robinson	17.3	9	38	3		32	7	105	2
Woakes	15	6	55	4		32	8	83	3
Overton	15	2	49	1		18.2	3	58	1
Ali						26	0	118	2
Root						7	1	16	1
INDIA									
Yadav	19	2	76	3		18.2	2	60	3
Bumrah	21	6	67	2		22	9	27	2
Thakur	15	2	54	1	(5)	8	1	22	2
Siraj	12	4	42	1		14	0	44	0
Jadeja	17	1	36	2	(3)	30	11	50	2

FALL OF WICKETS

	I	E	I	E
Wkt	*1st*	*1st*	*2nd*	*2nd*
1st	28	5	83	100
2nd	28	6	236	120
3rd	39	52	237	141
4th	69	53	296	146
5th	105	62	296	146
6th	117	151	312	147
7th	127	222	412	182
8th	190	250	414	193
9th	190	255	450	202
10th	191	290	466	210

Umpires: R.K.Illingworth (*England*) (57) and A.G.Wharf (*England*) (2).
Referee: B.C.Broad (*England*) (113). **Test No. 2430/130 (E1040/I555)**

The fifth Test, scheduled for 10-14 September at Old Trafford, Manchester, was cancelled following a Covid outbreak in the Indian touring party.

WEST INDIES v PAKISTAN (1st Test)

At Sabina Park, Kingston, Jamaica, on 12, 13, 14, 15 August 2021.
Toss: West Indies. Result: **WEST INDIES** won by one wicket.
Debuts: None.

PAKISTAN

Imran Butt	b Roach	11	lbw b Roach	0
Abid Ali	c Da Silva b Seales	9	c Holder b Seales	34
Azhar Ali	c Holder b Seales	17	b Roach	23
*Babar Azam	c Da Silva b Roach	30	c Holder b Mayers	55
Fawad Alam	b Holder	56	c Da Silva b Seales	0
†Mohammad Rizwan	c Chase b Holder	23	c Da Silva b Holder	30
Faheem Ashraf	run out	44	c Da Silva b Roach	20
Yasir Shah	c Da Silva b Mayers	0	c Da Silva b Seales	4
Hasan Ali	c Mayers b Seales	14	c Roach b Seales	28
Shaheen Shah Afridi	not out	0	lbw b Seales	0
Mohammad Abbas	c Da Silva b Holder	0	not out	1
Extras	(B 4, LB 5, NB 4)	13	(B 4, LB 2, NB 2)	8
Total	**(70.3 overs)**	**217**	**(83.4 overs)**	**203**

WEST INDIES

*K.C.Brathwaite	run out	97	c Rizwan b Afridi	2
K.O.A.Powell	c Butt b Abbas	0	lbw b Afridi	4
N.E.Bonner	lbw b Abbas	0	b Afridi	5
R.L.Chase	c Rizwan b Hasan	21	c Butt b Ashraf	22
J.Blackwood	c Abbas b Afridi	22	c Butt b Hasan	55
K.R.Mayers	lbw b Afridi	0	c Butt b Ashraf	0
J.O.Holder	c Rizwan b Ashraf	58	b Hasan	16
†J.Da Silva	lbw b Afridi	21	c Rizwan b Afridi	13
K.A.J.Roach	lbw b Abbas	13	not out	30
J.A.Warrican	b Afridi	1	c Rizwan b Hasan	6
J.N.T.Seales	not out	0	not out	2
Extras	(B 3, LB 11, NB 6)	20	(B 2, LB 10, NB 1)	13
Total	**(89.4 overs)**	**253**	**(9 wkts; 56.5 overs)**	**168**

WEST INDIES	*O*	*M*	*R*	*W*		*O*	*M*	*R*	*W*
Roach	16	4	47	2		19	8	30	3
Seales	16	3	70	3		15.4	3	55	5
Mayers	14	5	28	1		15	5	33	1
Holder	15.3	3	26	3		18	6	36	1
Chase	8	1	33	0	(6)	6	2	12	0
Warrican	1	0	4	0	(5)	7	2	28	0
Brathwaite						3	1	3	0
PAKISTAN									
Mohammad Abbas	22	9	43	3		12	5	27	0
Shaheen Shah Afridi	21.4	6	59	4		17	4	50	4
Yasir Shah	13	1	46	0	(5)	3	0	13	0
Faheem Ashraf	14	6	37	1		8	1	29	2
Hasan Ali	19	4	54	1	(3)	16.5	5	37	3

FALL OF WICKETS

Wkt	P *1st*	WI *1st*	P *2nd*	WI *2nd*
1st	21	1	1	4
2nd	21	1	56	15
3rd	68	51	65	16
4th	68	100	65	84
5th	101	100	121	92
6th	186	196	168	111
7th	190	221	170	114
8th	217	249	180	142
9th	217	252	192	151
10th	217	253	203	–

Umpires: G.O.Brathwaite (*West Indies*) (5) and J.S.Wilson (*West Indies*) (24).
Referee: Sir R.B.Richardson (*West Indies*) (34). **Test No. 2431/53 (WI557/P438)**

WEST INDIES v PAKISTAN (2nd Test)

At Sabina Park, Kingston, Jamaica, on 20, 21 (*no play*), 22, 23, 24 August 2021.
Toss: West Indies. Result: **PAKISTAN** won by 109 runs.
Debuts: None.

PAKISTAN

Abid Ali	c Blackwood b Roach	1	(2) c sub (S.D.Hope) b Joseph	29
Imran Butt	c Da Silva b Seales	1	(1) c Bonner b Mayers	37
Azhar Ali	c Da Silva b Roach	0	c Blackwood b Brathwaite	22
*Babar Azam	c Holder b Roach	75	c Bonner b Joseph	33
Fawad Alam	not out	124		
†Mohammad Rizwan	lbw b Holder	31	(7) not out	10
Faheem Ashraf	lbw b Seales	26	(6) lbw b Holder	9
Nauman Ali	c Da Silva b Holder	0		
Hasan Ali	run out	9	(5) c Da Silva b Holder	17
Shaheen Shah Afridi	c Powell b Seales	19		
Mohammad Abbas	not out	0		
Extras	(B 1, LB 9, NB 6)	16	(B 5, LB 6, NB 1, W 7)	19
Total	**(9 wkts dec; 110 overs)**	**302**	**(6 wkts dec; 27.2 overs)**	**176**

WEST INDIES

*K.C.Brathwaite	b Afridi	4	c Alam b Nauman	39
K.O.A.Powell	lbw b Afridi	5	run out	23
N.E.Bonner	c Rizwan b Abbas	37	(4) lbw b Hasan	2
R.L.Chase	b Ashraf	10	(5) c Butt b Hasan	0
A.S.Joseph	c Azam b Afridi	4	(3) c Rizwan b Afridi	17
J.Blackwood	c Alam b Afridi	33	c Rizwan b Nauman	25
K.R.Mayers	c Rizwan b Abbas	0	c Rizwan b Afridi	32
J.O.Holder	c Rizwan b Afridi	26	c Alam b Nauman	47
†J.Da Silva	lbw b Abbas	6	c Ashraf b Afridi	15
K.A.J.Roach	c Azam b Afridi	8	lbw b Afridi	7
J.N.T.Seales	not out	0	not out	0
Extras	(LB 10, NB 6, W 1)	17	(B 4, LB 2, NB 5, W 1)	12
Total	**(51.3 overs)**	**150**	**(83.2 overs)**	**219**

WEST INDIES	*O*	*M*	*R*	*W*		*O*	*M*	*R*	*W*
Roach	27	9	68	3		3	1	11	0
Seales	15	4	31	3		3	0	32	0
Joseph	18	1	75	0	(4)	4.2	0	24	2
Holder	23	9	46	2	(3)	6	0	27	2
Mayers	17	5	34	0		7	0	43	1
Chase	8	0	32	0					
Bonner	1	0	6	0					
Brathwaite	1	1	0	0	(6)	4	0	28	1
PAKISTAN									
Mohammad Abbas	18	6	44	3		14	3	42	0
Shaheen Shah Afridi	17.3	7	51	6		17.2	5	43	4
Hasan Ali	8	1	30	0		14	6	37	2
Faheem Ashraf	7	4	14	1		13	5	36	0
Nauman Ali	1	0	1	0		22	7	52	3
Fawad Alam						3	1	3	0

FALL OF WICKETS

	P	WI	P	WI
Wkt	*1st*	*1st*	*2nd*	*2nd*
1st	2	8	70	34
2nd	2	9	90	65
3rd	2	34	107	69
4th	168	45	145	73
5th	218	105	160	101
6th	231	105	176	113
7th	231	109	–	159
8th	267	116	–	199
9th	302	143	–	212
10th	–	150	–	219

Umpires: G.O.Brathwaite (*West Indies*) (6) and J.S.Wilson (*West Indies*) (25).
Referee: Sir R.B.Richardson (*West Indies*) (35). **Test No. 2432/534 (WI558/P439)**
Fawad Alam (76*) retired hurt at 160-3 and resumed at 218-5.

SRI LANKA v WEST INDIES (1st Test)

At Galle International Stadium, on 21, 22, 23, 24, 25 November 2021.
Toss: Sri Lanka. Result: **SRI LANKA** won by 187 runs.
Debut: West Indies – J.L.Solozano.

SRI LANKA

P.N.Silva	c Cornwall b Gabriel	56		c Hope b Cornwall	3
*F.D.M.Karunaratne	st Da Silva b Chase	147		c Blackwood b Cornwall	83
B.O.P.Fernando	c Bonner b Chase	3		lbw b Warrican	14
A.D.Mathews	c Holder b Chase	3		not out	69
D.M.de Silva	hit wkt b Gabriel	61		c and b Warrican	1
†L.D.Chandimal	c Cornwall b Chase	45		not out	10
R.T.M.Wanigamuni	c Da Silva b Warrican	13			
R.A.S.Lakmal	lbw b Warrican	11			
P.V.D.Chameera	c Brathwaite b Warrican	3			
L.Ambuldeniya	c Blackwood b Chase	17			
P.A.K.P.Jayawickrama	not out	8			
Extras	(B 5, LB 6, NB 8)	19		(B 8, LB 2, NB 1)	11
Total	**(133.5 overs)**	**386**		**(4 wkts dec; 40.5 overs)**	**191**

WEST INDIES

*K.C.Brathwaite	c Silva b Wanigamuni	41		lbw b Wanigamuni	0
J.Blackwood	lbw b Ambuldeniya	20		c Mathews b Ambuldeniya	9
N.E.Bonner	c de Silva b Jayawickrama	1		not out	68
S.D.Hope	c Fernando b Wanigamuni	10		b Wanigamuni	3
R.L.Chase	c Fernando b Wanigamuni	2		b Ambuldeniya	1
J.A.Warrican	c Chandimal b Jayawickrama	1	(10)	c Fernando b Ambuldeniya	1
K.R.Mayers	c Karunaratne b de Silva	45	(6)	lbw b Wanigamuni	2
J.O.Holder	c Chameera b Jayawickrama	36	(7)	b Wanigamuni	0
†J.Da Silva	not out	15	(8)	c de Silva b Ambuldeniya	54
R.R.S.Cornwall	c Wanigamuni b Lakmal	39	(9)	c Lakmal b Jayawickrama	13
S.T.Gabriel	lbw b Jayawickrama	2		c de Silva b Ambuldeniya	0
Extras	(B 8, LB 5, NB 2, W 3)	18		(LB 5, NB 2, W 2)	9
Total	**(85.5 overs)**	**230**		**(79 overs)**	**160**

WEST INDIES	*O*	*M*	*R*	*W*		*O*	*M*	*R*	*W*
Gabriel	19	2	69	2	(5)	4	0	23	0
Holder	19	9	24	0		5	0	19	0
Cornwall	27	3	91	0	(1)	15.5	0	60	2
Mayers	3	0	9	0					
Warrican	32	5	87	3	(4)	9	1	42	2
Chase	28.5	3	83	5	(3)	6	1	28	0
Blackwood	1	0	6	0					
Brathwaite	4	0	6	0	(6)	1	0	9	0
SRI LANKA									
Lakmal	6	1	10	1					
Chameera	8	0	14	0	(5)	4	0	12	0
Ambuldeniya	32	11	67	1	(1)	29	12	46	5
Jayawickrama	19.5	6	40	4	(3)	14	6	28	1
Wanigamuni	17	1	75	3	(2)	31	5	64	4
De Silva	3	0	11	1	(4)	1	0	5	0

FALL OF WICKETS

	SL	WI	SL	WI
Wkt	*1st*	*1st*	*2nd*	*2nd*
1st	139	46	4	3
2nd	164	51	39	11
3rd	170	80	162	14
4th	281	83	163	15
5th	296	86	–	18
6th	331	100	–	18
7th	355	163	–	118
8th	361	175	–	149
9th	361	224	–	156
10th	386	230	–	160

Umpires: H.D.P.K.Dharmasena (*Sri Lanka*) (70) and R.S.A.Palliyaguruge (*Sri Lanka*) (8).
Referee: R.S.Madugalle (*Sri Lanka*) (200). **Test No. 2433/23 (SL298/WI559)**
S.D.Hope replaced J.L.Solozano (concussion) after 116.1 overs of Sri Lanka's 1st innings.

SRI LANKA v WEST INDIES (2nd Test)

At Galle International Stadium, on 29, 30 November, 1, 2, 3 December 2021.
Toss: Sri Lanka. Result: **SRI LANKA** won by 164 runs.
Debut: Sri Lanka – K.I.C.Asalanka. ‡ (C.Karunaratne)

SRI LANKA

P.N.Silva	lbw b Permaul	73	(2)	lbw b Chase	66
*F.D.M.Karunaratne	c and b Chase	42	(1)	run out	6
B.O.P.Fernando	c Da Silva b Warrican	18		run out	14
A.D.Mathews	b Warrican	29	(9)	c Blackwood b Permaul	1
D.M.de Silva	c Da Silva b Permaul	2		not out	155
K.I.C.Asalanka	c Bonner b Permaul	10	(4)	c Bonner b Permaul	19
†L.D.Chandimal	lbw b Warrican	2	(6)	c and b Chase	2
R.T.M.Wanigamuni	c Hope b Warrican	5	(7)	c Roach b Brathwaite	25
R.A.S.Lakmal	c Warrican b Permaul	12	(8)	lbw b Permaul	7
L.Ambuldeniya	b Permaul	1		b Holder	39
P.A.K.P.Jayawickrama	not out	0			
Extras	(LB 7, NB 3)	10		(B 4, LB 4, NB 2, W 1)	11
Total	**(61.3 overs)**	**204**		**(9 wkts dec; 121.4 overs)**	**345**

WEST INDIES

*K.C.Brathwaite	b Ambuldeniya	72	lbw b Wanigamuni	6
J.Blackwood	lbw b Jayawickrama	44	c de Silva b Ambuldeniya	36
N.E.Bonner	lbw b Wanigamuni	35	b Ambuldeniya	44
S.D.Hope	lbw b Wanigamuni	22	c Lakmal b Wanigamuni	16
R.L.Chase	c Silva b Wanigamuni	10	c Fernando b Wanigamuni	0
K.R.Mayers	not out	36	c de Silva b Wanigamuni	0
J.O.Holder	lbw b Wanigamuni	4	c de Silva b Ambuldeniya	3
†J.Da Silva	b Wanigamuni	0	not out	4
K.A.J.Roach	c de Silva b Jayawickrama	8	lbw b Ambuldeniya	13
V.Permaul	b Ambuldeniya	15	lbw b Wanigamuni	1
J.A.Warrican	c sub‡ b Wanigamuni	1	c de Silva b Ambuldeniya	3
Extras	(NB 6)	6	(B 4, LB 2)	6
Total	**(104.2 overs)**	**253**	**(56.1 overs)**	**132**

WEST INDIES	*O*	*M*	*R*	*W*		*O*	*M*	*R*	*W*
Roach	6	2	12	0	(4)	8	0	27	0
Holder	8	2	23	0	(5)	9.4	1	26	1
Mayers	2	0	13	0					
Permaul	13	3	35	5	(1)	40	4	106	3
Chase	14	0	64	1	(2)	27	2	82	2
Warrican	18.3	5	50	4	(3)	29	5	76	0
Brathwaite					(6)	5	0	11	1
Bonner					(7)	3	1	9	0
SRI LANKA									
Lakmal	9	3	22	0					
Ambuldeniya	35	13	94	2	(1)	20.1	6	35	5
Wanigamuni	34.2	8	70	6	(2)	25	6	66	5
Jayawickrama	25	4	59	2	(3)	10	3	23	0
De Silva	1	0	8	0					
Asalanka					(4)	1	0	2	0

FALL OF WICKETS

Wkt	SL *1st*	WI *1st*	SL *2nd*	WI *2nd*
1st	106	62	7	15
2nd	139	137	39	65
3rd	152	166	73	92
4th	154	180	151	92
5th	169	191	157	92
6th	169	197	208	103
7th	178	197	219	108
8th	187	208	221	128
9th	200	246	345	129
10th	204	253	–	132

Umpires: H.D.P.K.Dharmasena (*Sri Lanka*) (71) and R.S.A.Palliyaguruge (*Sri Lanka*) (9).
Referee: R.S.Madugalle (*Sri Lanka*) (201). **Test No. 2434/24 (SL299/WI560)**
A.D.Mathews retired hurt at 162-4 and resumed at 187-8.

INDIA v NEW ZEALAND (1st Test)

At Green Park, Kanpur, on 25, 26, 27, 28, 29 November 2021.
Toss: India. Result: **MATCH DRAWN**.
Debuts: India – S.S.Iyer; New Zealand – R.Ravindra. ‡ (K.Srikar Bharat)

INDIA

M.A.Agarwal	c Blundell b Jamieson	13		c Latham b Southee	17
S.Gill	b Jamieson	52		b Jamieson	1
C.A.Pujara	c Blundell b Southee	26		c Blundell b Jamieson	22
*A.M.Rahane	b Jamieson	35		lbw b Patel	4
S.S.Iyer	c Young b Southee	105		c Blundell b Southee	65
R.A.Jadeja	b Southee	50		lbw b Southee	0
†W.P.Saha	c Blundell b Southee	1	(8)	not out	61
R.Ashwin	b Patel	38	(7)	b Jamieson	32
A.R.Patel	c Blundell b Southee	3		not out	28
U.T.Yadav	not out	10			
I.Sharma	lbw b Patel	0			
Extras	(B 5, LB 2, NB 4, W 1)	12		(B 3, LB 1)	4
Total	**(111.1 overs)**	**345**		**(7 wkts dec; 81 overs)**	**234**

NEW ZEALAND

T.W.M.Latham	st sub‡ b Patel	95		b Ashwin	52
W.A.Young	c sub‡ b Ashwin	89		lbw b Ashwin	2
*K.S.Williamson	lbw b Yadav	18	(4)	lbw b Jadeja	24
L.R.P.L.Taylor	c sub‡ b Patel	11	(5)	lbw b Jadeja	2
H.M.Nicholls	lbw b Patel	2	(6)	lbw b Patel	1
†T.A.Blundell	b Patel	13	(7)	b Ashwin	2
R.Ravindra	b Jadeja	13	(8)	not out	18
K.A.Jamieson	c Patel b Ashwin	23	(9)	lbw b Jadeja	5
T.G.Southee	b Patel	5	(10)	lbw b Jadeja	4
W.E.R.Somerville	b Ashwin	6	(3)	c Gill b Yadav	36
A.Y.Patel	not out	5		not out	2
Extras	(B 6, LB 4, NB 5, W 1)	16		(B 12, LB 1, NB 4)	17
Total	**(142.3 overs)**	**296**		**(9 wkts; 98 overs)**	**165**

NEW ZEALAND	*O*	*M*	*R*	*W*		*O*	*M*	*R*	*W*
Southee	27.4	6	69	5		22	2	75	3
Jamieson	23.2	6	91	3		17	6	40	3
Patel	29.1	7	90	2		17	3	60	1
Somerville	24	2	60	0	(5)	16	2	38	0
Ravindra	7	1	28	0	(4)	9	3	17	0
INDIA									
Sharma	15	5	35	0	(4)	7	1	20	0
Yadav	18	3	50	1	(3)	12	2	34	1
Ashwin	42.3	10	82	3	(1)	30	12	35	3
Jadeja	33	10	57	1	(5)	28	10	40	4
Patel	34	6	62	5	(2)	21	12	23	1

FALL OF WICKETS

	I	NZ	I	NZ
Wkt	*1st*	*1st*	*2nd*	*2nd*
1st	21	151	2	3
2nd	82	197	32	79
3rd	106	214	41	118
4th	145	218	51	125
5th	266	227	51	126
6th	288	241	103	128
7th	305	258	167	138
8th	313	270	–	147
9th	339	284	–	155
10th	345	296	–	–

Umpires: N.N.Menon (*India*) (8) and V.K.Sharma (*India*) (3).
Referee: J.Srinath (*India*) (58). **Test No. 2435/51 (I556/NZ450)**

INDIA v NEW ZEALAND (2nd Test)

At Wankhede Stadium, Mumbai, on 3, 4, 5, 6, December 2021.
Toss: India. Result: **INDIA** won by 372 runs.
Debuts: None.

INDIA

M.A.Agarwal	c Blundell b Patel	150		c Young b Patel	62
S.Gill	c Taylor b Patel	44	(3)	c Latham b Ravindra	47
C.A.Pujara	b Patel	0	(2)	c Taylor b Patel	47
*V.Kohli	lbw b Patel	0		b Ravindra	36
S.S.Iyer	c Blundell b Patel	18		st Blundell b Patel	14
†W.P.Saha	lbw b Patel	27		c Jamieson b Ravindra	13
R.Ashwin	b Patel	0			
A.R.Patel	lbw b Patel	52	(7)	not out	41
J.Yadav	c Ravindra b Patel	12	(8)	c and b Patel	6
U.T.Yadav	not out	0			
M.Siraj	c Ravindra b Patel	4			
Extras	(B 13, LB 5)	18		(B 6, LB 3, NB 1)	10
Total	**(109.5 overs)**	**325**		**(7 wkts dec; 70 overs)**	**276**

NEW ZEALAND

*T.W.M.Latham	c Iyer b Siraj	10		lbw b Ashwin	6
W.A.Young	c Kohli b Siraj	4		c sub (S.A.Yadav) b Ashwin	20
D.J.Mitchell	lbw b Patel	8		c J.Yadav b Patel	60
L.R.P.L.Taylor	b Siraj	1		c Pujara b Ashwin	6
H.M.Nicholls	b Ashwin	7		st Saha b Ashwin	44
†T.A.Blundell	c Pujara b Ashwin	8		run out	0
R.Ravindra	c Kohli b J.Yadav	4	(8)	c Pujara b J.Yadav	18
K.A.Jamieson	c Iyer b Patel	17		lbw b J.Yadav	0
T.G.Southee	c sub (S.A.Yadav) b Ashwin	0		b J.Yadav	0
W.E.R.Somerville	c Siraj b Ashwin	0	(3)	c Agarwal b J.Yadav	1
A.Y.Patel	not out	0		not out	0
Extras	(LB 1, NB 2)	3		(B 9, LB 1, NB 2)	12
Total	**(28.1 overs)**	**62**		**(56.3 overs)**	**167**

NEW ZEALAND	*O*	*M*	*R*	*W*		*O*	*M*	*R*	*W*
Southee	22	6	43	0		13	1	31	0
Jamieson	12	3	36	0	(3)	8	2	15	0
Patel	47.5	12	119	10	(2)	26	3	106	4
Somerville	19	0	80	0		10	0	59	0
Ravindra	4	0	20	0		13	2	56	3
Mitchell	5	3	9	0					
INDIA									
U.T.Yadav	5	2	7	0	(5)	5	1	19	0
Siraj	4	0	19	3	(1)	5	2	13	0
Patel	9.1	3	14	2		10	2	42	1
Ashwin	8	2	8	4	(2)	22.3	9	34	4
J.Yadav	2	0	13	1	(4)	14	4	49	4

FALL OF WICKETS

	I	NZ	I	NZ
Wkt	*1st*	*1st*	*2nd*	*2nd*
1st	80	10	107	13
2nd	80	15	115	45
3rd	80	17	197	55
4th	160	27	211	128
5th	224	31	217	129
6th	224	38	238	162
7th	291	53	276	165
8th	316	53	–	165
9th	321	62	–	167
10th	325	62	–	167

Umpires: A.K.Chaudhary (*India*) (3) and N.N.Menon (*India*) (9).
Referee: J.Srinath (*India*) (59). **Test No. 2436/52 (I557/NZ451)**

BANGLADESH v PAKISTAN (1st Test)

At Zohur Ahmed Chowdhury Stadium, Chittagong, on 26, 27, 28, 29, 30 November 2021.
Toss: Bangladesh. Result: **PAKISTAN** won by eight wickets.
Debuts: Bangladesh – Yasir Ali; Pakistan – Abdullah Shafiq.

BANGLADESH

Shadman Islam	lbw b Hasan	14		lbw b Afridi	1
Saif Hasan	c Abid b Afridi	14		c and b Afridi	18
Nazmul Hossain	c Khan b Ashraf	14		c Shafiq b Afridi	0
*Mominul Haque	c Rizwan b Khan	6		c Azhar b Hasan	0
Mushfiqur Rahim	c Rizwan b Ashraf	91		b Hasan	16
†Liton Das	lbw b Hasan	114	(7)	lbw b Afridi	59
Yasir Ali	b Hasan	4	(6)	retired hurt	36
Mehedi Hasan	not out	38		lbw b Khan	11
Taijul Islam	c Shafiq b Afridi	11	(10)	st Rizwan b Khan	0
Abu Jayed	c Shafiq b Hasan	8	(11)	c Rizwan b Afridi	0
Ebadat Hossain	b Hasan	0	(12)	not out	0
Nurul Hasan			(9)	c Ashraf b Khan	15
Extras	(LB 14, NB 1, W 1)	16		(B 1)	1
Total	**(114.4 overs)**	**330**		**(56.2 overs)**	**157**

PAKISTAN

Abid Ali	lbw b Taijul	133	lbw b Taijul	91
Abdullah Shafiq	lbw b Taijul	52	lbw b Mehedi	73
Azhar Ali	lbw b Taijul	0	not out	24
*Babar Azam	b Mehedi	10	not out	13
Fawad Alam	c Liton b Taijul	8		
†Mohammad Rizwan	lbw b Ebadat	5		
Faheem Ashraf	c Liton b Taijul	38		
Hasan Ali	st Liton b Taijul	12		
Sajid Khan	b Ebadat	5		
Nauman Ali	lbw b Taijul	8		
Shaheen Shah Afridi	not out	13		
Extras	(B 1, LB 1)	2	(B 2)	2
Total	**(115.4 overs)**	**286**	**(2 wkts; 58.3 overs)**	**203**

PAKISTAN	*O*	*M*	*R*	*W*		*O*	*M*	*R*	*W*
Shaheen Shah Afridi	27	8	70	2		15	8	32	5
Hasan Ali	20.4	5	51	5		11	0	52	2
Faheem Ashraf	14	2	54	2		8	3	16	0
Sajid Khan	27	5	79	1	(5)	13.2	1	33	3
Nauman Ali	26	6	62	0	(4)	9	3	23	0
BANGLADESH									
Abu Jayed	12	0	41	0	(4)	4	0	23	0
Ebadat Hossain	26	7	47	2		8	2	30	0
Taijul Islam	44.4	9	116	7	(1)	28	4	89	1
Mehedi Hasan	30	7	68	1	(3)	18.3	4	59	1
Mominul Haque	3	0	12	0					

FALL OF WICKETS

	B	P	B	P
Wkt	*1st*	*1st*	*2nd*	*2nd*
1st	19	146	14	151
2nd	33	146	14	171
3rd	47	169	15	–
4th	49	182	25	–
5th	255	207	43	–
6th	267	217	115	–
7th	276	229	153	–
8th	304	240	157	–
9th	330	257	157	–
10th	330	286	157	–

Umpires: M.A.Gough (*England*) (23) and Sharfuddoula (*Bangladesh*) (3).
Referee: Niamur Rashid (*Bangladesh*) (3). **Test No. 2437/12 (B125/P440)**
Nurul Hasan concussion replacement for Yasir Ali (Bangladesh 2nd innings, 37.1 overs).

BANGLADESH v PAKISTAN (2nd Test)

At Shere Bangla National Stadium, Mirpur, Dhaka, on 4, 5, 6 (*no play*), 7, 8 December 2021.
Toss: Pakistan. Result: **PAKISTAN** won by an innings and 8 runs.
Debut: Bangladesh – Mahmudul Hasan.

PAKISTAN

Abid Ali	b Taijul	39
Abdullah Shafiq	b Taijul	25
Azhar Ali	c Liton b Ebadat	56
*Babar Azam	lbw b Khaled	76
Fawad Alam	not out	50
†Mohammad Rizwan	not out	53
Faheem Ashraf		
Nauman Ali		
Hasan Ali		
Sajid Khan		
Shaheen Shah Afridi		
Extras	(LB 1)	1
Total	**(4 wkts dec; 98.3 overs)**	**300**

BANGLADESH

Shadman Islam	c Hasan b Khan	3	lbw b Afridi	2
Mahmudul Hasan	c Azam b Khan	0	b Hasan	6
Nazmul Hossain	lbw b Khan	30	c Alam b Afridi	6
*Mominul Haque	run out	1	lbw b Hasan	7
Mushfiqur Rahim	c Alam b Khan	5	run out	48
†Liton Das	c and b Khan	6	c Alam b Khan	45
Shakib Al Hasan	c Azhar b Khan	33	b Khan	63
Mehedi Hasan	b Khan	0	lbw b Azam	14
Taijul Islam	lbw b Khan	0	lbw b Khan	5
Khaled Ahmed	b Afridi	0	c Rizwan b Khan	0
Ebadat Hossain	not out	0	not out	0
Extras	(B 5, LB 3, NB 1)	9	(B 8, LB 1)	9
Total	**(32 overs)**	**87**	**(84.4 overs)**	**205**

BANGLADESH	*O*	*M*	*R*	*W*		*O*	*M*	*R*	*W*
Ebadat Hossain	23	3	88	1					
Khaled Ahmed	17.3	5	49	1					
Shakib Al Hasan	19	7	52	0					
Taijul Islam	25	6	73	2					
Mehedi Hasan	14	2	37	0					
PAKISTAN									
Shaheen Shah Afridi	4	3	3	1		15	5	31	2
Nauman Ali	12	2	33	0	(3)	20	5	41	0
Sajid Khan	15	4	42	8	(5)	32.4	8	86	4
Babar Azam	1	0	1	0	(6)	2	1	1	1
Hasan Ali					(2)	11	3	37	2
Faheem Ashraf					(4)	4	4	0	0

FALL OF WICKETS

	P	B	B
Wkt	*1st*	*1st*	*2nd*
1st	59	1	12
2nd	70	20	12
3rd	193	22	19
4th	197	31	25
5th	–	46	98
6th	–	65	147
7th	–	71	198
8th	–	76	200
9th	–	77	204
10th	–	87	205

Umpires: M.A.Gough (*England*) (24) and Sharfuddoula (*Bangladesh*) (4).
Referee: Niamur Rashid (*Bangladesh*) (4). **Test No. 2438/13 (B126/P441)**

AUSTRALIA v ENGLAND (1st Test)

At Woolloongabba, Brisbane, on 8, 9, 10, 11 December 2021.
Toss: England. Result: **AUSTRALIA** won by nine wickets.
Debut: Australia – A.T.Carey.

ENGLAND

R.J.Burns	b Starc	0	(2) c Carey b Cummins	13
H.Hameed	c Smith b Cummins	25	(1) c Carey b Starc	27
D.J.Malan	c Carey b Hazlewood	6	c Labuschagne b Lyon	82
*J.E.Root	c Warner b Hazlewood	0	c Carey b Green	89
B.A.Stokes	c Labuschagne b Cummins	5	c Green b Cummins	14
O.J.D.Pope	c Hazlewood b Green	35	c Smith b Lyon	4
†J.C.Buttler	c Carey b Starc	39	c Carey b Hazlewood	23
C.R.Woakes	c Hazlewood b Cummins	21	c Carey b Green	16
O.E.Robinson	c Carey b Cummins	0	c Head b Lyon	8
M.A.Wood	c Harris b Cummins	8	b Lyon	6
M.J.Leach	not out	2	not out	0
Extras	(LB 5, W 1)	6	(B 4, LB 5, W 6)	15
Total	**(50.1 overs)**	**147**	**(103 overs)**	**297**

AUSTRALIA

D.A.Warner	c Stokes b Robinson	94		
M.S.Harris	c Malan b Robinson	3	not out	9
M.Labuschagne	c Wood b Leach	74	not out	0
S.P.D.Smith	c Buttler b Wood	12		
T.M.Head	b Wood	152		
C.D.Green	b Robinson	0		
†A.T.Carey	c Pope b Woakes	12	(1) c Buttler b Robinson	9
*P.J.Cummins	c Hameed b Root	12		
M.A.Starc	c Burns b Woakes	35		
N.M.Lyon	c Robinson b Wood	15		
J.R.Hazlewood	not out	0		
Extras	(B 4, LB 6, NB 4, W 2)	16	(NB 2)	2
Total	**(104.3 overs)**	**425**	**(1 wkt; 5.1 overs)**	**20**

AUSTRALIA	*O*	*M*	*R*	*W*		*O*	*M*	*R*	*W*
Starc	12	2	35	2		20	3	77	1
Hazlewood	13	4	42	2		14	6	32	1
Cummins	13.1	3	38	5		20	6	51	2
Lyon	9	2	21	0		34	5	91	4
Green	3	1	6	1		12	3	23	2
Labuschagne						3	0	14	0
ENGLAND									
Woakes	25	8	76	2	(2)	2	0	3	0
Robinson	23	8	58	3	(1)	3	0	13	1
Wood	25.3	4	85	3		0.1	0	4	0
Stokes	12	0	65	0					
Leach	13	0	102	1					
Root	6	0	29	1					

FALL OF WICKETS

	E	A	E	A
Wkt	*1st*	*1st*	*2nd*	*2nd*
1st	0	10	23	16
2nd	11	166	61	–
3rd	11	189	223	–
4th	29	195	229	–
5th	60	195	234	–
6th	112	236	266	–
7th	118	306	268	–
8th	122	391	286	–
9th	144	420	296	–
10th	147	425	297	–

Umpires: P.R.Reiffel (*Australia*) (52) and R.J.Tucker (*Australia*) (72).
Referee: D.C.Boon (*Australia*) (62). **Test No. 2439/352 (A835/E1041)**

AUSTRALIA v ENGLAND (2nd Test)

At Adelaide Oval, on 16, 17, 18, 19, 20 December 2021 (day/night).
Toss: Australia. Result: **AUSTRALIA** won by 275 runs.
Debut: Australia – M.G.Neser.

AUSTRALIA

M.S.Harris	c Buttler b Broad	3	(2)	c Buttler b Broad	23
D.A.Warner	c Broad b Stokes	95	(1)	run out	13
M.Labuschagne	lbw b Robinson	103	(4)	c Stokes b Malan	51
*S.P.D.Smith	lbw b Anderson	93	(5)	c Buttler b Robinson	6
T.M.Head	b Root	18	(6)	c Stokes b Robinson	51
C.D.Green	b Stokes	2	(7)	not out	33
†A.T.Carey	c Hameed b Anderson	51	(8)	b Root	6
M.A.Starc	not out	39	(9)	c Pope b Root	19
M.G.Neser	c Broad b Stokes	35	(3)	b Anderson	3
J.A.Richardson	c Buttler b Woakes	9		c Buttler b Malan	8
N.M.Lyon					
Extras	(LB 9, NB 11, W 5)	25		(B 3, LB 8, NB 5, W 1)	17
Total	**(9 wkts dec; 150.4 overs)**	**473**		**(9 wkts dec; 61 overs)**	**230**

ENGLAND

H.Hameed	c Starc b Neser	6	(2)	c Carey b Richardson	0
R.J.Burns	c Smith b Starc	4	(1)	c Smith b Richardson	34
D.J.Malan	c Smith b Starc	80		lbw b Neser	20
*J.E.Root	c Smith b Green	62		c Carey b Starc	24
B.A.Stokes	b Green	34		lbw b Lyon	12
O.J.D.Pope	c Labuschagne b Lyon	5		c Smith b Starc	4
†J.C.Buttler	c Warner b Starc	0		hit wkt b Richardson	26
C.R.Woakes	b Lyon	24		b Richardson	44
O.E.Robinson	lbw b Lyon	0		c Smith b Lyon	8
S.C.J.Broad	c Head b Starc	9		not out	9
J.M.Anderson	not out	5		c Green b Richardson	2
Extras	(LB 6, NB 1)	7		(B 2, LB 3, NB 4)	9
Total	**(84.1 overs)**	**236**		**(113.1 overs)**	**192**

ENGLAND	*O*	*M*	*R*	*W*		*O*	*M*	*R*	*W*
Anderson	29	10	58	2		10	6	8	1
Broad	26	6	73	1		10	3	27	1
Woakes	23.4	6	103	1	(4)	12	3	46	0
Robinson	27	13	45	1	(3)	15	2	54	2
Stokes	25	2	113	3	(6)	2	0	24	0
Root	20	2	72	1	(5)	6	1	27	2
Malan						6	0	33	2
AUSTRALIA									
Starc	16.1	6	37	4		27	10	43	2
Richardson	19	4	78	0		19.1	9	42	5
Neser	11	0	33	1	(4)	13	5	28	1
Lyon	28	11	58	3	(3)	39	16	55	2
Green	10	3	24	2		9	5	9	0
Labuschagne						4	2	10	0
Smith						1	1	0	0
Head						1	1	0	0

FALL OF WICKETS

	A	E	A	E
Wkt	*1st*	*1st*	*2nd*	*2nd*
1st	4	7	41	4
2nd	176	12	48	48
3rd	241	150	48	70
4th	291	157	55	82
5th	294	164	144	86
6th	385	169	173	105
7th	390	202	180	166
8th	448	204	216	178
9th	473	220	230	182
10th	–	236	–	192

Umpires: R.J.Tucker (*Australia*) (73) and P.Wilson (*Australia*) (5).
Referee: D.C.Boon (*Australia*) (63). **Test No. 2440/353 (A836/E1042)**

AUSTRALIA v ENGLAND (3rd Test)

At Melbourne Cricket Ground, on 26, 27, 28 December 2021.
Toss: Australia. Result: **AUSTRALIA** won by an innings and 14 runs.
Debut: Australia – S.M.Boland.

ENGLAND

H.Hameed	c Carey b Cummins	0		c Carey b Boland	7
Z.Crawley	c Green b Cummins	12		c Carey b Starc	5
D.J.Malan	c Warner b Cummins	14		lbw b Starc	0
*J.E.Root	c Carey b Starc	50		c Warner b Boland	28
B.A.Stokes	c Lyon b Green	25	(6)	b Starc	11
J.M.Bairstow	c Green b Starc	35	(7)	lbw b Boland	5
†J.C.Buttler	c Boland b Lyon	3	(8)	not out	5
M.A.Wood	lbw b Boland	6	(9)	c and b Boland	0
O.E.Robinson	c Boland b Lyon	22	(10)	c Labuschagne b Boland	0
M.J.Leach	c Smith b Lyon	13	(5)	b Boland	0
J.M.Anderson	not out	0		b Green	2
Extras	(LB 4, NB 1)	5		(LB 5)	5
Total	**(65.1 overs)**	**185**		**(27.4 overs)**	**68**

AUSTRALIA

M.S.Harris	c Root b Anderson	76
D.A.Warner	c Crawley b Anderson	38
N.M.Lyon	c Buttler b Robinson	10
M.Labuschagne	c Root b Wood	1
S.P.D.Smith	b Anderson	16
T.M.Head	c Root b Robinson	27
C.D.Green	lbw b Leach	17
†A.T.Carey	c Buttler b Stokes	19
*P.J.Cummins	c Hameed b Anderson	21
M.A.Starc	not out	24
S.M.Boland	c Crawley b Wood	6
Extras	(B 2, LB 4, NB 5, W 1)	12
Total	**(87.5 overs)**	**267**

AUSTRALIA	*O*	*M*	*R*	*W*	*O*	*M*	*R*	*W*
Starc	15	3	54	2	10	3	29	3
Cummins	15	2	36	3	10	4	19	0
Boland	13	2	48	1	4	1	7	6
Green	8	4	7	1	3.4	0	8	1
Lyon	14.1	3	36	3				
ENGLAND								
Anderson	23	10	33	4				
Robinson	19.2	4	64	2				
Wood	19.5	2	71	2				
Stokes	10.4	1	47	1				
Leach	15	0	46	1				

FALL OF WICKETS

	E	A	E
Wkt	*1st*	*1st*	*2nd*
1st	4	57	7
2nd	13	76	7
3rd	61	84	22
4th	82	110	22
5th	115	171	46
6th	128	180	60
7th	141	207	61
8th	159	219	65
9th	176	253	65
10th	185	267	68

Umpires: P.R.Reiffel (*Australia*) (53) and P.Wilson (*Australia*) (6).
Referee: D.C.Boon (*Australia*) (64). **Test No. 2441/354 (A837/E1043)**

AUSTRALIA v ENGLAND (4th Test)

At Sydney Cricket Ground, on 5, 6, 7, 8, 9 January 2022.
Toss: Australia. Result: **MATCH DRAWN.**
Debuts: None.

AUSTRALIA

D.A.Warner	c Crawley b Broad	30	(2) c sub (O.J.D.Pope) b Wood	3
M.S.Harris	c Root b Anderson	38	(1) c sub (O.J.D.Pope) b Leach	27
M.Labuschagne	c Buttler b Wood	28	c sub (O.J.D.Pope) b Wood	29
S.P.D.Smith	c Buttler b Broad	67	b Leach	23
U.T.Khawaja	b Broad	137	not out	101
C.D.Green	c Crawley b Broad	5	c Root b Leach	74
†A.T.Carey	c Bairstow b Root	13	c sub (O.J.D.Pope) b Leach	0
*P.J.Cummins	c Buttler b Broad	24		
M.A.Starc	not out	34		
N.M.Lyon	not out	16		
S.M.Boland				
Extras	(LB 8, NB 4, W 12)	24	(LB 3, W 5)	8
Total	**(8 wkts dec; 134 overs)**	**416**	**(6 wkts dec; 68.5 overs)**	**265**

ENGLAND

H.Hameed	b Starc	6	(2) c Carey b Boland	9
Z.Crawley	b Boland	18	(1) lbw b Green	77
D.J.Malan	c Khawaja b Green	3	b Lyon	4
*J.E.Root	c Smith b Boland	0	c Carey b Boland	24
B.A.Stokes	lbw b Lyon	66	c Smith b Lyon	60
J.M.Bairstow	c Carey b Boland	113	c Labuschagne b Boland	41
†J.C.Buttler	c Khawaja b Cummins	0	lbw b Cummins	11
M.A.Wood	c Lyon b Cummins	39	lbw b Cummins	0
M.J.Leach	c Cummins b Lyon	10	c Warner b Smith	26
S.C.J.Broad	c Carey b Boland	15	not out	8
J.M.Anderson	not out	4	not out	0
Extras	(B 9, LB 6, NB 2, W 3)	20	(LB 7, NB 3)	10
Total	**(79.1 overs)**	**294**	**(9 wkts; 102 overs)**	**270**

ENGLAND	*O*	*M*	*R*	*W*		*O*	*M*	*R*	*W*
Anderson	30	9	54	1		12	1	34	0
Broad	29	5	101	5		11	3	31	0
Stokes	13.5	3	37	0					
Wood	26.1	6	76	1	(3)	15	0	65	2
Leach	24	2	89	0	(4)	21.5	1	84	4
Malan	3	0	15	0		2	0	13	0
Root	8	0	36	1	(5)	7	0	35	0
AUSTRALIA									
Cummins	20	6	68	2	(2)	22	5	80	2
Starc	16	2	56	1	(1)	18	2	68	0
Boland	14.1	6	36	4		24	11	30	3
Green	9	4	24	1	(5)	10	1	38	1
Lyon	17	0	88	2	(4)	22	10	28	2
Labuschagne	3	0	7	0		2	0	9	0
Smith						4	1	10	1

FALL OF WICKETS

	A	E	A	E
Wkt	*1st*	*1st*	*2nd*	*2nd*
1st	51	22	12	46
2nd	111	36	52	74
3rd	117	36	68	96
4th	232	36	86	156
5th	242	164	265	193
6th	285	173	265	218
7th	331	245	–	218
8th	398	266	–	237
9th	–	289	–	270
10th	–	294	–	–

Umpires: P.R.Reiffel (*Australia*) (54) and R.J.Tucker (*Australia*) (74).
Referee: S.R.Bernard (*Australia*) (1). **Test No. 2442/355 (A838/E1044)**

AUSTRALIA v ENGLAND (5th Test)

At Bellerive Oval, Hobart, on 14, 15, 16 January 2022 (day/night).
Toss: England. Result: **AUSTRALIA** won by 146 runs.
Debut: England – S.W.Billings.

AUSTRALIA

D.A.Warner	c Crawley b Robinson	0		c Pope b Broad	0
U.T.Khawaja	c Root b Broad	6		c Billings b Wood	11
M.Labuschagne	b Broad	44		c Billings b Woakes	5
S.P.D.Smith	c Crawley b Robinson	0		c Malan b Wood	27
T.M.Head	c Robinson b Woakes	101	(6)	c Billings b Wood	8
C.D.Green	c Crawley b Wood	74	(7)	lbw b Broad	23
†A.T.Carey	b Woakes	24	(8)	c Billings b Broad	49
M.A.Starc	c Burns b Wood	3	(9)	c Pope b Wood	1
*P.J.Cummins	c Crawley b Wood	2	(10)	b Wood	13
N.M.Lyon	b Broad	31	(11)	not out	4
S.M.Boland	not out	10	(5)	c Billings b Wood	8
Extras	(B 3, LB 3, W 2)	8		(B 1, LB 3, NB 1, W 1)	6
Total	**(75.4 overs)**	**303**		**(56.3 overs)**	**155**

ENGLAND

R.J.Burns	run out	0		b Green	26
Z.Crawley	c Head b Cummins	18		c Carey b Green	36
D.J.Malan	c Carey b Cummins	25		b Green	10
*J.E.Root	lbw b Cummins	34		b Boland	11
B.A.Stokes	c Lyon b Starc	4		c Lyon b Starc	5
O.J.D.Pope	c Carey b Boland	14		b Cummins	5
†S.W.Billings	c Boland b Green	29		c Cummins b Boland	1
C.R.Woakes	c Carey b Starc	36		c Carey b Boland	5
M.A.Wood	b Cummins	16		b Cummins	11
S.C.J.Broad	b Starc	0	(11)	not out	1
O.E.Robinson	not out	0	(10)	b Cummins	0
Extras	(B 4, LB 8)	12		(LB 13)	13
Total	**(47.4 overs)**	**188**		**(38.5 overs)**	**124**

ENGLAND	*O*	*M*	*R*	*W*		*O*	*M*	*R*	*W*
Broad	24.4	4	59	3		18	2	51	3
Robinson	8	3	24	2	(3)	11	4	23	0
Wood	18	1	115	3	(4)	16.3	2	37	6
Woakes	15	2	64	2	(2)	11	3	40	1
Root	10	1	35	0					
AUSTRALIA									
Starc	10	1	53	3		8	0	30	1
Cummins	13.4	2	45	4		12.5	3	42	3
Boland	14	6	33	1		12	5	18	3
Green	10	0	45	1		6	1	21	3

FALL OF WICKETS

	A	E	A	E
Wkt	*1st*	*1st*	*2nd*	*2nd*
1st	3	2	0	68
2nd	7	29	5	82
3rd	12	78	33	83
4th	83	81	47	92
5th	204	85	59	101
6th	236	110	63	107
7th	246	152	112	107
8th	252	182	121	115
9th	280	182	151	123
10th	303	188	155	124

Umpires: R.J.Tucker (*Australia*) (75) and P.Wilson (*Australia*) (7).
Referee: D.C.Boon (*Australia*) (65). **Test No. 2443/356 (A839/E1045)**

SOUTH AFRICA v INDIA (1st Test)

At SuperSport Park, Centurion, on 26, 27 (*no play*), 28, 29, 30 December 2021.
Toss: India. Result: **INDIA** won by 113 runs.
Debut: South Africa – M.Jansen.

INDIA

K.L.Rahul	c de Kock b Rabada	123		c Elgar b Ngidi	23
M.A.Agarwal	lbw b Ngidi	60		c de Kock b Jansen	4
C.A.Pujara	c Petersen b Ngidi	0	(4)	c de Kock b Ngidi	16
*V.Kohli	c Mulder b Ngidi	35	(5)	c de Kock b Jansen	18
A.M.Rahane	c de Kock b Ngidi	48	(6)	c van der Dussen b Jansen	20
†R.R.Pant	c van der Dussen b Ngidi	8	(7)	c Ngidi b Rabada	34
R.Ashwin	c Maharaj b Rabada	4	(8)	c Petersen b Rabada	14
S.N.Thakur	c de Kock b Rabada	4	(3)	c Mulder b Rabada	10
Mohammed Shami	c de Kock b Ngidi	8		c Mulder b Rabada	1
J.J.Bumrah	c Mulder b Jansen	14		not out	7
M.Siraj	not out	4		b Jansen	0
Extras	(B 4, LB 4, NB 11)	19		(B 17, LB 4, NB 6)	27
Total	**(105.3 overs)**	**327**		**(50.3 overs)**	**174**

SOUTH AFRICA

*D.Elgar	c Pant b Bumrah	1	(2)	lbw b Bumrah	77
A.K.Markram	b Shami	13	(1)	b Shami	1
K.D.Petersen	b Shami	15		c Pant b Siraj	17
H.E.van der Dussen	c Rahane b Siraj	3		b Bumrah	11
T.Bavuma	c Pant b Shami	52	(6)	not out	35
†Q.de Kock	b Thakur	34	(7)	b Siraj	21
P.W.A.Mulder	c Pant b Shami	12	(8)	c Pant b Shami	1
M.Jansen	lbw b Thakur	19	(9)	c Pant b Shami	13
K.Rabada	c Pant b Shami	25	(10)	c Shami b Ashwin	0
K.A.Maharaj	c Rahane b Bumrah	12	(5)	b Bumrah	8
L.T.Ngidi	not out	0		c Pujara b Ashwin	0
Extras	(B 4, LB 7)	11		(LB 2, NB 5)	7
Total	**(62.3 overs)**	**197**		**(68 overs)**	**191**

SOUTH AFRICA	*O*	*M*	*R*	*W*		*O*	*M*	*R*	*W*
Rabada	26	5	72	3		17	4	42	4
Ngidi	24	5	71	6		10	2	31	2
Jansen	18.3	4	69	1		13.3	4	55	4
Mulder	19	4	49	0		10	4	25	0
Maharaj	18	2	58	0					
INDIA									
Bumrah	7.2	2	16	2		19	4	50	3
Siraj	15.1	3	45	1	(3)	18	5	47	2
Mohammed Shami	16	5	44	5	(2)	17	3	63	3
Thakur	11	1	51	2		5	0	11	0
Ashwin	13	2	37	0		9	2	18	2

FALL OF WICKETS

	I	SA	I	SA
Wkt	*1st*	*1st*	*2nd*	*2nd*
1st	117	2	12	1
2nd	117	25	34	34
3rd	199	30	54	74
4th	278	32	79	94
5th	291	104	109	130
6th	296	133	111	161
7th	296	144	146	164
8th	304	181	166	190
9th	308	193	169	191
10th	327	197	174	191

Umpires: M.Erasmus (*South Africa*) (68) and A.T.Holdstock (*South Africa*) (3).
Referee: A.J.Pycroft (*Zimbabwe*) (82). **Test No. 2444/40 (SA446/I558)**

SOUTH AFRICA v INDIA (2nd Test)

At New Wanderers Stadium, Johannesburg, on 3, 4, 5, 6 January 2022.
Toss: India. Result: **SOUTH AFRICA** won by seven wickets.
Debuts: None.

INDIA

*K.L.Rahul	c Rabada b Jansen	50	c Markram b Jansen	8
M.A.Agarwal	c Verreynne b Jansen	26	lbw b Olivier	23
C.A.Pujara	c Bavuma b Olivier	3	lbw b Rabada	53
A.M.Rahane	c Petersen b Olivier	0	c Verreynne b Rabada	58
G.H.Vihari	c van der Dussen b Rabada	20	not out	40
†R.R.Pant	c Verreynne b Jansen	17	c Verreynne b Rabada	0
R.Ashwin	c Petersen b Jansen	46	c Verreynne b Ngidi	16
S.N.Thakur	c Petersen b Olivier	0	c Maharaj b Jansen	28
Mohammed Shami	c and b Rabada	9	c Verreynne b Jansen	0
J.J.Bumrah	not out	14	c Jansen b Ngidi	7
M.Siraj	c Verreynne b Rabada	1	b Ngidi	0
Extras	(B 8, LB 3, NB 5)	16	(B 16, LB 4, NB 8, W 5)	33
Total	**(63.1 overs)**	**202**	**(60.1 overs)**	**266**

SOUTH AFRICA

*D.Elgar	c Pant b Thakur	28	(2) not out	96
A.K.Markram	lbw b Shami	7	(1) lbw b Thakur	31
K.D.Petersen	c Agarwal b Thakur	62	lbw b Ashwin	28
H.E.van der Dussen	c Pant b Thakur	1	c Pujara b Shami	40
T.Bavuma	c Pant b Thakur	51	not out	23
†K.Verreynne	lbw b Thakur	21		
M.Jansen	c Ashwin b Thakur	21		
K.Rabada	c Siraj b Shami	0		
K.A.Maharaj	b Bumrah	21		
D.Olivier	not out	1		
L.T.Ngidi	c Pant b Thakur	0		
Extras	(B 4, LB 4, NB 3, W 5)	16	(B 1, LB 7, NB 1, W 16)	25
Total	**(79.4 overs)**	**229**	**(3 wkts; 67.4 overs)**	**243**

SOUTH AFRICA	*O*	*M*	*R*	*W*		*O*	*M*	*R*	*W*
Rabada	17.1	2	64	3		20	3	77	3
Olivier	17	1	64	3		12	1	51	1
Ngidi	11	4	26	0		10.1	2	43	3
Jansen	17	5	31	4		17	4	67	3
Maharaj	1	0	6	0		1	0	8	0
INDIA									
Bumrah	21	5	49	1		17	2	70	0
Mohammed Shami	21	5	52	2		17	3	55	1
Siraj	9.5	2	24	0	(4)	6	0	37	0
Thakur	17.5	3	61	7	(3)	16	2	47	1
Ashwin	10	1	35	0		11.4	2	26	1

FALL OF WICKETS

	I	SA	I	SA
Wkt	*1st*	*1st*	*2nd*	*2nd*
1st	36	14	24	47
2nd	49	88	44	93
3rd	49	101	155	175
4th	91	102	163	–
5th	116	162	167	–
6th	156	177	184	–
7th	157	179	225	–
8th	185	217	228	–
9th	187	228	245	–
10th	202	229	266	–

Umpires: M.Erasmus (*South Africa*) (69) and A.Paleker (*South Africa*) (1).
Referee: A.J.Pycroft (*Zimbabwe*) (83). **Test No. 2445/41 (SA447/I559)**

SOUTH AFRICA v INDIA (3rd Test)

At Newlands, Cape Town, on 11, 12, 13, 14 January 2022.
Toss: India. Result: **SOUTH AFRICA** won by seven wickets.
Debuts: None.

INDIA

K.L.Rahul	c Verreynne b Olivier	12		c Markram b Jansen	10
M.A.Agarwal	c Markram b Rabada	15		c Elgar b Rabada	7
C.A.Pujara	c Verreynne b Jansen	43		c Petersen b Jansen	9
*V.Kohli	c Verreynne b Rabada	79		c Markram b Ngidi	29
A.M.Rahane	c Verreynne b Rabada	9		c Elgar b Rabada	1
†R.R.Pant	c Petersen b Jansen	27		not out	100
R.Ashwin	c Verreynne b Jansen	2		c Jansen b Ngidi	7
S.N.Thakur	c Petersen b Maharaj	12		c Verreynne b Ngidi	5
J.J.Bumrah	c Elgar b Rabada	0	(11)	c Bavuma b Jansen	2
U.T.Yadav	not out	4	(9)	c Verreynne b Rabada	0
Mohammed Shami	c Bavuma b Ngidi	7	(10)	c van der Dussen b Jansen	0
Extras	(B 5, LB 1, NB 7)	13		(B 8, LB 9, NB 9, W 2)	28
Total	**(77.3 overs)**	**223**		**(67.3 overs)**	**198**

SOUTH AFRICA

*D.Elgar	c Pujara b Bumrah	3	(2)	c Pant b Shami	30
A.K.Markram	b Bumrah	8	(1)	c Rahul b Shami	16
K.A.Maharaj	b Yadav	25			
K.D.Petersen	c Pujara b Bumrah	72	(3)	b Thakur	82
H.E.van der Dussen	c Kohli b Yadav	21	(4)	not out	41
T.Bavuma	c Kohli b Shami	28	(5)	not out	32
†K.Verreynne	c Pant b Shami	0			
M.Jansen	b Bumrah	7			
K.Rabada	c Bumrah b Thakur	15			
D.Olivier	not out	10			
L.T.Ngidi	c Ashwin b Bumrah	3			
Extras	(B 4, LB 4, NB 4, W 1, Pen 5)	18		(LB 8, NB 3)	11
Total	**(76.3 overs)**	**210**		**(3 wkts; 63.3 overs)**	**212**

SOUTH AFRICA	*O*	*M*	*R*	*W*		*O*	*M*	*R*	*W*
Rabada	22	4	73	4		17	5	53	3
Olivier	18	5	42	1		10	1	38	0
Jansen	18	6	55	3		19.3	6	36	4
Ngidi	14.3	7	33	1		14	5	21	3
Maharaj	5	2	14	1		7	1	33	0
INDIA									
Bumrah	23.3	8	42	5		17	5	54	1
Yadav	16	3	64	2	(3)	9	0	36	0
Mohammed Shami	16	4	39	2	(2)	15	3	41	1
Thakur	12	2	37	1		11	3	22	1
Ashwin	9	3	15	0		11.3	1	51	0

FALL OF WICKETS

	I	SA	I	SA
Wkt	*1st*	*1st*	*2nd*	*2nd*
1st	31	10	20	23
2nd	33	17	24	101
3rd	95	45	57	155
4th	116	112	58	–
5th	167	159	152	–
6th	175	159	162	–
7th	205	176	170	–
8th	210	179	180	–
9th	211	200	189	–
10th	223	210	198	–

Umpires: M.Erasmus (*South Africa*) (70) and A.T.Holdstock (*South Africa*) (4).
Referee: A.J.Pycroft (*Zimbabwe*) (84). **Test No. 2446/42 (SA448/I560)**

NEW ZEALAND v BANGLADESH (1st Test)

At Bay Oval, Mount Maunganui, on 1, 2, 3, 4, 5 January 2022.
Toss: Bangladesh. Result: **BANGLADESH** won by eight wickets.
Debuts: None.

NEW ZEALAND

*T.W.M.Latham	c Liton b Shoriful	1	b Taskin	14
W.A.Young	run out	52	b Ebadat	69
D.P.Conway	c Liton b Mominul	122	c Shadman b Ebadat	13
L.R.P.L.Taylor	c Shadman b Shoriful	31	b Ebadat	40
H.M.Nicholls	c Shadman b Mominul	75	b Ebadat	0
†T.A.Blundell	b Ebadat	11	lbw b Ebadat	0
R.Ravindra	c Shadman b Shoriful	4	c Liton b Taskin	16
K.A.Jamieson	c Shadman b Mehedi	6	c Shoriful b Ebadat	0
T.G.Southee	c Mominul b Mehedi	6	b Taskin	0
N.Wagner	c Liton b Mehedi	0	not out	0
T.A.Boult	not out	9	c sub (Taijul Islam) b Mehedi	8
Extras	(B 1, LB 4, NB 3, W 3)	11	(B 2, LB 5, NB 1, W 1)	9
Total	**(108.1 overs; 487 mins)**	**328**	**(73.4 overs; 340 mins)**	**169**

BANGLADESH

Shadman Islam	c and b Wagner	22		c Blundell b Southee	3
Mahmudul Hasan	c Nicholls b Wagner	78			
Nazmul Hossain	c Young b Wagner	64	(2)	c Taylor b Jamieson	17
*Mominul Haque	lbw b Boult	88	(3)	not out	13
Mushfiqur Rahim	b Boult	12	(4)	not out	5
†Liton Das	c Blundell b Boult	86			
Yasir Ali	c Blundell b Jamieson	26			
Mehedi Hasan	c Blundell b Southee	47			
Taskin Ahmed	lbw b Southee	5			
Shoriful Islam	b Boult	7			
Ebadat Hossain	not out	0			
Extras	(LB 8, NB 3, W 7, Pen 5)	23		(LB 1, NB 1, W 2)	4
Total	**(176.2 overs; 772 mins)**	**458**		**(2 wkts; 16.5 overs; 72 mins)**	**42**

BANGLADESH	*O*	*M*	*R*	*W*		*O*	*M*	*R*	*W*
Taskin Ahmed	26	7	77	0		14	3	36	3
Shoriful Islam	26	7	69	3		12	2	30	0
Ebadat Hossain	18	3	75	1	(4)	21	6	46	6
Mehedi Hasan	32	9	86	3	(3)	22.4	5	43	1
Nazmul Hossain	2	0	10	0					
Mominul Haque	4.1	0	6	2	(5)	4	0	7	0
NEW ZEALAND									
Southee	38	4	114	2	(2)	5	2	21	1
Boult	35.2	11	85	4	(1)	5	3	4	0
Jamieson	35	11	78	1		3.5	1	12	1
Wagner	40	9	101	3		3	1	4	0
Ravindra	28	5	67	0					

FALL OF WICKETS	NZ	B	NZ	B
Wkt	*1st*	*1st*	*2nd*	*2nd*
1st	1	43	29	3
2nd	139	147	63	34
3rd	189	184	136	–
4th	227	203	136	–
5th	258	361	136	–
6th	265	370	154	–
7th	297	445	160	–
8th	316	450	160	–
9th	316	458	161	–
10th	328	458	169	–

Umpires: C.M.Brown (*New Zealand*) (3) and C.B.Gaffaney (*New Zealand*) (38).
Referee: J.J.Crowe (*New Zealand*) (104). **Test No. 2447/16 (NZ452/B127)**

NEW ZEALAND v BANGLADESH (2nd Test)

At Hagley Oval, Christchurch, on 9, 10, 11 January 2022.
Toss: Bangladesh. Result: **NEW ZEALAND** won by an innings and 117 runs.
Debut: Bangladesh – Mohammad Naim.

NEW ZEALAND

*T.W.M.Latham	c Yasir b Mominul	252
W.A.Young	c Naim b Shoriful	54
D.P.Conway	run out	109
L.R.P.L.Taylor	c Shoriful b Ebadat	28
H.M.Nicholls	c Nurul b Ebadat	0
D.J.Mitchell	c Nurul b Shoriful	3
†T.A.Blundell	not out	57
K.A.Jamieson	not out	4
T.G.Southee		
N.Wagner		
T.A.Boult		
Extras	(LB 8, NB 1, W 5)	14
Total	**(6 wkts dec; 128.5 overs; 566 mins)**	**521**

BANGLADESH

Shadman Islam	c Latham b Boult	7	c Blundell b Jamieson	21
Mohammad Naim	b Southee	0	c Latham b Southee	24
Nazmul Hossain	c Latham b Boult	4	c Boult b Wagner	29
*Mominul Haque	b Southee	0	c Taylor b Wagner	37
Liton Das	c Blundell b Boult	8	lbw b Jamieson	102
Yasir Ali	c Mitchell b Jamieson	55	c Latham b Wagner	2
†Nurul Hasan	lbw b Southee	41	c Wagner b Mitchell	36
Mehedi Hasan	b Boult	5	c Latham b Jamieson	3
Taskin Ahmed	c Young b Jamieson	2	not out	9
Shoriful Islam	b Boult	2	c Southee b Jamieson	0
Ebadat Hossain	not out	0	c Latham b Taylor	4
Extras	(NB 1, W 1)	2	(B 4, LB 1, NB 4, W 2)	11
Total	**(41.2 overs; 194 mins)**	**126**	**(79.3 overs; 369 mins)**	**278**

BANGLADESH	*O*	*M*	*R*	*W*	*O*	*M*	*R*	*W*
Taskin Ahmed	32.5	5	117	0				
Shoriful Islam	28	9	79	2				
Ebadat Hossain	30	3	143	2				
Mehedi Hasan	31	2	125	0				
Nazmul Hossain	4	0	15	0				
Mominul Haque	3	0	34	1				
NEW ZEALAND								
Southee	12	4	28	3	17	6	54	1
Boult	13.2	3	43	5	16	6	42	0
Jamieson	9	3	32	2	18	4	82	4
Wagner	7	1	23	0	22	7	77	3
Mitchell					6	1	18	1
Taylor					0.3	0	0	1

FALL OF WICKETS

	NZ	B	B
Wkt	*1st*	*1st*	*2nd*
1st	148	7	27
2nd	363	11	71
3rd	411	11	105
4th	414	11	123
5th	423	27	128
6th	499	87	229
7th	–	109	244
8th	–	118	269
9th	–	126	269
10th	–	126	278

Umpires: C.B.Gaffaney (*New Zealand*) (39) and W.R.Knights (*New Zealand*) (3).
Referee: J.J.Crowe (*New Zealand*) (105). **Test No. 2448/17 (NZ453/B128)**

NEW ZEALAND v SOUTH AFRICA (1st Test)

At Hagley Oval, Christchurch, on 17, 18, 19 February 2022.
Toss: New Zealand. Result: **NEW ZEALAND** won by an innings and 276 runs.
Debuts: South Africa – S.J.Erwee, G.A.Stuurman.

SOUTH AFRICA

*D.Elgar	c Southee b Henry	1	(2)	c Blundell b Henry	0
S.J.Erwee	c Mitchell b Jamieson	10	(1)	lbw b Southee	0
A.K.Markram	c Blundell b Henry	15		c Mitchell b Southee	2
H.E.van der Dussen	c Southee b Henry	8		b Henry	9
T.Bavuma	c Conway b Southee	7		lbw b Wagner	41
M.Z.Hamza	c Blundell b Henry	25		c Mitchell b Jamieson	6
†K.Verreynne	lbw b Henry	18		c de Grandhomme b Southee	30
M.Jansen	not out	2		c Blundell b Wagner	10
K.Rabada	c Blundell b Henry	0		c Jamieson b Southee	0
G.A.Stuurman	c Blundell b Henry	0		lbw b Southee	11
D.Olivier	c Latham b Wagner	1		not out	0
Extras	(B 4, LB 4)	8		(LB 1, NB 1)	2
Total	**(49.2 overs; 217 mins)**	**95**		**(41.4 overs; 192 mins)**	**111**

NEW ZEALAND

*T.W.M.Latham	b Olivier	15
W.A.Young	c Verreynne b Jansen	8
D.P.Conway	b Olivier	36
H.M.Nicholls	c Markram b Olivier	105
N.Wagner	c van der Dussen b Rabada	49
D.J.Mitchell	c Elgar b Stuurman	16
†T.A.Blundell	c Verreynne b Jansen	96
C.de Grandhomme	c Jansen b Markram	45
K.A.Jamieson	c Rabada b Markram	15
T.G.Southee	c Erwee b Rabada	4
M.J.Henry	not out	58
Extras	(B 9, LB 13, NB 7, W 6)	35
Total	**(117.5 overs; 517 mins)**	**482**

NEW ZEALAND	*O*	*M*	*R*	*W*	*O*	*M*	*R*	*W*
Southee	12	2	33	1	17.4	6	35	5
Henry	15	7	23	7	11	4	32	2
Jamieson	11	4	19	1	6	0	24	1
Wagner	9.2	2	11	1	7	2	19	2
De Grandhomme	2	1	1	0				
SOUTH AFRICA								
Rabada	30	6	113	2				
Stuurman	29	5	124	1				
Jansen	29.5	3	96	2				
Olivier	21	1	100	3				
Markram	8	0	27	2				

FALL OF WICKETS

Wkt	SA *1st*	NZ *1st*	SA *2nd*
1st	1	18	0
2nd	20	36	2
3rd	36	111	4
4th	37	191	34
5th	52	239	46
6th	85	273	87
7th	88	349	91
8th	88	368	97
9th	88	388	105
10th	95	482	111

Umpires: C.M.Brown (*New Zealand*) (4) and C.B.Gaffaney (*New Zealand*) (40).
Referee: J.J.Crowe (*New Zealand*) (106). **Test No. 2449/46 (NZ454/SA449)**

NEW ZEALAND v SOUTH AFRICA (2nd Test)

At Hagley Oval, Christchurch, on 25, 26, 27, 28 February, 1 March 2022.
Toss: South Africa. Result: **SOUTH AFRICA** won by 198 runs.
Debuts: None.

SOUTH AFRICA

*D.Elgar	b Southee	41	(2)	c Blundell b Southee	13
S.J.Erwee	c Blundell b Henry	108	(1)	lbw b Southee	8
A.K.Markram	c Mitchell b Wagner	42		b Henry	14
H.E.van der Dussen	c Mitchell b Wagner	35		c and b Wagner	45
T.Bavuma	b Henry	29		c Southee b Wagner	23
†K.Verreynne	c Latham b Henry	4		not out	136
P.W.A.Mulder	c Blundell b Wagner	14		c Blundell b Jamieson	35
M.Jansen	not out	37		c Young b de Grandhomme	9
K.Rabada	c Mitchell b Wagner	6		c de Grandhomme b Henry	47
K.A.Maharaj	c Nicholls b Jamieson	36		c de Grandhomme b Jamieson	4
L.L.Sipamla	c Southee b Jamieson	0		not out	10
Extras	(LB 7, NB 4 W 1)	12		(LB 5, NB 2, W 3)	10
Total	**(133 overs; 559 mins)**	**364**		**(9 wkts dec; 100 overs; 447 mins)**	**354**

NEW ZEALAND

*T.W.M.Latham	c Verreynne b Rabada	0	c van der Dussen b Rabada	1
W.A.Young	c Verreynne b Rabada	3	c Bavuma b Rabada	0
D.P.Conway	c Verreynne b Jansen	16	lbw b Sipamla	92
H.M.Nicholls	c Erwee b Jansen	39	b Maharaj	7
D.J.Mitchell	lbw b Maharaj	60	b Maharaj	24
†T.A.Blundell	b Rabada	6	c Bavuma b Jansen	44
C.de Grandhomme	not out	120	c Mulder b Jansen	18
K.A.Jamieson	c Mulder b Jansen	13	c Rabada b Jansen	12
T.G.Southee	c Bavuma b Jansen	5	c Sipamla b Rabada	17
N.Wagner	c Jansen b Rabada	21	not out	10
M.J.Henry	c van der Dussen b Rabada	0	lbw b Maharaj	0
Extras	(LB 6, NB 2, W 2)	10	(LB 1, NB 1)	2
Total	**(80 overs; 346 mins)**	**293**	**(93.5 overs; 397 mins)**	**227**

NEW ZEALAND	*O*	*M*	*R*	*W*		*O*	*M*	*R*	*W*
Southee	32	11	75	1		26	5	90	2
Henry	35	10	90	3		24	5	81	2
Jamieson	27	10	74	2		21	2	81	2
De Grandhomme	8	3	16	0	(5)	6	2	16	1
Wagner	31	10	102	4	(4)	23	3	81	2
SOUTH AFRICA									
Rabada	19	3	60	5		19	5	46	3
Jansen	22	2	98	4		23	6	63	3
Sipamla	16	4	49	0	(4)	14	5	29	1
Mulder	7	2	34	0	(5)	6	1	13	0
Maharaj	16	2	46	1	(3)	31.5	9	75	3

FALL OF WICKETS	SA	NZ	SA	NZ
Wkt	*1st*	*1st*	*2nd*	*2nd*
1st	111	4	12	1
2nd	199	9	23	6
3rd	199	51	38	25
4th	257	83	103	81
5th	261	91	114	166
6th	277	224	192	187
7th	296	249	219	188
8th	302	255	297	201
9th	364	293	322	220
10th	364	293	–	227

Umpires: C.M.Brown (*New Zealand*) (5) and W.R.Knights (*New Zealand*) (4).
Referee: J.J.Crowe (*New Zealand*) (107). **Test No. 2450/47 (NZ455/SA450)**

INTERNATIONAL UMPIRES AND REFEREES 2022

ELITE PANEL OF UMPIRES 2022

The Elite Panel of ICC Umpires and Referees was introduced in April 2002 to raise standards and guarantee impartial adjudication. Two umpires from this panel stand in Test matches while one officiates with a home umpire from the Supplementary International Panel in limited-overs internationals.

Full Names	*Birthdate*	*Birthplace*	*Tests*	*Debut*	*LOI*	*Debut*
ALIM Sarwar DAR	06.06.68	Jhang, Pakistan	136	2003-04	211	1999-00
DHARMASENA, H.D.P.Kumar	24.04.71	Colombo, Sri Lanka	71	2010-11	114	2008-09
ERASMUS, Marais	27.02.64	George, South Africa	70	2009-10	102	2007-08
GAFFANEY, Christopher Blair	30.11.75	Dunedin, New Zealand	40	2014	71	2010
GOUGH, Michael Andrew	18.12.79	Hartlepool, England	24	2016	65	2013
ILLINGWORTH, Richard Keith	23.08.63	Bradford, England	57	2012-13	71	2010
KETTLEBOROUGH, Richard Allan	15.03.73	Sheffield, England	72	2010-11	92	2009
MENON, Nitin Narendra	02.11.83	Indore, India	9	2019-20	30	2016-17
REIFFEL, Paul Ronald	19.04.66	Box Hill, Australia	54	2012	71	2008-09
TUCKER, Rodney James	28.08.64	Sydney, Australia	75	2009-10	85	2008-09
WILSON, Joel Sheldon	30.12.66	Trinidad, West Indies	25	2015	75	2011

ELITE PANEL OF REFEREES 2022

Full Names	*Birthdate*	*Birthplace*	*Tests*	*Debut*	*LOI*	*Debut*
BOON, David Clarence	29.12.60	Launceston, Australia	65	2011	146	2011
BROAD, Brian Christopher	29.09.57	Bristol, England	113	2003-04	332	2003-04
CROWE, Jeffrey John	14.09.58	Auckland, New Zealand	107	2004-05	301	2003-04
MADUGALLE, Ranjan Senerath	22.04.59	Kandy, Sri Lanka	201	1993-94	372	1993-94
PYCROFT, Andrew John	06.06.56	Harare, Zimbabwe	84	2009	188	2009
RICHARDSON, Sir Richard Benjamin	12.01.62	Five Islands, Antigua	35	2016	63	2016
SRINATH, Javagal	31.08.69	Mysore, India	59	2006	227	2006-07

INTERNATIONAL UMPIRES PANEL 2022

Nominated by their respective cricket boards, members from this panel officiate in home LOIs and supplement the Elite panel for Test matches. The number of Test matches/LOI in which they have stood is shown in brackets.

Afghanistan	Ahmed Shah Pakteen (2/30)	Ahmed Shah Durrani (-/7)	Bismillah Jan Shinwari (-/9) Izafullah Safi (-/3)
Australia	S.A.J.Craig (-/-)	P.Wilson (7/32)	S.J.Nogajski (-/6) G.A.Abood (-/2)
Bangladesh	Tanvir Ahmed (-/4)	Sharfuddoula (4/48)	Masudur Rahman (-/12) Gazi Sohel (-/4)
England	A.G.Wharf (2/8)	D.J.Millns (-/5)	M.Burns (-/1) M.J.Saggers (-/2)
India	J.Madanagopal (-/1)	A.K.Chaudhary (3/22)	V.K.Sharma (3/4) K.N.Ananthapadmanabhan (-/2)
Ireland	M.Hawthorne (-/33)	R.E.Black (-/17)	J.McCready (-/-) P.A.Reynolds (-/6)
New Zealand	W.R.Knights (4/17)	C.M.Brown (5/18)	S.B.Haig (-/6)
Pakistan	Shozab Raza (-/24)	Ahsan Raza (2/37)	Asif Yaqoob (-/2) Rashid Riaz (-/2)
South Africa	A.T.Holdstock (4/32)	S.George (-/56)	B.P.Jele (-/13) A.Paleker (1/4)
Sri Lanka	R.M.P.J.Rambukwella (-/1)	R.S.A.Palliyaguruge (9/81)	R.R.Wimalasiri (-/17) L.E.Hannibal (-/10)
West Indies	G.O.Brathwaite (6/47)	L.S.Reifer (-/7)	P.A.Gustard (-/-) N.Duguid (-/10)
Zimbabwe	L.Rusere (3/15)	I.Chabi (-/3)	C.Phiri (-/-) F.Mutizwa (-/-)

Test Match and LOI statistics to 3 March 2022.

TEST MATCH CAREER RECORDS

These records, complete to 3 March 2022, contain all players registered for county cricket or The Hundred in 2022 at the time of going to press, plus those who have played Test cricket since 3 December 2020 (Test No. 2393). Some players who may return to Test action have also been listed, even if their most recent game was earlier than this date.

ENGLAND – BATTING AND FIELDING

	M	*I*	*NO*	*HS*	*Runs*	*Avge*	*100*	*50*	*Ct/St*
M.M.Ali	64	111	8	155*	2914	28.29	5	14	40
J.M.Anderson	169	239	103	81	1262	9.27	–	1	99
J.C.Archer	13	20	–	30	155	7.75	–	–	2
J.M.Bairstow	80	142	8	167*	4575	34.14	7	22	196/13
J.T.Ball	4	8	–	31	67	8.37	–	–	1
G.S.Ballance	23	42	2	156	1498	37.45	4	7	22
D.M.Bess	14	19	5	57	319	22.78	–	1	3
S.W.Billings	1	2	–	29	30	15.00	–	–	5
R.S.Bopara	13	19	1	143	575	31.94	3	–	6
S.G.Borthwick	1	2	–	4	5	2.50	–	–	2
J.R.Bracey	2	3	–	8	8	2.66	–	–	6
S.C.J.Broad	152	224	39	169	3412	18.44	1	13	51
R.J.Burns	32	59	–	133	1789	30.32	3	11	24
J.C.Buttler	57	100	9	152	2907	31.94	2	18	153/1
A.N.Cook	161	291	16	294	12472	45.35	33	57	175
M.S.Crane	1	2	–	4	6	3.00	–	–	–
Z.Crawley	18	32	–	267	903	28.21	1	5	21
S.M.Curran	24	38	5	78	815	24.69	–	3	5
T.K.Curran	2	3	1	39	66	33.00	–	–	–
L.A.Dawson	3	6	2	66*	84	21.00	–	1	2
J.L.Denly	15	28	–	94	827	29.53	–	6	7
B.M.Duckett	4	7	–	56	110	15.71	–	1	1
S.T.Finn	36	47	22	56	279	11.16	–	1	8
B.T.Foakes	8	16	3	107	410	31.53	1	1	14/5
A.D.Hales	11	21	–	94	573	27.28	–	5	8
H.Hameed	10	19	1	82	439	24.38	–	4	7
K.K.Jennings	17	32	1	146*	781	25.19	2	1	17
C.J.Jordan	8	11	1	35	180	18.00	–	–	14
D.W.Lawrence	8	15	2	81*	354	27.23	–	3	1
M.J.Leach	19	34	10	92	324	13.50	–	1	9
A.Lyth	7	13	–	107	265	20.38	1	–	8
D.J.Malan	22	39	–	140	1074	27.53	1	9	13
E.J.G.Morgan	16	24	1	130	700	30.43	2	3	11
C.Overton	6	11	2	41*	167	18.55	–	–	4
S.R.Patel	6	9	–	42	151	16.77	–	–	3
O.J.D.Pope	23	40	4	135*	1032	28.66	1	6	24
A.U.Rashid	19	33	5	61	540	19.28	–	2	4
O.E.Robinson	9	16	2	42	125	8.92	–	–	4
S.D.Robson	7	11	–	127	336	30.54	1	1	5
T.S.Roland-Jones	4	6	2	25	82	20.50	–	–	–
J.E.Root	114	210	15	254	9600	49.23	23	53	148
J.J.Roy	5	10	–	72	187	18.70	–	1	1
D.P.Sibley	22	39	3	133*	1042	28.94	2	5	12
B.A.Stokes	76	140	5	258	4867	36.05	10	26	84
O.P.Stone	3	6	–	20	55	9.16	–	–	1
M.D.Stoneman	11	20	1	60	526	27.68	–	5	1
J.M.Vince	13	22	–	83	548	24.90	–	3	8
T.Westley	5	9	1	59	193	24.12	–	1	1
C.R.Woakes	42	68	12	137*	1535	27.41	1	6	18
M.A.Wood	25	43	7	52	563	15.63	–	1	8

ENGLAND – BOWLING

	O	*M*	*R*	*W*	*Avge*	*Best*	*5wI*	*10wM*
M.M.Ali	1975.4	278	7149	195	36.66	6- 53	5	1
J.M.Anderson	6066	1581	17014	640	26.58	7- 42	31	3
J.C.Archer	434.5	95	1304	42	31.04	6- 45	3	–
J.T.Ball	102	23	343	3	114.33	1- 47	–	–
G.S.Ballance	2	1	5	0	–	–	–	–
D.M.Bess	417	82	1223	36	33.97	5- 30	2	–
R.S.Bopara	72.2	10	290	1	290.00	1- 39	–	–
S.G.Borthwick	13	0	82	4	20.50	3- 33	–	–
S.C.J.Broad	5095.5	1206	14932	537	27.80	8- 15	19	3
A.N.Cook	3	0	7	1	7.00	1- 6	–	–
M.S.Crane	48	3	193	1	193.00	1-193	–	–
S.M.Curran	515.1	96	1669	47	35.51	4- 58	–	–
T.K.Curran	66	14	200	2	100.00	1- 65	–	–
L.A.Dawson	87.4	12	298	7	42.57	4-101	–	–
J.L.Denly	65	11	219	2	109.50	2- 42	–	–
S.T.Finn	1068.4	190	3800	125	30.40	6- 79	5	–
A.D.Hales	3	1	2	0	–	–	–	–
K.K.Jennings	12.1	1	55	0	–	–	–	–
C.J.Jordan	255	74	752	21	35.80	4- 18	–	–
D.W.Lawrence	6	0	33	1	33.00	1- 16	–	–
M.J.Leach	691	104	2180	68	32.05	5- 83	2	–
A.Lyth	1	1	0	0	–	–	–	–
D.J.Malan	37	4	131	2	65.50	2- 33	–	–
C.Overton	180.2	31	571	17	33.58	3- 14	–	–
S.R.Patel	143	23	421	7	60.14	2- 27	–	–
A.U.Rashid	636	50	2390	60	39.83	5- 49	2	–
O.E.Robinson	314.4	92	830	39	21.28	5- 65	2	–
T.S.Roland-Jones	89.2	23	334	17	19.64	5- 57	1	–
J.E.Root	619.5	113	1977	44	44.93	5- 8	1	–
D.P.Sibley	1	0	7	0	–	–	–	–
B.A.Stokes	1609.2	292	5401	167	32.34	6- 22	4	–
O.P.Stone	59.4	14	194	10	19.40	3- 29	–	–
J.M.Vince	4	1	13	0	–	–	–	–
T.Westley	4	0	12	0	–	–	–	–
C.R.Woakes	1221	276	3752	125	30.01	6- 17	4	1
M.A.Wood	772	154	2572	81	31.75	6- 37	3	–

AUSTRALIA – BATTING AND FIELDING

	M	*I*	*NO*	*HS*	*Runs*	*Avge*	*100*	*50*	*Ct/St*
J.M.Bird	9	9	6	19*	43	14.33	–	–	2
S.M.Boland	3	3	1	10*	24	12.00	–	–	4
A.T.Carey	5	9	–	51	183	20.22	–	1	23
P.J.Cummins	38	55	7	63	780	16.25	–	2	18
C.D.Green	9	15	1	84	464	33.14	–	3	9
P.S.P.Handscomb	16	29	5	110	934	38.91	2	4	28
M.S.Harris	14	26	2	79	607	25.29	–	3	8
J.R.Hazlewood	56	69	32	39	445	12.02	–	–	21
T.M.Head	23	37	2	161	1510	43.14	4	8	15
U.T.Khawaja	46	81	7	174	3142	42.45	10	14	37
M.Labuschagne	23	40	1	215	2220	56.92	6	12	20
N.M.Lyon	105	134	41	47	1177	12.65	–	–	54
G.J.Maxwell	7	14	1	104	339	26.07	1	–	5
M.G.Neser	1	2	–	35	38	19.00	–	–	–
T.D.Paine	35	57	10	92	1534	32.63	–	9	150/7

	M	I	NO	HS	Runs	Avge	100	50	Ct/St
J.L.Pattinson	21	25	9	47*	417	26.06	–	–	6
W.J.Pucovski	1	2	–	62	72	36.00	–	–	–
M.T.Renshaw	11	20	1	184	636	33.47	1	3	8
J.A.Richardson	3	3	–	9	18	6.00	–	–	–
P.M.Siddle	67	94	15	51	1164	14.73	–	2	19
S.P.D.Smith	82	147	17	239	7784	59.87	27	33	134
M.A.Starc	66	98	22	99	1751	23.03	–	10	32
M.S.Wade	36	63	9	117	1613	29.87	4	5	74/11
D.A.Warner	91	167	7	335*	7584	47.40	24	32	74

AUSTRALIA – BOWLING

	O	M	R	W	Avge	Best	5wI	10wM
J.M.Bird	322.2	80	1042	34	30.64	5- 59	1	–
S.M.Boland	81.1	31	172	18	9.55	6- 7	1	–
P.J.Cummins	1415.4	349	3921	185	21.19	6- 23	6	1
C.D.Green	124.4	29	323	13	24.84	4- 66	–	–
J.R.Hazlewood	2008.1	525	5512	215	25.63	6- 67	9	–
T.M.Head	22	5	76	0	–	–	–	–
U.T.Khawaja	2	0	5	0	–	–	–	–
M.Labuschagne	149	14	540	12	45.00	3- 45	–	–
N.M.Lyon	4444.5	862	13193	415	31.79	8- 50	18	3
G.J.Maxwell	77	4	341	8	42.62	4-127	–	–
M.G.Neser	24	5	61	2	30.50	1- 28	–	–
J.L.Pattinson	660.3	142	2133	81	26.33	5- 27	4	–
M.T.Renshaw	4	0	13	0	–	–	–	–
J.A.Richardson	89.1	28	243	11	22.09	5- 42	1	–
P.M.Siddle	2317.5	615	6777	221	30.66	6- 54	8	–
S.P.D.Smith	235.1	27	970	18	53.88	3- 18	–	–
M.A.Starc	2248	447	7513	274	27.41	6- 50	13	2
M.S.Wade	5	1	28	0	–	–	–	–
D.A.Warner	57	1	269	4	67.25	2- 45	–	–

SOUTH AFRICA – BATTING AND FIELDING

	M	I	NO	HS	Runs	Avge	100	50	Ct/St
K.J.Abbott	11	14	–	17	95	6.78	–	–	4
H.M.Amla	124	215	16	311*	9282	46.64	28	41	108
T.Bavuma	49	83	11	102*	2418	33.58	1	17	26
Q.de Kock	54	91	6	141*	3300	38.82	6	22	221/11
M.de Lange	2	2	–	9	9	4.50	–	–	1
F.du Plessis	69	118	14	199	4163	40.02	10	21	63
D.Elgar	74	130	11	199	4637	38.96	13	19	79
S.J.Erwee	2	4	–	108	126	31.50	1	–	2
M.Z.Hamza	6	12	–	62	212	17.66	–	1	5
S.R.Harmer	5	6	1	13	58	11.60	–	–	1
B.E.Hendricks	1	2	1	5*	9	9.00	–	–	–
M.Jansen	5	8	2	37*	118	19.66	–	–	4
G.F.Linde	3	6	–	37	135	22.50	–	–	–
K.A.Maharaj	40	63	6	73	845	14.82	–	3	12
A.K.Markram	31	57	1	152	1973	35.23	5	9	29
P.W.A.Mulder	8	13	–	36	205	15.76	–	–	13
L.T.Ngidi	13	20	8	14*	52	4.33	–	–	6
A.A.Nortje	12	21	4	40	115	6.76	–	–	4
D.Olivier	13	16	8	10*	38	4.75	–	–	2
D.Paterson	2	4	3	39*	43	43.00	–	–	1

SOUTH AFRICA – BATTING AND FIELDING (continued)

	M	I	NO	HS	Runs	Avge	100	50	Ct/St
K.D.Petersen	5	9	–	82	320	35.55	–	3	11
K.Rabada	52	79	13	47	786	11.90	–	–	27
L.L.Sipamla	3	4	1	10*	15	5.00	–	–	2
G.A.Stuurman	1	2	–	11	11	5.50	–	–	–
H.E.van der Dussen	15	27	2	98	824	32.96	–	6	22
K.Verreynne	6	9	1	136*	248	31.00	1	–	21
D.J.Vilas	6	9	–	26	94	10.44	–	–	13

SOUTH AFRICA – BOWLING

	O	M	R	W	Avge	Best	5wI	10wM
K.J.Abbott	346.5	95	886	39	22.71	7- 29	3	–
H.M.Amla	9	0	37	0	–	–	–	–
T.Bavuma	16	1	61	1	61.00	1- 29	–	–
M.de Lange	74.4	10	277	9	30.77	7- 81	1	–
F.du Plessis	13	0	69	0	–	–	–	–
D.Elgar	171.4	12	665	15	44.33	4- 22	–	–
S.R.Harmer	191.2	34	588	20	29.40	4- 61	–	–
B.E.Hendricks	38.3	5	175	6	29.16	5- 64	1	–
M.Jansen	178.2	40	570	28	20.35	4- 31	–	–
G.F.Linde	78.5	17	252	9	28.00	5- 64	1	–
K.A.Maharaj	1385.3	262	4407	134	32.88	9-129	7	1
A.K.Markram	41.2	5	130	2	65.00	2- 27	–	–
P.W.A.Mulder	141	37	416	14	29.71	3- 1	–	–
L.T.Ngidi	324.4	84	971	47	20.65	6- 39	3	–
A.A.Nortje	363.4	64	1321	47	28.10	6- 56	3	–
D.Olivier	318	52	1219	56	21.76	6- 37	3	1
D.Paterson	57.5	11	166	4	41.50	2- 86	–	–
K.Rabada	1651.2	341	5446	243	22.41	7-112	11	4
L.L.Sipamla	69.5	14	245	11	22.27	4- 76	–	–
G.A.Stuurman	29	5	124	1	124.00	1-124	–	–

WEST INDIES – BATTING AND FIELDING

	M	I	NO	HS	Runs	Avge	100	50	Ct/St
J.Blackwood	43	79	4	112*	2277	30.36	2	15	34
N.E.Bonner	9	16	2	113*	577	41.21	1	3	9
C.R.Brathwaite	3	5	1	69	181	45.25	–	3	–
K.C.Brathwaite	74	142	7	212	4402	32.60	9	23	34
D.M.Bravo	56	102	5	218	3538	36.47	8	17	51
S.S.J.Brooks	8	15	–	111	422	28.13	1	3	8
J.D.Campbell	15	30	3	68	640	22.70	–	2	8
R.L.Chase	43	79	4	137*	2009	26.78	5	9	19
R.R.S.Cornwall	9	15	2	73	238	18.30	–	2	15
J.Da Silva	11	21	3	92	445	24.72	–	3	38/2
S.O.Dowrich	35	62	8	125*	1570	29.07	3	9	85/5
S.T.Gabriel	56	84	32	20*	221	4.25	–	–	16
C.K.Holder	1	2	2	13*	21	–	–	–	–
J.O.Holder	53	95	15	202*	2477	30.96	3	11	55
S.D.Hope	38	72	3	147	1726	25.01	2	5	53/1
A.S.Joseph	17	28	–	86	394	14.07	–	2	8
K.R.Mayers	10	20	2	210*	636	35.33	1	2	5
S.A.R.Moseley	2	4	–	12	28	7.00	–	–	3
S.P.Narine	6	7	2	22*	40	8.00	–	–	2
V.Permaul	7	11	1	23*	114	11.40	–	–	2
K.O.A.Powell	44	83	1	134	2113	25.76	3	7	31

WEST INDIES – BATTING AND FIELDING (continued)

	M	I	NO	HS	Runs	Avge	100	50	Ct/St
K.A.J.Roach	68	111	23	41	1042	11.84	–	–	18
J.N.T.Seales	4	8	5	7	12	4.00	–	–	1
J.L.Solozano	1	–	–	–	–	–	–	–	–
J.A.Warrican	13	23	9	41	163	11.64	–	–	5

WEST INDIES – BOWLING

	O	M	R	W	Avge	Best	5wI	10wM
J.Blackwood	66	10	236	3	78.66	2- 14	–	–
N.E.Bonner	12	1	61	1	61.00	1- 16	–	–
C.R.Brathwaite	68	9	242	1	242.00	1- 30	–	–
K.C.Brathwaite	382.2	30	1227	24	51.12	6- 29	1	–
D.M.Bravo	1	0	2	0	–	–	–	–
J.D.Campbell	10.1	0	30	0	–	–	–	–
R.L.Chase	980.1	114	3377	79	42.74	8- 60	4	–
R.R.S.Cornwall	444.1	79	1284	34	37.76	7- 75	2	1
S.T.Gabriel	1509.1	265	5127	161	31.84	8- 62	6	1
C.K.Holder	26	1	110	2	55.00	2-110	–	–
J.O.Holder	1487.4	400	3745	138	27.13	6- 42	8	1
A.S.Joseph	469.3	95	1598	40	39.95	3- 53	–	–
K.R.Mayers	134	42	327	13	25.15	3- 24	–	–
S.P.Narine	275	60	851	21	40.52	6- 91	2	–
V.Permaul	281.3	41	929	26	35.73	5- 35	1	–
K.O.A.Powell	1	1	0	0	–	–	–	–
K.A.J.Roach	2050.2	460	6289	231	27.22	6- 48	9	1
J.N.T.Seales	100.4	23	341	16	21.31	5- 55	1	–
J.A.Warrican	449.3	64	1444	41	35.21	4- 50	–	–

NEW ZEALAND – BATTING AND FIELDING

	M	I	NO	HS	Runs	Avge	100	50	Ct/St
T.A.Blundell	17	27	3	121	809	33.70	2	4	39/1
T.A.Boult	75	88	43	52*	704	15.64	–	1	40
D.P.Conway	7	12	–	200	767	63.91	3	3	1
C.de Grandhomme	28	42	6	120*	1390	38.61	2	8	19
M.J.Henry	16	20	5	66	294	19.60	–	2	6
K.A.Jamieson	14	18	3	51*	351	23.40	–	1	5
T.W.M.Latham	65	113	5	264*	4502	41.68	12	22	76
D.J.Mitchell	9	11	1	102*	403	40.30	1	3	11
J.D.S.Neesham	12	22	1	137*	709	33.76	2	4	12
H.M.Nicholls	46	69	6	174	2544	40.38	8	12	29
A.Y.Patel	11	15	7	20	80	10.00	–	–	6
R.Ravindra	3	6	1	18*	73	14.60	–	–	2
M.J.Santner	24	32	1	126	766	24.70	1	2	16
W.E.R.Somerville	6	10	2	40*	115	14.37	–	–	–
T.G.Southee	85	120	11	77*	1769	16.22	–	5	65
L.R.P.L.Taylor	112	196	24	290	7683	44.66	19	35	163
N.Wagner	58	74	21	66*	775	14.62	–	1	15
B.J.Watling	75	117	16	205	3790	37.52	8	19	267/8
K.S.Williamson	86	150	14	251	7272	53.47	24	33	72
W.A.Young	9	14	–	89	439	31.35	–	5	6

NEW ZEALAND – BOWLING

	O	M	R	W	Avge	Best	5wI	10wM
T.A.Blundell	3	0	13	0	–	–	–	–
T.A.Boult	2781.3	634	8254	301	27.42	6- 30	9	1
C.de Grandhomme	663.5	160	1588	48	33.08	6- 41	1	–
M.J.Henry	615.1	121	1938	51	38.00	7- 23	1	–
K.A.Jamieson	478.3	158	1236	66	18.72	6- 48	5	1
D.J.Mitchell	58	13	160	2	80.00	1- 7	–	–
J.D.S.Neesham	179.2	18	675	14	48.21	3- 42	–	–
A.Y.Patel	413.5	89	1167	43	27.13	10-119	3	1
R.Ravindra	61	11	188	3	62.66	3- 56	–	–
M.J.Santner	672.5	140	1871	41	45.63	3- 53	–	–
W.E.R.Somerville	244.2	34	724	15	48.26	4- 75	–	–
T.G.Southee	3225.2	742	9530	338	28.19	7- 64	14	1
L.R.P.L.Taylor	16.3	3	48	3	16.00	2- 4	–	–
N.Wagner	2140.5	459	6464	244	26.49	7- 39	9	–
K.S.Williamson	358.3	48	1207	30	40.23	4- 44	–	–

INDIA – BATTING AND FIELDING

	M	I	NO	HS	Runs	Avge	100	50	Ct/St
M.A.Agarwal	19	33	–	243	1429	43.30	4	6	13
R.Ashwin	84	120	14	124	2844	26.83	5	11	29
J.J.Bumrah	27	43	15	34*	174	6.21	–	–	7
S.Gill	10	19	2	91	558	32.82	–	4	6
S.S.Iyer	2	4	–	105	202	50.50	1	1	2
R.A.Jadeja	57	84	19	100*	2195	33.76	1	17	39
V.Kohli	99	168	10	254*	7962	50.39	27	28	100
Kuldeep Yadav	7	8	–	26	54	6.75	–	–	3
Mohammed Shami	57	79	23	56*	615	10.98	–	2	14
S.Nadeem	2	3	1	1*	1	0.50	–	–	1
T.Natarajan	1	1	1	1*	1	–	–	–	–
R.R.Pant	28	48	4	159*	1735	39.43	4	7	102/8
A.R.Patel	5	8	2	52	179	29.83	–	1	2
C.A.Pujara	95	162	9	206*	6713	43.87	18	32	64
A.M.Rahane	82	140	12	188	4931	38.52	12	25	99
K.L.Rahul	43	74	2	199	2547	35.37	7	13	50
W.P.Saha	40	56	10	117	1353	29.41	3	6	92/12
N.Saini	2	3	1	5	8	4.00	–	–	1
I.Sharma	105	142	47	57	785	8.26	–	1	23
R.G.Sharma	43	74	9	212	3047	46.87	8	14	45
P.P.Shaw	5	9	1	134	339	42.37	1	2	2
M.Siraj	12	17	7	16*	62	6.20	–	–	7
S.N.Thakur	7	12	1	67	249	22.63	–	3	2
G.H.Vihari	13	23	3	111	684	34.20	1	4	3
M.S.Washington Sundar	4	6	2	96*	265	66.25	–	3	1
J.Yadav	5	8	1	104	246	35.14	1	1	2
U.T.Yadav	52	61	26	31	408	11.65	–	–	17

INDIA – BOWLING

	O	M	R	W	Avge	Best	5wI	10wM
R.Ashwin	3778.5	778	10485	430	24.38	7-59	30	7
J.J.Bumrah	971.4	238	2583	113	22.85	6-27	7	–
R.A.Jadeja	2388.5	603	5765	232	24.84	7-48	9	1
V.Kohli	29.1	2	84	0	–	–	–	–
Kuldeep Yadav	177.1	24	620	26	23.84	5-57	2	–
Mohammed Shami	1735.3	328	5670	209	27.12	6-56	6	–

INDIA – BOWLING (continued)

	O	M	R	W	Avge	Best	5wI	10wM
S.Nadeem	76.2	11	273	8	34.12	2-18	–	–
T.Natarajan	38.2	7	119	3	39.66	3-78	–	–
A.R.Patel	201.5	50	427	36	11.86	6-38	5	1
C.A.Pujara	1	0	2	0	–	–	–	–
N.Saini	41.5	5	172	4	43.00	2-54	–	–
I.Sharma	3193.2	640	10078	311	32.40	7-74	11	1
R.G.Sharma	63.5	5	224	2	112.00	1-26	–	–
M.Siraj	345.1	73	1067	36	29.63	5-73	1	–
S.N.Thakur	166.3	26	547	26	21.03	7-61	1	–
G.H.Vihari	57.3	10	180	5	36.00	3-37	–	–
M.S.Washington Sundar	87.4	10	299	6	49.83	3-89	–	–
J.Yadav	120.3	23	429	16	26.81	4-49	–	–
U.T.Yadav	1372.3	228	4867	158	30.80	6-88	3	1

PAKISTAN – BATTING AND FIELDING

	M	I	NO	HS	Runs	Avge	100	50	Ct/St
Abdullah Shafiq	2	3	–	73	150	50.00	–	2	3
Abid Ali	16	26	2	215*	1180	49.16	4	3	6
Azhar Ali	91	169	11	302*	6721	42.53	18	34	65
Babar Azam	37	66	9	143	2451	43.17	5	19	25
Faheem Ashraf	13	19	1	91	632	35.11	–	4	4
Fawad Alam	15	24	4	168	953	47.65	5	2	11
Haris Sohail	16	27	1	147	847	32.57	2	3	14
Hasan Ali	17	25	5	30	299	14.95	–	–	6
Iftikhar Ahmed	3	5	–	27	48	9.60	–	–	1
Imam-ul-Haq	11	21	2	76	485	25.52	–	3	7
Imran Butt	6	10	–	91	178	17.80	–	–	16
Mohammad Abbas	25	36	16	29	110	5.50	–	–	7
Mohammad Rizwan	19	28	5	115*	972	42.26	1	7	52/2
Naseem Shah	9	12	5	12	28	4.00	–	–	1
Nauman Ali	7	7	–	97	182	26.00	–	1	–
Sajid Khan	4	3	–	20	32	10.66	–	–	3
Shaheen Shah Afridi	21	28	7	19	121	5.76	–	–	2
Shan Masood	25	47	–	156	1378	29.31	4	6	16
Tabish Khan	1	–	–	–	–	–	–	–	–
Yasir Shah	46	69	7	113	847	13.66	1	–	23
Zafar Gohar	1	2	–	37	71	35.50	–	–	–

PAKISTAN – BOWLING

	O	M	R	W	Avge	Best	5wI	10wM
Azhar Ali	142.3	8	611	8	76.37	2-35	–	–
Babar Azam	3	1	2	1	2.00	1- 2	–	–
Faheem Ashraf	258	71	750	22	34.09	3-42	–	–
Fawad Alam	16	1	54	2	27.00	2-46	–	–
Haris Sohail	105	12	294	13	22.61	3- 1	–	–
Hasan Ali	502	121	1555	72	21.59	5-27	6	1
Iftikhar Ahmed	31.2	1	141	1	141.00	1- 1	–	–
Mohammad Abbas	855.4	261	2072	90	23.02	5-33	4	1
Naseem Shah	224.4	33	849	20	42.45	5-31	1	–
Nauman Ali	216.3	58	529	19	27.84	5-35	2	–
Sajid Khan	121.4	26	355	18	19.72	8-42	1	1
Shaheen Shah Afridi	684.3	150	2055	86	23.89	6-51	4	1
Shan Masood	24	6	92	2	46.00	1- 6	–	–

PAKISTAN – BOWLING (continued)

	O	M	R	W	Avge	Best	5wI	10wM
Tabish Khan	26	11	68	1	68.00	1-22	–	–
Yasir Shah	2282.5	349	7306	235	31.08	8-41	16	3
Zafar Gohar	32	0	159	0	–	–	–	–

SRI LANKA – BATTING AND FIELDING

	M	I	NO	HS	Runs	Avge	100	50	Ct/St
L.Ambuldeniya	13	19	1	40	178	9.88	–	–	2
K.I.C.Asalanka	1	2	–	19	29	14.50	–	–	1
P.V.D.Chameera	12	21	2	22	104	5.47	–	–	5
L.D.Chandimal	64	117	10	164	4217	39.41	11	20	79/10
D.M.de Silva	38	68	6	173	2472	39.87	8	9	46
P.W.H.de Silva	4	7	–	59	196	28.00	–	1	2
D.P.D.N.Dickwella	45	80	5	96	2443	32.57	–	18	112/23
A.M.Fernando	3	6	3	4	4	1.33	–	–	–
B.O.P.Fernando	13	24	3	102	726	34.57	1	4	12
M.V.T.Fernando	14	20	11	38	58	6.44	–	–	3
P.A.K.P.Jayawickrama	3	3	3	8*	11	–	–	–	–
F.D.M.Karunaratne	74	143	5	244	5454	39.52	13	27	55
C.B.R.L.S.Kumara	23	30	15	10	52	3.46	–	–	4
R.A.S.Lakmal	68	105	25	42	928	11.60	–	–	21
A.D.Mathews	92	165	23	200*	6338	44.63	11	37	69
B.K.G.Mendis	47	91	4	196	3022	34.73	7	11	71
M.D.K.Perera	43	77	8	95	1303	18.88	–	7	19
M.D.K.J.Perera	22	41	3	153*	1177	30.97	2	7	19/8
C.A.K.Rajitha	9	12	2	12	35	3.50	–	–	4
M.B.Ranasinghe	1	2	–	5	6	3.00	–	–	–
M.D.Shanaka	6	12	2	66*	140	14.00	–	1	4
P.N.Silva	6	10	–	103	427	42.70	1	4	2
H.D.R.L.Thirimanne	42	81	6	155*	2063	27.50	3	10	34
R.T.M.Wanigamuni	4	7	–	33	100	14.28	–	–	1

SRI LANKA – BOWLING

	O	M	R	W	Avge	Best	5wI	10wM
L.Ambuldeniya	654.4	126	2065	62	33.30	7-137	5	1
K.I.C.Asalanka	1	0	2	0	–	–	–	–
P.V.D.Chameera	337	28	1321	32	41.28	5- 47	1	–
D.M.de Silva	439.1	55	1465	25	58.60	3- 25	–	–
P.W.H.de Silva	112.2	8	403	4	100.75	4-171	–	–
A.M.Fernando	47	9	156	4	39.00	2- 44	–	–
B.O.P.Fernando	3	0	19	0	–	–	–	–
M.V.T.Fernando	397	51	1403	40	35.07	5-101	1	–
P.A.K.P.Jayawickrama	132.5	36	328	18	18.22	6- 92	2	1
F.D.M.Karunaratne	47.2	4	191	2	95.50	1- 12	–	–
C.B.R.L.S.Kumara	700	97	2642	69	38.28	6-122	1	–
R.A.S.Lakmal	2030.5	433	6096	168	36.28	5- 47	4	–
A.D.Mathews	655	159	1766	33	53.51	4- 44	–	–
B.K.G.Mendis	21	1	110	1	110.00	1- 10	–	–
M.D.K.Perera	1800.5	239	5780	161	35.90	6- 32	8	2
C.A.K.Rajitha	235.4	44	779	25	31.16	3- 20	–	–
M.D.Shanaka	127	19	431	13	33.15	3- 46	–	–
H.D.R.L.Thirimanne	14	1	51	0	–	–	–	–
R.T.M.Wanigamuni	192.2	30	560	26	21.53	6- 70	2	1

M.B.Ranasinghe is also known as M.Bhanuka; P.N.Silva is also known as P.Nissanka; R.T.M.Wanigamuni is also known as W.R.T.Mendis.

ZIMBABWE – BATTING AND FIELDING

	M	I	NO	HS	Runs	Avge	100	50	Ct/St
R.P.Burl	3	5	–	16	24	4.80	–	–	1
R.W.Chakabva	22	43	4	101	1061	27.20	1	5	46/5
T.S.Chisoro	3	5	–	9	27	5.40	–	–	1
L.M.Jongwe	1	2	–	37	56	28.00	–	–	–
R.Kaia	3	6	–	48	59	9.83	–	–	1
T.Kaitano	1	2	–	87	94	47.00	–	1	–
K.T.Kasuza	7	12	1	63	249	22.63	–	1	3
W.N.Madhevere	2	3	–	0	0	0.00	–	–	1
T.H.Maruma	4	7	–	41	68	9.71	–	–	1
P.S.Masvaure	8	15	1	65	346	24.71	–	3	1
T.K.Musakanda	5	9	–	43	134	14.88	–	–	4
B.Muzarabani	6	11	4	30*	102	14.57	–	–	–
D.N.Myers	1	2	–	27	53	26.50	–	–	3
R.Ngarava	3	6	1	15*	31	6.20	–	–	1
V.M.Nyauchi	6	10	4	11	40	6.66	–	–	2
M.Shumba	3	6	–	41	101	16.83	–	–	1
Sikandar Raza	17	33	–	127	1187	35.96	1	8	5
B.R.M.Taylor	34	68	4	171	2320	36.25	6	12	30
D.T.Tiripano	15	29	6	95	508	22.08	–	2	4
S.C.Williams	14	27	2	151*	1034	41.36	4	3	13

ZIMBABWE – BOWLING

	O	M	R	W	Avge	Best	5wI	10wM
R.P.Burl	38	3	107	4	26.75	2- 16	–	–
T.S.Chisoro	115.3	23	333	6	55.50	3-113	–	–
L.M.Jongwe	17	1	68	1	68.00	1- 68	–	–
R.Kaia	30	2	165	0	–	–	–	–
W.N.Madhevere	13	1	42	0	–	–	–	–
P.S.Masvaure	14	0	61	0	–	–	–	–
B.Muzarabani	169.1	37	473	19	24.89	4- 48	–	–
D.N.Myers	3	1	13	0	–	–	–	–
R.Ngarava	85	14	281	5	56.20	2-104	–	–
V.M.Nyauchi	168.5	29	567	15	37.80	3- 30	–	–
M.Shumba	57.4	8	233	1	233.00	1- 64	–	–
Sikandar Raza	442.5	56	141	34	42.38	7-113	2	–
B.R.M.Taylor	7	0	38	0	–	–	–	–
D.T.Tiripano	435.5	97	1247	26	47.96	3- 23	–	–
S.C.Williams	337.3	39	1072	21	51.04	3- 20	–	–

BANGLADESH – BATTING AND FIELDING

	M	I	NO	HS	Runs	Avge	100	50	Ct/St
Abu Jayed	13	22	8	8	36	2.57	–	–	1
Ebadat Hossain	12	18	9	4	8	0.88	–	–	1
Khaled Ahmed	3	4	1	4*	4	1.33	–	–	2
Liton Das	29	49	1	114	1649	34.35	2	11	53/5
Mahmudul Hasan	2	3	–	78	84	28.00	–	1	–
Mahmudullah	50	94	7	150*	2914	33.49	5	16	38/1
Mehedi Hasan	31	57	7	103	1012	20.24	1	3	21
Mithun Ali	10	18	–	67	333	18.50	–	2	6
Mohammad Naim	1	2	–	24	24	12.00	–	–	1
Mominul Haque	49	91	6	181	3501	41.18	11	15	30
Mushfiqur Rahim	78	144	12	219*	4873	36.91	7	24	107/15
Mustafizur Rahman	14	20	7	16	59	4.53	–	–	1
Nayeem Hasan	7	10	3	26	109	15.57	–	–	4

BANGLADESH – BATTING AND FIELDING (continued)

	M	I	NO	HS	Runs	Avge	100	50	Ct/St
Nazmul Hossain	13	25	1	163	713	29.70	2	2	11
Nurul Hasan	5	9	–	64	207	23.00	–	1	7/3
Saif Hasan	6	11	–	43	159	14.45	–	–	–
Shadman Islam	12	23	1	115*	550	25.00	1	2	9
Shakib Al Hasan	59	109	7	217	4029	39.50	5	26	25
Shoriful Islam	3	5	1	7	9	2.25	–	–	3
Soumya Sarkar	16	30	–	149	831	27.70	1	4	23
Taijul Islam	35	59	8	39*	483	9.47	–	–	18
Tamim Iqbal	64	123	2	206	4788	39.57	9	31	18
Taskin Ahmed	10	17	2	75	172	11.46	–	1	1
Yasir Ali	3	5	1	55	123	30.75	–	1	1

BANGLADESH – BOWLING

	O	M	R	W	Avge	Best	5wI	10wM
Abu Jayed	327.2	64	1118	30	37.26	4-71	–	–
Ebadat Hossain	321	64	1161	20	58.05	6-46	1	–
Khaled Ahmed	77.3	22	291	1	291.00	1-49	–	–
Mahmudullah	570.3	56	1958	43	45.53	5-51	1	–
Mehedi Hasan	1302.1	189	4153	119	34.89	7-58	8	2
Mominul Haque	119.2	8	456	7	65.14	3-27	–	–
Mustafizur Rahman	335.3	68	1102	30	36.73	4-37	–	–
Nayeem Hasan	220.2	35	656	25	26.24	5-61	2	–
Nazmul Hossain	6.4	0	38	0	–	–	–	–
Saif Hasan	6	0	27	1	27.00	1-22	–	–
Shakib Al Hasan	2254.5	420	6731	215	31.30	7-36	18	2
Shoriful Islam	96	24	277	6	46.16	3-69	–	–
Soumya Sarkar	84.4	3	336	4	84.00	2-68	–	–
Taijul Islam	1520.1	251	4697	144	32.61	8-39	9	1
Tamim Iqbal	5	0	20	0	–	–	–	–
Taskin Ahmed	344.1	58	1305	23	56.73	4-82	–	–

IRELAND – BATTING AND FIELDING

	M	I	NO	HS	Runs	Avge	100	50	Ct/St
M.R.Adair	1	2	–	8	11	5.50	–	–	1
A.Balbirnie	3	6	–	82	146	24.33	–	2	3
G.H.Dockrell	1	2	–	39	64	32.00	–	–	–
A.R.McBrine	2	4	–	11	18	4.50	–	–	–
J.A.McCollum	2	4	–	39	73	18.25	–	–	2
T.J.Murtagh	3	6	2	54*	109	27.25	–	1	–
K.J.O'Brien	3	6	1	118	258	51.60	1	1	–
W.T.S.Porterfield	3	6	–	32	58	9.66	–	–	2
S.W.Poynter	1	2	–	1	1	0.50	–	–	2/1
P.R.Stirling	3	6	–	36	104	17.33	–	–	4
S.R.Thompson	3	6	–	53	64	10.66	–	1	–

IRELAND – BOWLING

	O	M	R	W	Avge	Best	5wI	10wM
M.R.Adair	27.4	8	98	6	16.33	3-32	–	–
A.Balbirnie	1	0	8	0	–	–	–	–
G.H.Dockrell	40	11	121	2	60.50	2-63	–	–
A.R.McBrine	50	10	159	3	53.00	2-77	–	–
T.J.Murtagh	95	25	213	13	16.38	5-13	1	–
K.J.O'Brien	10	2	31	0	–	–	–	–

IRELAND – BOWLING (continued)

	O	M	R	W	Avge	Best	5wI	10wM
P.R.Stirling	2	0	11	0	–	–	–	–
S.R.Thompson	68.2	14	204	10	20.40	3-28	–	–

Ireland have not played a Test match since 26 July 2019. The players listed include all those who played in some format of the game since the start of the 2021 season.

AFGHANISTAN – BATTING AND FIELDING

	M	I	NO	HS	Runs	Avge	100	50	Ct/St
Abdul Malik	1	2	–	0	0	0.00	–	–	2
Abdul Wasi	1	2	–	9	12	6.00	–	–	–
Afsar Zazai	5	8	1	48*	172	24.57	–	–	9/1
Asghar Stanikzai	6	10	–	164	440	44.00	1	3	2
Hamza Hotak	3	4	2	34	72	36.00	–	–	1
Hashmatullah Shahidi	5	10	4	200*	353	58.83	1	1	2
Ibrahim Zadran	4	8	–	87	356	44.50	–	3	6
Javed Ahmadi	3	6	–	62	113	18.83	–	1	1
Mujeeb Zadran	1	2	–	15	18	9.00	–	–	–
Munir Ahmad	1	2	–	12	13	6.50	–	–	–
Nasir Ahmadzai	2	4	2	55*	76	38.00	–	–	2
Qais Ahmad	1	2	–	14	23	11.50	–	–	–
Rahmat Shah	6	12	–	102	385	32.08	1	3	4
Rashid Khan	5	7	–	51	106	15.14	–	1	–
Sayed Shirzad	1	–	–	–	–	–	–	–	–
Shahidullah	1	1	–	0	0	0.00	–	–	–
Yamin Ahmadzai	5	9	–	18	32	3.55	–	–	–
Zahir Khan	3	6	3	0*	0	0.00	–	–	–

AFGHANISTAN – BOWLING

	O	M	R	W	Avge	Best	5wI	10wM
Abdul Wasi	8.5	0	23	0	–	–	–	–
Asghar Stanikzai	3	0	17	0	–	–	–	–
Hamza Hotak	123.5	21	342	16	21.37	6- 75	2	–
Ibrahim Zadran	2	0	13	1	13.00	1- 13	–	–
Javed Ahmadi	25	6	69	1	69.00	1- 40	–	–
Mujeeb Zadran	15	1	75	1	75.00	1- 75	–	–
Qais Ahmad	9	2	28	1	28.00	1- 22	–	–
Rahmat Shah	3	0	9	0	–	–	–	–
Rashid Khan	255.4	48	760	30	22.35	7-137	4	2
Sayed Shirzad	42	10	97	3	32.33	2- 48	–	–
Shahidullah	5	1	6	0	–	–	–	–
Yamin Ahmadzai	88.3	18	264	11	24.00	3- 41	–	–
Zahir Khan	56	3	239	7	34.14	3- 59	–	–

INTERNATIONAL TEST MATCH RESULTS

Complete to 3 March 2022.

	Opponents	*Tests*	*Won by*												*Tied*	*Drawn*
			E	*A*	*SA*	*WI*	*NZ*	*I*	*P*	*SL*	*Z*	*B*	*Ire*	*Afg*		
England	Australia	356	110	150	–	–	–	–	–	–	–	–	–	–	–	96
	South Africa	153	64	–	34	–	–	–	–	–	–	–	–	–	–	55
	West Indies	160	51	–	–	58	–	–	–	–	–	–	–	–	–	51
	New Zealand	107	48	–	–	–	12	–	–	–	–	–	–	–	–	47
	India	130	49	–	–	–	–	31	–	–	–	–	–	–	–	50
	Pakistan	86	26	–	–	–	–	–	21	–	–	–	–	–	–	39
	Sri Lanka	36	17	–	–	–	–	–	–	8	–	–	–	–	–	11
	Zimbabwe	6	3	–	–	–	–	–	–	–	0	–	–	–	–	3
	Bangladesh	10	9	–	–	–	–	–	–	–	–	1	–	–	–	0
	Ireland	1	1	–	–	–	–	–	–	–	–	–	0	–	–	0
Australia	South Africa	98	–	52	26	–	–	–	–	–	–	–	–	–	–	20
	West Indies	116	–	58	–	32	–	–	–	–	–	–	–	–	1	25
	New Zealand	60	–	34	–	–	8	–	–	–	–	–	–	–	–	18
	India	102	–	43	–	–	–	30	–	–	–	–	–	–	1	28
	Pakistan	66	–	33	–	–	–	–	15	–	–	–	–	–	–	18
	Sri Lanka	31	–	19	–	–	–	–	–	4	–	–	–	–	–	8
	Zimbabwe	3	–	3	–	–	–	–	–	–	0	–	–	–	–	0
	Bangladesh	6	–	5	–	–	–	–	–	–	–	1	–	–	–	0
S Africa	West Indies	30	–	–	20	3	–	–	–	–	–	–	–	–	–	7
	New Zealand	47	–	–	26	–	5	–	–	–	–	–	–	–	–	16
	India	42	–	–	17	–	–	15	–	–	–	–	–	–	–	10
	Pakistan	28	–	–	15	–	–	–	6	–	–	–	–	–	–	7
	Sri Lanka	31	–	–	16	–	–	–	–	9	–	–	–	–	–	6
	Zimbabwe	9	–	–	8	–	–	–	–	–	0	–	–	–	–	1
	Bangladesh	12	–	–	10	–	–	–	–	–	–	0	–	–	–	2
W Indies	New Zealand	49	–	–	–	13	17	–	–	–	–	–	–	–	–	19
	India	98	–	–	–	30	–	22	–	–	–	–	–	–	–	46
	Pakistan	54	–	–	–	18	–	–	21	–	–	–	–	–	–	15
	Sri Lanka	24	–	–	–	4	–	–	–	11	–	–	–	–	–	9
	Zimbabwe	10	–	–	–	7	–	–	–	–	0	–	–	–	–	3
	Bangladesh	18	–	–	–	12	–	–	–	–	–	4	–	–	–	2
	Afghanistan	1	–	–	–	1	–	–	–	–	–	–	–	0	–	0
N Zealand	India	62	–	–	–	–	13	22	–	–	–	–	–	–	–	27
	Pakistan	60	–	–	–	–	14	–	25	–	–	–	–	–	–	21
	Sri Lanka	36	–	–	–	–	16	–	–	9	–	–	–	–	–	11
	Zimbabwe	17	–	–	–	–	11	–	–	–	0	–	–	–	–	6
	Bangladesh	17	–	–	–	–	13	–	–	–	–	1	–	–	–	3
India	Pakistan	59	–	–	–	–	–	9	12	–	–	–	–	–	–	38
	Sri Lanka	44	–	–	–	–	–	20	–	7	–	–	–	–	–	17
	Zimbabwe	11	–	–	–	–	–	7	–	–	2	–	–	–	–	2
	Bangladesh	11	–	–	–	–	–	9	–	–	–	0	–	–	–	2
	Afghanistan	1	–	–	–	–	–	1	–	–	–	–	–	0	–	0
Pakistan	Sri Lanka	55	–	–	–	–	–	–	20	16	–	–	–	–	–	19
	Zimbabwe	19	–	–	–	–	–	–	12	–	3	–	–	–	–	4
	Bangladesh	13	–	–	–	–	–	–	12	–	–	0	–	–	–	1
	Ireland	1	–	–	–	–	–	–	1	–	–	–	0	–	–	0
Sri Lanka	Zimbabwe	20	–	–	–	–	–	–	–	14	0	–	–	–	–	6
	Bangladesh	22	–	–	–	–	–	–	–	17	–	1	–	–	–	4
Zimbabwe	Bangladesh	18	–	–	–	–	–	–	–	–	7	8	–	–	–	3
	Afghanistan	2	–	–	–	–	–	–	–	–	1	–	–	1	–	0
Bangladesh	Afghanistan	1	–	–	–	–	–	–	–	–	–	0	–	1	–	0
Ireland	Afghanistan	1	–	–	–	–	–	–	–	–	–	–	0	1	–	0
		2450	378	397	172	178	109	166	145	95	13	16	0	3	2	776

	Tests	Won	Lost	Drawn	Tied	Toss Won
England	1045	378	315	352	–	511
Australia	839†	398†	226	213	2	421†
South Africa	450	172	154	124	–	211
West Indies	560	178	204	177	1	295
New Zealand	455	109	178	168	–	225
India	560	166	173	220	1	280
Pakistan	441	145	134	162	–	209
Sri Lanka	299	95	113	91	–	163
Zimbabwe	115	13	74	28	–	64
Bangladesh	128	16	95	17	–	67
Ireland	3	–	3	–	–	2
Afghanistan	6	3	3	–	–	4

† total includes Australia's victory against the ICC World XI.

INTERNATIONAL TEST CRICKET RECORDS

(To 3 March 2022)

TEAM RECORDS
HIGHEST INNINGS TOTALS

952-6d	Sri Lanka v India	Colombo (RPS)	1997-98
903-7d	England v Australia	The Oval	1938
849	England v West Indies	Kingston	1929-30
790-3d	West Indies v Pakistan	Kingston	1957-58
765-6d	Pakistan v Sri Lanka	Karachi	2008-09
760-7d	Sri Lanka v India	Ahmedabad	2009-10
759-7d	India v England	Chennai	2016-17
758-8d	Australia v West Indies	Kingston	1954-55
756-5d	Sri Lanka v South Africa	Colombo (SSC)	2006
751-5d	West Indies v England	St John's	2003-04
749-9d	West Indies v England	Bridgetown	2008-09
747	West Indies v South Africa	St John's	2004-05
735-6d	Australia v Zimbabwe	Perth	2003-04
730-6d	Sri Lanka v Bangladesh	Dhaka	2013-14
729-6d	Australia v England	Lord's	1930
726-9d	India v Sri Lanka	Mumbai	2009-10
715-6d	New Zealand v Bangladesh	Hamilton	2018-19
713-3d	Sri Lanka v Zimbabwe	Bulawayo	2003-04
713-9d	Sri Lanka v Bangladesh	Chittagong	2017-18
710-7d	England v India	Birmingham	2011
708	Pakistan v England	The Oval	1987
707	India v Sri Lanka	Colombo (SSC)	2010
705-7d	India v Australia	Sydney	2003-04
701	Australia v England	The Oval	1934
699-5	Pakistan v India	Lahore	1989-90
695	Australia v England	The Oval	1930
692-8d	West Indies v England	The Oval	1995
690	New Zealand v Pakistan	Sharjah	2014-15
687-8d	West Indies v England	The Oval	1976
687-6d	India v Bangladesh	Hyderabad	2016-17
682-6d	South Africa v England	Lord's	2003
681-8d	West Indies v England	Port-of-Spain	1953-54
680-8d	New Zealand v India	Wellington	2013-14
679-7d	Pakistan v India	Lahore	2005-06

676-7	India v Sri Lanka	Kanpur	1986-87
675-5d	India v Pakistan	Multan	2003-04
674	Australia v India	Adelaide	1947-48
674-6	Pakistan v India	Faisalabad	1984-85
674-6d	Australia v England	Cardiff	2009
671-4	New Zealand v Sri Lanka	Wellington	1990-91
668	Australia v West Indies	Bridgetown	1954-55
664	India v England	The Oval	2007
662-9d	Australia v England	Perth	2017-18
660-5d	West Indies v New Zealand	Wellington	1994-95
659-8d	Australia v England	Sydney	1946-47
659-4d	Australia v India	Sydney	2011-12
659-6d	New Zealand v Pakistan	Christchurch	2020-21
658-8d	England v Australia	Nottingham	1938
658-9d	South Africa v West Indies	Durban	2003-04
657-8d	Pakistan v West Indies	Bridgetown	1957-58
657-7d	India v Australia	Calcutta	2000-01
656-8d	Australia v England	Manchester	1964
654-5	England v South Africa	Durban	1938-39
653-4d	England v India	Lord's	1990
653-4d	Australia v England	Leeds	1993
652-8d	West Indies v England	Lord's	1973
652	Pakistan v India	Faisalabad	1982-83
652-7d	England v India	Madras	1984-85
652-7d	Australia v South Africa	Johannesburg	2001-02
651	South Africa v Australia	Cape Town	2008-09
650-6d	Australia v West Indies	Bridgetown	1964-65

The highest for Zimbabwe is 563-9d (v WI, Harare, 2001), and for Bangladesh 638 (v SL, Galle, 2012-13).

LOWEST INNINGS TOTALS

† One batsman absent

26	New Zealand v England	Auckland	1954-55
30	South Africa v England	Port Elizabeth	1895-96
30	South Africa v England	Birmingham	1924
35	South Africa v England	Cape Town	1898-99
36	Australia v England	Birmingham	1902
36	South Africa v Australia	Melbourne	1931-32
36	India v Australia	Adelaide	2020-21
38	Ireland v England	Lord's	2019
42	Australia v England	Sydney	1887-88
42	New Zealand v Australia	Wellington	1945-46
42†	India v England	Lord's	1974
43	South Africa v England	Cape Town	1888-89
43	Bangladesh v West Indies	North Sound	2018
44	Australia v England	The Oval	1896
45	England v Australia	Sydney	1886-87
45	South Africa v Australia	Melbourne	1931-32
45	New Zealand v South Africa	Cape Town	2012-13
46	England v West Indies	Port-of-Spain	1993-94
47	South Africa v England	Cape Town	1888-89
47	New Zealand v England	Lord's	1958
47	West Indies v England	Kingston	2003-04
47	Australia v South Africa	Cape Town	2011-12
49	Pakistan v South Africa	Johannesburg	2012-13

The lowest for Sri Lanka is 71 (v P, Kandy, 1994-95) and for Zimbabwe 51 (v NZ, Napier, 2011-12).

BATTING RECORDS
5000 RUNS IN TESTS

Runs			*M*	*I*	*NO*	*HS*	*Avge*	*100*	*50*
15921	S.R.Tendulkar	I	200	329	33	248*	53.78	51	68
13378	R.T.Ponting	A	168	287	29	257	51.85	41	62
13289	J.H.Kallis	SA/ICC	166	280	40	224	55.37	45	58
13288	R.S.Dravid	I/ICC	164	286	32	270	52.31	36	63
12472	A.N.Cook	E	161	291	16	294	45.35	33	57
12400	K.C.Sangakkara	SL	134	233	17	319	57.40	38	52
11953	B.C.Lara	WI/ICC	131	232	6	400*	52.88	34	48
11867	S.Chanderpaul	WI	164	280	49	203*	51.37	30	66
11814	D.P.M.D.Jayawardena	SL	149	252	15	374	49.84	34	50
11174	A.R.Border	A	156	265	44	205	50.56	27	63
10927	S.R.Waugh	A	168	260	46	200	51.06	32	50
10122	S.M.Gavaskar	I	125	214	16	236*	51.12	34	45
10099	Younus Khan	P	118	213	19	313	52.05	34	33
9600	J.E.Root	E	114	210	15	254	49.23	23	53
9282	H.M.Amla	SA	124	215	16	311*	46.64	28	41
9265	G.C.Smith	SA/ICC	117	205	13	277	48.25	27	38
8900	G.A.Gooch	E	118	215	6	333	42.58	20	46
8832	Javed Miandad	P	124	189	21	280*	52.57	23	43
8830	Inzamam-ul-Haq	P/ICC	120	200	22	329	49.60	25	46
8781	V.V.S.Laxman	I	134	225	34	281	45.97	17	56
8765	A.B.de Villiers	SA	114	191	18	278*	50.66	22	46
8643	M.J.Clarke	A	115	198	22	329*	49.10	28	27
8625	M.L.Hayden	A	103	184	14	380	50.73	30	29
8586	V.Sehwag	I/ICC	104	180	6	319	49.34	23	32
8540	I.V.A.Richards	WI	121	182	12	291	50.23	24	45
8463	A.J.Stewart	E	133	235	21	190	39.54	15	45
8231	D.I.Gower	E	117	204	18	215	44.25	18	39
8181	K.P.Pietersen	E	104	181	8	227	47.28	23	35
8114	G.Boycott	E	108	193	23	246*	47.72	22	42
8032	G.St A.Sobers	WI	93	160	21	365*	57.78	26	30
8029	M.E.Waugh	A	128	209	17	153*	41.81	20	47
7962	V.Kohli	I	99	168	10	254*	50.39	27	28
7784	S.P.D.Smith	A	82	147	17	239	59.87	27	33
7728	M.A.Atherton	E	115	212	7	185*	37.70	16	46
7727	I.R.Bell	E	118	205	24	235	42.69	22	46
7696	J.L.Langer	A	105	182	12	250	45.27	23	30
7683	L.R.P.L.Taylor	NZ	112	196	24	290	44.66	19	35
7624	M.C.Cowdrey	E	114	188	15	182	44.06	22	38
7584	D.A.Warner	A	91	167	7	335*	47.40	24	32
7558	C.G.Greenidge	WI	108	185	16	226	44.72	19	34
7530	Mohammad Yousuf	P	90	156	12	223	52.29	24	33
7525	M.A.Taylor	A	104	186	13	334*	43.49	19	40
7515	C.H.Lloyd	WI	110	175	14	242*	46.67	19	39
7487	D.L.Haynes	WI	116	202	25	184	42.29	18	39
7422	D.C.Boon	A	107	190	20	200	43.65	21	32
7289	G.Kirsten	SA	101	176	15	275	45.27	21	34
7272	K.S.Williamson	NZ	86	150	14	251	53.47	24	33
7249	W.R.Hammond	E	85	140	16	336*	58.45	22	24
7214	C.H.Gayle	WI	103	182	11	333	42.18	15	37
7212	S.C.Ganguly	I	113	188	17	239	42.17	16	35
7172	S.P.Fleming	NZ	111	189	10	274*	40.06	9	46
7110	G.S.Chappell	A	87	151	19	247*	53.86	24	31
7037	A.J.Strauss	E	100	178	6	177	40.91	21	27

Runs			M	I	NO	HS	Avge	100	50
6996	D.G.Bradman	A	52	80	10	334	99.94	29	13
6973	S.T.Jayasuriya	SL	110	188	14	340	40.07	14	31
6971	L.Hutton	E	79	138	15	364	56.67	19	33
6868	D.B.Vengsarkar	I	116	185	22	166	42.13	17	35
6806	K.F.Barrington	E	82	131	15	256	58.67	20	35
6744	G.P.Thorpe	E	100	179	28	200*	44.66	16	39
6721	Azhar Ali	P	91	169	11	302*	42.53	18	34
6713	C.A.Pujara	I	95	162	9	206*	43.87	18	32
6453	B.B.McCullum	NZ	101	176	9	302	38.64	12	31
6361	P.A.de Silva	SL	93	159	11	267	42.97	20	22
6338	A.D.Mathews	SL	92	165	23	200*	44.63	11	37
6235	M.E.K.Hussey	A	79	137	16	195	51.52	19	29
6227	R.B.Kanhai	WI	79	137	6	256	47.53	15	28
6215	M.Azharuddin	I	99	147	9	199	45.03	22	21
6167	H.H.Gibbs	SA	90	154	7	228	41.95	14	26
6149	R.N.Harvey	A	79	137	10	205	48.41	21	24
6080	G.R.Viswanath	I	91	155	10	222	41.93	14	35
5949	R.B.Richardson	WI	86	146	12	194	44.39	16	27
5842	R.R.Sarwan	WI	87	154	8	291	40.01	15	31
5825	M.E.Trescothick	E	76	143	10	219	43.79	14	29
5807	D.C.S.Compton	E	78	131	15	278	50.06	17	28
5768	Salim Malik	P	103	154	22	237	43.69	15	29
5764	N.Hussain	E	96	171	16	207	37.19	14	33
5762	C.L.Hooper	WI	102	173	15	233	36.46	13	27
5719	M.P.Vaughan	E	82	147	9	197	41.44	18	18
5570	A.C.Gilchrist	A	96	137	20	204*	47.60	17	26
5515	M.V.Boucher	SA/ICC	147	206	24	125	30.30	5	35
5502	M.S.Atapattu	SL	90	156	15	249	39.02	16	17
5492	T.M.Dilshan	SL	87	145	11	193	40.98	16	23
5462	T.T.Samaraweera	SL	81	132	20	231	48.76	14	30
5454	F.D.M.Karunaratne	SL	74	143	5	244	39.52	13	27
5444	M.D.Crowe	NZ	77	131	11	299	45.36	17	18
5410	J.B.Hobbs	E	61	102	7	211	56.94	15	28
5357	K.D.Walters	A	74	125	14	250	48.26	15	33
5345	I.M.Chappell	A	75	136	10	196	42.42	14	26
5334	J.G.Wright	NZ	82	148	7	185	37.82	12	23
5312	M.J.Slater	A	74	131	7	219	42.84	14	21
5248	Kapil Dev	I	131	184	15	163	31.05	8	27
5234	W.M.Lawry	A	67	123	12	210	47.15	13	27
5222	Misbah-ul-Haq	P	75	132	20	161*	46.62	10	39
5200	I.T.Botham	E	102	161	6	208	33.54	14	22
5138	J.H.Edrich	E	77	127	9	310*	43.54	12	24
5105	A.Ranatunga	SL	93	155	12	135*	35.69	4	38
5062	Zaheer Abbas	P	78	124	11	274	44.79	12	20

The most for Zimbabwe is 4794 by A.Flower (112 innings), and for Bangladesh 4873 by Mushfiqur Rahim (144 innings).

750 RUNS IN A SERIES

Runs			Series	M	I	NO	HS	Avge	100	50
974	D.G.Bradman	A v E	1930	5	7	–	334	139.14	4	–
905	W.R.Hammond	E v A	1928-29	5	9	1	251	113.12	4	–
839	M.A.Taylor	A v E	1989	6	11	1	219	83.90	2	5
834	R.N.Harvey	A v SA	1952-53	5	9	–	205	92.66	4	3
829	I.V.A.Richards	WI v E	1976	4	7	–	291	118.42	3	2

Runs			Series	M	I	NO	HS	Avge	100	50
827	C.L.Walcott	WI v A	1954-55	5	10	–	155	82.70	5	2
824	G.St A.Sobers	WI v P	1957-58	5	8	2	365*	137.33	3	3
810	D.G.Bradman	A v E	1936-37	5	9	–	270	90.00	3	1
806	D.G.Bradman	A v SA	1931-32	5	5	1	299*	201.50	4	–
798	B.C.Lara	WI v E	1993-94	5	8	–	375	99.75	2	2
779	E.de C.Weekes	WI v I	1948-49	5	7	–	194	111.28	4	2
774	S.M.Gavaskar	I v WI	1970-71	4	8	3	220	154.80	4	3
774	S.P.D.Smith	A v E	2019	4	7	–	211	110.57	3	3
769	S.P.D.Smith	A v I	2014-15	4	8	2	192	128.16	4	2
766	A.N.Cook	E v A	2010-11	5	7	1	235*	127.66	3	2
765	B.C.Lara	WI v E	1995	6	10	1	179	85.00	3	3
761	Mudassar Nazar	P v I	1982-83	6	8	2	231	126.83	4	1
758	D.G.Bradman	A v E	1934	5	8	–	304	94.75	2	1
753	D.C.S.Compton	E v SA	1947	5	8	–	208	94.12	4	2
752	G.A.Gooch	E v I	1990	3	6	–	333	125.33	3	2

HIGHEST INDIVIDUAL INNINGS

400*	B.C.Lara	WI v E	St John's	2003-04
380	M.L.Hayden	A v Z	Perth	2003-04
375	B.C.Lara	WI v E	St John's	1993-94
374	D.P.M.D.Jayawardena	SL v SA	Colombo (SSC)	2006
365*	G.St A.Sobers	WI v P	Kingston	1957-58
364	L.Hutton	E v A	The Oval	1938
340	S.T.Jayasuriya	SL v I	Colombo (RPS)	1997-98
337	Hanif Mohammed	P v WI	Bridgetown	1957-58
336*	W.R.Hammond	E v NZ	Auckland	1932-33
335*	D.A.Warner	A v P	Adelaide	2019-20
334*	M.A.Taylor	A v P	Peshawar	1998-99
334	D.G.Bradman	A v E	Leeds	1930
333	G.A.Gooch	E v I	Lord's	1990
333	C.H.Gayle	WI v SL	Galle	2010-11
329*	M.J.Clarke	A v I	Sydney	2011-12
329	Inzamam-ul-Haq	P v NZ	Lahore	2001-02
325	A.Sandham	E v WI	Kingston	1929-30
319	V.Sehwag	I v SA	Chennai	2007-08
319	K.C.Sangakkara	SL v B	Chittagong	2013-14
317	C.H.Gayle	WI v SA	St John's	2004-05
313	Younus Khan	P v SL	Karachi	2008-09
311*	H.M.Amla	SA v E	The Oval	2012
311	R.B.Simpson	A v E	Manchester	1964
310*	J.H.Edrich	E v NZ	Leeds	1965
309	V.Sehwag	I v P	Multan	2003-04
307	R.M.Cowper	A v E	Melbourne	1965-66
304	D.G.Bradman	A v E	Leeds	1934
303*	K.K.Nair	I v E	Chennai	2016-17
302*	Azhar Ali	P v WI	Dubai (DSC)	2016-17
302	L.G.Rowe	WI v E	Bridgetown	1973-74
302	B.B.McCullum	NZ v I	Wellington	2013-14
299*	D.G.Bradman	A v SA	Adelaide	1931-32
299	M.D.Crowe	NZ v SL	Wellington	1990-91
294	A.N.Cook	E v I	Birmingham	2011
293	V.Sehwag	I v SL	Mumbai	2009-10
291	I.V.A.Richards	WI v E	The Oval	1976
291	R.R.Sarwan	WI v E	Bridgetown	2008-09

290	L.R.P.L.Taylor	NZ v A	Perth	2015-16
287	R.E.Foster	E v A	Sydney	1903-04
287	K.C.Sangakkara	SL v SA	Colombo (SSC)	2006
285*	P.B.H.May	E v WI	Birmingham	1957
281	V.V.S.Laxman	I v A	Calcutta	2000-01
280*	Javed Miandad	P v I	Hyderabad	1982-83
278*	A.B.de Villiers	SA v P	Abu Dhabi	2010-11
278	D.C.S.Compton	E v P	Nottingham	1954
277	B.C.Lara	WI v A	Sydney	1992-93
277	G.C.Smith	SA v E	Birmingham	2003
275*	D.J.Cullinan	SA v NZ	Auckland	1998-99
275	G.Kirsten	SA v E	Durban	1999-00
275	D.P.M.D.Jayawardena	SL v I	Ahmedabad	2009-10
274*	S.P.Fleming	NZ v SL	Colombo (SSC)	2002-03
274	R.G.Pollock	SA v A	Durban	1969-70
274	Zaheer Abbas	P v E	Birmingham	1971
271	Javed Miandad	P v NZ	Auckland	1988-89
270*	G.A.Headley	WI v E	Kingston	1934-35
270	D.G.Bradman	A v E	Melbourne	1936-37
270	R.S.Dravid	I v P	Rawalpindi	2003-04
270	K.C.Sangakkara	SL v Z	Bulawayo	2004
269*	A.C.Voges	A v WI	Hobart	2015-16
268	G.N.Yallop	A v P	Melbourne	1983-84
267*	B.A.Young	NZ v SL	Dunedin	1996-97
267	P.A.de Silva	SL v NZ	Wellington	1990-91
267	Younus Khan	P v I	Bangalore	2004-05
267	Z.Crawley	E v P	Southampton	2020
266	W.H.Ponsford	A v E	The Oval	1934
266	D.L.Houghton	Z v SL	Bulawayo	1994-95
264*	T.W.M.Latham	NZ v SL	Wellington	2018-19
263	A.N.Cook	E v P	Abu Dhabi	2015-16
262*	D.L.Amiss	E v WI	Kingston	1973-74
262	S.P.Fleming	NZ v SA	Cape Town	2005-06
261*	R.R.Sarwan	WI v B	Kingston	2004
261	F.M.M.Worrell	WI v E	Nottingham	1950
260	C.C.Hunte	WI v P	Kingston	1957-58
260	Javed Miandad	P v E	The Oval	1987
260	M.N.Samuels	WI v B	Khulna	2012-13
259*	M.J.Clarke	A v SA	Brisbane	2012-13
259	G.M.Turner	NZ v WI	Georgetown	1971-72
259	G.C.Smith	SA v E	Lord's	2003
258	T.W.Graveney	E v WI	Nottingham	1957
258	S.M.Nurse	WI v NZ	Christchurch	1968-69
258	B.A.Stokes	E v SA	Cape Town	2015-16
257*	Wasim Akram	P v Z	Sheikhupura	1996-97
257	R.T.Ponting	A v I	Melbourne	2003-04
256	R.B.Kanhai	WI v I	Calcutta	1958-59
256	K.F.Barrington	E v A	Manchester	1964
255*	D.J.McGlew	SA v NZ	Wellington	1952-53
254*	V.Kohli	I v SA	Pune	2019-20
254	D.G.Bradman	A v E	Lord's	1930
254	V.Sehwag	I v P	Lahore	2005-06
254	J.E.Root	E v P	Manchester	2016
253*	H.M.Amla	SA v I	Nagpur	2009-10
253	S.T.Jayasuriya	SL v P	Faisalabad	2004-05
253	D.A.Warner	A v NZ	Perth	2015-16
252	T.W.M.Latham	NZ v B	Christchurch	2021-22

251	W.R.Hammond	E v A	Sydney	1928-29
251	K.S.Williamson	NZ v WI	Hamilton	2020-21
250	K.D.Walters	A v NZ	Christchurch	1976-77
250	S.F.A.F.Bacchus	WI v I	Kanpur	1978-79
250	J.L.Langer	A v E	Melbourne	2002-03

The highest for Bangladesh is 219* by Mushfiqur Rahim (v Z, Dhaka, 2018-19).

20 HUNDREDS

					Opponents										
			200	*Inn*	*E*	*A*	*SA*	*WI*	*NZ*	*I*	*P*	*SL*	*Z*	*B*
51	S.R.Tendulkar	I	6	329	7	11	7	3	4	–	2	9	3	5
45	J.H.Kallis	SA	2	280	8	5	–	8	6	7	6	1	3	1
41	R.T.Ponting	A	6	287	8	–	8	7	2	8	5	1	1	1
38	K.C.Sangakkara	SL	11	233	3	1	3	3	4	5	10	–	2	7
36	R.S.Dravid	I	5	286	7	2	2	5	6	–	5	3	3	3
34	Younus Khan	P	6	213	4	4	4	3	2	5	–	8	1	3
34	S.M.Gavaskar	I	4	214	4	8	–	13	2	–	5	2	–	–
34	B.C.Lara	WI	9	232	7	9	4	–	1	2	4	5	1	1
34	D.P.M.D.Jayawardena	SL	7	252	8	2	6	1	3	6	2	–	1	5
33	A.N.Cook	E	5	291	–	5	2	6	3	7	5	3	–	2
32	S.R.Waugh	A	1	260	10	–	2	7	2	2	3	3	1	2
30	M.L.Hayden †	A	2	184	5	–	6	5	1	6	1	3	2	–
30	S.Chanderpaul	WI	2	280	5	5	5	–	2	7	1	–	1	4
29	D.G.Bradman	A	12	80	19	–	4	2	–	4	–	–	–	–
28	M.J.Clarke	A	4	198	7	–	5	1	4	7	1	3	–	–
28	H.M.Amla	SA	4	215	6	5	–	1	4	5	2	2	–	3
27	S.P.D.Smith	A	3	147	11	–	1	2	2	8	2	1	–	–
27	V.Kohli	I	7	168	5	7	3	2	3	–	–	5	–	2
27	G.C.Smith	SA	5	205	7	3	–	7	2	–	4	–	1	3
27	A.R.Border	A	2	265	8	–	–	3	5	4	6	1	–	–
26	G.St A.Sobers	WI	2	160	10	4	–	–	1	8	3	–	–	–
25	Inzamam-ul-Haq	P	2	200	5	1	–	4	3	3	–	5	2	2
24	K.S.Williamson	NZ	4	150	3	2	3	3	–	2	4	3	1	3
24	G.S.Chappell	A	4	151	9	–	–	5	3	1	6	–	–	–
24	Mohammad Yousuf	P	4	156	6	1	–	7	1	4	–	1	2	2
24	D.A.Warner	A	2	167	3	–	4	1	5	4	5	–	–	2
24	I.V.A.Richards	WI	3	182	8	5	–	–	1	8	2	–	–	–
23	V.Sehwag	I	6	180	2	3	5	2	2	–	4	5	–	–
23	K.P.Pietersen	E	3	181	–	4	3	3	2	6	2	3	–	–
23	J.L.Langer	A	3	182	5	–	2	3	4	3	4	2	–	–
23	Javed Miandad	P	6	189	2	6	–	2	7	5	–	1	–	–
23	J.E.Root	E	5	210	–	3	2	3	2	8	1	4	–	–
22	W.R.Hammond	E	7	140	–	9	6	1	4	2	–	–	–	–
22	M.Azharuddin	I	–	147	6	2	4	–	2	–	3	5	–	–
22	M.C.Cowdrey	E	–	188	–	5	3	6	2	3	3	–	–	–
22	A.B.de Villiers	SA	2	191	2	6	–	6	–	3	4	1	–	–
22	G.Boycott	E	1	193	–	7	1	5	2	4	3	–	–	–
22	I.R.Bell	E	1	205	–	4	2	2	1	4	4	2	–	3
21	R.N.Harvey	A	2	137	6	–	8	3	–	4	–	–	–	–
21	G.Kirsten	SA	3	176	5	2	–	3	2	3	2	1	1	2
21	A.J.Strauss	E	–	178	–	4	3	6	3	3	2	–	–	–
21	D.C.Boon	A	1	190	7	–	–	3	3	6	1	1	–	–
20	K.F.Barrington	E	1	131	–	5	2	3	3	3	4	–	–	–
20	P.A.de Silva	SL	2	159	2	1	–	–	2	5	8	–	1	1
20	M.E.Waugh	A	–	209	6	–	4	4	1	1	3	1	–	–
20	G.A.Gooch	E	2	215	–	4	–	5	4	5	1	1	–	–

† Includes century scored for Australia v ICC in 2005-06.

The most for Zimbabwe 12 by A.Flower (112), and for Bangladesh 11 by Mominul Haque (91).
The most double hundreds by batsmen not included above are 6 by M.S.Atapattu (16 hundreds for Sri Lanka), 4 by L.Hutton (19 for England), 4 by C.G.Greenidge (19 for West Indies), 4 by Zaheer Abbas (12 for Pakistan), and 4 by B.B.McCullum (12 for New Zealand).

HIGHEST PARTNERSHIP FOR EACH WICKET

1st	415	N.D.McKenzie/G.C.Smith	SA v B	Chittagong	2007-08
2nd	576	S.T.Jayasuriya/R.S.Mahanama	SL v I	Colombo (RPS)	1997-98
3rd	624	K.C.Sangakkara/D.P.M.D.Jayawardena	SL v SA	Colombo (SSC)	2006
4th	449	A.C.Voges/S.E.Marsh	A v WI	Hobart	2015-16
5th	405	S.G.Barnes/D.G.Bradman	A v E	Sydney	1946-47
6th	399	B.A.Stokes/J.M.Bairstow	E v SA	Cape Town	2015-16
7th	347	D.St E.Atkinson/C.C.Depeiza	WI v A	Bridgetown	1954-55
8th	332	I.J.L.Trott/S.C.J.Broad	E v P	Lord's	2010
9th	195	M.V.Boucher/P.L.Symcox	SA v P	Johannesburg	1997-98
10th	198	J.E.Root/J.M.Anderson	E v I	Nottingham	2014

BOWLING RECORDS
200 WICKETS IN TESTS

Wkts			*M*	*Balls*	*Runs*	*Avge*	*5wI*	*10wM*
800	M.Muralitharan	SL/ICC	133	44039	18180	22.72	67	22
708	S.K.Warne	A	145	40705	17995	25.41	37	10
640	J.M.Anderson	E	169	36396	17014	26.58	31	3
619	A.Kumble	I	132	40850	18355	29.65	35	8
563	G.D.McGrath	A	124	29248	12186	21.64	29	3
537	S.C.J.Broad	E	152	30575	14932	27.80	19	3
519	C.A.Walsh	WI	132	30019	12688	24.44	22	3
439	D.W.Steyn	SA	93	18608	10077	22.95	26	5
434	Kapil Dev	I	131	27740	12867	29.64	23	2
433	H.M.R.K.B.Herath	SL	93	25993	12157	28.07	34	9
431	R.J.Hadlee	NZ	86	21918	9612	22.30	36	9
430	R.Ashwin	I	84	22673	10485	24.38	30	7
421	S.M.Pollock	SA	108	24453	9733	23.11	16	1
417	Harbhajan Singh	I	103	28580	13537	32.46	25	5
415	N.M.Lyon	A	105	26669	13193	31.79	18	3
414	Wasim Akram	P	104	22627	9779	23.62	25	5
405	C.E.L.Ambrose	WI	98	22104	8500	20.98	22	3
390	M.Ntini	SA	101	20834	11242	28.82	18	4
383	I.T.Botham	E	102	21815	10878	28.40	27	4
376	M.D.Marshall	WI	81	17584	7876	20.94	22	4
373	Waqar Younis	P	87	16224	8788	23.56	22	5
362	Imran Khan	P	88	19458	8258	22.81	23	6
362	D.L.Vettori	NZ/ICC	113	28814	12441	34.36	20	3
355	D.K.Lillee	A	70	18467	8493	23.92	23	7
355	W.P.J.U.C.Vaas	SL	111	23438	10501	29.58	12	2
338	T.G.Southee	NZ	85	19352	9530	28.19	14	1
330	A.A.Donald	SA	72	15519	7344	22.25	20	3
325	R.G.D.Willis	E	90	17357	8190	25.20	16	–
313	M.G.Johnson	A	73	16001	8891	28.40	12	3
311	I.Sharma	I	105	19160	10078	32.40	11	1
311	Z.Khan	I	92	18785	10247	32.94	11	1
310	B.Lee	A	76	16531	9554	30.81	10	–
309	M.Morkel	SA	86	16498	8550	27.66	8	–
309	L.R.Gibbs	WI	79	27115	8989	29.09	18	2

Wkts			M	Balls	Runs	Avge	5wI	10wM
307	F.S.Trueman	E	67	15178	6625	21.57	17	3
301	T.A.Boult	NZ	75	16689	8254	27.42	9	1
297	D.L.Underwood	E	86	21862	7674	25.83	17	6
292	J.H.Kallis	SA/ICC	166	20232	9535	32.65	5	–
291	C.J.McDermott	A	71	16586	8332	28.63	14	2
274	M.A.Starc	A	66	13488	7513	27.41	13	2
266	B.S.Bedi	I	67	21364	7637	28.71	14	1
261	Danish Kaneria	P	61	17697	9082	34.79	15	2
259	J.Garner	WI	58	13169	5433	20.97	7	–
259	J.N.Gillespie	A	71	14234	6770	26.13	8	–
255	G.P.Swann	E	60	15349	7642	29.96	17	3
252	J.B.Statham	E	70	16056	6261	24.84	9	1
249	M.A.Holding	WI	60	12680	5898	23.68	13	2
248	R.Benaud	A	63	19108	6704	27.03	16	1
248	M.J.Hoggard	E	67	13909	7564	30.50	7	1
246	G.D.McKenzie	A	60	17681	7328	29.78	16	3
244	N.Wagner	NZ	58	12845	6464	26.49	9	–
243	K.Rabada	SA	52	9908	5446	22.41	11	4
242	B.S.Chandrasekhar	I	58	15963	7199	29.74	16	2
236	A.V.Bedser	E	51	15918	5876	24.89	15	5
236	J.Srinath	I	67	15104	7196	30.49	10	1
236	Abdul Qadir	P	67	17126	7742	32.80	15	5
235	Yasir Shah	P	46	13697	7306	31.08	16	3
235	G.St A.Sobers	WI	93	21599	7999	34.03	6	–
234	A.R.Caddick	E	62	13558	6999	29.91	13	1
233	C.S.Martin	NZ	71	14026	7878	33.81	10	1
232	R.A.Jadeja	I	57	14333	5765	24.84	9	1
231	K.A.J.Roach	WI	68	12302	6289	27.22	9	1
229	D.Gough	E	58	11821	6503	28.39	9	–
228	R.R.Lindwall	A	61	13650	5251	23.03	12	–
226	S.J.Harmison	E/ICC	63	13375	7192	31.82	8	1
226	A.Flintoff	E/ICC	79	14951	7410	32.78	3	–
224	V.D.Philander	SA	64	11391	5000	22.32	13	2
221	P.M.Siddle	A	67	13907	6777	30.66	8	–
218	C.L.Cairns	NZ	62	11698	6410	29.40	13	1
216	C.V.Grimmett	A	37	14513	5231	24.21	21	7
216	H.H.Streak	Z	65	13559	6079	28.14	7	–
215	J.R.Hazlewood	A	56	12049	5512	25.63	9	–
215	Shakib Al Hasan	B	59	13529	6731	31.30	18	2
212	M.G.Hughes	A	53	12285	6017	28.38	7	1
209	Mohammed Shami	I	57	10413	5670	27.12	6	–
208	S.C.G.MacGill	A	44	11237	6038	29.02	12	2
208	Saqlain Mushtaq	P	49	14070	6206	29.83	13	3
202	A.M.E.Roberts	WI	47	11136	5174	25.61	11	2
202	J.A.Snow	E	49	12021	5387	26.66	8	1
200	J.R.Thomson	A	51	10535	5601	28.00	8	–

35 OR MORE WICKETS IN A SERIES

Wkts			Series	M	Balls	Runs	Avge	5wI	10wM
49	S.F.Barnes	E v SA	1913-14	4	1356	536	10.93	7	3
46	J.C.Laker	E v A	1956	5	1703	442	9.60	4	2
44	C.V.Grimmett	A v SA	1935-36	5	2077	642	14.59	5	3
42	T.M.Alderman	A v E	1981	6	1950	893	21.26	4	–
41	R.M.Hogg	A v E	1978-79	6	1740	527	12.85	5	2
41	T.M.Alderman	A v E	1989	6	1616	712	17.36	6	1

Wkts			Series	M	Balls	Runs	Avge	5wI	10wM
40	Imran Khan	P v I	1982-83	6	1339	558	13.95	4	2
40	S.K.Warne	A v E	2005	5	1517	797	19.92	3	2
39	A.V.Bedser	E v A	1953	5	1591	682	17.48	5	1
39	D.K.Lillee	A v E	1981	6	1870	870	22.30	2	1
38	M.W.Tate	E v A	1924-25	5	2528	881	23.18	5	1
37	W.J.Whitty	A v SA	1910-11	5	1395	632	17.08	2	–
37	H.J.Tayfield	SA v E	1956-57	5	2280	636	17.18	4	1
37	M.G.Johnson	A v E	2013-14	5	1132	517	13.97	3	–
36	A.E.E.Vogler	SA v E	1909-10	5	1349	783	21.75	4	1
36	A.A.Mailey	A v E	1920-21	5	1465	946	26.27	4	2
36	G.D.McGrath	A v E	1997	6	1499	701	19.47	2	–
35	G.A.Lohmann	E v SA	1895-96	3	520	203	5.80	4	2
35	B.S.Chandrasekhar	I v E	1972-73	5	1747	662	18.91	4	–
35	M.D.Marshall	WI v E	1988	5	1219	443	12.65	3	1

The most for New Zealand is 33 by R.J.Hadlee (3 Tests v A, 1985-86), for Sri Lanka 30 by M.Muralitharan (3 Tests v Z, 2001-02), for Zimbabwe 22 by H.H.Streak (3 Tests v P, 1994-95), and for Bangladesh 19 by Mehedi Hasan (2 Tests v E, 2016-17).

15 OR MORE WICKETS IN A TEST († *On debut*)

19- 90	J.C.Laker	E v A	Manchester	1956
17-159	S.F.Barnes	E v SA	Johannesburg	1913-14
16-136†	N.D.Hirwani	I v WI	Madras	1987-88
16-137†	R.A.L.Massie	A v E	Lord's	1972
16-220	M.Muralitharan	SL v E	The Oval	1998
15- 28	J.Briggs	E v SA	Cape Town	1888-89
15- 45	G.A.Lohmann	E v SA	Port Elizabeth	1895-96
15- 99	C.Blythe	E v SA	Leeds	1907
15-104	H.Verity	E v A	Lord's	1934
15-123	R.J.Hadlee	NZ v A	Brisbane	1985-86
15-124	W.Rhodes	E v A	Melbourne	1903-04
15-217	Harbhajan Singh	I v A	Madras	2000-01

The best analysis for South Africa is 13-132 by M.Ntini (v WI, Port-of-Spain, 2004-05), for West Indies 14-149 by M.A.Holding (v E, The Oval, 1976), for Pakistan 14-116 by Imran Khan (v SL, Lahore, 1981-82), for Zimbabwe 11-257 by A.G.Huckle (v NZ, Bulawayo, 1997-98), and for Bangladesh 12-117 by Mehedi Hasan (v WI, Dhaka, 2018-19).

NINE OR MORE WICKETS IN AN INNINGS

10- 53	J.C.Laker	E v A	Manchester	1956
10- 74	A.Kumble	I v P	Delhi	1998-99
10-119	A.Y.Patel	NZ v I	Mumbai	2021-22
9- 28	G.A.Lohmann	E v SA	Johannesburg	1895-96
9- 37	J.C.Laker	E v A	Manchester	1956
9- 51	M.Muralitharan	SL v Z	Kandy	2001-02
9- 52	R.J.Hadlee	NZ v A	Brisbane	1985-86
9- 56	Abdul Qadir	P v E	Lahore	1987-88
9- 57	D.E.Malcolm	E v SA	The Oval	1994
9- 65	M.Muralitharan	SL v E	The Oval	1998
9- 69	J.M.Patel	I v A	Kanpur	1959-60
9- 83	Kapil Dev	I v WI	Ahmedabad	1983-84
9- 86	Sarfraz Nawaz	P v A	Melbourne	1978-79
9- 95	J.M.Noreiga	WI v I	Port-of-Spain	1970-71
9-102	S.P.Gupte	I v WI	Kanpur	1958-59
9-103	S.F.Barnes	E v SA	Johannesburg	1913-14
9-113	H.J.Tayfield	SA v E	Johannesburg	1956-57
9-121	A.A.Mailey	A v E	Melbourne	1920-21

9-127	H.M.R.K.B.Herath	SL v P	Colombo (SSC)	2014
9-129	K.A.Maharaj	SA v SL	Colombo (SSC)	2018

The best analysis for Zimbabwe is 8-109 by P.A.Strang (v NZ, Bulawayo, 2000-01), and for Bangladesh 8-39 by Taijul Islam (v Z, Dhaka, 2014-15).

HAT-TRICKS

F.R.Spofforth	Australia v England	Melbourne	1878-79
W.Bates	England v Australia	Melbourne	1882-83
J.Briggs[7]	England v Australia	Sydney	1891-92
G.A.Lohmann	England v South Africa	Port Elizabeth	1895-96
J.T.Hearne	England v Australia	Leeds	1899
H.Trumble	Australia v England	Melbourne	1901-02
H.Trumble	Australia v England	Melbourne	1903-04
T.J.Matthews (2)[2]	Australia v South Africa	Manchester	1912
M.J.C.Allom[1]	England v New Zealand	Christchurch	1929-30
T.W.J.Goddard	England v South Africa	Johannesburg	1938-39
P.J.Loader	England v West Indies	Leeds	1957
L.F.Kline	Australia v South Africa	Cape Town	1957-58
W.W.Hall	West Indies v Pakistan	Lahore	1958-59
G.M.Griffin[7]	South Africa v England	Lord's	1960
L.R.Gibbs	West Indies v Australia	Adelaide	1960-61
P.J.Petherick[1/7]	New Zealand v Pakistan	Lahore	1976-77
C.A.Walsh[3]	West Indies v Australia	Brisbane	1988-89
M.G.Hughes[3/7]	Australia v West Indies	Perth	1988-89
D.W.Fleming[1]	Australia v Pakistan	Rawalpindi	1994-95
S.K.Warne	Australia v England	Melbourne	1994-95
D.G.Cork	England v West Indies	Manchester	1995
D.Gough[7]	England v Australia	Sydney	1998-99
Wasim Akram[4]	Pakistan v Sri Lanka	Lahore	1998-99
Wasim Akram[4]	Pakistan v Sri Lanka	Dhaka	1998-99
D.N.T.Zoysa[5]	Sri Lanka v Zimbabwe	Harare	1999-00
Abdul Razzaq	Pakistan v Sri Lanka	Galle	2000-01
G.D.McGrath	Australia v West Indies	Perth	2000-01
Harbhajan Singh	India v Australia	Calcutta	2000-01
Mohammad Sami[7]	Pakistan v Sri Lanka	Lahore	2001-02
J.J.C.Lawson[7]	West Indies v Australia	Bridgetown	2002-03
Alok Kapali[7]	Bangladesh v Pakistan	Peshawar	2003
A.M.Blignaut	Zimbabwe v Bangladesh	Harare	2003-04
M.J.Hoggard	England v West Indies	Bridgetown	2003-04
J.E.C.Franklin	New Zealand v Bangladesh	Dhaka	2004-05
I.K.Pathan[6/7]	India v Pakistan	Karachi	2005-06
R.J.Sidebottom[7]	England v New Zealand	Hamilton	2007-08
P.M.Siddle	Australia v England	Brisbane	2010-11
S.C.J.Broad	England v India	Nottingham	2011
Sohag Gazi	Bangladesh v New Zealand	Chittagong	2013-14
S.C.J.Broad[7]	England v Sri Lanka	Leeds	2014
H.M.R.K.B.Herath	Sri Lanka v Australia	Galle	2016
M.M.Ali	England v South Africa	The Oval	2017
J.J.Bumrah	India v West Indies	Kingston	2019
Naseem Shah	Pakistan v Bangladesh	Rawalpindi	2019-20
K.A.Maharaj	South Africa v West Indies	Gros Islet	2021

[1] On debut. [2] Hat-trick in each innings. [3] Involving both innings. [4] In successive Tests. [5] His first 3 balls (second over of the match). [6] The fourth, fifth and sixth balls of the match. [7] On losing side.

WICKET-KEEPING RECORDS
150 DISMISSALS IN TESTS†

Total			*Tests*	*Ct*	*St*
555	M.V.Boucher	South Africa/ICC	147	532	23
416	A.C.Gilchrist	Australia	96	379	37
395	I.A.Healy	Australia	119	366	29
355	R.W.Marsh	Australia	96	343	12
294	M.S.Dhoni	India	90	256	38
270	B.J.Haddin	Australia	66	262	8
270†	P.J.L.Dujon	West Indies	81	265	5
269	A.P.E.Knott	England	95	250	19
265	B.J.Watling	New Zealand	75	257	8
256	M.J.Prior	England	79	243	13
241†	A.J.Stewart	England	133	227	14
232	Q.de Kock	South Africa	54	221	11
228	Wasim Bari	Pakistan	81	201	27
219	R.D.Jacobs	West Indies	65	207	12
219	T.G.Evans	England	91	173	46
217	D.Ramdin	West Indies	74	205	12
206	Kamran Akmal	Pakistan	53	184	22
201†	A.C.Parore	New Zealand	78	194	7
198	S.M.H.Kirmani	India	88	160	38
191†	J.M.Bairstow	England	80	178	13
189	D.L.Murray	West Indies	62	181	8
187	A.T.W.Grout	Australia	51	163	24
179†	B.B.McCullum	New Zealand	101	168	11
176	I.D.S.Smith	New Zealand	63	168	8
174	R.W.Taylor	England	57	167	7
167	Sarfraz Ahmed	Pakistan	49	146	21
165	R.C.Russell	England	54	153	12
157	T.D.Paine	Australia	35	150	7
156	H.A.P.W.Jayawardena	Sri Lanka	58	124	32
152	D.J.Richardson	South Africa	42	150	2
151†	K.C.Sangakkara	Sri Lanka	134	131	20
151†	A.Flower	Zimbabwe	63	142	9

The most for Bangladesh is 113 (98 ct, 15 st) by Mushfiqur Rahim in 78 Tests.

† *Excluding catches taken in the field*

25 OR MORE DISMISSALS IN A SERIES

29	B.J.Haddin	Australia v England	2013
28	R.W.Marsh	Australia v England	1982-83
27 (inc 2st)	R.C.Russell	England v South Africa	1995-96
27 (inc 2st)	I.A.Healy	Australia v England (6 Tests)	1997
26 (inc 3st)	J.H.B.Waite	South Africa v New Zealand	1961-62
26	R.W.Marsh	Australia v West Indies (6 Tests)	1975-76
26 (inc 5st)	I.A.Healy	Australia v England (6 Tests)	1993
26 (inc 1st)	M.V.Boucher	South Africa v England	1998
26 (inc 2st)	A.C.Gilchrist	Australia v England	2001
26 (inc 2st)	A.C.Gilchrist	Australia v England	2006-07
26 (inc 1st)	T.D.Paine	Australia v England	2017-18
25 (inc 2st)	I.A.Healy	Australia v England	1994-95
25 (inc 2st)	A.C.Gilchrist	Australia v England	2002-03
25	A.C.Gilchrist	Australia v India	2007-08

TEN OR MORE DISMISSALS IN A TEST

11	R.C.Russell	England v South Africa	Johannesburg	1995-96
11	A.B.de Villiers	South Africa v Pakistan	Johannesburg	2012-13
11	R.R.Pant	India v Australia	Adelaide	2018-19
10	R.W.Taylor	England v India	Bombay	1979-80
10	A.C.Gilchrist	Australia v New Zealand	Hamilton	1999-00
10	W.P.Saha	India v South Africa	Cape Town	2017-18
10	Sarfraz Ahmed	Pakistan v South Africa	Johannesburg	2018-19

SEVEN DISMISSALS IN AN INNINGS

7	Wasim Bari	Pakistan v New Zealand	Auckland	1978-79
7	R.W.Taylor	England v India	Bombay	1979-80
7	I.D.S.Smith	New Zealand v Sri Lanka	Hamilton	1990-91
7	R.D.Jacobs	West Indies v Australia	Melbourne	2000-01

FIVE STUMPINGS IN AN INNINGS

5	K.S.More	India v West Indies	Madras	1987-88

FIELDING RECORDS
100 CATCHES IN TESTS

Total			*Tests*	*Total*			*Tests*
210	R.S.Dravid	India/ICC	164	122	I.V.A.Richards	West Indies	121
205	D.P.M.D.Jayawardena	Sri Lanka	149	121†	A.B.de Villiers	South Africa	114
200	J.H.Kallis	South Africa/ICC	166	121	A.J.Strauss	England	100
196	R.T.Ponting	Australia	168	120	I.T.Botham	England	102
181	M.E.Waugh	Australia	128	120	M.C.Cowdrey	England	114
175	A.N.Cook	England	161	115	C.L.Hooper	West Indies	102
171	S.P.Fleming	New Zealand	111	115	S.R.Tendulkar	India	200
169	G.C.Smith	South Africa/ICC	117	112	S.R.Waugh	Australia	168
164	B.C.Lara	West Indies/ICC	131	110	R.B.Simpson	Australia	62
163	L.R.P.L.Taylor	New Zealand	112	110	W.R.Hammond	England	85
157	M.A.Taylor	Australia	104	109	G.St A.Sobers	West Indies	93
156	A.R.Border	Australia	156	108	H.M.Amla	South Africa	124
148	J.E.Root	England	114	108	S.M.Gavaskar	India	125
139	Younus Khan	Pakistan	118	105	I.M.Chappell	Australia	75
135	V.V.S.Laxman	India	134	105	M.Azharuddin	India	99
134	S.P.D.Smith	Australia	82	105	G.P.Thorpe	England	100
134	M.J.Clarke	Australia	115	103	G.A.Gooch	England	118
128	M.L.Hayden	Australia	103	100	V.Kohli	India	99
125	S.K.Warne	Australia	145	100	I.R.Bell	England	118
122	G.S.Chappell	Australia	87				

The most for Zimbabwe is 60 by A.D.R.Campbell (60) and for Bangladesh 38 by Mahmudullah (50).

† *Excluding catches taken when wicket-keeping.*

15 CATCHES IN A SERIES

15	J.M.Gregory	Australia v England	1920-21

SEVEN OR MORE CATCHES IN A TEST

8	A.M.Rahane	India v Sri Lanka	Galle	2015
7	G.S.Chappell	Australia v England	Perth	1974-75
7	Yajurvindra Singh	India v England	Bangalore	1976-77
7	H.P.Tillekeratne	Sri Lanka v New Zealand	Colombo (SSC)	1992-93
7	S.P.Fleming	New Zealand v Zimbabwe	Harare	1997-98

7	M.L.Hayden	Australia v Sri Lanka	Galle	2003-04
7	K.L.Rahul	India v England	Nottingham	2018

FIVE CATCHES IN AN INNINGS

5	V.Y.Richardson	Australia v South Africa	Durban	1935-36
5	Yajurvindra Singh	India v England	Bangalore	1976-77
5	M.Azharuddin	India v Pakistan	Karachi	1989-90
5	K.Srikkanth	India v Australia	Perth	1991-92
5	S.P.Fleming	New Zealand v Zimbabwe	Harare	1997-98
5	G.C.Smith	South Africa v Australia	Perth	2012-13
5	D.J.G.Sammy	West Indies v India	Mumbai	2013-14
5	D.M.Bravo	West Indies v Bangladesh	Kingstown	2014
5	A.M.Rahane	India v Sri Lanka	Galle	2015
5	J.Blackwood	West Indies v Sri Lanka	Colombo (PSS)	2015-16
5	S.P.D.Smith	Australia v South Africa	Cape Town	2017-18
5	B.A.Stokes	England v South Africa	Cape Town	2019-20
5	H.D.R.L.Thirimanne	Sri Lanka v England	Galle	2020-21

APPEARANCE RECORDS
100 TEST MATCH APPEARANCES

			Opponents									
			E	*A*	*SA*	*WI*	*NZ*	*I*	*P*	*SL*	*Z*	*B*
200	S.R.Tendulkar	India	32	39	25	21	24	–	18	25	9	7
169	J.M.Anderson	England	–	35	26	22	16	34	18	14	2	2
168†	R.T.Ponting	Australia	35	–	26	24	17	29	15	14	3	4
168	S.R.Waugh	Australia	46	–	16	32	23	18	20	8	3	2
166†	J.H.Kallis	South Africa/ICC	31	28	–	24	18	18	19	15	6	6
164	S.Chanderpaul	West Indies	35	20	24	–	21	25	14	7	8	10
164†	R.S.Dravid	India/ICC	21	32	21	23	15	–	15	20	9	7
161	A.N.Cook	England	–	35	19	20	15	30	20	16	–	6
156	A.R.Border	Australia	47	–	6	31	23	20	22	7	–	–
152*	S.C.J.Broad	England	–	35	22	19	18	23	19	12	–	3
149	D.P.M.D.Jayawardena	Sri Lanka	23	16	18	11	13	18	29	–	8	13
147†	M.V.Boucher	South Africa/ICC	25	20	–	24	17	14	15	17	6	8
145†	S.K.Warne	Australia	36	–	24	19	20	14	15	13	1	2
134	V.V.S.Laxman	India	17	29	19	22	10	–	15	13	6	3
134	K.C.Sangakkara	Sri Lanka	22	11	17	12	12	17	23	–	5	15
133†	M.Muralitharan	Sri Lanka/ICC	16	12	15	12	14	22	16	–	14	11
133	A.J.Stewart	England	–	33	23	24	16	9	13	9	6	–
132	A.Kumble	India	19	20	21	17	11	–	15	18	7	4
132	C.A.Walsh	West Indies	36	38	10	–	10	15	18	3	2	–
131	Kapil Dev	India	27	20	4	25	10	–	29	14	2	–
131†	B.C.Lara	West Indies/ICC	30	30	18	–	11	17	12	8	2	2
128	M.E.Waugh	Australia	29	–	18	28	14	14	15	9	1	–
125	S.M.Gavaskar	India	38	20	–	27	9	–	24	7	–	–
124	H.M.Amla	South Africa	21	21	–	9	14	21	14	14	2	8
124	Javed Miandad	Pakistan	22	24	–	17	18	28	–	12	3	–
124†	G.D.McGrath	Australia	30	–	17	23	14	11	17	8	1	2
121	I.V.A.Richards	West Indies	36	34	–	–	7	28	16	–	–	–
120†	Inzamam-ul-Haq	Pakistan/ICC	19	13	13	15	12	10	–	20	11	6
119	I.A.Healy	Australia	33	–	12	28	11	9	14	11	1	–
118	I.R.Bell	England	–	33	11	12	13	20	13	10	–	6
118	G.A.Gooch	England	–	42	3	26	15	19	10	3	–	–
118	Younus Khan	Pakistan	17	11	14	15	11	9	–	29	5	7
117	D.I.Gower	England	–	42	–	19	13	24	17	2	–	–
117†	G.C.Smith	South Africa/ICC	21	21	–	14	13	15	16	7	2	8

			Opponents									
			E	*A*	*SA*	*WI*	*NZ*	*I*	*P*	*SL*	*Z*	*B*
116	D.L.Haynes	West Indies	36	33	1	–	10	19	16	1	–	–
116	D.B.Vengsarkar	India	26	24	–	25	11	–	22	8	–	–
115	M.A.Atherton	England	–	33	18	27	11	7	11	4	4	–
115†	M.J.Clarke	Australia	35	–	14	12	11	22	10	8	–	2
114	M.C.Cowdrey	England	–	43	14	21	18	8	10	–	–	–
114	A.B.de Villiers	South Africa	20	24	–	13	10	20	12	7	4	4
114*	J.E.Root	England	–	29	12	11	13	24	12	10	–	2
113	S.C.Ganguly	India	12	24	17	12	8	–	12	14	9	5
113†	D.L.Vettori	New Zealand/ICC	17	18	14	10	–	15	9	11	9	9
112	L.R.P.L.Taylor	New Zealand	19	12	8	14	–	17	15	12	4	11
111	S.P.Fleming	New Zealand	19	14	15	11	–	13	9	13	11	6
111	W.P.J.U.C.Vaas	Sri Lanka	15	12	11	9	10	14	18	–	15	7
110	S.T.Jayasuriya	Sri Lanka	14	13	15	10	13	10	17	–	13	5
110	C.H.Lloyd	West Indies	34	29	–	–	8	28	11	–	–	–
108	G.Boycott	England	–	38	7	29	15	13	6	–	–	–
108	C.G.Greenidge	West Indies	29	32	–	–	10	23	14	–	–	–
108	S.M.Pollock	South Africa	23	13	–	16	11	12	12	13	5	3
107	D.C.Boon	Australia	31	–	6	22	17	11	11	9	–	–
105†	J.L.Langer	Australia	21	–	11	18	14	14	13	8	3	2
105	N.M.Lyon	Australia	28	–	15	8	10	22	9	11	–	2
105‡	I.Sharma	India	23	25	15	12	9	–	1	12	–	7
104	K.P.Pietersen	England	–	27	10	14	8	16	14	11	–	4
104†	V.Sehwag	India/ICC	17	23	15	10	12	–	9	11	3	4
104	M.A.Taylor	Australia	33	–	11	20	11	9	12	8	–	–
104	Wasim Akram	Pakistan	18	13	4	17	9	12	–	19	10	2
103	C.H.Gayle	West Indies	20	8	16	–	12	14	8	10	8	7
103	Harbhajan Singh	India	14	18	11	11	13	–	9	16	7	4
103†	M.L.Hayden	Australia	20	–	19	15	11	18	6	7	2	4
103	Salim Malik	Pakistan	19	15	1	7	18	22	–	15	6	–
102	I.T.Botham	England	–	36	–	20	15	14	14	3	–	–
102	C.L.Hooper	West Indies	24	25	10	–	2	19	14	6	2	–
101	G.Kirsten	South Africa	22	18	–	13	13	10	11	9	3	2
101	B.B.McCullum	New Zealand	16	16	13	13	–	10	8	12	4	9
101	M.Ntini	South Africa	18	15	–	15	11	10	9	12	3	8
100	A.J.Strauss	England	–	20	16	18	9	12	13	8	–	4
100	G.P.Thorpe	England	–	16	16	27	13	5	8	9	2	4

† Includes appearance in the Australia v ICC 'Test' in 2005-06; * includes appearance v Ireland in 2019; ‡ includes appearance v Afghanistan in 2018. The most for Zimbabwe is 67 by G.W.Flower, and for Bangladesh 78 by Mushfiqur Rahim.

100 CONSECUTIVE TEST APPEARANCES

159	A.N.Cook	England	May 2006 to September 2018
153	A.R.Border	Australia	March 1979 to March 1994
107	M.E.Waugh	Australia	June 1993 to October 2002
106	S.M.Gavaskar	India	January 1975 to February 1987
101	B.B.McCullum	New Zealand	March 2004 to February 2016

50 TESTS AS CAPTAIN

			Won	*Lost*	*Drawn*	*Tied*
109	G.C.Smith	South Africa	53	29	27	–
93	A.R.Border	Australia	32	22	38	1
80	S.P.Fleming	New Zealand	28	27	25	–
77	R.T.Ponting	Australia	48	16	13	–
74	C.H.Lloyd	West Indies	36	12	26	–

			Won	*Lost*	*Drawn*	*Tied*
68	V.Kohli	India	40	17	11	–
61	J.E.Root	England	27	25	9	–
60	M.S.Dhoni	India	27	18	15	–
59	A.N.Cook	England	24	22	13	–
57	S.R.Waugh	Australia	41	9	7	–
56	Misbah-ul-Haq	Pakistan	26	19	11	–
56	A.Ranatunga	Sri Lanka	12	19	25	–
54	M.A.Atherton	England	13	21	20	–
53	W.J.Cronje	South Africa	27	11	15	–
51	M.P.Vaughan	England	26	11	14	–
50	I.V.A.Richards	West Indies	27	8	15	–
50	M.A.Taylor	Australia	26	13	11	–
50	A.J.Strauss	England	24	11	15	–

The most for Zimbabwe is 21 by A.D.R.Campbell and H.H.Streak, and for Bangladesh 34 by Mushfiqur Rahim.

70 TEST UMPIRING APPEARANCES

136	Alim Dar	(Pakistan)	21.10.2003 to 14.03.2021
128	S.A.Bucknor	(West Indies)	28.04.1989 to 22.03.2009
108	R.E.Koertzen	(South Africa)	26.12.1992 to 24.07.2010
95	D.J.Harper	(Australia)	28.11.1998 to 23.06.2011
92	D.R.Shepherd	(England)	01.08.1985 to 07.06.2005
84	B.F.Bowden	(New Zealand)	11.03.2000 to 03.05.2015
78	D.B.Hair	(Australia)	25.01.1992 to 08.06.2008
75	R.J.Tucker	(Australia)	15.02.2010 to 16.01.2022
74	I.J.Gould	(England)	19.11.2008 to 23.02.2019
74	S.J.A.Taufel	(Australia)	26.12.2000 to 20.08.2012
73	S.Venkataraghavan	(India)	29.01.1993 to 20.01.2004
72	R.A.Kettleborough	(England)	15.11.2010 to 28.08.2021
71	H.D.P.K.Dharmasena	(Sri Lanka)	04.11.2010 to 03.12.2021
70	M.Erasmus	(South Africa)	17.01.2010 to 14.01.2022

THE FIRST-CLASS COUNTIES REGISTER, RECORDS AND 2021 AVERAGES

All statistics are to 9 March 2022.

ABBREVIATIONS – General

*	not out/unbroken partnership	IT20	International Twenty20
b	born	l-o	limited-overs
BB	Best innings bowling analysis	LOI	Limited-Overs Internationals
Cap	Awarded 1st XI County Cap	Tests	International Test Matches
f-c	first-class	F-c Tours	Overseas tours involving first-class appearances
HS	Highest Score		

Awards

PCA 2021	Professional Cricketers' Association Player of 2021
Wisden 2020	One of *Wisden Cricketers' Almanack*'s Five Cricketers of 2020
YC 2021	Cricket Writers' Club Young Cricketer of 2021

ECB Competitions

CB40	Clydesdale Bank 40 (2010-12)
CC	County Championship
FPT	Friends Provident Trophy (2007-09)
P40	NatWest PRO 40 League (2006-09)
RLC	Royal London One-Day Cup (2014-19)
T20	Twenty20 Competition
Y40	Yorkshire Bank 40 (2013)

Education

Ac	Academy
BHS	Boys' High School
C	College
CS	Comprehensive School
GS	Grammar School
HS	High School
I	Institute
S	School
SFC	Sixth Form College
SS	Secondary School
TC	Technical College
U	University

Playing Categories

LBG	Bowls right-arm leg-breaks and googlies
LF	Bowls left-arm fast
LFM	Bowls left-arm fast-medium
LHB	Bats left-handed
LM	Bowls left-arm medium pace
LMF	Bowls left-arm medium fast
OB	Bowls right-arm off-breaks
RF	Bowls right-arm fast
RFM	Bowls right-arm fast-medium
RHB	Bats right-handed
RM	Bowls right-arm medium pace
RMF	Bowls right-arm medium-fast
SLA	Bowls left-arm leg-breaks
SLC	Bowls left-arm 'Chinamen'
WK	Wicket-keeper

Teams (see also p 220)

AS	Adelaide Strikers
BH	Brisbane Heat
CC&C	Combined Campuses & Colleges
CD	Central Districts
CSK	Chennai Super Kings
DC	Deccan Chargers
DCa	Delhi Capitals
DD	Delhi Daredevils
EL	England Lions
EP	Eastern Province
FATA	Federally Administered Tribal Areas
FS	Free State
GW	Griqualand West
HB	Habib Bank Limited
HH	Hobart Hurricanes
KKR	Kolkata Knight Riders
KRL	Khan Research Laboratories
KXIP	Kings XI Punjab
KZN	KwaZulu-Natal Inland
ME	Mashonaland Eagles
MI	Mumbai Indians
MR	Melbourne Renegades
MS	Melbourne Stars
MSC	Mohammedan Sporting Club
MT	Matabeleland Tuskers
MWR	Mid West Rhinos
ND	Northern Districts
NSW	New South Wales
PDSC	Prime Doleshwar Sporting Club
PK	Punjab Kings
PS	Perth Scorchers
PT	Pakistan Television
PW	Pune Warriors
Q	Queensland
RCB	Royal Challengers Bangalore
RPS	Rising Pune Supergiant
RR	Rajasthan Royals
RS	Rising Stars
SA	South Australia
SGR	Speen Ghar Region
SH	Sunrisers Hyderabad
SJD	Sheikh Jamal Dhanmondi
SNGPL	Sui Northern Gas Pipelines Limited
SR	Southern Rocks
SS	Sydney Sixers
ST	Sydney Thunder
Tas	Tasmania
T&T	Trinidad & Tobago
Vic	Victoria
WA	Western Australia
WP	Western Province
ZT	Zarai Taraqiati Bank Limited

DERBYSHIRE

Formation of Present Club: 4 November 1870
Inaugural First-Class Match: 1871
Colours: Chocolate, Amber and Pale Blue
Badge: Rose and Crown
County Champions: (1) 1936
NatWest Trophy Winners: (1) 1981
Benson and Hedges Cup Winners: (1) 1993
Sunday League Winners: (1) 1990
Twenty20 Cup Winners: (0) best – Semi-Finalist 2019

Chief Executive: Ryan Duckett, Derbyshire County Cricket Club, The Incora County Ground, Nottingham Road, Derby, DE21 6DA • Tel: 01332 388101 • Email: info@derbyshireccc.com • Web: www.derbyshireccc.com • Twitter: @DerbyshireCCC (68,232 followers)

Head of Cricket: Mickey Arthur. **Assistant Coaches**: Ajmal Shahzad (bowling) and Mal Loye (batting). **Captain**: B.A.Godleman. **Overseas Players**: R.A.S.Lakmal, Shan Masood and D.J.Melton. **2022 Testimonial**: None. **Head Groundsman**: Neil Godrich. **Scorer**: John Brown. **Blast Team Name**: Derbyshire Falcons. ‡ New registration. NQ Not qualified for England.

AITCHISON, Benjamin William (Merchant Taylors' S; Ormskirk Range HS), b Southport, Lancs 6 Jul 1999. RHB, RFM. Squad No 11. Debut (Derbyshire) 2020. Lancashire 2nd XI 2019. Cheshire 2018-19. HS 50 v Notts (Derby) 2021. BB 6-28 v Durham (Derby) 2021. LO HS 19 v Surrey (Derby) 2021 (RLC). LO BB 2-51 v Leics (Leicester) 2021 (RLC).

CAME, Harry Robert Charles (Bradfield C), b Basingstoke, Hants 27 Aug 1998. Son of P.R.C.Came (Hampshire 2nd XI 1986-87); grandson of K.C.Came (Free Foresters 1957); great-grandson of R.W.V.Robins (Middlesex, Cambridge U & England 1925-58). 5'9". RHB, OB. Squad No 4. Hampshire 2019-20. Derbyshire debut 2021. Hampshire 2nd XI 2017-19. Kent 2nd XI 2017-18. HS 45 v Sussex (Hove) 2021. LO HS 57 v Notts (Derby) 2021 (RLC). T20 HS 56.

NQ**COHEN, Michael** Alexander Robert (Reddam House C), b Cape Town, South Africa 4 Aug 1998. LHB, LFM. Squad No 8. Western Province 2017-18 to 2018-19. Cape Cobras 2017-18. Derbyshire debut 2020. Nottinghamshire 2nd XI 2019. HS 30* v Notts (Nottingham) 2020. BB 5-40 WP v SW Districts (Rondebosch) 2017-18. De BB 5-43 v Warwks (Derby) 2021. LO HS 16 WP v Northerns (Rondebosch) 2017-18. LO BB 1-17 WP v SW Districts (Rondebosch) 2017-18. T20 HS 7*. T20 BB 2-17.

CONNERS, Samuel (George Spencer Ac), b Nottingham 13 Feb 1999. 6'0". RHB, RM. Squad No 59. Debut (Derbyshire) 2019. Derbyshire 2nd XI debut 2016. England U19 2018. HS 39 v Kent (Derby) 2021. BB 5-83 v Durham (Chester-le-St) 2021. LO HS 4 and LO BB 1-45 v Durham (Chester-le-St) 2019 (RLC). T20 HS 2*. T20 BB 2-38.

DAL, Anuj Kailash (Durban HS; Nottingham HS), b Newcastle-upon-Tyne, Northumb 8 Jul 1996. 5'9". RHB, RM. Squad No 65. Debut (Derbyshire) 2018. HS 106 v Leics (Derby) 2021, sharing De record 6th wkt partnership of 227 with B.D.Guest. BB 3-11 v Sussex (Derby) 2019. LO HS 52 v Lancs (Manchester) 2019 (RLC). T20 HS 35.

NQ**Du PLOOY,** Jacobus **Leus**, b Pretoria, South Africa 12 Jan 1995. LHB, SLA. Squad No 76. Free State 2014-15 to 2017-18. Knights 2015-16. Northerns 2018-19. Titans 2018-19. Derbyshire debut 2019. SW Districts 2021-22. Welsh Fire 2021. HS 186 SW Districts v Northern Cape (Kimberley) 2021-22. De HS 130 v Notts (Nottingham) 2020. BB 3-76 Northerns v WP (Pretoria, TU) 2018-19. De BB 2-24 v Glamorgan (Swansea) 2019. LO HS 155 Northerns v WP (Pretoria, TU) 2018-19. LO BB 3-19 Northerns v KZN (Pretoria, TU) 2018-19. T20 HS 92. T20 BB 4-15.

GODLEMAN, Billy Ashley (Islington Green S), b Islington, London 11 Feb 1989. 6'3". LHB, LB. Squad No 1. Middlesex 2005-09. Essex 2010-12. Derbyshire debut 2013; cap 2015; captain 2016 to date. F-c Tour (MCC): Nepal 2019-20. 1000 runs (2); most – 1087 (2019). HS 227 v Glamorgan (Swansea) 2016. BB –. LO HS 137 v Warwks (Birmingham) 2018 (RLC). T20 HS 92.

GUEST, Brooke David (Kent Street Senior HS, Perth, WA; Murdoch U, Perth), b Whitworth Park, Manchester, Lancs 14 May 1997. 5'11". RHB, WK. Squad No 29. Lancashire 2018-19. Derbyshire debut 2020. Lancashire 2nd XI 2016-19. HS 116 v Leics (Derby) 2021, sharing De record 6th wkt partnership of 227 with A.K.Dal. LO HS 74 v Somerset (Taunton) 2021 (RLC). T20 HS 34*.

HUGHES, Alex Lloyd (Ounsdale HS, Wolverhampton), b Wordsley, Staffs 29 Sep 1991. 5'10". RHB, RM. Squad No 18. Debut (Derbyshire) 2013; cap 2017. HS 142 v Glos (Bristol) 2017. BB 4-46 v Glamorgan (Derby) 2014. LO HS 96* v Leics (Leicester) 2016 (RLC). LO BB 4-44 v Northants (Derby) 2019 (RLC). T20 HS 43*. T20 BB 4-42.

‡NQ**LAKMAL**, Ranasinghe Arachchige **Suranga**, b Matara, Sri Lanka 10 Mar 1987. RHB, RMF. Squad No 82. Tamil Union 2007-08 to date. **Tests** (SL): 69 (2010-11 to 2021-22); HS 42 v B (Colombo, PSS) 2016-17; BB 5-47 v WI (North Sound) 2020-21. **LOI** (SL): 86 (2009-10 to 2020-21); HS 26 v P (Cardiff) 2017; BB 4-13 v I (Dharamsala) 2017-18. **IT20** (SL): 11 (2011 to 2018-19); HS 5* v I (Colombo, RPS) 2017-18; BB 2-26 v E (Bristol) 2011. F-c Tours (SL): E 2011, 2016; A 2011-12, 2018-19; SA 2008-09 (SL A), 2016-17, 2018-19; WI 2013 (SL A), 2018, 2020-21; NZ 2014-15, 2015-16, 2018-19; I 2017-18, 2021-22; Z 2016-17, 2019-20; B 2013-14; UAE (v P) 2011-12, 2013-14, 2017-18. HS 58* TU v SL Navy (Welisara) 2012-13. BB 6-68 TU v Nondescripts (Colombo, NCC) 2012-13. LO HS 38* SL A v The Rest (Pallekele) 2013. LO BB 5-31 TU v Nondescripts (Colombo, NCC) 2008-09. T20 HS 33. T20 BB 5-34.

McKIERNAN, Matthew Harry ('**Mattie**') (Lowton HS; St John Rigby C, Wigan), b Billinge, Lancs 14 Jun 1994. 6'0". RHB, LB. Squad No 21. Debut (Derbyshire) 2019. Cumberland 2016-17. HS 52 v Lancs (Liverpool) 2020. BB 2-3 v Notts (Nottingham) 2020. LO HS 38 and LO BB 1-26 v Surrey (Derby) 2021 (RLC). T20 HS 25. T20 BB 3-9.

MADSEN, Wayne Lee (Kearsney C, Durban; U of South Africa), b Durban, South Africa 2 Jan 1984. Nephew of M.B.Madsen (Natal 1967-68 to 1978-79), T.R.Madsen (Natal 1976-77 to 1989-90) and H.R.Fotheringham (Natal, Transvaal 1971-72 to 1989-90), cousin of G.S.Fotheringham (KwaZulu-Natal 2008-09 to 2009-10). 5'11". RHB, OB. Squad No 77. KwaZulu-Natal 2003-04 to 2007-08. Dolphins 2006-07 to 2007-08. Derbyshire debut 2009, scoring 170 v Glos (Cheltenham); cap 2011; captain 2012-15; testimonial 2017. Qualified for England by residence in February 2015. 1000 runs (5); most – 1292 (2016). HS 231* v Northants (Northampton) 2012. BB 3-45 KZN v EP (Pt Elizabeth) 2007-08. De BB 2-8 v Sussex (Hove) 2021. LO HS 138 v Hants (Derby) 2014 (RLC). LO BB 3-27 v Durham (Derby) 2013 (Y40). T20 HS 86*. T20 BB 2-20.

NQ**MELTON, Dustin** Renton (Pretoria BHS; U of Pretoria), b Harare, Zimbabwe 11 Apr 1995. RHB, RFM. Squad No 13. Debut (Derbyshire) 2019. HS 15 v Essex (Chelmsford) 2021. BB 4-22 v Leics (Leicester) 2020. T20 BB 2-37.

POTTS, Nicholas James (De Ferrers Ac), b Burton-on-Trent, Staffs 17 Jul 2002. RHB, RFM. Squad No 26. Derbyshire 2nd XI debut 2018. Awaiting 1st XI debut.

REECE, Luis Michael (St Michael's HS, Chorley; Leeds Met U), b Taunton, Somerset 4 Aug 1990. 6'1". LHB, LM. Squad No 10. Leeds/Bradford MCCU 2012-13. Lancashire 2013-15, no f-c appearances in 2016. Derbyshire debut 2017; cap 2019. MCC 2014. Unicorns 2011-12. London Spirit 2021. HS 184 v Sussex (Derby) 2019. 50 wkts (1): 55 (2019). BB 7-20 v Glos (Derby) 2018. LO HS 128 v Worcs (Derby) 2019 (RLC). LO BB 4-35 Unicorns v Glos (Exmouth) 2011 (CB40). T20 HS 97*. T20 BB 3-33.

SCRIMSHAW, George Louis Sheridan (John Taylor HS, Burton), b Burton-on-Trent, Staffs 10 Feb 1998. 6'7". RHB, RMF. Squad No 9. Worcestershire 2nd XI 2016-17. Debut (Derbyshire) 2021. Worcestershire 2017 (T20 only). HS 5* and BB 2-40 v Notts (Derby) 2021. LO HS 13* v Surrey (Derby) 2021 (RLC). LO BB 2-41 v Notts (Derby) 2021 (RLC). T20 HS 3*. T20 BB 3-23.

‡NQ**SHAN MASOOD**, b Kuwait 14 Oct 1989. LHB, RMF. Squad No 94. Karachi Whites 2007-08. Habib Bank 2009-10 to 2013-14. Durham MCCU 2011. Federal Areas 2011-12. Islamabad 2012-13. United Bank 2015-16 to 2017-18. National Bank 2018-19. Southern Punjab 2019-20 to 2020-21. Baluchistan 2021-22. **Tests** (P): 25 (2013-14 to 2020-21); HS 156 v E (Manchester) 2020; BB 1-6 v SA (Centurion) 2018-19. **LOI** (P): 5 (2018-19); HS 50 v A (Dubai) 2018-19. F-c Tours (P): E 2016, 2020; A 2019-20; SA 2018-19; WI 2010-11 (P A), 2016-17; NZ 2020-21; SL 2015 (P A). 1000 runs (0+1): 1123 (2012-13). HS 199 Islamabad v Karachi W (Islamabad) 2012-13. BB 2-52 DU v Warwks (Durham) 2011. LO HS 182* Islamabad v Rawalpindi (Rawalpindi) 2017-18. LO BB 2-0 HB v Islamabad Leopards (Islamabad) 2010-11. T20 HS 103*.

THOMSON, Alexander Thomas (Kings S, Macclesfield; Denstone C; Cardiff Met U), b Macclesfield, Cheshire 30 Oct 1993. 6'2". RHB, OB. Squad No 15. Cardiff MCCU 2014-16. Warwickshire 2017-20. Derbyshire debut 2021. Staffordshire 2013-16. F-c Tour (MCC): Nepal 2019-20. HS 46 Wa v Northants (Birmingham) 2020. De HS 18 and CC BB 3-71 v Middx (Lord's) 2021. BB 6-138 CfU v Hants (Southampton) 2016. LO HS 68* Wa v Derbys (Derby) 2019 (RLC). LO BB 3-27 Wa v Lancs (Birmingham) 2019 (RLC). T20 HS 28. T20 BB 4-35.

NQ**WATT, Mark** Robert James, b Edinburgh, Scotland 29 Jul 1996. LHB, SLA. Squad No 51. Scotland 2016 to 2017-18. Lancashire 2018 (T20 only). Derbyshire debut 2019 (white ball only). **LOI** (Scot): 33 (2016 to 2021-22); HS 31* v Ire (Harare) 2017-18; BB 4-42 v USA (Sharjah) 2019-20. **IT20** (Scot): 47 (2015 to 2021-22); HS 22 v B (Al Amerat) 2021-22; BB 5-27 v Netherlands (Dubai, ICCA) 2015-16. HS 81* Scot v PNG (Port Moresby) 2017-18. BB 3-60 Scot v Ire (Dubai, DSC) 2017-18. LO HS 36 Scot v Oman (Al Amerat) 2018-19. LO BB 4-42 (*see LOI*). T20 HS 22. T20 BB 5-27.

WOOD, Thomas Anthony (Heanor Gate Science C), b Derby 11 May 1994. 6'3". RHB, RM. Squad No 24. Debut (Derbyshire) 2016. HS 31 v Notts (Derby) 2020. LO HS 109 v Notts (Derby) 2021 (RLC). LO BB 1-13 v Surrey (Derby) 2021 (RLC). T20 HS 67.

RELEASED/RETIRED

(Having made a County 1st XI appearance in 2021, even if not formally contracted. Some may return in 2022.)

CRITCHLEY, M.J.J. – *see ESSEX.*

HOSEIN, Harvey Richard (Denstone C), b Chesterfield 12 Aug 1996. 5'10". RHB, WK. Derbyshire 2014-21, taking seven catches in an innings and UK record-equalling 11 in match v Surrey (Oval). HS 138* v Leeds/Brad MCCU (Derby) 2019. CC HS 108 v Worcs (Worcester) 2016. LO HS 41* v Lancs (Manchester) 2019 (RLC). T20 HS 10*.

HUDSON-PRENTICE, F.J. – *see SUSSEX.*

McDERMOTT, B.R. – *see HAMPSHIRE.*

MARSHALL, Connor Robert (Trent C), b Cardiff, Glamorgan 28 Jan 1998. LHB, LB. Derbyshire 2021 (l-o only). Nottinghamshire 2nd XI 2015-18. Derbyshire 2nd XI 2019-21. Lincolnshire 2015. Awaiting f-c debut. LO HS 19 v Surrey (Derby) 2021 (RLC). LO BB –.

PRIESTLEY, Nils Oscar (Blessed Robert Sutton S; Abbotsholme SFC), b Sutton Coldfield, Warwks 18 Sep 2000. LHB, RM. Derbyshire 2nd XI 2017-21. LO HS 25* v Northants (Northampton) 2021 (RLC).

NQ**RAMPAUL, Ravi**, b Preysal, Trinidad 15 Oct 1984. 6'1". LHB, RFM. Trinidad & Tobago 2001-02 to 2018-19. Surrey 2016-17. Derbyshire 2018-19; cap 2019. IPL: RCB 2013-14. **Tests** (WI): 18 (2009-10 to 2012-13); HS 40* v A (Adelaide) 2009-10; BB 4-48 v P (Providence) 2011. **LOI** (WI): 92 (2003-04 to 2015-16); HS 86* v I (Visakhapatnam) 2011-12; BB 5-49 v B (Khulna) 2012-13. **IT20** (WI): 27 (2007 to 2021-22); HS 8 v Ire (Providence) 2010; BB 3-16 v A (Colombo, RPS) 2012-13. F-c Tours (WI): E 2007, 2012; A 2009-10; SA 2003-04 (WI A); I 2011-12; B 2011-12, 2012-13. HS 64* WI A v SL A (Basseterre) 2006-07. De HS 30 v Glamorgan (Derby) 2019. BB 7-51 T&T v Barbados (Pointe-a-Pierre) 2006-07. De BB 5-77 v Durham (Chester-le-St) 2019. LO HS 86* (*see LOI*). LO BB 5-48 v Yorks (Derby) 2018 (RLC). T20 HS 23*. T20 BB 5-9.

NQ**SMIT, Daryn** (Northwood S; U of SA), b Durban, South Africa 28 Jan 1984. 5'11". RHB, LB, occ WK. KwaZulu Natal 2004-05 to 2016-17. Dolphins 2005-06 to 2016-17. Derbyshire 2017-18. 1000 runs (0+1): 1081 (2015-16). HS 156* KZN v NW (Durban) 2015-16. De HS 45* v Durham (Derby) 2017. BB 7-27 KZN v SW Districts (Durban) 2013-14. De BB –. LO HS 109 Dolphins v Warriors (East London) 2011-12. LO BB 4-39 KZN v GW (Kimberley) 2013-14. T20 HS 57. T20 BB 3-19.

NQ**STANLAKE, Billy**, b Hervey Bay, Queensland, Australia 4 Nov 1994. RHB, RFM. Queensland 2015-16 to 2019-20. Derbyshire 2021. IPL: RCB 2017. SH 2018. Big Bash: AS 2015-16 to 2019-20. MS 2020-21. **LOI** (A): 7 (2016-17 to 2018-19); HS 2 and BB 3-35 v E (Manchester) 2018. **IT20** (A): 19 (2016-17 to 2019-20); HS 7 v E (Birmingham) 2018; BB 4-8 v P (Harare) 2018. HS 8 and De BB 2-91 v Essex (Chelmsford) 2021. BB 3-50 Q v SA (Brisbane) 2015-16. LO HS 4* (twice). LO BB 4-24 Q v Tas (Hobart) 2020-21. T20 HS 7. T20 BB 4-8.

NQ**VAN BEEK, Logan** Verjus, b Christchurch, New Zealand 7 Sep 1990. Grandson of S.C.Guillen (Trinidad, Canterbury, West Indies and New Zealand 1947-48 to 1960-61). 6'1". RHB, RMF. Canterbury 2009-10 to 2016-17. Netherlands 2017. Wellington 2017-18 to date. Derbyshire 2019. **LOI** (Neth): 5 (2021); HS 29 v Ire (Utrecht) 2021; BB 3-29 v Ire (Utrecht) 2021 – separate matches. **IT20** (Neth): 10 (2013-14 to 2021-22); HS 11 v Ire (Abu Dhabi) 2021-22; BB 3-9 v E (Chattogram) 2013-14. F-c Tour (NZA): UAE 2018-19 (v P A). HS 111* Cant v Otago (Christchurch) 2015-16. De HS 34* v Glos (Derby) 2019. BB 6-46 Well v Auckland (Auckland) 2017-18. De BB 3-20 v Leics (Leicester) 2019. LO HS 64* Neth v Z (Amstelveen) 2017. LO BB 6-18 Neth v UAE (Voorburg) 2017. T20 HS 61*. T20 BB 4-17.

WAGSTAFF, Mitchell David (John Port S), b Derby 2 Sep 2003. LHB, LB. Derbyshire 2nd XI 2019-21. Awaiting f-c debut. LO HS 36 v Surrey (Derby) 2021 (RLC).

DERBYSHIRE 2021

RESULTS SUMMARY

	Place	Won	Lost	Tied	Drew	NR
LV= Insurance County Champ (Div 3)	5th	1	7		6	
Royal London One-Day Cup (Group 2)	9th	1	6			1
Vitality Blast (North Group)	8th	4	7	1		

LV= INSURANCE COUNTY CHAMPIONSHIP AVERAGES
BATTING AND FIELDING

Cap		*M*	*I*	*NO*	*HS*	*Runs*	*Avge*	*100*	*50*	*Ct/St*
2019	M.J.J.Critchley	14	26	3	109	1000	43.47	1	8	8
	H.R.Hosein	8	14	5	83*	371	41.22	–	4	11
2011	W.L.Madsen	11	20	–	111	675	33.75	1	4	20
2015	B.A.Godleman	10	18	2	100*	530	33.12	1	3	5
	A.K.Dal	8	13	2	106	333	30.27	1	1	6
	B.D.Guest	12	20	1	116	489	25.73	1	1	26/3
	J.L.du Plooy	13	24	1	98	428	18.60	–	2	5
	F.J.Hudson-Prentice	9	15	2	31*	209	16.07	–	–	2
	H.R.C.Came	3	5	–	45	68	13.60	–	–	1
2019	L.M.Reece	9	17	–	63	231	13.58	–	1	3
	B.W.Aitchison	13	20	4	50	200	12.50	–	1	12
	B.R.McDermott	2	4	–	25	49	12.25	–	–	1
	A.T.Thomson	4	6	–	18	65	10.83	–	–	1
2017	A.L.Hughes	5	9	1	25	84	10.50	–	–	1
	T.A.Wood	7	13	–	31	129	9.92	–	–	6
	S.Conners	10	16	3	39	114	8.76	–	–	1
	D.R.Melton	5	8	3	15	39	7.80	–	–	2
	M.A.R.Cohen	5	8	1	11	41	5.85	–	–	1
	G.L.S.Scrimshaw	3	5	3	5*	5	2.50	–	–	1

Also batted: M.H.McKiernan (1 match) 23 (1 ct); E.H.T.Moulton (2) 6*, 3; B.Stanlake (1) 0, 8.

BOWLING

	O	*M*	*R*	*W*	*Avge*	*Best*	*5wI*	*10wM*
B.W.Aitchison	275.4	50	792	34	23.29	6-28	1	–
F.J.Hudson-Prentice	182	47	548	23	23.82	5-68	1	–
M.A.R.Cohen	99.5	19	280	11	25.45	5-43	1	–
S.Conners	225.5	44	750	26	28.84	5-83	1	–
M.J.J.Critchley	343.3	42	1230	32	38.43	5-67	1	–
L.M.Reece	183.3	46	555	12	46.25	2-25	–	–
Also bowled:								
A.T.Thomson	53.2	6	186	7	26.57	3-71	–	–
A.K.Dal	110	18	298	9	33.11	2-17	–	–
D.R.Melton	93	15	390	9	43.33	3-57	–	–

J.L.du Plooy 8-1-21-0; A.L.Hughes 31-8-83-1; M.H.McKiernan 4-0-16-0; W.L.Madsen 43.5-8-130-4; E.H.T.Moulton 40-8-159-3; G.L.S.Scrimshaw 35-6-154-3; B.Stanlake 17-2-91-2.

The First-Class Averages (pp 220–232) give the records of Derbyshire players in all first-class county matches, with the exceptions of F.J.Hudson-Prentice and A.T.Thomson, whose first-class figures for Derbyshire are as above.

DERBYSHIRE RECORDS

FIRST-CLASS CRICKET

Highest Total	For 801-8d		v	Somerset	Taunton	2007
	V 677-7d		by	Yorkshire	Leeds	2013
Lowest Total	For 16		v	Notts	Nottingham	1879
	V 23		by	Hampshire	Burton upon T	1958
Highest Innings	For 274	G.A.Davidson	v	Lancashire	Manchester	1896
	V 343*	P.A.Perrin	for	Essex	Chesterfield	1904

Highest Partnership for each Wicket

1st	333	L.M.Reece/B.A.Godleman	v	Northants	Derby	2017
2nd	417	K.J.Barnett/T.A.Tweats	v	Yorkshire	Derby	1997
3rd	316*	A.S.Rollins/K.J.Barnett	v	Leics	Leicester	1997
4th	328	P.Vaulkhard/D.Smith	v	Notts	Nottingham	1946
5th	302*†	J.E.Morris/D.G.Cork	v	Glos	Cheltenham	1993
6th	227	B.D.Guest/A.K.Dal	v	Leics	Derby	2021
7th	258	M.P.Dowman/D.G.Cork	v	Durham	Derby	2000
8th	198	K.M.Krikken/D.G.Cork	v	Lancashire	Manchester	1996
9th	283	A.Warren/J.Chapman	v	Warwicks	Blackwell	1910
10th	132	A.Hill/M.Jean-Jacques	v	Yorkshire	Sheffield	1986

† *346 runs were added for this wicket in two separate partnerships*

Best Bowling	For	10- 40	W.Bestwick	v	Glamorgan	Cardiff	1921
(Innings)	V	10- 45	R.L.Johnson	for	Middlesex	Derby	1994
Best Bowling	For	17-103	W.Mycroft	v	Hampshire	Southampton	1876
(Match)	V	16-101	G.Giffen	for	Australians	Derby	1886

Most Runs – Season	2165	D.B.Carr	(av 48.11)	1959
Most Runs – Career	23854	K.J.Barnett	(av 41.12)	1979-98
Most 100s – Season	8	P.N.Kirsten		1982
Most 100s – Career	53	K.J.Barnett		1979-98
Most Wkts – Season	168	T.B.Mitchell	(av 19.55)	1935
Most Wkts – Career	1670	H.L.Jackson	(av 17.11)	1947-63
Most Career W-K Dismissals	1304	R.W.Taylor	(1157 ct; 147 st)	1961-84
Most Career Catches in the Field	563	D.C.Morgan		1950-69

LIMITED-OVERS CRICKET

Highest Total	**50ov**	366-4		v	Comb Univs	Oxford	1991
	40ov	321-5		v	Essex	Leek	2013
	T20	222-5		v	Yorkshire	Leeds	2010
		222-5		v	Notts	Nottingham	2017
Lowest Total	**50ov**	73		v	Lancashire	Derby	1993
	40ov	60		v	Kent	Canterbury	2008
	T20	72		v	Leics	Derby	2013
Highest Innings	**50ov**	173*	M.J.Di Venuto	v	Derbys CB	Derby	2000
	40ov	141*	C.J.Adams	v	Kent	Chesterfield	1992
	T20	111	W.J.Durston	v	Notts	Nottingham	2010
Best Bowling	**50ov**	8-21	M.A.Holding	v	Sussex	Hove	1988
	40ov	6- 7	M.Hendrick	v	Notts	Nottingham	1972
	T20	5-27	T.Lungley	v	Leics	Leicester	2009

DURHAM

Formation of Present Club: 23 May 1882
Inaugural First-Class Match: 1992
Colours: Navy Blue, Yellow and Maroon
Badge: Coat of Arms of the County of Durham
County Champions: (3) 2008, 2009, 2013
Friends Provident Trophy Winners: (1) 2007
Royal London One-Day Cup Winners: (1) 2014
Twenty20 Cup Winners: (0); best – Finalist 2016

Chief Executive: Tim Bostock, Emirates Riverside, Chester-le-Street, Co Durham DH3 3QR • Tel: 0191 387 1717 • Email: reception@durhamcricket.co.uk • Web: www.durhamcricket.co.uk • Twitter: @DurhamCricket (86,821 followers)

Director of Cricket: Marcus North. **Lead High Performance Coach**: James Franklin. **Bowling Coach**: Neil Killeen. **Assistant Coaches**: Alan Walker and Will Gidman. **Captain**: S.G.Borthwick. **Overseas Players**: D.G.Bedingham and K.D.Petersen. **2022 Testimonial**: None. **Head Groundsman**: Vic Demain. **Scorer**: William Dobson. **Blast Team Name**: Durham Jets. ‡ New registration. NQ Not qualified for England.

Durham initially awarded caps immediately after their players joined the staff but revised this policy in 1998, capping players on merit, past 'awards' having been nullified. Durham abolished both their capping and 'awards' systems after the 2005 season.

NQ**BEDINGHAM, David** Guy, b George, Cape Province, South Africa 22 Apr 1994. 5'9". RHB, OB, occ WK. Squad No 5. Western Province 2012-13 to date. Boland 2015-16 to 2018-19. Cape Cobras 2018-19 to 2019-20. Durham debut 2020. Birmingham Phoenix 2021. 1000 runs (1): 1029 (2021). HS 257 v Derbys (Chester-le-St) 2021. BB –. LO HS 104* Boland v Border (East London) 2017-18. LO BB –. T20 HS 73.

BORTHWICK, Scott George (Farringdon Community Sports C, Sunderland), b Sunderland 19 Apr 1990. 5'9". LHB, LBG. Squad No 16. Debut (Durham) 2009; captain 2021 to date. Chilaw Marians 2014-15. Wellington 2015-16 to 2016-17. Surrey 2017-20; cap 2018. **Tests**: 1 (2013-14); HS 4 and BB 3-33 v A (Sydney) 2013-14. **LOI**: 2 (2011 to 2011-12); HS 15 v Ire (Dublin) 2011; BB –. **IT20**: 1 (2011); HS 14 and BB 1-15 v WI (Oval) 2011. F-c Tours: A 2013-14; SL 2013-14 (EL). 1000 runs (5); most – 1390 (2015). HS 216 v Middx (Chester-le-St) 2014, sharing Du record 2nd wkt partnership of 274 with M.D.Stoneman. BB 6-70 v Surrey (Oval) 2013. LO HS 87 and LO BB 5-38 v Leics (Leicester) 2015 (RLC). T20 HS 62. T20 BB 4-18.

BUSHNELL, Jonathan James (Durham S), b Durham 6 Sep 2001. RHB, RM. Squad No 20. Durham 2nd XI debut 2019. Awaiting 1st XI debut.

CAMPBELL, Jack Oliver Ian (Churcher's C, Petersfield; Durham U), b Portsmouth, Hants 11 Nov 1999. 6'7". RHB, LMF. Squad No 21. Durham MCCU 2019. Durham debut 2019. Hampshire 2nd XI 2017. Kent 2nd XI 2018. Durham 2nd XI debut 2018. HS 2 DU v Durham (Chester-le-St) 2019. Du HS 0* and BB 1-43 v Leics (Leicester) 2019. LO BB 3-58 v Essex (Chester-le-St) 2021 (RLC). T20 HS 6. T20 BB 1-21.

CARSE, Brydon Alexander (Pearson HS, Pt Elizabeth), b Port Elizabeth, South Africa 31 Jul 1995. Son of J.A.Carse (Rhodesia, W Province, E Province, Northants, Border, Griqualand W 1977-78 to 1992-93). 6'1½". RHB, RF. Squad No 99. Debut (Durham) 2016. Northern Superchargers 2021. **LOI**: 3 (2021); HS 31 v P (Lord's) 2021; BB 5-61 v P (Birmingham) 2021. F-c Tour (EL): A 2019-20. HS 77* v Northants (Chester-le-St) 2019, sharing Du record 8th wkt partnership of 154 with B.A.Raine. BB 6-26 v Middx (Lord's) 2019. LO HS 31 (*see LOI*). LO BB 35-61 (*see LOI*). T20 HS 51. T20 BB 3-30.

CLARK, Graham (St Benedict's Catholic HS, Whitehaven), b Whitehaven, Cumbria 16 Mar 1993. Younger brother of J.Clark (*see SURREY*). 6'1". RHB, LB. Squad No 7. Debut (Durham) 2015. HS 109 v Glamorgan (Chester-le-St) 2017. BB 1-10 v Sussex (Arundel) 2018. LO HS 141 v Kent (Beckenham) 2021 (RLC). LO BB 3-18 v Leics (Leicester) 2018 (RLC). T20 HS 91*. T20 BB –.

COUGHLIN, Paul (St Robert of Newminster Catholic CS, Washington), b Sunderland 23 Oct 1992. Elder brother of J.Coughlin (Durham 2016-19); nephew of T.Harland (Durham 1974-78). 6'3". RHB, RM. Squad No 23. Debut (Durham) 2012. Nottinghamshire in 2019. Northumberland 2011. F-c Tour (EL): WI 2017-18. HS 90 v Derbys (Chester-le-St) 2020. BB 5-49 (10-133 match) v Northants (Chester-le-St) 2017. LO HS 22 v Notts (Nottingham) 2017 (RLC) and 22 v Lancs (Chester-le-St) 2017 (RLC). LO BB 3-36 v Worcs (Worcester) 2017 (RLC). T20 HS 53. T20 BB 5-42.

CRAWSHAW, Harry Michael (Q Ethelberga's Collegiate, York), b Middlesbrough, Yorks 16 Feb 2003. LHB, SLA. Squad No 3. Durham 2nd XI debut 2021. Awaiting f-c debut. T20 HS 5. T20 BB –.

DICKSON, Sean Robert, b Johannesburg, South Africa 2 Sep 1991. 5'10". RHB, RM. Squad No 58. Northerns 2013-14 to 2014-15. Kent 2015-19. Durham debut 2020. UK passport holder; England qualified. HS 318 K v Northants (Beckenham) 2017, 2nd highest score in K history. Du HS 56 v Notts (Nottingham) 2020. BB 1-15 Northerns v GW (Centurion) 2014-15. CC BB –. LO HS 103* v Lancs (Gosforth) 2021 (RLC). T20 HS 53. T20 BB 1-9.

DONEATHY, Luke (Prudhoe HS), b Newcastle upon Tyne 26 Jul 2001. RHB, RM. Squad No 24. Durham 2nd XI debut 2019. Awaiting f-c debut. LO HS 69* and LO BB 4-36 v Lancs (Gosforth) 2021 (RLC). T20 HS 5*. T20 BB 1-19.

DRISSELL, George Samuel (Bedminster Down SS; Filton C), b Bristol, Glos 20 Jan 1999. 6'1½". RHB, OB. Squad No 8. Gloucestershire 2017-19; cap 2017. Gloucestershire 2nd XI 2016-19. Worcestershire 2nd XI 2021. Somerset 2nd XI 2021. Durham 2nd XI debut 2021. HS 19 Gs v Warwks (Birmingham) 2018. BB 4-83 Gs v Glamorgan (Newport) 2019. LO HS 17* Sm v Warwks (Birmingham) 2021 (RLC). LO BB 1-21 Sm v Glamorgan (Taunton) 2021 (RLC).

ECKERSLEY, Edmund John Holden (**'Ned'**) (St Benedict's GS, Ealing), b Oxford 9 Aug 1989. 6'0". RHB, WK, occ OB. Squad No 66. Leicestershire 2011-18; cap 2013. Mountaineers 2011-12. Durham debut 2019; captain 2020. MCC 2013. 1000 runs (1): 1302 (2013). HS 158 Le v Derbys (Derby) 2017. Du HS 118 v Sussex (Hove) 2019, sharing Du record 6th wkt partnership of 282 with C.T.Bancroft. BB 2-29 Le v Lancs (Manchester) 2013. Du BB –. LO HS 108 Le v Yorks (Leicester) 2013 (Y40). T20 HS 50*.

GIBSON, Oliver James (Q Elizabeth GS, Hexham; Derwentside SFC), b Northallerton, Yorks 7 Jul 2000. RHB, RFM. Squad No 73. Durham 2nd XI debut 2018. Awaiting 1st XI debut.

[NQ]**JONES, Michael** Alexander (Ormskirk S; Myerscough C), b Ormskirk, Lancs 5 Jan 1998. 6'2". RHB, OB. Squad No 10. Debut (Durham) 2018. Durham 2nd XI debut 2017. Derbyshire 2nd XI 2017. Leicestershire 2nd XI 2017. **LOI** (Scot): 8 (2017-18 to 2019-20); HS 87 v Ire (Dubai, ICCA) 2017-18. HS 82 v Notts (Nottingham) 2020. LO HS 87 (*see LOI*).

LEES, Alexander Zak (Holy Trinity SS, Halifax), b Halifax, Yorks 14 Apr 1993. 6'3". LHB, LB. Squad No 19. Yorkshire 2010-18; cap 2014; captain (l-o) 2016. Durham debut 2018. MCC 2017. YC 2014. **Tests**: 1 (2021-22); HS 6 v WI (North Sound) 2021-22. F-c Tour: WI 2021-22. 1000 runs (2); most – 1199 (2016). HS 275* Y v Derbys (Chesterfield) 2013. Du HS 181 v Leics (Chester-le-St) 2019. BB 2-51 Y v Middx (Lord's) 2016. Du BB 1-12 v Yorks (Chester-le-St) 2020. LO HS 126* v Essex (Chester-le-St) 2021 (RLC). T20 HS 77*.

MACKINTOSH, Tomas Scott Sabater (Merchiston Castle S), b Madrid, Spain 11 Jan 2003. RHB, WK. Squad No 14. Durham 2nd XI debut 2021. Awaiting 1st XI debut.

‡NQ**PETERSEN, Keegan** Darryl, b Paarl, South Africa 8 Aug 1993. RHB, LB. Boland 2011-12 to 2016-17. Cape Cobras 2014-15 to 2016-17. Knights 2016-17 to 2019-20. Northern Cape 2017-18 to 2019-20. Dolphins 2020-21. KZN-Coastal 2021-22. **Tests** (SA): 5 (2021 to 2021-22); HS 82 v I (Cape Town) 2021-22. F-c Tour (SA): WI 2021. 1000 runs (0+1): 1263 (2018-19). HS 225* Boland v NW (Paarl) 2013-14. BB 3-49 Knights v Dolphins (Durban) 2017-18. LO HS 134* Boland v EP (Pt Elizabeth) 2012-13. LO BB 1-18 Boland v KZN (Pietermaritzburg) 2012-13. T20 HS 66*. T20 BB –.

POTTS, Matthew ('**Matty**') James (St Robert of Newminster Catholic S), b Sunderland 29 Oct 1998. 6'0". RHB, RM. Squad No 35. Debut (Durham) 2017. Northern Superchargers 2021. Durham 2nd XI debut 2016. England U19 2017. HS 81 v Northants (Northampton) 2021. BB 4-32 v Worcs (Worcester) 2021. LO HS 30 v Yorks (Chester-le-St) 2018 (RLC). LO BB 4-62 v Northants (Chester-le-St) 2019 (RLC). T20 HS 40*. T20 BB 3-8.

RAINE, Benjamin Alexander (St Aidan's RC SS, Sunderland) b Sunderland, 14 Sep 1991. 6'0". LHB, RMF. Squad No 44. Debut (Durham) 2011 – one game only. Leicestershire 2013-18; cap 2018. HS 82 v Northants (Chester-le-St) 2019, sharing Du record 8th wkt partnership of 154 with B.A.Carse. 50 wkts (2); most – 61 (2015). BB 6-27 v Sussex (Hove) 2019. LO HS 83 Le v Worcs (Worcester) 2018 (RLC). LO BB 3-31 Le v Northants (Northampton) 2018 (RLC). T20 HS 113.

RUSHWORTH, Christopher (Castle View CS, Sunderland), b Sunderland 11 Jul 1986. Cousin of P.Mustard (Durham, Mountaineers, Auckland, Lancashire and Gloucestershire 2002-17). 6'2". RHB, RMF. Squad No 22. Debut (Durham) 2010; testimonial 2019. MCC 2013, 2015. Northumberland 2004-05. PCA 2015. HS 57 v Kent (Canterbury) 2017. 50 wkts (6); most – 88 (2015) – Du record. BB 9-52 (15-95 match – Du record) v Northants (Chester-le-St) 2014. Hat-trick v Hants (Southampton) 2015. LO HS 38* v Derbys (Chester-le-St) 2015 (RLC). LO BB 5-31 v Notts (Chester-le-St) 2010 (CB40). T20 HS 5. T20 BB 3-14.

SALISBURY, Matthew Edward Thomas (Shenfield HS; Anglia Ruskin U), b Chelmsford, Essex 18 Apr 1993. 6'0½". RHB, RMF. Squad No 32. Cambridge MCCU 2012-13. Essex 2014-15. Hampshire 2017. Durham debut 2018. Suffolk 2016. HS 41 v Essex (Chelmsford) 2021. BB 6-37 v Middx (Chester-le-St) 2018. LO HS 5* Ex v Leics (Chelmsford) 2014 (RLC). LO BB 4-55 Ex v Lancs (Chelmsford) 2014 (RLC). T20 HS 1*. T20 BB 2-19.

STOKES, Benjamin Andrew (Cockermouth S), b Christchurch, Canterbury, New Zealand 4 Jun 1991. 6'1". LHB, RFM. Squad No 38. Debut (Durham) 2010. IPL: RPS 2017; RR 2018 to date. Big Bash: MR 2014-15. Northern Superchargers 2021. YC 2013. *Wisden* 2015. PCA 2019. BBC Sports Personality of the Year 2019. OBE 2020. **ECB Central Contract 2021-22. Tests**: 77 (2013-14 to 2021-22, 1 as captain); HS 258 v SA (Cape Town) 2015-16, setting E record fastest double century in 163 balls; BB 6-22 v WI (Lord's) 2017. **LOI**: 101 (2011 to 2021, 3 as captain); HS 102* v A (Birmingham) 2017; BB 5-61 v A (Southampton) 2013. **IT20**: 34 (2011 to 2020-21); HS 47* v SA (Durban) 2019-20; BB 3-26 v NZ (Delhi) 2015-16. F-c Tours: A 2013-14, 2021-22; SA 2015-16, 2019-20; WI 2010-11 (EL), 2014-15, 2018-19, 2021-22; NZ 2017-18, 2019-20; I 2016-17, 2020-21; SL 2018-19; B 2016-17; UAE 2015-16 (v P). HS 258 (*see Tests*). Du HS 185 v Lancs (Chester-le-St) 2011, sharing Du record 4th wkt partnership of 331 with D.M.Benkenstein. BB 7-67 (10-121 match) v Sussex (Chester-le-St) 2014. LO HS 164 v Notts (Chester-le-St) 2014 (RLC) – Du record. LO BB 5-61 (*see LOI*). T20 HS 107*. T20 BB 4-16.

TREVASKIS, Liam (Q Elizabeth GS, Penrith), b Carlisle, Cumberland 18 Apr 1999. 5'8". LHB, SLA. Squad No 80. Debut (Durham) 2017. Durham 2nd XI debut 2015. HS 77* v Northants (Northampton) 2021. BB 5-78 v Glos (Bristol) 2021. LO HS 23 v Middx (Radlett) 2021 (RLC). LO BB 3-38 v Worcs (Worcester) 2021 (RLC). T20 HS 31*. T20 BB 4-16.

WOOD, Mark Andrew (Ashington HS; Newcastle C), b Ashington 11 Jan 1990. 5'11". RHB, RF. Squad No 33. Debut (Durham) 2011. IPL: CSK 2018. Northumberland 2008-10. **ECB Central Contract 2021-22. Tests**: 26 (2015 to 2021-22); HS 52 v NZ (Christchurch) 2017-18; BB 6-37 v A (Hobart) 2021-22. **LOI**: 57 (2015 to 2021); HS 14 v I (Pune) 2020-21; BB 4-33 v A (Birmingham) 2017. **IT20**: 19 (2015 to 2021-22); HS 5* v A (Hobart) 2017-18 and 5* v NZ (Wellington) 2017-18; BB 3-9 v WI (Basseterre) 2018-19. F-c Tours: A 2021-22; SA 2014-15 (EL), 2019-20; WI 2018-19, 2021-22; NZ 2017-18; SL 2013-14 (EL), 2020-21; UAE 2015-16 (v P), 2018-19 (EL v P A). HS 72* v Kent (Chester-le-St) 2017. BB 6-46 v Derbys (Derby) 2018. LO HS 24 EL v Pakistan A (Abu Dhabi) 2018-19. LO BB 4-33 (*see LOI*). T20 HS 27*. T20 BB 4-25.

RELEASED/RETIRED

(Having made a County 1st XI appearance in 2021)

NQ**BANCROFT, Cameron** Timothy (Aquinas C, Perth), b Attadale, Perth, Australia 19 Nov 1992. 6'0". RHB, RM, occ WK. W Australia 2013-14 to date. Gloucestershire 2016-17; cap 2016. Durham 2019-21; captain 2019-20. Big Bash: PS 2014-15 to date. **Tests** (A): 10 (2017-18 to 2019); HS 82* v E (Brisbane) 2017-18. **IT20** (A): 1 (2015-16); HS 0* v I (Sydney) 2015-16. F-c Tours (A): E 2019; SA 2017-18; I 2015 (Aus A). HS 228* WA v SA (Perth) 2017-18. CC HS 206* Gs v Kent (Bristol) 2017. Du HS 158 v Sussex (Hove) 2019, sharing Du record 6th wkt partnership of 282 with E.J.H.Eckersley. BB 1-10 WA v Q (Brisbane) 2019-20. LO HS 176 WA v SA (Sydney, HO) 2015-16. T20 HS 87*.

BURNHAM, Jack Tony Arthur (Deerness Valley CS, Durham), b Durham 18 Jan 1997. 6'1". RHB, RM. Durham 2015-21. Northumberland 2015. HS 135 v Surrey (Oval) 2016. LO HS 45 v Derbys (Chester-le-St) 2019 (RLC). T20 HS 53*.

NQ**POYNTER, Stuart** William (Teddington S), b Hammersmith, London 18 Oct 1990. Younger brother of A.D.Poynter (Middlesex and Ireland 2005-11). 5'9". RHB, WK. Middlesex 2010. Ireland 2011 to 2018-19. Warwickshire 2013. Durham 2016-21. **Tests** (Ire): 1 (2018-19); HS 1 v Afg (Dehradun) 2018-19. **LOI** (Ire): 21 (2014 to 2018-19); HS 36 v SL (Dublin) 2016. **IT20** (Ire): 25 (2015 to 2018-19); HS 39 v Scotland (Dubai, DSC) 2016-17. F-c Tour (Ire): Z 2015-16. HS 170 v Derbys (Derby) 2018. LO HS 109 Ire v Sri Lanka A (Belfast) 2014. T20 HS 61*.

STEEL, C.T. – *see SURREY.*

VAN MEEKEREN, P.A. – *see GLOUCESTERSHIRE.*

YOUNG, W.A. – *see NORTHAMPTONSHIRE.*

DURHAM 2021

RESULTS SUMMARY

	Place	Won	Lost	Drew	NR
LV= Insurance County Champ (Div 2)	3rd	4	3	6	
Royal London One-Day Cup (Group 1)	Finalist	7	2		1
Vitality Blast (North Group)	7th	5	8		1

LV= INSURANCE COUNTY CHAMPIONSHIP AVERAGES
BATTING AND FIELDING

Cap		*M*	*I*	*NO*	*HS*	*Runs*	*Avge*	*100*	*50*	*Ct/St*
	L.Trevaskis	3	4	2	77*	135	67.50	–	2	2
	D.G.Bedingham	13	20	3	257	1029	60.52	3	3	11
	W.A.Young	4	7	–	124	278	39.71	2	–	1
	A.Z.Lees	11	17	1	129	625	39.06	1	5	6
	E.J.H.Eckersley	13	18	1	113*	520	30.58	1	3	28/1
	M.J.Potts	7	9	2	81	206	29.42	–	1	3
	M.A.Jones	8	13	1	81	337	28.08	–	2	2
	G.Clark	3	4	1	42	83	27.66	–	–	–
	J.T.A.Burnham	10	15	2	102*	357	27.46	1	1	3
	S.R.Dickson	3	4	1	46	79	26.33	–	–	–
	C.T.Bancroft	5	8	1	46*	183	26.14	–	–	4
	B.A.Raine	13	15	3	74	308	25.66	–	2	3
	S.G.Borthwick	13	20	–	100	474	23.70	1	1	14
	B.A.Carse	8	9	2	40*	161	23.00	–	–	2
	P.Coughlin	4	5	–	48	89	17.80	–	–	3
	M.E.T.Salisbury	4	5	–	41	75	15.00	–	–	–
	S.W.Poynter	6	8	2	52*	85	14.16	–	1	22
	C.Rushworth	13	13	6	31	91	13.00	–	–	3

Also played: B.A.Stokes (1 match) did not bat (1 ct); M.A.Wood (3) 17, 12, 1.

BOWLING

	O	*M*	*R*	*W*	*Avge*	*Best*	*5wI*	*10wM*
C.Rushworth	435.3	125	1073	59	18.18	6-49	3	–
B.A.Carse	203.2	26	724	34	21.29	5-49	2	–
B.A.Raine	406.1	128	968	43	22.51	5- 9	2	–
P.Coughlin	88.4	22	279	12	23.25	5-64	1	–
M.A.Wood	79	19	233	10	23.30	3-28	–	–
M.J.Potts	204.3	51	613	23	26.65	4-32	–	–
M.E.T.Salisbury	142.4	38	440	16	27.50	4-74	–	–
S.G.Borthwick	130.5	22	445	12	37.91	4-32	–	–
Also bowled:								
L.Trevaskis	81.4	27	176	9	19.55	5-78	1	–

E.J.H.Eckersley 4-1-7-0; B.A.Stokes 17-1-55-3.

The First-Class Averages (pp 220–232) give the records of Durham players in all first-class county matches, with the exception of M.A.Wood and W.A.Young, whose first-class figures for Durham are as above.

DURHAM RECORDS

FIRST-CLASS CRICKET

Highest Total	For 648-5d		v	Notts	Chester-le-St[2]	2009
	V 810-4d		by	Warwicks	Birmingham	1994
Lowest Total	For 61		v	Leics	Leicester	2018
	V 18		by	Durham MCCU	Chester-le-St[2]	2012
Highest Innings	For 273	M.L.Love	v	Hampshire	Chester-le-St[2]	2003
	V 501*	B.C.Lara	for	Warwicks	Birmingham	1994

Highest Partnership for each Wicket

1st	334*	S.Hutton/M.A.Roseberry	v	Oxford U	Oxford	1996
2nd	274	M.D.Stoneman/S.G.Borthwick	v	Middlesex	Chester-le-St[2]	2014
3rd	212	M.J.Di Venuto/D.M.Benkenstein	v	Essex	Chester-le-St[2]	2010
4th	331	B.A.Stokes/D.M.Benkenstein	v	Lancashire	Chester-le-St[2]	2011
5th	254*	D.G.Bedingham/E.J.H.Eckersley	v	Notts	Nottingham	2021
6th	282	C.T.Bancroft/E.J.H.Eckersley	v	Sussex	Hove	2019
7th	315	D.M.Benkenstein/O.D.Gibson	v	Yorkshire	Leeds	2006
8th	154	B.A.Raine/B.A.Carse	v	Yorkshire	Chester-le-St[2]	2019
9th	150	P.Mustard/P.Coughlin	v	Northants	Chester-le-St[2]	2014
10th	103	M.M.Betts/D.M.Cox	v	Sussex	Hove	1996

Best Bowling	For	10- 47	O.D.Gibson	v	Hampshire	Chester-le-St[2]	2007
(Innings)	V	9- 34	J.A.R.Harris	for	Middlesex	Lord's	2015
Best Bowling	For	15- 95	C.Rushworth	v	Northants	Chester-le-St[2]	2014
(Match)	V	13-103	J.A.R.Harris	for	Middlesex	Lord's	2015

Most Runs – Season	1654	M.J.Di Venuto	(av 78.76)	2009
Most Runs – Career	12030	P.D.Collingwood	(av 33.98)	1996-2018
Most 100s – Season	7	K.K.Jennings		2016
Most 100s – Career	25	P.D.Collingwood		1996-2018
Most Wkts – Season	88	C.Rushworth	(av 20.09)	2015
Most Wkts – Career	564	C.Rushworth	(av 22.22)	2010-21
Most Career W-K Dismissals	638	P.Mustard	(619 ct; 19 st)	2002-16
Most Career Catches in the Field	246	P.D.Collingwood		1996-2018

LIMITED-OVERS CRICKET

Highest Total	**50ov**	405-4		v	Kent	Beckenham	2021
	40ov	325-9		v	Surrey	The Oval	2011
	T20	225-2		v	Leics	Chester-le-St[2]	2010
Lowest Total	**50ov**	82		v	Worcs	Chester-le-St[1]	1968
	40ov	72		v	Warwicks	Birmingham	2002
	T20	78		v	Lancashire	Chester-le-St[2]	2009
Highest Innings	**50ov**	164	B.A.Stokes	v	Notts	Chester-le-St[2]	2014
	40ov	150*	B.A.Stokes	v	Warwicks	Birmingham	2011
	T20	108*	P.D.Collingwood	v	Worcs	Worcester	2017
Best Bowling	**50ov**	7-32	S.P.Davis	v	Lancashire	Chester-le-St[1]	1983
	40ov	6-31	N.Killeen	v	Derbyshire	Derby	2000
	T20	5- 6	P.D.Collingwood	v	Northants	Chester-le-St[2]	2011

[1] Chester-le-Street CC (Ropery Lane) [2] Emirates Riverside

ESSEX

Formation of Present Club: 14 January 1876
Inaugural First-Class Match: 1894
Colours: Blue, Gold and Red
Badge: Three Seaxes above Scroll bearing 'Essex'
County Champions: (8) 1979, 1983, 1984, 1986, 1991, 1992, 2017, 2019
NatWest/Friends Prov Trophy Winners: (3) 1985, 1997, 2008
Benson and Hedges Cup Winners: (2) 1979, 1998
Pro 40/National League (Div 1) Winners: (2) 2005, 2006
Sunday League Winners: (3) 1981, 1984, 1985
Twenty20 Cup Winners: (1) 2019
Bob Willis Trophy Winners: (1) 2020

Interim Chairman: John Stephenson, The Cloud County Ground, New Writtle Street, Chelmsford CM2 0PG • Tel: 01245 252420 • Email: questions@essexcricket.org.uk • Web: www.essexcricket.org.uk • Twitter: @EssexCricket (111,021 followers)

Head Coach: Anthony McGrath. **Bowling Coach**: Mick Lewis. **Batting Coach**: Tom Huggins. **Captains**: T.Westley (f-c and 50 ov) and S.R.Harmer (T20). **Overseas Players**: S.R.Harmer and M.T.Steketee. **2022 Testimonial**: None. **Head Groundsman**: Stuart Kerrison. **Scorer**: Tony Choat. **Blast Team Name**: Essex Eagles. ‡ New registration. [NQ] Not qualified for England.

ALLISON, Benjamin Michael John (New Hall S; Chelmsford C), b Colchester 18 Dec 1999. RHB, RFM. Squad No 65. Gloucestershire 2019; cap 2019. Essex debut 2021. Essex 2nd XI debut 2017. Bedfordshire 2018. Cambridgeshire 2019. HS 52 v Durham (Chelmsford) 2021. BB 3-109 Gs v Derbys (Derby) 2019. Ex BB 1-67 v Worcs (Chelmsford) 2021. LO HS 3 v Glamorgan (Cardiff) 2021 (RLC). LO BB 2-33 v Kent (Chelmsford) 2021 (RLC). T20 HS 1*. T20 BB 1-32.

BEARD, Aaron Paul (Boswells S, Chelmsford), b Chelmsford 15 Oct 1997. LHB, RFM. Squad No 14. Debut (Essex) 2016. England U19 2016 to 2016-17. HS 58* v Durham MCCU (Chelmsford) 2017. CC HS 41 v Yorks (Chelmsford) 2019. BB 4-21 v Middx (Chelmsford) 2020. LO HS 22* v Kent (Beckenham) 2019 (RLC). LO BB 3-51 v Glos (Chelmsford) 2019 (RLC). T20 HS 13. T20 BB 3-41.

BENKENSTEIN, Luc Martin (Hilton C; Seaford C), b Durban, South Africa 2 Nov 2004. Son of D.M.Benkenstein (Natal, KZN, Dolphins, Durham 1993-94 to 2013); grandson of M.M.Benkenstein (Rhodesia and Natal B 1970-71 to 1980-81); nephew of B.N.Benkenstein (Natal B and Griqualand W 1994-95 to 1996-97) and B.R.Benkenstein (Natal B 1993-94). RHB, LBG. Sussex 2nd XI 2021. Hampshire 2nd XI 2021. Essex 2nd XI debut 2021. Awaiting f-c debut. LO BB 1-30 v Durham (Chester-le-St) 2021 (RLC) – only 1st XI appearance.

BROWNE, Nicholas Lawrence Joseph (Trinity Catholic HS, Woodford Green), b Leytonstone 24 Mar 1991. 6'3½". LHB, LB. Squad No 10. Debut (Essex) 2013; cap 2015. MCC 2016. 1000 runs (3); most – 1262 (2016). HS 255 v Derbys (Chelmsford) 2016. BB –. LO HS 99 v Glamorgan (Chelmsford) 2016 (RLC). T20 HS 38.

BUTTLEMAN, William Edward Lewis (Felsted S), b Chelmsford 20 Apr 2000. Younger brother of J.E.L.Buttleman (Durham UCCE 2007-09). RHB, WK, occ OB. Squad No 9. Debut (Essex) 2019. Essex 2nd XI debut 2017. HS 0 v Yorks (Leeds) 2019. LO HS 23 v Middx (Chelmsford) 2021 (RLC). T20 HS 56*.

COOK, Sir Alastair Nathan (Bedford S), b Gloucester 25 Dec 1984. 6'3". LHB, OB. Squad No 26. Debut (Essex) 2003; cap 2005; benefit 2014. MCC 2004-07, 2015. YC 2005. *Wisden* 2011. Knighted in 2019 New Year's honours list. **Tests**: 161 (2005-06 to 2018, 59 as captain); 1000 runs (5); most – 1364 (2015); HS 294 v I (Birmingham) 2011. Scored 60 and 104* v I (Nagpur) 2005-06 on debut, and 71 and 147 in final Test v I (Oval) 2018. Second, after M.A.Taylor, to score 1000 runs in the calendar year of his debut. Finished career after appearing in world record 159 consecutive Tests. BB 1-6 v I (Nottingham) 2014. **LOI**: 92 (2006 to 2014-15, 69 as captain); HS 137 v P (Abu Dhabi) 2011-12. **IT20**: 4 (2007 to 2009-10); HS 26 v SA (Centurion) 2009-10. F-c Tours (C=Captain): A 2006-07, 2010-11, 2013-14C, 2017-18; SA 2009-10, 2015-16C; WI 2005-06 (Eng A), 2008-09, 2014-15C; NZ 2007-08, 2012-13C, 2017-18; I 2005-06, 2008-09, 2012-13C, 2016-17C; SL 2004-05 (Eng A), 2007-08, 2011-12; B 2009-10C, 2016-17C; UAE 2011-12 (v P), 2015-16C (v P). 1000 runs (8+1); most – 1466 (2005). HS 294 (*see Tests*). CC HS 195 v Northants (Northampton) 2005. BB 3-13 v Northants (Chelmsford) 2005. LO HS 137 (*see LOI*). BB –. T20 HS 100*.

COOK, Samuel James (Great Baddow HS & SFC; Loughborough U), b Chelmsford 4 Aug 1997. RHB, RFM. Squad No 16. Loughborough MCCU 2016-17. Essex debut 2017; cap 2020. MCC 2019. Trent Rockets 2021. Essex 2nd XI debut 2014. HS 37* v Yorks (Leeds) 2019. 50 wkts (1): 58 (2021). BB 7-23 (12-65 match) v Kent (Canterbury) 2019. LO HS 6 v Middx (Chelmsford) 2019 (RLC). LO BB 3-37 v Surrey (Oval) 2019 (RLC). T20 HS 18. T20 BB 4-15.

‡**CRITCHLEY, Matt**hew James John (St Michael's HS, Chorley), b Preston, Lancs 13 Aug 1996. 6'2". RHB, LB. Squad No 20. Derbyshire 2015-21; cap 2019. Welsh Fire 2021. 1000 runs (1): 1000 (2021). HS 137* De v Northants (Derby) 2015. BB 6-73 De v Leics (Leicester) 2020. LO HS 64* v Northants (Derby) 2019 (RLC). LO BB 4-48 v Northants (Derby) 2015 (RLC). T20 HS 80*. T20 BB 4-36.

DAS, Robin James (Brentwood S), b Leytonstone 27 Feb 2002. RHB. Squad No 47. Essex 2nd XI debut 2018. Awaiting f-c debut. T20 HS 7.

NQ**HARMER, Simon** Ross, b Pretoria, South Africa 10 Feb 1993. RHB, OB. Squad No 11. Eastern Province 2009-10 to 2011-12. Warriors 2010-11 to 2018-19. Essex debut 2017; cap 2018; captain 2020 to date (T20 only). Northerns 2021-22. *Wisden* 2019. **Tests** (SA): 5 (2014-15 to 2015-16); HS 13 v I (Nagpur) 2015-16; BB 4-61 v I (Mohali) 2015-16. F-c Tours (SA): A 2014 (SA A); I 2015-16; B 2015; Ire 2012 (SA A). HS 102* v Surrey (Oval) 2018. 50 wkts (4+1); most – 86 (2019). BB 9-80 (12-202 match) v Derbys (Chelmsford) 2021. LO HS 44* v Surrey (Oval) 2017 (RLC). LO BB 4-42 Warriors v Lions (Potchefstroom) 2011-12. T20 HS 43. T20 BB 4-19.

KALLEY, Eshun Singh (Barking Abbey S), b Ilford 23 Nov 2001. RHB, RM. Squad No 30. Essex 2nd XI debut 2017. Hertfordshire 2021. Awaiting 1st XI debut.

KHUSHI, Feroze Isa Nazir (Kelmscott S, Walthamstow; Leyton SFC), b Whipps Cross 23 Jun 1999. RHB. OB. Squad No 23. Debut (Essex) 2020. Essex 2nd XI debut 2015. Suffolk 2019-21. HS 66 v Surrey (Chelmsford) 2020. LO HS 109 v Durham (Chester-le-St) 2021 (RLC). T20 HS 17.

LAWRENCE, Daniel William (Trinity Catholic HS, Woodford Green), b Whipps Cross 12 Jul 1997. 6'2". RHB, LB. Squad No 28. Debut (Essex) 2015; cap 2017. MCC 2019. Big Bash: BH 2020-21. London Spirit 2021. Essex 2nd XI debut 2013. England U19 2015. **Tests**: 9 (2020-21 to 2021-22); HS 81* v NZ (Birmingham) 2021; BB 1-0 v WI (North Sound) 2021-22. F-c Tours: A 2019-20 (EL); WI 2021-22; I 2020-21; SL 2020-21. 1000 runs (1): 1070 (2016). HS 161 v Surrey (Oval) 2015. BB 2-28 v Durham (Chelmsford) 2021. LO HS 115 v Kent (Chelmsford) 2018 (RLC). LO BB 3-35 v Middx (Lord's) 2016 (RLC). T20 HS 86. T20 BB 3-21.

NIJJAR, Aron Stuart Singh (Ilford County HS), b Goodmayes 24 Sep 1994. LHB, SLA. Squad No 24. Debut (Essex) 2015. Cardiff MCCU 2017. Suffolk 2014. HS 53 v Northants (Chelmsford) 2015. BB 2-28 v Cambridge MCCU (Cambridge) 2019. CC BB 2-33 v Lancs (Chelmsford) 2015. LO HS 32* v Glos (Bristol) 2021 (RLC). LO BB 2-26 v Yorks (Chelmsford) 2021 (RLC). T20 HS 27*. T20 BB 3-22.

PEPPER, Michael-Kyle Steven (The Perse S), b Harlow 25 Jun 1998. Younger brother of C.A.Pepper (Cambridgeshire 2013-16). RHB, WK. Squad No 19. Debut (Essex) 2018. Essex 2nd XI debut 2017. Cambridgeshire 2014-19. HS 92 v Durham (Chester-le-St) 2021. LO HS 34 v Hants (Southampton) 2021 (RLC). T20 HS 55*.

PLOM, Jack Henry (Gable Hall S; S Essex C), b Basildon 27 Aug 1999. LHB, RFM. Squad No 77. Debut (Essex) 2018 – did not bat or bowl. Essex 2nd XI debut 2016. England U19 2018. LO HS 9* v Sussex (Chelmsford) 2021 (RLC). LO BB 3-34 v Yorks (Chelmsford) 2021 (RLC). T20 HS 12. T20 BB 3-31.

PORTER, James Alexander (Oak Park HS, Newbury Park; Epping Forest C), b Leytonstone 25 May 1993. 5'11½". RHB, RFM. Squad No 44. Debut (Essex) 2014, taking a wkt with his 5th ball; cap 2015. *Wisden* 2017. F-c Tours (EL): WI 2017-18; I 2018-19; UAE 2018-19 (v P A). HS 34 v Glamorgan (Cardiff) 2015. 50 wkts (5); most – 85 (2017). BB 7-41 (11-98 match) v Worcs (Chelmsford) 2018. LO HS 7* v Middx (Chelmsford) 2019 (RLC). LO BB 4-29 v Glamorgan (Chelmsford) 2018 (RLC). T20 HS 1*. T20 BB 4-20.

RICHARDS, Jamal Adrian (Norlington S; Waltham Forest C), b Edmonton, Middx 3 Mar 2004. RHB, RFM. Essex 2nd XI debut 2021. Awaiting 1st XI debut.

RYMELL, Joshua Sean (Ipswich S; Colchester SFC), b Ipswich, Suffolk 4 Apr 2001. RHB. Squad No 49. Debut (Essex) 2021. Essex 2nd XI debut 2017. Suffolk 2021. HS 14 v Glos (Chelmsford) 2021. LO HS 121 v Yorks (Chelmsford) 2021 (RLC). T20 HS 21.

[NQ]**SNATER, Shane** (St John's C, Harare), b Harare, Zimbabwe 24 Mar 1996. RHB, RM. Squad No 29. Netherlands 2016 to 2017-18. Southern Rocks 2020-21. Essex debut 2021. **LOI** (Neth): 2 (2018); HS 12 and BB 1-41 v Nepal (Amstelveen) 2018. **IT20** (Neth): 13 (2018 to 2019-20); HS 10 and BB 3-42 v Scotland (Dublin) 2019. HS 50* Neth v Namibia (Dubai, ICCA) 2017-18. Ex HS 48 v Glamorgan (Cardiff) 2021. BB 7-98 v Notts (Nottingham) 2021. LO HS 23* Neth v Nepal (Kwekwe) 2017-18. LO BB 5-60 v Somerset (Chelmsford) 2018 (RLC). T20 HS 16*. T20 BB 3-42.

‡[NQ]**STEKETEE, Mark** Thomas, b Warwick, Queensland, Australia 17 Jan 1994. RHB, RFM. Queensland 2014-15 to date. Big Bash: BH 2013-14 to date. HS 53 Q v NSW (Sydney) 2016-17. BB 7-44 (10-92 match) Q v SA (Adelaide) 2021-22. LO HS 30* Q v WA (Sydney, DO) 2015-16. LO BB 4-25 Q v Vic (Melbourne, St K) 2019-20. T20 HS 33. T20 BB 4-33.

WALTER, Paul Ian (Billericay S), b Basildon 28 May 1994. LHB, LMF. Squad No 22. Debut (Essex) 2016. HS 96 v Glos (Chelmsford) 2021. BB 3-44 v Derbys (Derby) 2016. LO HS 50 v Glamorgan (Cardiff) 2021 (RLC). LO BB 4-37 v Middx (Chelmsford) 2017 (RLC). T20 HS 76. T20 BB 3-24.

WESTLEY, Thomas (Linton Village C; Hills Road SFC), b Cambridge 13 March 1989. 6'2". RHB, OB. Squad No 21. Debut (Essex) 2007; cap 2013; captain 2020 to date. MCC 2007, 2009, 2016, 2019. Durham MCCU 2009-11. Bloomfield 2014-15. Cambridgeshire 2005. **Tests**: 5 (2017); HS 59 v SA (Oval) 2017. F-c Tours: SL 2016-17 (EL); Nepal 2019-20 (MCC). 1000 runs (1): 1435 (2016). HS 254 v Worcs (Chelmsford) 2016. BB 4-55 DU v Durham (Durham) 2010. CC BB 4-75 v Surrey (Colchester) 2015. LO HS 134 v Middx (Radlett) 2018 (RLC). LO BB 4-60 v Northants (Northampton) 2014 (RLC). T20 HS 109*. T20 BB 2-27.

WHEATER, Adam Jack Aubrey (Millfield S; Anglia Ruskin U), b Whipps Cross 13 Feb 1990. 5'6". RHB, WK. Squad No 31. Debut (Essex) 2008; cap 2020. Cambridge MCCU 2010. Matabeleland Tuskers 2010-11 to 2012-13. Badureliya Sports Club 2011-12. Northern Districts 2012-13. Hampshire 2013-16; cap 2016. HS 204* H v Warwks (Birmingham) 2016. Ex HS 164 v Northants (Chelmsford) 2011, sharing Ex record 6th wkt partnership of 253 with J.S.Foster. BB 1-86 v Leics (Leicester) 2012 – in contrived circumstances. LO HS 135 v Essex (Chelmsford) 2014 (RLC). T20 HS 78.

RELEASED/RETIRED

(Having made a County 1st XI appearance in 2021)

CHOPRA, Varun (Ilford County HS), b Barking 21 Jun 1987. 6'1". RHB, LB. Essex 2006-20, scoring 106 v Glos (Chelmsford) on CC debut; cap 2018. Warwickshire 2010-16; cap 2012; captain 2015. Tamil Union 2011-12. Sussex 2019. Middlesex 2021 (white ball only). F-c Tour (EL): SL 2013-14. 1000 runs (3); most – 1203 (2011). HS 233* TU v Sinhalese (Colombo, PSS) 2011-12. CC HS 228 Wa v Worcs (Worcester) 2011 (in 2nd CC game of season, having scored 210 v Somerset in 1st). Ex HS 155 v Glos (Bristol) 2008. BB –. LO HS 160 v Somerset (Chelmsford) 2018 (RLC). T20 HS 116.

NEESHAM, J.D.S. – *see NORTHAMPTONSHIRE.*

SIDDLE, P.M. – *see SOMERSET.*

NQ**Ten DOESCHATE, Ryan** Neil (Fairbairn C; Cape Town U), b Port Elizabeth, South Africa 30 Jun 1980. 5'10½". RHB, RMF. Essex 2003-21; cap 2006; captain (l-o) 2014-15; captain 2016-19. EU passport – Dutch ancestry. Netherlands 2005 to 2009-10. Otago 2012-13. IPL: KKR 2011-15. Big Bash: AS 2014-15. **LOI** (Neth): 33 (2006 to 2010-11); HS 119 v E (Nagpur) 2010-11; BB 4-31 v Canada (Nairobi) 2006-07. **IT20** (Neth): 22 (2008 to 2019-20); HS 59 v Namibia (Dubai, ICCA) 2019-20; BB 3-23 v Scotland (Belfast) 2008. F-c Tours (Ne): SA 2006-07, 2007-08; K 2005-06, 2009-10; Ireland 2005. 1000 runs (1): 1226 (2016). HS 259* and BB 6-20 Neth v Canada (Pretoria) 2006. Ex HS 173* v Somerset (Chelmsford) 2018. Ex BB 6-57 v New Zealanders (Chelmsford) 2008. CC BB 5-13 v Hants (Chelmsford) 2010. LO HS 180 v Scotland (Chelmsford) 2013 (Y40) – Ex 40-over record, inc 15 sixes. LO BB 5-50 v Glos (Bristol) 2007 (FPT). T20 HS 121*. T20 BB 4-24.

ESSEX 2021

RESULTS SUMMARY

	Place	*Won*	*Lost*	*Tied*	*Drew*	*NR*
LV= Insurance County Champ (Div 2)	1st	6	2		6	
Royal London One-Day Cup (Group 1)	SF	6	3	1		
Vitality Blast (South Group)	7th	5	8			1

LV= INSURANCE COUNTY CHAMPIONSHIP AVERAGES
BATTING AND FIELDING

Cap		*M*	*I*	*NO*	*HS*	*Runs*	*Avge*	*100*	*50*	*Ct/St*
2017	D.W.Lawrence	10	13	1	152*	640	53.33	1	4	8
2013	T.Westley	13	18	1	213	631	37.11	3	1	5
	P.I.Walter	13	16	1	96	544	36.26	–	4	5
2005	A.N.Cook	14	19	–	165	611	32.15	2	2	16
2015	N.L.J.Browne	14	19	2	102	524	30.82	1	4	6
	M.S.Pepper	6	7	–	92	204	29.14	–	2	3
2020	A.J.A.Wheater	14	16	–	87	434	27.12	–	2	23/4
2018	S.R.Harmer	14	16	4	82*	317	26.41	–	2	14
2006	R.N.ten Doeschate	10	12	–	56	314	26.16	–	3	9
	S.Snater	9	8	2	48	99	16.50	–	–	1
2015	J.A.Porter	12	13	7	30	73	12.16	–	–	1
2020	S.J.Cook	13	13	2	37	126	11.45	–	–	1
2021	P.M.Siddle	6	9	2	20	70	10.00	–	–	–

Also batted: B.M.J.Allison (2 matches) 13, 4, 52 (1 ct); J.D.S.Neesham (1) 10*; A.S.S.Nijjar (1) 2; J.S.Rymell (3) 0, 14, 9 (2 ct).

BOWLING

	O	*M*	*R*	*W*	*Avge*	*Best*	*5wI*	*10wM*
S.J.Cook	382.2	128	837	58	14.43	5-20	3	1
S.Snater	168.5	42	511	31	16.48	7-98	2	–
S.R.Harmer	558.4	182	1233	53	23.26	9-80	3	2
P.M.Siddle	176.2	37	488	20	24.40	6-38	1	–
J.A.Porter	299.4	73	842	34	24.76	4-31	–	–
Also bowled:								
D.W.Lawrence	49.1	7	155	5	31.00	2-28	–	–

B.M.J.Allison 36-7-94-1; A.N.Cook 1-0-5-0; J.D.S.Neesham 4.1-0-15-2; A.S.S.Nijjar 13-5-21-0; R.N.ten Doeschate 9-0-35-1; P.I.Walter 34-4-120-2; T.Westley 10-1-12-0.

The First-Class Averages (pp 220–232) give the records of Essex players in all first-class county matches, with the exception of D.W.Lawrence, whose first-class figures for Essex are as above.

ESSEX RECORDS

FIRST-CLASS CRICKET

Highest Total	For 761-6d		v	Leics	Chelmsford	1990
	V 803-4d		by	Kent	Brentwood	1934
Lowest Total	For 20		v	Lancashire	Chelmsford	2013
	V 14		by	Surrey	Chelmsford	1983
Highest Innings	For 343*	P.A.Perrin	v	Derbyshire	Chesterfield	1904
	V 332	W.H.Ashdown	for	Kent	Brentwood	1934

Highest Partnership for each Wicket

1st	373	N.L.J.Browne/A.N.Cook	v	Middlesex	Chelmsford	2017
2nd	403	G.A.Gooch/P.J.Prichard	v	Leics	Chelmsford	1990
3rd	347*	M.E.Waugh/N.Hussain	v	Lancashire	Ilford	1992
4th	314	Salim Malik/N.Hussain	v	Surrey	The Oval	1991
5th	339	J.C.Mickleburgh/J.S.Foster	v	Durham	Chester-le-St[2]	2010
6th	253	A.J.A.Wheater/J.S.Foster	v	Northants	Chelmsford	2011
7th	261	J.W.H.T.Douglas/J.R.Freeman	v	Lancashire	Leyton	1914
8th	263	D.R.Wilcox/R.M.Taylor	v	Warwicks	Southend	1946
9th	251	J.W.H.T.Douglas/S.N.Hare	v	Derbyshire	Leyton	1921
10th	218	F.H.Vigar/T.P.B.Smith	v	Derbyshire	Chesterfield	1947

Best Bowling	For	10- 32	H.Pickett	v	Leics	Leyton	1895
(Innings)	V	10- 40	E.G.Dennett	for	Glos	Bristol	1906
Best Bowling	For	17-119	W.Mead	v	Hampshire	Southampton[1]	1895
(Match)	V	17- 56	C.W.L.Parker	for	Glos	Gloucester	1925

Most Runs – Season	2559	G.A.Gooch	(av 67.34)	1984
Most Runs – Career	30701	G.A.Gooch	(av 51.77)	1973-97
Most 100s – Season	9	J.O'Connor		1929, 1934
	9	D.J.Insole		1955
Most 100s – Career	94	G.A.Gooch		1973-97
Most Wkts – Season	172	T.P.B Smith	(av 27.13)	1947
Most Wkts – Career	1610	T.P.B.Smith	(av 26.68)	1929-51
Most Career W-K Dismissals	1231	B.Taylor	(1040 ct; 191 st)	1949-73
Most Career Catches in the Field	519	K.W.R.Fletcher		1962-88

LIMITED-OVERS CRICKET

Highest Total	**50ov**	391-5		v	Surrey	The Oval	2008
	40ov	368-7		v	Scotland	Chelmsford	2013
	T20	242-3		v	Sussex	Chelmsford	2008
Lowest Total	**50ov**	57		v	Lancashire	Lord's	1996
	40ov	69		v	Derbyshire	Chesterfield	1974
	T20	74		v	Middlesex	Chelmsford	2013
Highest Innings	**50ov**	201*	R.S.Bopara	v	Leics	Leicester	2008
	40ov	180	R.N.ten Doeschate	v	Scotland	Chelmsford	2013
	T20	152*	G.R.Napier	v	Sussex	Chelmsford	2008
Best Bowling	**50ov**	5- 8	J.K.Lever	v	Middlesex	Westcliff	1972
		5- 8	G.A.Gooch	v	Cheshire	Chester	1995
	40ov	8-26	K.D.Boyce	v	Lancashire	Manchester	1971
	T20	6-16	T.G.Southee	v	Glamorgan	Chelmsford	2011

GLAMORGAN

Formation of Present Club: 6 July 1888
Inaugural First-Class Match: 1921
Colours: Blue and Gold
Badge: Gold Daffodil
County Champions: (3) 1948, 1969, 1997
Pro 40/National League (Div 1) Winners: (2) 2002, 2004
Sunday League Winners: (1) 1993
Royal London One-Day Cup Winners: (1) 2021
Twenty20 Cup Winners: (0); best – Semi-Finalist 2004, 2017

Chief Executive: Hugh Morris, Sophia Gardens, Cardiff, CF11 9XR • Tel: 02920 409380 • email: info@glamorgancricket.co.uk • Web: www.glamorgancricket.com • Twitter: @GlamCricket (76,972 followers)

Director of Cricket: Mark Wallace. **Head Coach**: Matthew Maynard. **2nd XI Coach**: Steve Watkin. **Player Development Manager**: Richard Almond. **Captain**: D.L.Lloyd (f-c & T20) and K.S.Carlson (50 ov). **Vice-captain**: K.S.Carlson. **Overseas Players**: C.A.Ingram, M.Labuschagne and M.G.Neser. **2022 Testimonial**: M.G.Hogan. **Head Groundsman**: Robin Saxton. **Scorer**: Andrew K.Hignell. ‡ New registration. NQ Not qualified for England.

BYROM, Edward James (St John's C, Harare; King's C, Taunton), b Harare, Zimbabwe 17 Jun 1997. 5'11". LHB, OB. Squad No 97. Irish passport. Somerset 2017-21. Rising Stars 2017-18. Glamorgan debut 2021. HS 152 RS v MT (Kwekwe) 2017-18. CC HS 117 Sm v Essex (Lord's) 2020. Gm HS 78 v Glos (Cardiff) 2021. BB 2-64 v Surrey (Oval) 2021. LO HS 18 Sm v Northants (Northampton) 2021 (RLC). T20 HS 54*.

CAREY, Lukas John (Pontarddulais CS; Gower SFC), b Carmarthen 17 Jul 1997. 6'0". RHB, RFM. Squad No 17. Debut (Glamorgan) 2016. Glamorgan 2nd XI debut 2014. Wales MC 2016. HS 62* v Derbys (Swansea) 2019. BB 4-54 v Middx (Cardiff) 2019. LO HS 39 v Somerset (Cardiff) 2019 (RLC). LO BB 2-24 v Notts (Cardiff) 2021 (RLC). T20 HS 5. T20 BB 1-15.

CARLSON, Kiran Shah (Whitchurch HS; Cardiff U), b Cardiff 16 May 1998. 5'8". RHB, OB. Squad No 5. Debut (Glamorgan) 2016; cap 2021; l-o captain 2022. Cardiff MCCU 2019. Glamorgan 2nd XI debut 2015. Wales MC 2014. HS 191 v Glos (Cardiff) 2017. BB 5-28 v Northants (Northampton) 2016 – on debut. Youngest ever to score a century & take five wkts in an innings in a f-c career, aged 18y 119d. LO HS 82 v Durham (Nottingham) 2021 (RLC). LO BB 1-30 v Middx (Radlett) 2017 (RLC). T20 HS 58.

COOKE, Christopher Barry (Bishops S, Cape Town; U of Cape Town), b Johannesburg, South Africa 30 May 1986. 5'11". RHB, WK, occ RM. Squad No 46. W Province 2009-10. Glamorgan debut 2013; cap 2016; captain 2019-21. Birmingham Phoenix 2021. HS 205* v Surrey (Oval) 2021. LO HS 161 v Glos (Bristol) 2019 (RLC). T20 HS 72.

COOKE, Joseph Michael (Durham U), b Hemel Hempstead, Herts 30 May 1997. LHB, RMF. Squad No 57. Durham MCCU 2017-18. Glamorgan debut 2020. Sussex 2nd XI 2018-19. Glamorgan 2nd XI debut 2019. Hertfordshire 2014-18. HS 68 v Surrey (Oval) 2020. BB 1-26 DU v Warwks (Birmingham) 2018. LO HS 66* and LO BB 5-61 v Essex (Cardiff) 2021 (RLC).

CULLEN, Thomas Nicholas (Aquinas C, Stockport; Cardiff Met U), b Perth, Australia 4 Jan 1992. RHB, WK. Squad No 54. Cardiff MCCU 2015-17. Glamorgan debut 2017. HS 63 v Northants (Northampton) 2019. LO HS 58* v Northants (Northampton) 2021 (RLC). T20 HS 5.

DOUTHWAITE, Daniel Alexander (Reed's S, Cobham; Cardiff Met U), b Kingston-upon-Thames, Surrey 8 Feb 1997. RHB, RMF. Squad No 88. Cardiff MCCU 2019. Glamorgan debut 2019. Warwickshire 2018 (l-o only). Manchester Originals 2021. HS 100* CfU v Sussex (Hove) 2019. Gm HS 96 v Durham (Chester-le-St) 2021. BB 4-48 v Derbys (Derby) 2019. LO HS 52* v Sussex (Hove) 2019 (RLC). LO BB 3-43 Wa v West Indies A (Birmingham) 2018. T20 HS 53. T20 BB 3-28.

GORVIN, Andrew William (Portsmouth HS; Cardiff Met U), b Winchester, Hants 10 May 1997. RHB, RM. Squad No 14. Hampshire 2nd XI 2014-16. Glamorgan 2nd XI debut 2021. Wales MC 2019 to date. Awaiting f-c debut. LO HS 12* v Somerset (Taunton) 2021 (RLC). LO BB 1-11 v Surrey (Cardiff) 2021 (RLC).

HARRIS, James Alexander Russell (Pontardulais CS; Gorseinon C), b Morriston, Swansea 16 May 1990. 6'0". RHB, RMF. Squad No 9. Debut (Glamorgan) 2007, aged 16y 351d – youngest Gm player to take a f-c wicket; cap 2010. Middlesex 2013-21; cap 2015. Kent 2017 (on loan). MCC 2016. Wales MC 2005-08. F-c Tours (EL): WI 2010-11; SL 2013-14. HS 87* v Notts (Swansea) 2007. 50 wkts (3); most – 73 (2015). BB 9-34 (13-103 match) M v Durham (Lord's) 2015 – record innings and match analysis v Durham. Gm BB 7-66 (12-118 match) v Glos (Bristol) 2007 – youngest (17y 3d) to take 10 wickets in any CC match. LO HS 117 M v Lancs (Lord's) 2019 (RLC). LO BB 4-38 M v Glamorgan (Lord's) 2015 (RLC). T20 HS 18. T20 BB 4-23.

HOGAN, Michael Garry, b Newcastle, New South Wales, Australia 31 May 1981. British passport. 6'5". RHB, RFM. Squad No 31. W Australia 2009-10 to 2015-16. Glamorgan debut/cap 2013; captain 2018; testimonial 2020-22. Big Bash: HH 2011-12 to 2012-13. HS 57 v Lancs (Colwyn Bay) 2015. 50 wkts (3); most – 67 (2013). BB 7-92 v Glos (Bristol) 2013. LO HS 27 WA v Vic (Melbourne) 2011-12. LO BB 5-44 WA v Vic (Melbourne) 2010-11. T20 HS 17*. T20 BB 5-17.

HORTON, Alex Jack (St Edward's, Oxford), b Newport, Monmouths 7 Jan 2004. RHB, WK. Squad No 12. Glamorgan 2nd XI debut 2019. Awaiting 1st XI debut.

[NQ]**INGRAM, Colin** Alexander, b Port Elizabeth, South Africa 3 Jul 1985. LHB, LB. Squad No 41. Free State 2004-05 to 2005-06. Eastern Province 2005-06 to 2008-09. Warriors 2006-07 to 2016-17. Somerset 2014. Glamorgan debut 2015; cap 2017; captain 2018-19 (T20 only). IPL: DD 2011. Big Bash: AS 2017-18 to 2018-19. HH 2020-21. Oval Invincibles 2021. **LOI** (SA): 31 (2010-11 to 2013-14); HS 124 v Z (Bloemfontein) 2010-11 – on debut; BB –. **IT20** (SA): 9 (2010-11 to 2011-12); HS 78 v I (Johannesburg) 2011-12. HS 190 EP v KZN (Port Elizabeth) 2008-09. Gm HS 155* v Notts (Cardiff) 2017. BB 4-16 EP v Boland (Port Elizabeth) 2005-06. Gm BB 3-90 v Essex (Chelmsford) 2015. LO HS 142 v Essex (Cardiff) 2017 (RLC). LO BB 4-39 v Middx (Radlett) 2017 (RLC). T20 HS 127*. T20 BB 4-32.

[NQ]**LABUSCHAGNE, Marnus**, b Klerksdorp, South Africa 22 Jun 1994. RHB, LB. Squad No 99. Queensland 2014-15 to date. Glamorgan debut 2019; cap 2019. Big Bash: BH 2016-17 to date. *Wisden* 2019. **Tests** (A): 245 (2018-19 to 2021-22); 1000 runs (1): 1104 (2019); HS 215 v NZ (Sydney) 2019-20; BB 3-45 v P (Abu Dhabi) 2018-19. **LOI** (A): 13 (2019-20 to 2020-21); HS 108 v SA (Potchefstroom) 2019-20; BB –. F-c Tours (A): E 2019; I 2018-19 (Aus A); P 2021-22; UAE 2018-19 (v P). 1000 runs (1+2); most – 1530 (2019). HS 215 (*see Tests*). Gm HS 182 v Sussex (Hove) 2019, sharing Gm record 2nd wkt partnership of 291 with N.J.Selman. BB 3-45 (*see Tests*). Gm BB 3-52 v Middx (Radlett) 2019. LO HS 135 Q v SA (Brisbane) 2019-20. LO BB 3-46 v Somerset (Cardiff) 2019 (RLC). T20 HS 93*. T20 BB 3-13.

LLOYD, David Liam (Darland HS; Shrewsbury S), b St Asaph, Denbighs 15 May 1992. 5'9". RHB, RM. Squad No 73. Debut (Glamorgan) 2012; cap 2019; captain 2022. Wales MC 2010-11. Welsh Fire 2021. HS 121 v Surrey (Oval) 2021. BB 4-11 v Kent (Cardiff) 2021. LO HS 92 v Middx (Cardiff) 2018 (RLC). LO BB 5-53 v Kent (Swansea) 2017 (RLC). T20 HS 97*. T20 BB 2-13.

McILROY, Jamie Peter (Builth Wells HS), b Hereford 19 Jun 1994. RHB, LFM. Squad No 35. Debut (Glamorgan) 2021. HS 0. BB 1-12 v Yorks (Leeds) 2021.

NQ**NESER, Michael** Gertges, b Pretoria, South Africa 29 Mar 1990. 6'0". RHB, RMF. Squad No 30. Queensland 2010-11 to date. Glamorgan debut/cap 2021. IPL: KXIP 2013. Big Bash: BH 2011-12 to 2021-22. AS 2012-13 to 2020-21. **Tests** (A): 1 (2021-22); HS 35 and BB 1-28 v E (Adelaide), taking wicket of H.Hameed with 2nd ball in Test cricket. **LOI** (A): 2 (2018); HS 6 and BB 2-46 v E (Oval) 2018. F-c Tours (Aus A): E 2019; I 2018-19; UAE (v P) 2018-19. HS 121 Q v Tas (Adelaide) 2020-21. Gm HS 24 and Gm BB 5-39 v Yorks (Cardiff) 2021. BB 6-57 Q v Tas (Hobart) 2017-18. LO HS 122 Q v WA (Sydney, DO) 2017-18. LO BB 4-41 Q v SA (Perth) 2016-17. T20 HS 40*. T20 BB 3-24.

‡**NORTHEAST, Sam** Alexander (Harrow S), b Ashford, Kent 16 Oct 1989. 5'11". RHB, LB. Squad No 16. Kent 2007-17; cap 2012; captain 2016-17. Hampshire 2018-21; cap 2019. Yorkshire 2021 (on loan). Nottinghamshire 2021 (on loan). MCC 2013, 2018. 1000 runs (4); most – 1402 (2016). HS 191 K v Derbys (Canterbury) 2016. BB 1-60 K v Glos (Cheltenham) 2013. LO HS 132 K v Somerset (Taunton) 2014 (RLC). T20 HS 114.

PEARCE, Samuel James (Archbishop McGrath Catholic HS), b Bridgend 2 Sep 1997. RHB, LB. Cardiff MCCU 2018-19. Glamorgan 2nd XI debut 2014. Wales MC 2015 to date. HS 35 CfU v Glos (Bristol) 2018. BB 1-74 CfU v Hants (Southampton) 2018. T20 HS 5. T20 BB –.

PHILLIPS, Tegid Daniel Canning (Melingriffith PS; Ysgol Glantaf; Cardiff U), b Cardiff 21 Feb 2002. RHB, OB. Squad No 23. Glamorgan 2nd XI debut 2021. Wales MC 2019-21. Awaiting 1st XI debut.

REINGOLD, Steven Jack (Jewish Free S), b Cape Town, South Africa 7 Aug 1998. RHB, OB. Cardiff MCCU 2019. Glamorgan debut 2021. Middlesex 2nd XI 2017. Glamorgan 2nd XI debut 2019. HS 22 CfU v Sussex (Hove) 2019. CC HS 9 and BB 3-15 v Essex (Cardiff) 2021. LO HS 40 and LO BB 1-16 v Surrey (Cardiff) 2021 (RLC).

ROOT, William ('**Billy**') Thomas (Worksop C; Leeds Beckett U), b Sheffield, Yorks 5 Aug 1992. Younger brother of J.E.Root (*see YORKSHIRE*). LHB, OB. Squad No 7. Leeds/Bradford MCCU 2015-16. Nottinghamshire 2015-18. Glamorgan debut 2019; cap 2021. Suffolk 2014. HS 229 v Northants (Northampton) 2019. BB 3-29 Nt v Sussex (Hove) 2017. Gm BB 2-63 v Northants (Cardiff) 2019. LO HS 113* v Surrey (Cardiff) 2019 (RLC). LO BB 2-36 v Middx (Lord's) 2019 (RLC). T20 HS 41*. T20 BB –.

SALTER, Andrew Graham (Milford Haven SFC; Cardiff Met U), b Haverfordwest 1 Jun 1993. 5'9". RHB, OB. Squad No 21. Cardiff MCCU 2012-14. Glamorgan debut 2013. Wales MC 2010-11. HS 90 v Durham (Chester-le-St) 2021. BB 4-18 v Northants (Cardiff) 2021. LO HS 51 v Pakistan A (Newport) 2016. LO BB 3-37 v Surrey (Cardiff) 2021 (RLC). T20 HS 39*. T20 BB 4-12.

SISODIYA, Prem (Clifton C; Cardiff Met U), b Cardiff 21 Sep 1998. RHB, SLA. Squad No 32. Debut (Glamorgan) 2018. Cardiff MCCU 2019. Wales MC 2017-19. HS 38 and CC BB 3-54 v Derbys (Swansea) 2018. BB 4-79 CfU v Somerset (Taunton) 2019. T20 HS 6*. T20 BB 3-26.

[NQ]**SMITH, Ruaidhri** Alexander James (Llandaff Cathedral S; Shrewsbury S; Bristol U), b Glasgow, Scotland 5 Aug 1994. 6'1". RHB, RM. Squad No 20. Debut (Glamorgan) 2013. Scotland 2017. Wales MC 2010-16. **LOI** (Scot): 2 (2016); HS 10 and BB 1-34 v Afg (Edinburgh) 2016. **IT20** (Scot): 2 (2018-19); HS 9* v Netherlands (Al Amerat) 2018-19; BB –. HS 57* v Glos (Bristol) 2014. BB 5-87 v Durham (Cardiff) 2018. LO HS 14 v Hants (Swansea) 2018 (RLC). LO BB 4-7 v Oman (Al Amerat) 2018-19. T20 HS 22*. T20 BB 4-6.

TAYLOR, Callum Zinzan (The Southport S), b Newport, Monmouths 19 Jun 1998. RHB, OB. Squad No 4. Debut (Glamorgan) 2020, scoring 106 v Northants (Northampton). Glamorgan 2nd XI debut 2017. Wales MC 2017. HS 106 (*see above*). BB 2-16 v Yorks (Leeds) 2020. LO HS 36 v Northants (Northampton) 2021 (RLC). LO BB 1-6 v Somerset (Taunton) 2021 (RLC). T20 HS 23. T20 BB 2-9.

[NQ]**van der GUGTEN, Timm**, b Hornsby, Sydney, Australia 25 Feb 1991. 6'1½". RHB, RFM. Squad No 64. New South Wales 2011-12. Netherlands 2012 to date. Glamorgan debut 2016; cap 2018. Big Bash: HH 2014-15. Trent Rockets 2021. **LOI** (Neth): 8 (2011-12 to 2021-22); HS 49 v Ire (Utrecht) 2021; BB 5-24 v Canada (King City, NW) 2013. **IT20** (Neth): 40 (2011-12 to 2021-22); HS 40* v PNG (Dubai, ICCA) 2019-20; BB 3-9 v Singapore (Dubai, ICCA) 2019-20. HS 85* v Yorks (Leeds) 2021. 50 wkts (1): 56 (2016). BB 7-42 v Kent (Cardiff) 2018. LO HS 49 (*see LOI*). LO BB 5-24 (*see LOI*). T20 HS 40*. T20 BB 5-21.

WEIGHELL, William **James** (Stokesley S), b Middlesbrough, Yorks 28 Jan 1994. 6'4". LHB, RMF. Squad No 29. Durham 2015-19. Leicestershire 2020. Glamorgan debut 2021. Northumberland 2012-15. HS 84 Du v Kent (Chester-le-St) 2018. Gm HS 21 v Sussex (Hove) 2021. BB 7-32 Du v Leics (Chester-le-St) 2018. Gm BB 2-46 v Lancs (Cardiff) 2021. LO HS 23 Du v Lancs (Manchester) 2018 (RLC). LO BB 5-57 Du v Warwks (Birmingham) 2017 (RLC). T20 HS 51. T20 BB 3-28.

RELEASED/RETIRED

(Having made a County 1st XI appearance in 2021)

BALBIRNIE, A. – *see IRELAND.*

[NQ]**RUTHERFORD, Hamish** Duncan, b Dunedin, New Zealand 27 Apr 1989. Son of K.R.Rutherford (Gauteng, Otago, Transvaal & New Zealand 1982-83 to 1999-00). Nephew of I.A.Rutherford (C Districts, Otago & Worcestershire 1974-75 to 1983-84). 5'10". LHB, SLA. Otago 2008-09 to date. Essex 2013. Derbyshire 2015-16. Worcestershire 2019. Glamorgan 2021. **Tests** (NZ): 16 (2012-13 to 2014-15); HS 171 v E (Dunedin) 2012-13 – on debut. **LOI** (NZ): 4 (2012-13 to 2013-14); HS 11 v E (Napier) 2012-13. **IT20** (NZ): 8 (2012-13 to 2019); HS 62 v E (Oval) 2013. F-c Tours (NZ): E 2013, 2014 (NZ A); WI 2014; B 2013-14. 1000 runs (0+1): 1077 (2012-13). HS 239 Otago v Wellington (Dunedin) 2011-12. CC HS 123 Wo v Leics (Leicester) 2019 – on Wo debut. Gm HS 71 v Durham (Chester-le-St) 2021. BB 1-26 v Surrey (Oval) 2021. LO HS 155 Otago v CD (Dunedin) 2019-20. LO BB 1-4 Otago v Wellington (Dunedin) 2017-18. T20 HS 106. T20 BB 1-6.

SELMAN, Nicholas James (Matthew Flinders Anglican C, Buderim), b Brisbane, Australia 18 Oct 1995. 6'4". RHB, RM. Glamorgan 2016-21. HS 150 v Glos (Newport) 2019. BB 1-22 v Northants (Cardiff) 2019. LO HS 92 v Leics (Leicester) 2021 (RLC). T20 HS 78.

WALKER, R.I. – *see LEICESTERSHIRE.*

C.R.Hemphrey left the staff without making a County 1st XI appearance in 2021.

GLAMORGAN 2021

RESULTS SUMMARY

	Place	Won	Lost	Drew	NR
LV= Insurance County Champ (Div 2)	6th	2	5	7	
Royal London One-Day Cup (Group 2)	**Winners**	6	2		2
Vitality Blast (South Group)	9th	3	9		2

LV= INSURANCE COUNTY CHAMPIONSHIP AVERAGES
BATTING AND FIELDING

Cap		*M*	*I*	*NO*	*HS*	*Runs*	*Avge*	*100*	*50*	*Ct/St*
2016	C.B.Cooke	14	21	7	205*	816	58.28	4	1	40/1
2021	K.S.Carlson	14	23	4	170*	928	48.84	3	5	3
	H.D.Rutherford	4	7	–	71	260	37.14	–	2	–
	C.Z.Taylor	6	8	2	84	215	35.83	–	2	2
2019	D.L.Lloyd	14	25	1	121	828	34.50	1	5	7
2019	M.Labuschagne	6	9	2	77	228	32.57	–	2	1
	D.A.Douthwaite	13	16	1	96	482	32.13	–	4	3
	A.G.Salter	10	11	4	90	221	31.57	–	1	3
	E.J.Byrom	3	5	–	78	151	30.20	–	1	1
2021	W.T.Root	11	18	2	110*	442	27.62	1	1	4
	J.M.Cooke	8	13	2	68	203	18.45	–	1	7
2018	T.van der Gugten	11	13	2	85*	194	17.63	–	1	5
	L.J.Carey	3	5	–	29	78	15.60	–	–	–
2013	M.G.Hogan	13	14	6	54	113	14.12	–	1	2
	N.J.Selman	5	10	–	69	121	12.10	–	1	3
	W.J.Weighell	4	5	–	21	52	10.40	–	–	2
	A.Balbirne	3	6	–	29	57	9.50	–	–	3

Also batted: J.A.R.Harris (2 matches – cap 2010) 17, 18* (1 ct); C.A.Ingram (1 – cap 2017) 7, 27; J.P.McIlroy (2) 0; M.G.Neser (5 – cap 2021) 17, 24, 17* (3 ct); S.J.Reingold (1) 9, 4 (1 ct); R.A.J.Smith (1) 8, 4.

BOWLING

	O	*M*	*R*	*W*	*Avge*	*Best*	*5wI*	*10wM*
M.G.Neser	127	29	386	23	16.78	5-39	1	–
M.G.Hogan	332.5	78	874	34	25.70	5-28	1	–
D.L.Lloyd	170.3	24	558	21	26.57	4-11	–	–
T.van der Gugten	274.3	54	823	27	30.48	4-34	–	–
A.G.Salter	218.5	41	687	15	45.80	4-18	–	–
D.A.Douthwaite	181.1	18	781	17	45.94	2-16	–	–
Also bowled:								
W.J.Weighell	80.1	9	359	7	51.28	2-46	–	–
C.Z.Taylor	146.2	16	484	5	96.80	2-16	–	–

A.Balbirnie 3-0-17-0; E.J.Byrom 16-0-64-2; L.J.Carey 54-9-179-4; K.S.Carlson 14.3-4-43-1; C.B.Cooke 3-0-19-0; J.M.Cooke 11-0-51-0; J.A.R.Harris 44.5-3-159-4; M.Labuschagne 32.2-3-127-2; J.P.McIlroy 38-10-131-1; S.J.Reingold 6-1-15-3; W.T.Root 13-0-64-0; H.D.Rutherford 8-1-26-1; R.A.J.Smith 22-3-84-1.

The First-Class Averages (pp 220–232) give the records of Glamorgan players in all first-class county matches, with the exception of E.J.Byrom and J.A.R.Harris, whose first-class figures for Glamorgan are as above.

GLAMORGAN RECORDS

FIRST-CLASS CRICKET

Highest Total	For 718-3d		v	Sussex	Colwyn Bay	2000
	V 750		by	Northants	Cardiff	2019
Lowest Total	For 22		v	Lancashire	Liverpool	1924
	V 33		by	Leics	Ebbw Vale	1965
Highest Innings	For 309*	S.P.James	v	Sussex	Colwyn Bay	2000
	V 322*	M.B.Loye	for	Northants	Northampton	1998

Highest Partnership for each Wicket

1st	374	M.T.G.Elliott/S.P.James	v	Sussex	Colwyn Bay	2000
2nd	291	N.J.Selman/M.Labuschagne	v	Sussex	Hove	2019
3rd	313	D.E.Davies/W.E.Jones	v	Essex	Brentwood	1948
4th	425*	A.Dale/I.V.A.Richards	v	Middlesex	Cardiff	1993
5th	307*	K.S.Carlson/C.B.Cooke	v	Northants	Cardiff	2021
6th	240	J.Allenby/M.A.Wallace	v	Surrey	The Oval	2009
7th	211	P.A.Cottey/O.D.Gibson	v	Leics	Swansea	1996
8th	202	D.Davies/J.J.Hills	v	Sussex	Eastbourne	1928
9th	203*	J.J.Hills/J.C.Clay	v	Worcs	Swansea	1929
10th	143	T.Davies/S.A.B.Daniels	v	Glos	Swansea	1982

Best Bowling	For	10- 51	J.Mercer	v	Worcs	Worcester	1936
(Innings)	V	10- 18	G.Geary	for	Leics	Pontypridd	1929
Best Bowling	For	17-212	J.C.Clay	v	Worcs	Swansea	1937
(Match)	V	16- 96	G.Geary	for	Leics	Pontypridd	1929

Most Runs – Season	2276	H.Morris	(av 55.51)	1990
Most Runs – Career	34056	A.Jones	(av 33.03)	1957-83
Most 100s – Season	10	H.Morris		1990
Most 100s – Career	54	M.P.Maynard		1985-2005
Most Wkts – Season	176	J.C.Clay	(av 17.34)	1937
Most Wkts – Career	2174	D.J.Shepherd	(av 20.95)	1950-72
Most Career W-K Dismissals	933	E.W.Jones	(840 ct; 93 st)	1961-83
Most Career Catches in the Field	656	P.M.Walker		1956-72

LIMITED-OVERS CRICKET

Highest Total	**50ov**	429		v	Surrey	The Oval	2002
	40ov	328-4		v	Lancashire	Colwyn Bay	2011
	T20	240-3		v	Surrey	The Oval	2015
Lowest Total	**50ov**	68		v	Lancashire	Manchester	1973
	40ov	42		v	Derbyshire	Swansea	1979
	T20	44		v	Surrey	The Oval	2019
Highest Innings	**50ov**	169*	J.A.Rudolph	v	Sussex	Hove	2014
	40ov	155*	J.H.Kallis	v	Surrey	Pontypridd	1999
	T20	116*	I.J.Thomas	v	Somerset	Taunton	2004
Best Bowling	**50ov**	6-20	S.D.Thomas	v	Comb Univs	Cardiff	1995
	40ov	7-16	S.D.Thomas	v	Surrey	Swansea	1998
	T20	5-14	G.G.Wagg	v	Worcs	Worcester	2013

GLOUCESTERSHIRE

Formation of Present Club: 1871
Inaugural First-Class Match: 1870
Colours: Blue, Gold, Brown, Silver, Green and Red
Badge: Coat of Arms of the City and County of Bristol
County Champions (since 1890): (0); best – 2nd 1930, 1931, 1947, 1959, 1969, 1986
Gillette/NatWest/C&G Trophy Winners: (5) 1973, 1999, 2000, 2003, 2004
Benson and Hedges Cup Winners: (3) 1977, 1999, 2000
Pro 40/National League (Div 1) Winners: (1) 2000
Royal London One-Day Cup Winners: (1) 2015
Twenty20 Cup Winners: (0); best – Finalist 2007

Chief Executive: Will Brown, Seat Unique Stadium, Nevil Road, Bristol BS7 9EJ • Tel: 0117 910 8000 • Email: reception@glosccc.co.uk • Web: www.gloscricket.co.uk • Twitter: @Gloscricket (71,870 followers)

Head Coach: Dale Benkenstein. **Assistant Coach**: Ian Harvey. **Performance Director**: Steve Snell. **Captain**: G.L.van Buuren (f-c & l-o) and J.M.R.Taylor (T20). **Overseas Players**: M.S.Harris, Naseem Shah and Zafar Gohar. **2022 Testimonial**: None. **Head Groundsman**: Sean Williams. **Scorer**: Adrian Bull. ‡ New registration. NQ Not qualified for England.

Gloucestershire revised their capping policy in 2004 and now award players with their County Caps when they make their first-class debut.

BRACEY, James Robert (Filton CS), b Bristol 3 May 1997. Younger brother of S.N.Bracey (Cardiff MCCU 2014-15). 6'1". LHB, WK, occ RM. Squad No 25. Debut (Gloucestershire) 2016; cap 2016. Loughborough MCCU 2017-18. **Tests**: 2 (2021); HS 8 v NZ (Birmingham) 2021. F-c Tour (EL): A 2019-20. HS 156 v Glamorgan (Cardiff) 2017. BB –. LO HS 113* and LO BB 1-23 v Essex (Chelmsford) 2019 (RLC). T20 HS 64.

CHARLESWORTH, Ben Geoffrey (St Edward's S), b Oxford 19 Nov 2000. Son of G.M.Charlesworth (Griqualand W and Cambridge U 1989-90 to 1993). 6'2½". LHB, RM/OB. Squad No 64. Debut (Gloucestershire) 2018; cap 2018. Gloucestershire 2nd XI debut 2016. Oxfordshire 2016. England U19 2018 to 2018-19. HS 77* and BB 3-25 v Middx (Bristol) 2018. HS 77* v Northants (Bristol) 2019. LO HS 99* v Hants (Bristol) 2021 (RLC). LO BB –.

COCKBAIN, Ian Andrew (Maghull HS), b Bootle, Liverpool 17 Feb 1987. Son of I.Cockbain (Lancs and Minor Cos 1979-94). 6'0". RHB, RM. Squad No 28. Debut (Gloucestershire) 2011; cap 2011; testimonial 2019. Big Bash: AS 2021-22. Welsh Fire 2021. HS 151* v Surrey (Bristol) 2014. BB 1-23 v Durham MCCU (Bristol) 2016. LO HS 108* v Middx (Lord's) 2017 (RLC). T20 HS 123.

DALE, Ajeet Singh (Wellington C), b Slough, Berks 3 Jul 2000. 6'1". RHB, RFM. Squad No 39. Hampshire 2020. Hampshire 2nd XI 2018-21. Gloucestershire 2nd XI debut 2021. HS 6 H v Kent (Canterbury) 2020. BB 3-20 H v Sussex (Hove) 2020.

DENT, Christopher David James (Backwell CS; Alton C), b Bristol 20 Jan 1991. 5'9". LHB, WK, occ SLA. Squad No 15. Debut (Gloucestershire) 2010; cap 2010; captain 2018-21. 1000 runs (4); most – 1336 (2016). HS 268 v Glamorgan (Bristol) 2015. BB 2-21 v Sussex (Hove) 2016. LO HS 151* v Glamorgan (Cardiff) 2013 (Y40). LO BB 4-43 v Leics (Bristol) 2012 (CB40). T20 HS 87. T20 BB 1-4.

GOODMAN, Dominic Charles (Dr Challenor's GS), b Ashford, Kent 23 Oct 2000. 6'6". RHB, RM. Squad No 83. Debut (Gloucestershire) 2021; cap 2021. Gloucestershire 2nd XI debut 2019. HS 9* v Hants (Southampton) 2021. BB 2-19 v Somerset (Taunton) 2021.

HAMMOND, Miles Arthur Halhead (St Edward's S, Oxford), b Cheltenham 11 Jan 1996. 5'11". LHB, OB. Squad No 88. Debut (Gloucestershire) 2013; cap 2013. Birmingham Phoenix 2021. F-c Tour (MCC): Nepal 2019-20. HS 123* v Middx (Bristol) 2018. BB 2-37 v Leics (Leicester) 2021. LO HS 95 v Sussex (Eastbourne) 2019 (RLC). LO BB 2-18 v Northants (Northampton) 2015 (RLC). T20 HS 63. T20 BB –.

‡[NQ]**HARRIS, Marcus** Sinclair, b Perth, W Australia 21 July 1992. 5'8". LHB, OB. Squad No 21. W Australia 2010-11 to 2015-16. Victoria 2016-17 to date. Leicestershire 2021. Big Bash: PS 2014-15 to 2015-16. MR 2016-17 to 2019-20. **Tests** (A): 14 (2018-19 to 2021-22); HS 79 v I (Sydney) 2018-19. HS 250* Vic v NSW (Melbourne) 2018-19. CC HS 185 Le v Middx (Leicester) 2021. BB –. LO HS 127 Le v Yorks (Leicester) 2021 (RLC). T20 HS 85.

HIGGINS, Ryan Francis (Bradfield C), b Harare, Zimbabwe 6 Jan 1995. 5'10". RHB, RM. Squad No 29. Middlesex 2017. Gloucestershire debut/cap 2018. Welsh Fire 2021. HS 199 v Leics (Leicester) 2019. 50 wkts (2); most – 51 (2021). BB 7-42 (11-96 match) v Warwks (Bristol) 2020. LO HS 81* v Surrey (Oval) 2018 (RLC). LO BB 4-50 ECB XI v India A (Leeds) 2018. T20 HS 77*. T20 BB 5-13.

HOWELL, Benny Alexander Cameron (The Oratory S), b Bordeaux, France 5 Oct 1988. Son of J.B.Howell (Warwickshire 2nd XI 1978). 5'11". RHB, RM. Squad No 13. Hampshire 2011. Gloucestershire debut/cap 2012. Big Bash: MR 2020-21. Birmingham Phoenix 2021. Berkshire 2007. HS 163 v Glamorgan (Cardiff) 2017. BB 5-57 v Leics (Leicester) 2013. LO HS 122 v Surrey (Croydon) 2011 (CB40). LO BB 3-37 v Yorks (Leeds) 2015 (RLC). T20 HS 57. T20 BB 5-18.

LACE, Thomas Cresswell (Millfield S), b Hammersmith, Middx 27 May 1998. 5'8". RHB, WK. Squad No 8. Derbyshire 2018-19 (on loan). Middlesex 2019. Gloucestershire debut/cap 2020. Middlesex 2nd XI 2015-18. HS 143 De v Glamorgan (Swansea) 2019. Gs HS 118 v Hants (Cheltenham) 2021. LO HS 48 De v Durham (Chester-le-St) 2019 (RLC).

NAISH, William Lewis (Wycliffe C; Clifton C), b Guildford, Surrey 19 Jun 2003. 5'11" RHB, RM. Squad No 22. Gloucestershire 2nd XI debut 2019. Wiltshire 2021. Awaiting 1st XI debut.

‡[NQ]**NASEEM SHAH**, b Lower Dir, NWFP, Pakistan 15 Feb 2003. 5'8". RHB, RF. Squad No 71. ZT Bank 2018-19. Central Punjab 2019-20. Southern Punjab 2021-22. **Tests** (P): 10 (2019-20 to 2021-22); HS 12 v NZ (Christchurch) 2020-21; BB 5-31 v SL (Karachi) 2019-20. F-c Tours (P): E 2020; A 2019-20; NZ 2020-21; SL 2021-22 (PA). HS 31 P Shaheens v Sri Lanka A (Pallekele) 2021-22. BB 6-59 ZT v PT (Rawalpindi) 2018-19. LO HS 1 ZT v PT (Rawalpindi) 2018-19. LO BB 2-26 P Shaheens v Sri Lanka A (Dambulla) 2021-22. T20 HS 11*. T20 BB 5-20.

PAYNE, David Alan (Lytchett Minster S), b Poole, Dorset, 15 Feb 1991. 6'2". RHB, LMF. Squad No 14. Debut (Gloucestershire) 2011; cap 2011. Welsh Fire 2021. Dorset 2009. HS 67* v Glamorgan (Cardiff) 2016. BB 6-26 v Leics (Bristol) 2011. LO HS 36* v Glamorgan (Bristol) 2019 (RLC). LO BB 7-29 v Essex (Chelmsford) 2010 (CB40), inc 4 wkts in 4 balls and 6 wkts in 9 balls – Gs record. T20 HS 10. T20 BB 5-24.

PRICE, Oliver James (Magdalen Coll S), b Oxford 12 Jun 2001. Younger brother of T.J.Price (*see below*). 6'3". RHB, OB. Squad No 67. Debut (Gloucestershire) 2021; cap 2021. Gloucestershire 2nd XI debut 2018. Oxfordshire 2018-19. HS 33 v Middx (Cheltenham) 2021. BB –. LO HS 24 and LO BB 1-9 v Kent (Beckenham) 2021 (RLC).

PRICE, Thomas James (Magdalen Coll S), b Oxford 2 Jan 2000. Elder brother of O.J.Price (*see above*). 6'1". RHB, RM. Squad No 53. Debut (Gloucestershire) 2020; cap 2020. Gloucestershire 2nd XI debut 2015. Oxfordshire 2018-19. HS 71 v Glamorgan (Cardiff) 2021. BB 4-72 v Northants (Bristol) 2021. LO HS 1 v Surrey (Oval) 2021 (RLC). LO BB –.

SCOTT, George Frederick Buchan (Beechwood Park S; St Albans S; Leeds U), b Hemel Hempstead, Herts 6 Nov 1995. Younger brother of J.E.B.Scott (Hertfordshire 2013-18); elder brother of C.F.B.Scott (Durham MCCU 2019) and P.E.B.Scott (Hertfordshire 2014-17). 6'2". RHB, RM. Squad No 17. Leeds/Bradford MCCU 2015-16. Middlesex 2018-19. Gloucestershire debut/cap 2020. Hertfordshire 2011-14. HS 55 M v Leics (Lord's) 2019. Gs HS 44* and BB 2-34 v Warwks (Bristol) 2020. LO HS 66* v Surrey (Oval) 2021 (RLC). LO BB 1-65 M v Lancs (Lord's) 2019 (RLC). T20 HS 38*. T20 BB 1-14.

SHAW, Joshua (Crofton HS, Wakefield; Skills Exchange C), b Wakefield, Yorks 3 Jan 1996. Son of C.Shaw (Yorkshire 1984-88). 6'1". RHB, RMF. Squad No 5. Debut (Gloucestershire) 2016 (on loan); cap 2016. Yorkshire 2016-19. HS 42 Y v Somerset (Leeds) 2018. Gs HS 41* v Leics (Bristol) 2021. BB 5-79 v Sussex (Bristol) 2016. LO HS 2 and LO BB 4-36 v Lancs (Bristol) 2021 (RLC). T20 HS 1*. T20 BB 3-32.

SMITH, Thomas Michael John (Seaford Head Community C; Sussex Downs C), b Eastbourne, Sussex 29 Aug 1987. 5'9". RHB, SLA. Squad No 6. Sussex 2007-09. Surrey 2009 (l-o only). Middlesex 2010-13. Gloucestershire debut/cap 2013. HS 84 v Leics (Cheltenham) 2019. BB 4-35 v Kent (Canterbury) 2014. LO HS 65 Sy v Leics (Leicester) 2009 (P40). LO BB 4-26 v Sussex (Cheltenham) 2016 (RLC). T20 HS 36*. T20 BB 5-16 v Warwks (Birmingham) 2020 – Gs record.

TAYLOR, Jack Martin Robert (Chipping Norton S), b Banbury, Oxfordshire 12 Nov 1991. Elder brother of M.D.Taylor (*see below*). 5'11". RHB, OB. Squad No 10. Debut (Gloucestershire) 2010; cap 2010. Oxfordshire 2009-11. HS 156 v Northants (Cheltenham) 2015. BB 4-16 v Glamorgan (Bristol) 2016. LO HS 75 v Glamorgan (Bristol) 2019 (RLC). LO BB 4-38 v Hants (Bristol) 2014 (RLC). T20 HS 80. T20 BB 4-16.

TAYLOR, Matthew David (Chipping Norton S), b Banbury, Oxfordshire 8 Jul 1994. Younger brother of J.M.R.Taylor (*see above*). 6'0". RHB, LMF. Squad No 36. Debut (Gloucestershire) 2013; cap 2013. Oxfordshire 2011-12. HS 56 v Somerset (Taunton) 2021. BB 5-15 v Cardiff MCCU (Bristol) 2018. CC BB 5-40 v Middx (Cheltenham) 2021. LO HS 51* v Lancs (Bristol) 2021 (RLC). LO BB 3-39 v Sussex (Eastbourne) 2019 (RLC). T20 HS 9*. T20 BB 3-16.

van BUUREN, Graeme Lourens, b Pretoria, South Africa 22 Aug 1990. 5'6". RHB, SLA. Squad No 12. Northerns 2009-10 to 2015-16. Titans 2012-13 to 2014-15. Gloucestershire debut/cap 2016; captain 2022. England resident since May 2019. HS 235 Northerns v EP (Centurion) 2014-15. Gs HS 172* v Worcs (Worcester) 2016. BB 4-12 Northerns v SW Districts (Oudtshoorn) 2012-13. Gs BB 4-18 v Durham MCCU (Bristol) 2017. CC BB 3-15 v Glamorgan (Bristol) 2016. LO HS 119* Northerns v EP (Pt Elizabeth, Grey HS) 2013-14. LO BB 5-35 Northerns v SW Districts (Pretoria) 2011-12. T20 HS 64. T20 BB 5-8.

‡NQ**VAN MEEKEREN, Paul** Adriaan, b Amsterdam, Netherlands 15 Jan 1993. 6'4". RHB, RMF. Squad No 47. Netherlands 2013 to date. Somerset 2016-18. Durham 2021 (white ball only). **LOI** (Neth): 7 (2013 to 2021); HS 15* v SA (Amstelveen) 2013; BB 2-28 v Scot (Rotterdam) 2021. **IT20** (Neth): 46 (2013 to 2021-22); HS 18 v Hong Kong (Dubai, DSC) 2016-17; BB 4-11 v Ire (Dharamsala) 2015-16. HS 34 Neth v PNG (Amstelveen) 2015. CC HS 6 Sm v Lancs (Manchester) 2018. BB 4-60 Sm v Essex (Chelmsford) 2017. LO HS 15* (*see LOI*). LO BB 3-22 Neth v UAE (Amstelveen) 2017. T20 HS 18. T20 BB 4-11.

WARNER, Jared David (Kettleborough Park HS; Silcoates SFC), b Wakefield, Yorks 14 Nov 1996. 6'1". RHB, RFM. Squad No 4. Sussex 2019 (on loan). Yorkshire 2020. Gloucestershire debut 2021; cap 2021. HS 13* Sx v Middx (Hove) 2019. Gs HS 10* v Glamorgan (Cardiff) 2021. BB 3-35 Sx v Glamorgan (Hove) 2019. Gs BB 2-54 v Northants (Bristol) 2021. LO HS 0. LO BB 3-42 v Sussex (Hove) 2021 (RLC).

WELLS, Ben Joseph James (Monkton Combe S), b Bath, Somerset 30 Jul 2000. RHB, WK. Debut (Gloucestershire) 2021. Somerset 2nd XI 2018-21. Warwickshire 2nd XI 2021. Gloucestershire 2nd XI debut 2021. Dorset 2018. HS 40 v Glamorgan (Cardiff) 2021. LO HS 7 v Surrey (Oval) 2021 (RLC).

NQ**ZAFAR GOHAR**, b Lahore, Pakistan 1 Feb 1995. 5'11". LHB, SLA. Squad No 77. ZT Bank 2013-14. State Bank 2014-15. SSGC 2015-16 to 2016-17. Lahore Blues 2018-19. Central Punjab 2019-20 to date. Gloucestershire debut 2021. **Tests** (P): 1 (2020-21); HS 37 and BB-v NZ (Christchurch) 2020-21. **LOI** (P): 1 (2015-16); HS 15 and BB 2-54 v E (Sharjah) 2015-16. F-c Tours (P): NZ 2020-21; SL 2015 (PA). HS 100* C Punjab v Baluchistan (Quetta) 2019-20. Gs HS 30 v Durham (Bristol) 2021. BB 7-79 (11-133 match) C Punjab v Northern (Faisalabad) 2019-20. Gs BB 6-43 v Glamorgan (Cardiff) 2021. LO HS 53 C Punjab v Sindh (Karachi) 2020-21. LO BB 5-56 ZT v SNGPL (Islamabad) 2013-14. T20 HS 32*. T20 BB 4-14.

RELEASED/RETIRED

(Having made a County 1st XI appearance in 2021)

NQ**BRATHWAITE, Kraigg** Clairmonte (Combermere S), b Belfield, St Michael, Barbados 1 Dec 1992. RHB, OB. Barbados 2008-09 to date. Sagicor HPC 2014. Yorkshire 2017. Nottinghamshire 2018; cap 2018. Glamorgan 2019. Gloucestershire 2021; cap 2021. **Tests** (WI): 75 (2011 to 2021-22, 16 as captain); HS 212 v B (Kingstown) 2014; BB 6-29 v SL (Colombo, PSS) 2015-16. **LOI** (WI): 10 (2016-17); HS 78 v Z (Bulawayo) 2016-17; BB 1-56 v SL (Bulawayo) 2016-17. F-c Tours (WI)(C=Captain): E 2010 (WI A), 2017, 2020; A 2015-16; SA 2014-15; NZ 2013-14, 2017-18, 2020-21; I 2011-12, 2013-14 (WI A), 2018-19, 2019-20 (v Afg); SL 2014-15 (WI A), 2015-16, 2021-22C; Z 2017-18; B 2011-12, 2018-19C, 2020-21C; UAE (v P) 2016-17. HS 276 Bar v Jamaica (Bridgetown) 2021-22. CC HS 103* Gm v Leics (Cardiff) 2019. Gs HS 60 v Hants (Southampton) 2021. BB 6-29 (*see Tests*). LO HS 108 Bar v ICC Americas (Lucas Street) 2016-17. LO BB 2-54 WI A v Sri Lanka A (Dambulla) 2014-15.

HANKINS, George Thomas (Millfield S), b Bath, Somerset 4 Jan 1997. Elder brother of H.J.Hankins (*see below*). 6'1½". RHB, OB. Gloucestershire 2016-21; cap 2016. HS 116 v Northants (Northampton) 2016. BB –. LO HS 92 v Kent (Beckenham) 2018 (RLC). T20 HS 14.

NQ**PHILLIPS, Glenn** Dominic, b East London, South Africa 6 Dec 1996. Elder brother of D.N.Phillips (Otago 2019-20 to date). RHB, WK, OB. Auckland 2016-17 to date. Gloucestershire 2021; cap 2021. Welsh Fire 2021. **Tests** (NZ): 1 (2019-20); HS 52 v A (Sydney) 2019-20. **IT20** (NZ): 35 (2016-17 to 2021-22); HS 108 v WI (Mt Maunganui) 2020-21; BB 1-11 v B (Auckland) 2020-21. F-c Tour (NZ): A 2019-20. HS 138* Auckland v ND (Whangarei) 2018-19. Gs HS 86* v Surrey (Oval) 2021. BB 4-70 Auckland v Wellington (Auckland) 2019-20. Gs BB 2-67 v Hants (Cheltenham) 2021. LO HS 156 Auckland v Otago (Lincoln) 2019-20. LO BB 3-40 Auckland v Otago (Auckland) 2019-20. T20 HS 116*. T20 BB 2-11.

WORRALL, D.J. – *see SURREY.*

H.J.Hankins left the staff without making a County 1st XI appearance in 2021.

GLOUCESTERSHIRE 2021

RESULTS SUMMARY

	Place	Won	Lost	Drew	NR
LV= Insurance County Champ (Div 2)	2nd	8	4	2	
Royal London One-Day Cup (Group 1)	QF	4	4		
Vitality Blast (South Group)	6th	6	6		2

LV= INSURANCE COUNTY CHAMPIONSHIP AVERAGES
BATTING AND FIELDING

Cap†		*M*	*I*	*NO*	*HS*	*Runs*	*Avge*	*100*	*50*	*Ct/St*
2021	J.A.Tattersall	2	4	1	86*	162	54.00	–	2	2
2016	G.L.van Buuren	6	9	2	110*	354	50.57	1	4	3
2016	J.R.Bracey	11	21	2	118	715	37.63	1	6	33
2013	M.A.H.Hammond	9	17	2	94	547	36.46	–	4	11
2020	T.J.Price	6	9	4	71	177	35.40	–	1	1
2011	I.A.Cockbain	6	11	1	117	302	30.20	1	2	1
2021	K.C.Brathwaite	6	11	–	60	295	26.81	–	1	6
2010	C.D.J.Dent	12	23	2	91*	560	26.66	–	5	5
2010	J.M.R.Taylor	3	5	–	40	133	26.60	–	–	1
2016	J.Shaw	4	6	2	41*	105	26.25	–	–	1
2020	T.C.Lace	14	26	4	118	573	26.04	1	3	9
2018	B.G.Charlesworth	3	5	–	49	112	22.40	–	–	–
2018	R.F.Higgins	13	19	1	73	376	20.88	–	1	3
2016	G.T.Hankins	5	7	1	37	120	20.00	–	–	6
2013	M.D.Taylor	9	12	3	56	166	18.44	–	1	–
2021	G.D.Phillips	3	6	–	47	109	18.16	–	–	5
2021	O.J.Price	4	7	–	33	110	15.71	–	–	4
2020	G.F.B.Scott	5	7	–	31	100	14.28	–	–	3
2021	Zafar Gohar	4	6	–	30	78	13.00	–	–	–
2011	D.A.Payne	10	12	3	34	102	11.33	–	–	6
2013	T.M.J.Smith	5	8	1	47	76	10.85	–	–	2
2021	D.C.Goodman	4	5	3	9*	20	10.00	–	–	–
2018	D.J.Worrall	8	12	3	24	75	8.33	–	–	–

Also batted: J.D.Warner (2 matches – cap 2021) 10, 10* (1 ct); B.J.Wells (1 – cap 2021) 40 (2 ct);

BOWLING

	O	*M*	*R*	*W*	*Avge*	*Best*	*5wI*	*10wM*
Zafar Gohar	117.3	32	287	20	14.35	6-43	3	1
D.A.Payne	258.2	59	719	34	21.14	6-56	2	1
R.F.Higgins	443	118	1143	51	22.41	5-46	2	–
D.J.Worrall	249.5	80	621	27	23.00	5-54	2	–
T.J.Price	128	37	368	15	24.53	4-72	–	–
M.D.Taylor	266.1	67	818	27	30.29	5-40	1	–
Also bowled:								
G.L.van Buuren	48.4	11	119	7	17.00	3-28	–	–
J.Shaw	86	10	333	9	37.00	4-48	–	–
D.C.Goodman	104	25	252	5	50.40	2-19	–	–

K.C.Brathwaite 4-0-16-0; B.G.Charlesworth 7.2-0-37-0; C.D.J.Dent 3-0-18-0; M.A.H.Hammond 19-2-85-3; G.D.Phillips 40-3-159-4; O.J.Price 33-5-100-0; G.F.B.Scott 51-13-149-2; T.M.J.Smith 104-8-303-4; J.D.Warner 37.3-7-118-4.

The First-Class Averages (pp 220–232) give the records of Gloucestershire players in all first-class county matches, with the exception of J.R.Bracey and J.A.Tattersall, whose first-class figures for Gloucestershire are as above.

† Gloucestershire revised their capping policy in 2004 and now award players with their County Caps when they make their first-class debut.

GLOUCESTERSHIRE RECORDS

FIRST-CLASS CRICKET

Highest Total	For	695-9d		v	Middlesex	Gloucester	2004
	V	774-7d		by	Australians	Bristol	1948
Lowest Total	For	17		v	Australians	Cheltenham	1896
	V	12		by	Northants	Gloucester	1907
Highest Innings	For	341	C.M.Spearman	v	Middlesex	Gloucester	2004
	V	319	C.J.L.Rogers	for	Northants	Northampton	2006

Highest Partnership for each Wicket

1st	395	D.M.Young/R.B.Nicholls	v	Oxford U	Oxford	1962
2nd	256	C.T.M.Pugh/T.W.Graveney	v	Derbyshire	Chesterfield	1960
3rd	392	G.H.Roderick/A.P.R.Gidman	v	Leics	Bristol	2014
4th	321	W.R.Hammond/W.L.Neale	v	Leics	Gloucester	1937
5th	261	W.G.Grace/W.O.Moberly	v	Yorkshire	Cheltenham	1876
6th	320	G.L.Jessop/J.H.Board	v	Sussex	Hove	1903
7th	248	W.G.Grace/E.L.Thomas	v	Sussex	Hove	1896
8th	239	W.R.Hammond/A.E.Wilson	v	Lancashire	Bristol	1938
9th	193	W.G.Grace/S.A.P.Kitcat	v	Sussex	Bristol	1896
10th	137	C.N.Miles/L.C.Norwell	v	Worcs	Cheltenham	2014

Best Bowling	For	10-40	E.G.Dennett	v	Essex	Bristol	1906
(Innings)	V	10-66	A.A.Mailey	for	Australians	Cheltenham	1921
		10-66	K.Smales	for	Notts	Stroud	1956
Best Bowling	For	17-56	C.W.L.Parker	v	Essex	Gloucester	1925
(Match)	V	15-87	A.J.Conway	for	Worcs	Moreton-in-M	1914

Most Runs – Season	2860	W.R.Hammond	(av 69.75)	1933
Most Runs – Career	33664	W.R.Hammond	(av 57.05)	1920-51
Most 100s – Season	13	W.R.Hammond		1938
Most 100s – Career	113	W.R.Hammond		1920-51
Most Wkts – Season	222	T.W.J.Goddard	(av 16.80)	1937
	222	T.W.J.Goddard	(av 16.37)	1947
Most Wkts – Career	3170	C.W.L.Parker	(av 19.43)	1903-35
Most Career W-K Dismissals	1054	R.C.Russell	(950 ct; 104 st)	1981-2004
Most Career Catches in the Field	719	C.A.Milton		1948-74

LIMITED-OVERS CRICKET

Highest Total	**50ov**	401-7		v	Bucks	Wing	2003
	40ov	344-6		v	Northants	Cheltenham	2001
	T20	254-3		v	Middlesex	Uxbridge	2011
Lowest Total	**50ov**	82		v	Notts	Bristol	1987
	40ov	49		v	Middlesex	Bristol	1978
	T20	68		v	Hampshire	Bristol	2010
Highest Innings	**50ov**	177	A.J.Wright	v	Scotland	Bristol	1997
	40ov	153	C.M.Spearman	v	Warwicks	Gloucester	2003
	T20	126*	M.Klinger	v	Essex	Bristol	2015
Best Bowling	**50ov**	6-13	M.J.Proctor	v	Hampshire	Southampton[1]	1977
	40ov	7-29	D.A.Payne	v	Essex	Chelmsford	2010
	T20	5-16	T.M.J.Smith	v	Warwicks	Birmingham	2020

HAMPSHIRE

Formation of Present Club: 12 August 1863
Inaugural First-Class Match: 1864
Colours: Blue, Gold and White
Badge: Tudor Rose and Crown
County Champions: (2) 1961, 1973
NatWest/C&G/FP Trophy Winners: (3) 1991, 2005, 2009
Benson and Hedges Cup Winners: (2) 1988, 1992
Sunday League Winners: (3) 1975, 1978, 1986
Clydesdale Bank Winners: (1) 2012
Royal London One-Day Cup: (1) 2018
Twenty20 Cup Winners: (2) 2010, 2012

CEO: David Mann, The Ageas Bowl, Botley Road, West End, Southampton SO30 3XH • Tel: 023 8047 2002 • Email: enquiries@ageasbowl.com • Web: www.ageasbowl.com • Twitter: @hantscricket (97,576 followers)

Cricket Operations Manager: Tim Tremlett. **Director of Cricket**: Giles White. **1st XI Manager**: Adrian Birrell. **1st XI Assistant Coach**: Jimmy Adams. **Batting Lead Coach**: Tony Middleton. **Bowling Lead Coach**: Graeme Welch. **Captain**: J.M.Vince. **Overseas Players**: K.J.Abbott and Mohammad Abbas. **2022 Testimonial**: None. **Head Groundsman**: Simon Lee. **Scorer**: Alan Mills. **Blast Team Name**: Hampshire Hawks. ‡ New registration. NQ Not qualified for England.

NQ**ABBOTT, Kyle** John (Kearnsey C, KZN), b Empangeni, South Africa 18 Jun 1987. 6'3½". RHB, RFM. Squad No 87. KwaZulu-Natal 2008-09 to 2009-10. Dolphins 2008-09 to 2014-15. Hampshire debut 2014; cap 2017. Worcestershire 2016. Boland 2021-22. IPL: KXIP 2016. Middlesex 2015 (T20 only). **Tests** (SA): 11 (2012-13 to 2016-17); HS 17 v A (Adelaide) 2016-17; BB 7-29 v P (Centurion) 2012-13. **LOI** (SA): 28 (2012-13 to 2016-17); HS 23 v Z (Bulawayo) 2014; BB 4-21 v Ire (Canberra) 2014-15. **IT20** (SA): 21 (2012-13 to 2015-16); HS 9* v NZ (Centurion) 2015; BB 3-20 v B (Dhaka) 2015. F-c Tours (SA): A 2016-17; I 2015-16. HS 97* v Lancs (Manchester) 2017. 50 wkts (3+1): 72 (2019). BB 9-40 (17-86 match) v Somerset (Southampton) 2019 – 4th best match figures in CC history. Hat-trick v Worcs (Worcester) 2018. LO HS 56 v Surrey (Oval) 2017 (RLC). LO BB 5-43 v Worcs (Southampton) 2021 (RLC). T20 HS 30. T20 BB 5-14.

ALBERT, Toby Edward (Park House S), b Basingstoke 12 Nov 2001. 6'1". RHB, WK. Squad No 15. Hampshire 2nd XI debut 2021. Awaiting f-c debut. T20 HS 13.

ALSOP, Thomas Philip (Lavington S), b High Wycombe, Bucks 26 Nov 1995. Younger brother of O.J.Alsop (Wiltshire 2010-12). 5'11". LHB, WK, occ SLA. Squad No 9. Debut (Hampshire) 2014; cap 2021. MCC 2017. F-c Tours (EL): SL 2016-17. UAE 2016-17 (v Afg). HS 150 v Warwks (Birmingham) 2019. BB 2-59 v Yorks (Leeds) 2016. LO HS 130* v Glamorgan (Southampton) 2019 (RLC). T20 HS 85.

BARKER, Keith Hubert Douglas (Moorhead HS; Fulwood C, Preston), b Manchester 21 Oct 1986. Son of K.H.Barker (British Guiana 1960-61 to 1963-64). Played football for Blackburn Rovers and Rochdale. 6'3". LHB, LMF. Squad No 13. Warwickshire 2009-18; cap 2013. Hampshire debut 2019; cap 2021. HS 125 Wa v Surrey (Guildford) 2013. H HS 84 v Middx (Lord's) 2021. 50 wkts (3); most – 62 (2016). BB 7-46 v Notts (Southampton) 2021. LO HS 56 Wa v Scotland (Birmingham) 2011 (CB40). LO BB 4-33 Wa v Scotland (Birmingham) 2010 (CB40). T20 HS 46. T20 BB 4-19.

‡**BROWN, Ben** Christopher (Ardingly C), b Crawley, Sussex 23 Nov 1988. 5'8". RHB, WK. Squad No 10. Sussex 2007-21; cap 2014; captain 2017-20. 1000 runs (2); most – 1031 (2015, 2018). HS 163 Sx v Durham (Hove) 2014. BB 1-48 Sx v Essex (Colchester) 2016. LO HS 105 Sx v Middx (Hove) 2021 (RLC). T20 HS 68.

CRANE, Mason Sidney (Lancing C), b Shoreham-by-Sea, Sussex 18 Feb 1997. 5'10". RHB, LB. Squad No 32. Debut (Hampshire) 2015; cap 2021. NSW 2016-17. MCC 2017. London Spirit 2021. **Test**: 1 (2017-18); HS 4 and BB 1-193 v A (Sydney) 2017-18. **IT20**: 2 (2017); HS – ; BB 1-38 v SA (Cardiff) 2017. F-c Tours: A 2017-18; WI 2017-18 (EL). HS 29 v Somerset (Taunton) 2017. BB 5-35 v Warwks (Southampton) 2015. LO HS 28* v Somerset (Lord's) 2019 (RLC). LO BB 4-30 v Middx (Southampton) 2015 (RLC). T20 HS 12*. T20 BB 3-15.

CURRIE, Scott William (St Edward's RC & C of E S), b Poole, Dorset 2 May 2001. Younger brother of B.J.Currie (Dorset 2016 to date). 6'5". RHB, RMF. Squad No 44. Debut (Hampshire) 2020. Hampshire 2nd XI debut 2018. Dorset 2017-19. HS 38 v Kent (Canterbury) 2020. BB 4-109 v Surrey (Oval) 2021. LO HS 8 and LO BB 3-58 v Essex (Southampton) 2021 (RLC). T20 HS 3. T20 BB 4-24.

DAWSON, Liam Andrew (John Bentley S, Calne), b Swindon, Wilts 1 Mar 1990. 5'8". RHB, SLA. Squad No 8. Debut (Hampshire) 2007; cap 2013. Mountaineers 2011-12. Essex 2015 (on loan). Wiltshire 2006-07. **Tests**: 3 (2016-17 to 2017); HS 66* v I (Chennai) 2016-17; BB 2-34 v SA (Lord's) 2017. **LOI**: 3 (2016 to 2018-19); HS 10 and BB 2-70 v P (Cardiff) 2016. **IT20**: 8 (2016 to 2021-22); HS 10 v NZ (Hamilton) 2017-18; BB 3-27 v SL (Southampton) 2016. F-c Tour: I 2016-17. HS 169 v Somerset (Southampton) 2011. BB 7-51 Mountaineers v ME (Mutare) 2011-12 (also scored 110* in same match). H BB 5-29 v Leics (Southampton) 2012. LO HS 113* SJD v Kalabagan (Savar) 2014-15. LO BB 6-47 v Sussex (Southampton) 2015 (RLC). T20 HS 82. T20 BB 5-17.

DONALD, Aneurin Henry Thomas (Pontarddulais CS), b Swansea, Glamorgan 20 Dec 1996. 6'2". RHB, OB. Squad No 12. Glamorgan 2014-18. Hampshire debut 2019. Wales MC 2012. No 1st XI appearances in 2020 and 2021 due to injury. 1000 runs (1): 1088 (2016). HS 234 Gm v Derbys (Colwyn Bay) 2016, in 123 balls, equalling world record for fastest 200, inc 15 sixes, going from 0-127* between lunch and tea, and 127-234 after tea. H HS 173 v Warwks (Southampton) 2019, sharing H record 5th wkt partnership of 262 with I.G.Holland. LO HS 57 v Somerset (Taunton) 2019 (RLC). T20 HS 76.

‡[NQ]**ELLIS, Nathan** Trevor, b Greenacre, NSW, Australia 22 Sep 1994. 6'0". RHB, RMF. Tasmania debut 2019-20. IPL: PK 2021. Big Bash: HH 2018-19 to date. **IT20** (A): 2 (2021); HS 1 v B (Mirpur) 2021; BB 3-34 v B (Mirpur) 2021 – separate matches. HS 41 Tas v WA (Adelaide, P25) 2020-21. BB 6-43 Tas v NSW (Hobart) 2019-20. LO HS 31 Tas v NSW (Hobart) 2020-21. LO BB 5-38 Tas v NSW (Sydney, NS) 2019-20. T20 HS 20. T20 BB 4-34.

FULLER, James Kerr (Otago U, NZ), b Cape Town, South Africa 24 Jan 1990. UK passport. 6'3". RHB, RFM. Squad No 26. Otago 2009-10 to 2012-13. Gloucestershire 2011-15; cap 2011. Middlesex 2016-18. Hampshire debut 2019. HS 93 M v Somerset (Taunton) 2016. H HS 54* v Yorks (Leeds) 2019. BB 6-24 (10-79 match) Otago v Wellington (Dunedin) 2012-13. CC BB 6-47 Gs v Surrey (Oval) 2014. H BB 4-17 v Surrey (Arundel) 2020. Hat-tricks (2): Gs v Worcs (Cheltenham) 2013; v Surrey (Arundel) 2020. LO HS 55* v Somerset (Lord's) 2019 (RLC). LO BB 6-35 M v Netherlands (Amstelveen) 2012 (CB40). T20 HS 53*. T20 BB 6-28 M v Hants (Southampton) 2018 – M record.

GUBBINS, Nicholas Richard Trail (Radley C; Leeds U), b Richmond, Surrey 31 Dec 1993. 6'0½". LHB, LB. Squad No 18. Leeds/Bradford MCCU 2013-15. Middlesex 2014-21; cap 2016. Hampshire debut 2021. Tuskers 2021-22. F-c Tours (EL): WI 2017-18; SL 2016-17; UAE 2016-17 (v Afg), 2018-19 (v PA). 1000 runs (1): 1409 (2016). HS 201* M v Lancs (Lord's) 2016. H HS 137* v Glos (Cheltenham) 2021. BB 4-41 Tuskers v ME (Harare) 2021-22. LO HS 141 M v Sussex (Hove) 2015 (RLC). LO BB 4-38 v Sussex (Southampton) 2021 (RLC). T20 HS 53. T20 BB 1-22.

HOLLAND, Ian Gabriel (Ringwood Secondary C, Melbourne), b Stevens Point, Wisconsin, USA 3 Oct 1990. 6'0". RHB, RMF. Squad No 22. England qualified at the start of the 2020 season. Victoria 2015-16. Hampshire debut 2017; cap 2021. **LOI** (USA): 8 (2019-20); HS 75 v Nepal (Kirtipur) 2019-20; BB 3-11 v UAE (Dubai, ICCA) 2019-20. **IT20** (USA): 6 (2021-22); HS 39* v Bahamas (Coolidge) 2021-22; BB 2-3 v Panama (Coolidge) 2021-22. HS 146* v Middx (Southampton) 2021. BB 4-16 v Somerset (Southampton) 2017. LO HS 75 (*see LOI*). LO BB 4-12 v Kent (Beckenham) 2021 (RLC). T20 HS 65. T20 BB 2-3.

‡NQ**McDERMOTT, Ben**jamin Reginald, b Caboolture, Queensland, Australia 12 Dec 1994. Son of C.J.McDermott (Queensland and Australia 1983-84 to 1995-96); younger brother of A.C.McDermott (Queensland 2009-10 to 2014-15). 6'0". RHB, WK, occ RM. Squad No 28. Queensland 2014-15. Tasmania 2015-16 to date. Derbyshire 2021. Big Bash: BH 2013-14; MR 2015-16; HH 2016-17 to date. **LOI** (A): 2 (2021); HS 28 v WI (Bridgetown) 2021. **IT20** (A): 22 (2018-19 to 2021-22); HS 53 v SL (Sydney) 2021-22. HS 107* Aus A v Indians (Sydney) 2020-21. CC HS 25 De v Worcs (Worcester) 2021. BB –. LO HS 133 Tas v WA (Hobart) 2021-22. T20 HS 127.

McMANUS, Lewis David (Clayesmore S, Bournemouth; Exeter U), b Poole, Dorset 9 Oct 1994. 5'10". RHB, WK. Squad No 18. Debut (Hampshire) 2015; cap 2021. Dorset 2011-19. HS 132* v Surrey (Southampton) 2016. LO HS 50 v Essex (Southampton) 2021 (RLC). T20 HS 60*.

MIDDLETON, Fletcha Scott (Wyvern C), b Winchester 21 Jan 2002. Son of T.C.Middleton (Hampshire 1984-95). 5'8½". RHB, OB. Squad No 19. Hampshire 2nd XI debut 2018. Awaiting f-c debut. LO HS 16 v Durham (Chester-le-St) 2021 (RLC) – only 1st XI appearance.

NQ**MOHAMMAD ABBAS**, b Sialkot, Pakistan 10 Mar 1990. 5'11". RHB, RMF. Squad No 38. Sialkot 2008-09 to 2012-13. KRL 2015-16 to 2016-17. SNGPL 2017-18 to 2018-19. Leicestershire 2018-19; cap 2018. Southern Punjab 2019-20 to date. Hampshire debut 2021. **Tests** (P): 25 (2017 to 2021); HS 29 v A (Adelaide) 2019-20; BB 5-33 v A (Abu Dhabi) 2018-19. **LOI** (P): 3 (2018-19); HS – ; BB 1-44 v A (Sharjah) 2018-19. F-c Tours (P): E 2018, 2020; A 2019-20; SA 2018-19; WI 2017, 2021; NZ 2020-21; Ire 2018. HS 40 and BB 8-46 (14-93 match) KRL v Karachi Whites (Karachi) 2016-17. CC HS 32* Le v Sussex (Hove) 2018. H HS 6 (twice). 50 wkts (1+2); most – 71 (2016-17). CC BB 6-11 v Middx (Southampton) 2021, inc hat-trick. LO HS 15* KRL v HB (Karachi) 2016-17. LO BB 4-31 KRL v SNGPL (Karachi) 2016-17. T20 HS 15*. T20 BB 3-22.

ORGAN, Felix Spencer (Canford S), b Sydney, Australia 2 Jun 1999. 5'9". RHB, OB. Squad No 3. Debut (Hampshire) 2017. Hampshire 2nd XI debut 2015. Dorset 2019. HS 100 v Kent (Southampton) 2019. BB 5-25 v Surrey (Southampton) 2019. LO HS 79 v Durham (Chester-le-St) 2021 (RLC). LO BB 2-43 v Sussex (Southampton) 2021 (RLC). T20 HS 9. T20 BB 2-21.

PETRIE, Harry William (Wellington C), b Wycombe, Bucks 6 Sep 2002. 6'3". RHB, RFM. Squad No 30. Hampshire 2nd XI debut 2021. Awaiting 1st XI debut.

PREST, Thomas James (Canford S), b Wimborne, Dorset 24 Mar 2003. 5'11". RHB, OB. Debut (Hampshire) 2021. Hampshire 2nd XI debut 2019. Dorset 2019. HS 18 v Glos (Cheltenham) 2021. LO HS 41 and LO BB 2-28 v Glos (Bristol) 2021 (RLC). T20 HS 59*.

TURNER, John Andrew (Hilton C, Johannesburg), b Johannesburg, South Africa 10 Apr 2001. 6'1". RHB, RFM. Squad No 6. Hampshire 2nd XI debut 2021. Awaiting f-c debut. LO HS 6* v Essex (Southampton) 2021 (RLC). LO BB 3-44 v Worcs (Southampton) 2021 (RLC).

VINCE, James Michael (Warminster S), b Cuckfield, Sussex 14 Mar 1991. 6'2". RHB, RM. Squad No 14. Debut (Hampshire) 2009; cap 2013; captain 2016 to date. Wiltshire 2007-08. Big Bash: ST 2016-17 to 2017-18; SS 2018-19 to date. Southern Brave 2021. **Tests**: 13 (2016 to 2017-18); HS 83 v A (Brisbane) 2017-18; BB –. **LOI**: 19 (2015 to 2021); HS 102 v P (Birmingham) 2021; BB 1-18 v Ire (Southampton) 2020. **IT20**: 17 (2015-16 to 2021-22); HS 59 v NZ (Christchurch) 2019-20. F-c Tours: A 2017-18; SA 2014-15 (EL); NZ 2017-18; SL 2013-14 (EL). 1000 runs (2); most – 1525 (2014). HS 240 v Essex (Southampton) 2014. BB 5-41 v Loughborough MCCU (Southampton) 2013. CC BB 2-2 v Lancs (Southport) 2013. LO HS 190 v Glos (Southampton) 2019 (RLC) – H record. LO BB 1-18 EL v Australia A (Sydney) 2012-13 and (*see LOI*). T20 HS 107*. T20 BB 1-5.

WEATHERLEY, Joe James (King Edward VI S, Southampton), b Winchester 19 Jan 1997. 6'1". RHB, OB. Squad No 5. Debut (Hampshire) 2016; cap 2021. Kent 2017 (on loan). HS 126* v Lancs (Manchester) 2018. BB 1-2 v Notts (Southampton) 2018. LO HS 105* v Kent (Southampton) 2018 (RLC). LO BB 4-25 v T&T (Cave Hill) 2017-18. T20 HS 71. T20 BB –.

WHEAL, Bradley Thomas James (Clifton C), b Durban, South Africa 28 Aug 1996. 5'9". RHB, RMF. Squad No 58. Debut (Hampshire) 2015; cap 2021. London Spirit 2021. **LOI** (Scot): 13 (2015-16 to 2019); HS 14 v Ire (Harare) 2017-18; BB 3-34 v WI (Harare) 2017-18. **IT20** (Scot): 14 (2015-16 to 2021-22); HS 2* (twice); BB 3-20 v Hong Kong (Mong Kok) 2015-16. HS 46* v Warwks (Birmingham) 2021. BB 6-51 v Notts (Nottingham) 2016. LO HS 18* v CC&C (Bridgetown) 2017-18. LO BB 4-38 v Kent (Southampton) 2016 (RLC). T20 HS 16. T20 BB 4-17.

WHITELEY, Ross Andrew (Repton S), b Sheffield, Yorks 13 Sep 1988. 6'2". LHB, LM. Squad No 4. Derbyshire 2008-13. Worcestershire 2013-21; cap 2013. Southern Brave 2021. HS 130* De v Kent (Derby) 2011. BB 2-6 De v Hants (Derby) 2012. LO HS 131 Wo v Leics (Leicester) 2019 (RLC). LO BB 4-58 Wo v West Indies A (Worcester) 2018. T20 HS 91*. T20 BB 1-10.

WOOD, Christopher Philip (Alton C), b Basingstoke 27 June 1990. 6'2". RHB, LM. Squad No 25. Debut (Hampshire) 2010; cap 2018. London Spirit 2021. HS 105* v Leics (Leicester) 2012. BB 5-39 v Kent (Canterbury) 2014. LO HS 41 v Essex (Southampton) 2013 (Y40). LO BB 5-22 v Glamorgan (Cardiff) 2012 (CB40). T20 HS 27. T20 BB 5-32.

RELEASED/RETIRED

(Having made a County 1st XI appearance in 2021)

[NQ]**De GRANDHOMME, Colin**, b Harare, Zimbabwe 22 Jul 1986. Son of L.L.de Grandhomme (Rhodesia B and Zimbabwe 1979-80 to 1987-88). RHB, RMF. Zimbabwe A 2005-06. Auckland 2006-07 to 2017-18. N Districts 2018-19 to date. Hampshire 2021. Warwickshire 2017-18 (T20 only). IPL: KKR 2017; RCB 2018-19. Southern Brave 2021. **Tests** (NZ): 28 (2016-17 to 2021-22); HS 120* v SA (Christchurch) 2021-22; BB 6-41 v P (Christchurch) 2016-17 – on debut. **LOI** (NZ): 42 (2011-12 to 2019-20); HS 74* v P (Hamilton) 2017-18; BB 3-26 v I (Hamilton) 2018-19. **IT20** (NZ): 41 (2011-12 to 2021); HS 59 v SL (Pallekele) 2019; BB 2-22 v SA (Auckland) 2016-17. F-c Tours (NZ): E 2014 (NZ A), 2021; A 2019-20; SA 2005-06 (Z U23); SL 2019; UAE 2018-19 (v P). HS 174* v Surrey (Southampton) 2021. BB 6-24 Auckland v Wellington (Auckland) 2013-14. LO HS 151 NZ A v Northants (Northampton) 2014. LO BB 4-37 Auckland v Wellington (Wellington) 2015-16. T20 HS 86. T20 BB 3-4.

NORTHEAST, S.A. – *see GLAMORGAN.*

SCRIVEN, T.A.R. – *see LEICESTERSHIRE.*

[NQ]**SHORT, D'Arcy** John Matthew, b Katherine, N Territory, Australia 9 Aug 1990. 5'11". LHB, SLC. W Australia 2016-17 to date. IPL: RR 2018. Big Bash: HH 2016-17 to date. Durham 2019 (T20 only). Hampshire 2021 (T20 only). Trent Rockets 2021. **LOI** (A): 8 (2018 to 2019-20); HS 69 v SA (Bloemfontein) 2019-20; BB –. **IT20** (A): 23 (2017-18 to 2020-21); HS 76 v NZ (Auckland) 2017-18 and 76 v P (Harare) 2018; BB 1-13 v P (Abu Dhabi) 2018-19. HS 67 WA v Tas (Hobart) 2021-22. BB 3-78 WA v Vic (Melbourne) 2017-18. LO HS 257 (inc world record 23 sixes) WA v Q (Sydney, HO) 2018-19 – 3rd highest l-o score on record. LO BB 3-53 WA v Vic (Perth) 2017-18. T20 HS 122*. T20 BB 5-21.

STEVENSON, Ryan Anthony (King Edward VI Community C), b Torquay, Devon 2 Apr 1992. 6'2". RHB, RMF. Hampshire 2015-20. Devon 2015. HS 51 v Surrey (Oval) 2019. BB 4-70 v Middx (Radlett) 2020. LO HS 0. LO BB 1-28 v Essex (Southampton) 2016 (RLC). T20 HS 17. T20 BB 2-28.

A.S.Dale and B.J.Taylor left the staff without making a County 1st XI appearance in 2021.

COUNTY CAPS AWARDED IN 2021

Derbyshire	–
Durham	–
Essex	P.M.Siddle
Glamorgan	K.S.Carlson, M.G.Neser, W.T.Root
Gloucestershire	K.C.Brathwaite, D.C.Goodman, G.D.Phillips, O.J.Price, J.A.Tattersall, J.D.Warner, B.J.Wells, Zafar Gohar
Hampshire	T.P.Alsop, K.H.D.Barker, M.S.Crane, I.G.Holland, L.D.McManus, J.J.Weatherley, B.T.J.Wheal
Kent	J.A.Leaning, M.E.Milnes
Lancashire	J.J.Bohannon, S.Mahmood
Leicestershire	L.J.Hill, C.J.C.Wright
Middlesex	–
Northamptonshire	R.S.Vasconcelos, G.G.White
Nottinghamshire	J.M.Clarke, B.A.Hutton, T.J.Moores, D.Paterson, B.T.Slater
Somerset	J.H.Davey, M.T.C.Waller
Surrey	H.M.Amla
Sussex	T.J.Haines
Warwickshire	T.T.Bresnan, D.R.Briggs, M.G.K.Burgess
Worcestershire (colours)	J.O.Baker, A.S.Joseph, G.H.Roderick, I.S.Sodhi
Yorkshire	H.C.Brook

Durham abolished their capping system after 2005. Gloucestershire award caps on first-class debut. Worcestershire award club colours on Championship debut. Glamorgan's capping system is now based on a player's number of appearances and not on his performances.

HAMPSHIRE 2021

RESULTS SUMMARY

	Place	Won	Lost	Drew	NR
LV= Insurance County Champ (Div 1)	4th	6	3	5	
Royal London One-Day Cup (Group 1)	6th	3	4		1
Vitality Blast (South Group)	SF	7	6		3

LV= INSURANCE COUNTY CHAMPIONSHIP AVERAGES
BATTING AND FIELDING

Cap		*M*	*I*	*NO*	*HS*	*Runs*	*Avge*	*100*	*50*	*Ct/St*
2013	J.M.Vince	13	20	–	231	816	40.80	1	4	13
2021	I.G.Holland	14	24	1	146*	766	33.30	2	4	8
2019	S.A.Northeast	8	13	2	118	358	32.54	1	2	–
	N.R.T.Gubbins	6	11	2	137*	255	28.33	1	1	6
2021	K.H.D.Barker	10	15	1	84	379	27.07	–	3	1
2021	L.D.McManus	11	14	2	91	320	26.66	–	2	28/1
2021	T.P.Alsop	14	24	2	149	564	25.63	2	–	14
	L.A.Dawson	12	20	2	152*	449	24.94	1	1	17
	F.S.Organ	6	10	–	67	213	21.30	–	1	6
2021	J.J.Weatherley	13	22	–	78	406	18.45	–	1	21
2021	B.T.J.Wheal	13	16	6	46*	181	18.10	–	–	2
	K.J.Abbott	11	12	3	58	148	16.44	–	1	1
2021	M.S.Crane	6	7	1	28	92	15.33	–	–	2
	J.K.Fuller	2	4	–	21	34	8.50	–	–	–
	Mohammad Abbas	10	14	7	6	28	4.00	–	–	2

Also batted: S.W.Currie (1 match) 4, 1 (1 ct); C.de Grandhomme (2) 174*, 0, 12* (2 ct); T.J.Prest (2) 18 (1 ct); C.T.Steel (1) 15, 14.

BOWLING

	O	*M*	*R*	*W*	*Avge*	*Best*	*5wI*	*10wM*
Mohammad Abbas	309.5	113	651	41	15.87	6-11	3	–
K.H.D.Barker	310	88	755	41	18.41	7-46	3	–
K.J.Abbott	329.3	87	996	46	21.65	6-44	3	1
M.S.Crane	195.5	39	587	23	25.52	5-41	1	–
B.T.J.Wheal	298.5	62	882	34	25.94	4-59	–	–
L.A.Dawson	257	55	624	18	34.66	5-45	1	–
Also bowled:								
C.de Grandhomme	37	20	68	6	11.33	4-31	–	–
F.S.Organ	73	20	205	8	25.62	3-22	–	–
I.G.Holland	147.1	35	433	6	72.16	3-19	–	–

S.W.Currie 27.5-2-109-4; J.K.Fuller 17-4-37-3; T.J.Prest 1-0-5-0; J.M.Vince 13-1-85-1; J.J.Weatherley 9-2-22-1.

The First-Class Averages (pp 220–232) give the records of Hampshire players in all first-class county matches, with the exception of C.de Grandhomme, N.R.T.Gubbins, S.A.Northeast and C.T.Steel, whose first-class figures for Hampshire are as above.

HAMPSHIRE RECORDS

FIRST-CLASS CRICKET

Highest Total	For 714-5d		v	Notts	Southampton[2]	2005
	V 742		by	Surrey	The Oval	1909
Lowest Total	For 15		v	Warwicks	Birmingham	1922
	V 23		by	Yorkshire	Middlesbrough	1965
Highest Innings	For 316	R.H.Moore	v	Warwicks	Bournemouth	1937
	V 303*	G.A.Hick	for	Worcs	Southampton[1]	1997

Highest Partnership for each Wicket

1st	347	V.P.Terry/C.L.Smith	v	Warwicks	Birmingham	1987
2nd	373	J.H.K.Adams/M.A.Carberry	v	Somerset	Taunton	2011
3rd	523	M.A.Carberry/N.D.McKenzie	v	Yorkshire	Southampton[2]	2011
4th	367	J.H.K.Adams/S.M.Ervine	v	Warwicks	Southampton[2]	2017
5th	262	I.G.Holland/A.H.T.Donald	v	Warwicks	Southampton[2]	2019
6th	411	R.M.Poore/E.G.Wynyard	v	Somerset	Taunton	1899
7th	325	G.Brown/C.H.Abercrombie	v	Essex	Leyton	1913
8th	257	N.Pothas/A.J.Bichel	v	Glos	Cheltenham	2005
9th	230	D.A.Livingstone/A.T.Castell	v	Surrey	Southampton[1]	1962
10th	192	H.A.W.Bowell/W.H.Livsey	v	Worcs	Bournemouth	1921

Best Bowling	For	9- 25	R.M.H.Cottam	v	Lancashire	Manchester	1965
(Innings)	V	10- 46	W.Hickton	for	Lancashire	Manchester	1870
Best Bowling	For	17- 86	K.J.Abbott	v	Somerset	Southampton[2]	2019
(Match)	V	17-103	W.Mycroft	for	Derbyshire	Southampton	1876

Most Runs – Season	2854	C.P.Mead	(av 79.27)	1928
Most Runs – Career	48892	C.P.Mead	(av 48.84)	1905-36
Most 100s – Season	12	C.P.Mead		1928
Most 100s – Career	138	C.P.Mead		1905-36
Most Wkts – Season	190	A.S.Kennedy	(av 15.61)	1922
Most Wkts – Career	2669	D.Shackleton	(av 18.23)	1948-69
Most Career W-K Dismissals	700	R.J.Parks	(630 ct; 70 st)	1980-92
Most Career Catches in the Field	629	C.P.Mead		1905-36

LIMITED-OVERS CRICKET

Highest Total	**50ov**	371-4		v	Glamorgan	Southampton[1]	1975
	40ov	353-8		v	Middlesex	Lord's	2005
	T20	249-8		v	Derbyshire	Derby	2017
Lowest Total	**50ov**	50		v	Yorkshire	Leeds	1991
	40ov	43		v	Essex	Basingstoke	1972
	T20	85		v	Sussex	Southampton[2]	2008
Highest Innings	**50ov**	190	J.M.Vince	v	Glos	Southampton[2]	2019
	40ov	172	C.G.Greenidge	v	Surrey	Southampton[1]	1987
	T20	124*	M.J.Lumb	v	Essex	Southampton[2]	2009
Best Bowling	**50ov**	7-30	P.J.Sainsbury	v	Norfolk	Southampton[1]	1965
	40ov	6-20	T.E.Jesty	v	Glamorgan	Cardiff	1975
	T20	6-19	Shaheen Shah Afridi	v	Middlesex	Southampton[2]	2020

[1] County Ground (Northlands Road) [2] Ageas Bowl

KENT

Formation of Present Club: 1 March 1859
Substantial Reorganisation: 6 December 1870
Inaugural First-Class Match: 1864
Colours: Maroon and White
Badge: White Horse on a Red Ground
County Champions: (6) 1906, 1909, 1910, 1913, 1970, 1978
Joint Champions: (1) 1977
Gillette Cup Winners: (2) 1967, 1974
Benson and Hedges Cup Winners: (3) 1973, 1976, 1978
Pro 40/National League (Div 1) Winners: (1) 2001
Sunday League Winners: (4) 1972, 1973, 1976, 1995
Twenty20 Cup Winners: (2) 2007, 2021

Cricket Chief Executive: Simon Storey, The Spitfire Ground, Old Dover Road, Canterbury, CT1 3NZ • Tel: 01227 456886 • Email: feedback@kentcricket.co.uk • Web: www.kentcricket.co.uk • Twitter: @kentcricket (100,334 followers)

Director of Cricket: Paul Downton. **Head Coach**: Matt Walker. **Batting Coach**: Ryan ten Doeschate. **Bowling Coach**: Simon Cook. **Captain**: S.W.Billings. **Vice-Captain**: D.J.Bell-Drummond. **Overseas Player**: J.M.Bird, M.J.Henry, G.F.Linde and Qais Ahmad. **2022 Testimonial**: None. **Head Groundsman**: Adrian Llong. **Scorers**: Lorne Hart. **Blast Team Name**: Kent Spitfires. ‡ New registration. [NQ] Not qualified for England.

BELL-DRUMMOND, Daniel James (Millfield S), b Lewisham, London 4 Aug 1993. 5'10". RHB, RMF. Squad No 23. Debut (Kent) 2011; cap 2015. MCC 2014, 2018. Birmingham Phoenix 2021. 1000 runs (1): 1058 (2014). HS 206* v Loughborough MCCU (Canterbury) 2016. CC HS 166 v Warwks (Canterbury) 2019. BB 3-47 v Middx (Canterbury) 2021. LO HS 171* EL v Sri Lanka A (Canterbury) 2016. LO BB 2-22 v Surrey (Oval) 2019 (RLC). T20 HS 112*. T20 BB 2-19.

BILLINGS, Samuel William (Haileybury S; Loughborough U), b Pembury 15 Jun 1991. 5'11". RHB, WK. Squad No 7. Loughborough MCCU 2011, scoring 131 v Northants (Loughborough) on f-c debut. Kent debut 2011; cap 2015; captain 2018 to date. MCC 2015. IPL: DD 2016-17; CSK 2018-19. Big Bash: SS 2016-17 to 2017-18; ST 2020-21 to date. Oval Invincibles 2021. **Tests**: 1 (2021-22); HS 29 v A (Hobart) 2021-22. **LOI**: 25 (2015 to 2021); HS 118 v A (Manchester) 2020. **IT20**: 37, inc 1 for ICC World XI (2015 to 2021-22); HS 87 v WI (Basseterre) 2018-19 – world record IT20 score by a No 6 batsman. F-c Tours (EL): I 2018-19; UAE 2018-19 (v P). HS 171 v Glos (Bristol) 2016. LO HS 175 EL v Pakistan A (Canterbury) 2016. T20 HS 95*.

‡[NQ]**BIRD, Jackson** Munro (St Pius X C, Sydney; St Ignatius C, Riverview), b Paddington, Sydney, Australia 11 Dec 1986. RHB, RFM. Tasmania 2011-12 to date. Hampshire 2015. Nottinghamshire 2016; cap 2016. Big Bash: MS 2011-12 to 2018-19; SS 2015-16 to date. **Tests** (A): 9 (2012-13 to 2017-18); HS 19* v P (Brisbane) 2016-17; BB 5-59 v NZ (Christchurch) 2015-16. F-c Tours (A): E 2012 (Aus A), 2013, 2019 (Aus A); NZ 2015-16; I 2016-17 (Aus A), SL 2016. HS 64 Tas v WA (Perth) 2020-21. CC HS 23 Nt v Yorks (Nottingham) 2016. 50 wkts (0+2): 53 (2011-12). BB 7-18 Tas v NSW (Hobart) 2020-21. CC BB 4-56 Nt v Surrey (Nottingham) 2016. LO HS 28* Tas v NSW (Hobart) 2020-21. LO BB 6-25 Tas v NSW (Hobart) 2019-20. T20 HS 14*. T20 BB 4-31.

BLAKE, Alexander James (Hayes SS; Leeds Met U), b Farnborough 25 Jan 1989. 6'1". LHB, RMF. Squad No 10. Debut (Kent) 2008; cap 2017. Oval Invincibles 2021. HS 105* v Yorks (Leeds) 2010. BB 2-9 v Pakistanis (Canterbury) 2010. CC BB 1-60 v Hants (Southampton) 2010. LO HS 116 v Somerset (Taunton) 2017 (RLC). LO BB 2-13 v Yorks (Leeds) 2011 (CB40). T20 HS 71*. T20 BB 1-17.

‡**COMPTON, Ben**jamin Garnet (Clifton C, Durban), b Durban, S Africa 29 Mar 1994. Son of P.M.D.Compton (Natal 1979-80); grandson of D.S.C.Compton (Middlesex and England 1936-58); cousin of N.R.D.Compton (Middlesex, Somerset, ME, Worcs and England 2004-17). LHB, OB. Squad No 2. Nottinghamshire 2019-21. Mountaineers 2021-22. Norfolk 2021. HS 109* Mountaineers v MT (Harare) 2021-22. CC HS 20 Nt v Durham (Chester-le-St) 2021. LO HS 102 Mountaineers v MWR (Mutare) 2021-22.

COX, Jordan Matthew (Felsted S), b Margate 21 Oct 2000. 5'8". RHB, WK. Squad No 22. Debut (Kent) 2019. Big Bash: HH 2021-22. Kent 2nd XI debut 2017. England U19 2018-19. HS 238* v Sussex (Canterbury) 2020, sharing K record 2nd wkt partnership of 423 with J.A.Leaning. LO HS 21 v Pakistanis (Beckenham) 2019. T20 HS 64.

CRAWLEY, Zak (Tonbridge S), b Bromley 3 Feb 1998. 6'6". RHB, RM. Squad No 16. Debut (Kent) 2017; cap 2019. London Spirit 2021. YC 2020. *Wisden* 2020. **ECB Central Contract 2021-22. Tests**: 19 (2019-20 to 2021-22); HS 267 v P (Southampton) 2020. **LOI**: 3 (2021); HS 58* v P (Cardiff) 2021. F-c Tours: A 2021-22; SA 2019-20; WI 2021-22; NZ 2019-20; I 2020-21; SL 2019-20, 2020-21. HS (*see Tests*). K HS 168 v Glamorgan (Canterbury) 2018. LO HS 120 v Middx (Canterbury) 2019 (RLC). T20 HS 108*.

DENLY, Joseph Liam (Chaucer TC), b Canterbury 16 Mar 1986. 6'0". RHB, LB. Squad No 6. Kent debut 2004; cap 2008; testimonial 2019. Middlesex 2012-14; cap 2012. MCC 2013. IPL: KKR 2019. Big Bash: SS 2017-18 to 2018-19; BH 2020-21. London Spirit 2021. PCA 2018. **Tests**: 15 (2018-19 to 2020); HS 94 v A (Oval) 2019; BB 2-42 v SA (Cape Town) 2019-20. **LOI**: 16 (2009 to 2019-20); HS 87 v SA (Cape Town) 2019-20; BB 1-24 v Ire (Dublin) 2019. **IT20**: 13 (2009 to 2020); HS 30 v WI (Gros Islet) 2018-19; BB 4-19 v SL (Colombo, RPS) 2018-19. F-c Tours: SA 2019-20; WI 2018-19; NZ 2008-09 (Eng A), 2019-20; I 2007-08 (Eng A); SL 2019-20. 1000 runs (4); most – 1266 (2017). HS 227 v Worcs (Worcester) 2017. BB 4-36 v Derbys (Derby) 2018. LO HS 150* v Glamorgan (Canterbury) 2018 (RLC) – K record. LO BB 4-35 v Jamaica (North Sound) 2017-18. T20 HS 127 v Essex (Chelmsford) 2017 – K record. T20 BB 4-19.

GILCHRIST, Nathan Nicholas (St Stithian's C; King's C, Taunton), b Harare, Zimbabwe 11 Jun 2000. 6'5". RHB, RFM. Squad No 17. Debut (Kent) 2020. Somerset 2nd XI 2016-19. HS 25 v Surrey (Oval) 2020. BB 5-38 v Worcs (Canterbury) 2021. LO HS 8 v Essex (Chelmsford) 2021 (RLC). LO BB 5-45 v Middx (Radlett) 2021.

HAMIDULLAH QADRI (Derby Moor S; Chellaston Ac), b Kandahar, Afghanistan 5 Dec 2000. 5'9". RHB, OB. Squad No 75. Derbyshire 2017-19, taking 5-60 v Glamorgan (Cardiff), the youngest to take 5 wkts on CC debut, and the first born this century to play f-c cricket in England. Kent debut 2020. England U19 2018-19. HS 30* and K BB 1-20 v Sussex (Canterbury) 2021. BB 5-60 (*see above*). LO HS 42* v Durham (Beckenham) 2021 (RLC). LO BB 3-47 v Middx (Radlett) 2021 (RLC). T20 BB –. Youngest to play domestic T20 Blast, aged 16y, 223d.

NQ**HENRY, Matt**hew James (St Bede's C), b Christchurch, New Zealand 14 Dec 1991. RHB, RFM. Canterbury 2010-11 to date. Worcestershire 2016. Kent debut 2018; cap 2018. Derbyshire 2017 (T20 only). IPL: KXIP 2017. **Tests** (NZ): 16 (2015 to 2021-22); HS 66 v A (Christchurch) 2015-16; BB 7-23 v SA (Christchurch) 2021-22. **LOI** (NZ): 55 (2013-14 to 2020-21); HS 48* v P (Wellington) 2015-16; BB 5-30 v P (Abu Dhabi) 2014-15. **IT20** (NZ): 6 (2014-15 to 2016-17); HS 10 v P (Auckland) 2015-16; BB 3-44 v SL (Mt Maunganui) 2015-16. F-c Tours (NZ): E 2014 (NZA), 2015, 2021; A 2015-16, 2019-20; I 2016-17, 2017-18 (NZA); SL 2013-14 (NZA). HS 81 v Derbys (Derby) 2018. 50 wkts (1): 75 (2018). BB 7-23 (*see Tests*). CC BB 7-42 (11-114 match) v Northants (Canterbury) 2018. LO HS 48* (*see LOI*). LO BB 6-45 Canterbury v Auckland (Auckland) 2012-13. T20 HS 44. T20 BB 4-43.

KLAASSEN, Frederick Jack (Sacred Heart C, Auckland, NZ), b Haywards Heath, Sussex 13 Nov 1992. 6'4". RHB, LMF. Squad No 18. England-qualified thanks to UK passport. Debut (Kent) 2019. Manchester Originals 2021. **LOI** (Neth): 10 (2018 to 2021-22); HS 13 v Nepal (Amstelveen) 2018; BB 3-23 v Ire (Utrecht) 2021. **IT20** (Neth): 24 (2018 to 2021-22); HS 13 v Z (Rotterdam) 2019; BB 3-31 v Ire (Al Amerat) 2018-19. HS 14* v Loughborough MCCU (Canterbury) 2019. CC HS 13 v Yorks (Canterbury) 2019. BB 4-44 v Middx (Canterbury) 2020. LO HS 13 (*see LOI*). LO BB 3-23 (*see LOI*). T20 HS 13. T20 BB 4-17.

LEANING, Jack Andrew (Archbishop Holgate's S, York; York C), b Bristol, Glos 18 Oct 1993. 5'10". RHB, RMF. Squad No 34. Yorkshire 2013-19; cap 2016. Kent debut 2020; cap 2021. YC 2015. HS 220* v Sussex (Canterbury) 2020, sharing K record 2nd wkt partnership of 423 with J.M.Cox. BB 2-20 Y v Hants (Southampton) 2019. K BB 2-101 v Lancs (Canterbury) 2021. LO HS 131* Y v Leics (Leicester) 2016 (RLC). LO BB 5-22 Y v Unicorns (Leeds) 2013 (Y40). T20 HS 81*. T20 BB 3-15.

‡[NQ]**LINDE, George** Fredrik (Pretoria U), b Cape Town, South Africa 4 Dec 1991. LHB, SLA. Squad No 27. W Province 2011-12 to date. Cape Cobras 2014-15 to 2020-21. **Tests** (SA): 3 (2019-20 to 2020-21); HS 37 v I (Ranchi) 2019-20; BB 5-64 v P (Rawalpindi) 2020-21. **LOI** (SA): 2 (2021); HS 18 and BB 2-32 v SL (Colombo, RPS) 2021. IT20 (SA): 14 (2020-21 to 2021); HS 29 v E (Paarl) 2020-21; BB 3-23 v P (Johannesburg) 2020-21. F-c Tours (SA): I 2019-20; P 2020-21. HS 148* Cobras v Titans (Cape Town) 2019-20. BB 7-29 Cobras v Knights (Cape Town) 2020-21. LO HS 93* WP v Northerns (Rondebosch) 2015-16. LO BB 6-47 Cobras v Warriors (Oudtshoorn) 2017-18. T20 HS 52*. T20 BB 4-19.

LOGAN, James Edwin Graham (Normanton Freestone HS; Pontefract New C), b Wakefield, Yorks 12 Oct 1997. 6'1". LHB, SLA. Squad No 11. Yorkshire 2018-19. Kent debut 2021. HS 21 and K BB 3-8 v Leics (Leicester) 2021. BB 4-22 Y v Warwks (York) 2019. LO HS 17* v Glos (Beckenham) 2021 (RLC). LO BB 2-45 v Worcs (Worcester) 2021 (RLC). T20 BB 1-4.

MILNES, Matthew Edward (West Bridgford CS; Durham U), b Nottingham 29 Jul 1994. 6'1". RHB, RMF. Squad No 8. Durham MCCU 2014. Nottinghamshire 2018. Kent debut 2019; cap 2021. Welsh Fire 2021. HS 78 v Yorks (Canterbury) 2021. 50 wkts (1): 58 (2019). BB 6-53 v Leics (Leicester) 2021. LO HS 26 and LO BB 5-79 v Hants (Canterbury) 2019 (RLC). T20 HS 13*. T20 BB 5-22.

[NQ]**MUYEYE, Tawanda** Sean (Eastbourne C), b Harare, Zimbabwe 5 March 2001. RHB, OB. Squad No 14. Wisden Schools Cricketer of the Year 2020. Debut (Kent) 2021. HS 89 v Middx (Canterbury) 2021. LO HS 30 v Glos (Beckenham) 2021 (RLC). LO BB –.

O'RIORDAN, Marcus Kevin (Tonbridge S), b Pembury 25 Jan 1998. 5'10". RHB, OB. Squad No 55. Debut (Kent) 2019. Kent 2nd XI debut 2014. HS 52* v Hants (Canterbury) 2020. BB 3-50 v Sussex (Canterbury) 2020. LO HS 60 v Middx (Radlett) 2021 (RLC). LO BB 1-77 v Durham (Beckenham) 2021 (RLC). T20 HS 13*. T20 BB 2-24.

PODMORE, Harry William (Twyford HS), b Hammersmith, London 23 Jul 1994. 6'3". RHB, RMF. Squad No 1. Glamorgan 2016-17 (on loan). Middlesex 2016 to 2016-17. Derbyshire 2017 (on loan). Kent debut 2018; cap 2019. HS 66* De v Sussex (Hove) 2017. K HS 54* v Essex (Canterbury) 2019. 50 wkts (1): 54 (2019). BB 6-36 v Middx (Canterbury) 2018. LO HS 40 v Hants (Canterbury) 2019 (RLC). LO BB 4-57 v Notts (Nottingham) 2018 (RLC). T20 HS 9. T20 BB 3-13.

[NQ]**QAIS AHMAD** Kamawal, b Nangarhar, Afghanistan 15 Aug 2000. RHB, LB. Squad No 32. Speen Ghar Region 2017-18 to 2018-19. Kent debut 2021 (T20 only). Big Bash: HH 2018-19 to 2019-20; MS 2021-22. Welsh Fire 2021. **Tests** (Afg): 1 (2019); HS 14 and BB 1-22 v B (Chittagong) 2019. **LOI** (Afg): 1 (2021-22); BB 3-32 v Neth (Doha) 2021-22. **IT20** (Afg): 2 (2019-20 to 2021-22); HS 8 v B (Mirpur) 2021-22; BB 3-25 v Ire (Greater Noida) 2019-20. HS 46* Afg A v Bangladesh A (Khulna) 2019. BB 7-41 SGR v Band-e-Amir (Ghazi Amanullah Khan) 2019. LO HS 66 Afg Emerging Players v Oman (Colombo, CCC) 2018-19. LO BB 3-21 SGR v Amo Region (Kandahar) 2020-21. T20 HS 50*. T20 BB 5-18.

QUINN, Matthew Richard, b Auckland, New Zealand 28 Feb 1993. RHB, RMF. Squad No 64. Auckland 2012-13 to 2015-16. Essex 2016-20. Kent debut 2021. UK passport. HS 50 Auckland v Canterbury (Auckland) 2013-14. CC HS 16 Ex v Notts (Chelmsford) 2018. K HS 13* v Lancs (Manchester) 2021. BB 7-76 (11-163 match) Ex v Glos (Cheltenham) 2016. K BB 4-54 v Sussex (Hove) 2021. LO HS 36 Auckland v CD (Auckland) 2013-14. LO BB 4-71 v Sussex (Hove) 2016 (RLC). T20 HS 8*. T20 BB 4-20.

ROBINSON, Oliver Graham (Hurtsmere S, Greenwich), b Sidcup 1 Dec 1998. 5'8". RHB, WK, occ RM. Squad No 21. Debut (Kent) 2018. Kent 2nd XI debut 2015. England U19 2017 to 2018. HS 143 v Warwks (Birmingham) 2019. LO HS 75 v Glos (Beckenham) 2021 (RLC). T20 HS 53.

SINGH, Jaskaran (Wilmington Ac), b Denmark Hill, London 19 Sep 2002. RHB, RFM. Squad No 19. Debut (Kent) 2021, dismissing A.G.H.Orr with his fifth ball in f-c cricket. Kent 2nd XI debut 2021. HS 2 and BB 4-51 v Sussex (Canterbury) 2021.

STEVENS, Darren Ian (Hinckley C), b Leicester 30 Apr 1976. 5'11". RHB, RM. Squad No 3. Leicestershire 1997-2004; cap 2002. Kent debut/cap 2005; benefit 2016. MCC 2002. *Wisden* 2020, the oldest to be given the honour since W.E.Astill in 1933. F-c Tour (ECB Acad): SL 2002-03. 1000 runs (3); most – 1304 (2013). HS 237 v Yorks (Leeds) 2019, sharing K record 6th wkt partnership of 346 with S.W.Billings. 50 wkts (4); most – 63 (2017). BB 8-75 v Leics (Canterbury) 2017. LO HS 147 v Glamorgan (Swansea) 2017 (RLC). LO BB 6-25 v Surrey (Beckenham) 2018 (RLC). T20 HS 90. T20 BB 4-14.

STEWART, Grant (All Saints C, Maitland; U of Newcastle), b Kalgoorlie, W Australia 19 Feb 1994. 6'2". RHB, RMF. Squad No 9. England qualified due to Italian mother. Debut (Kent) 2017. **IT20** (Italy): 6 (2021-22); HS 51 v Denmark (Almeria) 2021-22; BB 2-17 v Denmark (Almeria) 2021-22 – separate matches. HS 103 and BB 6-22 v Middx (Canterbury) 2018. LO HS 44 v USA (North Sound) 2017-18. LO BB 3-17 v Guyana (Coolidge) 2017-18. T20 HS 51. T20 BB 3-33.

RELEASED/RETIRED

(Having made a County 1st XI appearance in 2021, even if not formally contracted. Some may return in 2022.)

NQ**CUMMINS, Miguel** Lamar, b St Michael, Barbados 5 Sep 1990. 6'2". LHB, RF. Barbados 2011-12 to 2018-19. Sagicor HPC 2014. Worcestershire 2016. Middlesex 2019-20. Kent 2021. **Tests** (WI): 14 (2016 to 2019); HS 24* v I (Kingston) 2016; BB 6-48 v I (Gros Islet) 2016. **LOI** (WI): 11 (2013-14 to 2017); HS 5 v Afg (Gros Islet) 2017; BB 3-82 v E (Bristol) 2017. F-c Tours (WI): E 2017; NZ 2017-18; I 2013-14 (WIA); SL 2014-15 (WIA); UAE (v P) 2016-17. HS 29* Barbados v Leeward Is (Basseterre) 2015-16. CC HS 28* v Yorks (Leeds) 2021. BB 7-45 Barbados v T&T (Port of Spain) 2012-13. CC BB 7-84 (12-166 match) Wo v Sussex (Hove) 2016. K BB 2-100 v Lancs (Canterbury) 2021. LO HS 20 Barbados v CC&C (Cave Hill) 2018-19. LO BB 4-27 Barbados v Windward Is (Bridgetown) 2017-18. T20 HS 10. T20 BB 3-19.

FINCH, Harry Zachariah (St Richard's Catholic C, Bexhill; Eastbourne C), b Hastings, E.Sussex 10 Feb 1995. 5'8". RHB, RM. Sussex 2013-20. Kent 2021. HS 135* and BB 1-9 Sx v Leeds/Bradford MCCU (Hove) 2016. CC HS 115 v Sussex (Canterbury) 2021. CC BB 1-30 Sx v Northants (Arundel) 2016. LO HS 108 Sx v Hants (Hove) 2018 (RLC). LO BB –. T20 HS 47.

GORDON, Joseph Archie, b Coffs Harbour, NSW, Australia 18 May 2002. RHB, RM. Kent 2021. Kent 2nd XI debut 2019. HS 8 v Sussex (Canterbury) 2021. LO HS 9 v Hants (Beckenham) 2021 (RLC).

HOOPER, Elliot Owen (Bede's, Upper Dicker; Loughborough U), b Eastbourne, Sussex 22 Mar 1996. LHB, SLA. Sussex 2019. Kent 2021 (T20 only). HS 20 and BB 1-65 Sx v Middx (Hove) 2019. T20 HS 0*. T20 BB 3-24.

HOUILLON, Harry Fraser (Sevenoaks S; Fitzwilliam C, Cambridge), b 12 Dec 2001 Greenwich. RHB, WK. Kent 2021. Kent 2nd XI debut 2019. Cambridge U 2021 (not f-c). HS 9 v Sussex (Canterbury) 2021.

NQ**KUHN, Heino** Gunther, b Piet Relief, Mpumalanga, South Africa 1 Apr 1984. 5'10". RHB, WK. Northerns 2004-05 to 2015-16. Titans 2005-06 to 2018-19. Kent 2018-21; cap 2018. North West 2021-22. **Tests** (SA): 4 (2017); HS 34 v E (Nottingham) 2017. **IT20** (SA): 7 (2009-10 to 2016-17); HS 29 v SL (Johannesburg) 2016-17. F-c Tours (SAA): E 2017 (SA); A 2014; SL 2010; Z 2016; B 2010; Ire 2012. 1000 runs (0+1): 1159 (2015-16). HS 244* Titans v Lions (Benoni) 2014-15. Scored 200* SAA v Hants (Southampton) 2017 on UK debut. K HS 140 v Essex (Chelmsford) 2020. LO HS 141* SAA v Bangladesh A (Benoni) 2011. T20 HS 83*.

LINCOLN, Daniel John (Edgbarrow S, Crowthorne), b Frimley, Surrey 26 May 1995. 6'1". RHB, RM. Kent 2021. Berkshire 2012-21. Played as a goalkeeper for Reading and Arsenal junior sides, and as 12th man for England in 2019 Ashes. HS 41 v Sussex (Canterbury) 2021. T20 HS 30.

NQ**MacLEOD, Calum** Scott (Hillpark S, Glasgow), b Glasgow, Scotland 15 Nov 1988. 6'0". RHB, RMF. Scotland 2007 to date. Warwickshire 2008-09. Durham 2014-16. Derbyshire 2018 (T20 only). Sussex 2020 (T20 only). Kent 2021 (T20 only). **LOI** (Scot): 72 (2008 to 2021-22); HS 175 v Canada (Christchurch) 2013-14; BB 2-26 v Kenya (Aberdeen) 2013. **IT20** (Scot): 60 (2009 to 2021-22); HS 74 v Bermuda (Dubai, DSC) 2019-20; BB 2-17 v Kenya (Aberdeen) 2013. F-c Tours (Scot): UAE 2011-12, 2012-13; Namibia 2011-12. HS 84 Du v Lancs (Manchester) 2014. BB 4-66 Scot v Canada (Aberdeen) 2009. LO HS 175 (*see LOI*). LO BB 3-37 Scot v UAE (Queenstown) 2013-14. T20 HS 104*. T20 BB 2-17.

NQ**MILNE, Adam** Fraser, b Palmerston North, New Zealand 13 Apr 1992. RHB, RF. Central Districts 2009-10 to 2018-19. Kent 2017; cap 2019. IPL: RCB 2016-17; MI 2021. Big Bash: ST 2020-21. Birmingham Phoenix 2021. **LOI** (NZ): 40 (2012-13 to 2017-18); HS 36 v A (Wellington) 2015-16; BB 3-49 v P (Auckland) 2015-16. **IT20** (NZ): 31 (2010-11 to 2021-22); HS 10* v SA (Centurion) 2015; BB 4-37 v P (Auckland) 2015-16. F-c Tour (NZA): SL 2013-14. HS 97 and BB 5-47 CD v Otago (Napier) 2012-13. K HS 51 v Notts (Nottingham) 2017. K BB 4-68 v Durham (Chester-le-St) 2017. LO HS 50 CD v Otago (Dunedin) 2021-22. LO BB 5-61 NZA v Sri Lanka A (Pallekele) 2013-14. T20 HS 18*. T20 BB 5-11 v Somerset (Taunton) 2017 – K record.

NQ**MUNSEY,** Henry **George** (Loretto S), b Oxford 22 Feb 1993. LHB, RMF. Northamptonshire 2015. Scotland 2017 to 2017-18. Leicestershire 2019 (l-o only). Hampshire 2020 (T20 only). Kent 2021 (white ball only). **LOI** (Scot): 31 (2016-17 to 2021-22); HS 79* v Neth (Rotterdam) 2021. **IT20** (Scot): 51 (2015 to 2021-22); HS 127* v Neth (Dublin) 2019. HS 100* Scot v Namibia (Alloway) 2017. LO HS 108 v Worcs (Worcester) 2021. T20 HS 127*.

NQ**SHARIF, Safayaan** Mohammad (Buckhaven HS), b Huddersfield, Yorks 24 May 1991. RHB, RMF. Scotland 2011-12 to date. Derbyshire 2018 (white ball only). Kent 2021 (T20 only). **LOI** (Scot): 48 (2011 to 2021-22); HS 34 v Ire (Harare) 2017-18; BB 5-33 v Z (Bulawayo) 2017-18. **IT20** (Scot): 53 (2011-12 to 2021-22); HS 26 v Neth (Edinburgh) 2015; BB 4-24 v UAE (Dubai, ICCA) 2015-16 and 4-24 v Z (Edinburgh) 2021. HS 60 Scot v Ire (Dublin, CA) 2013. BB 4-94 Scot v PNG (Port Moresby) 2017-18. LO HS 34 (*see LOI*). LO BB 5-33 (*see LOI*). T20 HS 26. T20 BB 4-24.

WIGHTMAN, Bailey John (St Peter's C, Adelaide), b Warwick 16 June 1999. RHB, RM. Kent 2021. Warwickshire 2nd XI 2019. Derbyshire 2nd XI 2021. Cheshire 2018. HS 0* and BB-v Sussex (Canterbury) 2021.

T.D.Groenewald and Imran Qayyum left the staff without making a County 1st XI appearance in 2021.

KENT 2021

RESULTS SUMMARY

	Place	Won	Lost	Drew	NR
LV= Insurance County Champ (Div 3)	1st	4	3	7	
Royal London One-Day Cup (Group 1)	9th	1	5		2
Vitality Blast (South Group)	**Winners**	12	4		1

LV= INSURANCE COUNTY CHAMPIONSHIP AVERAGES
BATTING AND FIELDING

Cap		*M*	*I*	*NO*	*HS*	*Runs*	*Avge*	*100*	*50*	*Ct/St*
2021	J.A.Leaning	13	21	5	127*	745	46.56	1	6	11
2005	D.I.Stevens	12	18	3	190	650	43.33	3	2	4
	O.G.Robinson	13	21	1	120	725	36.25	2	3	38/1
	T.S.Muyeye	4	6	2	89	142	35.50	–	1	–
2019	Z.Crawley	12	21	2	90	637	33.52	–	6	9
2015	S.W.Billings	4	5	–	72	149	29.80	–	1	6
	J.M.Cox	13	23	2	90	579	27.57	–	4	10
2015	D.J.Bell-Drummond	10	17	1	114	419	26.18	1	2	2
2021	M.E.Milnes	8	14	4	78	244	24.40	–	1	2
2019	H.W.Podmore	5	6	1	37	107	21.40	–	–	–
	M.K.O'Riordan	7	7	–	47	140	20.00	–	–	4
	G.Stewart	6	9	2	40	134	19.14	–	–	–
2008	J.L.Denly	9	14	–	63	246	17.57	–	1	–
	M.R.Quinn	6	5	3	13*	32	16.00	–	–	–
	M.L.Cummins	8	10	2	28*	108	13.50	–	–	1
2018	H.G.Kuhn	4	8	–	32	108	13.50	–	–	4
	J.E.G.Logan	4	6	1	21	51	10.20	–	–	1
	N.N.Gilchrist	9	8	1	13	52	7.42	–	–	2
	F.J.Klaassen	2	4	1	5	8	2.66	–	–	–

Also batted: H.Z.Finch (1 match) 24, 115; J.A.Gordon (1) 8, 0; Hamidullah Qadri (1) 30*, 4; H.F.Houillon (1) 0, 9 (3 ct); D.J.Lincoln (1) 0, 41 (1 ct); J.Singh (2) 2, 0 (1 ct); B.J.Wightman (1) 0, 0*.

BOWLING

	O	*M*	*R*	*W*	*Avge*	*Best*	*5wI*	*10wM*
D.I.Stevens	284	93	725	39	18.58	5- 53	2	–
N.N.Gilchrist	160.1	26	620	30	20.66	5- 38	1	–
M.E.Milnes	205.3	42	687	32	21.46	6- 53	2	–
G.Stewart	120	31	384	17	22.58	5- 23	1	–
M.R.Quinn	149.3	34	413	18	22.94	4- 54	–	–
H.W.Podmore	114.3	16	419	12	34.91	4- 77	–	–
Also bowled:								
J.E.G.Logan	47.1	11	119	8	14.87	3- 8	–	–
J.Singh	40	5	140	7	20.00	4- 51	–	–
J.A.Leaning	103.5	12	356	6	59.33	2-101	–	–
M.L.Cummins	162.2	19	622	6	103.66	2-100	–	–

D.J.Bell-Drummond 19-3-70-3; J.M.Cox 1-0-3-0; J.L.Denly 89.2-12-274-4; Hamidullah Qadri 17-2-44-1; F.J.Klaassen 42.5-3-172-3; M.K.O'Riordan 50-9-145-2; B.J.Wightman 12-4-24-0.

The First-Class Averages (pp 220–232) give the records of Kent players in all first-class county matches, with the exception of Z.Crawley, whose first-class figures for Kent are as above.

KENT RECORDS

FIRST-CLASS CRICKET

Highest Total	For 803-4d		v	Essex	Brentwood	1934
	V 676		by	Australians	Canterbury	1921
Lowest Total	For 18		v	Sussex	Gravesend	1867
	V 16		by	Warwicks	Tonbridge	1913
Highest Innings	For 332	W.H.Ashdown	v	Essex	Brentwood	1934
	V 344	W.G.Grace	for	MCC	Canterbury	1876

Highest Partnership for each Wicket

1st	300	N.R.Taylor/M.R.Benson	v	Derbyshire	Canterbury	1991
2nd	423	J.M.Cox/J.A.Leaning	v	Sussex	Canterbury	2020
3rd	323	R.W.T.Key/M.van Jaarsveld	v	Surrey	Tunbridge Wells	2005
4th	368	P.A.de Silva/G.R.Cowdrey	v	Derbyshire	Maidstone	1995
5th	277	F.E.Woolley/L.E.G.Ames	v	N Zealanders	Canterbury	1931
6th	346	S.W.Billings/D.I.Stevens	v	Yorkshire	Leeds	2019
7th	248	A.P.Day/E.Humphreys	v	Somerset	Taunton	1908
8th	222	S.A.Northeast/J.C.Tredwell	v	Essex	Chelmsford	2016
9th	171	M.A.Ealham/P.A.Strang	v	Notts	Nottingham	1997
10th	235	F.E.Woolley/A.Fielder	v	Worcs	Stourbridge	1909

Best Bowling	For	10- 30	C.Blythe	v	Northants	Northampton	1907
(Innings)	V	10- 48	C.H.G.Bland	for	Sussex	Tonbridge	1899
Best Bowling	For	17- 48	C.Blythe	v	Northants	Northampton	1907
(Match)	V	17-106	T.W.J.Goddard	for	Glos	Bristol	1939

Most Runs – Season	2894	F.E.Woolley	(av 59.06)	1928
Most Runs – Career	47868	F.E.Woolley	(av 41.77)	1906-38
Most 100s – Season	10	F.E.Woolley		1928, 1934
Most 100s – Career	122	F.E.Woolley		1906-38
Most Wkts – Season	262	A.P.Freeman	(av 14.74)	1933
Most Wkts – Career	3340	A.P.Freeman	(av 17.64)	1914-36
Most Career W-K Dismissals	1253	F.H.Huish	(901 ct; 352 st)	1895-1914
Most Career Catches in the Field	773	F.E.Woolley		1906-38

LIMITED-OVERS CRICKET

Highest Total	**50ov**	384-6		v	Berkshire	Finchampstead	1994
		384-8		v	Surrey	Beckenham	2018
	40ov	337-7		v	Sussex	Canterbury	2013
	T20	236-3		v	Essex	Canterbury	2021
Lowest Total	**50ov**	60		v	Somerset	Taunton	1979
	40ov	83		v	Middlesex	Lord's	1984
	T20	72		v	Hampshire	Southampton[2]	2011
Highest Innings	**50ov**	150*	J.L.Denly	v	Glamorgan	Canterbury	2018
	40ov	146	A.Symonds	v	Lancashire	Tunbridge Wells	2004
	T20	127	J.L.Denly	v	Essex	Chelmsford	2017
Best Bowling	**50ov**	8-31	D.L.Underwood	v	Scotland	Edinburgh	1987
	40ov	6- 9	R.A.Woolmer	v	Derbyshire	Chesterfield	1979
	T20	5-11	A.F.Milne	v	Somerset	Taunton	2017

LANCASHIRE

Formation of Present Club: 12 January 1864
Inaugural First-Class Match: 1865
Colours: Red, Green and Blue
Badge: Red Rose
County Champions (since 1890): (8) 1897, 1904, 1926, 1927, 1928, 1930, 1934, 2011
Joint Champions: (1) 1950
Gillette/NatWest Trophy Winners: (7) 1970, 1971, 1972, 1975, 1990, 1996, 1998
Benson and Hedges Cup Winners: (4) 1984, 1990, 1995, 1996
Pro 40/National League (Div 1) Winners: (1) 1999.
Sunday League Winners: (4) 1969, 1970, 1989, 1998
Twenty20 Cup Winners: (1) 2015

Chief Executive: Daniel Gidney, Emirates Old Trafford, Talbot Road, Manchester M16 0PX • Tel: 0161 282 4000 • Email: enquiries@lancashirecricket.co.uk • Web: www.lancashirecricket.co.uk • Twitter: @lancscricket (130,814 followers)

Head Coach: Glen Chapple. **Assistant Head Coach**: Carl Crowe. **Director of Cricket Performance**: Mark Chilton. **Bowling Coach**: Graham Onions. **Captain**: D.J.Vilas. **Overseas Players**: T.H.David, Hasan Ali and D.J.Vilas. **2022 Testimonial**: None. **Head Groundsman**: Matthew Merchant. **Scorer**: Chris Rimmer. **Blast Team Name**: Lancashire Lightning. ‡ New registration. [NQ] Not qualified for England.

ANDERSON, James Michael (St Theodore RC HS and SFC, Burnley), b Burnley 30 Jul 1982. 6'2". LHB, RFM. Squad No 9. Debut (Lancashire) 2002; cap 2003; benefit 2012. Auckland 2007-08. YC 2003. *Wisden* 2008. OBE 2015. **ECB Central Contract 2021-22. Tests**: 160 (2003 to 2021-22); HS 81 v I (Nottingham) 2014, sharing a world Test record 10th wkt partnership of 198 with J.E.Root; 50 wkts (3); most – 57 (2010); BB 7-42 v WI (Lord's) 2017. **LOI**: 194 (2002-03 to 2014-15); HS 28 v NZ (Southampton) 2013; BB 5-23 v SA (Port Elizabeth) 2009-10. Hat-trick v P (Oval) 2003 – 1st for E in 373 LOI. **IT20**: 19 (2006-07 to 2009-10); HS 1* v A (Sydney) 2006-07; BB 3-23 v Netherlands (Lord's) 2009. F-c Tours: A 2006-07, 2010-11, 2013-14, 2017-18, 2021-22; SA 2004-05, 2009-10, 2015-16, 2019-20; WI 2003-04, 2005-06 (Eng A) (*part*), 2008-09, 2014-15, 2018-19; NZ 2007-08, 2012-13, 2017-18; I 2005-06 (*part*), 2008-09, 2012-13, 2016-17, 2020-21; SL 2003-04, 2007-08, 2011-12, 2018-19, 2020-21; UAE 2011-12 (v P), 2015-16 (v P). HS 81 (*see Tests*). La HS 42 v Surrey (Manchester) 2015. 50 wkts (4); most – 60 (2005, 2017). BB 7-19 v Kent (Manchester) 2021. Hat-trick v Essex (Manchester) 2003. LO HS 28 (*see LOI*). LO BB 5-23 (*see LOI*). T20 HS 16. T20 BB 3-23.

BAILEY, Thomas Ernest (Our Lady's Catholic HS, Preston), b Preston 21 Apr 1991. 6'4". RHB, RMF. Squad No 8. Debut (Lancashire) 2012; cap 2018. F-c Tour (EL): I 2018-19. HS 68 v Northants (Manchester) 2019. 50 wkts (2); most – 65 (2018). BB 7-37 v Hants (Liverpool) 2021. LO HS 45 v Sussex (Sedbergh) 2021 (RLC). LO BB 3-23 v Hants (Southampton) 2021 (RLC). T20 HS 10. T20 BB 5-17.

BALDERSON, George Philip (Cheadle Hulme HS), b Manchester 11 Oct 2000. 5'11". LHB, RM. Squad No 10. Debut (Lancashire) 2020. Lancashire 2nd XI debut 2018. England U19 2018-19. HS 77 v Notts (Nottingham) 2021. BB 3-21 v Hants (Liverpool) 2021. LO HS 19 v Middx (Manchester) 2021 (RLC). LO BB 3-25 v Hants (Southampton) 2021 (RLC).

BELL, George Joseph (Manchester GS), b Manchester 25 Sep 2002. RHB, WK. Squad No 17. Lancashire 2nd XI debut 2021. Awaiting 1st XI debut.

BLATHERWICK, Jack Morgan (Holgate Ac, Hucknall; Central C, Nottingham), b Nottingham 4 June 1998. 6'2". RHB, RMF. Squad No 4. Nottinghamshire 2019. Lancashire debut 2021. Northamptonshire 2019 (l-o only). England U19 2017. HS 11 v Warwks (Lord's) 2021. CC HS 4* Nt v Warwks (Nottingham) 2019. BB 4-28 v Somerset (Taunton) 2021. LO HS 3* Nt v Warwks (Nottingham) 2018 (RLC). LO BB 1-55 Nh v Australia A (Northampton) 2019.

BOHANNON, Joshua James (Harper Green HS), b Bolton 9 Apr 1997. 5'8". RHB, RM. Squad No 20. Debut (Lancashire) 2018; cap 2021. HS 174 v Derbys (Manchester) 2019. BB 3-46 v Hants (Southampton) 2018. LO HS 55* v Yorks (Leeds) 2019 (RLC). LO BB 1-33 v Notts (Nottingham) 2019. T20 HS 23.

BUTTLER, Joseph Charles (King's C, Taunton), b Taunton, Somerset 8 Sep 1990. 6'0". RHB, WK. Squad No 6. Somerset 2009-13; cap 2013. Lancashire debut 2014; cap 2018. IPL: MI 2016-17; RR 2018 to date. Big Bash: MR 2013-14; ST 2017-18 to 2018-19. Manchester Originals 2021. *Wisden* 2018. MBE 2020. **ECB Central Contract 2021-22. Tests**: 57 (2014 to 2021-22); HS 152 v P (Southampton) 2020. **LOI**: 148 (2011-12 to 2020-21); HS 150 v WI (St George's) 2018-19. **IT20**: 88 (2011 to 2021-22); HS 101* v SL (Sharjah) 2021-22. F-c Tours: A 2021-22; SA 2019-20; WI 2015, 2018-19; NZ 2019-20; I 2016-17, 2020-21; SL 2018-19, 2019-20, 2020-21; UAE 2015-16 (v P). HS 144 Sm v Hants (Southampton) 2010. La HS 100* v Durham (Chester-le-St) 2014. BB –. LO HS 150 (*see LOI*). T20 HS 124.

CROFT, Steven John (Highfield HS, Blackpool; Myerscough C), b Blackpool 11 Oct 1984. 5'10". RHB, OB. Squad No 15. Debut (Lancashire) 2005; cap 2010; captain 2017; testimonial 2018. Auckland 2008-09. HS 156 v Northants (Manchester) 2014. BB 6-41 v Worcs (Manchester) 2012. LO HS 127 v Warwks (Birmingham) 2017 (RLC). LO BB 4-24 v Scotland (Manchester) 2008 (FPT). T20 HS 94*. T20 BB 3-6.

NQ**DAVID, Tim**othy Hays, b Singapore 16 Mar 1996. Son of R.David (Singapore 1996-97). 6'5". RHB, RMF. Squad No 16. Surrey 2021 (white ball only). IPL: RCB 2021. Big Bash: PS 2017-18 to 2019-20; HH 2020-21 to date. **IT20** (Sing): 14 (2019 to 2019-20); HS 92* v Malaysia (Bangkok) 2019-20; BB 1-18 v Namibia (Dubai, DSC) 2019-20 and 1-18 v Hong Kong (Bangkok) 2019-20. LO HS 140* Sy v Warwks (Oval) 2021 (RLC). LO BB 3-26 Sing v Canada (Kuala Lumpur) 2019-20. T20 HS 92*. T20 BB 1-4.

GLEESON, Richard James (Baines HS), b Blackpool, Lancs 2 Dec 1987. 6'3". RHB, RFM. Squad No 11. Northamptonshire 2015-18. Lancashire debut 2018. MCC 2018. Big Bash: MR 2019-20. Cumberland 2010-15. F-c Tour (EL): WI 2017-18. HS 31 Nh v Glos (Bristol) 2016. La HS 11 v Leics (Liverpool) 2019. BB 6-43 v Leics (Leicester) 2019. Hat-trick MCC v Essex (Bridgetown) 2017-18. LO HS 13 EL v West Indies A (Coolidge) 2017-18. LO BB 5-47 Nh v Worcs (Worcester) 2016 (RLC). T20 HS 7*. T20 BB 3-12.

HARTLEY, Tom William (Merchant Taylors S), b Ormskirk 3 May 1999. 6'3". LHB, SLA. Squad No 2. Debut (Lancashire) 2020. Manchester Originals 2021. Lancashire 2nd XI debut 2018. HS 25 v Northants (Manchester) 2021. BB 4-42 v Kent (Manchester) 2021. T20 HS 16*. T20 BB 4-16.

‡NQ**HASAN ALI**, b Mandi Bahauddin, Pakistan 7 Feb 1994. RHB, RMF. Squad No 32. Sialkot 2013-14. Sialkot Stallions 2014-15. Islamabad 2015-16 to 2016-17. Central Punjab 2019-20 to date. **Tests** (P): 17 (2017 to 2021-22); HS 30 v Z (Harare) 2021; BB 5-27 v Z (Harare) 2021 – separate matches. **LOI** (P): 57 (2016 to 2021); HS 59 v SA (Durban) 2018-19; BB 5-34 v SL (Abu Dhabi) 2017-18. **IT20** (P): 48 (2016 to 2021-22); HS 23 v NZ (Wellington) 2017-18; BB 4-18 v Z (Harare) 2021. F-c Tours (P): E 2016 (PA), 2018; SA 2018-19; WI 2017, 2021; Z 2020-21; B 2021-22. HS 106* C Punjab v Khyber Paktunkhwa (Karachi) 2020-21. 50 wkts (0+1): 55 (2020-21). BB 8-107 Siakot S v State Bank (Sialkot) 2014-15. LO HS 59 (*see LOI*). LO BB 5-34 (*see LOI*). T20 HS 45. T20 BB 5-20.

HURT, Liam Jack (Balshaw's CE HS, Leyland), b Preston 15 Mar 1994. 6'4". RHB, RMF. Squad No 22. Debut (Lancashire) 2019. Leicestershire 2015 (l-o only). HS 38 v Leics (Leicester) 2019. BB 4-27 v Durham (Chester-le-St) 2020. LO HS 15* v Yorks (Leeds) 2019 (RLC). LO BB 3-55 v Sussex (Sedbergh) 2021 (RLC). T20 HS 0. T20 BB 3-22.

JENNINGS, Keaton Kent (King Edward VII S, Johannesburg), b Johannesburg, South Africa 19 Jun 1992. Son of R.V.Jennings (Transvaal 1973-74 to 1992-93), brother of D.Jennings (Gauteng and Easterns 1999 to 2003-04), nephew of K.E.Jennings (Northern Transvaal 1981-82 to 1982-83). 6'4". LHB, RM. Squad No 1. Gauteng 2011-12. Durham 2012-17; captain 2017 (l-o only). Lancashire debut/cap 2018. **Tests**: 17 (2016-17 to 2018-19); HS 146* v SL (Galle) 2018-19; scored 112 v I (Mumbai) on debut; BB –. F-c Tours (C=Captain): A 2019-20 (EL)C; WI 2017-18 (EL)C, 2018-19; I 2016-17; SL 2016-17 (EL), 2018-19. 1000 runs (1): 1602 (2016), inc seven hundreds (Du record). HS 221* Du v Yorks (Chester-le-St) 2016. La HS 177 v Worcs (Worcester) 2018. BB 3-37 Du v Sussex (Chester-le-St) 2017. La BB 1-8 v Durham (Sedbergh) 2019. LO HS 139 Du v Warwks (Birmingham) 2017 (RLC). LO BB 2-19 v Worcs (Worcester) 2018 (RLC). T20 HS 108 v Durham (Chester-le-St) 2020 – La record. T20 BB 4-37.

JONES, Robert Peter (Bridgewater HS), b Warrington, Cheshire 3 Nov 1995. 5'10". RHB, LB. Squad No 12. Debut (Lancashire) 2016. Cheshire 2014. HS 122 v Middx (Lord's) 2019. BB 1-4 v Northants (Manchester) 2021. LO HS 72 v Middx (Manchester) 2021 (RLC). LO BB 1-3 v Leics (Manchester) 2019 (RLC). T20 HS 61*.

LAMB, Daniel John (St Michael's HS, Chorley; Cardinal Newman C, Preston), b Preston 7 Sep 1995. 6'0". RHB, RMF. Squad No 26. Debut (Lancashire) 2018. HS 125 v Kent (Canterbury) 2021, sharing La record 8th wkt partnership of 187 with L.Wood. BB 4-55 v Yorks (Leeds) 2019. LO HS 86* v Sussex (Sedbergh) 2021 (RLC). LO BB 5-30 v Glos (Bristol) 2021 (RLC). T20 HS 29*. T20 BB 3-23.

LAVELLE, George Isaac Davies (Merchant Taylors S), b Ormskirk 24 Mar 2000. 5'8". RHB. WK. Squad No 24. Debut (Lancashire) 2020. Lancashire 2nd XI debut 2017. England U19 2018. HS 32 v Notts (Nottingham) 2021. LO HS 52 v Essex (Manchester) 2021 (RLC). T20 HS 12.

LIVINGSTONE, Liam Stephen (Chetwynde S, Barrow-in-Furness), b Barrow-in-Furness, Cumberland 4 Aug 1993. 6'1". RHB, LB. Squad No 23. Debut (Lancashire) 2016; cap 2017; captain 2018. IPL: RR 2019 to 2021. Big Bash: PS 2019-20 to 2020-21. Birmingham Phoenix 2021. **ECB Incremental Contract 2021-22. LOI**: 3 (2020-21 to 2021); HS 36 and BB 1-20 v I (Pune) 2020-21, taking wkt of K.L.Rahul with 2nd delivery in international cricket. **IT20**: 17 (2017 to 2021-22); HS 103 v P (Nottingham) 2021; BB 2-15 v B (Abu Dhabi) 2021-22. F-c Tours (EL): WI 2017-18; SL 2016-17. HS 224 v Warwks (Manchester) 2017. BB 6-52 v Surrey (Manchester) 2017. LO HS 129 EL v South Africa A (Northampton) 2017. LO BB 3-51 v Yorks (Manchester) 2016 (RLC). T20 HS 103. T20 BB 4-17.

MAHMOOD, Saqib (Matthew Moss HS, Rochdale), b Birmingham, Warwks 25 Feb 1997. 6'3". RHB, RFM. Squad No 25. Debut (Lancashire) 2016. Big Bash: ST 2021-22. Oval Invincibles 2021. **ECB Pace Bowling Development Contract 2021-22. LOI**: 7 (2019-20 to 2021); HS 12 v Ire (Southampton) 2020; BB 4-42 v P (Cardiff) 2021. **IT20**: 12 (2019-20 to 2021-22); HS 7* v WI (Bridgetown) 2021-22; BB 3-33 v PZ (Leeds) 2021. F-c Tours (EL): A 2021-22; WI 2017-18. HS 34 v Middx (Manchester) 2019. BB 5-47 v Yorks (Manchester) 2021. LO HS 45 v Warwks (Birmingham) 2019 (RLC). LO BB 6-37 v Northants (Manchester) 2019 (RLC). T20 HS 11*. T20 BB 4-14.

MORLEY, Jack Peter (Siddal Moor Sports C), b Rochdale 25 Jun 2001. 5'10". LHB, SLA. Squad No 18. Debut (Lancashire) 2020. Lancashire 2nd XI debut 2018. England U19 2018-19. HS 3 and BB 4-62 v Derbys (Liverpool) 2020. LO HS 6 v Durham (Gosforth) 2021 (RLC). LO BB 2-22 v Glos (Bristol) 2021 (RLC).

PARKINSON, Matthew William (Bolton S), b Bolton 24 Oct 1996. Twin brother of C.F.Parkinson (*see LEICESTERSHIRE*). 6'0". RHB, LB. Squad No 28. Debut (Lancashire) 2016; cap 2019. Manchester Originals 2021. Staffordshire 2014. **LOI**: 5 (2019-20 to 2021); HS 7* v P (Lord's) 2021; BB 2-28 v P (Cardiff) 2021. **IT20**: 4 (2019-20 to 2021); HS 5 v P (Nottingham) 2021; BB 4-47 v NZ (Napier) 2019-20. HS 21* v Northants (Manchester) 2021. BB 7-126 v Kent (Canterbury) 2021. LO HS 15* EL v West Indies A (Coolidge) 2017-18. LO BB 5-51 v Worcs (Manchester) 2019 (RLC). T20 HS 7*. T20 BB 4-9.

‡**SALT, Phil**ip Dean (Reed's S, Cobham), b Bodelwyddan, Denbighs 28 Aug 1996. 5'10". RHB, OB. Squad No 7. Sussex 2013-20. Big Bash: AS 2019-20 to 2020-21. Manchester Originals 2021. **LOI**: 3 (2021); HS 60 v P (Lord's) 2021. **IT20**: 3 (2021-22); HS 57 v WI (Bridgetown) 2021-22. HS 148 Sx v Derbys (Hove) 2018. BB 1-32 Sx v Warwks (Hove) 2018. LO HS 137* Sx v Kent (Beckenham) 2019 (RLC). T20 HS 78*.

NQ**VILAS, Dane** James, b Johannesburg, South Africa 10 Jun 1985. 6'2". RHB, WK. Squad No 33. Gauteng 2006-07 to 2009-10. Lions 2008-09 to 2009-10. W Province 2010-11. Cape Cobras 2011-12 to 2016-17. Lancashire debut 2017; cap 2018; captain 2019 to date. Dolphins 2017-18 to 2018-19. Northern Superchargers 2021. **Tests** (SA): 6 (2015 to 2015-16); HS 26 v E (Johannesburg) 2015-16. **IT20** (SA): 1 (2011-12); HS –. F-c Tours (SA): A 2016 (SA A), I 2015 (SA A), 2015-16; Z 2016 (SA A), B 2015. 1000 runs (1): 1036 (2019). HS 266 v Glamorgan (Colwyn B) 2019. LO HS 166 v Notts (Nottingham) 2019 (RLC). T20 HS 75*.

WELLS, Luke William Peter (St Bede's S, Upper Dicker), b Eastbourne, E Sussex 29 Dec 1990. Son of A.P.Wells (Border, Kent, Sussex and England 1981-2000); elder brother of D.A.C.Wells (Oxford MCCU 2017); nephew of C.M.Wells (Border, Derbyshire, Sussex and WP 1979-96). 6'4". LHB, LB. Squad No 3. Sussex 2010-19; cap 2016. Colombo CC 2011-12. Lancashire debut 2021. 1000 runs (2); most – 1292 (2017). HS 258 Sx v Durham (Hove) 2017. La HS 103 and La BB 3-8 v Somerset (Taunton) 2021. BB 5-63 Sx v Glamorgan (Hove) 2019. LO HS 66* v Hants (Southampton) 2021 (RLC). BB 3-19 Sx v Netherlands (Amstelveen) 2011 (CB40). T20 HS 30. T20 BB 1-15.

WOOD, Luke (Portland CS, Worksop), b Sheffield, Yorks 2 Aug 1995. 5'9". LHB, LFM. Squad No 14. Nottinghamshire 2014-19. Worcestershire 2018 (on loan). Northamptonshire 2019 (on loan). Lancashire debut 2020. Trent Rockets 2021. HS 119 v Kent (Canterbury), sharing La record 8th wkt partnership of 187 with D.J.Lamb. BB 5-40 Nt v Cambridge MCCU (Cambridge) 2016. CC BB 5-67 Nt v Yorks (Scarborough) 2019. La BB 3-31 v Northants (Manchester) 2021. LO HS 52 Nt v Leics (Leicester) 2016 (RLC). LO BB 2-36 Nt v Worcs (Worcester) 2019 (RLC). T20 HS 33*. T20 BB 4-20.

RELEASED/RETIRED

(Having made a County 1st XI appearance in 2021)

NQ**ALLEN, Finn**ley Hugh (St Kentigern C), b Auckland, New Zealand 22 Apr 1999. RHB, WK. Auckland 2017-18 to 2019-20. Wellington 2020-21 to date. Lancashire 2021 (T20 only). Birmingham Phoenix 2021. **IT20** (NZ): 6 (2020-21 to 2021); HS 71 v B (Auckland) 2020-21. HS 66 Auckland v Wellington (Auckland) 2019-20. BB 1-15 Wellington v Otago (Wellington) 2020-21. LO HS 128 (in 59 balls) Wellington v Otago (Wellington) 2020-21. LO BB 1-32 Auckland v ND (Whangarei) 2019-20. T20 HS 92*.

CORNALL, T.R. – *see WORCESTERSHIRE.*

DAVIES, A.L. – *see WARWICKSHIRE.*

MOULTON, Edwin Henry Taylor (Bishop Rawstone C of E Ac; Myerscough C), Preston 18 Apr 1999. RHB, RMF. Lancashire 2020. Derbyshire 2021 (on loan). Lancashire 2nd XI debut 2017. HS 6* De v Leics (Derby) 2021. BB 2-24 De v Sussex (Hove) 2021.

G.D.Burrows and S.M.O.Shah left the staff without making a County 1st XI appearance in 2021.

LANCASHIRE 2021

RESULTS SUMMARY

	Place	Won	Lost	Tied	Drew	NR
LV= Insurance County Champ (Div 1)	2nd	6	2		6	
Royal London One-Day Cup (Group 1)	4th	3	2	1		2
Vitality Blast (North Group)	QF	7	6	1		1

LV= INSURANCE COUNTY CHAMPIONSHIP AVERAGES
BATTING AND FIELDING

Cap		*M*	*I*	*NO*	*HS*	*Runs*	*Avge*	*100*	*50*	*Ct/St*
2021	J.J.Bohannon	14	18	2	170	853	53.31	2	5	7
2018	K.K.Jennings	10	13	1	132	577	48.08	2	3	8
	L.W.P.Wells	12	16	2	103	572	40.85	1	3	16
2017	A.L.Davies	13	19	2	84	652	38.35	–	6	17/3
2018	D.J.Vilas	14	16	1	189	559	37.26	1	2	20
	L.Wood	9	11	1	119	357	35.70	1	1	3
2010	S.J.Croft	10	12	2	103*	327	32.70	1	1	8
	M.W.Parkinson	11	10	8	21*	59	29.50	–	–	1
	D.J.Lamb	11	14	1	125	365	28.07	1	2	5
	G.P.Balderson	5	7	1	77	145	24.16	–	1	–
2018	T.E.Bailey	12	14	–	63	306	21.85	–	2	1
	T.W.Hartley	3	4	1	25	61	20.33	–	–	2
	R.P.Jones	8	9	–	58	180	20.00	–	1	11
2017	L.S.Livingstone	6	7	–	25	77	11.00	–	–	5
2021	S.Mahmood	8	11	4	20	73	10.42	–	–	2

Also batted: J.M.Anderson (4 matches – cap 2003) 5*, 8* (1 ct); J.M.Blatherwick (3) 1, 4, 1 (1 ct); G.I.D.Lavelle (2) 4, 32, 0 (5 ct).

BOWLING

	O	*M*	*R*	*W*	*Avge*	*Best*	*5wI*	*10wM*
J.M.Anderson	46	19	83	11	7.54	7- 19	1	–
T.E.Bailey	340	108	843	50	16.86	7- 37	1	–
M.W.Parkinson	321.2	87	740	36	20.55	7-126	1	–
S.Mahmood	233.1	52	669	28	23.89	5- 47	1	–
G.P.Balderson	128.5	28	344	12	28.66	3- 21	–	–
L.Wood	189	30	596	18	33.11	3- 31	–	–
D.J.Lamb	280.5	67	780	23	33.91	4- 60	–	–
Also bowled:								
L.W.P.Wells	46	10	109	7	15.57	3- 8	–	–
J.M.Blatherwick	40.1	8	156	6	26.00	4- 28	–	–

J.J.Bohannon 31.1-5-94-3; S.J.Croft 22-3-77-0; T.W.Hartley 83-32-143-4; R.P.Jones 3-0-7-1; L.S.Livingstone 91-17-248-4; D.J.Vilas 1-0-6-0.

The First-Class Averages (pp 220–232) give the records of Lancashire players in all first-class county matches, with the exception of J.M.Anderson, whose first-class figures for Lancashire are as above.

LANCASHIRE RECORDS

FIRST-CLASS CRICKET

Highest Total	For 863		v	Surrey	The Oval	1990
	V 707-9d		by	Surrey	The Oval	1990
Lowest Total	For 25		v	Derbyshire	Manchester	1871
	V 20		by	Essex	Chelmsford	2013
Highest Innings	For 424	A.C.MacLaren	v	Somerset	Taunton	1895
	V 315*	T.W.Hayward	for	Surrey	The Oval	1898

Highest Partnership for each Wicket

1st	368	A.C.MacLaren/R.H.Spooner	v	Glos	Liverpool	1903
2nd	371	F.B.Watson/G.E.Tyldesley	v	Surrey	Manchester	1928
3rd	501	A.N.Petersen/A.G.Prince	v	Glamorgan	Colwyn Bay	2015
4th	358	S.P.Titchard/G.D.Lloyd	v	Essex	Chelmsford	1996
5th	360	S.G.Law/C.L.Hooper	v	Warwicks	Birmingham	2003
6th	278	J.Iddon/H.R.W.Butterworth	v	Sussex	Manchester	1932
7th	248	G.D.Lloyd/I.D.Austin	v	Yorkshire	Leeds	1997
8th	187	L.Wood/D.J.Lamb	v	Kent	Canterbury	2021
9th	142	L.O.S.Poidevin/A.Kermode	v	Sussex	Eastbourne	1907
10th	173	J.Briggs/R.Pilling	v	Surrey	Liverpool	1885

Best Bowling	For	10-46	W.Hickton	v	Hampshire	Manchester	1870
(Innings)	V	10-40	G.O.B.Allen	for	Middlesex	Lord's	1929
Best Bowling	For	17-91	H.Dean	v	Yorkshire	Liverpool	1913
(Match)	V	16-65	G.Giffen	for	Australians	Manchester	1886

Most Runs – Season	2633	J.T.Tyldesley	(av 56.02)	1901
Most Runs – Career	34222	G.E.Tyldesley	(av 45.20)	1909-36
Most 100s – Season	11	C.Hallows		1928
Most 100s – Career	90	G.E.Tyldesley		1909-36
Most Wkts – Season	198	E.A.McDonald	(av 18.55)	1925
Most Wkts – Career	1816	J.B.Statham	(av 15.12)	1950-68
Most Career W-K Dismissals	925	G.Duckworth	(635 ct; 290 st)	1923-38
Most Career Catches in the Field	556	K.J.Grieves		1949-64

LIMITED-OVERS CRICKET

Highest Total	**50ov**	406-9		v	Notts	Nottingham	2019
	40ov	324-4		v	Worcs	Worcester	2012
	T20	231-4		v	Yorkshire	Manchester	2015
Lowest Total	**50ov**	59		v	Worcs	Worcester	1963
	40ov	68		v	Yorkshire	Leeds	2000
		68		v	Surrey	The Oval	2002
	T20	83		v	Durham	Manchester	2020
Highest Innings	**50ov**	166	D.J.Vilas	v	Notts	Nottingham	2019
	40ov	143	A.Flintoff	v	Essex	Chelmsford	1999
	T20	108	K.K.Jennings	v	Durham	Chester-le-St[2]	2020
Best Bowling	**50ov**	6-10	C.E.H.Croft	v	Scotland	Manchester	1982
	40ov	6-25	G.Chapple	v	Yorkshire	Leeds	1998
	T20	5-13	S.D.Parry	v	Worcs	Manchester	2016

LEICESTERSHIRE

Formation of Present Club: 25 March 1879
Inaugural First-Class Match: 1894
Colours: Dark Green and Scarlet
Badge: Gold Running Fox on Green Ground
County Champions: (3) 1975, 1996, 1998
Benson and Hedges Cup Winners: (3) 1972, 1975, 1985
Sunday League Champions: (2) 1974, 1977
Twenty20 Cup Winners: (3) 2004, 2006, 2011

Chief Executive: Sean Jarvis, Uptonsteel County Ground, Grace Road, Leicester LE2 8EB • Tel: 0116 283 2128 • Email: enquiries@leicestershireccc.co.uk • Web: www.leicestershireccc.co.uk • Twitter: @leicsccc (67,092 followers)

Director of Cricket: Claude Henderson. **Head Coach**: Paul Nixon. **Captains**: C.N.Ackermann (f-c & T20) and L.J.Hill (50 ov). **Vice-captain**: C.F.Parkinson. **Overseas Players**: B.E.Hendricks, P.W.A.Mulder, Naveen-ul-Haq (T20 only) and Rahmanullah Gurbaz (T20 only). **2022 Testimonial**: None. **Head Groundsman**: Andy Ward. **Scorer**: Paul Rogers. **Blast Team Name**: Leicestershire Foxes. ‡ New registration. [NQ] Not qualified for England.

[NQ]**ACKERMANN, Colin** Neil (Grey HS, Port Elizabeth; U of SA), b George, South Africa 4 Apr 1991. RHB, OB. Squad No 48. Eastern Province 2010-11 to 2015-16. Warriors 2013-14 to 2018-19. Leicestershire debut 2017; cap 2019; captain 2020 to date (T20 only in 2020). **LOI** (Neth); 4 (2021-22); HS 81 v Afg (Doha) 2021-22; BB 1-10 v Afg (Doha) 2021-22 – separate matches. **IT20** (Neth): 14 (2019-20 to 2021-22); HS 43* and BB 1-6 v Bermuda (Dubai, DSC) 2019-20. 1000 runs (0+1): 1200 (2013-14). HS 196* v Middx (Leicester) 2018. BB 5-69 v Sussex (Hove) 2019. LO HS 152* v Worcs (Leicester) 2019 (RLC). LO BB 4-48 Warriors v Dolphins (Durban) 2017-18. T20 HS 79*. T20 BB 7-18 v Warwks (Leicester) 2019 – world record T20 figures.

AHMED, Rehan (Bluecoat Aspley SFC), b Nottingham 13 Aug 2004. RHB, LB. Squad No 16. Leicestershire 2nd XI debut 2021. Awaiting f-c debut. LO 40* v Northants (Northampton) 2021 (RLC). LO 2-25 v Surrey (Leicester) 2021 (RLC).

AZAD, Mohammad **Hasan** (Fernwood S, Nottingham; Bilborough SFC; Loughborough U), b Quetta, Pakistan 7 Jan 1994. Son of Imran Azad (Public Works 1986-87). LHB, OB. Squad No 42. Loughborough MCCU 2015-19. Leicestershire debut 2019, scoring 139 v Loughborough MCCU (Leicester). 1000 runs (1): 1189 (2019). HS 152 v Sussex (Leicester) 2021. BB 1-15 v Durham (Leicester) 2020.

BARNES, Edward (King James S, Knaresborough), b York 26 Nov 1997. 6'0". RHB, RFM. Squad No 62. Derbyshire 2020. Leicestershire debut 2021. Yorkshire 2nd XI 2016-19. England U19 2016. HS 83* v Somerset (Taunton) 2021. BB 4-61 v Hants (Southampton) 2021. LO HS 33* and LO BB 2-34 v Surrey (Leicester) 2021 (RLC). T20 HS 7. T20 BB 2-27.

BATES, Samuel David (Groby C; Gateway C), b Leicester 14 Sep 1999. 6'3". LHB, WK. Squad No 14. Debut (Leicestershire) 2021. Leicestershire 2nd XI debut 2018. HS 6 v Worcs (Worcester) 2021 – only 1st XI appearance.

BOWLEY, Nathan John (Woodvale S, Loughborough; Loughborough C), b Nottingham 3 Aug 2001. LHB, OB. Squad No 33. Leicestershire 2nd XI debut 2018. Awaiting 1st XI debut.

DAVIS, William Samuel (Stafford GS), b Stafford 6 Mar 1996. 6'1". RHB, RFM. Squad No 44. Derbyshire 2015-18. Leicestershire debut 2019. HS 42 v Kent (Leicester) 2021. BB 7-146 De v Glamorgan (Colwyn Bay) 2016. Le BB 5-66 v Middx (Northwood) 2021. LO HS 15* v Durham (Chester-le-St) 2019 (RLC) and 15* v Surrey (Leicester) 2021 (RLC). LO BB 2-40 v Northants (Northampton) 2021 (RLC). T20 HS 4*. T20 BB 3-24.

EVANS, Huw **Alex**ander (Bedford Modern S; Loughborough U), b Bedford 9 Aug 2000. 6'3". LHB, RFM. Squad No 72. Loughborough MCCU 2019. Leicestershire debut 2019. Leicestershire 2nd XI debut 2018. Bedfordshire 2017. HS 15 v Yorks (Leeds) 2020. BB 3-49 LU v Kent (Canterbury) 2019. Le BB 2-50 v Hants (Southampton) 2021.

EVANS, Samuel Thomas (Lancaster S, Leicester; Wyggeston & QE I C; Leicester U), b Leicester 20 Dec 1997. 5'8". RHB, OB. Squad No 21. Loughborough MCCU 2017-18. Leicestershire debut 2017. Leicestershire 2nd XI debut 2015. HS 138 v Surrey (Oval) 2021. BB –. LO HS 20 v India A (Leicester) 2018.

GRIFFITHS, Gavin Timothy (St Mary's C, Crosby), b Ormskirk, Lancs 19 Nov 1993. 6'2". RHB, RMF. Squad No 93. Debut (Leicestershire) 2017. Lancashire 2014-15 (l-o only). Hampshire 2016 (T20 only). HS 40 v Middx (Leicester) 2018. BB 6-49 (10-83 match) v Durham (Chester-le-St) 2018. LO HS 15* v Notts (Leicester) 2018 (RLC). LO BB 4-30 v Northants (Northampton) 2018 (RLC). T20 HS 12. T20 BB 4-24.

‡[NQ]**HENDRICKS, Beuran** Eric, b Cape Town, South Africa 8 Jun 1990. LHB, LFM. Squad No 18. W Province 2009-10 to date. Cape Cobras 2010-11 to 2016-17. Lions 2016-17 to 2020-21. IPL: KXIP 2014-15. **Tests** (SA): 1 (2019-20); HS 5* and BB 5-64 v E (Johannesburg) 2019-20. **LOI** (SA): 8 (2018-19 to 2020-21); HS 3 and BB 3-59 v E (Johannesburg) 2019-20. **IT20** (SA): 19 (2013-14 to 2021); HS 12* v A (Centurion) 2013-14; BB 4-14 v P (Centurion) 2018-19. F-c Tours (SAA): E 2017; I 2015, 2018. HS 68 Lions v Dolphins (Johannesburg) 2017-18. 50 wkts (0+1): 60 (2012-13). BB 7-29 (10-83 match) Lions v Cobras (Johannesburg) 2020-21. LO HS SA A v Australia A (Darwin) 2014. LO BB 5-31 Cobras v Titans (Benoni) 2015-16. T20 HS 12*. T20 BB 6-29.

HILL, Lewis John (Hastings HS, Hinckley; John Cleveland C), b Leicester 5 Oct 1990. 5'7½". RHB, WK, occ RM. Squad No 23. Debut (Leicestershire) 2015; cap 2021. Unicorns 2012-13. HS 145 v Sussex (Leicester) 2021. LO HS 118 v Worcs (Leicester) 2019 (RLC). T20 HS 59.

KIMBER, Louis Philip James (William Farr C of E S; Loughborough U), b Lincoln 24 Feb 1997. Elder brother of J.F.Kimber (Lincolnshire 2016-18). RHB, OB, occ WK. Squad No 17. Loughborough MCCU 2019. Leicestershire debut 2021. Lincolnshire 2015-19. HS 71 v Worcs (Worcester) 2021. BB LU 1-34 v Kent (Canterbury) 2019. LO HS 85 v Somerset (Taunton) 2021 (RLC). T20 HS 53.

LILLEY, Arron Mark (Mossley Hollins HS; Ashton SFC), b Tameside, Lancs 1 Apr 1991. 6'1". RHB, OB. Squad No 7. Lancashire 2013-18. Leicestershire debut 2019. White-ball contract in 2021. HS 63 and BB 5-23 La v Derbys (Southport) 2015. Le HS 13 and Le BB 3-21 v Yorks (Leeds) 2020. LO HS 46 v Northants (Northampton) 2021 (RLC). LO BB 4-30 La v Derbys (Manchester) 2013 (Y40). T20 HS 99*. T20 BB 3-26.

MIKE, Benjamin Wentworth Munro (Loughborough GS), b Nottingham 24 Aug 1998. Son of G.W.Mike (Nottinghamshire 1989-96). 6'1". RHB, RM. Squad No 8. Debut (Leicestershire) 2018. Warwickshire 2019 (on loan). Leicestershire 2nd XI debut 2017. HS 74 v Surrey (Leicester) 2021. BB 5-37 (9-94 match) v Sussex (Hove) 2018 – on debut. LO HS 41 v Northants (Leicester) 2019 (RLC). LO BB 3-34 v Surrey (Leicester) 2021 (RLC). T20 HS 37. T20 BB 4-22.

‡[NQ]**MULDER**, Peter Willem Adriaan ('**Wiaan**'), b Johannesburg, South Africa 19 Feb 1998. RHB, RM. Squad No 24. Lions 2016-17 to 2020-21. Gauteng 2017-18 to date. Kent 2019. **Tests** (SA): 8 (2018-19 to 2021-22); HS 36 v SL (Centurion) 2020-21; BB 3-1 v WI (Gros Islet) 2021. **LOI** (SA): 12 (2017-18 to 2021); HS 19* v SL (Dambulla) 2018; BB 2-59 v SL (Colombo, RPS) 2018. **IT20** (SA): 5 (2021); HS 36 v Ire (Belfast) 2021; BB 2-10 v Ire (Belfast) 2021 – separate matches. F-c Tours (SA): E 2017 (SA A); WI 2021; NZ 2021-22; P 2020-21. HS 146 Lions v Knights (Bloemfontein) 2018-19. CC HS 68* and CC BB 4-118 K v Surrey (Beckenham) 2019. BB 7-25 Lions v Dolphins (Potchefstroom) 2016-17. LO HS 66 SA A v India A (Pretoria) 2017. LO BB 3-32 Lions v Knights (Potchefstroom) 2017-18. T20 HS 63. T20 BB 2-10.

[NQ]**NAVEEN-UL-HAQ** Murid, b Logar, Afghanistan 23 Sep 1999. RHB, RMF. Squad No 78. Kabul Region 2017-18 to 2018-19. Leicestershire debut 2021 (T20 only). **LOI** (Afg): 7 (2016 to 2020-21); HS 10* v Ire (Abu Dhabi) 2020-21; BB 4-42 v Ire (Abu Dhabi) 2020-21 – separate matches. **IT20** (Afg): 13 (2019 to 2021-22); HS 5 v WI (Lucknow) 2019-20; BB 3-21 v Ire (Greater Noida) 2019-20. HS 34 Kabul v Mis Ainak (Asadabad) 2017-18. BB 8-35 Kabul v Mis Ainak (Kabul) 2018-19. LO HS 30 Kabul v Band-e-Amir (Kabul) 2018. LO BB 5-40 Afg A v Bangladesh A (Savar) 2019. T20 HS 20*. T20 BB 4-14.

PARKINSON, Callum Francis (Bolton S), b Bolton, Lancs 24 Oct 1996. Twin brother of M.W.Parkinson (*see LANCASHIRE*). 5'8". RHB, SLA. Squad No 10. Derbyshire 2016. Leicestershire debut 2017. Northern Superchargers 2021. Staffordshire 2015-16. HS 75 v Kent (Canterbury) 2017. BB 8-148 (10-185 match) v Worcs (Worcester) 2017. LO HS 52* v Notts (Leicester) 2018 (RLC). LO BB 1-34 v Derbys (Derby) 2018 (RLC). T20 HS 27*. T20 BB 4-20.

PATEL, Rishi Ketan (Brentwood S), b Chigwell, Essex 26 Jul 1998. 6'2". RHB, LB. Squad No 26. Cambridge MCCU 2019. Essex 2019. Leicestershire debut 2020. Essex 2nd XI 2015-19. Hertfordshire 2019. HS 44 v Glos (Bristol) 2021. LO HS 118 v Warwks (Birmingham) 2021 (RLC). T20 HS 35.

‡[NQ]**RAHMANULLAH GURBAZ**, b Afghanistan 28 Nov 2001. RHB, WK. Squad No 1. Mis Ainak Region 2017-18. Kabul Region 2018-19. **LOI** (Afg): 9 (2020-21 to 2021-22); HS 127 v Ire (Abu Dhabi) 2020-21 – on debut. **IT20** (Afg): 20 (2019 to 2021-22); HS 87 v Z (Abu Dhabi) 2020-21. HS 153 Kabul v Mis Ainak (Kabul) 2018-19. LO HS 128 Mis Ainak v Amo (Kandahar) 2020-21. T20 HS 99.

RHODES, George Harry (Chase HS & SFC, Malvern), b Birmingham 26 Oct 1993. Son of S.J.Rhodes (Yorkshire, Worcestershire & England 1981-2004) and grandson of W.E.Rhodes (Nottinghamshire 1961-64). 6'0". RHB, OB. Squad No 34. Worcestershire 2016-19. Leicestershire debut 2019. HS 90 v Worcs (Worcester) 2021. BB 2-83 Wo v Kent (Canterbury) 2016. Le BB –. LO HS 106 Wo v Yorks (Worcester) 2019 (RLC). LO BB 3-44 v Glamorgan (Leicester) 2021 (RLC). T20 HS 30*. T20 BB 4-13.

SAKANDE, Abidine (Ardingly C; St John's C, Oxford), b Chester 22 Sep 1994. 6'1". RHB, RFM. Squad No 20. Oxford U 2014-15. Oxford MCCU 2015-16. Sussex 2016-19. Leicestershire debut 2021. HS 33 OU v Cambridge U (Cambridge) 2015. CC HS 15 Sx v Lancs (Manchester) 2019. Le HS 9 v Middx (Northwood) 2021. BB 5-43 Sx v South Africa A (Arundel) 2017. CC BB 3-44 Sx v Northants (Northampton) 2018. Le BB 3-66 v Worcs (Worcester) 2021. LO HS 7* Sx v South Africans (Hove) 2017. LO BB 2-53 Sx v Somerset (Taunton) 2018 (RLC).

‡**SCRIVEN, Thomas** Antony Rhys (Magdalen Coll S), b Oxford 18 Nov 1998. 6'0½". RHB, RMF. Squad No 88. Hampshire 2020. Hampshire 2nd XI 2016-21. HS 68 and BB 2-24 H v Kent (Canterbury) 2020. LO HS 42 H v Durham (Chester-le-S) 2021 (RLC). LO BB 1-6 H v Kent (Beckenham) 2021 (RLC). T20 HS 2. T20 BB –.

STEEL, Scott (Belmont Community S), b Durham 20 Apr 1999. 6'0". RHB, OB. Squad No 55. Durham 2019. Leicestershire debut 2021 (T20 only). Durham 2nd XI 2016-19. Northumberland 2017. HS 39 Du v Middx (Lord's) 2019. BB –. LO HS 68 Du v Northants (Chester-le-St) 2019 (RLC) and 68 Du v Yorks (Leeds) 2019 (RLC). LO BB 1-38 Du v Derbys (Chester-le-St) 2019 (RLC). T20 HS 70. T20 BB 3-20.

SWINDELLS, Harry John (Brockington C; Lutterworth C), b Leicester 21 Feb 1999. 5'7". RHB, WK. Squad No 28. Debut (Leicestershire) 2019. Leicestershire 2nd XI debut 2015. England U19 2017. HS 171* v Somerset (Taunton) 2021. LO HS 75 v Surrey (Leicester) 2021 (RLC). T20 HS 63.

‡**WALKER, Roman** Isaac (Ysgol Bryn Alyn), b Wrexham, Denbighs 6 Aug 2000. RHB, RFM. Squad No 49.Glamorgan 2019-21 (white ball only). Glamorgan 2nd XI 2016-21. Wales MC 2018. Awaiting f-c debut. LO HS 15* and LO BB 1-53 Gm v Warwks (Cardiff) 2021 (RLC). T20 HS 2. T20 BB 3-15.

WELCH, Nicholas Roy (St John's C, Harare; Loughborough U), b Harare, Zimbabwe 5 Feb 1998. 5'11". RHB, LBG. Squad No 67. Mashonaland Eagles 2013-14. Loughborough MCCU 2019. Sussex 2nd XI 2016-17. Northamptonshire 2nd XI 2017. Surrey 2nd XI 2017-19. Essex 2nd XI 2017. Leicestershire 2nd XI debut 2019. HS 83 ME v SR (Harare) 2013-14. LO HS 52 ME v MT (Bulawayo) 2013-14. T20 HS 43.

WRIGHT, Christopher Julian Clement (Eggars S, Alton; Anglia Ruskin U), b Chipping Norton, Oxon 14 Jul 1985. 6'3". RHB, RFM. Squad No 31. Cambridge UCCE 2004-05. Middlesex 2004-07. Tamil Union 2005-06. Essex 2008-11. Warwickshire 2011-18; cap 2013. Leicestershire debut 2019; cap 2021. F-c Tour (MCC): Nepal 2019-20. HS 77 Ex v Cambridge MCCU (Cambridge) 2011. CC HS 87 v Derbys (Derby) 2021. 50 wkts (2); most – 67 (2012). BB 7-53 v Glos (Bristol) 2021. LO HS 42 Ex v Glos (Cheltenham) 2011 (CB40). LO BB 4-20 Ex v Unicorns (Chelmsford) 2011 (CB40). T20 HS 6*. T20 BB 4-24.

RELEASED/RETIRED

(Having made a County 1st XI appearance in 2021)

DEARDEN, Harry Edward (Tottington HS), b Bury, Lancs 7 May 1997. LHB, OB. Leicestershire 2016-21. Cheshire 2016. HS 87 v Glamorgan (Leicester) 2017. BB 1-0 v Kent (Leicester) 2017. LO HS 91 v Worcs (Leicester) 2019 (RLC). T20 HS 61.

HARRIS, M.S. – *see GLOUCESTERSHIRE.*

NQ**INGLIS, Josh**ua Patrick (St Mary's S, Menston; Mindarie Sen HS, Perth), b Leeds, Yorks 4 Mar 1995. RHB, WK. W Australia 2016-17 to date. Leicestershire 2021. Big Bash: PS 2017-18 to date. London Spirit 2021. HS 153* WA v SA (Adelaide) 2020-21. Le HS 52 v Middx (Northwood) 2021. LO HS 91 WA v Vic (Perth) 2020-21. T20 HS 118*.

NQ**KLEIN, Dieter** (Hoerskool, Lichtenburg), b Lichtenburg, South Africa 31 Oct 1988. 5'10". RHB, LMF. North West 2007-08 to 2015-16. Lions 2012-13 to 2013-14. Leicestershire 2016-21. **IT20** (Ger): 13 (2019-20 to 2021-22); HS 31* v Spain (Almeria) 2019-20; BB 3-31 v Canada (Al Amerat) 2021-22. HS 94 v Glamorgan (Cardiff) 2018. BB 8-72 NW v Northerns (Potchefstroom) 2014-15. Le BB 6-80 v Northants (Northampton) 2017. LO HS 46 v Durham (Chester-le-St) 2019 (RLC). LO BB 5-35 NW v Northerns (Pretoria) 2012-13. T20 HS 31*. T20 BB 3-27.

LEICESTERSHIRE 2021

RESULTS SUMMARY

	Place	Won	Lost	Drew	NR
LV= Insurance County Champ (Div 3)	4th	3	6	5	
Royal London One-Day Cup (Group 2)	4th	4	3		1
Vitality Blast (South Group)	6th	6	8		

LV= INSURANCE COUNTY CHAMPIONSHIP AVERAGES
BATTING AND FIELDING

Cap		*M*	*I*	*NO*	*HS*	*Runs*	*Avge*	*100*	*50*	*Ct/St*
	M.S.Harris	8	13	1	185	655	54.58	3	1	7
	G.H.Rhodes	3	4	–	90	208	52.00	–	2	2
2021	L.J.Hill	14	22	1	145	944	44.95	3	5	3
	H.J.Swindells	13	19	3	171*	693	43.31	2	3	27/1
2019	C.N.Ackermann	10	15	1	126*	485	34.64	1	3	20
	S.T.Evans	11	18	–	138	591	32.83	3	1	3
	E.Barnes	10	12	4	83*	259	32.37	–	2	4
	L.P.J.Kimber	4	6	1	71	151	30.20	–	2	6
	M.H.Azad	12	20	2	152	518	28.77	2	1	4
	B.W.M.Mike	13	19	1	74	495	27.50	–	4	2
	H.E.Dearden	3	6	–	62	126	21.00	–	1	1
	R.K.Patel	5	7	–	44	143	20.42	–	–	4
2021	C.J.C.Wright	12	16	2	87	257	18.35	–	1	2
	C.F.Parkinson	13	18	2	41	253	15.81	–	–	2
	G.T.Griffiths	5	6	3	16	44	14.66	–	–	–
	W.S.Davis	6	7	3	42	54	13.50	–	–	3
	A.Sakande	3	4	2	9	23	11.50	–	–	2
	H.A.Evans	4	6	2	12	29	7.25	–	–	–
	D.Klein	3	4	–	12	12	3.00	–	–	–

Also batted: S.D.Bates (1 match) 0, 6 (2 ct, 1st); J.P.Inglis (2) 27, 49, 52 (4 ct).

BOWLING

	O	*M*	*R*	*W*	*Avge*	*Best*	*5wI*	*10wM*
C.J.C.Wright	351	74	1116	49	22.77	7-53	4	–
W.S.Davis	157.4	32	416	15	27.73	5-66	1	–
C.F.Parkinson	479.4	122	1452	50	29.04	5-45	3	1
E.Barnes	204.2	30	724	18	40.22	4-61	–	–
B.W.M.Mike	256	40	1002	23	43.56	4-34	–	–
Also bowled:								
C.N.Ackermann	96	22	324	9	36.00	3-44	–	–
A.Sakande	89.2	14	309	7	44.14	3-66	–	–
G.T.Griffiths	92	8	388	7	55.42	3-93	–	–

H.E.Dearden 0.5-0-8-0; H.A.Evans 79-8-297-4; L.J.Hill 4-0-22-0; L.P.J.Kimber 3-1-15-0; D.Klein 53.5-5-254-4; G.H.Rhodes 32-2-97-0.

The First-Class Averages (pp 220–232) give the records of Leicestershire players in all first-class county matches.

LEICESTERSHIRE RECORDS

FIRST-CLASS CRICKET

Highest Total	For	701-4d		v	Worcs	Worcester	1906
	V	761-6d		by	Essex	Chelmsford	1990
Lowest Total	For	25		v	Kent	Leicester	1912
	V	24		by	Glamorgan	Leicester	1971
		24		by	Oxford U	Oxford	1985
Highest Innings	For	309*	H.D.Ackerman	v	Glamorgan	Cardiff	2006
	V	355*	K.P.Pietersen	for	Surrey	The Oval	2015

Highest Partnership for each Wicket

1st	390	B.Dudleston/J.F.Steele	v	Derbyshire	Leicester	1979
2nd	320	M.H.Azad/N.J.Dexter	v	Glos	Leicester	2019
3rd	436*	D.L.Maddy/B.J.Hodge	v	L'boro UCCE	Leicester	2003
4th	360*	J.W.A.Taylor/A.B.McDonald	v	Middlesex	Leicester	2010
5th	330	J.W.A.Taylor/S.J.Thakor	v	L'boro MCCU	Leicester	2011
6th	284	P.V.Simmons/P.A.Nixon	v	Durham	Chester-le-St[2]	1996
7th	219*	J.D.R.Benson/P.Whitticase	v	Hampshire	Bournemouth	1991
8th	203*	H.J.Swindells/E.Barnes	v	Somerset	Taunton	2021
9th	160	R.T.Crawford/ W.W.Odell	v	Worcs	Leicester	1902
10th	228	R.Illingworth/K.Higgs	v	Northants	Leicester	1977

Best Bowling	For	10- 18	G.Geary	v	Glamorgan	Pontypridd	1929
(Innings)	V	10- 32	H.Pickett	for	Essex	Leyton	1895
Best Bowling	For	16- 96	G.Geary	v	Glamorgan	Pontypridd	1929
(Match)	V	16-102	C.Blythe	for	Kent	Leicester	1909

Most Runs – Season	2446	L.G.Berry	(av 52.04)	1937
Most Runs – Career	30143	L.G.Berry	(av 30.32)	1924-51
Most 100s – Season	7	L.G.Berry		1937
	7	W.Watson		1959
	7	B.F.Davison		1982
Most 100s – Career	45	L.G.Berry		1924-51
Most Wkts – Season	170	J.E.Walsh	(av 18.96)	1948
Most Wkts – Career	2131	W.E.Astill	(av 23.18)	1906-39
Most Career W-K Dismissals	905	R.W.Tolchard	(794 ct; 111 st)	1965-83
Most Career Catches in the Field	426	M.R.Hallam		1950-70

LIMITED-OVERS CRICKET

Highest Total	**50ov**	406-5		v	Berkshire	Leicester	1996
	40ov	344-4		v	Durham	Chester-le-St[2]	1996
	T20	229-5		v	Warwicks	Birmingham	2018
Lowest Total	**50ov**	56		v	Northants	Leicester	1964
		56		v	Minor Cos	Wellington	1982
	40ov	36		v	Sussex	Leicester	1973
	T20	90		v	Notts	Nottingham	2014
Highest Innings	**50ov**	201	V.J.Wells	v	Berkshire	Leicester	1996
	40ov	154*	B.J.Hodge	v	Sussex	Horsham	2004
	T20	118*	J.P.Inglis	v	Worcs	Leicester	2021
Best Bowling	**50ov**	6-16	C.M.Willoughby	v	Somerset	Leicester	2005
	40ov	6-17	K.Higgs	v	Glamorgan	Leicester	1973
	T20	7-18	C.N.Ackermann	v	Warwicks	Leicester	2019

MIDDLESEX

Formation of Present Club: 2 February 1864
Inaugural First-Class Match: 1864
Colours: Blue
Badge: Three Seaxes
County Champions (since 1890): (11) 1903, 1920, 1921, 1947, 1976, 1980, 1982, 1985, 1990, 1993, 2016
Joint Champions: (2) 1949, 1977
Gillette/NatWest Trophy Winners: (4) 1977, 1980, 1984, 1988
Benson and Hedges Cup Winners: (2) 1983, 1986
Sunday League Winners: (1) 1992
Twenty20 Cup Winners: (1) 2008

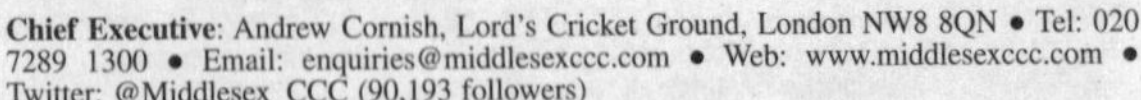

Chief Executive: Andrew Cornish, Lord's Cricket Ground, London NW8 8QN • Tel: 020 7289 1300 • Email: enquiries@middlesexccc.com • Web: www.middlesexccc.com • Twitter: @Middlesex_CCC (90,193 followers)

Head of Men's Cricket: Alan Coleman. **1st Team Coach**: Richard Johnson. **Club Coach**: Rory Coutts. **Batting Coach**: Mark Ramprakash. **T20 Bowling Coach**: Dimitri Mascarenhas. **Captains**: T.J.Murtagh (club), P.S.P.Handscomb (f-c and l-o) and E.J.G.Morgan (T20). **Overseas Players**: P.S.P.Handscomb, Mujeeb Zadran (T20 only) and Shaheen Shah Afridi. **2022 Testimonial**: E.J.G.Morgan. **Head Groundsman**: Karl McDermott. **Scorer**: Don Shelley. ‡ New registration. [NQ] Not qualified for England.

ANDERSSON, Martin Kristoffer (Reading Blue Coat S), b Reading, Berks 6 Sep 1996. 6'1". RHB, RM. Squad No 24. Debut (Leeds/Bradford MCCU) 2017. Derbyshire 2018 (on loan). Middlesex debut 2018. Berkshire 2015-16. HS 92 v Hants (Radlett) 2020. BB 4-25 De v Glamorgan (Derby) 2018. M BB 4-27 v Leics (Leicester) 2021. LO HS 44* and LO BB 1-83 v Sussex (Hove) 2021 (RLC). T20 HS 24. T20 BB –.

BAMBER, Ethan Read (Mill Hill S), b Westminster 17 Dec 1998. 5'11". RHB, RMF. Squad No 54. Debut (Middlesex) 2018. Gloucestershire 2019 (on loan). Middlesex 2nd XI debut 2015. Berkshire 2017. HS 27* v Glos (Bristol) 2018. 50 wkts (1): 52 (2021). BB 5-41 v Derbys (Lord's) 2021. T20 HS 0*. T20 BB 1-38.

CRACKNELL, Joseph Benjamin (London Oratory S), b Enfield 16 Mar 2000. 5'9". RHB, WK. Squad No 48. Debut (Middlesex) 2021. London Spirit 2021. Middlesex 2nd XI debut 2017. Berkshire 2018. HS 13 v Leics (Northwood) 2021. LO HS 2 v Essex (Chelmsford) 2021 (RLC). T20 HS 77.

CULLEN, Blake Carlton (Hampton S), b Hounslow 19 Feb 2002. 6'1". RHB, RMF. Squad No 19. Debut (Middlesex) 2020. London Spirit 2021. Middlesex 2nd XI debut 2017, aged 15y 142d. HS 34 v Sussex (Radlett) 2020. BB 3-30 v Surrey (Oval) 2021. T20 HS 20*. T20 BB 4-32.

DAVIES, Jack Leo Benjamin (Wellington C), b Reading, Berks 30 Mar 2000. Son of A.G.Davies (Cambridge U 1982-89). 5'10". LHB, WK. Squad No 17. Debut (Middlesex) 2020. Middlesex 2nd XI debut 2017. Berkshire 2017-19. England U19 2018. HS 24 v Hants (Lord's) 2021. LO HS 70 v Essex (Chelmsford) 2021 (RLC). T20 HS 23. T20 HS 23.

De CAIRES, Joshua Michael (St Albans S; Leeds U), b Paddington 25 Apr 2002. Son of M.A.Atherton (Lancashire, Cambridge U & England 1987-2001); great-grandson of F.I.de Caires (British Guiana & West Indies 1928/29-1938). 6'0". RHB, RM. Squad No 25. Middlesex 2nd XI debut 2017. HS 17 v Leics (Northwood) 2021. BB –. LO HS 43 and LO BB 1-13 v Kent (Radlett) 2021 (RLC). T20 HS 14.

ESKINAZI, Stephen Sean (Christ Church GS, Claremont; U of WA), b Johannesburg, South Africa 28 Mar 1994. 6'2". RHB, WK. Squad No 28. Debut (Middlesex) 2015; cap 2018; captain 2020. UK passport. HS 179 v Warwks (Birmingham) 2017. LO HS 130 v Worcs (Worcester) 2021 (RLC). T20 HS 102*.

GREATWOOD, Toby Louie (Reading Blue Coats S), b High Wycombe, Bucks 21 Oct 2001. 6'1". RHB, RMF. Squad No 31. Middlesex 2nd XI debut 2019. Berkshire 2018-21. Awaiting f-c debut. LO HS 7* and LO BB 2-30 v Kent (Radlett) 2021 (RLC) – only 1st XI appearance.

NQ**HANDSCOMB, Peter** Stephen Patrick (Mt Waverley SC; Deakin U, Melbourne), b Melbourne, Australia 26 Apr 1991. RHB, WK. Squad No 29. British passport (English parents). Victoria 2011-12 to date. Gloucestershire 2015; cap 2015. Yorkshire 2017. Durham 2019. Middlesex debut 2021; f-c and 50-over captain 2021 to date. IPL: RPS 2016. Big Bash: MS 2012-13 to 2019-20; HH 2020-21 to date. **Tests** (A): 16 (2016-17 to 2018-19); HS 110 v P (Sydney) 2016-17. **LOI** (A): 22 (2016-17 to 2019); HS 117 v I (Mohali) 2018-19. **IT20** (A): 2 (2018-19); HS 20* v I (Bengaluru) 2018-19. F-c Tours (A): SA 2017-18; I 2015 (Aus A), 2016-17, 2018-19; B 2017. HS 215 Vic v NSW (Sydney) 2016-17. CC HS 101* Y v Lancs (Manchester) 2017. M HS 70 v Surrey (Oval) 2021. LO HS 140 Y v Derbys (Leeds) 2017 (RLC). T20 HS 103*.

HARRIS, Max Benjamin, b London 17 Aug 2001. 5'11". RHB, RFM. Squad No 44. Middlesex 2nd XI debut 2019. Awaiting 1st XI debut.

HELM, Thomas George (Misbourne S, Gt Missenden), b Stoke Mandeville Hospital, Bucks 7 May 1994. 6'4". RHB, RMF. Squad No 7. Debut (Middlesex) 2013; cap 2019. Glamorgan 2014 (on loan). Birmingham Phoenix 2021. Buckinghamshire 2011. F-c Tour (EL): SL 2016-17. HS 52 v Derbys (Derby) 2018. BB 5-36 v Worcs (Worcester) 2019. LO HS 30 v Surrey (Lord's) 2018 (RLC). LO BB 5-33 EL v Sri Lanka A (Colombo, CCC) 2016-17. T20 HS 28*. T20 BB 5-11.

HOLDEN, Max David Edward (Sawston Village C; Hills Road SFC, Cambridge), b Cambridge 18 Dec 1997. 5'11". LHB, OB. Squad No 4. Northamptonshire 2017 (on loan). Middlesex debut 2017. Middlesex 2nd XI debut 2013. England U19 2014-15 to 2016-17. F-c Tour (EL): I 2018-19. HS 153 and BB 2-59 Nh v Kent (Beckenham) 2017. M HS 119* v Derbys (Lord's) 2018. M BB 1-15 v Leics (Leicester) 2018. LO HS 166 v Kent (Canterbury) 2019 (RLC) – M record. LO BB 1-29 v Australians (Lord's) 2018. T20 HS 102*. T20 BB –.

HOLLMAN, Luke Barnaby Kurt (Acland Burghley S), b Islington 16 Sep 2000. 6'2". LHB, LB. Squad No 56. Debut (Middlesex) 2021. Middlesex 2nd XI debut 2017. Berkshire 2019. England U19 2018 to 2018-19. HS 46 v Worcs (Lord's) 2021. BB 5-65 v Sussex (Hove) 2021. LO HS 14* v Worcs (Worcester) 2021 (RLC). LO BB 4-56 v Lancs (Manchester) 2021 (RLC). T20 HS 51. T20 BB 3-18.

KAUSHAL, Ishaan (Dovay Martyrs S; Brunel U), b Hillingdon 9 Feb 2002. 6'1". RHB, RM. Squad No 22. Middlesex 2nd XI debut 2021. Awaiting 1st XI debut.

MORGAN, Eoin Joseph Gerard (Catholic University S), b Dublin, Ireland 10 Sep 1986. 6'0". LHB, RM. Squad No 16. UK passport. Ireland 2004 to 2007-08. Middlesex debut 2006; cap 2008; testimonial 2022; l-o captain 2014-15; T20 captain 2020 to date. IPL: RCB 2009-10; KKR 2011 to date; SH 2015-16; KXIP 2017. Big Bash: ST 2013-14 to 2016-17. London Spirit 2021. *Wisden* 2010. CBE 2020. **ECB Central Contract 2021-22. Tests**: 16 (2010 to 2011-12); HS 130 v P (Nottingham) 2010. **LOI** (E/Ire): 246 (23 for Ire 2006 to 2008-09; 223 for E 2009 to 2021, 124 as captain); HS 148 v Afg (Manchester) 2019, inc world record 17 sixes. **IT20**: 115 (2009 to 2021-22, 72 as captain); HS 91 v NZ (Napier) 2019-20. F-c Tours (Ire): A 2010-11 (E); NZ 2008-09 (Eng A); Namibia 2005-06; UAE 2006-07, 2007-08, 2011-12 (v P). 1000 runs (1): 1085 (2008). HS 209* Ire v UAE (Abu Dhabi) 2006-07. M HS 191 v Notts (Nottingham) 2014. BB 2-24 v Notts (Lord's) 2007. LO HS 161 v Kent (Canterbury) 2009 (FPT). LO BB –. T20 HS 91.

[NQ]**MUJEEB ZADRAN** (also known as Mujeeb Ur Rahman), b Khost, Afghanistan 28 Mar 2001. 5'11". RHB, OB. Squad No 88. Afghanistan 2018. Hampshire 2018 (T20 only). Middlesex debut 2019 (T20 only). IPL: KXIP 2018 to 2020-21; SH 2021. Big Bash: BH 2018-19 to date. Northern Superchargers 2021. **Tests** (Afg): 1 (2018); HS 15 and BB 1-75 v I (Bengalaru) 2018. **LOI** (Afg): 49 (2017-18 to 2021-22); HS 18* v Ire (Abu Dhabi) 2020-21; BB 5-50 v Z (Sharjah) 2017-18. **IT20** (Afg): 23 (2017-18 to 2021-22); HS 8* v WI (Lucknow) 2019-20; BB 5-20 v Scot (Sharjah) 2021-22. F-c Tour (Afg): I 2018. HS 15 (*see Tests*). BB 1-75 (*see Tests*). LO HS 18* (*see LOI*). LO BB 5-50 (*see LOI*). T20 HS 27. T20 BB 5-15.

[NQ]**MURTAGH, Tim**othy James (John Fisher S; St Mary's C), b Lambeth, London 2 Aug 1981. Elder brother of C.P.Murtagh (Loughborough UCCE and Surrey 2005-09), nephew of A.J.Murtagh (Hampshire and EP 1973-77). 6'0". LHB, RMF. Squad No 34. British U 2000-03. Surrey 2001-06. Middlesex debut 2007; cap 2008; benefit 2015; captain 2022. Ireland 2012-13 to 2019. MCC 2010. **Tests** (Ire): 3 (2018 to 2019); HS 54* v Afg (Dehradun) 2018-19; BB 5-13 v E (Lord's) 2019. **LOI** (Ire): 58 (2012 to 2019); HS 23* v Scotland (Belfast) 2013; BB 5-21 v Z (Belfast) 2019. **IT20** (Ire): 14 (2012 to 2015-16); HS 12* v UAE (Abu Dhabi) 2015-16; BB 3-23 v PNG (Townsville) 2015-16. HS 74* Sy v Middx (Oval) 2004 and 74* Sy v Warwks (Croydon) 2005. M HS 55 v Leics (Leicester) 2011, sharing M record 9th wkt partnership of 172 with G.K.Berg. 50 wkts (9); most – 85 (2011). BB 7-82 v Derbys (Derby) 2009. LO HS 35* v Surrey (Lord's) 2008 (FPT). LO BB 5-21 (*see LOI*). T20 HS 40*. T20 BB 6-24 Sy v Middx (Lord's) 2005 – Sy record.

O'DRISCOLL, Daniel Mark (Ruislip HS), b Hillingdon 10 Oct 2002. 5'9". RHB, WK. Squad No 2. Middlesex 2nd XI debut 2019. Awaiting 1st XI debut.

ROBSON, Sam David (Marcellin C, Randwick), b Paddington, Sydney, Australia 1 Jul 1989. Elder brother of A.J.Robson Leicestershire, Sussex and Durham 2013-19). 6'0". RHB, LB. Squad No 12. Qualified for England in April 2013. Debut (Middlesex) 2009; cap 2013. **Tests**: 7 (2014); HS 127 v SL (Leeds) 2014. F-c Tours (EL): SA 2014-15; SL 2013-14. 1000 runs (2); most – 1180 (2013). HS 253 v Sussex (Hove) 2021, sharing M record 1st wkt partnership of 376 with M.D.Stoneman. BB 2-0 v Surrey (Oval) 2020. LO HS 106 v Somerset (Radlett) 2019 (RLC). LO BB 1-26 v Durham (Radlett) 2021 (RLC). T20 HS 60.

ROLAND-JONES, Tobias Skelton ('**Toby**') (Hampton S; Leeds U), b Ashford 29 Jan 1988. 6'4". RHB, RFM. Squad No 21. Debut (Middlesex) 2010; cap 2012. MCC 2011. *Wisden* 2016. Leeds/Bradford UCCE 2009 (not f-c). **Tests**: 4 (2017); HS 25 and BB 5-57 v SA (Oval) 2017. **LOI**: 1 (2017); HS 37* and BB 1-34 v SA (Lord's) 2017. F-c Tours (EL): WI 2017-18; SL 2016-17; UAE 2016-17 (v Afg). HS 103* v Yorks (Lord's) 2015. 50 wkts (2); most – 64 (2012). BB 7-52 (10-79 match) v Glos (Northwood) 2019. Hat-tricks (2): v Derbys (Lord's) 2013, and v Yorks (Lord's) 2016 – at end of match to secure the Championship. LO HS 65 v Glos (Lord's) 2017 (RLC). LO BB 4-10 v Hants (Southampton) 2017 (RLC). T20 HS 40. T20 BB 5-21.

‡[NQ]**SHAHEEN** Shah **AFRIDI**, b Khyber Agency, Pakistan 6 Apr 2000. 6'4½". LHB, LFM. Squad No 10. Khan Research Laboratories 2017-18. Northern Areas 2019-20. Hampshire 2020 (T20 only). **Tests** (P): 22 (2018-19 to 2021-22); HS 19 and BB 6-51 v WI (Kingston) 2021. **LOI** (P): 28 (2018-19 to 2021); HS 19* v E (Leeds) 2019; BB 6-35 v B (Lord's) 2019. **IT20** (P): 39 (2017-18 to 2021-22); HS 10* v NZ (Auckland) 2020-21; BB 3-20 v NZ (Dubai, DSC) 2018-19. F-c Tours (P): E 2020; A 2019-20; SA 2018-19; WI 2021; NZ 2020-21; B 2021-22. HS 25 P v Australia A (Perth, OS) 2019-20. BB 8-39 KRL v Rawalpindi (Rawalpindi) 2017-18 – on f-c debut, aged 17y 174d. LO HS 19* (*see LOI*). LO BB 6-35 (*see LOI*). T20 HS 39*. T20 BB 6-19 v Middx (Southampton) 2020 – H record.

SIMPSON, John Andrew (St Gabriel's RC HS), b Bury, Lancs 13 Jul 1988. 5'10". LHB, WK. Squad No 20. Debut (Middlesex) 2009; cap 2011. MCC 2018. Northern Superchargers 2021. Cumberland 2007. **LOI**: 3 (2021); HS 17 v P (Lord's) 2021. HS 167* v Lancs (Manchester) 2019. LO HS 82* v Sussex (Lord's) 2017 (RLC). T20 HS 84*.

SOWTER, Nathan Adam (Hill Sport HS, NSW), b Penrith, NSW, Australia 12 Oct 1992. 5'10". RHB, LB. Squad No 72. Debut (Middlesex) 2017. Oval Invincibles 2021. HS 57* v Glamorgan (Cardiff) 2019. BB 3-42 v Lancs (Manchester) 2017. LO HS 31 v Surrey (Oval) 2019 (RLC). LO BB 6-62 v Essex (Chelmsford) 2019 (RLC). T20 HS 37*. T20 BB 4-23.

STONEMAN, Mark Daniel (Whickham CS), b Newcastle upon Tyne, Northumb 26 Jun 1987. 5'10". LHB, OB. Squad No 11. Durham 2007-16; captain (l-o only) 2015-16. Surrey 2017-21; cap 2018. Middlesex debut 2021. Yorkshire 2021 (T20 only). **Tests**: 11 (2017 to 2018); HS 60 v NZ (Christchurch) 2017-18. F-c Tour: A 2017-18; NZ 2017-18. 1000 runs (5); most – 1481 (2017). HS 197 Sy v Essex (Guildford) 2017. M HS 174 v Sussex (Hove) 2021, sharing M record 1st wkt partnership of 376 with S.D.Robson. BB –. LO HS 144* v Notts (Lord's) 2017 (RLC). LO BB 1-8 Du v Derbys (Derby) 2016 (RLC). T20 HS 89*.

WALALLAWITA, Thilan Nipuna (Oaklands S), b Colombo, Sri Lanka 23 Jun 1998. 5'9". LHB, SLA. Squad No 32. Moved to UK in 2004. Debut (Middlesex) 2020. Middlesex 2nd XI debut 2015. HS 20* v Derbys (Lord's) 2021. BB 3-28 v Hants (Radlett) 2020. LO HS 29 v Lancs (Manchester) 2021 (RLC). LO BB 2-54 v Worcs (Worcester) 2021 (RLC). T20 HS 0. T20 BB 3-19.

WHITE, Robert George (Harrow S; Loughborough U), b Ealing 15 Sep 1995. 5'9". RHB, WK, occ RM. Squad No 14. Loughborough MCCU 2015-17. Middlesex debut 2018. Essex 2019 (on loan). HS 120 v Derbys (Lord's) 2021. LO HS 55 v Durham (Radlett) 2021 (RLC). T20 HS 11*.

RELEASED/RETIRED

(Having made a County 1st XI appearance in 2021)

FINN, S.T. – *see SUSSEX.*

[NQ]**GREEN, Chris**topher James (Knox GS, Wahroonga), b Durban, South Africa 1 Oct 1993. RHB, OB. Awaiting f-c debut. New South Wales (l-o only) 2014-15 to 2018-19. Warwickshire 2019 (T20 only). Middlesex 2021 (T20 only). IPL: KKR 2020-21. Big Bash: ST 2014-15 to date. LO HS 24 NSW v Tas (Sydney, NS) 2018-19. LO BB 5-53 NSW v Q (Sydney, DO) 2018-19. T20 HS 50. T20 BB 5-32.

GUBBINS, N.R.T. – *see HAMPSHIRE.*

HARRIS, J.A.R. – *see GLAMORGAN.*

[NQ]**MITCHELL, Daryl** Joseph, b Hamilton, New Zealand 20 May 1991. RHB, RM. N Districts 2011-12 to 2019-20. Canterbury 2020-21. Middlesex 2021. **Tests** (NZ): 9 (2019-20 to 2021-22); HS 102* v P (Christchurch) 2020-21; BB 1-7 v WI (Hamilton) 2020-21. **LOI** (NZ): 3 (2020-21); HS 100* v B (Wellington) 2020-21; BB –. **IT20** (NZ): 25 (2018-19 to 2021-22); HS 72* v E (Abu Dhabi) 2021-22; BB 2-27 v I (Hamilton) 2018-19. F-c Tours (NZ): E 2021; I/SL 2013-14 (NZA); I 2021-22. HS 170* ND v Canterbury (Christchurch) 2019-20. M HS 73 v Glos (Cheltenham) 2021. BB 5-44 Cant v Otago (Alexandra) 2020-21. LO HS 126* ND v Wellington (Wellington) 2017-18. LO BB 3-34 ND v Wellington (Mt Maunganui) 2014-15. T20 HS 88*. T20 BB 4-32.

STIRLING, P.R. – *see IRELAND.*

MIDDLESEX 2021

RESULTS SUMMARY

	Place	Won	Lost	Drew	NR
LV= Insurance County Champ (Div 3)	2nd	5	8	1	
Royal London One-Day Cup (Group 1)	8th	2	4		1
Vitality Blast (South Group)	8th	4	9		1

LV= INSURANCE COUNTY CHAMPIONSHIP AVERAGES
BATTING AND FIELDING

Cap		*M*	*I*	*NO*	*HS*	*Runs*	*Avge*	*100*	*50*	*Ct/St*
	M.D.Stoneman	4	7	–	174	354	50.57	2	1	–
2013	S.D.Robson	14	27	1	253	1047	40.26	3	2	16
	R.G.White	14	26	4	120	765	34.77	2	4	19
2016	N.R.T.Gubbins	8	15	–	124	514	34.26	1	4	1
	D.J.Mitchell	2	4	–	73	134	33.50	–	1	–
2018	S.S.Eskinazi	9	17	2	102	453	30.20	1	2	8
2011	J.A.Simpson	13	22	2	95*	535	26.75	–	3	50/3
	L.B.K.Hollman	6	9	1	46	176	22.00	–	–	3
	M.K.Andersson	13	24	–	88	439	18.29	–	2	6
	M.D.E.Holden	10	19	1	52	325	18.05	–	1	6
	T.N.Walallawita	4	6	3	20*	54	18.00	–	–	2
	P.S.P.Handscomb	7	13	–	70	227	17.46	–	1	3
2012	T.S.Roland-Jones	6	11	2	46*	138	15.33	–	–	–
	B.C.Cullen	4	5	–	27	55	11.00	–	–	–
	N.A.Sowter	3	6	1	24*	46	9.20	–	–	3
2015	J.A.R.Harris	3	6	–	26	55	9.16	–	–	1
	J.L.B.Davies	2	4	–	24	35	8.75	–	–	1
	E.R.Bamber	12	22	4	25	151	8.38	–	–	2
2019	T.G.Helm	4	8	2	17	49	8.16	–	–	1
	J.M.De Caires	2	4	–	17	28	7.00	–	–	1
2008	T.J.Murtagh	12	20	7	31	88	6.76	–	–	3
2009	S.T.Finn	2	4	1	13*	17	5.66	–	–	–

Also batted: J.B.Cracknell (1 match) 13, 7 (2 ct).

BOWLING

	O	*M*	*R*	*W*	*Avge*	*Best*	*5wI*	*10wM*
T.S.Roland-Jones	167.4	38	460	25	18.40	5-36	1	–
T.J.Murtagh	402.4	113	1079	58	18.60	5-64	1	–
E.R.Bamber	407	111	1084	52	20.84	5-41	1	–
S.T.Finn	68.2	4	266	12	22.16	5-77	1	–
J.A.R.Harris	65.3	3	230	10	23.00	3-50	–	–
L.B.K.Hollman	105.4	16	363	13	27.92	5-65	2	1
M.K.Andersson	250.1	41	916	29	31.58	4-27	–	–
B.C.Cullen	109.2	19	393	10	39.30	3-30	–	–
Also bowled:								
D.J.Mitchell	44	8	142	9	15.77	4-42	–	–
T.G.Helm	131.1	21	413	8	51.62	3-47	–	–

J.M.De Caires 3-0-7-0; N.R.T.Gubbins 1-0-2-0; M.D.E.Holden 1-0-8-0; S.D.Robson 17-0-72-2; N.A.Sowter 68-7-237-2; T.N.Walallawita 102.2-20-326-3.

The First-Class Averages (pp 220–232) give the records of Middlesex players in all first-class county matches, with the exception of N.R.T.Gubbins, J.A.R.Harris, D.J.Mitchell and M.D.Stoneman, whose first-class figures for Middlesex are as above.

MIDDLESEX RECORDS

FIRST-CLASS CRICKET

Highest Total	For 676-5d		v	Sussex	Hove	2021
	V 850-7d		by	Somerset	Taunton	2007
Lowest Total	For 20		v	MCC	Lord's	1864
	V 31		by	Glos	Bristol	1924
Highest Innings	For 331*	J.D.B.Robertson	v	Worcs	Worcester	1949
	V 341	C.M.Spearman	for	Glos	Gloucester	2004

Highest Partnership for each Wicket

1st	376	S.D.Robson/M.D.Stoneman	v	Sussex	Hove	2021
2nd	380	F.A.Tarrant/J.W.Hearne	v	Lancashire	Lord's	1914
3rd	424*	W.J.Edrich/D.C.S.Compton	v	Somerset	Lord's	1948
4th	325	J.W.Hearne/E.H.Hendren	v	Hampshire	Lord's	1919
5th	338	R.S.Lucas/T.C.O'Brien	v	Sussex	Hove	1895
6th	270	J.D.Carr/P.N.Weekes	v	Glos	Lord's	1994
7th	271*	E.H.Hendren/F.T.Mann	v	Notts	Nottingham	1925
8th	182*	M.H.C.Doll/H.R.Murrell	v	Notts	Lord's	1913
9th	172	G.K.Berg/T.J.Murtagh	v	Leics	Leicester	2011
10th	230	R.W.Nicholls/W.Roche	v	Kent	Lord's	1899

Best Bowling	For	10- 40	G.O.B.Allen	v	Lancashire	Lord's	1929
(Innings)	V	9- 38	R.C.R-Glasgow†	for	Somerset	Lord's	1924
Best Bowling	For	16-114	G.Burton	v	Yorkshire	Sheffield	1888
(Match)		16-114	J.T.Hearne	v	Lancashire	Manchester	1898
	V	16-100	J.E.B.B.P.Q.C.Dwyer	for	Sussex	Hove	1906

Most Runs – Season	2669	E.H.Hendren	(av 83.41)	1923
Most Runs – Career	40302	E.H.Hendren	(av 48.81)	1907-37
Most 100s – Season	13	D.C.S.Compton		1947
Most 100s – Career	119	E.H.Hendren		1907-37
Most Wkts – Season	158	F.J.Titmus	(av 14.63)	1955
Most Wkts – Career	2361	F.J.Titmus	(av 21.27)	1949-82
Most Career W-K Dismissals	1223	J.T.Murray	(1024 ct; 199 st)	1952-75
Most Career Catches in the Field	561	E.H.Hendren		1907-37

LIMITED-OVERS CRICKET

Highest Total	**50ov**	380-5		v	Kent	Canterbury	2019
	40ov	350-6		v	Lancashire	Lord's	2012
	T20	227-4		v	Somerset	Taunton	2019
Lowest Total	**50ov**	41		v	Essex	Westcliff	1972
	40ov	23		v	Yorkshire	Leeds	1974
	T20	80		v	Kent	Lord's	2021
Highest Innings	**50ov**	166	M.D.E.Holden	v	Kent	Canterbury	2019
	40ov	147*	M.R.Ramprakash	v	Worcs	Lord's	1990
	T20	129	D.T.Christian	v	Kent	Canterbury	2014
Best Bowling	**50ov**	7-12	W.W.Daniel	v	Minor Cos E	Ipswich	1978
	40ov	6- 6	R.W.Hooker	v	Surrey	Lord's	1969
	T20	6-28	J.K.Fuller	v	Hampshire	Southampton[2]	2018

† R.C.Robertson-Glasgow

NORTHAMPTONSHIRE

Formation of Present Club: 31 July 1878
Inaugural First-Class Match: 1905
Colours: Maroon
Badge: Tudor Rose
County Champions: (0); best – 2nd 1912, 1957, 1965, 1976
Gillette/NatWest/C&G/FP Trophy Winners: (2) 1976, 1992
Benson and Hedges Cup Winners: (1) 1980
Twenty20 Cup Winners: (2) 2013, 2016

Chief Executive: Ray Payne, County Ground, Abington Avenue, Northampton, NN1 4PR • Tel: 01604 514455 • Email: info@nccc.co.uk • Web: www.nccc.co.uk • Twitter: @NorthantsCCC (66,087 followers)

Head Coach: John Sadler. **Batting Coach**: Ben Smith. **Assistant Coach/Bowling Lead**: Chris Liddle. **Captains**: A.M.Rossington (f-c) and J.J.Cobb (T20). **Overseas Players**: M.L.Kelly, J.D.S.Neesham and W.A.Young. **2022 Testimonial**: None. **Head Groundsman**: Craig Harvey. **Scorer**: Tony Kingston. **Blast Team Name**: Northamptonshire Steelbacks. ‡ New registration. [NQ] Not qualified for England.

BERG, Gareth Kyle (South African College S), b Cape Town, South Africa 18 Jan 1981. 6'0". RHB, RMF. Squad No 13. England qualified through residency. Middlesex 2008-14; cap 2010. Hampshire 2015-19; cap 2016. Northamptonshire debut 2019. Italy 2011-12 to date (l-o and T20 only). **IT20** (Italy): 6 (2021-22); HS 12* v Denmark (Almeria) 2021-22; BB 2-23 v Denmark (Almeria) 2021-22 – separate matches. HS 130* M v Leics (Leicester) 2011, sharing M record 9th wkt partnership of 172 with T.J.Murtagh. Nh HS 69* v Glamorgan (Northampton) 2021. BB 6-56 H v Yorks (Southampton) 2016. Nh BB 5-18 v Sussex (Northampton) 2021. LO HS 75 M v Glamorgan (Lord's) 2013 (Y40). LO BB 5-26 H v Lancs (Southampton) 2019 (RLC). T20 HS 90. T20 BB 4-20.

BUCK, Nathan Liam (Newbridge HS; Ashby S), b Leicester 26 Apr 1991. 6'2". RHB, RMF. Squad No 11. Leicestershire 2009-14; cap 2011. Lancashire 2015-16. Northamptonshire debut 2017. F-c Tour (EL): WI 2010-11. HS 53 v Glamorgan (Cardiff) 2019. BB 6-34 v Durham (Chester-le-St) 2017. LO HS 21 Le v Glamorgan (Leicester) 2009 (P40). LO BB 4-39 EL v Sri Lanka A (Dambulla) 2011-12. T20 HS 26*. T20 BB 4-26.

COBB, Joshua James (Oakham S), b Leicester 17 Aug 1990. Son of R.A.Cobb (Leics and N Transvaal 1980-89). 5'11½". RHB, OB. Squad No 4. Leicestershire 2007-14; l-o captain 2014. Northamptonshire debut 2015; cap 2018; captain 2020 to date (white ball only). Welsh Fire 2021. HS 148* Le v Middx (Lord's) 2008. Nh HS 139 v Durham MCCU (Northampton) 2019. BB 2-11 Le v Glos (Leicester) 2008. Nh BB 2-44 v Loughborough MCCU (Northampton) 2017. LO HS 146* v Pakistanis (Northampton) 2019. LO BB 3-34 Le v Glos (Leicester) 2013 (Y40). T20 HS 103. T20 BB 4-22.

CURRAN, Benjamin Jack (Wellington C), b Northampton 7 Jun 1996. Son of K.M.Curran (Glos, Natal, Northants, Boland and Zimbabwe 1980-81 to 1999); grandson of K.P.Curran (Rhodesia 1947-48 to 1954-55); younger brother of T.K.Curran (*see SURREY*) and elder brother of S.M.Curran (*see SURREY*). 5'8". LHB, OB. Squad No 17. Debut (Northamptonshire) 2018. Southern Rocks 2021-22. HS 83* v Sussex (Northampton) 2018. LO HS 94 v Somerset (Northampton) 2021 (RLC). T20 HS 62.

GAY, Emilio Nico (Bedford S), b Bedford May 2000. 6'2". LHB, RM. Squad No 19. Debut (Northamptonshire) 2019. Northamptonshire 2nd XI debut 2018. HS 101 v Kent (Canterbury) 2021. BB 1-8 v Kent (Northampton) 2021. LO HS 84* v Derbys (Northampton) 2021 (RLC). LO BB –. T20 HS 15.

[NQ]**GLOVER, Brandon** Dale (St Stithians C), b Johannesburg, South Africa 3 Apr 1997. 6'2½". RHB, RFM. Squad No 20. Boland 2016-17 to 2018-19. **LOI** (Neth): 6 (2019 to 2021-22); HS 18 v Ire (Utrecht) 2021; BB 3-43 v Afg (Doha) 2021-22. **IT20** (Neth): 21 (2019 to 2021-22); HS 1* (twice); BB 4-12 v UAE (Dubai, DSC) 2019-20. HS 12* Boland v Gauteng (Paarl) 2018-19. Nh HS 0. BB 4-83 Boland v FS (Bloemfontein) 2017-18. Nh BB 2-45 v Somerset (Northampton) 2020. LO HS 27 Boland v Easterns (Benoni) 2017-18. LO BB 3-43 (*see LOI*). T20 HS 6*. T20 BB 4-12.

GOULDSTONE, Harry Oliver Michael (Bedford S), b Kettering 26 Mar 2001. RHB, WK. Debut (Northamptonshire) 2020. Northamptonshire 2nd XI debut 2019. HS 67* v Glamorgan (Cardiff) 2021.

HELDREICH, Frederick James (Framlingham C), b Ipswich, Suffolk 12 Sep 2001. 6'3". RHB, SLC. Northamptonshire 2nd XI debut 2021. Awaiting f-c debut. LO HS 5 and LO BB 2-69 v Glamorgan (Northampton) 2021 (RLC). T20 BB 2-17.

‡[NQ]**KELLY, Matt** Liam, b Durban, South Africa 7 Dec 1994. RHB, RMF. W Australia 2017-18 to date. Big Bash: PS 2017-18 to date. HS 89 WA v NSW (Adelaide P25) 2020-21. BB 6-67 WA v SA (Perth) 2018-19. LO HS 27* WA v NSW (Melbourne, St K) 2021-22. LO BB 4-25 WA v Q (Sydney, DO) 2017-18. T20 HS 23*. T20 BB 4-25.

KEOGH, Robert Ian (Queensbury S; Dunstable C), b Luton, Beds 21 Oct 1991. 5'11". RHB, OB. Squad No 21. Debut (Northamptonshire) 2012; cap 2019. Bedfordshire 2009-10. HS 221 v Hants (Southampton) 2013. BB 9-52 (13-125 match) v Glamorgan (Northampton) 2016. LO HS 134 v Durham (Northampton) 2016 (RLC). LO BB 2-26 v Yorks (Leeds) 2018 (RLC). T20 HS 59*. T20 BB 3-30.

KERRIGAN, Simon Christopher (Corpus Christi RC HS, Preston), b Preston, Lancs 10 May 1989. 5'9". RHB, SLA. Squad No 10. Lancashire 2010-17; cap 2013. Northamptonshire debut 2017. MCC 2013. **Tests**: 1 (2013); HS 1* and BB – v A (Oval) 2013. F-c Tour (EL): SL 2013-14. HS 62* La v Hants (Southport) 2013. Nh HS 62 v Glamorgan (Cardiff) 2017. 50 wkts (2); most – 58 (2013). BB 9-51 (12-192 match) La v Hants (Liverpool) 2011. Nh BB 5-39 v Yorks (Northampton) 2021. LO HS 10 La v Middx (Lord's) 2012 (CB40). LO BB 4-48 v Somerset (Northampton) 2021 (RLC). T20 HS 4*. T20 BB 3-17.

MILLER, Augustus ('**Gus**') Horatio (Bedford S), b Oxford 8 Jan 2002. 6'1". RHB, RFM. Northamptonshire 2nd XI debut 2021. Bedfordshire 2018-21. Awaiting 1st XI debut.

‡[NQ]**NEESHAM, James** Douglas Sheahan, b Auckland, New Zealand 17 Sep 1990. LHB, RM. Auckland 2009-10 to 2010-11. Otago 2011-12 to 2017-18. Wellington 2018-19 to date. Essex 2021. Derbyshire 2016 (white ball only). Kent 2017 (T20 only). IPL: DD 2014; KXIP 2020-21; MI 2021. Welsh Fire 2021. **Tests** (NZ): 12 (2013-14 to 2016-17); HS 137* v I (Wellington) 2013-14; BB 3-42 v SL (Wellington) 2014-15. **LOI** (NZ): 66 (2012-13 to 2020-21); HS 97* v P (Birmingham) 2019; BB 5-27 v B (Wellington) 2020-21. **IT20** (NZ): 38 (2012-13 to 2021-22); HS 48* v WI (Auckland) 2020-21; BB 3-16 v WI (Auckland) 2013-14. F-c Tours (NZ): A 2015-16; WI 2014; I 2013-14 (NZ A), 2016-17; UAE (v P) 2014-15. HS 147 Otago v CD (Nelson) 2013-14. BB 5-65 Otago v ND (Whangarei) 2013-14. LO HS 120* Wellington v Auckland (Auckland) 2018-19. LO BB 5-27 (*see LOI*). T20 HS 59*. T20 BB 4-24.

PROCTER, Luke Anthony (Counthill S, Oldham), b Oldham, Lancs 24 June 1988. 5'11". LHB, RM. Squad No 2. Lancashire 2010-17. Northamptonshire debut 2017; cap 2020. Cumberland 2007. HS 137 La v Hants (Manchester) 2016. Nh HS 112* v Warwks (Birmingham) 2020. BB 7-71 La v Surrey (Liverpool) 2012. Nh BB 5-33 v Durham (Chester-le-St) 2017. LO HS 97 La v West Indies A (Manchester) 2010. LO BB 3-29 La v Unicorns (Colwyn Bay) 2010 (CB40). T20 HS 25*. T20 BB 3-22.

ROSSINGTON, Adam Matthew (Mill Hill S), b Edgware, Middx 5 May 1993. 5'11". RHB, WK, occ RM. Squad No 7. Middlesex 2010-14. Northamptonshire debut 2014; cap 2019; captain 2020 to date. London Spirit 2021. HS 138* v Sussex (Arundel) 2016. Won 2013 Walter Lawrence Trophy with 55-ball century v Cambridge MCCU (Cambridge). LO HS 97 v Notts (Nottingham) 2016 (RLC). T20 HS 85.

SALES, James John Grimwood (Wellingborough S), b Northampton 11 Feb 2003. Son of D.J.G.Sales (Northamptonshire and Wellington 1996-2014). RHB, RM. Debut (Northamptonshire) 2021. Northamptonshire 2nd XI debut 2021. HS 53 and BB 2-61 v Durham (Northampton) 2021. LO HS 28 v Leics (Northampton) 2021 (RLC).

SANDERSON, Ben William (Ecclesfield CS; Sheffield C), b Sheffield, Yorks 3 Jan 1989. 6'0". RHB, RMF. Squad No 26. Yorkshire 2008-10. Northamptonshire debut 2015; cap 2018. Shropshire 2013-15. HS 42 v Kent (Canterbury) 2015. 50 wkts (3); most – 61 (2019). BB 8-73 v Glos (Northampton) 2016. LO HS 31 v Derbys (Derby) 2019 (RLC). LO BB 3-29 v Derbys (Northampton) 2021 (RLC). T20 HS 12*. T20 BB 4-21.

TAYLOR, Thomas Alex Ian (Trentham HS, Stoke-on-Trent), b Stoke-on-Trent, Staffs 21 Dec 1994. Elder brother of J.P.A.Taylor (*see SURREY*). 6'2". RHB, RMF. Squad No 12. Derbyshire 2014-17. Leicestershire 2018-20. Northamptonshire debut 2021. HS 80 De v Kent (Derby) 2016. Nh HS 50 v Yorks (Leeds) 2021. BB 6-47 (10-122 match) Le v Sussex (Hove) 2019. Nh BB 5-41 v Surrey (Northampton) 2021. LO HS 98* Le v Warwks (Leicester) 2019 (RLC). LO BB 3-24 v Notts (Grantham) 2021 (RLC). T20 HS 50*. T20 BB 3-33.

THURSTON, Charles Oliver (Bedford S; Loughborough U), b Cambridge 17 Aug 1996. 5'11½". RHB, RM. Squad No 96. Loughborough MCCU 2016-18. Northamptonshire debut 2018. Bedfordshire 2014-17. HS 126 LU v Northants (Northampton) 2017. Nh HS 115 v Glamorgan (Northampton) 2020. BB –. LO HS 53 v Yorks (Leeds) 2018 (RLC). T20 HS 41.

NQ**VASCONCELOS, Ricardo** Surrador (St Stithians C), b Johannesburg, South Africa 27 Oct 1997. 5'5". LHB, WK. Squad No 27. Boland 2016-17 to 2017-18. Northamptonshire debut 2018; cap 2021. South Africa U19 2016. Portuguese passport. HS 185* v Glamorgan (Northampton) 2021. LO HS 112 v Yorks (Northampton) 2019 (RLC). T20 HS 78*.

WHITE, Curtley-**Jack** (Ullswater Comm C; Queen Elizabeth GS, Penrith), b Kendal, Cumberland 19 Feb 1992. 6'2". LHB, RFM. Squad No 9. Debut (Northamptonshire) 2020. Cumberland 2013. Cheshire 2016-17. HS 15* v Glos (Bristol) 2021. BB 4-35 v Glamorgan (Northampton) 2020. LO HS 10* v Leics (Northampton) 2021 (RLC). LO BB 4-20 v Derbys (Northampton) 2021 (RLC).

WHITE, Graeme Geoffrey (Stowe S), b Milton Keynes, Bucks 18 Apr 1987. 5'11". RHB, SLA. Squad No 87. Debut (Northamptonshire) 2006; cap 2021. Nottinghamshire 2010-13. Welsh Fire 2021. HS 65 v Glamorgan (Colwyn Bay) 2007. BB 6-44 v Glamorgan (Northampton) 2016. LO HS 41* v Yorks (Leeds) 2018 (RLC). LO BB 6-37 v Lancs (Northampton) 2016 (RLC). T20 HS 37*. T20 BB 5-22 Nt v Lancs (Nottingham) 2013 – Nt record.

‡NQ**YOUNG, Will**iam Alexander, New Plymouth, New Zealand 22 Nov 1992. RHB, OB. Central Districts 2011-12 to date. Durham 2021. **Tests** (NZ): 9 (2020-21 to 2021-22); HS 89 v I (Kanpur) 2021-22. **LOI** (NZ): 2 (2020-21); HS 11* v B (Dunedin) 2020-21. **IT20** (NZ): 8 (2020-21 to 2021); HS 53 v B (Hamilton) 2020-21. F-c Tours (NZ A) E 2021; I 2017-18, 2021-22; UAE 2018-19 (v P A). HS 162 CD v Auckland (Auckland) 2017-18. CC HS Du v Warwks (Chester-le-St) 2021. LO HS 136 NZ A v Pakistan A (Abu Dhabi) 2018-19. T20 HS 101.

ZAIB, Saif Ali (RGS High Wycombe), b High Wycombe, Bucks 22 May 1998. 5'7½". LHB, SLA. Squad No 18. Debut (Northamptonshire) 2015. Northamptonshire 2nd XI debut 2013, aged 15y 90d. HS 135 v Sussex (Northampton) 2021. BB 6-115 v Loughborough MCCU (Northampton) 2017 CC BB 5-148 v Leics (Northampton) 2016. LO HS 43 and LO BB 3-37 v Leics (Northampton) 2021 (RLC). T20 HS 36. T20 BB 1-20.

RELEASED/RETIRED

(Having made a County 1st XI appearance in 2021)

NQ**LEVI, Richard** Ernst, b Johannesburg, South Africa 14 Jan 1988. 5'11". RHB, RM. W Province 2006-07 to 2016-17. Cape Cobras 2008-09 to 2015-16. Northamptonshire 2014-20; cap 2017. IPL: MI 2012. **IT20** (SA): 13 (2011-12 to 2012-13); HS 117* v NZ (Hamilton) 2011-12. HS 168 v Essex (Northampton) 2015. LO HS 166 Cobras v Titans (Paarl) 2012-13. T20 HS 117*.

NQ**MOHAMMAD NABI** Eisakhil, b Peshawar, Pakistan 7 Mar 1985. 6'3". RHB, OB. Pakistan Customs 2007-08 to 2009-10. MCC 2007-11. Afghanistan 2009 to date. IPL: SH 2017-18 to date. Big Bash: MR 2017-18 to date. Leicestershire 2018 (T20 only). Kent 2019 (T20 only). Northamptonshire 2021 (T20 only). London Spirit 2021. **Tests** (Afg): 3 (2018 to 2019); HS 24 v I (Bengalaru) 2018; BB 3-36 v Ire (Dehradun) 2018-19. **LOI** (Afg): 130 (2009 to 2021-22); HS 116 v Z (Bulawayo) 2015-16; BB 4-30 v Ire (Greater Noida) 2016-17 and 4-30 v SL (Cardiff) 2019. **IT20** (Afg): 88 (2009-10 to 2021-22); HS 89 v Ire (Greater Noida) 2016-17; BB 4-10 v Ire (Dubai, DSC) 2016-17. HS 117 Afg v UAE (Sharjah) 2011-12. BB 6-33 Afg v Namibia (Windhoek) 2013. LO HS 146 MSC v PDSC (Bogra) 2013-14. LO BB 5-12 Afg v Namibia (Windhoek) 2013. T20 HS 89. T20 BB 5-15.

NQ**PARNELL, Wayne** Dillon (Grey HS), b Port Elizabeth, South Africa 30 Jul 1989. 6'2". LHB, LFM. E Province 2006-07 to 2010-11. Warriors 2008-09 to 2014-15. Kent 2009-17. Sussex 2011. Cape Cobras 2015-16 to 2016-17. Worcestershire 2018-19. Northamptonshire 2021. W Province 2021-22. IPL: PW 2011-13; DD 2014. Glamorgan 2015 (T20 only). **Tests** (SA): 6 (2009-10 to 2017-18); HS 23 and BB 4-51 v SL (Johannesburg) 2016-17. **LOI** (SA): 66 (2008-09 to 2021-22); HS 56 v P (Sharjah) 2013-14; BB 5-48 v E (Cape Town) 2009-10. **IT20** (SA): 40 (2008-09 to 2017); HS 29* v A (Johannesburg) 2011-12; BB 4-13 v WI (Oval) 2009. F-c Tours (SA A): A 2016; I 2009-10 (SA), 2015; Ire 2012. HS 111* Cobras v Warriors (Paarl) 2015-16. CC HS 90 K v Glamorgan (Canterbury) 2009. Nh HS 54 v Glamorgan (Northampton) 2021. BB 7-51 Cobras v Dolphins (Cape Town) 2015-16. CC BB 5-47 Wo v Lancs (Manchester) 2019. Nh BB 5-64 (10-143 match) v Yorks (Leeds) 2021. LO HS 129 Warriors v Lions (Potchefstroom) 2013-14. LO BB 6-51 Warriors v Knights (Kimberley) 2013-14. T20 HS 99. T20 BB 4-13.

WAKELY, Alexander George (Bedford S), b Hammersmith, London 3 Nov 1988. 6'2". RHB, RM. Northamptonshire 2007-21; cap 2012; captain 2015-19; testimonial 2020-21. Bedfordshire 2004-05. HS 123 v Leics (Northampton) 2015. BB 2-62 v Somerset (Taunton) 2007. LO HS 109* v Lancs (Liverpool) 2017 (RLC). LO BB 2-14 v Lancs (Northampton) 2007 (P40). T20 HS 64. T20 BB –.

NORTHAMPTONSHIRE 2021

RESULTS SUMMARY

	Place	Won	Lost	Drew	NR
LV= Insurance County Champ (Div 2)	4th	4	5	5	
Royal London One-Day Cup (Group 2)	8th	2	4		2
Vitality Blast (North Group)	9th	4	8		1

LV= INSURANCE COUNTY CHAMPIONSHIP AVERAGES
BATTING AND FIELDING

Cap		*M*	*I*	*NO*	*HS*	*Runs*	*Avge*	*100*	*50*	*Ct/St*
2021	R.S.Vasconcelos	14	24	1	185*	845	36.73	2	2	32/1
2019	A.M.Rossington	11	16	1	94	537	35.80	–	4	24/2
2019	R.I.Keogh	14	24	2	126	766	34.81	2	4	1
2020	L.A.Procter	13	21	2	93	597	31.42	–	5	2
	G.K.Berg	9	10	3	69*	216	30.85	–	1	3
	J.J.G.Sales	3	6	2	53	112	28.00	–	1	1
	S.A.Zaib	13	22	1	135	576	27.42	1	3	4
	H.O.M.Gouldstone	4	8	2	67*	155	25.83	–	1	–
	E.N.Gay	9	17	–	101	391	23.00	1	1	5
	T.A.I.Taylor	11	17	2	50	316	21.06	–	1	6
	S.C.Kerrigan	11	19	6	45*	224	17.23	–	–	3
	W.D.Parnell	6	7	–	54	107	15.28	–	1	–
	B.J.Curran	7	10	–	36	148	14.80	–	–	6
	C.J.White	4	7	5	15*	29	14.50	–	–	–
	C.O.Thurston	6	10	–	48	142	14.20	–	–	3
	N.L.Buck	4	6	1	21*	69	13.80	–	–	1
2018	B.W.Sanderson	13	17	3	20	72	5.14	–	–	2

Also batted (1 match each): J.J.Cobb (cap 2018) 1, 0 (1 ct); A.G.Wakely (cap 2012) 4 (1 ct).

BOWLING

	O	*M*	*R*	*W*	*Avge*	*Best*	*5wI*	*10wM*
W.D.Parnell	114.4	26	427	18	23.72	5-64	2	1
G.K.Berg	199.4	48	600	24	25.00	5-18	1	–
S.C.Kerrigan	298.5	57	766	29	26.41	5-39	2	–
B.W.Sanderson	435.2	117	1155	43	26.86	5-28	3	1
T.A.I.Taylor	263.2	63	783	29	27.00	5-41	1	–
L.A.Procter	115.5	29	352	13	27.07	5-42	1	–
N.L.Buck	107.4	11	436	10	43.60	3-65	–	–
Also bowled:								
C.J.White	94	10	319	5	63.80	4-40	–	–
R.I.Keogh	126.4	15	462	5	92.40	2- 8	–	–

E.N.Gay 5-0-22-1; J.J.G.Sales 40-9-154-3; S.A.Zaib 43.1-6-139-3.

The First-Class Averages (pp 220–232) give the records of Northamptonshire players in all first-class county matches.

NORTHAMPTONSHIRE RECORDS

FIRST-CLASS CRICKET

Highest Total	For 781-7d		v	Notts	Northampton	1995
	V 701-7d		by	Kent	Beckenham	2017
Lowest Total	For 12		v	Glos	Gloucester	1907
	V 33		by	Lancashire	Northampton	1977
Highest Innings	For 331*	M.E.K.Hussey	v	Somerset	Taunton	2003
	V 333	K.S.Duleepsinhji	for	Sussex	Hove	1930

Highest Partnership for each Wicket

1st	375	R.A.White/M.J.Powell	v	Glos	Northampton	2002
2nd	344	G.Cook/R.J.Boyd-Moss	v	Lancashire	Northampton	1986
3rd	393	A.Fordham/A.J.Lamb	v	Yorkshire	Leeds	1990
4th	370	R.T.Virgin/P.Willey	v	Somerset	Northampton	1976
5th	401	M.B.Loye/D.Ripley	v	Glamorgan	Northampton	1998
6th	376	R.Subba Row/A.Lightfoot	v	Surrey	The Oval	1958
7th	293	D.J.G.Sales/D.Ripley	v	Essex	Northampton	1999
8th	179	A.J.Hall/J.D.Middlebrook	v	Surrey	The Oval	2011
9th	156	R.Subba Row/S.Starkie	v	Lancashire	Northampton	1955
10th	148	B.W.Bellamy/J.V.Murdin	v	Glamorgan	Northampton	1925

Best Bowling	For	10-127	V.W.C.Jupp	v	Kent	Tunbridge W	1932
(Innings)	V	10- 30	C.Blythe	for	Kent	Northampton	1907
Best Bowling	For	15- 31	G.E.Tribe	v	Yorkshire	Northampton	1958
(Match)	V	17- 48	C.Blythe	for	Kent	Northampton	1907

Most Runs – Season	2198	D.Brookes	(av 51.11)	1952
Most Runs – Career	28980	D.Brookes	(av 36.13)	1934-59
Most 100s – Season	8	R.A.Haywood		1921
Most 100s – Career	67	D.Brookes		1934-59
Most Wkts – Season	175	G.E.Tribe	(av 18.70)	1955
Most Wkts – Career	1102	E.W.Clark	(av 21.26)	1922-47
Most Career W-K Dismissals	810	K.V.Andrew	(653 ct; 157 st)	1953-66
Most Career Catches in the Field	469	D.S.Steele		1963-84

LIMITED-OVERS CRICKET

Highest Total	**50ov**	425		v	Notts	Nottingham	2016
	40ov	324-6		v	Warwicks	Birmingham	2013
	T20	231-5		v	Warwicks	Birmingham	2018
Lowest Total	**50ov**	62		v	Leics	Leicester	1974
	40ov	41		v	Middlesex	Northampton	1972
	T20	47		v	Durham	Chester-le-St[2]	2011
Highest Innings	**50ov**	161	D.J.G.Sales	v	Yorkshire	Northampton	2006
	40ov	172*	W.Larkins	v	Warwicks	Luton	1983
	T20	111*	L.Klusener	v	Worcs	Kidderminster	2007
Best Bowling	**50ov**	7-10	C.Pietersen	v	Denmark	Brondby	2005
	40ov	7-39	A.Hodgson	v	Somerset	Northampton	1976
	T20	6-21	A.J.Hall	v	Worcs	Northampton	2008

NOTTINGHAMSHIRE

Formation of Present Club: March/April 1841
Substantial Reorganisation: 11 December 1866
Inaugural First-Class Match: 1864
Colours: Green and Gold
County Champions (since 1890): (6) 1907, 1929, 1981, 1987, 2005, 2010
NatWest Trophy Winners: (1) 1987
Benson and Hedges Cup Winners: (1) 1989
Sunday League Winners: (1) 1991
Yorkshire Bank 40 Winners: (1) 2013
Royal London Cup Winners: (1) 2017
Twenty20 Cup Winners: (2) 2017, 2020

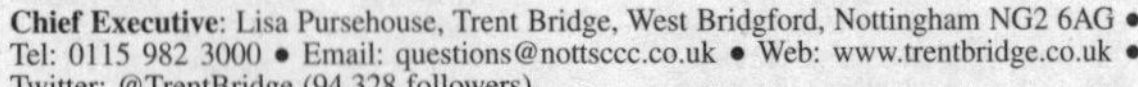

Chief Executive: Lisa Pursehouse, Trent Bridge, West Bridgford, Nottingham NG2 6AG • Tel: 0115 982 3000 • Email: questions@nottsccc.co.uk • Web: www.trentbridge.co.uk • Twitter: @TrentBridge (94,328 followers)

Director of Cricket: Mick Newell. **Head Coach**: Peter Moores. **Assistant Head Coach**: Paul Franks. **Assistant Coach**: Kevin Shine. **Captains**: S.J.Mullaney (f-c), H.Hameed (l-o) and D.T.Christian (T20). **Vice-captain**: H.Hameed. **Overseas Players**: D.T.Christian (T20 only), D.Paterson and J.L.Pattinson. **2022 Testimonial**: None. **Head Groundsman**: Steve Birks. **Scorer**: Roger Marshall and Anne Cusworth. **Blast Team Name**: Nottinghamshire Outlaws. ‡ New registration. [NQ] Not qualified for England.

BALL, Jacob Timothy (**'Jake'**) (Meden CS), b Mansfield 14 Mar 1991. Nephew of B.N.French (Notts and England 1976-95). 6'0". RHB, RFM. Squad No 28. Debut (Nottinghamshire) 2011; cap 2016. MCC 2016. Big Bash: SS 2020-21. Welsh Fire 2021. **Tests**: 4 (2016 to 2017-18); HS 31 and BB 1-47 v I (Mumbai) 2016-17. **LOI**: 18 (2016-17 to 2018); HS 28 v B (Dhaka) 2016-17; BB 5-51 v B (Dhaka) 2016-17 – separate matches. **IT20**: 2 (2018); HS – ; BB 1-39 v I (Bristol) 2018. F-c Tours: A 2017-18; I 2016-17. HS 49* v Warwks (Nottingham) 2015. 50 wkts (1): 54 (2016). BB 6-49 v Sussex (Nottingham) 2015. Hat-trick v Middx (Nottingham) 2016. LO HS 28 (*see LOI*). BB 5-51 (*see LOI*). T20 HS 18*. T20 BB 4-11.

BROAD, Stuart Christopher John (Oakham S), b Nottingham 24 Jun 1986. Son of B.C.Broad (Glos, Notts, OFS and England 1979-94). 6'6". LHB, RFM. Squad No 8. Debut (Leicestershire) 2005; cap 2007. Nottinghamshire debut/cap 2008; testimonial 2019. MCC 2019. Big Bash: HH 2016-17. YC 2006. *Wisden* 2009. **ECB Central Contract 2021-22. Tests**: 152 (2007-08 to 2021-22); HS 169 v P (Lord's) 2010, sharing in record Test and UK f-c 8th wkt partnership of 332 with I.J.L.Trott; 50 wkts (2); most – 62 (2013); BB 8-15 v A (Nottingham) 2015. Hat-tricks (2): v I (Nottingham) 2011, and v SL (Leeds) 2014. **LOI**: 121 (2006 to 2015-16, 3 as captain); HS 45* v I (Manchester) 2007; BB 5-23 v SA (Nottingham) 2008. **IT20**: 56 (2006 to 2013-14, 27 as captain); HS 18* v SA (Chester-le-St) 2012 and 18* v A (Melbourne) 2013-14; BB 4-24 v NZ (Auckland) 2012-13. F-c Tours: A 2010-11, 2013-14, 2017-18, 2021-22; SA 2009-10, 2015-16, 2019-20; WI 2005-06 (Eng A), 2008-09, 2014-15, 2018-19; NZ 2007-08, 2012-13, 2017-18, 2019-20; I 2008-09, 2012-13, 2016-17, 2020-21; SL 2007-08, 2011-12, 2018-19, 2020-21; B 2006-07 (Eng A), 2009-10, 2016-17; UAE 2011-12 (v P), 2015-16 (v P). HS 169 (*see Tests*). CC HS 91* Le v Derbys (Leicester) 2007. Nt HS 60 v Worcs (Nottingham) 2009. BB 8-15 (*see Tests*). CC BB 8-52 (11-131 match) v Warwks (Birmingham) 2010. LO HS 45* (*see LOI*). LO BB 5-23 (*see LOI*). T20 HS 18*. T20 BB 4-24.

BUDINGER, Soloman George (Southport S), b Colchester, Essex 21 Aug 1999. LHB, OB, occ WK. Squad No 1. Sussex 2nd XI 2016-17. Nottinghamshire 2nd XI debut 2018. Awaiting f-c debut. LO HS 71 v Yorks (York) 2021 (RLC). T20 HS 21.

CARTER, Matthew (Branston S), b Lincoln 26 May 1996. Younger brother of A.Carter (*see WORCESTERSHIRE*). RHB, OB. Squad No 20. Debut (Nottinghamshire) 2015, taking 7-56 v Somerset (Taunton) – the best debut figures for Nt since 1914. Trent Rockets 2021. Lincolnshire 2013-17. HS 33 v Sussex (Hove) 2017. BB 7-56 (10-195 match) (*see above*). LO HS 21* v Warwks (Birmingham) 2019 (RLC). LO BB 4-40 v Warwks (Nottingham) 2018 (RLC). T20 HS 23*. T20 BB 3-14.

CHAPPELL, Zachariah John ('**Zak**') (Stamford S), b Grantham, Lincs 21 Aug 1996. 6'4". RHB, RFM. Squad No 32. Leicestershire 2015-18. Nottinghamshire debut 2019. HS 96 Le v Derbys (Derby) 2015. Nt HS 29 v Warwks (Nottingham) 2019. BB 6-44 Le v Northants (Northampton) 2018. Nt BB 4-59 v Yorks (Nottingham) 2020. LO HS 59* Le v Durham (Gosforth) 2017 (RLC). LO BB 3-45 Le v Durham (Leicester) 2018 (RLC). T20 HS 16. T20 BB 3-23.

NQ**CHRISTIAN, Dan**iel Trevor, b Camperdown, NSW, Australia 4 May 1983. RHB, RFM. Squad No 54. S Australia 2007-08 to 2012-13. Hampshire 2010. Gloucestershire 2013; cap 2013. Victoria 2013-14 to 2017-18. Nottinghamshire debut 2016, having joined in 2015 for l-o and T20 only; cap 2015; captain 2016 to date (T20 only). IPL: DC 2011-12; RCB 2013 to 2021; RPS 2017; DD 2018. Big Bash: BH 2011-12 to 2014-15. HH 2015-16 to 2017-18. MR 2018-19 to 2019-20. SS 2020-21 to date. **LOI** (A): 20 (2011-12 to 2021); HS 39 v I (Adelaide) 2011-12; BB 5-31 v SL (Melbourne) 2011-12. **IT20** (A): 23 (2009-10 to 2021); HS 39 v B (Mirpur) 2021; BB 3-27 v WI (Gros Islet) 2011-12. HS 131* SA v NSW (Adelaide) 2011-12. CC HS 36 and CC BB 2-115 H v Somerset (Taunton) 2010. Nt HS 31 v Hants (Southampton) 2016. BB 5-24 SA v WA (Perth) (2009-10). Nt BB 1-22 v Warwks (Birmingham) 2016. LO HS 117 Vic v NSW (Sydney) 2013-14. LO BB 6-48 SA v Vic (Geelong) 2010-11. T20 HS 129 M v Kent (Canterbury) 2014 – M record. T20 BB 5-14.

CLARKE, Joe Michael (Llanfyllin HS), b Shrewsbury, Shrops 26 May 1996. 5'11". RHB, WK. Squad No 33. Worcestershire 2015-18. Nottinghamshire debut 2019. MCC 2017. Big Bash: PS 2020-21; MS 2021-22. Manchester Originals 2021. Shropshire 2012-13. F-c Tours (EL): WI 2017-18; UAE 2016-17 (v Afg). 1000 runs (1): 1325 (2016). HS 194 Wo v Derbys (Worcester) 2016. Nt HS 133 v Durham (Nottingham) 2020. BB –. LO HS 139 v Lancs (Nottingham) 2019 (RLC). T20 HS 136 v Northants (Northampton) 2021 – Nt record.

DUCKETT, Ben Matthew (Stowe S), b Farnborough, Kent 17 Oct 1994. 5'7". LHB, WK, occ OB. Squad No 17. Northamptonshire 2013-18; cap 2016. Nottinghamshire debut 2018; cap 2019. MCC 2017. Big Bash: HH 2018-19; BH 2021-22. Welsh Fire 2021. PCA 2016. YC 2016. *Wisden* 2016. **Tests**: 4 (2016-17); HS 56 v B (Dhaka) 2016-17. **LOI**: 3 (2016-17); HS 63 v B (Chittagong) 2016-17. **IT20**: 1 (2019); HS 9 v P (Cardiff) 2019. F-c Tours: I 2016-17; B 2016-17. 1000 runs (2); most – 1338 (2016). HS 282* Nh v Sussex (Northampton) 2016. Nt HS 216 v Cambridge MCCU (Cambridge) 2019. BB 1-21 Nh v Kent (Beckenham) 2017. LO HS 220* EL v Sri Lanka A (Canterbury) 2016. T20 HS 96.

EVISON, Joseph David Michael (Stamford S), b Peterborough, Cambs 14 Nov 2001. Son of G.M.Evison (Lincolnshire 1993-97); younger brother of S.H.G.Evison (Lincolnshire 2017-18). RHB, RM. Squad No 90. Debut (Nottinghamshire) 2019. Nottinghamshire 2nd XI debut 2017. HS 58 v Yorks (Nottingham) 2021. BB 5-21 v Durham (Chester-le-St) 2021. LO HS 54 v Surrey (Guildford) 2021 (RLC). LO BB 2-33 v Warwks (Birmingham) 2021 (RLC).

FLETCHER, Luke Jack (Henry Mellish S, Nottingham), b Nottingham 18 Sep 1988. 6'6". RHB, RMF. Squad No 19. Debut (Nottinghamshire) 2008; cap 2014. Surrey 2015 (on loan). Derbyshire 2016 (on loan). Welsh Fire 2021. HS 92 v Hants (Southampton) 2009 and 92 v Durham (Chester-le-St) 2017. 50 wkts (1): 66 (2021). BB 7-37 (10-57 match) v Worcs (Nottingham) 2021. LO HS 53* v Kent (Nottingham) 2018 (RLC). LO BB 5-56 v Derbys (Derby) 2019 (RLC). T20 HS 27. T20 BB 5-43.

HALES, Alexander Daniel (Chesham HS), b Hillingdon, Middx 3 Jan 1989. 6'5". RHB, OB, occ WK. Squad No 10. Debut (Nottinghamshire) 2008; cap 2011. Agreed white-ball-only contract in 2018. Worcestershire 2014 (1 game, on loan). Buckinghamshire 2006-07. IPL: SH 2018. Big Bash: MR 2012-13; AS 2013-14; HH 2014-15; ST 2019-20 to date. Trent Rockets 2021. **Tests**: 11 (2015-16 to 2016); HS 94 v SL (Lord's) 2016; BB –. **LOI**: 70 (2014 to 2018-19); HS 171 v P (Nottingham) 2016. **IT20**: 60 (2011 to 2018-19); HS 116* v SL (Chittagong) 2013-14 – E record. 1000 runs (3); most – 1127 (2011). HS 236 v Yorks (Nottingham) 2015. BB 2-63 v Yorks (Nottingham) 2009. LO HS 187* v Surrey (Lord's) 2017 (RLC) – Nt record. T20 HS 116*.

HAMEED, Haseeb (Bolton S), b Bolton, Lancs 17 Jan 1997. 6'2". RHB, LB. Squad No 99. Lancashire 2015-19; cap 2016. Nottinghamshire debut/cap 2020. Lancashire 2nd XI debut 2013. England U19 2014-15 to 2015. **Tests**: 10 (2016-17 to 2021-22); HS 82 v I (Rajkot) 2016-17 – on debut. F-c Tours: A 2021-22; WI 2017-18 (EL); I 2016-17; SL 2016-17 (EL). 1000 runs (1): 1198 (2016). HS 122 La v Notts (Nottingham) 2016. Nt HS 114* v Worcs (Worcester) 2021. BB –. LO HS 103 v Warwks (Birmingham) 2021 (RLC).

HARRISON, Calvin Grant (King's C, Taunton; Oxford Brookes U), b Durban, S Africa 29 Apr 1998. 6'4". RHB, LBG. Oxford MCCU 2019. Hampshire 2020 (T20 only). Nottinghamshire debut 2021 (T20 only). Manchester Originals 2021. Somerset 2nd XI 2015-17. Warwickshire 2nd XI 2017. Surrey 2nd XI 2018. Gloucestershire 2nd XI 2018-19. Hampshire 2nd XI 2019. HS 37* and BB 1-30 OU v Middx (Northwood) 2019. T20 HS 23. T20 BB 4-17.

HAYES, James Philip Henry (King's C, Taunton; Richard Huish C), b Haywards Heath, Sussex 27 Jun 2001. RHB, RFM. Nottinghamshire 2nd XI debut 2021. Awaiting 1st XI debut.

HUTTON, Brett Alan (Worksop C), b Doncaster, Yorks 6 Feb 1993. 6'2". RHB, RM. Squad No 16. Debut (Nottinghamshire) 2011. Northamptonshire 2018-20. HS 74 v Durham (Nottingham) 2016. BB 8-57 Nh v Glos (Northampton) 2018. Nt BB 5-29 v Durham (Nottingham) 2015. LO HS 46 v Derbys (Derby) 2021 (RLC). LO BB 3-72 v Kent (Nottingham) 2015 (RLC). T20 HS 18*. T20 BB 2-28.

JAMES, Lyndon Wallace (Oakham S), b Worksop 27 Dec 1998. RHB, RMF. Squad No 45. Debut (Nottinghamshire) 2018. Nottinghamshire 2nd XI debut 2017. HS 91 v Lancs (Nottingham) 2021. BB 4-51 v Essex (Nottingham) 2021. LO HS 16* v Leics (Welbeck) 2021 (RLC). LO BB 5-48 v Warwks (Birmingham) 2021 (RLC). T20 HS 7.

KING, Samuel Isaac Michael (Nottingham HS; Nottingham U), b Nottingham 12 Jan 2003. RHB, RM. Nottinghamshire 2nd XI debut 2021. Awaiting f-c debut. LO HS 11 v Glam (Cardiff) 2021 (RLC) – only 1st XI appearance.

MONTGOMERY, Matthew (Clifton C; Loughborough U), b Johannesburg, South Africa 10 May 2000. RHB, OB. KwaZulu-Natal 2018-19. Nottinghamshire 2nd XI debut 2021. S Africa U19 2018-19. HS 50* KZN v SW Districts (Oudtshoorn) 2018-19. LO HS 104 KZN v WP (Chatsworth) 2018-19 – on debut. LO BB –.

MOORES, Thomas James (Loughborough GS), b Brighton, Sussex 4 Sep 1996. Son of P.Moores (Worcestershire, Sussex & OFS 1983-98); nephew of S.Moores (Cheshire 1995). LHB, WK. Squad No 23. Lancashire 2016 (on loan). Nottinghamshire debut 2016; cap 2021. Trent Rockets 2021. HS 106 v Yorks (Nottingham) 2020. LO HS 76 v Leics (Leicester) 2018 (RLC). T20 HS 80*.

MULLANEY, Steven John (St Mary's RC S, Astley), b Warrington, Cheshire 19 Nov 1986. 5'9". RHB, RM. Squad No 5. Lancashire 2006-08. Nottinghamshire debut 2010, scoring 100* v Hants (Southampton); cap 2013; captain 2018 to date. Trent Rockets 2021. F-c Tour (EL): I 2018-19. 1000 runs (1): 1148 (2016). HS 179 v Warwks (Nottingham) 2019. BB 5-32 v Glos (Nottingham) 2017. LO HS 124 v Durham (Chester-le-St) 2018 (RLC). LO BB 4-29 v Kent (Nottingham) 2013 (Y40). T20 HS 55. T20 BB 4-19.

PATEL, Samit Rohit (Worksop C), b Leicester 30 Nov 1984. Elder brother of A.Patel (Derbyshire and Notts 2007-11). 5'8". RHB, SLA. Squad No 21. Debut (Nottinghamshire) 2002; cap 2008; testimonial 2017. Glamorgan 2019 (on loan). Big Bash: MR 2019-20. Trent Rockets 2021. MCC 2014, 2016. PCA 2017. **Tests**: 6 (2011-12 to 2015-16); HS 42 v P (Sharjah) 2015-16; BB 2-27 v SL (Galle) 2011-12. **LOI**: 36 (2008 to 2012-13); HS 70* v I (Mohali) 2011-12; BB 5-41 v SA (Oval) 2008. **IT20**: 18 (2011 to 2012-13); HS 67 v SL (Pallekele) 2012-13; BB 2-6 v Afg (Colombo, RPS) 2012-13. F-c Tours: NZ 2008-09 (Eng A); I 2012-13; SL 2011-12; UAE 2015-16 (v P). 1000 runs (2); most – 1125 (2014). HS 257* v Glos (Bristol) 2017. BB 7-68 (11-111 match) v Hants (Southampton) 2011. LO HS 136* v Northants (Northampton) 2019 (RLC). LO BB 6-13 v Ireland (Dublin) 2009 (FPT). T20 HS 90*. T20 BB 4-5.

NQ**PATERSON, Dane**, b Cape Town, South Africa 4 Apr 1989. RHB, RFM. Squad No 4. Western Province 2009-10 to 2014-15. Dolphins 2010-11 to 2012-13. KwaZulu-Natal 2011-12 to 2012-13. Cape Cobras 2013-14 to 2019-20. Eastern Province 2021-22. **Tests** (SA): 2 (2019-20); HS 39* v E (Port Elizabeth) 2019-20; BB 2-86 v E (Johannesburg) 2019-20. **LOI** (SA): 4 (2017-18 to 2018-19); HS – ; BB 3-44 v B (East London) 2017-18. **IT20** (SA): 8 (2016-17 to 2018-19); HS 4* v E (Taunton) 2017; BB 4-32 v E (Cardiff) 2017. F-c Tour (SA A): E 2017. HS 59 KZN v FS (Bloemfontein) 2012-13. Nt HS 22 v Warwks (Nottingham) 2021. 50 wkts (1+2); most – 67 (2013-14). BB 7-20 (10-62 match) WP v FS (Rondebosch) 2013-14. Nt BB 5-90 v Warwks (Birmingham) 2021. LO HS 29 Cape Cobras v Dolphins (Cape Town) 2017-18. LO BB 5-19 SA A v India A (Bangalore) 2018. T20 HS 24*. T20 BB 4-24.

PATTERSON-WHITE, Liam Anthony (Worksop C), b Sunderland, Co Durham 8 Nov 1998. LHB, SLA. Squad No 22. Debut (Nottinghamshire) 2019, taking 5-73 v Somerset (Taunton). Nottinghamshire 2nd XI debut 2016. England U19 2016-17. HS 101 v Somerset (Taunton) 2021. BB 5-41 v Hants (Southampton) 2021. LO HS 27 v Derbys (Derby) 2021 (RLC). LO BB 5-19 v Northants (Grantham) 2021 (RLC).

NQ**PATTINSON, James** Lee, b Melbourne, Australia 3 May 1990. Younger brother of D.J.Pattinson (Victoria, Nottinghamshire and England 2006-07 to 2011-12). LHB, RFM. Victoria 2008-09 to date. Nottinghamshire debut/cap 2017. IPL: MI 2020-21. Big Bash: MR 2013-14 to date; BH 2018-19 to 2019-20. **Tests** (A): 21 (2011-12 to 2019-20); HS 47* v E (Birmingham) 2019; BB 5-27 v NZ (Brisbane) 2011-12 and 5-27 v WI (Hobart) 2015-16. **LOI** (A): 15 (2011 to 2015); HS 13 v E (Manchester) 2012; BB 4-51 v SL (Melbourne) 2011-12. **IT20** (A): 4 (2011-12); HS 5* and BB 2-17 v SA (Johannesburg) 2011-12. F-c Tours (A): E 2013, 2019; SA 2013-14; WI 2011-12; NZ 2015-16; I 2012-13. HS 89* v Leics (Leicester) 2017. BB 6-32 Vic v Q (Brisbane) 2012-13. Nt BB 6-73 v Kent (Tunbridge W) 2019. LO HS 54 Vic v NSW (N Sydney) 2020-21. LO BB 6-48 Vic v NSW (Sydney) 2009-10. T20 HS 27*. T20 BB 5-33.

PETTMAN, Toby Henry Somerville (Tonbridge S; Jesus C, Oxford), b Kingston-upon-Thames, Surrey 11 May 1998. 6'7". RHB, RFM. Squad No 15. Oxford University 2017-20. HS 54* OU v Cambridge U (Oxford) 2018. BB 5-19 OU v Cambridge (Cambridge) 2019. Awaiting Nt 1st XI debut.

NQ**SCHADENDORF, Dane** J., b Harare, Zimbabwe 31 Jul 2002. RHB, WK. Squad No 89. Debut (Nottinghamshire) 2021. Zimbabwe U19 2019-20. HS 24 v Derbys (Nottingham) 2021. LO HS 44* v Surrey (Guildford) 2021.

SINGH, Fateh (Trent C), b Nottingham 20 Apr 2004. LHB, SLA. Nottinghamshire 2nd XI debut 2021. Awaiting f-c debut. LO HS 21 v Glamorgan (Cardiff) 2021 (RL). LO BB –.

SLATER, Benjamin Thomas (Netherthorpe S; Leeds Met U), b Chesterfield, Derbys 26 Aug 1991. 5'10". LHB, OB. Squad No 26. Debut (Leeds/Bradford MCCU) 2012. Southern Rocks 2012-13. Derbyshire 2013-18. Nottinghamshire debut 2018; cap 2021. Leicestershire 2020 (on loan). HS 172 Le v Lancs (Worcester) 2020. Nt HS 142 v Lancs (Nottingham) 2020. BB –. LO HS 148* De v Northants (Northampton) 2016 (RLC). T20 HS 57.

RELEASED/RETIRED

(Having made a County 1st XI appearance in 2021)

BARBER, Thomas Edward (Bournemouth GS), b Poole, Dorset 31 May 1994. 6'3". RHB, LFM. Middlesex 2018. Nottinghamshire 2020. Hampshire 2014 (l-o only). Dorset 2016. HS 3 M v Sussex (Hove) 2018. Nt HS 2* and BB 3-42 v Lancs (Nottingham) 2020. LO HS 1 South v North (Cave Hill) 2017-18. LO BB 3-62 M v Australians (Lord's) 2018. T20 HS 2. T20 BB 4-28.

COMPTON, B.G. – *see KENT*.

TREGO, Peter David (Wyvern CS, W-s-M), b Weston-super-Mare, Somerset 12 Jun 1981. 6'0". RHB, RMF. Somerset 2000-18; cap 2007; benefit 2015. Kent 2003. Middlesex 2005. C Districts 2013-14. Nottinghamshire 2020. MCC 2013, 2019. Herefordshire 2005. 1000 runs (1): 1070 (2016). HS 154* Sm v Lancs (Manchester) 2016, sharing Sm record 8th wkt partnership of 236 with R.C.Davies. Nt HS 39 v Yorks (Nottingham) 2020. 50 wkts (1): 50 (2012). BB 7-84 (11-153 match) Sm v Yorks (Leeds) 2014. Nt BB 3-33 v Lancs (Nottingham) 2020. LO HS 147 Sm v Glamorgan (Taunton) 2010 (CB40). LO BB 5-40 EL v West Indies A (Worcester) 2010. T20 HS 94*. T20 BB 4-27.

H.F.Gurney left the staff without making a County 1st XI appearance in 2021.

NOTTINGHAMSHIRE 2021

RESULTS SUMMARY

	Place	Won	Lost	Tied	Drew	NR
LV= Insurance County Champ (Div 1)	3rd	7	3		4	
Royal London One-Day Cup (Group 2)	6th	3	3			2
Vitality Blast (North Group)	QF	9	3	3		

LV= INSURANCE COUNTY CHAMPIONSHIP AVERAGES
BATTING AND FIELDING

Cap		*M*	*I*	*NO*	*HS*	*Runs*	*Avge*	*100*	*50*	*Ct/St*
2021	B.T.Slater	14	24	3	114*	837	39.85	2	5	8
2020	H.Hameed	11	19	1	114*	679	37.72	2	4	11
2019	B.M.Duckett	13	21	2	177*	705	37.10	1	4	15
2021	J.M.Clarke	13	22	1	109	760	36.19	1	7	8
	L.W.James	12	18	1	91	558	32.82	–	5	1
	L.A.Patterson-White	14	20	3	101	538	31.64	1	3	4
2021	T.J.Moores	12	19	3	97	486	30.37	–	3	52/2
2013	S.J.Mullaney	14	22	–	117	657	29.86	1	3	6
	J.D.M.Evison	4	6	–	58	121	20.16	–	1	–
2021	D.Paterson	12	15	11	22	64	16.00	–	–	4
2021	B.A.Hutton	8	11	–	51	174	15.81	–	1	8
	Z.J.Chappell	3	5	1	22	61	15.25	–	–	–
2008	S.C.J.Broad	5	7	–	41	87	12.42	–	–	–
2014	L.J.Fletcher	13	17	5	51	140	11.66	–	1	1
	B.G.Compton	3	5	–	20	55	11.00	–	–	2

Also batted: J.T.Ball (1 match – cap 2016) 4; S.A.Northeast (2) 34, 65, 13 (2 ct); D.J.Schadendorf (1) 24 (4 ct).

BOWLING

	O	*M*	*R*	*W*	*Avge*	*Best*	*5wI*	*10wM*
L.J.Fletcher	420.5	135	984	66	14.90	7-37	4	1
S.C.J.Broad	150	34	368	23	16.00	4-37	–	–
J.D.M.Evison	82.1	23	249	14	17.78	5-21	1	–
D.Paterson	352.5	98	971	54	17.98	5-90	1	–
B.A.Hutton	254	75	679	29	23.41	5-62	2	–
L.W.James	139	27	424	14	30.28	4-51	–	–
L.A.Patterson-White	285	70	749	24	31.20	5-41	1	–
Also bowled:								
Z.J.Chappell	100	21	306	6	51.00	3-64	–	–
S.J.Mullaney	151.2	29	423	7	60.42	2-37	–	–

J.T.Ball 17.3-7-43-2; B.M.Duckett 3-0-17-0; B.T.Slater 2-0-8-0.

The First-Class Averages (pp 220–232) give the records of Nottinghamshire players in all first-class county matches, with the exception of S.C.J.Broad, H.Hameed, L.W.James, S.A.Northeast and L.A.Patterson-White, whose first-class figures for Nottinghamshire are as above.

NOTTINGHAMSHIRE RECORDS

FIRST-CLASS CRICKET

Highest Total	For 791		v	Essex	Chelmsford	2007
	V 781-7d		by	Northants	Northampton	1995
Lowest Total	For 13		v	Yorkshire	Nottingham	1901
	V 16		by	Derbyshire	Nottingham	1879
	16		by	Surrey	The Oval	1880
Highest Innings	For 312*	W.W.Keeton	v	Middlesex	The Oval	1939
	V 345	C.G.Macartney	for	Australians	Nottingham	1921

Highest Partnership for each Wicket

1st	406*	D.J.Bicknell/G.E.Welton	v	Warwicks	Birmingham	2000
2nd	398	A.Shrewsbury/W.Gunn	v	Sussex	Nottingham	1890
3rd	367	W.Gunn/J.R.Gunn	v	Leics	Nottingham	1903
4th	361	A.O.Jones/J.R.Gunn	v	Essex	Leyton	1905
5th	359	D.J.Hussey/C.M.W.Read	v	Essex	Nottingham	2007
6th	372*	K.P.Pietersen/J.E.Morris	v	Derbyshire	Derby	2001
7th	301	C.C.Lewis/B.N.French	v	Durham	Chester-le-St[2]	1993
8th	220	G.F.H.Heane/R.Winrow	v	Somerset	Nottingham	1935
9th	170	J.C.Adams/K.P.Evans	v	Somerset	Taunton	1994
10th	152	E.B.Alletson/W.Riley	v	Sussex	Hove	1911
	152	U.Afzaal/A.J.Harris	v	Worcs	Nottingham	2000

Best Bowling	For	10-66	K.Smales	v	Glos	Stroud	1956
(Innings)	V	10-10	H.Verity	for	Yorkshire	Leeds	1932
Best Bowling	For	17-89	F.C.L.Matthews	v	Northants	Nottingham	1923
(Match)	V	17-89	W.G.Grace	for	Glos	Cheltenham	1877

Most Runs – Season	2620	W.W.Whysall	(av 53.46)	1929
Most Runs – Career	31592	G.Gunn	(av 35.69)	1902-32
Most 100s – Season	9	W.W.Whysall		1928
	9	M.J.Harris		1971
	9	B.C.Broad		1990
Most 100s – Career	65	J.Hardstaff jr		1930-55
Most Wkts – Season	181	B.Dooland	(av 14.96)	1954
Most Wkts – Career	1653	T.G.Wass	(av 20.34)	1896-1920
Most Career W-K Dismissals	983	C.M.W.Read	(939 ct; 44 st)	1998-2017
Most Career Catches in the Field	466	A.O.Jones		1892-1914

LIMITED-OVERS CRICKET

Highest Total	**50ov**	445-8		v	Northants	Nottingham	2016
	40ov	296-7		v	Somerset	Taunton	2002
	T20	227-3		v	Derbyshire	Nottingham	2017
Lowest Total	**50ov**	74		v	Leics	Leicester	1987
	40ov	57		v	Glos	Nottingham	2009
	T20	91		v	Lancashire	Manchester	2006
Highest Innings	**50ov**	187*	A.D.Hales	v	Surrey	Lord's	2017
	40ov	150*	A.D.Hales	v	Worcs	Nottingham	2009
	T20	136	J.M.Clarke	v	Northants	Northampton	2021
Best Bowling	**50ov**	6-10	K.P.Evans	v	Northumb	Jesmond	1994
	40ov	6-12	R.J.Hadlee	v	Lancashire	Nottingham	1980
	T20	5-22	G.G.White	v	Lancashire	Nottingham	2013

SOMERSET

SOMERSET CCC

Formation of Present Club: 18 August 1875
Inaugural First-Class Match: 1882
Colours: Black, White and Maroon
Badge: Somerset Dragon
County Champions: (0); best – 2nd (Div 1) 2001, 2010, 2012, 2016, 2018, 2019
Gillette/NatWest/C&G Trophy Winners: (3) 1979, 1983, 2001
Benson and Hedges Cup Winners: (2) 1981, 1982
Sunday League Winners: (1) 1979
Royal London One-Day Cup Winners: (1) 2019
Twenty20 Cup Winners: (1) 2005

Chief Executive: Gordon Hollins, Cooper Associates County Ground, Taunton TA1 1JT • Tel: 01823 425301 • Email: enquiries@somersetcountycc.co.uk • Web: www.somersetcountycc.co.uk • Twitter: @SomersetCCC (156,209 followers)

Director of Cricket: Andy Hurry. **Head Coach**: Jason Kerr. **Assistant Coaches**: Greg Kennis, Steve Kirby and Paul Tweddle. **Captain**: T.B.Abell. **Overseas Players**: M.de Lange, M.T.Renshaw and P.M.Siddle. **2022 Testimonial**: None. **Groundsman**: Scott Hawkins. **Scorer**: Polly Rhodes. ‡ New registration. NQ Not qualified for England.

ABELL, Thomas Benjamin (Taunton S; Exeter U), b Taunton 5 Mar 1994. 5'10". RHB, RM. Squad No 28. Debut (Somerset) 2014; captain 2017 to date; cap 2018. MCC 2019. Big Bash: BH 2021-22. Birmingham Phoenix 2021. F-c Tour (EL): A 2019-20. HS 135 v Lancs (Manchester) 2016. BB 4-39 v Warwks (Birmingham) 2019. Hat-trick v Notts (Nottingham) 2018. LO HS 106 v Sussex (Taunton) 2016 (RLC). LO BB 2-19 v Hants (Lord's) 2019 (RLC). T20 HS 101*. T20 BB 1-11.

ALDRIDGE, Kasey Luke (Millfield S), b Bristol 24 Dec 2000. RHB, RM. Squad No 5. Debut (Somerset) 2021. Somerset 2nd XI debut 2019. Devon 2019. England U19 2018-19. BB-. LO HS 12 v Surrey (Oval) 2021 (RLC). LO BB 3-39 v Glamorgan (Taunton) 2021 (RLC).

BAKER, Sonny (Torquay Boys' GS; King's C, Taunton), b Torbay 13 Mar 2003. Nephew of A.K.Hele (Devon 1998-2001). RHB, RM. Somerset 2nd XI debut 2019. Awaiting f-c debut. LO HS 7* v Surrey (Oval) 2021 (RLC). LO BB 3-46 v Derbys (Taunton) 2021 (RLC).

BANTON, Thomas (Bromsgrove S; King's C, Taunton), b Chiltern, Bucks 11 Nov 1998. Son of C.Banton (Nottinghamshire 1995); elder brother of J.Banton (*see WORCESTERSHIRE*). 6'2". RHB, WK. Squad No 18. Debut (Somerset) 2018. Big Bash: BH 2019-20. Welsh Fire 2021. Warwickshire 2nd XI 2015. Somerset 2nd XI debut 2016. England U19 2018. **LOI**: 6 (2019-20 to 2020); HS 58 v Ire (Southampton) 2020. **IT20**: 14 (2019-20 to 2021-22); HS 73 v WI (Bridgetown) 2021-22. HS 79 v Hants (Taunton) 2019. LO HS 112 v Worcs (Worcester) 2019 (RLC). T20 HS 107*.

BARTLETT, George Anthony (Millfield S), b Frimley, Surrey 14 Mar 1998. 6'0". RHB, OB. Squad No 14. Debut (Somerset) 2017. Somerset 2nd XI debut 2015. England U19 2016 to 2017. HS 137 v Surrey (Guildford) 2019. BB –. LO HS 108 v Leics (Taunton) 2021 (RLC). T20 HS 24.

BROOKS, Jack Alexander (Wheatley Park S), b Oxford 4 Jun 1984. 6'2". RHB, RFM. Squad No 70. Northamptonshire 2009-12; cap 2012. Yorkshire 2013-18; cap 2013. Somerset debut 2019. Oxfordshire 2004-09. F-c Tour (EL): SA 2014-15. HS 109* Y v Lancs (Manchester) 2017. Sm HS 72 v Glamorgan (Taunton) 2020. 50 wkts (4); most – 71 (2014). BB 6-65 Y v Middx (Lord's) 2016. Sm BB 5-33 v Surrey (Guildford) 2019. LO HS 10 Nh v Middx (Uxbridge) 2009 (P40). LO BB 3-30 Y v Hants (Southampton) 2014 (RLC). T20 HS 33*. T20 BB 5-21.

NQ**DAVEY, Josh**ua Henry (Culford S), b Aberdeen, Scotland 3 Aug 1990. 5'11". RHB, RMF. Squad No 38. Middlesex 2010-12. Scotland 2011-12 to 2016. Somerset debut 2015; cap 2021. Suffolk 2014. **LOI** (Scot): 31 (2010 to 2019-20); HS 64 v Afg (Sharjah) 2012-13; BB 6-28 v Afg (Abu Dhabi) 2014-15 – Scot record. **IT20** (Scot): 28 (2012 to 2021-22); HS 24 v Z (Nagpur) 2015-16; BB 4-18 v PNG (Al Amerat) 2021-22. HS 75* v Leics (Taunton) 2021. BB 5-21 v Yorks (Taunton) 2019. LO HS 91 Scot v Warwks (Birmingham) 2011 (CB40). LO BB 6-28 (*see LOI*). T20 HS 24. T20 BB 4-18.

DAVIES, Steven Michael (King Charles I S, Kidderminster), b Bromsgrove, Worcs 17 Jun 1986. 5'10". LHB, WK. Squad No 11. Worcestershire 2005-09. Surrey 2010-16; cap 2011. Somerset debut/cap 2017. MCC 2006-07, 2011. **LOI**: 8 (2009-10 to 2010-11); HS 87 v P (Chester-le-St) 2010. **IT20**: 5 (2008-09 to 2010-11); HS 33 v P (Cardiff) 2010. F-c Tours: A 2010-11; B 2006-07 (Eng A); UAE 2011-12 (v P). 1000 runs (6); most – 1147 (2016). HS 200* Sy v Glamorgan (Cardiff) 2015. Sm HS 142 v Surrey (Taunton) 2017. LO HS 127* Sy v Hants (Oval) 2013 (Y40). T20 HS 99*.

NQ**De LANGE, Marchant**, b Tzaneen, South Africa 13 Oct 1990. RHB, RF. Squad No 90. Easterns 2010-11 to 2015-16. Titans 2010-11 to 2015-16. Knights 2016-17 to 2017-18. Free State 2016-17. Glamorgan 2017-20; cap 2019. Somerset debut 2021. IPL: KKR 2012; MI 2014-15. Trent Rockets 2021. **Tests** (SA): 2 (2011-12); HS 9 and BB 7-81 v SL (Durban) 2011-12 – on debut. **LOI** (SA): 4 (2011-12 to 2015-16); HS – ; BB 4-46 v NZ (Auckland) 2011-12. **IT20** (SA): 6 (2011-12 to 2015-16); HS – ; BB 2-26 v WI (Durban) 2014-15. F-c Tours (SA): A 2014 (SA A); NZ 2011-12. HS 113 Gm v Northants (Northampton) 2020. Sm HS 75 v Leics (Taunton) 2021. BB 7-23 Knights v Titans (Centurion) 2016-17. CC BB 5-62 Gm v Glos (Bristol) 2018. Sm BB 4-55 v Yorks (Scarborough) 2021. LO HS 58* Gm v Surrey (Cardiff) 2019 (RLC). LO BB 5-49 Gm v Hants (Southampton) 2017 (RLC). T20 HS 28*. T20 BB 5-20.

GOLDSWORTHY, Lewis Peter (Cambourne Science & Int Ac), b Truro, Cornwall 8 Jan 2001. RHB, SLA. Squad No 44. Debut (Somerset) 2021. Somerset 2nd XI debut 2017. Cornwall 2017-19. England U19 2018-19. HS 48 v Surrey (Oval) 2021. BB –. LO HS 96 v Surrey (Oval) 2021 (RLC). LO BB 1-17 v Yorks (Taunton) 2021 (RLC). T20 HS 48. T20 BB 3-14.

GREEN, Benjamin George Frederick (Exeter S), b Exeter, Devon 28 Sep 1997. 6'2". RHB, RFM. Squad No 54. Debut (Somerset) 2018. Somerset 2nd XI debut 2014. Devon 2014-18. England U19 2014-15 to 2017. HS 54 v Glamorgan (Taunton) 2020. BB 1-8 v Hants (Southampton) 2018. LO HS 87 v Glamorgan (Taunton 2021 (RLC). LO BB 3-64 v Derbys (Taunton) 2021 (RLC). T20 HS 43*. T20 BB 4-26.

GREGORY, Lewis (Hele's S, Plympton), b Plymouth, Devon 24 May 1992. 6'0". RHB, RMF. Squad No 24. Debut (Somerset) 2011; cap 2015; T20 captain 2018-21. MCC 2017. Devon 2008. Big Bash: BH 2020-21. Trent Rockets 2021. LOI: 3 (2021); HS 77 v P (Birmingham) 2021; BB 3-44 v P (Lord's) 2021. **IT20**: 9 (2019-20 to 2021); HS 15 and BB 1-10 v NZ (Wellington) 2019-20. HS 137 v Middx (Lord's) 2017. 50 wkts (1): 59 (2019). BB 6-32 (11-53 match) v Kent (Canterbury) 2019. LO HS 105* v Durham (Taunton) 2014 (RLC). LO BB 4-23 v Essex (Chelmsford) 2016 (RLC). T20 HS 76*. T20 BB 5-24.

HILDRETH, James Charles (Millfield S), b Milton Keynes, Bucks 9 Sep 1984. 5'10", RHB, RMF. Squad No 25. Debut (Somerset) 2003; cap 2007; testimonial 2017. MCC 2015. F-c Tour (EL): WI 2010-11. 1000 runs (7); most – 1620 (2015). HS 303* v Warwks (Taunton) 2009. BB 2-39 v Hants (Taunton) 2004. LO HS 159 v Glamorgan (Taunton) 2018 (RLC). LO BB 2-26 v Worcs (Worcester) 2008 (FPT). T20 HS 107*. T20 BB 3-24.

LAMMONBY, Thomas Alexander (Exeter S), b Exeter, Devon 2 Jun 2000. LHB, LM. Squad No 15. Debut (Somerset) 2020. Big Bash: HH 2021-22. Manchester Originals 2021. Somerset 2nd XI debut 2015. Devon 2016-18. England U19 2018-19. HS 116 v Essex (Lord's) 2020. BB 1-4 v Glos (Taunton) 2020. T20 HS 90. T20 BB 2-32.

LEACH, Matthew **Jack** (Bishop Fox's Community S, Taunton; Richard Huish C; UWIC), b Taunton 22 Jun 1991. 6'0". LHB, SLA. Squad No 17. Cardiff MCCU 2012. Somerset debut 2012; cap 2017. MCC 2017. Dorset 2011. **ECB Central Contract 2021-22. Tests**: 20 (2017-18 to 2021-22); HS 92 v Ire (Lord's) 2019; BB 5-83 v SL (Pallekele) 2018-19. F-c Tours: A 2021-22; WI 2017-18 (EL), 2021-22; NZ 2017-18, 2019-20; I 2020-21; SL 2016-17 (EL), 2018-19, 2019-20, 2020-21; UAE 2016-17 (v Afg)(EL). HS 92 (*see Tests*). Sm HS 66 v Lancs (Manchester) 2018. 50 wkts (2); most – 68 (2016). BB 8-85 (10-112 match) v Essex (Taunton) 2018. LO HS 18 v Surrey (Oval) 2014 (RLC). LO BB 3-7 EL v UAE (Dubai, DSC) 2016-17. T20 BB 3-28.

LEONARD, Edward Owen ('**Ned**') (Millfield S), b Hammersmith, Middx 15 Aug 2002. RHB, RMF. Squad No 19. Debut (Somerset) 2021. Somerset 2nd XI debut 2018. HS 6 and BB 1-68 v Lancs (Taunton) 2021. LO HS 1* v Warwks (Birmingham) 2021 (RLC). LO BB 2-84 v Leics (Taunton) 2021 (RLC).

OVERTON, Craig (West Buckland S), b Barnstaple, Devon 10 Apr 1994. Twin brother of Jamie Overton (*see SURREY*). 6'5". RHB, RMF. Squad No 7. Debut (Somerset) 2012; cap 2016. MCC 2017. Southern Brave 2021. Devon 2010-11. **ECB Pace Bowling Development Contract 2021-22. Tests**: 7 (2017-18 to 2021-22); HS 41* v A (Adelaide) 2017-18; BB 3-14 v I (Leeds) 2021. F-c Tours: A 2017-18, 2019-20 (EL); WI 2021-22; NZ 2017-18. HS 138 v Hants (Taunton) 2016. BB 6-24 v Cardiff MCCU (Taunton) 2019. CC BB 6-74 v Warwks (Birmingham) 2015. LO HS 66* and LO BB 5-18 v Kent (Taunton) 2019 (RLC). T20 HS 35*. T20 BB 3-17.

NQ**RENSHAW, Matt**hew Thomas, b Middlesbrough, Yorks 28 Mar 1996. 6'0". LHB, OB. Queensland 2014-15 to date. Somerset debut 2018. Kent 2019. Big Bash: BH 2017-18 to 2019-20; AS 2020-21 to date. **Tests** (A): 11 (2016-17 to 2017-18); HS 184 v P (Sydney) 2016-17; BB –. F-c Tours (A): SA 2017-18; I 2016-17, 2018-19 (Aus A); B 2017; UAE 2018-19 (v P). HS 184 (*see Tests*). Sm HS 112 v Yorks (Taunton) 2018. BB 2-26 Aus A v EL (Brisbane) 2021-22. LO HS 156* Q v SA (Adelaide) 2021-22. LO BB 2-17 v Surrey (Oval) 2019 (RLC). T20 HS 90*. T20 BB 1-2.

REW, James Edward Kenneth (King's C, Taunton), b Lambeth, London 11 Jan 2004. LHB, WK. County Select XI 2021. Somerset 2nd XI debut 2019. HS 2 CS v Indians (Chester-le-St) 2021. LO HS 20 v Yorks (Taunton) 2021 (RLC).

SALE, Oliver Richard Trethowan (Sherborne S), b Newcastle-under-Lyme, Staffs 30 Sep 1995. 6'1". RHB, RFM. Squad No 82. Awaiting f-c debut. No 1st XI appearances in 2021 due to injury. T20 HS 14*. T20 BB 3-32.

‡NQ**SIDDLE, Peter** Matthew, b Traralgon, Victoria, Australia 25 Nov 1984. 6'1½". RHB, RFM. Victoria 2005-06 to 2019-20. Nottinghamshire 2014; cap 2014. Lancashire 2015. Essex 2018-21; cap 2021. Tasmania 2020-21 to date. Big Bash: MR 2013-14 to 2014-15. AS 2017-18 to date. **Tests** (A): 67 (2008-09 to 2019); HS 51 v I (Delhi) 2012-13; BB 6-54 v E (Brisbane) 2010-11. **LOI** (A): 20 (2008-09 to 2018-19); HS 10* v I (Melbourne) 2018-19; BB 3-55 v E (Centurion) 2009-10. **IT20** (A): 2 (2008-09 to 2010-11); HS 1* and BB 2-24 v NZ (Sydney) 2008-09. F-c Tours (A): E 2009, 2013, 2015, 2019; SA 2008-09, 2011-12, 2013-14; WI 2011-12; NZ 2015-16; I 2008-09 (Aus A), 2008-09, 2012-13; SL 2011; Z 2011 (Aus A); UAE 2014-15 (v P), 2018-19 (v P). HS 103* Aus A v Scotland (Edinburgh) 2013. CC HS 89 La v Northants (Northampton) 2015. 50 wkts (0+1): 54 (2011-12). BB 8-54 Vic v SA (Adelaide) 2014-15. CC BB 6-38 Ex v Warwks (Chelmsford) 2021. LO HS 62 Vic v Q (N Sydney) 2017-18. LO BB 4-22 Tas v Vic (Hobart) 2021-22. T20 HS 11. T20 BB 5-16.

SMEED, William Conrad Francis (King's C, Taunton), b Cambridge 26 Oct 2001. RHB, OB. Squad No 23. Birmingham Phoenix 2021. Somerset 2nd XI debut 2017. Awaiting f-c debut. T20 HS 99.

THOMAS, George William (King's C, Taunton), b Musgrove, Taunton 14 Nov 2003. RHB, RM. Somerset 2nd XI debut 2021. Awaiting f-c debut. LO HS 75 v Leics (Taunton) 2021 (RLC). LO BB –.

[NQ]**VAN DER MERWE, Roelof** Erasmus (Pretoria HS), b Johannesburg, South Africa 31 Dec 1984. RHB, SLA. Squad No 52. Northerns 2006-07 to 2013-14. Titans 2007-08 to 2014-15. Netherlands 2015 to 2017-18. Somerset debut 2016; cap 2018. IPL: RCB 2009 to 2009-10; DD 2011-13. Big Bash: BH 2011-12. London Spirit 2021. **LOI** (SA/Neth): 16 (13 for SA 2008-09 to 2010; 3 for Neth 2019 to 2021-22); HS 57 v Z (Deventer) 2019; BB 3-27 v Z (Centurion) 2009-10. **IT20** (SA/Neth): 46 (13 for SA 2008-09 to 2010; 33 for Neth 2015 to 2021-22); HS 75* v Z (Rotterdam) 2019; BB 4-35 v Z (Rotterdam) 2019 – separate matches. HS 205* Titans v Warriors (Benoni) 2014-15. Sm HS 102* v Hants (Taunton) 2016. BB 4-22 v Middx (Taunton) 2017. LO HS 165* v Surrey (Taunton) 2017 (RLC). LO BB 5-26 Titans v Knights (Centurion) 2012-13. T20 HS 89*. T20 BB 5-32.

WALLER, Maximilian Thomas Charles (Millfield S; Bournemouth U), b Salisbury, Wiltshire 3 March 1988. 6'0". RHB, LB. Squad No 10. Debut (Somerset) 2009; cap 2021. Dorset 2007-08. HS 28 v Hants (Southampton) 2009. BB 3-33 v Cardiff MCCU (Taunton Vale) 2012. CC BB 2-27 v Sussex (Hove) 2009. LO HS 25* v Glamorgan (Taunton) 2013 (Y40). LO BB 3-37 v Glos (Bristol) 2017 (RLC). T20 HS 17. T20 BB 4-16.

RELEASED/RETIRED

(Having made a County 1st XI appearance in 2021)

AZHAR ALI – *see WORCESTERSHIRE.*

BYROM, E.J. – *see GLAMORGAN.*

[NQ]**CONWAY, Devon** Philip, b Johannesburg, South Africa 8 Jul 1991. LHB, RM, occ WK. Gauteng 2008-09 to 2016-17. KwaZulu-Natal Inland 2010-11 to 2011-12. Dolphins 2010-11 to 2011-12. Lions 2013-14 to 2016-17. Wellington 2017-18 to date. Somerset 2021. **Tests** (NZ): 3 (2021 to 2021-22); HS 200 v E (Lord's) 2021 – on debut. **LOI** (NZ): 3 (2020-21); HS 126 v B (Wellington) 2020-21. **IT20** (NZ): 20 (2020-21 to 2021-22); HS 99* v A (Christchurch) 2020-21. F-c Tour (NZ): E 2021. HS 327* Wellington v Canterbury (Wellington) 2019-20. Sm HS 88 v Leics (Taunton) 2021. BB 3-36 Gauteng v EP (Johannesburg) 2016-17. LO HS 152 Gauteng v Border (East London) 2013-14. LO BB 1-7 Gauteng v Namibia (Windhoek) 2015-16. T20 HS 105*. T20 BB 1-10.

DRISSELL, G.S. – *see DURHAM.*

YOUNG, Samuel Jack (Millfield S), b Plymouth, Devon 30 Jul 2000. RHB, OB. Somerset 2nd XI debut 2018. LO HS 25 v Yorks (Taunton) 2021 (RLC).

SOMERSET 2021

RESULTS SUMMARY

	Place	*Won*	*Lost*	*Tied*	*Drew*	*NR*
LV= Insurance County Champ (Div 1)	6th	4	5		5	
Royal London One-Day Cup (Group 2)	7th	3	3			2
Vitality Blast (South Group)	Finalist	10	5			2

LV= INSURANCE COUNTY CHAMPIONSHIP AVERAGES
BATTING AND FIELDING

Cap		*M*	*I*	*NO*	*HS*	*Runs*	*Avge*	*100*	*50*	*Ct/St*
2015	L.Gregory	9	10	2	107	389	48.62	1	3	7
2018	T.B.Abell	12	20	2	132*	711	39.50	1	4	11
2017	S.M.Davies	13	22	2	87	634	31.70	–	5	37/1
2018	R.E.van der Merwe	6	8	–	88	241	30.12	–	2	4
	Azhar Ali	3	6	–	60	177	29.50	–	2	2
2021	J.H.Davey	12	16	7	75*	238	26.44	–	1	2
2017	M.J.Leach	10	15	4	49	276	25.09	–	–	2
	G.A.Bartlett	11	16	1	100	373	24.86	1	2	2
2016	C.Overton	8	11	1	74	237	23.70	–	2	9
2007	J.C.Hildreth	13	20	–	107	456	22.80	1	1	14
	B.G.F.Green	4	8	1	43	154	22.00	–	–	2
	M.de Lange	10	14	–	75	297	21.21	–	2	4
	L.P.Goldsworthy	10	15	1	48	297	21.21	–	–	1
	T.A.Lammonby	13	22	2	100	392	19.60	1	2	7
	T.Banton	8	14	1	51*	245	18.84	–	1	5
	E.J.Byrom	4	5	1	38	55	13.75	–	–	1
	J.A.Brooks	6	10	4	15	47	7.83	–	–	–

Also played: K.L.Aldridge (1 match) did not bat; D.P.Conway (2) 88, 21, 12 (3 ct); E.O.Leonard (1) 4*, 6 (1 ct).

BOWLING

	O	*M*	*R*	*W*	*Avge*	*Best*	*5wI*	*10wM*
C.Overton	270.3	93	650	42	15.47	5-25	4	–
J.H.Davey	292.2	84	781	35	22.31	5-30	2	–
L.Gregory	209.3	60	645	21	30.71	5-68	1	–
M.J.Leach	241	77	562	18	31.22	6-43	1	–
M.de Lange	231.5	49	685	20	34.25	4-55	–	–
J.A.Brooks	142	28	499	12	41.58	4-77	–	–
T.B.Abell	168.3	44	558	13	42.92	3-63	–	–
Also bowled:								
R.E.van der Merwe	96.1	26	241	8	30.12	4-54	–	–

K.L.Aldridge 22-2-101-0; L.P.Goldsworthy 24-8-45-0; B.G.F.Green 40-11-93-1; T.A.Lammonby 77-13-287-4; E.O.Leonard 18-2-85-1.

The First-Class Averages (pp 220–232) give the records of Somerset players in all first-class county matches, with the exception of E.J.Byrom, D.P.Conway and C.Overton, whose first-class figures for Somerset are as above.

SOMERSET RECORDS

FIRST-CLASS CRICKET

Highest Total	For 850-7d		v	Middlesex	Taunton	2007
	V 811		by	Surrey	The Oval	1899
Lowest Total	For 25		v	Glos	Bristol	1947
	V 22		by	Glos	Bristol	1920
Highest Innings	For 342	J.L.Langer	v	Surrey	Guildford	2006
	V 424	A.C.MacLaren	for	Lancashire	Taunton	1895

Highest Partnership for each Wicket

1st	346	L.C.H.Palairet/ H.T.Hewett	v	Yorkshire	Taunton	1892
2nd	450	N.R.D.Compton/J.C.Hildreth	v	Cardiff MCCU	Taunton Vale	2012
3rd	319	P.M.Roebuck/M.D.Crowe	v	Leics	Taunton	1984
4th	310	P.W.Denning/I.T.Botham	v	Glos	Taunton	1980
5th	320	J.D.Francis/I.D.Blackwell	v	Durham UCCE	Taunton	2005
6th	265	W.E.Alley/K.E.Palmer	v	Northants	Northampton	1961
7th	279	R.J.Harden/G.D.Rose	v	Sussex	Taunton	1997
8th	236	P.D.Trego/R.C.Davies	v	Lancashire	Manchester	2016
9th	183	C.H.M.Greetham/H.W.Stephenson	v	Leics	Weston-s-Mare	1963
	183	C.J.Tavaré/N.A.Mallender	v	Sussex	Hove	1990
10th	163	I.D.Blackwell/N.A.M.McLean	v	Derbyshire	Taunton	2003

Best Bowling	For	10-49	E.J.Tyler	v	Surrey	Taunton	1895
(Innings)	V	10-35	A.Drake	for	Yorkshire	Weston-s-Mare	1914
Best Bowling	For	16-83	J.C.White	v	Worcs	Bath	1919
(Match)	V	17-86	K.J.Abbott	for	Hampshire	Southampton[2]	2019

Most Runs – Season	2761	W.E.Alley	(av 58.74)	1961
Most Runs – Career	21142	H.Gimblett	(av 36.96)	1935-54
Most 100s – Season	11	S.J.Cook		1991
Most 100s – Career	52	M.E.Trescothick		1993-2018
Most Wkts – Season	169	A.W.Wellard	(av 19.24)	1938
Most Wkts – Career	2165	J.C.White	(av 18.03)	1909-37
Most Career W-K Dismissals	1007	H.W.Stephenson	(698 ct; 309 st)	1948-64
Most Career Catches in the Field	443	M.E.Trescothick		1993-2019

LIMITED-OVERS CRICKET

Highest Total	**50ov**	413-4		v	Devon	Torquay	1990
	40ov	377-9		v	Sussex	Hove	2003
	T20	250-3		v	Glos	Taunton	2006
Lowest Total	**50ov**	58		v	Middlesex	Southgate	2000
	40ov	58		v	Essex	Chelmsford	1977
	T20	82		v	Kent	Taunton	2010
Highest Innings	**50ov**	177	S.J.Cook	v	Sussex	Hove	1990
	40ov	184	M.E.Trescothick	v	Glos	Taunton	2008
	T20	151*	C.H.Gayle	v	Kent	Taunton	2015
Best Bowling	**50ov**	8-66	S.R.G.Francis	v	Derbyshire	Derby	2004
	40ov	6-16	Abdur Rehman	v	Notts	Taunton	2012
	T20	6- 5	A.V.Suppiah	v	Glamorgan	Cardiff	2011

SURREY

Formation of Present Club: 22 August 1845
Inaugural First-Class Match: 1864
Colours: Chocolate
Badge: Prince of Wales' Feathers
County Champions (since 1890): (19) 1890, 1891, 1892, 1894, 1895, 1899, 1914, 1952, 1953, 1954, 1955, 1956, 1957, 1958, 1971, 1999, 2000, 2002, 2018
Joint Champions: (1) 1950
NatWest Trophy Winners: (1) 1982
Benson and Hedges Cup Winners: (3) 1974, 1997, 2001
Pro 40/National League (Div 1) Winners: (1) 2003
Sunday League Winners: (1) 1996
Clydesdale Bank 40 Winners: (1) 2011
Twenty20 Cup Winners: (1) 2003

Chief Executive: Steve Elworthy, The Kia Oval, London, SE11 5SS • Tel: 0203 946 0100 • Email: enquiries@surreycricket.com • Web: www.kiaoval.com • Twitter: @surreycricket (108,977 followers)

Director of Cricket: Alec Stewart. **Interim Head Coach**: Gareth Batty. **Interim Assistant Coaches**: Azhar Mahmood and Jim Troughton. **Captains**: R.J.Burns (f-c and l-o), C.J.Jordan (T20). **Overseas Players**: H.M.Amla, S.P.Narine and K.A.J.Roach. **2022 Testimonial**: None. **Head Groundsman**: Lee Fortiss. **Scorer**: Debbie Beesley. ‡ New registration. [NQ] Not qualified for England.

[NQ]**AMLA, Hashim** Mahomed, b Durban, South Africa 31 Mar 1983. Younger brother of A.M.Amla (Natal B, KZN, Dolphins 1997-98 to 2012-13). 6'0". RHB, RM/OB. Squad No 1. KZN 1999-00 to 2003-04. Dolphins 2004-05 to 2011-12. Essex 2009. Nottinghamshire 2010; cap 2010. Surrey debut 2013; cap 2021. Derbyshire 2015. Cape Cobras 2015-16 to 2018-19. Hampshire 2018. IPL: KXIP 2016-17. *Wisden* 2012. **Tests** (SA): 124 (2004-05 to 2018-19, 14 as captain); 1000 runs (3); most – 1249 (2010); HS 311* v E (Oval) 2012; BB –. **LOI** (SA): 181 (2007-08 to 2019, 9 as captain); 1000 runs (2); most – 1062 (2015); HS 159 v Ire (Canberra) 2014-15. **IT20** (SA): 44 (2008-09 to 2018, 2 as captain); HS 97* v A (Cape Town) 2015-16. F-c Tours (SA) (C=Captain): E 2008, 2012, 2017; A 2008-09, 2012-13, 2016-17; WI 2010; NZ 2011-12, 2016-17; I 2004-05, 2007-08 (SA A), 2007-08, 2009-10, 2015-16C; P 2007-08; SL 2005-06 (SA A), 2006, 2014C, 2018; Z 2004 (SA A), 2007 (SA A), 2014C; B 2007-08, 2015C; UAE 2010-11, 2013-14 (v P). 1000 runs (0+2); most – 1126 (2005-06). HS 311* (*see Tests*). CC HS 215* v Hants (Oval) 2021. BB 1-10 SA A v India A (Kimberley) 2001-02. LO HS 159 (*see LOI*). T20 HS 104*.

ATKINSON, Angus ('**Gus**') Alexander Patrick (Bradfield C), b Chelsea, Middx 19 Jan 1998. 6'2". RHB, RM. Squad No 37. Debut (Surrey) 2020. Surrey 2nd XI debut 2016. HS 41* v Northants (Northampton) 2021. BB 3-78 v Glos (Bristol) 2021. LO HS 15 v Notts (Guildford) 2021 (RLC). LO BB 4-43 v Yorks (Scarborough) 2021 (RLC). T20 HS 14. T20 BB 4-36.

BARNWELL, Nathan André (Caterham S), b Ashford, Kent 3 Feb 2003. 6'0". RHB, RFM. Squad No 29. Surrey 2nd XI debut 2018. Awaiting 1st XI debut.

BURNS, Rory Joseph (City of London Freemen's S), b Epsom 26 Aug 1990. 5'10". LHB, WK, occ RM. Squad No 17. Debut (Surrey) 2011; cap 2014; captain 2018 to date. MCC 2016. MCC Univs 2010. *Wisden* 2018. **ECB Central Contract 2021-22. Tests**: 32 (2018-19 to 2021-22); HS 133 v A (Birmingham) 2019. F-c Tours: A 2021-22; SA 2019-20; WI 2018-19; NZ 2019-20; I 2020-21; SL 2018-19. 1000 runs (7); most – 1402 (2018). HS 219* v Hants (Oval) 2017. BB 1-18 v Middx (Lord's) 2013. LO HS 95 v Glos (Bristol) 2015 (RLC). T20 HS 56*.

CLARK, Jordan (Sedbergh S), b Whitehaven, Cumbria 14 Oct 1990. Elder brother of G.Clark (*see DURHAM*). 6'4". RHB, RMF, occ WK. Squad No 8. Lancashire 2015-18. Surrey debut 2019. Big Bash: HH 2018-19. Oval Invincibles 2021. HS 140 La v Surrey (Oval) 2017. Sy HS 61* v Leics (Oval) 2021. BB 6-21 v Hants (Oval) 2021. Hat-trick La v Yorks (Manchester) 2018, dismissing J.E.Root, K.S.Williamson and J.M.Bairstow. LO HS 79* and LO BB 4-34 La v Worcs (Manchester) 2017 (RLC). T20 HS 60. T20 BB 4-22.

CURRAN, Samuel Matthew (Wellington C), b Northampton 3 Jun 1998. Son of K.M.Curran (Glos, Natal, Northants, Boland and Zimbabwe 1980-81 to 1999), grandson of K.P.Curran (Rhodesia 1947-48 to 1954-55), younger brother of T.K.Curran (*see below*) and B.J.Curran (*see NORTHAMPTONSHIRE*). 5'9". LHB, LMF. Squad No 58. Debut (Surrey) 2015, taking 5-101 v Kent (Oval); cap 2018. IPL: KXIP 2019; CSK 2020-21 to date. Oval Invincibles 2021. YC 2018. *Wisden* 2018. **ECB Central Contract 2021-22. Tests**: 24 (2018 to 2021); HS 78 v I (Southampton) 2018; BB 4-58 v SA (Centurion) 2019-20. **LOI**: 11 (2018 to 2021); HS 95* v I (Pune) 2020-21; BB 5-48 v SL (Oval) 2021. **IT20**: 16 (2019-20 to 2021); HS 24 v NZ (Auckland) 2019-20; BB 3-28 v SA (Cape Town) 2020-21. F-c Tours: SA 2019-20; WI 2018-19; NZ 2019-20; SL 2016-17 (EL), 2018-19, 2019-20, 2020-21; UAE 2016-17 (v Afg)(EL). HS 96 v Lancs (Oval) 2016. BB 7-58 v Durham (Chester-le-St) 2016. LO HS 95* (*see LOI*). LO BB 5-48 (*see LOI*). T20 HS 72*. T20 BB 4-11.

CURRAN, Thomas Kevin (Hilton C, Durban), b Cape Town, South Africa 12 Mar 1995. Son of K.M.Curran (Glos, Natal, Northants, Boland and Zimbabwe 1980-81 to 1999), grandson of K.P.Curran (Rhodesia 1947-48 to 1954-55), elder brother of S.M.Curran (*see above*) and B.J.Curran (*see NORTHAMPTONSHIRE*). 6'0". RHB, RFM. Squad No 59. Debut (Surrey) 2014; cap 2016. IPL: KKR 2018; RR 2020-21; DC 2021. Big Bash: SS 2018-19 to date. Oval Invincibles 2021. **ECB Increment Contract 2021-22. Tests**: 2 (2017-18); HS 39 v A (Sydney) 2017-18; BB 1-65 v A (Melbourne) 2017-18. **LOI**: 28 (2017 to 2021); HS 47* v Ire (Dublin) 2019; BB 5-35 v A (Perth) 2017-18. **IT20**: 30 (2017 to 2021); HS 14* v NZ (Nelson) 2019-20; BB 4-36 v WI (Gros Islet) 2018-19. F-c Tours: A 2017-18; SL 2016-17 (EL); UAE 2016-17 (v Afg)(EL). HS 60 v Leics (Leicester) 2015. 50 wkts (1): 76 (2015). BB 7-20 v Glos (Oval) 2015. LO HS 47* (*see LOI*). LO BB 5-16 EL v UAE (Dubai, DSC) 2016-17. T20 HS 62. T20 BB 4-22.

DUNN, Matthew Peter (Bearwood C, Wokingham), b Egham 5 May 1992. 6'1". LHB, RFM. Squad No 4. Debut (Surrey) 2010. MCC 2015. HS 31* v Kent (Guildford) 2014. BB 5-43 v Somerset (Guildford) 2019. LO HS 8* v Glamorgan (Cardiff) 2021 (RLC). LO BB 2-32 Eng Dev XI v Sri Lanka A (Manchester) 2011. T20 HS 2. BB 3-8.

EVANS, Laurie John (Whitgift S; The John Fisher S; St Mary's C, Durham U), b Lambeth, London 12 Oct 1987. 6'0". RHB, RM. Squad No 10. Durham UCCE 2007. Surrey debut 2009; signed white-ball contract in 2022. Warwickshire 2010-16. Northamptonshire 2016 (on loan). Sussex 2017-19. MCC 2007. Big Bash: PS 2021-22. Oval Invincibles 2021. HS 213* and BB 1-29 Wa v Sussex (Birmingham) 2015, sharing Wa 6th wkt record partnership of 327 with T.R.Ambrose. Sy HS 98 and Sy BB 1-30 v Bangladeshis (Oval) 2010. LO HS 134* Sx v Kent (Canterbury) 2017 (RLC). LO BB 1-29 Sx v Middx (Lord's) 2019 (RLC). T20 HS 108*. T20 BB 1-5.

FOAKES, Benjamin Thomas (Tendring TC), b Colchester, Essex 15 Feb 1993. 6'1". RHB, WK. Squad No 7. Essex 2011-14. Surrey debut 2015; cap 2016. MCC 2016. **Tests**: 9 (2018-19 to 2021-22); HS 107 v SL (Galle) 2018-19 – on debut. **LOI**: 1 (2019); HS 61* v Ire (Dublin) 2019. **IT20**: 1 (2019) did not bat. F-c Tours: WI 2017-18 (EL), 2018-19, 2021-22; I 2020-21; SL 2013-14 (EL), 2016-17 (EL), 2018-19; UAE 2016-17 (v Afg)(EL). HS 141* v Hants (Southampton) 2016, sharing Sy record 8th wkt partnership of 222* with G.J.Batty. LO HS 92 v Somerset (Taunton) 2016 (RLC). T20 HS 75*.

GEDDES, Benedict Brodie Albert (St John's S, Leatherhead), b Epsom 31 Jul 2001. 6'1". RHB. Squad No 14. Debut (Surrey) 2021. Surrey 2nd XI debut 2019. HS 15 v Hants (Southampton) 2021. LO HS 32 v Warwks (Oval) 2021 (RLC). T20 HS 28.

JACKS, William George (St George's C, Weybridge), b Chertsey 21 Nov 1998. 6'1". RHB, OB. Squad No 9. Debut (Surrey) 2018. Big Bash: HH 2020-21. Oval Invincibles 2021. Surrey 2nd XI debut 2016. England U19 2016-17 to 2017. F-c Tour (EL): I 2018-19. HS 120 v Kent (Beckenham) 2019. BB 1-7 v Glos (Oval) 2021. LO HS 121 v Glos (Oval) 2018 (RLC). LO BB 2-32 v Middx (Oval) 2019 (RLC). T20 HS 92*. T20 BB 4-15.

JORDAN, Christopher James (Comber Mere S, Barbados; Dulwich C), b Christ Church, Barbados 4 Oct 1988. 6'1". RHB, RFM. Squad No 34. Debut (Surrey) 2007; returns in 2022 as T20 captain. Barbados 2011-12 to 2012-13. Sussex 2013-19; cap 2014. IPL: RCB 2016; SH 2017-18; KXIP 2020-21; PK 2021. Big Bash: AS 2016-17; ST 2018-19; PS 2019-20; SS 2021-22. Southern Brave 2021. **ECB Increment Contract 2021-22. Tests**: 8 (2014 to 2014-15); HS 35 v SL (Lord's) 2014; BB 4-18 v I (Oval) 2014. **LOI**: 34 (2013 to 2019-20); HS 38* v SL (Oval) 2014; BB 5-29 v SL (Manchester) 2014. **IT20**: 75 (2013-14 to 2021-22); HS 36 v NZ (Wellington) 2019-20; BB 4-6 v WI (Basseterre) 2018-19 – E record. F-c Tour: WI 2014-15. HS 166 Sx v Northants (Northampton) 2019. Sy HS 79* and Sy BB 4-57 v Essex (Chelmsford) 2011. 50 wkts (1): 61 (2013). BB 7-43 Barbados v CC&C (Bridgetown) 2012-13. CC BB 6-48 Sx v Yorks (Leeds) 2013. LO HS 55 Sx v Surrey (Guildford) 2016 (RLC). LO BB 5-28 Sx v Middx (Hove) 2016 (RLC). T20 HS 45*. T20 BB 4-6.

KIMBER, Nicholas John Henry (William Farr C of E S), b Lincoln 16 Jan 2001. Younger brother of L.P.J.Kimber (*see LEICESTERSHIRE*) (Loughborough MCCU 2019) and J.F.Kimber (Lincolnshire 2016-18). 5'11". RHB, RMF. Squad No 12. Nottinghamshire 2nd XI 2019. Awaiting f-c debut. LO HS 16 v Glamorgan (Cardiff) 2021 (RLC). LO BB 2-57 v Somerset (Oval) 2021 (RLC).

LAWES, Thomas Edward (Cranleigh S), b Singapore 25 Dec 2002. 6'0". RHB, RMF. Squad No 30. Surrey 2nd XI debut 2021. Awaiting 1st XI debut.

McKERR, Conor (St John's C, Johannesburg), b Johannesburg, South Africa 19 Jan 1998. 6'6". RHB, RFM. Squad No 3. UK passport, qualified for England in March 2020. Derbyshire 2017 (on loan), taking wkt of J.D.Libby with 4th ball in f-c cricket. Surrey debut 2017. Surrey 2nd XI debut 2016. HS 29 v Yorks (Oval) 2018. BB 5-54 (10-141 match) De v Northants (Northampton) 2017. Sy BB 4-26 v Notts (Oval) 2018. LO HS 26* v Glamorgan (Cardiff) 2019 (RLC). LO BB 4-64 v Warwks (Oval) 2021 (RLC).

MORIARTY, Daniel Thornhill (Rondesbosch Boys' HS), b Reigate 2 Dec 1999. 6'0". LHB, SLA. Squad No 21. Debut (Surrey) 2020, taking 5-64 v Middx (Oval). Surrey 2nd XI debut 2019. Essex 2nd XI 2019. MCC YC 2019. South Africa U19 2016. HS 8 v Essex (Oval) 2021. BB 6-60 v Glos (Oval) 2021. LO HS 5 v Glamorgan (Cardiff) 2021 (RLC). LO BB 4-30 v Somerset (Oval) 2021 (RLC). T20 HS 9*. T20 BB 3-25.

‡[NQ]**NARINE, Sunil** Philip, b Arima, Trinidad 26 May 1988. LHB, OB. Trinidad & Tobago 2008-09 to 2012-13. IPL: KKR 2012 to date. Big Bash: SS 2012-13; MR 2016-17. Oval Invincibles 2021. **Tests** (WI): 6 (2012 to 2013-14); HS 22* v B (Dhaka) 2012-13; BB 6-91 v NZ (Hamilton) 2013-14. **LOI** (WI): 65 (2011-12 to 2016-17); HS 36 v B (Khulna) 2012-13; BB 6-27 v SA (Providence) 2016. **IT20** (WI): 51 (2011-12 to 2019); HS 30 v P (Dubai, DSC) 2016-17; BB 4-12 v NZ (Lauderhill) 2012. F-c Tours (WI): E 2012; NZ 2013-14; B 2012-13. HS 40* WI A v Bangladesh A (Gros Islet) 2011-12. BB 8-17 (13-39 match) T&T v CC&C (Cave Hill) 2011-12. LO HS 51 T&T v Barbados (Bridgetown) 2017-18. LO BB 6-9 T&T v Guyana (Port of Spain) 2014-15. T20 HS 79. T20 BB 5-19.

OVERTON, Jamie (West Buckland S), b Barnstaple, Devon 10 Apr 1994. Twin brother of Craig Overton (*see SOMERSET*). 6'5". RHB, RFM. Squad No 88. Somerset 2012-20; cap 2019. Northamptonshire 2019 (on loan). Surrey debut 2020. Devon 2011. F-c Tour (EL): UAE 2018-19 (v PA). HS 120 Sm v Warwks (Birmingham) 2020. Sy HS 55 v Sussex (Oval) 2020. BB 6-95 Sm v Middx (Taunton) 2013. Sy BB 2-36 v Glos (Oval) 2021. Hat-trick Sm v Notts (Nottingham) 2018. LO HS 40* Sm v Glos (Taunton) 2016 (RLC). LO BB 4-42 Sm v Durham (Chester-le-St) 2012 (CB40). T20 HS 40*. T20 BB 5-47.

PATEL, Ryan Samir (Whitgift S), b Sutton 26 Oct 1997. 5'10". LHB, RMF. Squad No 26. Debut (Surrey) 2017. Surrey 2nd XI debut 2016. England U19 2017. HS 100* v Essex (Oval) 2019. BB 6-5 v Somerset (Guildford) 2018. LO HS 131 v Notts (Guildford) 2021 (RLC). LO BB 2-65 v Hants (Oval) 2019 (RLC). T20 HS 5*. T20 BB –.

POPE, Oliver John Douglas (Cranleigh S), b Chelsea, Middx 2 Jan 1998. 5'9". RHB, WK. Squad No 32. Debut (Surrey) 2017; cap 2018. Surrey 2nd XI debut 2015. England U19 2016 to 2016-17. **ECB Central Contract 2021-22. Tests**: 23 (2018 to 2021-22); HS 135* v SA (Port Elizabeth) 2019-20. F-c Tours: A 2021-22; SA 2019-20; NZ 2019-20; I 2018-19 (EL), 2020-21; SL 2019-20. 1000 runs (2); most – 1098 (2018). HS 274 v Glamorgan (Oval) 2021. LO HS 93* EL v Pakistan A (Abu Dhabi) 2018-19. T20 HS 60.

REIFER, Nico Malik Julian (Queen's C, Bridgetown; Whitgift S), b Bridgetown, Barbados 11 Nov 2000. 5'11". RHB, RM. Squad No 27. Surrey 2nd XI debut 2018. Awaiting f-c debut. LO HS 28 v Durham (Chester-le-St) 2021 (RLC).

NQ**ROACH, Kemar** Andre Jamal, b St Lucy, Barbados 30 Jun 1988. RHB, RFM. Squad No 66. Barbados 2007-08 to date. Worcestershire 2011. Surrey debut 2021. IPL: DC 2009-10. Big Bash: BH 2012-13 to 2013-14. **Tests** (WI): 69 (2009 to 2021-22); HS 41 v NZ (Kingston) 2012; BB 6-48 v B (St George's) 2009. **LOI** (WI): 95 (2008 to 2021-22); HS 34 v I (Port of Spain) 2013; BB 6-27 v Netherlands (Delhi) 2010-11. **IT20** (WI): 11 (2008 to 2012-13); HS 3* and BB 2-25 v SA (North Sound) 2010. F-c Tours (WI): E 2012, 2017, 2020; A 2009-10, 2015-16; SA 2014-15; NZ 2008-09, 2017-18, 2020-21; I 2011-12, 2019-20 (v Afg); SL 2010-11, 2015-16, 2021-22; Z 2017-18; B 2011-12, 2018-19, 2020-21. HS 53 Barbados v Leeward Is (Basseterre) 2015-16. CC HS 8 v Middx (Lord's) 2021. BB 8-40 (10-80 match) v Hants (Oval) 2021. LO HS 34 (*see LOI*). LO BB 6-27 (*see LOI*). T20 HS 12. T20 BB 3-18.

ROY, Jason Jonathan (Whitgift S), b Durban, South Africa 21 Jul 1990. 6'0". RHB, RM. Squad No 20. Debut (Surrey) 2010; cap 2014. IPL: GL 2017; DD 2018; SH 2021. Big Bash: ST 2014-15; SS 2016-17 to 2017-18; PS 2020-21. Oval Invincibles 2021. **ECB Central Contract 2021-22. Tests**: 5 (2019); HS 72 v Ire (Lord's) 2019. **LOI**: 98 (2015 to 2021); HS 180 v A (Melbourne) 2017-18 – E record. **IT20**: 58 (2014 to 2021-22); HS 78 v NZ (Delhi) 2015-16. 1000 runs (1): 1078 (2014). HS 143 v Lancs (Oval) 2015. BB 3-9 v Glos (Bristol) 2014. LO HS 180 (*see LOI*). LO BB –. T20 HS 122*. T20 BB 1-23.

SMITH, Jamie Luke (Whitgift S), b Epsom 12 Jul 2000. 5'10". RHB, WK. Squad No 11. Debut (Surrey) 2018-19, scoring 127 v MCC (Dubai, ICCA). Surrey 2nd XI debut. England U19 2018-19. HS 138 v Glamorgan (Oval). LO HS 40 v Durham (Chester-le-St) 2021 (RLC). T20 HS 60.

STEEL, Cameron Tate (Scotch C, Perth, Australia; Millfield S; Durham U), b San Francisco, USA 13 Sep 1995. 5'10". RHB, LB. Squad No 44. Durham MCCU 2014-16. Durham 2017-20. Hampshire 2021 (on loan). Surrey debut 2021. HS 224 Du v Leics (Leicester) 2017. Sy HS 28 v Essex (Oval) 2021. BB 2-7 Du v Glamorgan (Cardiff) 2018. Sy BB 1-9 v Northants (Northampton) 2021. LO HS 77 Du v Notts (Nottingham) 2017 (RLC). LO BB 4-33 v Leics (Leicester) 2021 (RLC). T20 HS 37. T20 BB 2-60.

TAYLOR, James Philip Arthur (Trentham HS), b Stoke-on-Trent, Staffs 19 Jan 2001. Younger brother of T.A.I.Taylor (*see NORTHAMPTONSHIRE*). 6'3". RHB, RM. Squad No 25. Derbyshire 2017-19. Surrey debut 2020. Derbyshire 2nd XI 2016-19. HS 22 and Sy BB 2-31 v Essex (Chelmsford) 2020. BB 3-26 De v Leeds/Brad MCCU (Derby) 2019. LO HS 6* and LO BB 2-66 De v Australia A (Derby) 2019. T20 HS 3. T20 BB 1-6.

TOPLEY, Reece James William (Royal Hospital S, Ipswich), b Ipswich, Suffolk 21 February 1994. Son of T.D.Topley (Surrey, Essex, GW 1985-94) and nephew of P.A.Topley (Kent 1972-75). 6'7". RHB, LFM. Squad No 24. Essex 2011-15; cap 2013. Hampshire 2016-17. Sussex 2019. Surrey debut 2021. Oval Invincibles 2021. **LOI**: 13 (2015 to 2020-21); HS 6 v A (Manchester) 2015; BB 4-50 v SA (Port Elizabeth) 2015-16. **IT20**: 10 (2015 to 2021-22); HS 2* v WI (Bridgetown) 2021-22; BB 3-24 v P (Dubai, DSC) 2015-16. F-c Tour (EL): SL 2013-14. HS 16 H v Yorks (Southampton) 2017. Sy HS 10 v Middx (Lord's) 2021. BB 6-29 (11-85 match) Ex v Worcs (Chelmsford) 2013. Sy BB 5-66 v Glos (Bristol) 2021. LO HS 19 Ex v Somerset (Taunton) 2011 (CB40). LO BB 4-16 EL v West Indies A (Northampton) 2018. T20 HS 14*. T20 BB 4-20.

VIRDI, Guramar Singh ('**Amar**') (Guru Nanak Sikh Ac, Hayes), b Chiswick, Middx 19 Jul 1998. 5'10". RHB, OB. Squad No 19. Debut (Surrey) 2017. Surrey 2nd XI debut 2016. England U19 2016 to 2017. HS 47 v Northants (Northampton) 2021. BB 8-61 (14-139 match) v Notts (Nottingham) 2019.

‡[NQ]**WORRALL, Daniel** James (Kardina International C; U of Melbourne), b Melbourne, Australia 10 Jul 1991. 6'0". RHB, RFM. Squad No 40. S Australia 2012-13 to date. Gloucestershire 2018-21; cap 2018. Big Bash: MS 2013-14 to 2019-20; AS 2020-21 to date. **LOI** (A): 3 (2016-17); HS 6* v SA (Centurion) 2016-17; BB 1-43 v SA (Benoni) 2016-17. CC HS 50 Gs v Glamorgan (Bristol) 2018. BB 7-64 (10-148 match) SA v WA (Adelaide) 2018-19. CC BB 5-54 Gs v Middx (Cheltenham) 2021. LO HS 31* SA v WA (Perth) 2021-22. LO BB 5-62 SA v Vic (Hobart) 2017-18. T20 HS 62*. T20 BB 4-23.

RELEASED/RETIRED

(Having made a County 1st XI appearance in 2021)

[NQ]**ABBOTT, Sean** Anthony, b Windsor, NSW, Australia 29 Feb 1992. RHB, RMF. New South Wales 2011-12 to date. Surrey 2021. IPL: RCB 2015. Big Bash: ST 2011-12 to 2012-13; SS 2013-14 to date. **LOI** (A): 2 (2014-15 to 2020-21); HS 4 v I (Canberra) 2020-21; BB 1-25 v P (Sharjah) 2014-15. **IT20** (A): 7 (2014-15 to 2020-21); HS 12* v I (Canberra) 2020-21; BB 2-14 v P (Perth) 2019-20. F-c Tour (Aus A): I 2015. HS 102* NSW v Tas (Adelaide) 2020-21. Sy HS 40 and Sy BB 2-5 v Glos (Oval) 2021. BB 7-45 NSW v Tas (Hobart) 2018-19. LO HS 50 NSW v SA (Sydney, DO) 2013-14. LO BB 5-43 NSW v Tas (N Sydney) 2018-19. T20 HS 41. T20 BB 5-16.

[NQ]**ASHWIN, Ravi**chandran, b Madras, India 17 Sep 1986. 6'2". RHB, OB. Tamil Nadu 2006-07 to date. Worcestershire 2017. Nottinghamshire 2019; cap 2019. Surrey 2021. IPL: CSK 2009-15; RPS 2016; KXIP 2018-19; DC 2020-21 to date. **Tests** (I): 85 (2011-12 to 2021-22); HS 124 v WI (Kolkata) 2013-14; 50 wkts (3); most 72 (2016); BB 7-59 (13-140 match) v NZ (Indore) 2016-17. **LOI** (I): 111 (2010 to 2021-22); HS 65 v NZ (Auckland) 2013-14; BB 4-25 v UAE (Perth) 2014-15. **IT20** (I): 51 (2010 to 2021-22); HS 31* v SL (Pune) 2015-16; BB 4-8 v SL (Visakhapatnam) 2015-16. F-c Tours (I): E 2014, 2018, 2021 (v NZ); A 2011-12, 2014-15, 2018-19, 2020-21; SA 2013-14, 2017-18, 2021-22; WI 2016; NZ 2019-20; SL 2007-08 (TN), 2015, 2017; B 2015. HS 124 (*see Tests*). CC HS 82 Wo v Durham (Worcester) 2017. 50 wkts (0+1): 82 (2016-17). BB 7-59 (*see Tests*). CC BB 6-27 v Somerset (Oval) 2021. LO HS 79 South Zone v Central Zone (Vadodara) 2009-10. LO BB 4-25 (*see LOI*). T20 HS 46. T20 BB 4-8.

BATTY, Gareth Jon (Bingley GS), b Bradford, Yorks 13 Oct 1977. Younger brother of J.D.Batty (Yorkshire and Somerset 1989-96). 5'11". RHB, OB. Yorkshire 1997. Surrey 1999-2019; cap 2011; captain 2015-17; testimonial 2017. Worcestershire 2002-09. MCC 2012. **Tests**: 9 (2003-04 to 2016-17); HS 38 v SL (Kandy) 2003-04; BB 3-55 v SL (Galle) 2003-04. Took wicket with his third ball in Test cricket. **LOI**: 10 (2002-03 to 2008-09); HS 17 v WI (Bridgetown) 2008-09; BB 2-40 v WI (Gros Islet) 2003-04. **IT20**: 1 (2008-09); HS 4 v WI (Port of Spain) 2008-09. F-c Tours: WI 2003-04, 2005-06; NZ 2008-09 (Eng A); I

2016-17; SL 2002-03 (ECB Acad), 2003-04; B 2003-04, 2016-17. HS 133 Wo v Surrey (Oval) 2004. Sy HS 110* v Hants (Southampton) 2016, sharing Sy record 8th wkt partnership of 222* with B.T.Foakes. 50 wkts (2); most – 60 (2003). BB 8-64 (10-111 match) v Warwks (Birmingham) 2019. Hat-tricks (2): v Derbys (Oval) 2015 and v Warwks (Birmingham) 2019. LO HS 83* v Yorks (Oval) 2001 (NL). LO BB 5-35 Wo v Hants (Southampton) 2009 (FPT). T20 HS 87. T20 BB 4-13.

CLARKE, Rikki (Broadwater SS; Godalming C), b Orsett, Essex 29 Sep 1981. 6'4". RHB, RMF. Surrey 2002-21, scoring 107* v Cambridge U (Cambridge) on debut; cap 2005; testimonial 2021. Derbyshire cap/captain 2008. Warwickshire 2008-17; cap 2011. MCC 2006, 2016. YC 2002. **Tests**: 2 (2003-04); HS 55 and BB 2-7 v B (Chittagong) 2003-04. **LOI**: 20 (2003 to 2006); HS 39 v P (Lord's) 2006; BB 2-28 v B (Dhaka) 2003-04. F-c Tours: WI 2003-04, 2005-06; SL 2002-03 (ECB Acad), 2004-05; B 2003-04. 1000 runs (1): 1027 (2006). HS 214 v Somerset (Guildford) 2006. BB 7-55 v Somerset (Oval) 2017. Took seven catches in an innings Wa v Lancs (Liverpool) 2011 to equal world record. LO HS 98* v Derbys (Derby) 2002 (NL). LO BB 5-26 Wa v Worcs (Birmingham) 2016 (RLC). T20 HS 79*. T20 BB 4-16.

DAVID, T.H. – *see LANCASHIRE.*

DERNBACH, Jade Winston (St John the Baptist S, Woking), b Johannesburg, South Africa 3 Mar 1986. 6'1½". RHB, RFM. Italian passport. UK resident since 1998. Surrey 2003-18; cap 2011; captain 2018-19 (T20 only); testimonial 2019. Derbyshire 2021 (T20 only). Big Bash: MS 2011-12. London Spirit 2021. **LOI**: 24 (2011 to 2013); HS 5 v SL (Leeds) 2011; BB 4-45 v P (Dubai) 2011-12. **IT20**: 34 (2011 to 2013-14); HS 12 v I (Colombo, RPS) 2012-13; BB 4-22 v I (Manchester) 2011. F-c Tour (EL): WI 2010-11. HS 56* v Northants (Northampton) 2010. 50 wkts (1): 51 (2010). BB 6-47 v Leics (Leicester) 2009. LO HS 31 v Somerset (Taunton) 2010 (CB40). LO BB 6-35 v Glos (Lord's) 2015 (RLC). T20 HS 24*. T20 BB 4-22.

NQ**JAMIESON, Kyle** Alex, b 30 Dec 1994. RHB, RFM. Canterbury 2014-15 to 2018-19. Auckland 2019-20 to date. Surrey 2021. IPL: RCB 2021. **Tests** (NZ): 14 (2019-20 to 2021-22); HS 51* v WI (Hamilton) 2020-21; BB 6-48 (11-117 match) v P (Christchurch) 2020-21. **LOI** (NZ): 5 (2019-20 to 2020-21); HS 25* and BB 2-42 v I (Auckland) 2019-20. **IT20** (NZ): 8 (2020-21); HS 30 v A (Wellington) 2020-21; BB 2-15 v WI (Mt Maunganui) 2020-21. F-c Tours (NZ): E 2021; I 2021-22; UAE (v I & P) 2018-19 (NZA). HS 67 Cant v Otago (Dunedin) 2018-19. BB 8-74 (11-160 match) Cant v Auckland (Rangiora) 2016-17. LO HS 67 Cant v CD (Palmerston N) 2017-18. LO BB 4-49 NZA v India A (Christchurch) 2019-20. T20 HS 33*. T20 BB 6-7 – joint 4th best analysis in all T20 cricket.

STONEMAN, M.D. – *see MIDDLESEX.*

L.E.Plunkett left the staff without making a County 1st XI appearance in 2021.

SURREY 2021

RESULTS SUMMARY

	Place	Won	Lost	Drew	NR
LV= Insurance County Champ (Div 2)	5th	2	3	8	
Royal London One-Day Cup (Group 2)	SF	5	3		2
Vitality Blast (South Group)	5th	6	5		3

LV= INSURANCE COUNTY CHAMPIONSHIP AVERAGES
BATTING AND FIELDING

Cap		*M*	*I*	*NO*	*HS*	*Runs*	*Avge*	*100*	*50*	*Ct/St*
2018	O.J.D.Pope	9	13	2	274	861	78.27	3	–	6
2021	H.M.Amla	13	20	3	215*	994	58.47	3	2	2
2014	R.J.Burns	9	14	1	104*	617	47.46	1	7	5
2016	B.T.Foakes	8	10	2	133	350	43.75	1	2	16/2
	J.L.Smith	12	17	2	138	656	43.73	3	1	15/1
	W.G.Jacks	6	5	1	60	146	36.50	–	2	4
2018	M.D.Stoneman	10	15	–	119	473	31.53	1	3	2
	R.S.Patel	6	10	–	62	250	25.00	–	2	3
	J.Overton	8	9	1	50	154	19.25	–	1	6
2005	R.Clarke	11	13	3	65	192	19.20	–	1	13
	A.A.P.Atkinson	2	4	1	41*	52	17.33	–	–	–
	J.Clark	12	14	1	61*	208	16.00	–	2	2
	C.T.Steel	2	4	–	28	45	11.25	–	–	1
	G.S.Virdi	11	12	6	47	59	9.83	–	–	1
	R.J.W.Topley	7	9	2	10	31	4.42	–	–	–

Also batted: S.A.Abbott (1 match) 40 (1 ct); R.Ashwin (1) 0, 0* (1 ct); M.P.Dunn (1) 23 (1 ct); L.J.Evans (2) 6, 4, 11 (2 ct); B.B.A.Geddes (1) 4, 15; K.A.Jamieson (1) 0*; D.T.Moriarty (4) 4, 0, 8 (2 ct); K.A.J.Roach (5) 8, 0*, 5; J.A.Tattersall (1) 4 (5 ct); J.P.A.Taylor (1) 19.

BOWLING

	O	*M*	*R*	*W*	*Avge*	*Best*	*5wI*	*10wM*
K.A.J.Roach	134	28	452	22	20.54	8- 40	2	1
J.Clark	276	36	904	32	28.25	6- 21	2	–
D.T.Moriarty	181.4	31	521	18	28.94	6- 60	1	–
R.J.W.Topley	199.3	46	616	21	29.33	5- 66	1	–
G.S.Virdi	299.4	48	961	28	34.32	6-171	1	–
R.Clarke	197.5	45	582	16	36.37	3- 34	–	–
Also bowled:								
R.Ashwin	58	13	126	7	18.00	6- 27	1	–
A.A.P.Atkinson	47	7	172	5	34.40	3- 78	–	–
J.Overton	142.1	30	454	6	75.66	2- 36	–	–

S.A.Abbott 15-8-27-2; R.J.Burns 7-1-22-0; M.P.Dunn 36-2-145-0; W.G.Jacks 64-9-216-4; K.A.Jamieson 6-3-10-0; R.S.Patel 23-5-80-0; C.T.Steel 24-1-120-1; M.D.Stoneman 3-0-13-0; J.P.A.Taylor 15.1-5-44-2.

The First-Class Averages (pp 220–232) give the records of Surrey players in all first-class county matches, with the exception of R.Ashwin, R.J.Burns, K.A.Jamieson, O.J.D.Pope, C.T.Steel and J.A.Tattersall, whose first-class figures for Surrey are as above.

SURREY RECORDS

FIRST-CLASS CRICKET

Highest Total	For	811		v	Somerset	The Oval	1899
	V	863		by	Lancashire	The Oval	1990
Lowest Total	For	14		v	Essex	Chelmsford	1983
	V	16		by	MCC	Lord's	1872
Highest Innings	For	357*	R.Abel	v	Somerset	The Oval	1899
	V	366	N.H.Fairbrother	for	Lancashire	The Oval	1990

Highest Partnership for each Wicket

1st	428	J.B.Hobbs/A.Sandham	v	Oxford U	The Oval	1926
2nd	371	J.B.Hobbs/E.G.Hayes	v	Hampshire	The Oval	1909
3rd	413	D.J.Bicknell/D.M.Ward	v	Kent	Canterbury	1990
4th	448	R.Abel/T.W.Hayward	v	Yorkshire	The Oval	1899
5th	318	M.R.Ramprakash/Azhar Mahmood	v	Middlesex	The Oval	2005
6th	298	A.Sandham/H.S.Harrison	v	Sussex	The Oval	1913
7th	262	C.J.Richards/K.T.Medlycott	v	Kent	The Oval	1987
8th	222*	B.T.Foakes/G.J.Batty	v	Hampshire	Southampton[2]	2016
9th	168	E.R.T.Holmes/E.W.J.Brooks	v	Hampshire	The Oval	1936
10th	173	A.Ducat/A.Sandham	v	Essex	Leyton	1921

Best Bowling	For	10-43	T.Rushby	v	Somerset	Taunton	1921
(Innings)	V	10-28	W.P.Howell	for	Australians	The Oval	1899
Best Bowling	For	16-83	G.A.R.Lock	v	Kent	Blackheath	1956
(Match)	V	15-57	W.P.Howell	for	Australians	The Oval	1899

Most Runs – Season	3246	T.W.Hayward	(av 72.13)	1906
Most Runs – Career	43554	J.B.Hobbs	(av 49.72)	1905-34
Most 100s – Season	13	T.W.Hayward		1906
	13	J.B.Hobbs		1925
Most 100s – Career	144	J.B.Hobbs		1905-34
Most Wkts – Season	252	T.Richardson	(av 13.94)	1895
Most Wkts – Career	1775	T.Richardson	(av 17.87)	1892-1904
Most Career W-K Dismissals	1221	H.Strudwick	(1035 ct; 186 st)	1902-27
Most Career Catches in the Field	605	M.J.Stewart		1954-72

LIMITED-OVERS CRICKET

Highest Total	**50ov**	496-4		v	Glos	The Oval	2007
	40ov	386-3		v	Glamorgan	The Oval	2010
	T20	250-6		v	Kent	Canterbury	2018
Lowest Total	**50ov**	74		v	Kent	The Oval	1967
	40ov	64		v	Worcs	Worcester	1978
	T20	88		v	Kent	The Oval	2012
Highest Innings	**50ov**	268	A.D.Brown	v	Glamorgan	The Oval	2002
	40ov	203	A.D.Brown	v	Hampshire	Guildford	1997
	T20	131*	A.J.Finch	v	Sussex	Hove	2018
Best Bowling	**50ov**	7-33	R.D.Jackman	v	Yorkshire	Harrogate	1970
	40ov	7-30	M.P.Bicknell	v	Glamorgan	The Oval	1999
	T20	6-24	T.J.Murtagh	v	Middlesex	Lord's	2005

SUSSEX

Formation of Present Club: 1 March 1839
Substantial Reorganisation: August 1857
Inaugural First-Class Match: 1864
Colours: Dark Blue, Light Blue and Gold
Badge: County Arms of Six Martlets
County Champions: (3) 2003, 2006, 2007
Gillette/NatWest/C&G Trophy Winners: (5) 1963, 1964, 1978, 1986, 2006
Pro 40/National League (Div 1) Winners: (2) 2008, 2009
Sunday League Winners: (1) 1982
Twenty20 Cup Winners: (1) 2009

Chief Executive: Rob Andrew, The 1st Central County Ground, Eaton Road, Hove BN3 3AN • Tel: 01273 827100 • Email: info@sussexcricket.co.uk • Web: www.sussexcricket.co.uk • Twitter: @SussexCCC (113,479 followers)

Performance Director: Keith Greenfield. **Head Coach**: Ian Salisbury. **Batting Coach**: Grant Flower. **T20 Head Coach**: James Kirtley. **Captains**: T.J.Haines (l-o) and L.J.Wright (T20). **Overseas Players**: Mohammad Rizwan, J.R.Philippe, C.A.Pujara and Rashid Khan (T20 only). **2022 Testimonial**: None. **Head Groundsman**: Ben Gibson. **Scorer**: Graham Irwin. **Vitality Blast Name**: Sussex Sharks. ‡ New registration. [NQ] Not qualified for England.

ARCHER, Jofra Chioke (Christchurch Foundation), b Bridgetown, Barbados 1 Apr 1995. 6'3". RHB, RF. Squad No 22. Debut (Sussex) 2016; cap 2017. IPL: RR 2018 to 2020-21. Big Bash: HH 2017-18 to 2018-19. *Wisden* 2019. **ECB Central Contract 2021-22. Tests**: 13 (2019 to 2020-21); HS 30 v NZ (Mt Maunganui) 2019-20; BB 6-45 v A (Leeds) 2019. **LOI**: 17 (2019 to 2020); HS 8* v A (Manchester) 2020; BB 3-27 v SA (Oval) 2019. **IT20**: 12 (2019 to 2020-21); HS 18* and BB 4-33 v I (Ahmedabad) 2020-21. F-c Tours: SA 2019-20; NZ 2019-20; I 2020-21. HS 81* v Northants (Northampton) 2017. 50 wkts (1): 61 (2017). BB 7-67 v Kent (Hove) 2017. LO HS 45 v Essex (Chelmsford) 2017 (RLC). LO BB 5-42 v Somerset (Taunton) 2016 (RLC). T20 HS 36. T20 BB 4-18.

ATKINS, Jamie Ardley (Eastbourne C), b Redhill, Surrey 20 May 2002. 6'6". RHB, RMF. Squad No 32. Debut (Sussex) 2021. HS 10* v Yorks (Leeds) 2021. BB 5-51 v Kent (Canterbury) 2021.

BEER, William Andrew Thomas (Reigate GS; Collyer's C, Horsham), b Crawley 8 Oct 1988. 5'10". RHB, LB. Squad No 18. Debut (Sussex) 2008. HS 97 v Glos (Arundel) 2019. BB 6-29 (11-91 match) v South Africa A (Arundel) 2017. CC BB 3-31 v Worcs (Worcester) 2010. LO HS 75 v Essex (Chelmsford) 2019 (RLC). LO BB 3-27 v Warwks (Hove) 2012 (CB40). T20 HS 37. T20 BB 3-14.

BOPARA, Ravinder Singh (Brampton Manor S; Barking Abbey Sports C), b Newham, London 4 May 1985. 5'8". RHB, RM. Squad No 23. Essex 2002-19; cap 2005; benefit 2015; captain (l-o only) 2016. Auckland 2009-10. Dolphins 2010-11. Sussex debut 2020 (T20 only). MCC 2006, 2008. IPL: KXIP 2009 to 2009-10; SH 2015. Big Bash: SS 2013-14. London Spirit 2021. YC 2008. **Tests**: 13 (2007-08 to 2012); HS 143 v WI (Lord's) 2009; BB 1-39 v SL (Galle) 2007-08. **LOI**: 120 (2006-07 to 2014-15); HS 101* v Ire (Dublin) 2013; BB 4-38 v B (Birmingham) 2010. **IT20**: 38 (2008 to 2014); HS 65* v A (Hobart) 2013-14; BB 4-10 v WI (Oval) 2011. F-c Tours: WI 2008-09, 2010-11 (EL); SL 2007-08, 2011-12. 1000 runs (1): 1256 (2008). HS 229 Ex v Northants (Chelmsford) 2007. BB 5-49 Ex v Derbys (Chelmsford) 2016. LO HS 201* Ex v Leics (Leicester) 2008 (FPT) – Ex record. LO BB 5-63 Dolphins v Warriors (Pietermaritzburg) 2010-11. T20 HS 105*. T20 BB 6-16.

CARSON, Jack Joshua (Bainbridge Ac; Hurstpierpoint C), b Craigavon, Co Armagh 3 Dec 2000. 6'2". RHB, OB. Squad No 16. Debut (Sussex) 2020. Sussex 2nd XI debut 2018. HS 87 v Worcs (Worcester) 2021. BB 5-85 v Yorks (Hove) 2021.

CARTER, Oliver James (Eastbourne C), b Eastbourne 2 Nov 2001. 5'8½". RHB, WK. Squad No 11. Debut (Sussex) 2021. Sussex 2nd XI debut 2018. HS 51 v Derbys (Hove) 2021. LO HS 59 v Glos (Hove) 2021 (RLC). T20 HS 0*.

CLARK, Thomas Geoffrey Reeves (Ardingly C), b Haywards Heath 27 Feb 2001. 6'2". LHB, RM. Squad No 27. Debut (Sussex) 2019. Sussex 2nd XI debut 2017. HS 65 v Kent (Canterbury) 2020. BB 1-37 v Kent (Hove) 2021. LO HS 44 v Kent (Hove) 2021 (RLC).

COLES, James Matthew (Magdalen Coll S), b Aylesbury, Bucks 2 Apr 2004. 6'0½". RHB, SLA. Squad No 30. Debut (Sussex) 2020, aged 16y 157d – youngest ever player for the county. HS 36 v Kent (Canterbury) 2021. BB 2-32 v Surrey (Oval) 2020. LO HS 32 v Essex (Chelmsford) 2021 (RLC). LO BB 3-27 v Worcs (Worcester) 2021 (RLC).

CROCOMBE, Henry Thomas (Bede's S, Upper Dicker), b Eastbourne 20 Sep 2001. 6'2". RHB, RMF. Squad No 5. Debut (Sussex) 2020. Sussex 2nd XI debut 2018. HS 46* v Northants (Hove) 2021. BB 4-92 v Derbys (Hove) 2021. LO HS 9* and LO BB 1-33 v Glos (Hove) 2021 (RLC). T20 BB –.

‡**FINN, Steven** Thomas (Parmiter's S, Garston), b Watford, Herts 4 Apr 1989. 6'7½". RHB, RFM. Squad No 44. Middlesex 2005-21; cap 2009. Otago 2011-12. Manchester Originals 2021. YC 2010. **Tests**: 36 (2009-10 to 2016-17); HS 56 v NZ (Dunedin) 2012-13; BB 6-79 v A (Birmingham) 2015. **LOI**: 69 (2010-11 to 2017); HS 35 v A (Brisbane) 2010-11; BB 5-33 v I (Brisbane) 2014-15. **IT20**: 21 (2011 to 2015); HS 8* v I (Colombo, RPS) 2012-13; BB 3-16 v NZ (Pallekele) 2012-13. F-c Tours: A 2010-11, 2013-14; SA 2015-16; NZ 2012-13; I 2012-13; SL 2011-12; B 2009-10, 2016-17; UAE 2011-12 (v P). HS 56 (*see Tests*) and 56 M v Sussex (Hove) 2019. 50 wkts (2); most – 64 (2010). BB 9-37 (14-106 match) M v Worcs (Worcester) 2010. LO HS 42* M v Glamorgan (Cardiff) 2014 (RLC). LO BB (*see LOI*) and 5-33 M v Derbys (Lord's) 2011 (CB40). T20 HS 11*. T20 BB 5-16.

GARTON, George Henry Simmons (Hurstpierpoint C), b Brighton 15 Apr 1997. 5'10½". LHB, LF. Squad No 15. Debut (Sussex) 2016. IPL: RCB 2021. Big Bash: AS 2021-22. Southern Brave 2021. **IT20**: 1 (2021-22); HS 2 and BB 1-57 v WI (Bridgetown) 2021-22. HS 97 v Glamorgan (Cardiff) 2021. BB 5-26 v Essex (Hove) 2020. LO HS 38 v Essex (Chelmsford) 2019 (RLC). LO BB 4-43 EL v Sri Lanka A (Canterbury) 2016. T20 HS 46. T20 BB 4-16.

HAINES, Thomas Jacob (Tanbridge House S, Horsham; Hurstpierpoint C), b Crawley 28 Oct 1998. 5'10". LHB, RM. Squad No 20. Debut (Sussex) 2016. Sussex 2nd XI debut 2014. 1000 runs (1): 1176 (2021). HS 156 v Middx (Hove) 2021. BB 1-9 v Durham (Chester-le-St) 2019. LO HS 123 v Middx (Hove) 2021 (RLC).

HINLEY, Tom Ian (Warden Park Ac; Eastbourne C), b Frimley, Surrey 5 Feb 2003. 6'1". LHB, SLA. Squad No 42. Debut (Sussex) 2021. Sussex 2nd XI debut 2021. HS 19 v Leics (Leicester) 2021 – only 1st XI appearance.

HUDSON-PRENTICE, Fynn Jake (Warden Park S, Cuckfield; Bede's S, Upper Dicker), b Haywards Heath, 12 Jan 1996. RHB, RMF. Squad No 33. Debut (Sussex) 2015. Derbyshire 2019-21. HS 99 De v Middx (Derby) 2019. Sx HS 67 v Middx (Hove) 2021. BB 5-68 De v Notts (Nottingham) 2021. Sx BB 2-49 v Worcs (Worcester) 2021. LO HS 93 De v Somerset (Taunton) 2021 (RLC). LO BB 3-37 De v Notts (Derby) 2021 (RLC). T20 HS 41. T20 BB 3-36.

HUNT, Sean Frank (Howard of Effingham S), b Guildford, Surrey 7 Dec 2001. RHB, LMF. Squad No 21. Debut (Sussex) 2021. Surrey 2nd XI 2019. HS 7 and BB 3-47 v Lancs (Manchester) 2021.

IBRAHIM, Danial Kashif (Eastbourne C; Bede's S, Upper Dicker), b Burnley, Lancs 8 Aug 2004. 5'10". RHB, RM. Squad No 40. Debut (Sussex) 2021, aged 16y 298d, scoring 55 v Yorks (Leeds) on 2nd day to become the youngest-ever to score a fifty in the County Championship. Sussex 2nd XI debut 2021. HS 119 v Kent (Canterbury) 2021. BB 2-9 v Worcs (Worcester) 2021. LO HS 46 v Lancs (Sedbergh) 2021 (RLC). BB 2-54 v Essex (Chelmsford) 2021 (RLC).

LENHAM, Archie David (Bede's S, Upper Dicker), b Eastbourne 23 Jul 2004. Grandson of L.J.Lenham (Sussex 1956-70); son of N.J.Lenham (Sussex 1984-97); younger brother of S.H.Lenham (Sussex 2nd XI debut 2018). 5'8½". RHB, LBG. Squad No 41. Debut (Sussex) 2021. Sussex 2nd XI debut 2021. HS 20 and BB 1-60 v Worcs (Worcester) 2021. LO HS 16 v Essex (Chelmsford) 2021 (RLC). LO BB 4-59 v Lancs (Sedbergh) 2021 (RLC) – on debut. T20 HS 5*. T20 BB 4-26. Became second youngest debutant in Blast aged 16y, 323d.

MILLS, Tymal Solomon (Mildenhall TC), b Dewsbury, Yorks 12 Aug 1992. 6'1". RHB, LF. Squad No 7. Essex 2011-14. Sussex debut 2015; has played T20 only since start of 2016. IPL: RCB 2017. Big Bash: BH 2016-17; HH 2017-18; PS 2021-22. Southern Brave 2021. **IT20**: 11 (+1 ICC World XI 2018) (2016 to 2021-22); HS 1* v WI (Bridgetown) 2021-22; BB 3-27 v B (Abu Dhabi) 2021-22. F-c Tour (EL): SL 2013-14. HS 31* EL v Sri Lanka A (Colombo, RPS) 2013-14. CC HS 30 Ex v Kent (Canterbury) 2014. Sx HS 8 v Worcs (Hove) 2015. BB 4-25 Ex v Glamorgan (Cardiff) 2012. Sx BB 2-28 v Hants (Southampton) 2015. LO HS 3* v Notts (Hove) 2015 (RLC). LO BB 3-23 Ex v Durham (Chelmsford) 2013 (Y40). T20 HS 27. T20 BB 4-22.

‡NQ**MOHAMMAD RIZWAN**, b Peshawar, Pakistan 1 Jun 1992. 5'7". RHB, WK, occ RM. Squad No 116. Peshawar 2008-09 to 2012-13. SNGP 2012-13 to 2018-19. Khyber Pakhtunkhwa 2019-20. *Wisden* 2020. **Tests** (P): 20 (2016-17 to 2021-22, 2 as captain); HS 115* v SA (Rawalpindi) 2020-21. **LOI** (P): 41 (2015 to 2021); HS 115 v A (Sharjah) 2018-19. **IT20** (P): 55 (2015 to 2021-22); HS 104* v SA (Lahore) 2020-21. F-c Tours (P)(C=Captain): E 2020; A 2019-20; WI 2021; NZ 2016-17, 2020-21C; Z 2020-21; B 2021-22. HS 224 SNGP v NB (Karachi) 2014-15. BB 2-10 SNGP v FATA (Abbottabad) 2018-19. LO HS 141* Pakistan A v EL (Abu Dhabi) 2018-19. T20 HS 104*. T20 BB 1-22.

ORR, Alistair Graham Hamilton (Bede's S, Upper Dicker), b Eastbourne 6 Apr 2001. LHB, RM. Squad No 6. Debut (Sussex) 2021. Sussex 2nd XI debut 2018. HS 119 v Kent (Canterbury) 2021. LO HS 108 v Worcs (Worcester) 2021 (RLC).

‡NQ**PHILIPPE, Josh**ua Ryan (Carine HS), b Subiaco, W Australia 1 Jun 1997. RHB, WK. W Australia 2017-18 to date. IPL: RCB 2020-21. Big Bash: PS 2017-18; SS 2018-19 to date. **LOI** (A): 3 (2021); HS 39 v WI (Bridgetown) 2021. **IT20** (A): 10 (2020-21 to 2021); HS 45 v NZ (Dunedin) 2020-21. HS 129 WA v Q (Brisbane) 2021-22. LO HS 137 WA v SA (Adelaide, KR) 2021-22. T20 HS 99*.

‡NQ**PUJARA, Cheteshwar** Arvindbhai, b Rajkot, India 25 Jan 1988. 5'11". RHB, LB. Son of A.S.Pujara (Saurashtra 1976-77 to 1979-80), nephew of B.S.Pujara (Saurashtra 1983-84 to 1996-97). Saurashtra 2005-06 to date. Derbyshire 2014. Yorkshire 2015-18. Nottinghamshire 2017; cap 2017. IPL: KKR 2009-10; RCB 2011-13; KXIP 2014. **Tests** (I): 95 (2010-11 to 2021-22); 1000 runs (1): 1140 (2017); HS 206* v E (Ahmedabad) 2012-13. **LOI** (I): 5 (2013 to 2014); HS 27 v B (Dhaka) 2014. F-c Tours (I): E 2010 (I A), 2014, 2018, 2021; A 2006 (I A), 2014-15, 2018-19, 2020-21; SA 2010-11, 2013 (I A), 2013-14, 2017-18, 2021-22; WI 2012 (I A), 2016, 2019; NZ 2013-14, 2019-20; SL 2015, 2017; Z/Ken 2007-08 (I A). 1000 runs (0+3); most – 2064 (2016-17). HS 352 Saur v Karnataka (Rajkot) 2012-13. CC HS 133* Y v Hants (Leeds) 2015. BB 2-4 Saur v Rajasthan (Jaipur) 2007-08. LO HS 158* Ind B v India A (Rajkot) 2012-13. T20 HS 100*.

NQ**RASHID KHAN** Arman, b Nangarhar, Afghanistan 20 Sep 1998. RHB, LBG. Squad No 1. Afghanistan 2016-17 to date. Sussex debut 2018 (T20 only). IPL: SH 2017 to date. Big Bash: AS 2017-18 to date. Trent Rockets 2021. **Tests** (Afg): 5 (2018 to 2020-21); HS 51 v B (Chittagong) 2019; BB 7-137 v Z (Abu Dhabi) 2020-21. **LOI** (Afg): 80 (2015-16 to 2021-22); HS 60* v Ire (Belfast) 2016; BB 7-18 v WI (Gros Islet) 2017 – 4th best analysis in all LOI. **IT20** (Afg): 58 (2015-16 to 2021-22); HS 33 v WI (Basseterre) 2017; BB 5-3 v Ire (Greater Noida) 2016-17. HS 52 and BB 8-74 (12-122 match) Afg v EL (Abu Dhabi) 2016-17. LO HS 60* (*see LOI*). LO BB 7-18 (*see LOI*). T20 HS 56*. T20 BB 6-17.

RAWLINS, Delray Millard Wendell (Bede's S, Upper Dicker), b Bermuda 14 Sep 1997. 6'1". LHB, SLA. Squad No 9. Debut (Sussex) 2017. MCC 2018. Bermuda (l-o and T20) 2019 to date. Southern Brave 2021. Sussex 2nd XI debut 2015. Oxfordshire 2017. England U19 2016-17. **IT20** (Ber): 17 (2019 to 2021-22); HS 63 v USA (Hamilton) 2019; BB 2-18 v Panama (Coolidge) 2021-22. HS 100 v Lancs (Manchester) 2019. BB 3-19 v Durham (Hove) 2019. LO HS 53 South v North (Bridgetown) 2017-18 and 53 Bermuda v Uganda (Al Amerat) 2019-20. LO BB 1-27 Bermuda v Italy (Al Amerat) 2019-20. T20 HS 69. T20 BB 3-21.

ROBINSON, Oliver Edward (King's S, Canterbury), b Margate, Kent 1 Dec 1993. 6'5". RHB, RMF. Squad No 25. Debut (Sussex) 2015; cap 2019. Yorkshire 2013 (l-o only). Hampshire 2014 (l-o only). **ECB Central Contract 2021-22. Tests**: 9 (2021 to 2021-22); HS 42 v NZ (Lord's) 2021; BB 5-65 v I (Leeds) 2021. F-c Tours: A 2019-20 (EL), 2021-22. HS 110 v Durham (Chester-le-St) 2015, on debut, sharing Sx record 10th wkt partnership of 164 with M.E.Hobden. 50 wkts (3); most – 81 (2018). BB 9-78 (13-128 match) v Glamorgan (Cardiff) 2021. LO HS 30 v Kent (Canterbury) 2015 (RLC). LO BB 3-31 v Kent (Hove) 2018 (RLC). T20 HS 31. T20 BB 4-15.

WARD, Harrison David (St Edward's S, Oxford), b Oxford 25 Oct 1999. 6'1½". LHB, OB. Squad No 35. Debut (Sussex) 2021. Sussex 2nd XI debut 2016. Hampshire 2nd XI 2019. Oxfordshire 2015-18. England U19 2018. HS 19 v Derbys (Hove) 2021. LO HS 20 v Hants (Southampton) 2021 (RLC). T20 HS 22.

WRIGHT, Luke James (Belvoir HS; Ratcliffe C; Loughborough U), b Grantham, Lincs 7 Mar 1985. Younger brother of A.S.Wright (Leicestershire 2001-02). 5'11". RHB, RMF. Squad No 10. Leicestershire 2003 (one f-c match). Sussex debut 2004; cap 2007; T20 captain & benefit 2015; captain 2016-17; captain 2020 to date (T20 only). IPL: PW 2012-13. Big Bash: MS 2011-12 to 2017-18. **LOI**: 50 (2007 to 2013-14); HS 52 v NZ (Birmingham) 2008; BB 2-34 v NZ (Bristol) 2008 and 2-34 v A (Southampton) 2010. **IT20**: 51 (2007-08 to 2013-14); HS 99* v Afg (Colombo, RPS) 2012-13; BB 2-24 v NZ (Hamilton) 2012-13. F-c Tour (EL): NZ 2008-09. 1000 runs (1): 1220 (2015). HS 226* v Worcs (Worcester) 2015, sharing Sx record 6th wkt partnership of 335 with B.C.Brown. BB 5-65 v Derbys (Derby) 2010. LO HS 166 v Middx (Lord's) 2019 (RLC). LO BB 4-12 v Middx (Hove) 2004 (NL). T20 HS 153* v Essex (Chelmsford) 2014 – Sx record. T20 BB 3-17.

RELEASED/RETIRED

(Having made a County 1st XI appearance in 2021)

BROWN, B.C. – *see HAMPSHIRE.*

CLAYDON, Mitchell Eric (Westfield Sports HS, Sydney), b Fairfield, NSW, Australia 25 Nov 1982. 6'4". LHB, RMF. Yorkshire 2005-06. Durham 2007-13. Canterbury 2010-11. Kent 2013-19; cap 2016. Sussex 2020-21. HS 77 K v Leics (Leicester) 2014. Sx HS 24 v Kent (Canterbury) 2020. 50 wkts (2); most – 59 (2014). BB 6-104 Du v Somerset (Taunton) 2011. Sx BB 3-23 v Middx (Radlett) 2020. LO HS 19 Du v Glos (Bristol) 2009 (FPT) and 19 K v Middx (Canterbury) 2017 (RLC). LO BB 5-31 K v Guyana (North Sound) 2017-18. T20 HS 19. T20 BB 5-26.

[NQ]**HEAD, Travis** Michael, b Adelaide, Australia 29 Dec 1993. 5'9". LHB, OB. S Australia 2011-12 to date. Yorkshire 2016. Worcestershire 2018. Sussex 2021. IPL: RCB 2016-17. Big Bash: AS 2012-13 to date. **Tests (A)**: 24 (2018-19 to 2021-22); HS 161 v SL (Canberra) 2018-19; BB –. **LOI** (A): 42 (2016 to 2018-19); HS 128 v P (Adelaide) 2016-17; BB 2-22 v SL (Pallekele) 2016. **IT20** (A): 16 (2015-16 to 2018); HS 48* v I (Guwahati) 2017-18; BB 1-16 v SL (Adelaide) 2016-17. F-c Tours (A): E 2019; I 2015 (Aus A), 2018-19 (Aus A); P 2021-22; UAE 2018-19 (v P). HS 223 SA v WA (Perth) 2020-21. CC HS 62 Wo v Essex (Worcester) 2018. Sx HS 49* v Kent (Canterbury) 2021. BB 3-42 SA v NSW (Adelaide) 2015-16. Sx BB 1-23 v Northants (Northampton) 2021. LO HS 230 SA v Q (Adelaide, KR) 2021-22. LO BB 2-9 SA v NSW (Brisbane) 2014-15. T20 HS 101*. T20 BB 3-16.

JORDAN, C.J. – *see SURREY.*

MEAKER, Stuart Christopher (Cranleigh S), b Durban, South Africa 21 Jan 1989. Moved to UK in 2001. 6'1". RHB, RFM. Surrey 2008-18; cap 2012. Auckland 2017-18. Sussex 2020-21. **LOI**: 2 (2011-12); HS 1 (twice); BB 1-45 v I (Mumbai) 2011-12. **IT20**: 2 (2012-13); BB 1-28 v I (Pune) 2013-14. F-c Tour: I 2012-13. HS 94 Sy v Bangladeshis (Oval) 2010. CC HS 72 Sy v Essex (Colchester) 2009. Sx HS 42 v Surrey (Oval) 2020. 50 wkts (1): 51 (2012). BB 8-52 (11-167 match) Sy v Somerset (Oval) 2012. Sx BB 3-22 v Lancs (Hove) 2021. LO HS 50 v Glamorgan (Cardiff) 2019 (RLC). LO BB 4-37 Sy v Kent (Oval) 2017 (RLC). T20 HS 17. T20 BB 4-30.

SALT, P.D. – *see LANCASHIRE.*

THOMASON, Aaron Dean (Barr Beacon S, Walsall), b Birmingham 26 Jun 1997. 5'10". RHB, RMF. Sussex 2019-21. Warwickshire (l-o and T20 only) 2014-19. HS 90 v Worcs (Kidderminster) 2019 – on debut. BB 2-107 v Australia A (Arundel) 2019. CC BB 1-33 v Northants (Hove) 2019. LO HS 28 Wa v Durham (Birmingham) 2017 (RLC). LO BB 4-45 Wa v Notts (Nottingham) 2018 (RLC). T20 HS 47. T20 BB 3-33.

[NQ]**VAN ZYL, Stiaan**, b Cape Town, South Africa 19 Sep 1987. 5'11½". LHB, RM. Boland 2006-07 to date. Cape Cobras 2007-08 to 2017-18. W Province 2014-15 to 2016-17. Sussex 2017-21; cap 2019. **Tests** (SA): 12 (2014-15 to 2016); HS 101* v WI (Centurion) 2014-15 – on debut; BB 3-20 v E (Durban) 2015-16. F-c Tours (SA): A 2016 (SA A), I 2015 (SA A), 2015-16; SL 2010 (SA A); B 2010 (SA A), 2015; Ire 2012 (SA A). 1000 runs (1): 1023 (2017). HS 228 Cobras v Lions (Paarl) 2017-18. Sx HS 173 v Middx (Lord's) 2019. BB 5-32 Boland v Northerns (Paarl) 2010-11. Sx BB 3-16 v Glos (Hove) 2018. LO HS 114* Cobras v Eagles (Kimberley) 2009-10. LO BB 4-24 Boland v Gauteng (Stellenbosch) 2010-11. T20 HS 86*. T20 BB 2-14.

[NQ]**WIESE, David** (Witbank HS), b Roodepoort, South Africa 18 May 1985. 6'3". RHB, RMF. Easterns 2005-06 to 2011-12. Titans 2009-10 to 2016-17. Sussex debut/cap 2016. IPL: RCB 2015-16. **LOI** (SA/Nam): 10 (6 for SA 2015 to 2015-16; 4 for Nam 2021-22); HS 67 Nam v UAE (Dubai) 2021-22; BB 3-50 SA v E (Cape Town) 2015-16. **IT20** (SA): 31 (20 for SA 2013 to 2015-16; 11 for Nam 2021-22); HS 66* Nam v Neth (Abu Dhabi) 2021-22; BB 5-23 SA v WI (Durban) 2014-15. F-c Tour (SA A): A 2014. HS 208 Easterns v GW (Benoni) 2008-09. Sx HS 139 v Cardiff MCCU (Hove) 2019. CC HS 106 v Warwks (Birmingham) 2018. BB 6-58 Titans v Knights (Centurion) 2014-15. Sx BB 5-26 v Middx (Lord's) 2019. LO HS 171 v Hants (Southampton) 2019 (RLC) – Sx record. LO BB 5-25 Easterns v Boland (Benoni) 2010-11. T20 HS 79*. T20 BB 5-19.

SUSSEX 2021

RESULTS SUMMARY

	Place	Won	Lost	Drew	NR
LV= Insurance County Champ (Div 3)	6th	1	9	4	
Royal London One-Day Cup (Group 1)	7th	2	4		2
Vitality Blast (South Group)	SF	7	4		5

LV= INSURANCE COUNTY CHAMPIONSHIP AVERAGES
BATTING AND FIELDING

Cap		*M*	*I*	*NO*	*HS*	*Runs*	*Avge*	*100*	*50*	*Ct/St*
2014	B.C.Brown	12	21	2	157	976	51.36	4	2	27/3
2021	T.J.Haines	13	25	–	156	1176	47.04	3	6	2
	A.G.H.Orr	7	14	–	119	548	39.14	1	4	1
	F.J.Hudson-Prentice	3	5	1	67	145	36.25	–	1	3
2019	O.E.Robinson	6	8	1	67	250	35.71	–	2	2
	D.K.Ibrahim	6	11	–	94	328	29.81	–	3	3
	A.D.Thomason	9	17	2	78*	379	25.26	–	3	16
	S.van Zyl	9	17	–	113	422	24.82	1	3	4
	J.M.Coles	2	4	1	36	72	24.00	–	–	–
	G.H.S.Garton	7	11	–	97	247	22.45	–	1	4
	T.G.R.Clark	7	13	2	54*	240	21.81	–	1	6
	O.J.Carter	6	12	1	51	235	21.36	–	1	14
	J.J.Carson	14	23	4	87	385	20.26	–	3	3
	T.M.Head	6	11	1	49*	183	18.30	–	–	3
	S.C.Meaker	6	9	1	30*	113	14.12	–	–	2
	D.M.W.Rawlins	10	17	–	58	233	13.70	–	1	3
	H.T.Crocombe	9	17	2	46*	83	5.53	–	–	–
	J.A.Atkins	5	9	5	10*	21	5.25	–	–	–
	H.D.Ward	3	6	–	19	30	5.00	–	–	2
	J.P.Sarro	3	6	3	7*	8	2.66	–	–	1
	S.F.Hunt	6	10	4	7	12	2.00	–	–	–

Also batted (1 match each): J.C.Archer (cap 2017) 2, W.A.T.Beer 19, 23*; M.E.Claydon 22*; T.I.Hinley 19, 1; A.D.Lenham 20, 9.

BOWLING

	O	*M*	*R*	*W*	*Avge*	*Best*	*5wI*	*10wM*
O.E.Robinson	207	49	547	33	16.57	9-78	2	1
J.A.Atkins	137.4	14	469	20	23.45	5-51	2	–
J.J.Carson	449.4	65	1336	37	36.10	5-85	1	–
S.F.Hunt	127.5	18	487	13	37.46	3-47	–	–
H.T.Crocombe	211	29	756	20	37.80	4-92	–	–
G.H.S.Garton	134.5	11	559	13	43.00	4-69	–	–
Also bowled:								
S.C.Meaker	135.4	11	525	9	58.33	3-22	–	–

J.C.Archer 18-4-43-3; W.A.T.Beer 29-6-70-3; T.G.R.Clark 33-3-120-1; M.E.Claydon 17-3-54-2; J.M.Coles 22-0-92-0; T.J.Haines 41-4-114-1; T.M.Head 27.4-4-109-1; T.I.Hinley 6-0-35-0; F.J.Hudson-Prentice 58.2-5-204-3; D.K.Ibrahim 67.4-11-236-3; A.D.Lenham 13-0-71-1; D.M.W.Rawlins 171-17-573-4; J.P.Sarro 43-3-220-4; A.D.Thomason 3-0-30-0; S.van Zyl 11-2-22-1; H.D.Ward 1-0-2-0.

The First-Class Averages (pp 220–232) give the records of Sussex players in all first-class county matches, with the exception of J.J.Carson, F.J.Hudson-Prentice and O.E.Robinson, whose first-class figures for Sussex are as above.

SUSSEX RECORDS

FIRST-CLASS CRICKET

Highest Total	For 742-5d		v	Somerset	Taunton	2009
	V 726		by	Notts	Nottingham	1895
Lowest Total	For 19		v	Surrey	Godalming	1830
	19		v	Notts	Hove	1873
	V 18		by	Kent	Gravesend	1867
Highest Innings	For 344*	M.W.Goodwin	v	Somerset	Taunton	2009
	V 322	E.Paynter	for	Lancashire	Hove	1937

Highest Partnership for each Wicket

1st	490	E.H.Bowley/J.G.Langridge	v	Middlesex	Hove	1933
2nd	385	E.H.Bowley/M.W.Tate	v	Northants	Hove	1921
3rd	385*	M.H.Yardy/M.W.Goodwin	v	Warwicks	Hove	2006
4th	363	M.W.Goodwin/C.D.Hopkinson	v	Somerset	Taunton	2009
5th	297	J.H.Parks/H.W.Parks	v	Hampshire	Portsmouth	1937
6th	335	L.J.Wright/B.C.Brown	v	Durham	Hove	2014
7th	344	K.S.Ranjitsinhji/W.Newham	v	Essex	Leyton	1902
8th	291	R.S.C.Martin-Jenkins/M.J.G.Davis	v	Somerset	Taunton	2002
9th	178	H.W.Parks/A.F.Wensley	v	Derbyshire	Horsham	1930
10th	164	O.E.Robinson/M.E.Hobden	v	Durham	Chester-le-St[2]	2015

Best Bowling	For	10- 48	C.H.G.Bland	v	Kent	Tonbridge	1899
(Innings)	V	9- 11	A.P.Freeman	for	Kent	Hove	1922
Best Bowling	For	17-106	G.R.Cox	v	Warwicks	Horsham	1926
(Match)	V	17- 67	A.P.Freeman	for	Kent	Hove	1922

Most Runs – Season	2850	J.G.Langridge	(av 64.77)	1949
Most Runs – Career	34150	J.G.Langridge	(av 37.69)	1928-55
Most 100s – Season	12	J.G.Langridge		1949
Most 100s – Career	76	J.G.Langridge		1928-55
Most Wkts – Season	198	M.W.Tate	(av 13.47)	1925
Most Wkts – Career	2211	M.W.Tate	(av 17.41)	1912-37
Most Career W-K Dismissals	1176	H.R.Butt	(911 ct; 265 st)	1890-1912
Most Career Catches in the Field	779	J.G.Langridge		1928-55

LIMITED-OVERS CRICKET

Highest Total	**50ov**	384-9		v	Ireland	Belfast	1996
	40ov	399-4		v	Worcs	Horsham	2011
	T20	242-5		v	Glos	Bristol	2016
Lowest Total	**50ov**	49		v	Derbyshire	Chesterfield	1969
	40ov	59		v	Glamorgan	Hove	1996
	T20	67		v	Hampshire	Hove	2004
Highest Innings	**50ov**	171	D.Wiese	v	Hampshire	Southampton[2]	2019
	40ov	163	C.J.Adams	v	Middlesex	Arundel	1999
	T20	153*	L.J.Wright	v	Essex	Chelmsford	2014
Best Bowling	**50ov**	6- 9	A.I.C.Dodemaide	v	Ireland	Downpatrick	1990
	40ov	7-41	A.N.Jones	v	Notts	Nottingham	1986
	T20	5-11	Mushtaq Ahmed	v	Essex	Hove	2005

WARWICKSHIRE

Formation of Present Club: 8 April 1882
Substantial Reorganisation: 19 January 1884
Inaugural First-Class Match: 1894
Colours: Dark Blue, Gold and Silver
Badge: Bear and Ragged Staff
County Champions: (8) 1911, 1951, 1972, 1994, 1995, 2004, 2012, 2021
Gillette/NatWest Trophy Winners: (5) 1966, 1968, 1989, 1993, 1995
Benson and Hedges Cup Winners: (2) 1994, 2002
Sunday League Winners: (3) 1980, 1994, 1997
Clydesdale Bank 40 Winners: (1) 2010
Royal London Cup Winners: (1) 2015
Twenty20 Cup Winners: (1) 2014

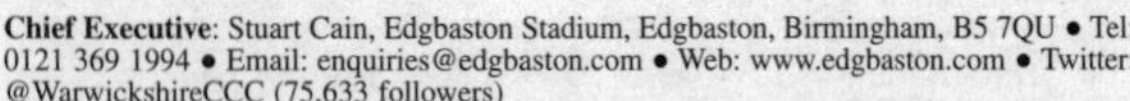

Chief Executive: Stuart Cain, Edgbaston Stadium, Edgbaston, Birmingham, B5 7QU • Tel: 0121 369 1994 • Email: enquiries@edgbaston.com • Web: www.edgbaston.com • Twitter: @WarwickshireCCC (75,633 followers)

Director of Cricket: Paul Farbrace. **1st Team Coach**: Mark Robinson. **Batting Coach**: Tony Frost. **Bowling Coach**: Matt Mason. **Assistant Coaches**: Jonathan Trott and Mohammed Sheikh. **Captains**: W.H.M.Rhodes (f-c and l-o) and C.R.Brathwaite (T20). **Overseas Player**: C.R.Brathwaite (T20 only). **2022 Testimonial**: None. **Head Groundsman**: Gary Barwell. **Scorer**: Mel Smith. **T20 Blast Name**: Birmingham Bears. ‡ New registration. [NQ] Not qualified for England.

BENJAMIN, Christopher Gavin (St Andrew's C, Johannesburg; Durham U), b Johannesburg, South Africa 29 Apr 1999. 5'11". RHB, RMF, WK. Squad No 13. Durham MCCU 2019. Warwickshire debut 2021, scoring 127 v Lancs (Manchester); also scored fifties on RLC and T20 debuts. Essex 2nd XI 2018-19. Derbyshire 2nd XI 2021. HS 33 DU v Durham (Chester-le-St) 2019. HS 127 (*see above*). LO HS 50 v Glamorgan (Cardiff) 2021 (RLC). T20 HS 60*.

BETHELL, Jacob Graham (Rugby S), b Bridgetown, Barbados 23 Oct 2003. 5'10". LHB, SLA. Squad No 2. Debut (Warwickshire) 2021. Warwickshire 2nd XI debut 2019. HS 15 v Yorks (Leeds) 2021. LO HS 66 v Yorks (York) 2021 (RLC). LO BB 4-36 v Glamorgan (Cardiff) 2021 (RLC). T20 HS 7. T20 BB –.

[NQ]**BRATHWAITE, Carlos** Ricardo, b Christ Church, Barbados 18 Jul 1988. RHB, RFM. Squad No 26. CC&C 2010-11. Barbados 2011-12 to 2015-16. Sagicor HPC 2014. Kent 2018 (T20 only). Warwickshire debut 2021 (T20 only); T20 captain 2022. IPL: DD 2016-17; SH 2018; KKR 2019. Big Bash: ST 2016-17; SS 2017-18 to 2020-21. Manchester Originals 2021. **Tests** (WI): 3 (2015-16 to 2016); HS 69 v A (Sydney) 2015-16; BB 1-30 v A (Melbourne) 2015-16. **LOI** (WI): 44 (2011-12 to 2019); HS 101 v NZ (Manchester) 2019; BB 5-27 v PNG (Harare) 2017-18. **IT20** (WI): 41 (2011-12 to 2019); HS 37* v P (Port of Spain) 2016-17; BB 3-20 v E (Chester-le-St) 2017. F-c Tours (WI): A 2015-16; SL 2014-15 (WI A). HS 109 Bar v T&T (Bridgetown) 2013-14. BB 7-90 CC&C v T&T (St Augustine) 2010-11 – on debut. LO HS 113 WI v SL Board Pres (Colombo, CC) 2015-16. LO BB 5-27 (*see LOI*). T20 HS 64*. T20 BB 4-15.

BRIGGS, Danny Richard (Isle of Wight C), b Newport, IoW, 30 Apr 1991. 6'2". RHB, SLA. Squad No 14. Hampshire 2009-15; cap 2012. Sussex 2016-19. Warwickshire debut 2021; cap 2021. Big Bash: AS 2020-21. Southern Brave 2021. **LOI**: 1 (2011-12); BB 2-39 v P (Dubai) 2011-12. **IT20**: 7 (2012 to 2013-14); HS 0*; BB 2-25 v A (Chester-le-St) 2013. F-c Tours (EL): WI 2010-11; I 2018-19. HS 120* v South Africa A (Arundel) 2017. CC HS 66* v Essex (Birmingham) 2021. BB 6-45 EL v Windward Is (Roseau) 2010-11. CC BB 6-65 H v Notts (Southampton) 2011. Wa BB 4-36 v Notts (Birmingham) 2021. LO HS 37* Sx v Essex (Chelmsford) 2019 (RLC). LO BB 4-32 H v Glamorgan (Cardiff) 2012 (CB40). T20 HS 35*. T20 BB 5-19.

BROOKES, Ethan Alexander (Solihull S & SFC), b Solihull 23 May 2001. Younger brother of H.J.H.Brookes (*see below*). 6'1". RHB, RMF. Squad No 77. Debut (Warwickshire) 2019. Warwickshire 2nd XI debut 2018. Staffordshire 2019. HS 15* v Glamorgan (Cardiff) 2020. BB –. LO HS 63 v Leics (Birmingham) 2021 (RLC). LO BB 3-15 v Northants (Birmingham) 2021 (RLC).

BROOKES, Henry James Hamilton (Tudor Grange Acad, Solihull), b Solihull 21 Aug 1999. Elder brother of E.A.Brookes (*see above*). 6'3". RHB, RMF. Squad No 10. Debut (Warwickshire) 2017. Warwickshire 2nd XI debut 2016. England U19 2016-17 to 2017. No 1st XI appearances in 2021 due to injury. HS 84 v Kent (Birmingham) 2019. BB 4-54 v Northants (Birmingham) 2018. LO HS 12* v Derbys (Derby) 2019 (RLC). LO BB 3-50 v Yorks (Birmingham) 2019 (RLC). T20 HS 31*. T20 BB 3-26.

BURGESS, Michael Gregory Kerran (Cranleigh S; Loughborough U), b Epsom, Surrey 8 Jul 1994. 6'1". RHB, WK, occ RM. Squad No 61. Loughborough MCCU 2014-15. Leicestershire 2016. Sussex 2017-19. Warwickshire debut 2019; cap 2021. HS 146 Sx v Notts (Hove) 2017. Wa HS 101 v Worcs (Birmingham) 2021. BB –. LO HS 73 v Glamorgan (Cardiff) 2021 (RLC) and 73 v Northants (Birmingham) 2021 (RLC). T20 HS 56.

‡**DAVIES, Alex**ander Luke (Queen Elizabeth GS, Blackburn), b Darwen, Lancs 23 Aug 1994. 5'7". RHB, WK. Squad No 71. Lancashire 2012-21; cap 2017. Southern Brave 2021. F-c Tour (EL): WI 2017-18. 1000 runs (1): 1046 (2017). HS 147 La v Northants (Northampton) 2019. LO HS 147 La v Durham (Manchester) 2018 (RLC). T20 HS 94*.

GARRETT, George Anthony (Shrewsbury S), Harpenden, Herts 4 Mar 2000. 6'3". RHB, RM. Squad No 44. Debut (Warwickshire) 2019. Warwickshire 2nd XI debut 2019. No 1st XI appearances in 2020. HS 24 v Essex (Birmingham) 2019. BB 2-53 v Notts (Nottingham) 2019. LO HS 7 v Glamorgan (Cardiff) 2021 (RLC). LO BB 3-50 v Leics (Birmingham) 2021 (RLC). T20 BB 1-19.

HAIN, Samuel Robert (Southport S, Gold Coast), b Hong Kong 16 July 1995. 5'10". RHB, OB. Squad No 16. Debut (Warwickshire) 2014; cap 2018. MCC 2018. Manchester Originals 2021. UK passport (British parents). HS 208 v Northants (Birmingham) 2014. BB –. LO HS 161* v Worcs (Worcester) 2019 (RLC). T20 HS 95.

HANNON-DALBY, Oliver James (Brooksbank S, Leeds Met U), b Halifax, Yorkshire 20 Jun 1989. 6'7". LHB, RMF. Squad No 20. Yorkshire 2008-12. Warwickshire debut 2013; cap 2019. F-c Tour (MCC): Nepal 2019-20. HS 40 v Somerset (Taunton) 2014. BB 6-33 (12-110 match) v Glos (Bristol) 2020. LO HS 21* Y v Warwks (Scarborough) 2012 (CB40). LO BB 5-27 v Glamorgan (Birmingham) 2015 (RLC). T20 HS 14*. T20 BB 4-20.

HOSE, Adam John (Carisbrooke S), b Newport, IoW 25 Oct 1992. 6'2". RHB, RMF. Squad No 21. Somerset 2016-17. Warwickshire debut 2018. HS 111 v Notts (Birmingham) 2019. LO HS 101* Sm v Glos (Bristol) 2017 (RLC). T20 HS 119.

JOHAL, Manraj Singh (Sandwell C; Oldbury Ac), b Birmingham 12 Oct 2001. 6'0". RHB, RFM. Squad No 5. Debut (Warwickshire) 2021. Staffordshire 2019. HS 19 and BB 3-29 v Lancs (Lord's) 2021 (Bob Willis Trophy). LO HS 10 v Yorks (York) 2021 (RLC). LO BB 2-35 v Northants (Birmingham) 2021 (RLC).

LAMB, Matthew James (North Bromsgrove HS; Bromsgrove S), b Wolverhampton, Staffs 19 July 1996. 6'1". RHB, RM. Squad No 7. Debut (Warwickshire) 2016. HS 173 and BB 2-38 v Worcs (Worcester 2021. LO HS 119* v Leics (Birmingham) 2021 (RLC). LO BB 4-35 v Somerset (Birmingham) 2021 (RLC). T20 HS 39.

LINTOTT, Jacob (**'Jake'**) Benedict (Queen's C, Taunton), b Taunton, Somerset 22 Apr 1993. 5'11". RHB, SLA. Squad No 23. Debut (Warwickshire) 2021. Hampshire 2017 (T20 only). Gloucestershire 2018 (T20 only). Southern Brave 2021. Dorset 2011-15. Wiltshire 2016-19. HS 15 v Worcs (Worcester) 2021. BB –. T20 HS 41. T20 BB 4-20.

MILES, Craig Neil (Bradon Forest S, Swindon; Filton C, Bristol), b Swindon, Wilts 20 July 1994. Brother of A.J.Miles (Cardiff MCCU 2012). 6'4". RHB, RMF. Squad No 18. Gloucestershire 2011-18; cap 2011. Warwickshire debut 2019. HS 62* Gs v Worcs (Cheltenham) 2014. Wa HS 30* and Wa BB 5-28 v Lancs (Lord's) 2021. 50 wkts (3); most – 58 (2018). BB 6-63 Gs v Northants (Northampton) 2015. Hat-trick Gs v Essex (Cheltenham) 2016. LO HS 31* v Surrey (Oval) 2021 (RLC). LO BB 4-29 Gs v Yorks (Scarborough) 2015 (RLC). T20 HS 8. T20 BB 3-25.

MOUSLEY, Daniel Richard (Bablake S, Coventry), b Birmingham 8 Jul 2001. 5'11". LHB, OB. Squad No 80. Debut (Warwickshire) 2019. Staffordshire 2019. England U19 2018-19. HS 71 v Glamorgan (Cardiff) 2020. BB –. LO HS 105 Burgher Rec v Nugegoda (Colombo) 2021-22. LO BB 3-32 Burgher Rec v SL Air Force (Colombo) 2021-22. T20 HS 58*. T20 BB 1-3.

NORWELL, Liam Connor (Redruth SS), b Bournemouth, Dorset 27 Dec 1991. 6'3". RHB, RMF. Squad No 24. Gloucestershire 2011-18, taking 6-46 v Derbys (Bristol) on debut; cap 2011. Warwickshire debut 2019. HS 102 Gs v Derbys (Bristol) 2016. Wa HS 64 v Surrey (Birmingham) 2019. 50 wkts (3); most – 68 (2015). BB 8-43 (10-95 match) Gs v Leics (Leicester) 2017. Wa BB 7-41 v Somerset (Taunton) 2019. LO HS 16 Gs v Somerset (Bristol) 2017 (RLC). LO BB 6-52 Gs v Leics (Leicester) 2012 (CB40). T20 HS 2*. T20 BB 3-27.

RHODES, William Michael Henry (Cottingham HS, Cottingham SFC, Hull), b Nottingham 2 Mar 1995. 6'2". LHB, RMF. Squad No 35. Yorkshire 2014-15 to 2016. Essex 2016 (on loan). Warwickshire debut 2018; cap 2020; captain 2020 to date. MCC 2019. F-c Tour (MCC): Nepal 2019-20. HS 207 v Worcs (Worcester) 2020. BB 5-17 v Essex (Chelmsford) 2019. LO HS 69 v Worcs (Birmingham) 2018 (RLC) and 69 v West Indies A (Birmingham) 2018. LO BB 3-40 v Notts (Birmingham) 2021 (RLC). T20 HS 79. T20 BB 4-34.

SIBLEY, Dominic Peter (Whitgift S, Croydon), b Epsom, Surrey 5 Sep 1995. 6'3". RHB, OB. Squad No 45. Surrey 2013-17. Warwickshire debut 2017; cap 2019. MCC 2019. *Wisden* 2020. **Tests**: 22 (2019-20 to 2021); HS 133* v SA (Cape Town) 2019-20. F-c Tours: SA 2019-20; NZ 2019-20; I 2020-21; SL 2019-20, 2020-21. 1000 runs (1): 1428 (2019). HS 244 v Kent (Canterbury) 2019. BB 2-103 Sy v Hants (Southampton) 2016. Wa BB –. LO HS 115 v West Indies A (Birmingham) 2018. LO BB 1-20 Sy v Essex (Chelmsford) 2016 (RLC). T20 HS 74*. T20 BB 2-33.

SIDEBOTTOM, Ryan Nathan, b Shepparton, Victoria, Australia 14 Aug 1989. UK passport. 6'0". RHB, RMF. Squad No 22. Victoria 2012-13. Warwickshire debut 2017. HS 27* v Kent (Birmingham) 2019. BB 6-35 (10-96 match) v Northants (Northampton) 2018. LO HS 9* and LO B 1-41 v Glamorgan (Cardiff) 2021 (RLC). T20 HS 3. T20 BB 1-37.

STONE, Oliver Peter (Thorpe St Andrew HS), b Norwich, Norfolk 9 Oct 1993. 6'1". RHB, RF. Squad No 6. Northamptonshire 2012-16. Warwickshire debut 2017; cap 2020. Norfolk 2011. **ECB Pace Bowling Development Contract 2021-22. Tests**: 3 (2019 to 2021); HS 20 v NZ (Birmingham) 2021; BB 3-29 v Ire (Lord's) 2019. **LOI**: 4 (2018-19); HS 9* and BB 1-23 v SL (Dambulla) 2018-19. HS 60 Nh v Kent (Northampton) 2016. Wa HS 43 v Notts (Nottingham) 2021. BB 8-80 v Sussex (Birmingham) 2018. LO HS 24* Nh v Derbys (Derby) 2015 (RLC). LO BB 4-71 v Worcs (Birmingham) 2018 (RLC). T20 HS 22*. T20 BB 3-22.

WOAKES, Christopher Roger (Barr Beacon Language S, Walsall), b Birmingham 2 March 1989. 6'2". RHB, RFM. Squad No 19. Debut (Warwickshire) 2006; cap 2009. Wellington 2012-13. MCC 2009. IPL: KKR 2017; RCB 2018; DC 2021. Big Bash: ST 2013-14. Herefordshire 2006-07. *Wisden* 2016. PCA 2020. **ECB Central Contract 2021-22. Tests**: 43 (2013 to 2021-22); HS 137* v I (Lord's) 2018; BB 6-17 v Ire (Lord's) 2019. **LOI**: 106 (2010-11 to 2021); HS 95* v SL (Nottingham) 2016; BB 6-45 v A (Brisbane) 2010-11. **IT20**: 16 (2010-11 to 2021-22); HS 37 v P (Sharjah) 2015-16; BB 2-23 v A (Dubai, DSC) 2021-22. F-c Tours: A 2017-18, 2021-22; SA 2015-16, 2019-20; WI 2010-11 (EL), 2021-22; NZ 2017-18, 2019-20; I 2016-17; SL 2013-14 (EL), 2019-20; B 2016-17; UAE 2015-16 (v P). HS 152* v Derbys (Derby) 2013. 50 wkts (3); most – 59 (2016). BB 9-36 v Durham (Birmingham) 2016. LO HS 95* (*see LOI*). LO BB 6-45 (*see LOI*). T20 HS 57*. T20 BB 4-21.

YATES, Robert Michael (Warwick S), b Solihull 19 Sep 1999. 6'0". LHB, OB. Squad No 17. Debut (Warwickshire) 2019. Warwickshire 2nd XI debut 2017. Staffordshire 2018. HS 141 v Somerset (Birmingham) 2019. BB 2-54 v Worcs (Worcester) 2021. LO HS 103 v Notts (Birmingham) 2019 (RLC). LO BB 1-27 v Surrey (Oval) 2021 (RLC). T20 HS 37. T20 BB 1-13.

RELEASED/RETIRED

(Having made a County 1st XI appearance in 2021, even if not formally contracted. Some may return in 2022.)

BRESNAN, Timothy Thomas (Castleford HS and TC; Pontefract New C), b Pontefract, Yorks 28 Feb 1985. 6'0". RHB, RFM. Yorkshire 2003-19; cap 2006; benefit 2014. Warwickshire 2020-21; cap 2021. MCC 2006, 2009. Big Bash: HH 2014-15; PS 2016-17 to 2017-18. *Wisden* 2011. **Tests**: 23 (2009 to 2013-14); HS 91 v B (Dhaka) 2009-10; BB 5-48 v I (Nottingham) 2011. **LOI**: 85 (2006 to 2015); HS 80 v SA (Centurion) 2009-10; BB 5-48 v I (Bangalore) 2010-11. **IT20**: 34 (2006 to 2013-14); HS 47* v WI (Bridgetown) 2013-14; BB 3-10 v P (Cardiff) 2010. F-c Tours: A 2010-11, 2013-14; I 2012-13; SL 2011-12; B 2006-07 (Eng A), 2009-10. HS 169* Y v Durham (Chester-le-St) 2015, sharing Y record 7th wkt partnership of 366* with J.M.Bairstow. Wa HS 105 v Northants (Birmingham) 2020 – on debut. BB 5-28 v Hants (Leeds) 2018. Wa BB 4-99 v Somerset (Birmingham) 2020. LO HS 95* Y v Notts (Scarborough) 2016 (RLC). BB 5-48 (*see LOI*). T20 HS 51. T20 BB 6-19 Y v Lancs (Leeds) 2017 – Y record.

BULPITT, Jordan (Walton HS; Stafford C; Anglia Ruskin U), b Stafford 19 Apr 1998. LHB, LM. Cambridge MCCU 2018. Warwickshire 2021 (l-o only). BB – and did not bat CU v Essex (Cambridge) 2018. LO HS –. LO BB 2-33 v Northants (Birmingham) 2021 (RLC).

CARVER, Karl (Thirsk S & SFC), b Northallerton, Yorks 26 Mar 1996. 5'10". LHB, SLA. Yorkshire 2014-18. Warwickshire 2021 (l-o only). Northumberland 2021. HS 20 Y v Somerset (Taunton) 2017. BB 4-106 Y v MCC (Abu Dhabi) 2015-16. CC BB 2-10 Y v Essex (Chelmsford) 2017. LO HS 35* Y v Somerset (Scarborough) 2015 (RLC). LO BB 3-5 Y v Lancs (Manchester) 2016 (RLC). T20 HS 2. T20 BB 3-40.

CHAKRAPANI, Ashish Mohan (Solihull S), b Birmingham 3 Apr 2004. LHB, OB. Warwickshire 2021 (l-o only). LO HS 18 v Glamorgan (Cardiff) 2021 (RLC).

[NQ]**HOLDER, Chemar** Keron, b Barbados 3 Mar 1998. RHB, RFM. Barbados 2017-18 to date. Warwickshire 2021. **Tests** (WI): 1 (2020-21); HS 13* and BB 2-110 v NZ (Wellington) 2020-21. **LOI** (WI): 1 (2020-21); HS 0* and BB-v B (Dhaka) 2020-21. F-c Tours (WI): E 2018 (WIA); NZ 2020-21. HS 34* Barb v T&T (Tarouba) 2019-20. Wa HS 6 v Lancs (Manchester) 2021. BB 6-47 (11-92 match) Barb v Jamaica (Kingston) 2019-20. Wa BB 1-23 v Hants (Birmingham) 2021. LO HS 6 WIA v India A (Leicester) 2018. LO BB 5-22 CC&C v Windward Is (Basseterre) 2015-16. T20 HS 4*. T20 BB 2-32.

[NQ]**MALAN, Pieter** Jacobus (Waterkloof Hoer S), b Nelspruit, South Africa 13 Aug 1989. Elder brother of J.N.Malan (North West, Cape Cobras & South Africa 2015-15 to date) and A.J.Malan (Northerns, North West, W Province & Cape Cobras 2010-11 to 2019-20). RHB, RMF. Northerns 2006-07 to 2012-13. Titans 2008-09 to 2012-13. Western Province 2013-14 to 2019-20. Cape Cobras 2014-15 to 2020-21. Warwickshire 2021. Boland 2021-22. **Tests** (SA): 3 (2019-20); HS 84 v E (Cape Town) 2019-20; BB –. F-c Tours (SA A): I 2018, 2019. 1000 runs (0+2); most – 1114 (2017-18). HS 264 Cobras v Knights (Cape Town) 2020-21. Wa HS 141 v Worcs (Worcester) 2021. BB 5-35 WP v EP (Port Elizabeth) 2017-18. LO HS 169* Northerns v WP (Pretoria) 2008-09. LO BB –. T20 HS 140*. T20 BB 2-30.

[NQ]**MAYERS, Kyle** Rico, b Barbados 8 Sep 1992. LHB, RM. Windward Is 2015-16 to 2017-18. Barbados 2019-20. Warwickshire 2021 (T20 only). **Tests** (WI): 10 (2020-21 to 2021-22); HS 210* v B (Chittagong) 2020-21 – on debut; BB 3-24 v SA (Gros Islet) 2021. **LOI** (WI): 3 (2020-21); HS 40 v B (Dhaka) 2020-21; BB 1-34 v B (Chittagong) 2020-21. **IT20** (WI): 7 (2020-21 to 2021-22); HS 40 v E (Bridgetown) 2021-22; BB –. F-c Tours (WI): NZ 2020-21 (WIA); SL 2021-22; B 2020-21. HS 210* (*see Tests*). BB 6-29 Wind Is v Jamaica (Kingstown) 2016-17. LO HS 113 Bar v Leeward Is (Basseterre) 2019-20. LO BB 4-15 CC&C v Leeward Is (Port of Spain) 2013-14. T20 HS 85. T20 BB 3-39.

POLLOCK, E.J. – *see WORCESTERSHIRE.*

Van VOLLENHOVEN, Kiel Thomas (Pretoria BHS), b 6 Jun 1998. Grandson of T.van Vollenhoven (St Helens and South Africa rugby league 1955-68). RHB, LB. Northerns 2020-21. Warwickshire 2021 (l-o only). MCC YC 2017-18. Sussex 2nd XI 2017. Somerset 2nd XI 2018. HS 23 and BB 1-18 Northerns v WP (Kimberley) 2020-21. LO HS 20 v Glamorgan (Cardiff) 2021 (RLC).

[NQ]**VIHARI**, Gade **Hanuma**, b Kakinada, India 13 Oct 1993. RHB, OB. Hyderabad 2010-11 to date. Andhra 2016-17 to 2019-20. Warwickshire 2021. IPL: SH 2013-15. DCa 2019. **Tests** (I): 14 (2018 to 2021-22); HS 111 v WI (Kingston) 2019; BB 3-37 v E (Oval) 2018. F-c Tours (I): E 2018; A 2018-19, 2020-21; SA 2017 (IA), 2021-22; WI 2019; NZ 2018-19 (IA), 2019-20. 1000 runs (0+1): 1056 (2017-18). HS 302* Andhra v Orissa (Vizianagram) 2017-18. Wa HS 52 v Essex (Birmingham) 2021. BB 3-17 Andhra v Goa (Dhanbad) 2016-17. LO HS 169 Andhra v Mumbai (Chennai) 2017-18. LO BB 3-31 Andhra v Madhya Pradesh (Delhi, MSC) 2018-19. T20 HS 81. T20 BB 3-21.

V.V.Kelley, A.T.Thomson left the staff without making a County 1st XI appearance in 2021.

WARWICKSHIRE 2021

RESULTS SUMMARY

	Place	Won	Lost	Drew	NR
LV= Insurance County Champ (Div 1)	**1st**	6	2	6	
Royal London One-Day Cup (Group 2)	5th	4	4		
Vitality Blast (North Group)	QF	7	7		1

LV= INSURANCE COUNTY CHAMPIONSHIP AVERAGES
BATTING AND FIELDING

Cap		*M*	*I*	*NO*	*HS*	*Runs*	*Avge*	*100*	*50*	*Ct/St*
	R.M.Yates	13	23	2	132*	793	37.76	4	2	21
	P.J.Malan	6	10	1	141	339	37.66	1	1	–
2019	D.P.Sibley	9	15	2	80	470	36.15	–	4	1
2018	S.R.Hain	14	25	2	118	826	35.91	1	6	18
	C.G.Benjamin	3	6	–	127	198	33.00	1	–	1
	M.J.Lamb	13	23	5	67	565	31.38	–	3	5
2021	M.G.K.Burgess	14	21	–	101	607	28.90	1	3	40/4
2021	D.R.Briggs	12	19	4	66*	411	27.40	–	3	4
2020	W.M.H.Rhodes	14	26	2	91	633	26.37	–	5	13
2021	T.T.Bresnan	10	15	2	68*	311	23.92	–	2	16
	G.H.Vihari	3	6	–	52	100	16.66	–	1	3
2020	O.P.Stone	4	5	1	43	63	15.75	–	–	–
	C.N.Miles	11	16	2	25	146	10.42	–	–	3
	L.C.Norwell	12	17	5	30*	118	9.83	–	–	1
2019	O.J.Hannon-Dalby	8	11	6	26	48	9.60	–	–	2

Also played: J.G.Bethell (1 match) 15, 8; E.A.Brookes (1) did not bat; C.K.Holder (2) 6, 0*, 0; J.B.Lintott (1) 15 (1 ct); R.N.Sidebottom (2) 0, 1; C.R.Woakes (2 – cap 2009) 9, 0, 10 (1 ct).

BOWLING

	O	*M*	*R*	*W*	*Avge*	*Best*	*5wI*	*10wM*
C.R.Woakes	72.3	23	205	12	17.08	3-26	–	–
L.C.Norwell	346.4	97	895	49	18.26	6-57	2	–
W.M.H.Rhodes	178	51	481	26	18.50	5-23	1	–
C.N.Miles	277.4	62	807	37	21.81	5-30	2	–
D.R.Briggs	290	81	664	30	22.13	4-36	–	–
O.J.Hannon-Dalby	258.5	73	698	24	29.08	5-76	1	–
O.P.Stone	124.3	20	395	13	30.38	4-89	–	–
T.T.Bresnan	163	57	417	12	34.75	3-35	–	–

Also bowled:

E.A.Brookes 7-2-22-0; C.K.Holder 45-9-177-2; M.J.Lamb 21-2-50-2; J.B.Lintott 39-2-103-0; R.N.Sidebottom 46-9-113-0; G.H.Vihari 1-0-11-0; R.M.Yates 47-7-108-3.

The First-Class Averages (pp 220–232) give the records of Warwickshire players in all first-class county matches, with the exception of C.N.Miles, W.M.H.Rhodes, C.R.Woakes and R.M.Yates, whose first-class figures for Warwickshire are as above, and:

D.P.Sibley 10-16-2-80-527-37.64-0-5-2ct. Did not bowl.

WARWICKSHIRE RECORDS

FIRST-CLASS CRICKET

Highest Total	For 810-4d		v	Durham	Birmingham	1994
	V 887		by	Yorkshire	Birmingham	1896
Lowest Total	For 16		v	Kent	Tonbridge	1913
	V 15		by	Hampshire	Birmingham	1922
Highest Innings	For 501*	B.C.Lara	v	Durham	Birmingham	1994
	V 322	I.V.A.Richards	for	Somerset	Taunton	1985

Highest Partnership for each Wicket

1st	377*	N.F.Horner/K.Ibadulla	v	Surrey	The Oval	1960
2nd	465*	J.A.Jameson/R.B.Kanhai	v	Glos	Birmingham	1974
3rd	327	S.P.Kinneir/W.G.Quaife	v	Lancashire	Birmingham	1901
4th	470	A.I.Kallicharran/G.W.Humpage	v	Lancashire	Southport	1982
5th	335	J.O.Troughton/T.R.Ambrose	v	Hampshire	Birmingham	2009
6th	327	L.J.Evans/T.R.Ambrose	v	Sussex	Birmingham	2015
7th	289*	I.R.Bell/T.Frost	v	Sussex	Horsham	2004
8th	228	A.J.W.Croom/R.E.S.Wyatt	v	Worcs	Dudley	1925
9th	233	I.J.L.Trott/J.S.Patel	v	Yorkshire	Birmingham	2009
10th	214	N.V.Knight/A.Richardson	v	Hampshire	Birmingham	2002

Best Bowling	For	10-41	J.D.Bannister	v	Comb Servs	Birmingham	1959
(Innings)	V	10-36	H.Verity	for	Yorkshire	Leeds	1931
Best Bowling	For	15-76	S.Hargreave	v	Surrey	The Oval	1903
(Match)	V	17-92	A.P.Freeman	for	Kent	Folkestone	1932

Most Runs – Season	2417	M.J.K.Smith	(av 60.42)	1959
Most Runs – Career	35146	D.L.Amiss	(av 41.64)	1960-87
Most 100s – Season	9	A.I.Kallicharran		1984
	9	B.C.Lara		1994
Most 100s – Career	78	D.L.Amiss		1960-87
Most Wkts – Season	180	W.E.Hollies	(av 15.13)	1946
Most Wkts – Career	2201	W.E.Hollies	(av 20.45)	1932-57
Most Career W-K Dismissals	800	E.J.Smith	(662 ct; 138 st)	1904-30
Most Career Catches in the Field	422	M.J.K.Smith		1956-75

LIMITED-OVERS CRICKET

Highest Total	**50ov**	392-5		v	Oxfordshire	Birmingham	1984
	40ov	321-7		v	Leics	Birmingham	2010
	T20	242-2		v	Derbyshire	Birmingham	2015
Lowest Total	**50ov**	94		v	Glos	Bristol	2000
	40ov	59		v	Yorkshire	Leeds	2001
	T20	63		v	Notts	Birmingham	2021
Highest Innings	**50ov**	206	A.I.Kallicharran	v	Oxfordshire	Birmingham	1984
	40ov	137	I.R.Bell	v	Yorkshire	Birmingham	2005
	T20	158*	B.B.McCullum	v	Derbyshire	Birmingham	2015
Best Bowling	**50ov**	7-32	R.G.D.Willis	v	Yorkshire	Birmingham	1981
	40ov	6-15	A.A.Donald	v	Yorkshire	Birmingham	1995
	T20	5-19	N.M.Carter	v	Worcs	Birmingham	2005

WORCESTERSHIRE

Formation of Present Club: 11 March 1865
Inaugural First-Class Match: 1899
Colours: Dark Green and Black
Badge: Shield Argent a Fess between three Pears Sable
County Championships: (5) 1964, 1965, 1974, 1988, 1989
NatWest Trophy Winners: (1) 1994
Benson and Hedges Cup Winners: (1) 1991
Pro 40/National League (Div 1) Winners: (1) 2007
Sunday League Winners: (3) 1971, 1987, 1988
Twenty20 Cup Winners: (1) 2018

Chief Executive: tba, County Ground, New Road, Worcester, WR2 4QQ • Tel: 01905 748474 Email: info@wccc.co.uk • Web: www.wccc.co.uk • Twitter: @WorcsCCC (82,944 followers)

Head of Player and Coaches Development: Kevin Sharp. **1st Team Coach**: Alex Gidman. **Asst/Bowling Coach**: Alan Richardson. **Captains**: B.L.D'Oliveira (f-c and l-o) and M.M.Ali (T20). **Overseas Player**: Azhar Ali. **2022 Testimonial**: None. **Head Groundsman**: Tim Packwood. **Scorer**: Sue Drinkwater. **Vitality Blast Name**: Worcestershire Rapids. ‡ New registration. [NQ] Not qualified for England.

Worcestershire revised their capping policy in 2002 and now award players with their County Colours when they make their Championship debut.

ALI, Moeen Munir (Moseley S), b Birmingham, Warwks 18 Jun 1987. Brother of A.K.Ali (Worcs, Glos and Leics 2000-12), cousin of Kabir Ali (Worcs, Rajasthan, Hants and Lancs 1999-2014). 6'0". LHB, OB. Squad No 8. Warwickshire 2005-06. Worcestershire debut 2007; captain 2020 to date (T20 only). Moors SC 2011-12. MT 2012-13. MCC 2012. IPL: RCB 2018 to 2020-21; CSK 2021. Birmingham Phoenix 2021. PCA 2013. *Wisden* 2014. **ECB Central Contract 2021-22. Tests**: 64 (2014 to 2021); 1000 runs (1): 1078 (2016); HS 155* v SL (Chester-le-St) 2016; BB 6-53 v SA (Lord's) 2017. Hat-trick v SA (Oval) 2017. **LOI**: 112 (2013-14 to 2021); HS 128 v Scotland (Christchurch) 2014-15; BB 4-46 v A (Manchester) 2018. **IT20**: 49 (2013-14 to 2021-22); HS 72* v A (Cardiff) 2015; BB 3-24 v WI (Bridgetown) 2021-22. F-c Tours: A 2017-18; SA 2015-16; WI 2014-15, 2018-19; NZ 2017-18; I 2016-17, 2020-21; SL 2013-14 (EL), 2018-19; B 2016-17; UAE 2015-16 (v P). 1000 runs (2); most – 1420 (2013). HS 250 v Glamorgan (Worcester) 2013. BB 6-29 (12-96 match) v Lancs (Manchester) 2012. LO HS 158 v Sussex (Horsham) 2011 (CB40). LO BB 4-33 v Notts (Nottingham) 2018 (RLC). T20 HS 121*. T20 BB 5-34.

‡[NQ]**AZHAR ALI**, b Lahore, Pakistan 19 Feb 1985. RHB, LB. Lahore Blues 2001-02. KRL 2002-03 to 2011-12. Lahore 2003-04. SNGPL 2012-13 to 2018-19. Somerset 2018-21; cap 2019. Central Punjab 2019-20 to date. **Tests** (P): 93 (2010 to 2021-22, 9 as captain); 1000 runs (1): 1198 (2016); HS 302* v WI (Dubai, DSC) 2016-17; BB 2-35 v SL (Pallekele) 2015. **LOI** (P): 53 (2011 to 2017-18, 31 as captain); HS 102 v Z (Lahore) 2015; BB 2-26 v E (Dubai, DSC) 2015-16. F-c Tours (P)(C=Captain): E 2010, 2016, 2018, 2020C; A 2009 (PA), 2016-17, 2019-20C; SA 2012-13, 2018-19; WI 2011, 2016-17, 2021; NZ 2010-11, 2016-17, 2020-21; SL 2009 (PA), 2012, 2014, 2015; Z 2011, 2013, 2021; B 2011-12, 2014-15, 2021-22; Ire 2018. HS 302* (*see Tests*). CC HS 125 Sm v Worcs (Worcester) 2018 – on debut. BB 4-34 KRL v Peshawar (Peshawar) 2002-03. CC BB 1-5 Sm v Essex (Taunton) 2018. LO HS 132* SNGPL v Lahore Blues (Islamabad) 2015-16. LO BB 5-23 Lahore Whites v Peshawar (Karachi) 2001 – on debut. T20 HS 72. T20 BB 3-10.

BAKER, Josh Oliver (Warkwood Middle S; Malvern C), b Redditch 16 May 2003. 6'3". RHB, SLA. Squad No 33. Debut (Worcestershire) 2021. HS 61* v Middx (Lord's) 2021. BB 3-49 v Sussex (Worcester). LO HS 25 v Durham (Worcester) 2021 (RLC). LO BB 2-53 v Sussex (Worcester) 2021 (RLC).

BANTON, Jacques (Bromsgrove S; King's C, Taunton), b Perpignan, France 6 Jul 2001. Son of C.Banton (Nottinghamshire 1995); younger brother of T. Banton (*see SOMERSET*). 5'10". RHB, SLA. Squad No 77. Worcestershire 2nd XI debut 2019. Awaiting f-c debut. LO HS 33 and LO BB 3-15 v Sussex (Worcester) 2021 (RLC).

BARNARD, Edward George (Shrewsbury S), b Shrewsbury, Shrops 20 Nov 1995. Younger brother of M.R.Barnard (Oxford MCCU 2010). 6'1". RHB, RMF. Squad No 30. Debut (Worcestershire) 2015. Shropshire 2012. HS 128 v Essex (Chelmsford) 2021. BB 6-37 (11-89 match) v Somerset (Taunton) 2018. LO HS 61 v Leics (Leicester) 2019 (RLC). LO BB 3-26 v Yorks (Worcester) 2019 (RLC). T20 HS 43*. T20 BB 3-29.

BROWN, Patrick Rhys (Bourne GS, Lincs), b Peterborough, Cambs 23 Aug 1998. 6'2". RHB, RMF. Squad No 36. Debut (Worcestershire) 2017. Birmingham Phoenix 2021. Worcestershire 2nd XI debut 2016. Lincolnshire 2016. **IT20**: 4 (2019-20); HS 4* v NZ (Wellington) 2019-20; BB 1-29 v NZ (Napier) 2019-20. HS 5* v Sussex (Worcester) 2017. BB 2-15 v Leics (Worcester) 2017. LO HS 3 v Somerset (Worcester) 2019 (RLC). LO BB 3-53 v Kent (Worcester) 2018 (RLC). T20 HS 7*. T20 BB 4-21.

CORNALL, Taylor Ryan, b Lytham St Anne's, Lancs 9 Oct 1998. 6'0". LHB. Squad No 57. Leeds/Bradford MCCU 2019. Lancashire 2021 (l-o only). Lancashire 2nd XI 2018-21. Kent 2nd XI 2021. Worcestershire 2nd XI debut 2021. HS 19 LBU v Derbys (Derby) 2019. LO HS 23* La v Durham (Gosforth) 2021 (RLC).

COX, Oliver **Ben** (Bromsgrove S), b Wordsley, Stourbridge 2 Feb 1992. 5'10". RHB, WK. Squad No 10. Debut (Worcestershire) 2009. MCC 2017, 2019. HS 124 v Glos (Cheltenham) 2017. LO HS 122* v Kent (Worcester) 2018 (RLC). T20 HS 59*.

DELL, Joshua Jamie (Cheltenham C), b Tenbury Wells 26 Sep 1997. 6'3". RHB, RMF. Squad No 52. Debut (Worcestershire) 2019. Worcestershire 2nd XI debut 2015. England U19 2016. HS 61 v Durham (Worcester) 2019. LO HS 46 v West Indies A (Worcester) 2018.

D'OLIVEIRA, Brett Louis (Worcester SFC), b Worcester 28 Feb 1992. Son of D.B.D'Oliveira (Worcs 1982-95), grandson of B.L.D'Oliveira (Worcs, EP and England 1964-80). 5'9". RHB, LB. Squad No 15. Debut (Worcestershire) 2012; captain 2022. MCC 2018. HS 202* v Glamorgan (Cardiff) 2016. BB 7-92 v Glamorgan (Cardiff) 2019. LO HS 123 and LO BB 3-8 v Essex (Chelmsford) 2021 (RLC). T20 HS 69. T20 BB 4-26.

FELL, Thomas Charles (Oakham S; Oxford Brookes U), b Hillingdon, Middx 17 Oct 1993. 6'1". RHB, WK, occ OB. Squad No 29. Oxford MCCU 2013. Worcestershire debut 2013. 1000 runs (1): 1127 (2015). HS 171 v Middx (Worcester) 2015. LO HS 116* v Lancs (Worcester) 2016 (RLC). T20 HS 28.

FINCH, Adam William (Kingswinford S; Oldswinford Hospital SFC), b Wordsley, Stourbridge 28 May 2000. 6'4". RHB, RMF. Squad No 61. Debut (Worcestershire) 2019. Surrey 2020 (on loan). Worcestershire 2nd XI debut 2017. England U19 2018 to 2018-19. HS 31 v Warwks (Worcester) 2021. Wo BB 2-23 v Glos (Worcester) 2019. BB 4-38 Sy v Essex (Chelmsford) 2020. LO HS 23* v Sussex (Worcester) 2021 (RLC). LO BB 2-54 v Durham (Worcester) 2021 (RLC). T20 HS 3*. T20 BB 1-22.

GIBBON, Benjamin James, b Chester 9 Jun 2000. 6'3". RHB, LMF. Squad No 21. Lancashire 2nd XI 2019-21. Worcestershire 2nd XI debut 2021. Cheshire 2019-21. Awaiting 1st XI debut.

HAYNES, Jack Alexander (Malvern C), b Worcester 30 Jan 2001. Son of G.R.Haynes (Worcestershire 1991-99); younger brother of J.L.Haynes (Worcestershire 2nd XI 2015-16). 6'1". RHB, OB. Squad No 17. Debut (Worcestershire) 2019. Worcestershire 2nd XI debut 2016. England U19 2018. HS 97 v Derbys (Worcester) 2021. LO HS 153 v Essex (Chelmsford) 2021 (RLC). T20 HS 41.

LEACH, Joseph (Shrewsbury S; Leeds U), b Stafford 30 Oct 1990. Elder brother of S.G.Leach (Oxford MCCU 2014-16). 6'1". RHB, RMF. Squad No 23. Leeds/Bradford MCCU 2012. Worcestershire debut 2012; captain 2017-21. Staffordshire 2008-09. HS 114 v Glos (Cheltenham) 2013. 50 wkts (3); most – 69 (2017). BB 6-73 v Warwks (Birmingham) 2015. LO HS 88 v Kent (Worcester) 2021 (RLC). LO BB 4-30 v Northants (Worcester) 2015 (RLC). T20 HS 24. T20 BB 5-33.

LIBBY, Jacob ('**Jake**') Daniel (Plymouth C; UWIC), b Plymouth, Devon 3 Jan 1993. 5'9". RHB, OB. Squad No 2. Cardiff MCCU 2014. Nottinghamshire 2014-19, scoring 108 v Sussex (Nottingham) on debut. Northamptonshire 2016 (on loan). Worcestershire debut 2020. Cornwall 2011-14. 1000 runs (1): 1104 (2021). HS 184 and BB 2-45 v Glamorgan (Worcester) 2020. LO HS 76 v Durham (Worcester) 2021 (RLC). T20 HS 78*. T20 BB 1-11.

MORRIS, Charles Andrew John (King's C, Taunton; Oxford Brookes U), b Hereford 6 Jul 1992. 6'0". RHB, RMF. Squad No 31. Oxford MCCU 2012-14. Worcestershire debut 2013. MCC Univs 2012. Devon 2011-12. HS 53* v Australians (Worcester) 2019. CC HS 50 v Leics (Worcester) 2021. 50 wkts (2); most – 56 (2014). BB 7-45 v Leics (Leicester) 2019. LO HS 25* v Durham (Worcester) 2021 (RLC). LO BB 4-33 v Durham (Gosforth) 2018 (RLC). T20 HS 3. T20 BB 3-21.

PENNINGTON, Dillon Young (Wrekin C), b Shrewsbury, Shrops 26 Feb 1999. 6'2". RHB, RMF. Squad No 22. Debut (Worcestershire) 2018. Birmingham Phoenix 2021. Worcestershire 2nd XI debut 2017. Shropshire 2017. HS 56 v Essex (Chelmsford) 2021. BB 5-32 v Derbys (Worcester) 2021. LO HS 4* and LO BB 5-67 v West Indies A (Worcester) 2018. T20 HS 10*. T20 BB 4-9.

‡**POLLOCK, Ed**ward John (RGS Worcester; Shrewsbury S; Collingwood C, Durham U), b High Wycombe, Bucks 10 Jul 1995. Son of A.J.Pollock (Cambridge U 1982-84); younger brother of A.W.Pollock (Cambridge MCCU & U 2013-15). 5'10". LHB, OB. Squad No 7. Durham MCCU 2015-17. Warwickshire 2017-21 (white-ball only). Herefordshire 2014-16. HS 52 DU v Glos (Bristol) 2017. LO HS 103* Wa v Derbys (Derby) 2021 (RLC). T20 HS 77.

RODERICK, Gareth Hugh (Maritzburg C), b Durban, South Africa 29 Aug 1991. 6'0". RHB, WK. Squad No 9. UK passport, qualifying for England in October 2018. KZN 2010-11 to 2011-12. Gloucestershire 2013-20; cap 2013; captain 2016-17. Worcestershire debut 2021. HS 171 Gs v Leics (Bristol) 2014. Wo HS 42* v Middx (Lord's) 2021. LO HS 104 Gs v Leics (Leicester) 2015 (RLC). T20 HS 32.

STANLEY, Mitchell Terry (Idsall S, Shifnal; Shrewsbury SFC), b Telford, Shrops 17 Mar 2001. RHB, RFM. Squad No 38. Worcestershire 2nd XI debut 2021. Shropshire 2021. Awaiting 1st XI debut.

TONGUE, Joshua Charles (King's S, Worcester; Worcester SFC), b Redditch 15 Nov 1997. 6'5". RHB, RM. Squad No 24. Debut (Worcestershire) 2016. Worcestershire 2nd XI debut 2015. HS 41 and BB 6-97 v Glamorgan (Worcester) 2017. LO HS 34 v Warwks (Worcester) 2019 (RLC). LO BB 2-35 v Lancs (Manchester) 2019 (RLC). T20 HS 2*. T20 BB 2-32.

RELEASED/RETIRED

(Having made a County 1st XI appearance in 2021)

[NQ]**DWARSHUIS, Ben**jamin James, b Kareela, NSW, Australia 23 June 1994. LHB, LFM. New South Wales 2016-17 to date (l-o only). Worcestershire 2021 (T20 only). Big Bash: SS 2014-15 to date. Awaiting f-c debut. LO HS 31* NSW v WA (Sydney, NS) 2021-22. LO BB 4-50 NSW v Tas (Hobart) 2020-21. T20 HS 66. T20 BB 5-26.

[NQ]**JOSEPH, Alzarri** Shaheim, b Antigua 20 Nov 1996. RHB, RFM. Leeward Is 2014-15 to date. Worcestershire 2021. Big Bash: MI 2019. **Tests** (WI): 18 (2016 to 2021-22); HS 86 v NZ (Hamilton) 2020-21; BB 3-53 v P (Roseau) 2017. **LOI** (WI): 43 (2016-17 to 2021-22); HS 29* v B (Providence) 2018; BB 5-56 v E (Oval) 2017. F-c Tours (WI): E 2017, 2020; NZ 2020-21; SL 2020-21; UAE 2016-17 (v P). HS 89 Leeward Is v Jamaica (North Sound) 2019-20. Wo HS 61 v Notts (Worcester) 2021. BB 7-46 Leeward Is v Windward Is (Roseau) 2015-16. Wo BB 2-22 v Warwks (Birmingham) 2021. LO HS 51* WI B v T&T (Port of Spain) 2018-19. LO BB 6-31 Leeward Is v Windward Is (Coolidge) 2016-17. T20 HS 21*. T20 BB 6-12.

MITCHELL, Daryl Keith Henry (Prince Henry's HS; University C, Worcester), b Badsey, near Evesham 25 Nov 1983. 5'10". RHB, RM. Worcestershire 2005-21; captain 2011-16; benefit 2016. Mountaineers 2011-12. MCC 2015. 1000 runs (5); most – 1334 (2014). HS 298 v Somerset (Taunton) 2009. BB 4-49 v Yorks (Leeds) 2009. LO HS 107 v Sussex (Hove) 2013 (Y40). LO BB 4-19 v Northants (Milton Keynes) 2014 (RLC). T20 HS 68*. T20 BB 5-28.

[NQ]**SODHI**, Inderbir Singh (**'Ish'**), b Ludhiana, Punjab, India 31 Oct 1992. RHB, LBG. Northern Districts 2012-13 to date. Worcestershire 2021. Nottinghamshire 2017-18 (T20 only). IPL: RR 2018-19. Big Bash: AS 2016-17. **Tests** (NZ): 17 (2013-14 to 2018-19); HS 63 v P (Abu Dhabi) 2014-15; BB 4-60 v Z (Bulawayo) 2016. **LOI** (NZ): 33 (2015 to 2019-20); HS 24 v P (Abu Dhabi) 2018-19; BB 4-58 v E (Dunedin) 2017-18. **IT20** (NZ): 66 (2014 to 2021-22); HS 16* v I (Mt Maunganui) 2019-20; BB 4-28 v A (Christchurch) 2020-21 and 4-28 v B (Hamilton) 2020-21. F-c Tours (NZ): WI 2014; I 2013-14, 2016-17, 2017-18 (NZ A); SL 2013-14 (NZ A); Z 2016; B 2013-14; UAE 2014-15 (v P), 2018-19 (v P). HS 82* ND v Otago (Dunedin) 2014-15. Wo HS 13 and Wo BB 6-89 v Warwks (Worcester) 2021. BB 7-30 (12-62 match) ND v Wellington (Wellington) 2017-18. LO HS 44* ND v CD (Whangarei) 2017-18. LO BB 4-10 NZ A v Sri Lanka A (Bristol) 2014. T20 HS 51. T20 BB 6-11.

WESSELS, Mattheus Hendrik (**'Riki'**) (Woodridge C, Pt Elizabeth; Northampton U), b Marogudoore, Queensland, Australia 12 Nov 1985. Left Australia when 2 months old. Qualified for England after gaining a UK passport in July 2016. Son of K.C.Wessels (OFS, Sussex, WP, NT, Q, EP, GW, Australia and South Africa 1973-74 to 1999-00). 5'11". RHB, WK. MCC 2004. Northamptonshire 2005-09. Nondescripts 2007-08. MWR 2009-10 to 2011-12. Nottinghamshire 2011-18; cap 2014. Worcestershire 2019-21. Big Bash: SS 2014-15. 1000 runs (2); most – 1213 (2014). HS 202* Nt v Sussex (Nottingham) 2017. Wo HS 118 v Durham (Worcester) 2019. BB 1-10 MWR v MT (Bulawayo) 2009-10. LO HS 146 Nt v Northants (Nottingham) 2016 (RLC). LO BB 1-0 MWR v MT (Bulawayo) 2009-10. T20 HS 110.

WHITELEY, R.A. – *see HAMPSHIRE.*

A.G.Milton left the staff without making a County 1st XI appearance in 2021.

WORCESTERSHIRE 2021

RESULTS SUMMARY

	Place	Won	Lost	Tied	Drew	NR
LV= Insurance County Champ (Div 3)	3rd	3	5		6	
Royal London One-Day Cup (Group 1)	5th	3	4			1
Vitality Blast (North Group)	5th	6	6	1		1

LV= INSURANCE COUNTY CHAMPIONSHIP AVERAGES
BATTING AND FIELDING

Cap†		*M*	*I*	*NO*	*HS*	*Runs*	*Avge*	*100*	*50*	*Ct/St*
2020	J.D.Libby	14	23	4	180*	1075	56.57	4	4	6
2015	E.G.Barnard	13	18	3	128	746	49.73	2	3	12
2019	J.A.Haynes	9	14	–	97	491	35.07	–	4	8
2012	J.Leach	13	19	5	84	377	26.92	–	1	2
2012	B.L.D'Oliveira	14	21	2	71	480	25.26	–	3	4
2009	O.B.Cox	14	21	2	60*	413	21.73	–	2	42/2
2005	D.K.H.Mitchell	14	23	1	113	470	21.36	1	3	13
2019	M.H.Wessels	7	10	–	60	202	20.20	–	2	3
2014	C.A.J.Morris	6	8	2	50	116	19.33	–	1	–
2021	G.H.Roderick	7	11	2	42*	167	18.55	–	–	1
2021	A.S.Joseph	6	8	–	61	148	18.50	–	1	–
2013	T.C.Fell	12	19	–	69	324	17.05	–	2	9
2021	J.O.Baker	5	7	2	61*	84	16.80	–	1	4
2018	D.Y.Pennington	10	14	4	56	156	15.60	–	1	1
2017	J.C.Tongue	4	6	1	17	66	13.20	–	–	–
2019	A.W.Finch	3	4	1	31	37	12.33	–	–	–

Also batted: I.S.Sodhi (1 match – cap 2021) 13; R.A.Whiteley (2 – cap 2013) 22, 8, 4 (1 ct).

BOWLING

	O	*M*	*R*	*W*	*Avge*	*Best*	*5wI*	*10wM*
J.C.Tongue	115.5	18	358	14	25.57	5-39	1	–
J.Leach	428	108	1141	38	30.02	5-68	1	–
D.Y.Pennington	282.4	57	898	29	30.96	5-32	1	–
C.A.J.Morris	189.3	45	621	19	32.68	6-52	1	–
J.O.Baker	144.2	30	408	12	34.00	3-49	–	–
A.S.Joseph	158	21	574	15	38.26	2-22	–	–
E.G.Barnard	368.1	83	1052	25	42.08	4-43	–	–
B.L.D'Oliveira	253.4	29	808	15	53.86	3-95	–	–
Also bowled:								
I.S.Sodhi	49.2	3	148	6	24.66	6-89	1	–
A.W.Finch	76	13	250	8	31.25	2-32	–	–

J.D.Libby 38.2-5-129-1; D.K.H.Mitchell 93.5-15-291-4; R.A.Whiteley 10-1-33-1.

The First-Class Averages (pp 220–232) give the records of Worcestershire players in all first-class county matches, with the exception of J.D.Libby, whose first-class figures for Worcestershire are as above.

† Worcestershire revised their capping policy in 2002 and now award players with their County Colours when they make their Championship debut.

WORCESTERSHIRE RECORDS

FIRST-CLASS CRICKET

Highest Total	For 701-6d		v	Surrey	Worcester	2007
	V 701-4d		by	Leics	Worcester	1906
Lowest Total	For 24		v	Yorkshire	Huddersfield	1903
	V 30		by	Hampshire	Worcester	1903
Highest Innings	For 405*	G.A.Hick	v	Somerset	Taunton	1988
	V 331*	J.D.B.Robertson	for	Middlesex	Worcester	1949

Highest Partnership for each Wicket

1st	309	H.K.Foster/F.L.Bowley	v	Derbyshire	Derby	1901
2nd	316	S.C.Moore/V.S.Solanki	v	Glos	Cheltenham	2008
3rd	438*	G.A.Hick/T.M.Moody	v	Hampshire	Southampton[1]	1997
4th	330	B.F.Smith/G.A.Hick	v	Somerset	Taunton	2006
5th	393	E.G.Arnold/W.B.Burns	v	Warwicks	Birmingham	1909
6th	265	G.A.Hick/S.J.Rhodes	v	Somerset	Taunton	1988
7th	256	D.A.Leatherdale/S.J.Rhodes	v	Notts	Nottingham	2002
8th	184	S.J.Rhodes/S.R.Lampitt	v	Derbyshire	Kidderminster	1991
9th	181	J.A.Cuffe/R.D.Burrows	v	Glos	Worcester	1907
10th	136	A.G.Milton/S.J.Magoffin	v	Somerset	Worcester	2018

Best Bowling	For	9- 23	C.F.Root	v	Lancashire	Worcester	1931
(Innings)	V	10- 51	J.Mercer	for	Glamorgan	Worcester	1936
Best Bowling	For	15- 87	A.J.Conway	v	Glos	Moreton-in-M	1914
(Match)	V	17-212	J.C.Clay	for	Glamorgan	Swansea	1937

Most Runs – Season	2654	H.H.I.H.Gibbons	(av 52.03)	1934
Most Runs – Career	34490	D.Kenyon	(av 34.18)	1946-67
Most 100s – Season	10	G.M.Turner		1970
	10	G.A.Hick		1988
Most 100s – Career	106	G.A.Hick		1984-2008
Most Wkts – Season	207	C.F.Root	(av 17.52)	1925
Most Wkts – Career	2143	R.T.D.Perks	(av 23.73)	1930-55
Most Career W-K Dismissals	1095	S.J.Rhodes	(991 ct; 104 st)	1985-2004
Most Career Catches in the Field	528	G.A.Hick		1984-2008

LIMITED-OVERS CRICKET

Highest Total	**50ov**	404-3		v	Devon	Worcester	1987
	40ov	376-6		v	Surrey	The Oval	2010
	T20	227-6		v	Northants	Kidderminster	2007
Lowest Total	**50ov**	58		v	Ireland	Worcester	2009
	40ov	86		v	Yorkshire	Leeds	1969
	T20	53		v	Lancashire	Manchester	2016
Highest Innings	**50ov**	192	C.J.Ferguson	v	Leics	Worcester	2018
	40ov	160	T.M.Moody	v	Kent	Worcester	1991
	T20	127	T.Kohler-Cadmore	v	Durham	Worcester	2016
Best Bowling	**50ov**	7-19	N.V.Radford	v	Beds	Bedford	1991
	40ov	6-16	Shoaib Akhtar	v	Glos	Worcester	2005
	T20	5-24	A.Hepburn	v	Notts	Worcester	2017

YORKSHIRE

Formation of Present Club: 8 January 1863
Substantial Reorganisation: 10 December 1891
Inaugural First-Class Match: 1864
Colours: Dark Blue, Light Blue and Gold
Badge: White Rose
County Championships (since 1890): (32) 1893, 1896, 1898, 1900, 1901, 1902, 1905, 1908, 1912, 1919, 1922, 1923, 1924, 1925, 1931, 1932, 1933, 1935, 1937, 1938, 1939, 1946, 1959, 1960, 1962, 1963, 1966, 1967, 1968, 2001, 2014, 2015
Joint Champions: (1) 1949
Gillette/C&G Trophy Winners: (3) 1965, 1969, 2002
Benson and Hedges Cup Winners: (1) 1987
Sunday League Winners: (1) 1983
Twenty20 Cup Winners: (0); best – Finalist 2012

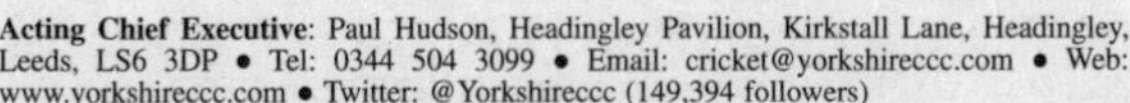
Acting Chief Executive: Paul Hudson, Headingley Pavilion, Kirkstall Lane, Headingley, Leeds, LS6 3DP • Tel: 0344 504 3099 • Email: cricket@yorkshireccc.com • Web: www.yorkshireccc.com • Twitter: @Yorkshireccc (149,394 followers)

Interim MD Cricket: Darren Gough. **Head Coach**: Ottis Gibson. **Assistant Coaches**: Kabir Ali and Alastair Maiden. **Captains**: S.A.Patterson (f-c and l-o) and D.J.Willey (T20). **Overseas Player**: Haris Rauf. **2022 Testimonial**: None. **Head Groundsman**: Andy Fogarty. **Scorers**: John Potter and John Virr. **Vitality Blast Name**: Yorkshire Vikings. ‡ New registration. [NQ] Not qualified for England.

BAIRSTOW, Jonathan Marc (St Peter's S, York; Leeds Met U), b Bradford 26 Sep 1989. Son of D.L.Bairstow (Yorkshire, GW and England 1970-90); brother of A.D.Bairstow (Derbyshire 1995). 6'0". RHB, WK, occ RM. Squad No 21. Debut (Yorkshire) 2009; cap 2011. Inaugural winner of Young Wisden Schools Cricketer of the Year 2008. YC 2011. **ECB Central Contract 2021-22. Tests**: 81 (2012 to 2021-22); 1000 runs (1): 1470 (2016); HS 167* v SL (Lord's) 2016. Took a world record 70 dismissals in 2016, as well as scoring a record number of runs in a calendar year for a keeper. **LOI**: 89 (2011 to 2021); 1000 runs (1): 1025 (2018); HS 141* v WI (Southampton) 2017. **IT20**: 63 (2011 to 2021-22): HS 86* v SA (Cape Town) 2020-21. F-c Tours: A 2013-14, 2017-18, 2021-22; SA 2014-15 (EL), 2015-16, 2019-20; WI 2010-11 (EL), 2018-19, WI 2021-22; NZ 2017-18; I 2012-13, 2016-17, 2020-21; SL 2013-14 (EL), 2018-19, 2020-21; B 2016-17; UAE 2015-16 (v P). 1000 runs (3); most – 1286 (2016). HS 246 v Hants (Leeds) 2016. LO HS 174 v Durham (Leeds) 2017 (RLC). T20 HS 114.

BALLANCE, Gary Simon (Peterhouse S, Marondera, Zimbabwe; Harrow S; Leeds Met U), b Harare, Zimbabwe 22 Nov 1989. Nephew of G.S.Ballance (Rhodesia B 1978-79) and D.L.Houghton (Rhodesia/Zimbabwe 1978-79 to 1997-98). 6'0". LHB, LB. Squad No 19. Debut (Yorkshire) 2008; cap 2012; captain 2017 to 2018 (*part*). MWR 2010-11 to 2011-12. No 1st XI appearances in 2020. *Wisden* 2014. **Tests**: 23 (2013-14 to 2017); HS 156 v I (Southampton) 2014; BB –. **LOI**: 16 (2013 to 2014-15); HS 79 v A (Melbourne) 2013-14. F-c Tours: A 2013-14; WI 2014-15; B 2016-17. 1000 runs (4+1); most – 1363 (2013). HS 210 MWR v SR (Masvingo) 2011-12. Y HS 203* v Hants (Southampton) 2017. BB –. LO HS 156 v Leics (Leeds) 2019 (RLC). T20 HS 79.

BESS, Dominic Mark (Blundell's S), b Exeter, Devon 22 Jul 1997. Cousin of Z.G.G.Bess (Devon 2015 to date), J.J.Bess (Devon 2007-18) and L.F.O.Bess (Devon 2017 to date). 5'11". RHB, OB. Squad No 47. Somerset 2016-19. Yorkshire debut 2019 (on loan). MCC 2018, 2019. Devon 2015-16. **ECB Increment Contract 2021-22. Tests**: 14 (2018 to 2020-21); HS 57 v P (Lord's) 2018; BB 5-30 v SL (Galle) 2020-21. F-c Tours: A 2019-20 (EL), 2021-22 (EL); SA 2019-20; WI 2017-18 (EL); I 2018-19 (EL), 2020-21; SL 2019-20, 2020-21. HS 107 MCC v Essex (Bridgetown) 2018. CC HS 92 Sm v Hants (Taunton) 2018. Y HS 91* v Essex (Leeds) 2019. BB 7-43 v Northants (Northampton) 2021. LO HS 24* South v North (Cave Hill) 2017-18. LO BB 3-35 EL v Pakistan A (Abu Dhabi) 2018-19. T20 HS 24. T20 BB 3-17.

BIRKHEAD, Benjamin David (Huddersfield New C), b Halifax 28 Oct 1998. 5'9½". RHB, WK. Squad No 30. Yorkshire 2nd XI debut 2016. Awaiting f-c debut. LO HS –. T20 HS –.

BROOK, Harry Cherrington (Sedbergh S), b Keighley 22 Feb 1999. 5'11". RHB, RM. Squad No 88. Debut (Yorkshire) 2016. Big Bash: HH 2021-22. Northern Superchargers 2021. Yorkshire 2nd XI debut 2015. England U19 2016-17 to 2017. YC 2021. **IT20**: 1 (2021-22); HS 10 v WI (Bridgetown) 2021-22. F-c Tour (EL): A 2021-22. HS 124 v Essex (Chelmsford) 2018. BB 3-15 v Glamorgan (Cardiff) 2021. LO HS 103 v Leics (Leeds) 2019 (RLC). T20 HS 102*. T20 BB 1-13.

COAD, Benjamin Oliver (Thirsk S & SFC), b Harrogate 10 Jan 1994. 6'2". RHB, RM. Squad No 10. Debut (Yorkshire) 2016; cap 2018. HS 48 v Surrey (Scarborough) 2019. 50 wkts (1): 53 (2017). BB 6-25 v Lancs (Leeds) 2017. LO HS 10 v Surrey (Scarborough) 2021 (RLC). LO BB 4-63 v Derbys (Leeds) 2017 (RLC). T20 HS 7. T20 BB 3-40.

DUKE, Harry George (QEGS, Wakefield), b Wakefield 6 Sep 2001. 5'8". RHB, WK. Squad No 22. Debut (Yorkshire) 2021. Yorkshire 2nd XI debut 2019. HS 54 v Sussex (Leeds) 2021. LO HS 125 v Leics (Leicester) 2021 (RLC). T20 HS –.

FISHER, Matthew David (Easingwold SS), b York 9 Nov 1997. 6'1". RHB, RFM. Squad No 7. Debut (Yorkshire) 2015. MCC 2018. Northern Superchargers 2021. Yorkshire 2nd XI debut 2013, aged 15y 201d. England U19 2014. F-c Tour (EL): A 2021-22. HS 47* v Kent (Leeds) 2019. BB 5-41 v Somerset (Scarborough) 2021. LO HS 36* v Worcs (Worcester) 2017 (RLC). LO BB 3-32 v Leics (Leeds) 2015 (RLC). T20 HS 19. T20 BB 5-22.

FRAINE, William Alan Richard (Silcoates S; Bromsgrove SFC; Durham U), b Huddersfield, Yorks 13 Jun 1996. 6'2". RHB, RM. Squad No 31. Durham MCCU 2017-18. Nottinghamshire 2018. Yorkshire debut 2019. Herefordshire 2016. HS 106 v Surrey (Scarborough) 2019. LO HS 69* v Derbys (Chesterfield) 2021 (RLC). T20 HS 44*.

‡[NQ]**HARIS RAUF**, b Rawalpindi, Pakistan 7 Nov 1993. 5'11". RHB, RFM. Northern 2019-20 to date. Big Bash: MS 2019-20 to date. **LOI** (P): 8 (2020-21 to 2021); HS 1* v SA (Johannesburg) 2020-21; BB 4-65 v E (Birmingham) 2021. **IT20** (P): 34 (2019-20 to 2021-22); HS 6 v Z (Harare) 2021; BB 4-22 v NZ (Sharjah) 2021-22. HS 9* Northern v Baluchistan (Rawalpindi) 2019-20. BB 6-47 Northern v Central Punjab (Karachi) 2021-22. LO HS 8 Baluchistan v Khyber Pakhtunkhwa (Rawalpindi) 2018-19. LO BB 4-65 (*see LOI*). T20 HS 19. T20 BB 5-27.

HILL, George Christopher Hindley (Sedbergh S), b Keighley 24 Jan 2001. 6'2½". RHB, RMF. Squad No 18. Debut (Yorkshire) 2020. Yorkshire 2nd XI debut 2018. England U19 2018-19. HS 71 v Northants (Northampton) 2021. BB 2-12 v Somerset (Scarborough) 2021. LO HS 90* v Leics (Leicester) 2021 (RLC). LO BB 3-47 v Warwks (York) 2021 (RLC). T20 HS 19*. T20 BB 1-9.

KOHLER-CADMORE, Tom (Malvern C), b Chatham, Kent 19 Aug 1994. 6'2". RHB, OB. Squad No 32. Worcestershire 2014-17. Yorkshire debut 2017; cap 2019. Northern Superchargers 2021. 1000 runs (1): 1004 (2019). HS 176 v Leeds/Brad MCCU (Leeds) 2019. CC HS 169 Wo v Glos (Worcester) 2016. LO HS 164 v Durham (Chester-le-St) 2018 (RLC). T20 HS 127 Wo v Durham (Worcester) 2016 – Wo record, winning Walter Lawrence Trophy for fastest 100 (43 balls).

LEECH, Dominic James (Nunthorpe Ac; Q Ethelburga's S, York), b Middlesbrough 10 Jan 2001. 6'2½". RHB, RMF. Squad No 8. Debut (Yorkshire) 2020. Yorkshire 2nd XI debut 2018. HS 1 v Notts (Nottingham) 2020. BB 2-72 v Derbys (Leeds) 2020.

LOTEN, Thomas William (Pocklington S), b York 8 Jan 1999. 6'5". RHB, RMF. Squad No 40. Debut (Yorkshire) 2019. Yorkshire 2nd XI debut 2018. HS 58 v Warwks (Birmingham) 2019. LO HS –.

LUXTON, William Andrew (Bradford GS), b Keighley 6 May 2003. RHB. Yorkshire 2nd XI debut 2021. Awaiting f-c debut. LO HS 68 v Northants (Scarborough) 2021 (RLC).

LYTH, Adam (Caedmon S, Whitby; Whitby Community C), b Whitby 25 Sep 1987. 5'8". LHB, RM. Squad No 9. Debut (Yorkshire) 2007; cap 2010; testimonial 2020-21. MCC 2017. Northern Superchargers 2021. PCA 2014. *Wisden* 2014. **Tests**: 7 (2015); HS 107 v NZ (Leeds) 2015. F-c Tours (EL): SA 2014-15; WI 2010-11. 1000 runs (3); most – 1619 (2014). HS 251 v Lancs (Manchester) 2014, sharing in Y record 6th wicket partnership of 296 with A.U.Rashid. BB 2-9 v Middx (Scarborough) 2016. LO HS 144 v Lancs (Manchester) 2018 (RLC). LO BB 2-27 v Derbys (Leeds) 2019 (RLC). T20 HS 161 v Northants (Leeds) 2017 – Y & UK record; 5th highest score in all T20 cricket. T20 BB 5-31.

MALAN, Dawid Johannes (Paarl HS), b Roehampton, Surrey 3 Sep 1987. Son of D.J.Malan (WP B and Transvaal B 1978-79 to 1981-82), elder brother of C.C.Malan (Loughborough MCCU 2009-10). 6'0". LHB, LB. Squad No 29. Boland 2005-06. Middlesex 2008-19, scoring 132* v Northants (Uxbridge) on debut; cap 2010; T20 captain 2016-19; captain 2018-19. Yorkshire debut/cap 2020. MCC 2010-11, 2013. IPL: PK 2021. Big Bash: HH 2020-21. Trent Rockets 2021. **ECB Central Contract 2021-22. Tests**: 22 (2017 to 2021-22); HS 140 v A (Perth) 2017-18; BB –. **LOI**: 6 (2019 to 2021); HS 68* v P (Cardiff) 2021. **IT20**: 36 (2017 to 2021-22); HS 103* v NZ (Napier) 2019-20; BB 1-27 v NZ (Hamilton) 2017-18. F-c Tours: A 2017-18, 2021-22; NZ 2017-18. 1000 runs (3); most – 1137 runs (2014). HS 219 v Derbys (Leeds) 2020. BB 5-61 M v Lancs (Liverpool) 2012. Y BB 2-24 v Notts (Nottingham) 2020. LO HS 185* EL v Sri Lanka A (Northampton) 2016. LO BB 4-25 PDSC v Partex (Savar) 2014-15. T20 HS 117. T20 BB 2-10.

PATTERSON, Steven Andrew (Malet Lambert CS; St Mary's SFC, Hull; Leeds U), b Beverley 3 Oct 1983. 6'4". RHB, RMF. Squad No 17. Debut (Yorkshire) 2005; cap 2012; testimonial 2017; captain 2018 (*part*) to date. Bradford/Leeds UCCE 2003 (not f-c). HS 63* v Warwks (Birmingham) 2016. 50 wkts (2); most – 53 (2012). BB 6-40 v Essex (Chelmsford) 2018. LO HS 25* v Worcs (Leeds) 2006 (P40). LO BB 6-32 v Derbys (Leeds) 2010. T20 HS 3*. T20 BB 4-30.

RASHID, Adil Usman (Belle Vue S, Bradford), b Bradford 17 Feb 1988. 5'8". RHB, LBG. Squad No 3. Debut (Yorkshire) 2006; cap 2008; testimonial 2018. Signed white ball only contract in 2020. MCC 2007-09. IPL: PK 2021. Big Bash: AS 2015-16. Northern Superchargers 2021. YC 2007. Match double (114, 48, 8-157 and 2-45) for England U19 v India U19 (Taunton) 2006. **ECB Central Contract 2021-22**. **Tests**: 19 (2015-16 to 2018-19), taking 5-64 v P (Abu Dhabi) on debut; HS 61 v P (Dubai, DSC) 2015-16; BB 5-49 v SL (Colombo, SSC) 2018-19. **LOI**: 112 (2009 to 2021); HS 69 v NZ (Birmingham) 2015; BB 5-27 v Ire (Bristol) 2017. **IT20**: 73 (2009 to 2021-22); HS 22 v WI (Bridgetown) 2021-22; BB 4-2 v WI (Dubai) 2021-22 – E record. F-c Tours: WI 2010-11 (EL), 2018-19; I 2007-08 (EL), 2016-17; SL 2018-19; B 2006-07 (Eng A), 2016-17; UAE 2015-16 (v P). HS 180 v Somerset (Leeds) 2013. 50 wkts (2); most – 65 (2008). BB 7-107 v Hants (Southampton) 2008. LO HS 71 v Glos (Leeds) 2014 (RLC). LO BB 5-27 (*see LOI*). T20 HS 36*. T20 BB 4-2.

REVIS, Matthew Liam (Ilkley GS), b Steeton 15 Nov 2001. 6'4½". RHB, RM. Squad No 77. Debut (Yorkshire) 2019. Yorkshire 2nd XI debut 2019. HS 34 and BB 2-19 v Notts (Nottingham) 2021. LO HS 58* v Somerset (Taunton) 2021 (RLC). LO BB 2-43 v Glamorgan (Cardiff) 2021 (RLC). T20 HS 0*.

ROOT, Joseph Edward (King Ecgbert S, Sheffield; Worksop C), b Sheffield 30 Dec 1990. Elder brother of W.T.Root (*see GLAMORGAN*). 6'0". RHB, OB. Squad No 66. Debut (Yorkshire) 2010; cap 2012. YC 2012. *Wisden* 2013. PCA 2021. **ECB Central Contract 2021-22. Tests**: 115 (2012-13 to 2021-22, 62 as captain); 1000 runs (3); most – 1708 (2021); HS 254 v P (Manchester) 2016; BB 5-8 v I (Ahmedabad) 2020-21. **LOI**: 152 (2012-13 to 2021); HS 133* v B (Oval) 2017; BB 3-52 v Ire (Lord's) 2017. **IT20**: 32 (2012-13 to 2019); HS 90* v A (Southampton) 2013; BB 2-9 v WI (Kolkata) 2015-16. F-c Tours(C=Captain): A 2013-14, 2017-18C, 2021-22C; SA 2015-16, 2019-20C; WI 2014-15, 2018-19C, 2021-22C; NZ 2012-13, 2017-18C, 2019-20C; I 2012-13, 2016-17, 2020-21C; SL 2018-19C, 2019-20C, 2020-21C; B 2016-17; UAE 2015-16 (v P). 1000 runs (3); most – 1228 (2013). HS 254 (*see Tests*). CC HS 236 v Derbys (Leeds) 2013. BB 5-8 (*see Tests*). Y BB 4-5 v Lancs (Manchester) 2018. LO HS 133* (*see LOI*). LO BB 3-52 (*see LOI*). T20 HS 92*. T20 BB 2-7.

SHUTT, Jack William (Kirk Balk S; Thomas Rotherham C), b Barnsley 24 Jun 1997. 6'0". RHB, OB. Squad No 24. Debut (Yorkshire) 2020. Yorkshire 2nd XI debut 2016. HS 7* v Durham (Chester-le-St) 2020. BB 2-14 v Notts (Nottingham) 2020. LO HS 1* (twice). LO BB 1-33 v Somerset (Taunton) 2021 (RLC). T20 HS 0*. T20 BB 5-11.

SULLIVAN, Joshua Richard (Temple Moor S), b Leeds 4 Aug 2000. 5'11½". RHB, LBG. Squad No 4. Yorkshire 2nd XI debut 2018. Awaiting f-c debut. LO HS 6 v Glamorgan (Cardiff) 2021 (RLC). LO BB 4-11 v Derbys (Chesterfield) 2021 (RLC).

TATTERSALL, Jonathan Andrew (King James S, Knaresborough), b Harrogate 15 Dec 1994. 5'8". RHB, WK, occ LB. Squad No 12. Debut (Yorkshire) 2018. Gloucestershire 2021 (on loan). Surrey 2021 (on loan). HS 135* v Leeds/Brad MCCU (Leeds) 2019. CC HS 92 v Notts (Scarborough) 2019. LO HS 89 v Hants (Southampton) 2018 (RLC). T20 HS 53*.

THOMPSON, Jordan Aaron (Benton Park S), b Leeds 9 Oct 1996. 5'11". LHB, RM. Squad No 44. Debut (Yorkshire) 2019. Big Bash: HH 2021-22. Northern Superchargers 2021. HS 98 v Notts (Nottingham) 2020. BB 5-31 Leics (Leeds) 2020. LO BB –. T20 HS 74. T20 BB 4-44.

WAITE, Matthew James (Brigshaw HS), b Leeds 24 Dec 1995. 6'0". RHB, RFM. Squad No 6. Debut (Yorkshire) 2017. No 1st XI appearances in 2020. HS 42 and CC BB 3-91 v Notts (Nottingham) 2018. BB 5-16 v Leeds/Brad MCCU (Leeds) 2019. LO HS 71 v Warwks (Birmingham) 2017 (RLC). LO BB 5-59 v Leics (Leicester) 2021 (RLC). T20 HS 19*. T20 BB 2-17.

WHARTON, James Henry (Holmfirth HS; Greenhead C), b Huddersfield 1 Feb 2001. 6'4". RHB, OB. Squad No 23. Yorkshire 2nd XI debut 2018. Awaiting f-c debut. T20 HS 8.

WILLEY, David Jonathan (Northampton S), b Northampton 28 Feb 1990. Son of P.Willey (Northants, Leics and England 1966-91). 6'1". LHB, LMF. Squad No 15. Northamptonshire 2009-15; cap 2013. Yorkshire debut/cap 2016; captain 2020 to date (T20 only). Bedfordshire 2008. IPL: CSK 2018. Big Bash: PS 2015-16 to 2018-19. **LOI**: 52 (2015 to 2021); HS 51 v Ire (Southampton) 2020; BB 5-30 v Ire (Southampton) 2020 – separate matches. **IT20**: 32 (2015 to 2021); HS 29* v I (Manchester) 2018; BB 4-7 v WI (Basseterre) 2018-19. HS 104* Nh v Glos (Northampton) 2015. Y HS 46 v Warwks (York) 2019. BB 5-29 (10-75 match) Nh v Glos (Northampton) 2011. Y BB 5-61 v Kent (Canterbury) 2021. LO HS 167 Nh v Warwks (Birmingham) 2013 (Y40). LO BB 5-30 (*see LOI*). T20 HS 118. T20 BB 4-7.

WISNIEWSKI, Sam Alex (Yorkshire Foundation Cricket C), b Huddersfield 2 Oct 2001. 5'7½". LHB, SLA. Awaiting f-c debut. T20 BB –.

RELEASED/RETIRED

(Having made a County 1st XI appearance in 2021)

NQ**FERGUSON**, Lachlan Hammond ('**Lockie**'), b Auckland, New Zealand 13 Jun 1991. RHB, RF. Auckland 2012-13 to date. Derbyshire 2018. Yorkshire 2021 (T20 only). IPL: RPS 2017; KKR 2019 to date. Manchester Originals 2021. **Tests** (NZ): 1 (2019-20); HS 1* and BB – v A (Perth) 2019-20. **LOI** (NZ): 37 (2016-17 to 2019-20); HS 19 v E (Mt Maunganui) 2017-18; BB 5-45 v P (Dubai, DSC) 2018-19. **IT20** (NZ): 15 (2016-17 to 2021-22); HS 14 v I (Kolkata) 2021-22; BB 5-21 v WI (Auckland) 2020-21. F-c Tour (NZ): A 2019-20; I 2017-18 (NZA). HS 41 Auckland v Canterbury (Rangiora) 2016-17. CC HS 16 De v Kent (Derby) 2018 and 16 De v Middx (Lord's) 2018. BB 7-34 (12-78 match) Auckland v Otago (Auckland) 2017-18. CC BB 4-56 De v Glos (Derby) 2018. LO HS 24 Auckland v Otago (Auckland) 2016-17. LO BB 6-27 Auckland v ND (Auckland) 2016-17. T20 HS 30. T20 BB 5-21.

NQ**OLIVIER, Duanne**, b Groblersdal, South Africa 9 May 1992. 6'4". RHB, RFM. Free State 2010-11 to 2017-18. Knights 2013-14 to 2018-19. Derbyshire 2018. Yorkshire 2019-21; cap 2020. Gauteng 2021-22. **Tests** (SA): 10 (2016-17 to 2021-22); HS 10* v P (Cape Town) 2018-19 and 10* v I (Cape Town) 2021-22; BB 6-37 (11-96 match) v P (Centurion) 2018-19. **LOI** (SA): 2 (2018-19); HS – ; BB 2-73 v P (Port Elizabeth) 2018-19. F-c Tours (SA): E 2017; A 2016 (SAA); NZ 2021-22; I 2018 (SAA); Z 2016 (SAA). HS 72 FS v Namibia (Bloemfontein) 2014-15. CC HS 40* De v Warwks (Birmingham) 2018. Y HS 24 v Kent (Leeds) 2019. 50 wkts (0+3); most – 64 (2016-17). BB 6-37 (*see Tests*). CC BB 5-20 (10-125 match) De v Durham (Chester-le-St) 2018. Y BB 5-96 v Notts (Nottingham) 2019. LO HS 25* and LO BB 4-34 Knights v Lions (Kimberley) 2017-18. T20 HS 15*. T20 BB 4-28.

NQ**PILLANS, Mathew** William (Pretoria BHS; U of Pretoria), b Durban, South Africa 4 Jul 1991. Qualifies for England in 2023, ancestral visa. 6'6". RHB, RF. Northerns 2012-13. KwaZulu-Natal Inland 2013-14 to 2015-16. Dolphins 2013-14 to 2015-16. Surrey 2016-18. Leicestershire 2017 (on loan). Yorkshire 2018-19. HS 56 Le v Northants (Northampton) 2017. Y HS 8 v Notts (Nottingham) 2018. BB 6-67 (10-129 match) Dolphins v Knights (Durban) 2014-15. CC BB 3-63 Le v Sussex (Arundel) 2017. Y BB 2-34 v Leeds/Brad MCCU (Leeds) 2019. LO HS 40 v Northants (Scarborough) 2021 (RLC). LO BB 5-29 v Leics (Leeds) 2019 (RLC). T20 HS 34*. T20 BB 3-15.

POYSDEN, Joshua Edward (Cardinal Newman S, Hove; Anglia RU), b Shoreham-by-Sea, Sussex 8 Aug 1991. 5'9". LHB, LB. Cambridge MCCU 2011-13. Warwickshire 2015-18. Yorkshire 2018. Unicorns (l-o) 2013. HS 47 CU v Surrey (Cambridge) 2011. CC HS 20* v Lancs (Manchester) 2018. BB 5-29 Wa v Glamorgan (Birmingham) 2018. Y BB 3-128 v Worcs (Scarborough) 2018. LO HS 10* Unicorns v Glos (Wormsley) 2013 (Y40). LO BB 3-33 Unicorns v Middx (Lord's) 2013 (Y40). T20 BB 9*. T20 BB 4-51.

YORKSHIRE 2021

RESULTS SUMMARY

	Place	*Won*	*Lost*	*Drew*	*NR*
LV= Insurance County Champ (Div 1)	5th	6	3	5	
Royal London One-Day Cup (Group 2)	QF	4	3		2
Vitality Blast (North Group)	QF	7	6		1

LV= INSURANCE COUNTY CHAMPIONSHIP AVERAGES
BATTING AND FIELDING

Cap		*M*	*I*	*NO*	*HS*	*Runs*	*Avge*	*100*	*50*	*Ct/St*
2012	G.S.Ballance	10	14	1	101*	594	45.69	1	4	3
2016	D.J.Willey	6	8	4	41*	165	41.25	–	–	1
2010	A.Lyth	14	22	1	153	819	39.00	3	3	25
2021	H.C.Brook	14	22	1	118	797	37.95	2	5	17
2012	J.E.Root	5	8	–	101	291	36.37	1	1	4
	G.C.H.Hill	7	11	–	71	263	23.90	–	2	1
	D.M.Bess	14	20	1	56	399	21.00	–	2	4
	J.A.Thompson	13	20	–	57	411	20.55	–	1	4
2019	T.Kohler-Cadmore	11	18	–	89	353	19.61	–	1	21
	H.G.Duke	9	13	1	54	197	16.41	–	2	31
	J.A.Tattersall	5	8	1	26	101	14.42	–	–	16
	T.W.Loten	2	4	–	27	57	14.25	–	–	–
2012	S.A.Patterson	13	17	2	47*	191	12.73	–	–	3
	M.D.Fisher	5	7	2	17	55	11.00	–	–	1
2018	B.O.Coad	10	13	5	33*	84	10.50	–	–	–
2020	D.Olivier	7	11	5	21	61	10.16	–	–	1
	W.A.R.Fraine	3	6	–	12	35	5.83	–	–	1

Also played: D.J.Leech (1 match) did not bat; D.J.Malan (2 – cap 2020) 199, 9, 12 (2 ct); S.A.Northeast (2) 3, 1.

BOWLING

	O	*M*	*R*	*W*	*Avge*	*Best*	*5wI*	*10wM*
M.D.Fisher	121	29	393	20	19.65	5-41	1	–
J.A.Thompson	329.5	91	949	46	20.63	5-52	1	–
B.O.Coad	287.1	79	766	35	21.88	4-48	–	–
D.J.Willey	148.3	30	479	20	23.95	5-61	1	–
S.A.Patterson	364	111	815	32	25.46	4-26	–	–
D.M.Bess	405.4	122	912	28	32.57	7-43	2	–
D.Olivier	175.1	26	610	18	33.88	4-61	–	–
Also bowled:								
G.C.H.Hill	48	12	128	7	18.28	2-12	–	–
H.C.Brook	82.1	18	194	7	27.71	3-15	–	–

D.J.Leech 17-1-79-0; A.Lyth 13-8-6-0; M.L.Revis 9-2-19-2; J.E.Root 27-4-74-1.

The First-Class Averages (pp 220–232) give the records of Yorkshire players in all first-class county matches, with the exception of D.J.Malan, S.A.Northeast, J.E.Root and J.A.Tattersall, whose first-class figures for Yorkshire are as above.

YORKSHIRE RECORDS

FIRST-CLASS CRICKET

Highest Total	For 887		v	Warwicks	Birmingham	1896
	V 681-7d		by	Leics	Bradford	1996
Lowest Total	For 23		v	Hampshire	Middlesbrough	1965
	V 13		by	Notts	Nottingham	1901
Highest Innings	For 341	G.H.Hirst	v	Leics	Leicester	1905
	V 318*	W.G.Grace	for	Glos	Cheltenham	1876

Highest Partnership for each Wicket

1st	555	P.Holmes/H.Sutcliffe	v	Essex	Leyton	1932
2nd	346	W.Barber/M.Leyland	v	Middlesex	Sheffield	1932
3rd	346	J.J.Sayers/A.McGrath	v	Warwicks	Birmingham	2009
4th	372	J.E.Root/J.M.Bairstow	v	Surrey	Leeds	2016
5th	340	E.Wainwright/G.H.Hirst	v	Surrey	The Oval	1899
6th	296	A.Lyth/A.U.Rashid	v	Lancashire	Manchester	2014
7th	366*	J.M.Bairstow/T.T.Bresnan	v	Durham	Chester-le-St[2]	2015
8th	292	R.Peel/Lord Hawke	v	Warwicks	Birmingham	1896
9th	246	T.T.Bresnan/J.N.Gillespie	v	Surrey	The Oval	2007
10th	149	G.Boycott/G.B.Stevenson	v	Warwicks	Birmingham	1982

Best Bowling	For	10-10	H.Verity	v	Notts	Leeds	1932
(Innings)	V	10-37	C.V.Grimmett	for	Australians	Sheffield	1930
Best Bowling	For	17-91	H.Verity	v	Essex	Leyton	1933
(Match)	V	17-91	H.Dean	for	Lancashire	Liverpool	1913

Most Runs – Season	2883	H.Sutcliffe	(av 80.08)	1932
Most Runs – Career	38558	H.Sutcliffe	(av 50.20)	1919-45
Most 100s – Season	12	H.Sutcliffe		1932
Most 100s – Career	112	H.Sutcliffe		1919-45
Most Wkts – Season	240	W.Rhodes	(av 12.72)	1900
Most Wkts – Career	3597	W.Rhodes	(av 16.02)	1898-1930
Most Career W-K Dismissals	1186	D.Hunter	(863 ct; 323 st)	1888-1909
Most Career Catches in the Field	665	J.Tunnicliffe		1891-1907

LIMITED-OVERS CRICKET

Highest Total	**50ov**	411-6		v	Devon	Exmouth	2004
	40ov	352-6		v	Notts	Scarborough	2001
	T20	260-4		v	Northants	Leeds	2017
Lowest Total	**50ov**	76		v	Surrey	Harrogate	1970
	40ov	54		v	Essex	Leeds	2003
	T20	81		v	Warwicks	Birmingham	2021
Highest Innings	**50ov**	175	T.M.Head	v	Leics	Leicester	2016
	40ov	191	D.S.Lehmann	v	Notts	Scarborough	2001
	T20	161	A.Lyth	v	Northants	Leeds	2017
Best Bowling	**50ov**	7-27	D.Gough	v	Ireland	Leeds	1997
	40ov	7-15	R.A.Hutton	v	Worcs	Leeds	1969
	T20	6-19	T.T.Bresnan	v	Lancashire	Leeds	2017

PROFESSIONAL UMPIRES' TEAM 2022

† New appointment. See page 81 for key to abbreviations.

BAILEY, Robert John (Biddulph HS), b Biddulph, Staffs 28 Oct 1963. 6'3". RHB, OB. Northamptonshire 1982-99; cap 1985; benefit 1993; captain 1996-97. Derbyshire 2000-01; cap 2000. Staffordshire 1980. YC 1984. **Tests:** 4 (1988 to 198990); HS 43 v WI (Oval) 1988. **LOI**: 4 (1984-85 to 1989-90); HS 43* v SL (Oval) 1988. F-c Tours: SA 199192 (Nh); WI 198990; Z 1994-95 (Nh). 1000 runs (13); most – 1987 (1990). HS 224* Nh v Glamorgan (Swansea) 1986. BB 554 Nh v Notts (Northampton) 1993. Fc career: 374 matches; 21844 runs @ 40.52, 47 hundreds; 121 wickets @ 42.51; 272 ct. Appointed 2006. Umpired 24 LOI (2011 to 2021). **ICC International Panel 2011-19.**

BAINTON, Neil Laurence, b Romford, Essex 2 October 1970. No f-c appearances. Appointed 2006.

BALDWIN, Paul Kerr, b Epsom, Surrey 18 Jul 1973. No f-c appearances. Umpired 18 LOI (2006 to 2009). Reserve List 2010-14. Appointed 2015.

BLACKWELL, Ian David (Brookfield Community S), b Chesterfield, Derbys 10 Jun 1978. 6'2". LHB, SLA. Derbyshire 1997-99. Somerset 2000-08; cap 2001; captain 2006 (*part*). Durham 2009-12. Warwickshire 2012 (on loan). MCC 2012. **Tests**: 1 (2005-06); HS 4 and BB-v I (Nagpur) 2005-06. **LOI**: 34 (2002-03 to 2005-06); HS 82 v I (Colombo) 2002-03; BB 3-26 v A (Adelaide) 2002-03. F-c Tour: I 2005-06. 1000 runs (3); most – 1256 (2005). HS 247* Sm v Derbys (Taunton) 2003 – off 156 balls and including 204 off 98 balls in reduced post-lunch session. BB 7-52 Du v Australia A (Chester-le-St) 2012. CC BB 7-85 Du v Lancs (Manchester) 2009. F-c career: 210 matches; 11595 runs @ 39.57, 27 hundreds; 398 wickets @ 35.91; 66 ct. Reserve List 2015-17. Appointed 2018.

BURNS, Michael (Walney CS), b Barrow-in-Furness, Lancs 6 Feb 1969. 6'0". RHB, RM, WK. Warwickshire 1992-96. Somerset 1997-2005; cap 1999; captain 2003-04. 1000 runs (2); most – 1133 (2003). HS 221 Sm v Yorks (Bath) 2001. BB 6-54 Sm v Leics (Taunton) 2001. F-c career: 154 matches; 7648 runs @ 32.68, 8 hundreds; 68 wickets @ 42.42; 142 ct, 7 st. Appointed 2016. Umpired 1 LOI (2020). **ICC International Panel 2020 to date.**

COOK, Nicholas Grant Billson (Lutterworth GS), b Leicester 17 Jun 1956. 6'0". RHB, SLA. Leicestershire 1978-85; cap 1982. Northamptonshire 1986-94; cap 1987; benefit 1995. **Tests:** 15 (1983 to 1989); HS 31 v A (Oval) 1989; BB 6-65 (11-83 match) v P (Karachi) 1983-84. **LOI:** 3 (1983-84 to 1989-90); HS –; BB 2-18 v P (Peshawar) 1987-88. F-c Tours: NZ 1979-80 (DHR), 1983-84; P 1983-84, 1987-88; SL 1985-86 (Eng B); Z 1980-81 (Le), 1984-85 (EC). HS 75 Le v Somerset (Taunton) 1980. 50 wkts (8); most – 90 (1982). BB 7-34 (10-97 match) Nh v Essex (Chelmsford) 1992. F-c career: 356 matches; 3137 runs @ 11.66; 879 wickets @ 29.01; 197 ct. Appointed 2009.

DEBENHAM, Benjamin John, b Chelmsford, Essex 11 Oct 1967. LHB. No f-c appearances. Reserve List 2012-17. Appointed 2018.

GOUGH, Michael Andrew (English Martyrs RCS; Hartlepool SFC), b Hartlepool, Co Durham 18 Dec 1979. Son of M.P.Gough (Durham 1974-77). 6'5". RHB, OB. Durham 1998-2003. F-c Tours (Eng A): NZ 1999-00; B 1999-00. HS 123 Du v CU (Cambridge) 1998. CC HS 103 Du v Essex (Colchester) 2002. BB 5-56 Du v Middx (Chester-le-St) 2001. F-c career: 67 matches; 2952 runs @ 25.44, 2 hundreds; 30 wickets @ 45.00; 57 ct. Reserve List 2006-08. Appointed 2009. Umpired 24 Tests (2016 to 2021-22) and 65 LOI (2013 to 2021). **ICC Elite Panel 2020 to date.**

†**HARRIS, Anthony** Charles, b Durban, South Africa 23 Nov 1973. No f-c appearances. Appointed 2022.

HARTLEY, Peter John (Greenhead GS; Bradford C), b Keighley, Yorks 18 Apr 1960. 6'0". RHB, RMF. Warwickshire 1982. Yorkshire 1985-97; cap 1987; benefit 1996. Hampshire 1998-2000; cap 1998. F-c Tours (Y): SA 199192; WI 198687; Z 1995-96. HS 127* Y v Lancs (Manchester) 1988. 50 wkts (7); most – 81 (1995). BB 941 (inc hat-trick, 4 wkts in 5 balls and 5 in 9; 11-68 match) Y v Derbys (Chesterfield) 1995. Hat-trick 1995. Fc career: 232 matches; 4321 runs @ 19.91, 2 hundreds; 683 wickets @ 30.21; 68 ct. Appointed 2003. Umpired 6 LOI (2007 to 2009). **ICC International Panel 2006-09.**

†**HASSAN ADNAN** (MAO C, Lahore), b Lahore, Pakistan 15 May 1975. 5'9". RHB, OB. Islamabad 1994-95 to 2000-01. WAPDA 1997-98 to 2010-11. Gujranwala 1997-98 to 1998-99. Derbyshire 2003-07; cap 2004. Lahore 2003-04. Pakistan Customs 2009-10. Suffolk 2008-12. 1000 runs (1): 1380 (2004). HS 191 De v Somerset (Taunton) 2005. BB 1-4 De v Glos (Derby) 2006. F-c career: 137 matches; 7609 runs @ 37.11, 10 hundreds; 4 wickets @ 88.00; 76 ct. Reserve list 2020-21. Appointed 2022.

ILLINGWORTH, Richard Keith (Salts GS), b Bradford, Yorks 23 Aug 1963. 5'11". RHB, SLA. Worcestershire 1982-2000; cap 1986; benefit 1997. Natal 198889. Derbyshire 2001. Wiltshire 2005. **Tests:** 9 (1991 to 1995-96); HS 28 v SA (Pt Elizabeth) 1995-96; BB 4-96 v WI (Nottingham) 1995. Took wicket of P.V.Simmons with his first ball in Tests – v WI (Nottingham) 1991. **LOI:** 25 (1991 to 1995-96); HS 14 v P (Melbourne) 1991-92; BB 333 v Z (Albury) 1991-92. F-c Tours: SA 1995-96; NZ 199192; P 199091 (Eng A); SL 199091 (Eng A); Z 198990 (Eng A), 199091 (Wo), 199394 (Wo), 1996-97 (Wo). HS 120* Wo v Warwks (Worcester) 1987 – as night-watchman. Scored 106 for England A v Z (Harare) 1989-90 – also as night-watchman. 50 wkts (5); most – 75 (1990). BB 750 Wo v OU (Oxford) 1985. Fc career: 376 matches; 7027 runs @ 22.45, 4 hundreds; 831 wickets @ 31.54; 161 ct. Appointed 2006. Umpired 57 Tests (2012-13 to 2021) and 71 LOI (2010 to 2021). **ICC Elite Panel 2013 to date.**

KETTLEBOROUGH, Richard Allan (Worksop C), b Sheffield, Yorks 15 Mar 1973. 6'0". LHB, RM. Yorkshire 1994-97. Middlesex 1998-99. F-c Tour (Y): Z 1995-96. HS 108 Y v Essex (Leeds) 1996. BB 2-26 Y v Notts (Scarborough) 1996. Fc career: 33 matches; 1258 runs @ 25.16, 1 hundred; 3 wickets @ 81.00; 20 ct. Appointed 2006. Umpired 72 Tests (2010-11 to 2021) and 92 LOI (2009 to 2021). **ICC Elite Panel 2011 to date.**

LLONG, Nigel James (Ashford North S), b Ashford, Kent 11 Feb 1969. 6'0". LHB, OB. Kent 1990-98; cap 1993. F-c Tour (K): Z 199293. HS 130 K v Hants (Canterbury) 1996. BB 521 K v Middx (Canterbury) 1996. Fc career: 68 matches; 3024 runs @ 31.17, 6 hundreds; 35 wickets @ 35.97; 59 ct. Appointed 2002. Umpired 62 Tests (2007-08 to 2019-20) and 130 LOI (2006 to 2019-20). **ICC Elite Panel 2012-20.**

LLOYD, Graham David (Hollins County HS), b Accrington, Lancs 1 Jul 1969. Son of D.Lloyd (Lancs and England 1965-83). 5'9". RHB, RM. Lancashire 1988-2002; cap 1992; benefit 2001. **LOI:** 6 (1996 to 1998-99); HS 22 v A (Oval) 1997. F-c Tours: A 1992-93 (Eng A); WI 1995-96 (La). 1000 runs (5); most – 1389 (1992). HS 241 La v Essex (Chelmsford) 1996. BB 1-4. F-c career: 203 matches; 11279 runs @ 38.23, 24 hundreds; 2 wickets @ 220.00; 140 ct. Reserve List 2009-13. Appointed 2014.

†**LUNGLEY, Tom** (St John Houghton SS; SE Derbyshire C), b Derby 25 Jul 1979. 6'1". LHB, RM. Derbyshire 2000-10; cap 2007. HS 50 De v Warwks (Derby) 2008. 50 wkts (1): 59 (2007). BB 5-20 De v Leics (Derby) 2007. F-c career: 55 matches; 885 runs @ 14.50; 149 wickets @ 32.10; 25 ct. Reserve list 2015-21. Appointed 2022.

MALLENDER, Neil Alan (Beverley GS), b Kirk Sandall, Yorks 13 Aug 1961. 6'0". RHB, RFM. Northamptonshire 198086 and 1995-96; cap 1984. Somerset 198794; cap 1987; benefit 1994. Otago 198384 to 199293; captain 199091 to 199293. **Tests:** 2 (1992); HS 4 v P (Oval) 1992; BB 550 v P (Leeds) 1992 – on debut. F-c Tour (Nh): Z 1994-95. HS 100* Otago v CD (Palmerston N) 199192. UK HS 87* Sm v Sussex (Hove) 1990. 50 wkts (6); most – 56 (1983). BB 727 Otago v Auckland (Auckland) 198485. UK BB 741 Nh v Derbys (Northampton) 1982. Fc career: 345 matches; 4709 runs @ 17.18, 1 hundred; 937 wickets @ 26.31; 111 ct. Appointed 1999. Umpired 3 Tests (2003-04) and 22 LOI (2001 to 2003-04), including 2002-03 World Cup. **ICC Elite Panel 2004**.

†**MIDDLEBROOK, James** Daniel (Pudsey Crawshaw S), b Leeds, Yorks 13 May 1977. 6'1". RHB, OB. Yorkshire 1998-2015. Essex 2002-09; cap 2003. Northamptonshire 2010-14, cap 2011. MCC 2010, 2013. HS 127 Ex v Middx (Lord's) 2007. 50 wkts (1): 56 (2003). BB 6-78 Nh v Kent (Northampton) 2013. Hat-trick Ex v Kent (Canterbury) 2003. F-c career: 226 matches; 7873 runs @ 27.72, 10 hundreds; 475 wickets @ 38.15; 112 ct. Reserve list 2017-21. Appointed 2022.

MILLNS, David James (Garibaldi CS; N Notts C; Nottingham Trent U), b Clipstone, Notts 27 Feb 1965. 6'3". LHB, RF. Nottinghamshire 1988-89, 2000-01; cap 2000. Leicestershire 1990-99; cap 1991; benefit 1999. Tasmania 1994-95. Boland 1996-97. F-c Tours: A 1992-93 (Eng A); SA 1996-97 (Le). HS 121 Le v Northants (Northampton) 1997. 50 wkts (4); most – 76 (1994). BB 9-37 (12-91 match) Le v Derbys (Derby) 1991. F-c career: 171 matches; 3082 runs @ 22.01, 3 hundreds; 553 wickets @ 27.35; 76 ct. Reserve List 2007-08. Appointed 2009. Umpired 5 LOI (2020 to 2021). **ICC International Panel 2020 to date.**

†**NAEEM ASHRAF**, b Lahore, Pakistan 10 Nov 1972. LHB, LFM. Lahore City 1987-88 to 1998-99. National Bank of Pakistan 1992-93 to 1999-00. Lahore Whites 2000-01. **LOI** (P): 2 (1995); HS 16 v SL (Sharjah) 1995; BB –. HS 139 Lahore City v Gujranwala (Gujranwala) 1997-98. BB 7-41 (10-70 match) NBP v Allied Bank (Lahore) 1997-98. F-c career: 86 matches; 3009 runs @ 26.16, 5 hundreds; 289 wickets @ 24.12; 47 ct. Appointed 2022.

†**NEWELL, Mark** (Hazelwick SS; City of Westminster C), b Crawley, Sussex 19 Dec 1973. Brother of K.Newell (Sussex, Matabeleland and Glamorgan 1995-2001). 6'1½". RHB, OB. Sussex 1996-98. Derbyshire 1999. Buckinghamshire 2007. HS 135* Sx v Derbys (Horsham) 1998. BB –. 24 matches; 889 runs @ 23.39; 3 hundreds; 17 ct. Reserve list 2017-21. Appointed 2022.

O'SHAUGHNESSY, Steven Joseph (Harper Green SS, Franworth), b Bury, Lancs 9 Sep 1961. 5'10½". RHB, RM. Lancashire 1980-87; cap 1985. Worcestershire 1988-89. Scored 100 in 35 min to equal world record for La v Leics (Manchester) 1983. 1000 runs (1): 1167 (1984). HS 159* La v Somerset (Bath) 1984. BB 4-66 La v Notts (Nottingham) 1982. F-c career: 112 matches; 3720 runs @ 24.31, 5 hundreds; 114 wickets @ 36.03; 57 ct. Reserve List 2009-10. Appointed 2011.

POLLARD, Paul Raymond (Gedling CS), b Carlton, Nottingham 24 Sep 1968. 5'11". LHB, RM. Nottinghamshire 1987-98; cap 1992. Worcestershire 1999-2001. F-c Tour (Nt): SA 1996-97. 1000 runs (3); most – 1463 (1993). HS 180 Nt v Derbys (Nottingham) 1993. BB 2-79 Nt v Glos (Bristol) 1993. F-c career: 192 matches; 9685 runs @ 31.44, 15 hundreds; 4 wkts @ 68.00; 158 ct. Reserve List 2012-17. Appointed 2018.

†**PRATT, Neil**, b Bishop Auckland, Co Durham 8 Jun 1972. Brother of A.Pratt (Durham 1997-2004) and G.Pratt (Durham 2000-06). RHB, RM. No f-c appearances. Reserve list 2020-21. Appointed 2022.

†**REDFERN, Suzanne**, b Mansfield, Notts 26 Oct 1977. LHB, LM. MBE 2018. **Tests**: 6 (1995-96 to 1999); HS 30 v NZ (Worcester) 1996; BB 2-27 v I (Shenley) 1999. **LOI**: 15 (1995 to 1999); HS 27 v I (Nottingham) 1999; BB 4-21 v SA (Bristol) 1997. Test career: 6 matches; 146 runs @ 29.20; 6 wickets @ 64.50; 5 ct. Appointed 2022.

ROBINSON, Robert **Tim**othy (Dunstable GS; High Pavement SFC; Sheffield U), b Sutton in Ashfield, Notts 21 Nov 1958. 6'0". RHB, RM. Nottinghamshire 1978-99; cap 1983; captain 198895; benefit 1992. *Wisden* 1985. **Tests:** 29 (198485 to 1989); HS 175 v A (Leeds) 1985. **LOI**: 26 (1984-85 to 1988); HS 83 v P (Sharjah) 1986-87. F-c Tours: A 198788; SA 198990 (Eng XI), 1996-97 (Nt); NZ 198788; WI 198586; I/SL 198485; P 198788. 1000 runs (14) inc 2000 (1): 2032 (1984). HS 220* Nt v Yorks (Nottingham) 1990. BB 122. Fc career: 425 matches; 27571 runs @ 42.15, 63 hundreds; 4 wickets @ 72.25; 257 ct. Appointed 2007. Umpired 17 LOI (2013 to 2021). **ICC International Panel 2012-19.**

SAGGERS, Martin John (Springwood HS, King's Lynn; Huddersfield U), b King's Lynn, Norfolk 23 May 1972. 6'2". RHB, RMF. Durham 1996-98. Kent 1999-2009; cap 2001; benefit 2009. MCC 2004. Essex 2007 (on loan). Norfolk 1995-96. **Tests**: 3 (2003-04 to 2004); HS 1 and BB 2-29 v B (Chittagong) 2003-04 – on debut. F-c Tour: B 2003-04. HS 64 K v Worcs (Canterbury) 2004. 50 wkts (4); most – 83 (2002). BB 7-79 K v Durham (Chester-le-St) 2000. F-c career: 119 matches; 1165 runs @ 11.20; 415 wickets @ 25.33; 27 ct. Reserve List 2010-11. Appointed 2012. Umpired 2 LOI (2020). **ICC International Panel 2020 to date.**

†**SHANMUGAM**, Surendiran ('**Suri**') (Sri Krishna C of Engineering & Technology; Manchester U), b Coimbatore, Tamil Nadu, India 2 Jun 1984. Appointed 2022.

†**SHANTRY, Jack** David (Priory SS; Shrewsbury SFC; Liverpool U), b Shrewsbury, Shrops 29 Jan 1988. Son of B.K.Shantry (Gloucestershire 1978-79), brother of A.J.Shantry (Northants, Warwicks, Glamorgan 2003-11). 6'4". LHB, LM. Worcestershire 2009-17. Shropshire 2007-09. HS 106 v Glos (Worcester) 2016. 50 wkts (2); most – 67 (2015). BB 7-60 v Oxford MCCU (Oxford) 2013. CC BB 7-69 v Essex (Worcester) 2013. F-c career: 92 matches; 1640 runs @ 19.06, 2 hundreds; 266 wickets @ 29.25; 30 ct. Appointed 2022.

TAYLOR, Billy Victor (Bitterne Park S, Southampton), b Southampton 11 Jan 1977. Younger brother of J.L.Taylor (Wiltshire 1998-2002). 6'3". LHB, RMF. Sussex 1999-2003. Hampshire 2004-09; cap 2006; testimonial 2010. Wiltshire 1996-98. HS 40 v Essex (Southampton) 2004. BB 6-32 v Middlesex (Southampton) 2006 (inc hat-trick). F-c career: 54 matches; 431 runs @10.26; 136 wickets @ 33.34; 6 ct. Reserve list 2011-16. Appointed 2017.

WARREN, Russell John (Kingsthorpe Upper S), b Northampton 10 Sep 1971. 6'1". RHB, OB, WK. Northamptonshire 1992-2002; cap 1995. Nottinghamshire 2003-06; cap 2004. 1000 runs (1): 1030 (2001). HS 201* Nh v Glamorgan (Northampton) 2001. F-c career: 146 matches; 7776 runs @ 36.67, 15 hundreds; 128 ct, 5 st. Reserve List: 2015-17. Appointed 2018.

†**WATTS, Christopher** Mark (Stalham HS; Paston C), b Acle, Norfolk 3 Jul 1967. No f-c appearances. Reserve list 2015-21. Appointed 2022.

WHARF, Alexander George (Buttershaw Upper S; Thomas Danby C), b Bradford, Yorks 4 Jun 1975. 6'5". RHB, RMF. Yorkshire 1994-97. Nottinghamshire 1998-99. Glamorgan 2000-08, scoring 100* v OU (Oxford) on debut; cap 2000; benefit 2009. **LOI**: 13 (2004 to 2004-05); HS 9 v India (Lord's) 2004; BB 4-24 v Z (Harare) 2004-05. F-c Tour (Eng A): WI 2005-06. HS 128* Gm v Glos (Bristol) 2007. 50 wkts (1): 52 (2003). BB 6-59 Gm v Glos (Bristol) 2005. F-c career: 121 matches; 3570 runs @ 23.03, 6 hundreds; 293 wickets @ 37.34; 63 ct. Reserve List 2011-13. Appointed 2014. Umpired 2 Tests (2021) and 8 LOI (2018 to 2021). **ICC International Panel 2018 to date.**

†**WHITE, Rob**ert Allan (Stowe S; Durham U; Loughborough U), b Chelmsford, Essex 15 Oct 1979. 5'11". RHB, LB. Northamptonshire 2000-12; cap 2008. Loughborough UCCE 2003. British U 2003. 1000 runs (1): 1037 (2008). HS 277 and BB 2-30 v Glos (Northampton) 2002 – highest maiden f-c hundred in UK; included 107 before lunch on first day. F-c career: 112 matches; 5706 runs @ 32.98, 8 hundreds; 18 wickets @ 59.50; 67 ct. Reserve list 2018-21. Appointed 2022.

Test Match and LOI statistics to 6 March 2022.

TOURING TEAMS REGISTER 2021

NEW ZEALAND

Full Names	*Birthdate*	*Birthplace*	*Team*	*Type*	*F-C Debut*
BLUNDELL, Thomas Ackland	01.09.90	Wellington	Wellington	RHB/WK	2012-13
BOULT, Trent Alexander	22.07.89	Rotorua	Northern D	RHB/LFM	2008-09
CONWAY, Devon Philip	08.07.91	Johannesburg, SA	Wellington	LHB/RM	2008-09
DE GRANDHOMME, Colin	22.07.86	Harare, Zim	Northern D	RHB/RMF	2005-06
HENRY, Matthew James	14.12.91	Christchurch	Canterbury	RHB/RFM	2010-11
JAMIESON, Kyle Alex	30.12.94	Auckland	Auckland	RHB/RFM	2014-15
LATHAM, Thomas William Maxwell	02.04.92	Christchurch	Canterbury	LHB/WK	2010-11
MITCHELL, Daryl Joseph	20.05.91	Hamilton	Canterbury	RHB/RM	2011-12
NICHOLLS, Henry Michael	15.11.91	Christchurch	Canterbury	LHB/OB	2011-12
PATEL, Ajaz Yunus	21.10.88	Bombay, India	Central D	LHB/SLA	2012-13
SANTNER, Mitchell Josef	05.02.92	Hamilton	Northern D	LHB/SLA	2011-12
SOUTHEE, Timothy Grant	11.12.88	Whangarei	Northern D	RHB/RMF	2006-07
TAYLOR, Luteru Ross Poutoa Lote	08.03.84	Lower Hutt	Central D	RHB/OB	2002-03
WAGNER, Neil	13.03.86	Pretoria, SA	Northern D	LHB/LMF	2005-06
WATLING, Bradley-John	09.07.85	Durban, SA	Northern D	RHB/WK	2004-05
WILLIAMSON, Kane Stuart	08.08.90	Tauranga	Northern D	RHB/OB	2007-08
YOUNG, William Alexander	22.11.92	New Plymouth	Central D	RHB/OB	2011-12

INDIA

Full Names	*Birthdate*	*Birthplace*	*Team*	*Type*	*F-C Debut*
AGARWAL, Mayank Anurag	16.02.91	Bangalore	Karnataka	RHB/OB	2013-14
ASHWIN, Ravichandran	17.09.86	Madras	Tamil Nadu	RHB/OB	2006-07
BUMRAH, Jasprit Jasbirsingh	06.12.93	Ahmedabad	Gujarat	RHB/RFM	2013-14
GILL, Shubman	08.09.99	Firozpur	Punjab	RHB/OB	2017-18
JADEJA, Ravindrasinh Anirudsinh	06.12.88	Navagam-Khed	Saurashtra	LHB/SLA	2006-07
KOHLI, Virat	05.11.88	Delhi	Delhi	RHB/RM	2006-07
MOHAMMED SHAMI	03.09.90	Jonagar	Bengal	RHB/RFM	2010-11
PANT, Rishabh Rajendra	04.10.97	Haridwar	Delhi	LHB/WK	2015-16
PATEL, Axar Rajeshbhai	20.01.94	Anand	Gujarat	LHB/SLA	2012-13
PUJARA, Cheteshwar Arvindbhai	25.01.88	Rajkot	Saurashtra	RHB/LB	2005-06
RAHANE, Ajinkya Madhukar	06.06.88	Ashwi Khurd	Mumbai	RHB/RM	2007-08
RAHUL, Kannur Lokesh	18.04.92	Bangalore	Karnataka	RHB/OB	2010-11
SHARMA, Ishant	02.09.88	Delhi	Delhi	RHB/RFM	2006-07
SHARMA, Rohit Gurunath	30.04.87	Bansod	Mumbai	RHB/OB	2006-07
SIRAJ, Mohammed	13.03.94	Hyderabad	Hyderabad	RHB/RFM	2015-16
THAKUR, Shardul Narendra	16.10.91	Palghar	Mumbai	RHB/RFM	2012-13
VIHARI, Gade Hanuma	13.10.93	Kakinada	Hyderabad	RHB/OB	2010-11
YADAV, Umesh Tilak	25.10.87	Nagpur	Vidarbha	RHB/RFM	2008-09

THE 2021 FIRST-CLASS SEASON STATISTICAL HIGHLIGHTS

FIRST TO INDIVIDUAL TARGETS

1000 RUNS	R.J.Burns	Surrey and England	5 September
2000 RUNS	–	Most – 1176 T.J.Haines (Sussex)	
50 WICKETS	O.E.Robinson	Sussex and England	25 August
100 WICKETS	–	Most – 66 L.J.Fletcher (Nottinghamshire)	

TEAM HIGHLIGHTS († Team record)
HIGHEST INNINGS TOTALS

722-4d	Surrey v Glamorgan	The Oval
676-5d†	Middlesex v Sussex	Hove
672-8d	Surrey v Leicestershire	The Oval
672-6d	Glamorgan v Surrey	The Oval
612-5d	Hampshire v Leicestershire	Leicester
561-8d	Essex v Worcestershire	Worcester
560-7d	Surrey v Hampshire	The Oval
558	Yorkshire v Sussex	Leeds

HIGHEST FOURTH INNINGS TOTAL

378-5	Leicestershire (set 378) v Middlesex	Leicester
375-8	Kent (set 373) v Middlesex	Canterbury
357-3	Northamptonshire (set 355) v Glamorgan	Northampton

LOWEST INNINGS TOTALS

45	Northamptonshire v Essex (*2nd inns*)	Chelmsford
69	Somerset v Surrey	The Oval
72	Surrey v Hampshire	Southampton
73	Yorkshire v Nottinghamshire	Nottingham
74	Kent v Glamorgan	Cardiff
74	Kent v Lancashire	Manchester
76	Gloucestershire v Essex	Chelmsford
78	India v England	Leeds
78	Lancashire v Warwickshire	Lord's
79	Middlesex v Hampshire	Southampton
79	Hampshire v Somerset	Southampton
80	Worcestershire v Nottinghamshire	Nottingham

HIGHEST MATCH AGGREGATE

1439-28	Northants (407 & 311-5d) v Glamorgan (364 & 357-3)	Northampton

LOWEST MATCH AGGREGATE

296-30	Northamptonshire (81 & 45) v Essex (170)	Chelmsford

BATSMEN'S MATCH (Qualification: 1200 runs, average 60 per wicket)

(139.40)	1394-10	Glamorgan (672-6d) v Surrey (722-4)	The Oval
(63.90)	1342-21	Leicestershire (375 & 295-3) v Surrey (672-8d)	The Oval

LARGE MARGINS OF VICTORY

310 runs	Nottinghamshire (256 & 318) beat Derbyshire (105 & 159)	Derby
Inns & 289 runs	Surrey (560-7d) beat Hampshire (92 & 179)	The Oval

NARROW MARGINS OF VICTORY

1 run	Yorkshire (206 & 247) beat Northants (234 & 218)	Leeds
1 wkt	Lancashire (141 & 198-9) beat Hampshire (143 & 193)	Liverpool
2 wkts	Northamptonshire (171 & 322-8) beat Surrey (252 & 238)	Northampton
2 wkts	Kent (138 & 375-8) beat Middlesex (147 & 363)	Canterbury

MOST EXTRAS IN AN INNINGS

	B	*LB*	*W*	*NB*		
81	48	11	2	20	Hampshire (486-7d) v Gloucestershire	Cheltenham

Under ECB regulations, Test matches excluded, two penalty extras were scored for each no-ball.

BATTING HIGHLIGHTS
DOUBLE HUNDREDS

H.M.Amla	215*	Surrey v Hampshire	The Oval
D.G.Bedingham	257	Durham v Derbyshire	Chester-le-St
D.P.Conway	200	New Zealand v England	Lord's
C.B.Cooke	205*	Glamorgan v Surrey	The Oval
O.J.D.Pope (2)	245	Surrey v Leicestershire	The Oval
	274	Surrey v Glamorgan	The Oval
S.D.Robson	253	Middlesex v Sussex	Hove
J.M.Vince	231	Hampshire v Leicestershire	Leicester
T.Westley	213	Essex v Worcestershire	Chelmsford

HUNDRED IN EACH INNINGS OF A MATCH

K.S.Carlson	127*	132	Glamorgan v Sussex	Cardiff
H.Hameed	111	114*	Nottinghamshire v Worcestershire	Worcester

MOST SIXES IN AN INNINGS

15	D.I.Stevens (190)	Kent v Glamorgan	Canterbury

150 RUNS OR MORE FROM BOUNDARIES IN AN INNINGS

Runs	*6s*	*4s*			
156	2	36	J.M.Vince	Hampshire v Leicestershire	Leicester
150	15	15	D.I.Stevens	Kent v Glamorgan	Canterbury

HUNDRED ON FIRST-CLASS DEBUT IN BRITAIN

D.P.Conway	200	New Zealand v England	Lord's

CARRYING BAT THROUGH COMPLETED INNINGS

J.D.Libby	180*	Worcestershire (475) v Essex	Chelmsford

60% OF A COMPLETE INNINGS TOTAL

61.88%	D.I.Stevens	Kent (190/307) v Glamorgan	Canterbury

LONG INNINGS (Qualification 600 mins and/or 400 balls)

Mins	*Balls*			
540	410	D.G.Bedingham (257)	Durham v Derbyshire	Chester-le-St
681	496	J.D.Libby (180*)	Worcestershire v Essex	Chelmsford
538	408	T.Westley (213)	Essex v Worcestershire	Chelmsford

BATTING FOR AN HOUR OR MORE WITHOUT SCORING

M.L.Cummins (1*)	108 mins	Kent v Glamorgan	Canterbury

The longest scoreless spell in all first-class cricket in England.

FIRST-WICKET PARTNERSHIP OF 100 IN EACH INNINGS

115/236*	B.T.Slater/H.Hameed	Nottinghamshire v Worcestershire	Worcester

OTHER NOTABLE PARTNERSHIPS

Qualifications: 1st-4th wkts: 250 runs; 5th-6th: 225; 7th: 200; 8th: 175; 9th: 150; 10th: 100; highest partnership for that wicket otherwise. († Team record)

First Wicket

376†	S.D.Robson/M.D.Stoneman	Middlesex v Sussex	Hove

Second Wicket

228	I.G.Holland/T.P.Alsop	Hampshire v Gloucestershire	Southampton

Third Wicket

362	H.M.Amla/O.J.D.Pope	Surrey v Glamorgan	The Oval
257	H.M.Amla/O.J.D.Pope	Surrey v Hampshire	The Oval
257	I.G.Holland/S.A.Northeast	Hampshire v Middlesex	Southampton

Fourth Wicket

229	O.J.D.Pope/B.T.Foakes	Surrey v Leicestershire	The Oval

Fifth Wicket

307*†	K.S.Carlson/C.B.Cooke	Glamorgan v Northants	Cardiff
254*†	D.G.Bedingham/E.J.H.Eckersley	Durham v Nottinghamshire	Nottingham
234	O.J.D.Pope/J.L.Smith	Surrey v Leicestershire	The Oval

Sixth Wicket

227†	B.D.Guest/A.K.Dal	Derbyshire v Leicestershire	Derby

Seventh Wicket

244	J.D.Libby/E.G.Barnard	Worcestershire v Essex	Chelmsford

Eighth Wicket

203*†	H.J.Swindells/E.Barnes	Leicestershire v Somerset	Taunton
187†	L.Wood/D.J.Lamb	Lancashire v Kent	Canterbury

Ninth Wicket

166	D.I.Stevens/M.L.Cummins	Kent v Glamorgan	Canterbury

D.I.Stevens made 160 out of this partnership. At 96.39%, this was the highest share of any century-plus partnership on record; Cummins scored 1.

Tenth Wicket

114	C.de Grandhomme/B.T.J.Wheal	Hampshire v Surrey	Southampton

BOWLING HIGHLIGHTS
EIGHT OR MORE WICKETS IN AN INNINGS

S.R.Harmer	9-80	Essex v Derbyshire	Chelmsford
K.A.J.Roach	8-40	Surrey v Hampshire	The Oval
O.E.Robinson	9-78	Sussex v Glamorgan	Cardiff

TEN OR MORE WICKETS IN A MATCH

K.J.Abbott	11- 85	Hampshire v Middlesex	Lord's
S.J.Cook	10- 41	Essex v Northamptonshire	Chelmsford
L.J.Fletcher	10- 57	Nottinghamshire v Worcestershire	Nottingham
S.R.Harmer (2)	10-136	Essex v Durham	Chelmsford
	12-202	Essex v Derbyshire	Chelmsford
L.B.K.Hollman	10-155	Middlesex v Sussex	Hove
C.F.Parkinson	10-108	Leicestershire v Gloucestershire	Leicester
W.D.Parnell	10-143	Northamptonshire v Yorkshire	Leeds
D.A.Payne	11- 87	Gloucestershire v Middlesex	Lord's
K.A.J.Roach	10- 80	Surrey v Hampshire	The Oval
O.E.Robinson	13-128	Sussex v Glamorgan	Cardiff
B.W.Sanderson	10- 99	Northamptonshire v Sussex	Northampton
Zafar Gohar	11-101	Gloucestershire v Durham	Bristol

HAT-TRICK

Mohammad Abbas		Hampshire v Middlesex	Southampton

MOST RUNS CONCEDED IN AN INNINGS

J.J.Carson	46-4-183-2	Sussex v Middlesex	Hove

MOST OVERS BOWLED IN AN INNINGS

S.R.Harmer	61.3-20-126-3	Essex v Worcestershire	Chelmsford

WICKET-KEEPING HIGHLIGHTS
SIX WICKET-KEEPING DISMISSALS IN AN INNINGS

H.G.Duke	6ct	Yorkshire v Nottinghamshire	Nottingham

EIGHT WICKET-KEEPING DISMISSALS IN A MATCH

T.A.Blundell	8ct	New Zealand v England	Birmingham
M.G.K.Burgess	7ct, 1st	Warwickshire v Derbyshire	Derby
J.C.Buttler	8ct	England v India	Leeds
O.G.Robinson	8ct	Kent v Northamptonshire	Cantderbury
T.J.Moores	7ct, 1st	Nottinghamshire v Somerset	Taunton
J.A.Simpson	6ct, 2st	Middlesex v Sussex	Hove

FIELDING HIGHLIGHTS
FOUR OR MORE CATCHES IN THE FIELD IN AN INNINGS

M.M.Ali	4ct	England v India	The Oval
T.T.Bresnan	6ct	Warwickshire v Yorkshire	Leeds
L.A.Dawson	4ct	Hampshire v Leicestershire	Leicester
J.A.Leaning	4ct	Kent v Derbyshire	Derby
W.L.Madsen	4ct	Derbyshire v Warwickshire	Derby
J.A.Simpson	5ct	Middlesex v Gloucestershire	Cheltenham

SIX OR MORE CATCHES IN THE FIELD IN A MATCH

M.M.Ali	6ct	England v India	The Oval
T.T.Bresnan	7ct	Warwickshire v Yorkshire	Leeds
R.Clarke	6ct	Surrey v Hampshire	The Oval
R.N.ten Doeschate	6ct	Essex v Derbyshire	Chelmsford

LV= INSURANCE COUNTY CHAMPIONSHIP 2021
GROUP TABLES

GROUP 1

		P	W	L	T	D	Bonus Bat	Points Bowl	Deduct Points	Total Points
1	Nottinghamshire	10	4	2	–	4	26	29	–	151
2	Warwickshire	10	4	1	–	5	17	25	1	145
3	Durham	10	3	2	–	5	17	30	3	132
4	Essex	10	3	2	–	5	15	26	–	129
5	Worcestershire	10	1	3	–	6	24	21	–	109
6	Derbyshire	10	–	5	–	5	10	23	1	72

GROUP 2

		P	W	L	T	D	Bonus Bat	Points Bowl	Deduct Points	Total Points
1	Somerset	10	4	1	–	5	26	26	8	148
2	Hampshire	10	4	2	–	4	23	26	–	145
3	Gloucestershire	10	5	3	–	2	14	21	–	131
4	Surrey	10	2	2	–	6	19	24	–	123
5	Leicestershire	10	2	4	–	4	22	25	–	111
6	Middlesex	10	2	7	–	1	15	30	1	84

GROUP 3

		P	W	L	T	D	Bonus Bat	Points Bowl	Deduct Points	Total Points
1	Lancashire	10	4	1	–	5	22	24	–	150
2	Yorkshire	10	5	1	–	4	14	23	–	149
3	Glamorgan	10	2	2	–	6	18	29	–	127
4	Northamptonshire	10	3	3	–	4	22	21	–	123
5	Kent	10	–	3	–	7	15	26	–	97
6	Sussex	10	1	5	–	4	18	28	–	94

Derbyshire, Durham, Middlesex and Warwickshire deducted point(s) for a slow over rate. Somerset deducted 8 points for a poor pitch in 2019.

SCORING OF CHAMPIONSHIP POINTS 2021

(a) For a win, 16 points, plus any points scored in the first innings.

(b) In a tie, each side to score eight points, plus any points scored in the first innings.

(c) In a drawn match, each side to score eight points, plus any points scored in the first innings (see also paragraph (e) below).

(d) **First Innings Points** (awarded only for performances **in the first 110 overs** of each first innings and retained whatever the result of the match).

(i) A maximum of five batting points to be available as under:
200 to 249 runs – 1 point; 250 to 299 runs – 2 points; 300 to 349 runs – 3 points; 350 to 399 runs – 4 points; 400 runs or over – 5 points.

(ii) A maximum of three bowling points to be available as under:
3 to 5 wickets taken – 1 point; 6 to 8 wickets taken – 2 points; 9 to 10 wickets taken – 3 points.

(e) If a match is abandoned without a ball being bowled, each side to score five points.

(f) The top two sides from each Group went through to Division 1; the sides third and fourth went through to Division 2; the fifth and sixth went through to Division 3. Should any sides in the Championship table be equal on points, the following tie-breakers will be applied in the order stated: most wins, fewest losses, team achieving most points in contests between teams level on points, most wickets taken, most runs scored.

COUNTY CHAMPIONSHIP RESULTS 2021

DIVISION 1

	DERBYS	DURHAM	ESSEX	NOTTS	WARKS	WORCS
DERBYS		Derby	Derby	Derby	Derby	Derby
		Drawn	Drawn	Nt 310	Wa 191	Drawn
DURHAM	C-le-St		C-le-St	C-le-St	C-le-St	C-le-St
	Drawn		Ex 195	Drawn	Du I/127	Du 258
ESSEX	C'ford	C'ford		C'ford	C'ford	C'ford
	Ex I/15	Ex 44		Drawn	Drawn	Drawn
NOTTS	N'ham	N'ham	N'ham		N'ham	N'ham
	Nt I/36	Drawn	Nt I/30		Wa 3w	Nt I/170
WARKS	Birm	Birm	Birm	Birm		Birm
	Drawn	Drawn	Wa 7w	Wa 170		Drawn
WORCS	Worcs	Worcs	Worcs	Worcs	Worcs	
	Wo I/23	Du 10w	Drawn	Drawn	Drawn	

DIVISION 2

	GLOS	HANTS	LEICS	MIDDX	SOM'T	SURREY
GLOS		Chelt	Bristol	Chelt	Bristol	Bristol
		H 7w	Gs 4w	Gs 164	Drawn	Gs 8w
HANTS	So'ton		So'ton	So'ton	So'ton	So'ton
	Drawn		Drawn	H 249	Sm 10w	Drawn
LEICS	Leics	Leics		Leics	Leics	Leics
	Le I/93	H I/105		Le 5w	Sm 9w	Drawn
MIDDX	Lord's	Lord's	N'wood		Lord's	Lord's
	Gs 7w	H 7w	M 121		Sm 4w	M 10w
SOM'T	Taunton	Taunton	Taunton	Taunton		Taunton
	Gs 8w	Drawn	Drawn	Sm 4w		Drawn
SURREY	Oval	Oval	Oval	Oval	Oval	
	Sy I/47	Sy I/289	Drawn	Drawn	Drawn	

DIVISION 3

	GLAM	KENT	LANCS	N'HANTS	SUSSEX	YORKS
GLAM		Cardiff	Cardiff	Cardiff	Cardiff	Cardiff
		Gm 10w	Gm 6w	Drawn	Sx 8w	Drawn
KENT	Cant		Cant	Cant	Beck	Cant
	Drawn		La I/5	Drawn	Drawn	Y 200
LANCS	Man	Man		Man	Man	Man
	Drawn	Drawn		La 206	Drawn	La I/79
N'HANTS	No'ton	No'ton	No'ton		No'ton	No'ton
	Nh 7w	Drawn	Drawn		Nh I/120	Y 53
SUSSEX	Hove	Hove	Hove	Hove		Hove
	Drawn	Drawn	La 5w	Nh 7w		Y 48
YORKS	Leeds	Leeds	Leeds	Leeds	Leeds	
	Drawn	Drawn	Drawn	Y 1	Y I/30	

LV= INSURANCE COUNTY CHAMPIONSHIP 2021 DIVISIONAL TABLES

DIVISION 1

		P	W	L	T	D	Bonus Bat	Points Bowl	Adjust Points	Total Points
1	**Warwickshire**	4	2	1	–	1	6	10	21	77
2	Lancashire	4	2	1	–	1	7	10	16.5	73.5
3	Nottinghamshire	4	3	1	–	–	8	12	5	73
4	Hampshire	4	2	1	–	1	1	12	8.5	61.5
5	Yorkshire	4	1	2	–	1	4	12	4.5	44.5
6	Somerset	4	–	4	–	–	3	11	17.5	31.5

DIVISION 2

		P	W	L	T	D	Bonus Bat	Points Bowl	Adjust Points	Total Points
1	Essex	4	3	–	–	1	9	12	19	99
2	Gloucestershire	4	3	1	–	–	4	12	12	76
3	Durham	3	1	1	–	1	7	9	4	44
4	Northamptonshire	4	1	2	–	1	3	11	16	54
5	Surrey	3	–	1	–	2	6	5	13	40
6	Glamorgan	4	–	3	–	1	8	7	11.5	34.5

DIVISION 3

		P	W	L	T	D	Bonus Bat	Points Bowl	Adjust Points	Total Points
1	Kent	4	4	–	–	–	7	12	11	94
2	Middlesex	4	3	1	–	–	7	12	13	80
3	Worcestershire	4	2	2	–	–	5	12	18.5	67.5
4	Leicestershire	4	1	2	–	1	9	10	11.5	54.5
5	Derbyshire	4	1	2	–	1	8	10	9.5	51.5
6	Sussex	4	–	4	–	–	12	6	12	30

Each county did not play the team that was in their Group, but carried forward into the Division stage half the total points they scored in the two matches against that county in the Group stage.
Somerset were deducted one point for a slow over rate.
The top two sides progressed to compete in the Bob Willis Trophy final.

Bob Willis Trophy Final
At Lord's, 28 September-1 October. Toss: Warwickshire. **WARWICKSHIRE** won by an innings and 199 runs. Lancashire 78 (C.N.Miles 5-28) and 241 (G.P.Balderson 65). Warwickshire 518 (W.M.H.Rhodes 156, R.M.Yates 113, D.P.Sibley 57, S.R.Hain 55).

COUNTY CHAMPIONSHIP DIVISIONAL RESULTS

Division 1

At Southampton, 30 August-2 September, Hampshire drew with Yorkshire.
At Manchester, 30 August-2 September, Lancashire drew with Warwickshire.
At Taunton, 30 August-1 September, Nottinghamshire beat Somerset by an innings and 160 runs.
At Nottingham, 5-8 September, Nottinghamshire beat Lancashire by 102 runs.
At Birmingham, 5-8 September, Hampshire beat Warwickshire by 60 runs.
At Scarborough, 5-6 September, Yorkshire beat Somerset by an innings and 33 runs.
At Southampton, 12-14 September, Hampshire beat Nottinghamshire by 122 runs.
At Taunton, 12-14 September, Lancashire beat Somerset by ten wickets.
At Leeds, 12-15 September, Warwickshire beat Yorkshire by 106 runs.
At Liverpool, 21-3 September, Lancashire beat Hampshire by one wicket.
At Nottingham, 21-4 September, Nottinghamshire beat Yorkshire by five wickets.
At Birmingham, 21-4 September, Warwickshire beat Somerset by 118 runs.

Division 2

At Chester-le-Street, 30 August-2 September, Durham v Surrey abandoned (Covid outbreak).
At Cardiff, 30 August-1 September, Essex beat Glamorgan by an innings and 74 runs.
At Bristol, 30 August-2 September, Gloucestershire beat Northamptonshire by six wickets.
At Chester-le-Street, 5-8 September, Durham beat Glamorgan by an innings and 42 runs.
At Chelmsford, 5-7 September, Essex beat Gloucestershire by an innings and 3 runs.
At Northampton, 5-8 September, Northamptonshire beat Surrey by two wickets.
At Cardiff, 12-15 September, Gloucestershire beat Glamorgan by ten wickets.
At Northampton, 12-15 September, Northamptonshire drew with Durham.
At The Oval, 12-15 September, Surrey drew with Essex.
At Chelmsford, 21-2 September, Essex beat Northamptonshire by an innings and 44 runs.
At Bristol, 21-2 September, Gloucestershire beat Durham by seven wickets.
At The Oval, 21-4 September, Surrey drew with Glamorgan.

Division 3

At Leicester, 30 August-1 September, Kent beat Leicestershire by 132 runs.
At Lord's, 30 August-2September, Middlesex beat Derbyshire by 112 runs.
At Worcester, 30 August-2 September, Worcestershire beat Sussex by six wickets.
At Derby, 5-8 September, Derbyshire drew with Leicestershire.
At Canterbury, 5-7 September, Kent beat Worcestershire by an innings and 56 runs.
At Hove, 6-9 September, Middlesex beat Sussex by an innings and 54 runs.
At Derby, 12-15 September, Kent beat Derbyshire by 130 runs.
At Leicester, 12-15 September, Leicestershire beat Sussex by an innings and 5 runs.
At Lord's, 12-15 September, Middlesex beat Worcestershire by 101 runs.
At Canterbury, 21-4 September, Kent beat Middlesex by two wickets.
At Hove, 21-3 September, Derbyshire beat Sussex by nine wickets.
At Worcester, 21-3 September, Worcestershire beat Leicestershire by ten wickets.

COUNTY CHAMPIONS

The English County Championship was not officially constituted until December 1889. Prior to that date there was no generally accepted method of awarding the title; although the 'least matches lost' method existed, it was not consistently applied. Rules governing playing qualifications were agreed in 1873 and the first unofficial points system 15 years later.

Research has produced a list of champions dating back to 1826, but at least seven different versions exist for the period from 1864 to 1889 (see *The Wisden Book of Cricket Records*). Only from 1890 can any authorised list of county champions commence.

That first official Championship was contested between eight counties: Gloucestershire, Kent, Lancashire, Middlesex, Nottinghamshire, Surrey, Sussex and Yorkshire. The remaining counties were admitted in the following seasons: 1891 – Somerset, 1895 – Derbyshire, Essex, Hampshire, Leicestershire and Warwickshire, 1899 – Worcestershire, 1905 – Northamptonshire, 1921 – Glamorgan, and 1992 – Durham.

The Championship pennant was introduced by the 1951 champions, Warwickshire, and the Lord's Taverners' Trophy was first presented in 1973. The first sponsors, Schweppes (1977-83), were succeeded by Britannic Assurance (1984-98), PPP Healthcare (1999-2000), CricInfo (2001), Frizzell (2002-05), Liverpool Victoria (2006-15) and Specsavers (from 2016). Based on their previous season's positions, the 18 counties were separated into two divisions in 2000. From 2000 to 2005 the bottom three Division 1 teams were relegated and the top three Division 2 sides promoted. This was reduced to two teams from the end of the 2006 season.

1890	Surrey
1891	Surrey
1892	Surrey
1893	Yorkshire
1894	Surrey
1895	Surrey
1896	Yorkshire
1897	Lancashire
1898	Yorkshire
1899	Surrey
1900	Yorkshire
1901	Yorkshire
1902	Yorkshire
1903	Middlesex
1904	Lancashire
1905	Yorkshire
1906	Kent
1907	Nottinghamshire
1908	Yorkshire
1909	Kent
1910	Kent
1911	Warwickshire
1912	Yorkshire
1913	Kent
1914	Surrey
1919	Yorkshire
1920	Middlesex
1921	Middlesex
1922	Yorkshire
1923	Yorkshire
1924	Yorkshire
1925	Yorkshire
1926	Lancashire
1927	Lancashire
1928	Lancashire
1929	Nottinghamshire
1930	Lancashire
1931	Yorkshire
1932	Yorkshire
1933	Yorkshire
1934	Lancashire
1935	Yorkshire
1936	Derbyshire
1937	Yorkshire
1938	Yorkshire
1939	Yorkshire
1946	Yorkshire
1947	Middlesex
1948	Glamorgan
1949	Middlesex Yorkshire
1950	Lancashire Surrey
1951	Warwickshire
1952	Surrey
1953	Surrey
1954	Surrey
1955	Surrey
1956	Surrey
1957	Surrey
1958	Surrey
1959	Yorkshire
1960	Yorkshire
1961	Hampshire
1962	Yorkshire
1963	Yorkshire
1964	Worcestershire
1965	Worcestershire
1966	Yorkshire
1967	Yorkshire
1968	Yorkshire
1969	Glamorgan
1970	Kent
1971	Surrey
1972	Warwickshire
1973	Hampshire
1974	Worcestershire
1975	Leicestershire
1976	Middlesex
1977	Kent Middlesex
1978	Kent
1979	Essex
1980	Middlesex
1981	Nottinghamshire
1982	Middlesex
1983	Essex
1984	Essex
1985	Middlesex
1986	Essex
1987	Nottinghamshire
1988	Worcestershire
1989	Worcestershire
1990	Middlesex
1991	Essex
1992	Essex
1993	Middlesex
1994	Warwickshire
1995	Warwickshire
1996	Leicestershire
1997	Glamorgan
1998	Leicestershire
1999	Surrey
2000	Surrey
2001	Yorkshire
2002	Surrey
2003	Sussex
2004	Warwickshire
2005	Nottinghamshire
2006	Sussex
2007	Sussex
2008	Durham
2009	Durham
2010	Nottinghamshire
2011	Lancashire
2012	Warwickshire
2013	Durham
2014	Yorkshire
2015	Yorkshire
2016	Middlesex
2017	Essex
2018	Surrey
2019	Essex
2021	Warwickshire

COUNTY CHAMPIONSHIP FIXTURES 2022

DIVISION 1

	ESSEX	GLOS	HANTS	KENT	LANCS	N'HANTS	SOM'T	SURREY	WARKS	YORKS
ESSEX		C'ford	C'ford	C'ford	C'ford	C'ford	C'ford			C'ford
GLOS			Chelt		Bristol	Chelt	Bristol	Bristol	Bristol	Bristol
HANTS		So'ton		So'ton	So'ton	So'ton	So'ton		So'ton	So'ton
KENT	Cant	Cant	Cant		Cant	Cant	Cant	Beck		
LANCS	Man	Man		Man			S'port	Man	Man	Man
N'HANTS	No'ton	No'ton		No'ton	No'ton			No'ton	No'ton	No'ton
SOM'T	Taunton	Taunton	Taunton			Taunton		Taunton	Taunton	Taunton
SURREY	Oval		Oval	Oval		Oval	Oval		Oval	Oval
WARKS	Birm		Birm	Birm	Birm	Birm	Birm	Birm		
YORKS	Leeds	Leeds	Scarb	Leeds	Leeds			Scarb	Leeds	

DIVISION 2

	DERBYS	DURHAM	GLAM	LEICS	MIDDX	NOTTS	SUSSEX	WORCS
DERBYS		Derby	Derby	Derby	Cfield	Derby	Derby	Derby
DURHAM	C-le-St		C-le-St	C-le-St	C-le-St	C-le-St	C-le-St	C-le-St
GLAM	Cardiff	Cardiff		Cardiff	Cardiff	Cardiff	Cardiff	Cardiff
LEICS	Leics	Leics	Leics		Leics	Leics	Leics	Leics
MIDDX	Lord's	Lord's	Lord's	Lord's		Lord's	Lord's	N'wood
NOTTS	N'ham	N'ham	N'ham	N'ham	N'ham		N'ham	N'ham
SUSSEX	Hove	Hove	Hove	Hove	Hove	Hove		Hove
WORCS	Worcs	Worcs	Worcs	Worcs	Worcs	Worcs	Worcs	

ROYAL LONDON ONE-DAY CUP 2021

This latest format of limited-overs competition was launched in 2014, and is now the only List-A tournament played in the UK. The top team from each group went through to the semi-finals, with a home draw; the second team from each group (drawn at home) played off against the third team from the other division to qualify for the semi-finals. The winner was decided in the final at Trent Bridge.

GROUP 1	*P*	*W*	*L*	*T*	*NR*	*Pts*	*Net RR*
1 Durham	8	6	1	–	1	13	+0.92
2 Essex	8	5	2	1	–	11	+0.23
3 Gloucestershire	7	4	3	–	–	8	+0.09
4 Lancashire	8	3	2	1	2	9	+0.01
5 Worcestershire	8	3	4	–	1	7	+0.25
6 Hampshire	8	3	4	–	1	7	+0.16
7 Sussex	8	2	4	–	2	6	–0.68
8 Middlesex	7	2	4	–	1	5	–0.28
9 Kent	8	1	5	–	2	4	–1.25

GROUP 2	*P*	*W*	*L*	*T*	*NR*	*Pts*	*Net RR*
1 Glamorgan	8	4	2	–	2	10	+0.81
2 Surrey	8	4	2	–	2	10	+0.40
3 Yorkshire	8	4	2	–	2	10	+0.02
4 Leicestershire	8	4	3	–	1	9	–0.42
5 Warwickshire	8	4	4	–	–	8	–0.02
6 Nottinghamshire	8	3	3	–	2	8	+0.68
7 Somerset	8	3	3	–	2	8	–0.41
8 Northamptonshire	8	2	4	–	2	6	–0.41
9 Derbyshire	8	1	6	–	1	3	–0.55

Win = 2 points. Tie (T)/No Result (NR) = 1 point.

Positions of counties finishing equal on points are decided by most wins or, if equal, the team that achieved the most points in the matches played between them; if still equal, the team with the higher net run rate (ie deducting from the average runs per over scored by that team in matches where a result was achieved, the average runs per over scored against that team). In the event the teams still cannot be separated, the winner will be decided by drawing lots.

Group 1 standings decided on points per game after Middx v Glos was postponed due to a Covid outbreak.

Statistical Highlights in 2021

Highest total	405-4		Durham v Kent	Beckenham
Biggest victory (runs)	182	Worcs (338-7) beat Essex (156)		Chelmsford
Most runs	646 (ave 80.75)	G.Clark (Durham)		
Highest innings	153	J.A.Haynes	Worcestershire v Essex	Chelmsford
Most sixes (inns)	11	T.H.David	Surrey v Warwickshire	The Oval
Highest partnership	243	J.A.Haynes/B.L.D'Oliveira	Worcs v Essex	Chelmsford
Most wickets	20 (ave 14.30)	J.M.Cooke (Glamorgan)		
Best bowling	5-19	L.A.Patterson-White	Notts v Northants	Grantham
Most economical	10-3-18-1	M.G.Hogan	Glamorgan v Surrey	Cardiff
Most expensive	10-0-97-1	M.R.Quinn	Kent v Durham	Beckenham
Most w/k dismissals	19	T.N.Cullen (Glamorgan)		
Most w/k dismissals (inns)	5	J.R.Bracey	Gloucestershire v Kent	Beckenham
Most catches	10	S.G.Borthwick (Durham)		

2021 ROYAL LONDON ONE-DAY CUP FINAL
GLAMORGAN v DURHAM

At Trent Bridge, Nottingham, on 19 August.

Result: **GLAMORGAN** won by 58 runs.

Toss: Durham.

GLAMORGAN		*Runs*	*Balls*	*4/6*	*Fall*
H.D.Rutherford	c Lees b Rushworth	15	17	–/1	1- 20
N.J.Selman	c Lees b Potts	36	74	4	3-157
S.J.Reingold	c Bancroft b Raine	14	21	3	2- 51
* K.S.Carlson	c Bancroft b Potts	82	59	10/3	5-160
W.T.Root	lbw b Potts	0	1	–	4-157
† T.N.Cullen	c and b Doneathy	24	40	1	7-240
J.M.Cooke	c Potts b Borthwick	29	29	2/1	6-203
A.G.Salter	c Bancroft b Raine	33	22	3/1	8-250
W.J.Weighell	c Clark b Raine	15	12	–/1	9-263
L.J.Carey	not out	19	16	3	
M.G.Hogan	not out	12	10	1/1	
Extras	(B 2, LB 7, NB 2, W 6)	17			
Total	**(9 wkts; 50 overs)**	**296**			

DURHAM		*Runs*	*Balls*	*4/6*	*Fall*
G.Clark	c Weighell b Salter	40	55	7	2- 64
A.Z.Lees	b Salter	15	23	2	1- 47
* S.G.Borthwick	c Reingold b Weighell	10	15	1	3- 73
† C.T.Bancroft	c sub (A.W.Gorvin) b Reingold	55	54	5	5-159
D.G.Bedingham	c Weighell b Salter	0	5	–	4- 74
S.R.Dickson	not out	84	83	8/1	
B.A.Raine	c Hogan b Cooke	10	19	–	6-198
L.Doneathy	c Carlson b Carey	10	8	1	7-226
M.J.Potts	c Cullen b Carey	0	2	–	8-227
L.Trevaskis	c Selman b Cooke	9	6	2	9-238
C.Rushworth	c Cullen b Hogan	0	1	–	10-238
Extras	(LB 4, W 1)	5			
Total	**(45.1 overs)**	**238**			

DURHAM	*O*	*M*	*R*	*W*	**GLAMORGAN**	*O*	*M*	*R*	*W*
Rushworth	10	2	37	1	Hogan	7.1	0	27	1
Potts	10	2	55	3	Carey	8	1	47	2
Raine	10	0	58	3	Salter	10	0	42	3
Doneathy	2.5	0	32	1	Weighell	8	0	43	1
Trevaskis	9	0	53	0	Cooke	9	0	57	2
Borthwick	8.1	0	52	1	Reingold	3	0	18	1

Umpires: N.A.Mallender and S.J.O'Shaughnessy

SEMI-FINALS

At Sophia Gardens, Cardiff, on 16 August. Toss: Glamorgan. **GLAMORGAN** won by five wickets. Essex 289 (49.4; A.N.Cook 68, P.I.Walter 50, J.M.Cooke 5-61). Glamorgan 293-5 (48; H.D.Rutherford 67, J.M.Cooke 66*, N.J.Selman 59).

At Riverside Ground, Chester-le-Street, 17 August. Toss: Durham. **DURHAM** won by five wickets. Surrey 280-8 (50; M.D.Stoneman 117, J.L.Smith 85, C.Rushworth 3-49). Durham 281-5 (47.3; A.Z.Lees 75, S.G.Borthwick 71, D.G.Bedingham 56).

PRINCIPAL LIST A RECORDS 1963-2021

These records cover all the major limited-overs tournaments played by the counties since the inauguration of the Gillette Cup in 1963.

Record	Figure	Player(s)	Match	Venue	Year
Highest Totals	496-4		Surrey v Glos	The Oval	2007
	445-8		Notts v Northants	Nottingham	2016
Highest Total Batting Second	429		Glamorgan v Surrey	The Oval	2002
Lowest Totals	23		Middlesex v Yorks	Leeds	1974
	36		Leics v Sussex	Leicester	1973
Largest Victory (Runs)	346		Somerset beat Devon	Torquay	1990
	304		Sussex beat Ireland	Belfast	1996
Highest Scores	268	A.D.Brown	Surrey v Glamorgan	The Oval	2002
	206	A.I.Kallicharran	Warwicks v Oxfords	Birmingham	1984
	203	A.D.Brown	Surrey v Hampshire	Guildford	1997
	201*	R.S.Bopara	Essex v Leics	Leicester	2008
	201	V.J.Wells	Leics v Berkshire	Leicester	1996
Fastest Hundred	36 balls	G.D.Rose	Somerset v Devon	Torquay	1990
	43 balls	R.R.Watson	Scotland v Somerset	Edinburgh	2003
	44 balls	M.A.Ealham	Kent v Derbyshire	Maidstone	1995
	44 balls	T.C.Smith	Lancashire v Worcs	Worcester	2012
	44 balls	D.I.Stevens	Kent v Sussex	Canterbury	2013
Most Sixes (Inns)	15	R.N.ten Doeschate	Essex v Scotland	Chelmsford	2013
Highest Partnership for each Wicket					
1st	342	M.J.Lumb/M.H.Wessels	Notts v Northants	Nottingham	2016
2nd	302	M.E.Trescothick/C.Kieswetter	Somerset v Glos	Taunton	2008
3rd	309*	T.S.Curtis/T.M.Moody	Worcs v Surrey	The Oval	1994
4th	234*	D.Lloyd/C.H.Lloyd	Lancashire v Glos	Manchester	1978
5th	221*	R.R.Sarwan/M.A.Hardinges	Glos v Lancashire	Manchester	2005
6th	232	D.Wiese/B.C.Brown	Sussex v Hampshire	Southampton	2019
7th	170	D.R.Brown/A.F.Giles	Warwicks v Essex	Birmingham	2003
8th	174	R.W.T.Key/J.C.Tredwell	Kent v Surrey	The Oval	2007
9th	155	C.M.W.Read/A.J.Harris	Notts v Durham	Nottingham	1984
10th	82	G.Chapple/P.J.Martin	Lancashire v Worcs	Manchester	1996
Best Bowling	8-21	M.A.Holding	Derbyshire v Sussex	Hove	1988
	8-26	K.D.Boyce	Essex v Lancashire	Manchester	1971
	8-31	D.L.Underwood	Kent v Scotland	Edinburgh	1987
	8-66	S.R.G.Francis	Somerset v Derbys	Derby	2004
Four Wkts in Four Balls		A.Ward	Derbyshire v Sussex	Derby	1970
		S.M.Pollock	Warwickshire v Leics	Birmingham	1996
		V.C.Drakes	Notts v Derbyshire	Nottingham	1999
		D.A.Payne	Gloucestershire v Essex	Chelmsford	2010
		G.R.Napier	Essex v Surrey	Chelmsford	2013
Most Economical Analyses					
	8-8-0-0	B.A.Langford	Somerset v Essex	Yeovil	1969
	8-7-1-1	D.R.Doshi	Notts v Northants	Northampton	1977
	12-9-3-1	J.Simmons	Lancashire v Suffolk	Bury St Eds	1985
	8-6-2-3	F.J.Titmus	Middlesex v Northants	Northampton	1972
Most Expensive Analyses					
	9-0-108-3	S.D.Thomas	Glamorgan v Surrey	The Oval	2002
	10-0-107-0	J.W.Dernbach	Surrey v Essex	The Oval	2008
	11-0-103-0	G.Welch	Warwicks v Lancs	Birmingham	1995
	10-0-101-1	M.J.J.Critchley	Derbyshire v Worcs	Worcester	2016
Century and Five Wickets in an Innings					
	154*, 5-26	M.J.Procter	Glos v Somerset	Taunton	1972
	206, 6-32	A.I.Kallicharran	Warwicks v Oxfords	Birmingham	1984
	103, 5-41	C.L.Hooper	Kent v Essex	Maidstone	1993
	125, 5-41	I.R.Bell	Warwicks v Essex	Chelmsford	2003
Most Wicket-Keeping Dismissals in an Innings					
	8 (8 ct)	D.J.S.Taylor	Somerset v British Us	Taunton	1982
	8 (8 ct)	D.J.Pipe	Worcs v Herts	Hertford	2001
Most Catches in an Innings by a Fielder					
	5	J.M.Rice	Hampshire v Warwicks	Southampton	1978
	5	D.J.G.Sales	Northants v Essex	Northampton	2007

VITALITY BLAST 2021

In 2021, the Twenty20 competition was again sponsored by Vitality. Between 2003 and 2009, three regional leagues competed to qualify for the knockout stages, but this was reduced to two leagues in 2010, before returning to the three-division format in 2012. Since 2014, the competition has reverted to two regional leagues, except for 2020 when, due to Covid constraints, the three-division format applied.

NORTH GROUP

	P	*W*	*L*	*T*	*NR*	*Pts*	*Net RR*
1. Nottinghamshire	14	9	2	3	–	21	+1.50
2. Yorkshire	13	7	5	–	1	15	+0.30
3. Lancashire	14	7	5	1	1	16	+0.20
4. Warwickshire	14	7	6	–	1	15	+0.00
5. Worcestershire	14	6	6	1	1	14	–0.62
6. Leicestershire	14	6	8	–	–	12	–0.01
7. Durham	14	5	8	1	–	11	–0.22
8. Derbyshire	12	4	7	1	–	9	–0.32
9. Northamptonshire	13	4	8	–	1	9	–0.87

Derbyshire's final two fixtures were cancelled due to a Covid outbreak, so the final positions were decided on a points-per-game basis.

SOUTH GROUP

	P	*W*	*L*	*T*	*NR*	*Pts*	*Net RR*
1. Kent	14	9	4	–	1	19	+0.65
2. Somerset	14	8	4	–	2	18	+0.37
3. Sussex	14	6	3	–	5	17	+0.47
4. Hampshire	14	6	5	–	3	15	+0.38
5. Surrey	14	6	5	–	3	15	+0.33
6. Gloucestershire	14	6	6	–	2	14	+0.20
7. Essex	14	5	8	–	1	11	–0.46
8. Middlesex	14	4	9	–	1	9	–0.38
9. Glamorgan	14	3	9	–	2	8	–1.37

QUARTER-FINALS: SUSSEX beat Yorkshire by five wickets at Chester-le-Street.
HAMPSHIRE beat Nottinghamshire by 2 runs at Nottingham.
SOMERSET beat Lancashire by seven wickets at Taunton.
KENT beat Warwickshire by 21 runs at Canterbury.

SEMI-FINALS: SOMERSET beat Hampshire by two wickets at Birmingham.
KENT beat Sussex by 21 runs at Birmingham.

LEADING AGGREGATES AND RECORDS 2021

BATTING (500 runs)	*M*	*I*	*NO*	*HS*	*Runs*	*Avge*	*100*	*50*	*R/100b*	*Sixes*
J.P.Inglis (Leics)	14	14	3	118*	531	48.27	2	1	175.8	24
G.D.Phillips (Glos)	12	12	3	94*	500	55.55	–	3	163.3	36

BOWLING (22 wkts)	*O*	*M*	*R*	*W*	*Avge*	*BB*	*4w*	*R/Over*
Naveen-ul-Haq (Leics)	52.4	–	457	26	17.57	3-26	–	8.67
M.E.Milnes (Kent)	42.2	–	339	22	15.40	5-22	2	8.00

Highest total	240-4	Yorkshire v Leicestershire		Leeds
Highest innings	136	J.M.Clarke	Nottinghamshire v Northants	Northampton
Most sixes	36	G.D.Phillips (Gloucestershire)		
Most sixes (innings)	11	J.M.Clarke	Nottinghamshire v Northants	Northampton
Highest partnership	169*	T.Banton/D.P.Conway	Somerset v Kent	Canterbury
Best bowling	5-22	M.E.Milnes	Kent v Glamorgan	Cardiff
Most economical	4-1-4-3	S.R.Patel	Nottinghamshire v Worcs	Nottingham
Most expensive	3-0-60-0	G.T.Griffiths	Leicestershire v Yorkshire	Leeds
Most w/k dismissals	18	L.D.McManus (Hampshire)		
Most catches	13	A.M.Lilley (Leicestershire), S.J.Mullaney (Nottinghamshire)		

2021 VITALITY BLAST FINAL
KENT v SOMERSET

At Edgbaston, Birmingham, on 18 September (floodlit).
Result: **KENT** won by 25 runs.
Toss: Somerset. Award: J.M.Cox.

KENT		*Runs*	*Balls*	*4/6*	*Fall*
Z.Crawley	c Lammonby b Goldsworthy	41	33	4	4- 75
D.J.Bell-Drummond	c Smeed b van der Merwe	18	15	1/1	1- 44
J.L.Denly	c Abell b van der Merwe	0	1	–	2- 44
*†S.W.Billings	c Gregory b van der Merwe	2	5	–	3- 52
J.A.Leaning	c Green b Davey	27	29	2	5-111
J.M.Cox	not out	58	28	3/3	
D.I.Stevens	run out	12	8	–/1	6-141
G.Stewart	run out	2	2	–	7-151
Qais Ahmad	not out	0	–	–	
M.E.Milnes					
F.J.Klaassen					
Extras	(B 1, LB 2, NB 2, W 2)	7			
Total	**(7 wkts; 20 overs)**	**167**			

SOMERSET		*Runs*	*Balls*	*4/6*	*Fall*
† T.Banton	st Billings b Denly	0	2	–	1- 0
W.C.F.Smeed	c Cox b Denly	43	32	2/2	4- 79
L.P.Goldsworthy	c Bell-Drummond b Klaassen	3	7	–	2- 3
T.B.Abell	c Klaassen b Qais Ahmad	26	20	3	3- 61
T.A.Lammonby	lbw b Denly	9	11	–	5- 89
* L.Gregory	c Milnes b Stevens	6	8	–	6- 94
R.E.van der Merwe	c Denly b Qais Ahmad	4	5	–	7- 95
B.G.F.Green	c Bell-Drummond b Stewart	9	12	–	9-119
C.Overton	c Leaning b Milnes	13	8	1/1	8-113
J.H.Davey	not out	16	9	–/1	
M.de Lange	not out	8	6	–/1	
Extras	(W 5)	5			
Total	**(9 wkts; 20 overs)**	**142**			

SOMERSET	*O*	*M*	*R*	*W*	**KENT**	*O*	*M*	*R*	*W*
Overton	4	0	37	0	Denly	4	0	31	3
Davey	4	0	41	1	Klaassen	2	0	17	1
Van der Merwe	4	0	19	3	Stewart	3	0	28	1
Goldsworthy	4	0	27	1	Milnes	3	0	17	1
Green	2	0	17	0	Qais Ahmad	4	0	19	2
De Lange	2	0	23	0	Stevens	4	0	30	1

Umpires: M.Burns and M.J.Saggers

TWENTY20 CUP WINNERS

2003	Surrey	2010	Hampshire	2017	Nottinghamshire
2004	Leicestershire	2011	Leicestershire	2018	Worcestershire
2005	Somerset	2012	Hampshire	2019	Essex
2006	Leicestershire	2013	Northamptonshire	2020	Nottinghamshire
2007	Kent	2014	Warwickshire	2021	Kent
2008	Middlesex	2015	Lancashire		
2009	Sussex	2016	Northamptonshire		

PRINCIPAL TWENTY20 CUP RECORDS 2003-21

Highest Total	260-4		Yorkshire v Northants	Leeds	2017
Highest Total Batting 2nd	231-5		Warwickshire v Northants	Birmingham	2018
Lowest Total	44		Glamorgan v Surrey	The Oval	2019
Largest Victory (Runs)	143		Somerset v Essex	Chelmsford	2011
Largest Victory (Balls)	82		Nottinghamshire v Worcs	Nottingham	2021
Highest Scores	161	A.Lyth	Yorkshire v Northants	Leeds	2017
	158*	B.B.McCullum	Warwickshire v Derbys	Birmingham	2015
	153*	L.J.Wright	Sussex v Essex	Chelmsford	2014
	152*	G.R.Napier	Essex v Sussex	Chelmsford	2008
	151*	C.H.Gayle	Somerset v Kent	Taunton	2015
Fastest Hundred	34 balls	A.Symonds	Kent v Middlesex	Maidstone	2004
Most Sixes (Innings)	16	G.R.Napier	Essex v Sussex	Chelmsford	2008
Most Runs in Career	4868	L.J.Wright	Sussex		2004-21

Highest Partnership for each Wicket

1st	207	J.L.Denly/D.J.Bell-Drummond	Kent v Essex	Chelmsford	2017
2nd	186	J.L.Langer/C.L.White	Somerset v Glos	Taunton	2006
3rd	171	I.R.Bell/A.J.Hose	Warwickshire v Northants	Birmingham	2018
4th	159*	L.J.Wright/M.W.Machan	Sussex v Essex	Chelmsford	2014
5th	171	A.J.Hose/D.R.Mousley	Warwickshire v Northants	Birmingham	2020
6th	141*	H.C.Brook/J.A.Thompson	Yorkshire v Worcestershire	Leeds	2021
7th	88	D.A.Douthwaite/W.J.Weighell	Glamorgan v Middlesex	Radlett	2021
8th	86*	J.A.Simpson/T.G.Southee	Middlesex v Hampshire	Southampton	2017
9th	69	C.J.Anderson/J.H.Davey	Somerset v Surrey	The Oval	2017
10th	59	H.H.Streak/J.E.Anyon	Warwickshire v Worcs	Birmingham	2005

Best Bowling	7-18	C.N.Ackermann	Leics v Warwicks	Leicester	2019
	6- 5	A.V.Suppiah	Somerset v Glamorgan	Cardiff	2011
	6-16	T.G.Southee	Essex v Glamorgan	Chelmsford	2011
	6-19	T.T.Bresnan	Yorkshire v Lancashire	Leeds	2017
	6-19	Shaheen Shah Afridi	Hampshire v Middlesex	Southampton	2020
	6-21	A.J.Hall	Northants v Worcs	Northampton	2008
	6-24	T.J.Murtagh	Surrey v Middlesex	Lord's	2005
	6-28	J.K.Fuller	Middlesex v Hampshire	Southampton	2018
Most Wkts in Career	1878	D.R.Briggs	Hampshire, Sussex, Warwickshire		2010-21

Most Economical Innings Analyses (Qualification: 4 overs)

4-1-4-3	S.R.Patel	Nottinghamshire v Worcs	Nottingham	2021

Most Maiden Overs in an Innings

4-2-9-1	M.Morkel	Kent v Surrey	Beckenham	2007
4-2-5-2	A.C.Thomas	Somerset v Hampshire	Southampton	2010
4-2-14-1	S.M.Curran	Surrey v Sussex	Hove	2018

Most Expensive Innings Analyses

4-0-77-0	B.W.Sanderson	Northants v Yorkshire	Leeds	2017
4-0-67-1	R.J.Kirtley	Sussex v Essex	Chelmsford	2008
4-0-67-2	C.P.Wood	Hampshire v Glamorgan	Cardiff	2019

Most Wicket-Keeping Dismissals in Career

114	J.S.Foster	Essex		2003-17

Most Wicket-Keeping Dismissals in an Innings

5 (5 ct)	M.J.Prior	Sussex v Middlesex	Richmond	2006
5 (4 ct, 1 st)	G.L.Brophy	Yorkshire v Durham	Chester-le-St	2008
5 (3 ct, 2 st)	B.J.M.Scott	Worcs v Yorkshire	Worcester	2011
5 (4 ct, 1 st)	G.C.Wilson	Surrey v Hampshire	The Oval	2014
5 (5 ct)	N.J.O'Brien	Leics v Northants	Leicester	2014
5 (3 ct, 2 st)	J.A.Simpson	Middlesex v Surrey	Lord's	2014
5 (4 ct, 1 st)	C.B.Cooke	Glamorgan v Surrey	Cardiff	2016

Most Catches in Career

114	S.J.Croft	Lancashire		2006-21

Most Catches in an Innings by a Fielder

5	M.W.Machan	Sussex v Glamorgan	Hove	2016

YOUNG CRICKETER OF THE YEAR

This annual award, made by The Cricket Writers' Club, is currently restricted to players qualified for England, Andrew Symonds meeting that requirement at the time of his award, and under the age of 23 on 1st May. In 1986 their ballot resulted in a dead heat. Up to 7 March 2022 their selections have gained a tally of 2,897 international Test match caps (shown in brackets).

1950	R.Tattersall (16)	1975	A.Kennedy	1999	A.J.Tudor (10)		
1951	P.B.H.May (66)	1976	G.Miller (34)	2000	P.J.Franks		
1952	F.S.Trueman (67)	1977	I.T.Botham (102)	2001	O.A.Shah (6)		
1953	M.C.Cowdrey (114)	1978	D.I.Gower (117)	2002	R.Clarke (2)		
1954	P.J.Loader (13)	1979	P.W.G.Parker (1)	2003	J.M.Anderson (169)		
1955	K.F.Barrington (82)	1980	G.R.Dilley (41)	2004	I.R.Bell (118)		
1956	B.Taylor	1981	M.W.Gatting (79)	2005	A.N.Cook (161)		
1957	M.J.Stewart (8)	1982	N.G.Cowans (19)	2006	S.C.J.Broad (152)		
1958	A.C.D.Ingleby-Mackenzie	1983	N.A.Foster (29)	2007	A.U.Rashid (19)		
1959	G.Pullar (28)	1984	R.J.Bailey (4)	2008	R.S.Bopara (13)		
1960	D.A.Allen (39)	1985	D.V.Lawrence (5)	2009	J.W.A.Taylor (7)		
1961	P.H.Parfitt (37)	1986	A.A.Metcalfe	2010	S.T.Finn (36)		
1962	P.J.Sharpe (12)	1986	J.J.Whitaker (1)	2011	J.M.Bairstow (80)		
1963	G.Boycott (108)	1987	R.J.Blakey (2)	2012	J.E.Root (114)		
1964	J.M.Brearley (39)	1988	M.P.Maynard (4)	2013	B.A.Stokes (76)		
1965	A.P.E.Knott (95)	1989	N.Hussain (96)	2014	A.Z.Lees		
1966	D.L.Underwood (86)	1990	M.A.Atherton (115)	2015	J.A.Leaning		
1967	A.W.Greig (58)	1991	M.R.Ramprakash (52)	2016	B.M.Duckett (4)		
1968	R.M.H.Cottam (4)	1992	I.D.K.Salisbury (15)	2017	D.W.Lawrence (8)		
1969	A.Ward (5)	1993	M.N.Lathwell (2)	2018	S.M.Curran (24)		
1970	C.M.Old (46)	1994	J.P.Crawley (37)	2019	T.Banton		
1971	J.Whitehouse	1995	A.Symonds (26 – Australia)	2020	Z.Crawley (18)		
1972	D.R.Owen-Thomas	1996	C.E.W.Silverwood (6)	2021	H.C.Brook		
1973	M.Hendrick (30)	1997	B.C.Hollioake (2)				
1974	P.H.Edmonds (51)	1998	A.Flintoff (79)				

THE PROFESSIONAL CRICKETERS' ASSOCIATION

PLAYER OF THE YEAR

Founded in 1967, the Professional Cricketers' Association introduced this award, decided by their membership, in 1970. The award, now known as the Reg Hayter Cup, is presented at the PCA's Annual Awards Dinner in London.

1970	M.J.Procter	1987	R.J.Hadlee	2005	A.Flintoff
1970	J.D.Bond	1988	G.A.Hick	2006	M.R.Ramprakash
1971	L.R.Gibbs	1989	S.J.Cook	2007	O.D.Gibson
1972	A.M.E.Roberts	1990	G.A.Gooch	2008	M.van Jaarsveld
1973	P.G.Lee	1991	Waqar Younis	2009	M.E.Trescothick
1974	B.Stead	1992	C.A.Walsh	2010	N.M.Carter
1975	Zaheer Abbas	1993	S.L.Watkin	2011	M.E.Trescothick
1976	P.G.Lee	1994	B.C.Lara	2012	N.R.D.Compton
1977	M.J.Procter	1995	D.G.Cork	2013	M.M.Ali
1978	J.K.Lever	1996	P.V.Simmons	2014	A.Lyth
1979	J.K.Lever	1997	S.P.James	2015	C.Rushworth
1980	R.D.Jackman	1998	M.B.Loye	2016	B.M.Duckett
1981	R.J.Hadlee	1999	S.G.Law	2017	S.R.Patel
1982	M.D.Marshall	2000	M.E.Trescothick	2018	J.L.Denly
1983	K.S.McEwan	2001	D.P.Fulton	2019	B.A.Stokes
1984	R.J.Hadlee	2002	M.P.Vaughan	2020	C.R.Woakes
1985	N.V.Radford	2003	Mushtaq Ahmed	2021	J.E.Root
1986	C.A.Walsh	2004	A.Flintoff		

2021 FIRST-CLASS AVERAGES

These averages involve the 408 players who appeared in the 143 first-class matches played by 22 teams in England and Wales during the 2021 season.

'Cap' denotes the season in which the player was awarded a 1st XI cap by the county he represented in 2021. If he played for more than one county in 2021, the county(ies) who awarded him his cap is (are) underlined. Durham abolished both their capping and 'awards' system after the 2005 season. Glamorgan's capping system is based on a player's number of appearances. Gloucestershire now cap players on first-class debut. Worcestershire now award county colours when players make their Championship debut.

Team abbreviations: CS – County Select; De – Derbyshire; Du – Durham; E – England; Ex – Essex; Gm – Glamorgan; Gs – Gloucestershire; H – Hampshire; I – India(ns); K – Kent; La – Lancashire; Le – Leicestershire; M – Middlesex; NZ – New Zealand(ers); Nh – Northamptonshire; Nt – Nottinghamshire; Sm – Somerset; Sy – Surrey; Sx – Sussex; Wa – Warwickshire; Wo – Worcestershire; Y – Yorkshire.

† Left-handed batsman. Cap: a dash (–) denotes a non-county player. A blank denotes uncapped by his current county.

BATTING AND FIELDING

	Cap	*M*	*I*	*NO*	*HS*	*Runs*	*Avge*	*100*	*50*	*Ct/St*
Aavesh Khan (CS)	–	1	–	–	–	–	–	–	–	–
K.J.Abbott (H)	2017	11	12	3	58	148	16.44	–	1	1
S.A.Abbott (Sy)		1	1	–	40	40	40.00	–	–	1
T.B.Abell (Sm)	2018	12	20	2	132*	711	39.50	1	4	11
C.N.Ackermann (Le)	2019	10	15	1	126*	485	34.64	1	3	20
M.A.Agarwal (I)	–	1	2	–	47	75	37.50	–	–	–
B.W.Aitchison (De)		13	20	4	50	200	12.50	–	1	12
K.L.Aldridge (Sm)		1	–	–	–	–	–	–	–	–
† M.M.Ali (E)	–	3	5	–	35	83	16.60	–	–	7
B.M.J.Allison (Ex)		2	3	–	52	69	23.00	–	1	1
† T.P.Alsop (H)	2021	14	24	2	149	564	25.63	2	–	14
H.M.Amla (Sy)	2021	13	20	3	215*	994	58.47	3	2	2
† J.M.Anderson (E/La)	2003	10	12	7	8*	29	5.80	–	–	3
M.K.Andersson (M)		13	24	–	88	439	18.29	–	2	6
J.C.Archer (Sx)	2017	1	1	–	2	2	2.00	–	–	–
R.Ashwin (I/Sy)		2	4	1	22	29	9.66	–	–	1
J.A.Atkins (Sx)		5	9	5	10*	21	5.25	–	–	–
A.A.P.Atkinson (Sy)		2	4	1	41*	52	17.33	–	–	–
† M.H.Azad (Le)		12	20	2	152	518	28.77	2	1	4
Azhar Ali (Sm)		3	6	–	60	177	29.50	–	2	2
T.E.Bailey (La)	2018	13	16	–	63	330	20.62	–	2	1
J.M.Bairstow (E)	–	4	7	–	57	184	26.28	–	1	9
J.O.Baker (Wo)	2021	5	7	2	61*	84	16.80	–	1	4
A.Balbirnie (Gm)		3	6	–	29	57	9.50	–	–	3
† G.P.Balderson (La)		6	9	1	77	211	26.37	–	2	–
J.T.Ball (Nt)	2016	1	1	–	4	4	4.00	–	–	–
† G.S.Ballance (Y)	2012	10	14	1	101*	594	45.69	1	4	3
E.R.Bamber (M)		12	22	4	25	151	8.38	–	–	2
C.T.Bancroft (Du)		5	8	1	46*	183	26.14	–	–	4
T.Banton (Sm)		8	14	1	51*	245	18.84	–	1	5
† K.H.D.Barker (H)	2021	10	15	1	84	379	27.07	–	3	1
E.G.Barnard (Wo)	2015	13	18	3	128	746	49.73	2	3	12
E.Barnes (Le)		10	12	4	83*	259	32.37	–	2	4
G.A.Bartlett (Sm)		11	16	1	100	373	24.86	1	2	2
† S.D.Bates (Le)		1	2	–	6	6	3.00	–	–	2/1
D.G.Bedingham (Du)		13	20	3	257	1029	60.52	3	3	11
W.A.T.Beer (Sx)		1	2	1	23*	42	42.00	–	–	–

	Cap	M	I	NO	HS	Runs	Avge	100	50	Ct/St
D.J.Bell-Drummond (K)	2015	10	17	1	114	419	26.18	1	2	2
C.G.Benjamin (Wa)		3	6	–	127	198	33.00	1	–	1
G.K.Berg (Nh)		9	10	3	69*	216	30.85	–	1	3
D.M.Bess (Y)		14	20	1	56	399	21.00	–	2	4
† J.G.Bethell (Wa)		1	2	–	15	23	11.50	–	–	1
S.W.Billings (K)	2015	4	5	–	72	149	29.80	–	1	6
J.M.Blatherwick (La)		4	5	–	11	17	3.40	–	–	1
T.A.Blundell (NZ)	–	1	1	–	34	34	34.00	–	–	8
J.J.Bohannon (La)	2021	15	20	2	170	878	48.77	2	5	7
S.G.Borthwick (Du)		13	20	–	100	474	23.70	1	1	14
T.A.Boult (NZ)	–	2	2	2	12*	19	–	–	–	–
† J.R.Bracey (E/Gs)	2016	13	24	2	118	723	32.86	1	6	39
K.C.Brathwaite (Gs)	2021	6	11	–	60	295	26.81	–	1	6
T.T.Bresnan (Wa)	2021	11	16	2	68*	315	22.50	–	2	18
D.R.Briggs (Wa)	2021	13	20	4	66*	413	25.81	–	3	4
† S.C.J.Broad (E/Nt)	2008	8	12	–	41	102	8.50	–	–	2
H.C.Brook (Y)	2021	14	22	1	118	797	37.95	2	5	17
E.A.Brookes (Wa)		1	–	–	–	–	–	–	–	–
J.A.Brooks (Sm)		6	10	4	15	47	7.83	–	–	–
B.C.Brown (Sx)	2014	12	21	2	157	976	51.36	4	2	27/3
† N.L.J.Browne (Ex)	2015	14	19	2	102	524	30.82	1	4	6
N.L.Buck (Nh)		4	6	1	21*	69	13.80	–	–	1
J.J.Bumrah (I)	–	6	10	2	34*	92	11.50	–	–	1
M.G.K.Burgess (Wa)	2021	15	22	–	101	651	29.59	1	3	44/5
J.T.A.Burnham (Du)		10	15	2	102*	357	27.46	1	1	3
† R.J.Burns (E/Sy)	2014	15	25	1	132	1038	43.25	2	10	8
J.C.Buttler (E)	–	3	5	–	25	72	14.40	–	–	18
† E.J.Byrom (Gm/Sm)		7	10	1	78	206	22.88	–	1	2
H.R.C.Came (De)		3	5	–	45	68	13.60	–	–	1
L.J.Carey (Gm)		3	5	–	29	78	15.60	–	–	–
K.S.Carlson (Gm)	2021	14	23	4	170*	928	48.84	3	5	3
B.A.Carse (Du)		8	9	2	40*	161	23.00	–	–	2
J.J.Carson (CS/Sx)		15	24	4	87	388	19.40	–	3	4
O.J.Carter (Sx)		6	12	1	51	235	21.36	–	1	14
Z.J.Chappell (Nt)		3	5	1	22	61	15.25	–	–	–
† B.G.Charlesworth (Gs)	2018	3	5	–	49	112	22.40	–	–	–
G.Clark (Du)		3	4	1	42	83	27.66	–	–	–
J.Clark (Sy)		12	14	1	61*	208	16.00	–	2	2
† T.G.R.Clark (Sx)		7	13	2	54*	240	21.81	–	1	6
J.M.Clarke (Nt)	2021	13	22	1	109	760	36.19	1	7	8
R.Clarke (Sy)	2005	11	13	3	65	192	19.20	–	1	13
† M.E.Claydon (Sx)		1	1	1	22*	22	–	–	–	–
B.O.Coad (Y)	2018	10	13	5	33*	84	10.50	–	–	–
J.J.Cobb (Nh)	2018	1	2	–	1	1	0.50	–	–	1
I.A.Cockbain (Gs)	2011	6	11	1	117	302	30.20	1	2	1
† M.A.R.Cohen (De)		5	8	1	11	41	5.85	–	–	1
J.M.Coles (Sx)		2	4	1	36	72	24.00	–	–	–
B.G.Compton (Nt)		3	5	–	20	55	11.00	–	–	2
S.Conners (De)		10	16	3	39	114	8.76	–	–	1
† D.P.Conway (NZ/Sm)		5	9	–	200	500	55.55	1	3	3
† A.N.Cook (Ex)	2005	14	19	–	165	611	32.15	2	2	16
S.J.Cook (Ex)	2020	13	13	2	37	126	11.45	–	–	1
C.B.Cooke (Gm)	2016	14	21	7	205*	816	58.28	4	1	40/1
† J.M.Cooke (Gm)		8	13	2	68	203	18.45	–	1	7
P.Coughlin (Du)		4	5	–	48	89	17.80	–	–	3
J.M.Cox (K)		13	23	2	90	579	27.57	–	4	10

	Cap	M	I	NO	HS	Runs	Avge	100	50	Ct/St
O.B.Cox (Wo)	2009	14	21	2	60*	413	21.73	–	2	42/2
J.B.Cracknell (M)		1	2	–	13	20	10.00	–	–	2
M.S.Crane (H)	2021	6	7	1	28	92	15.33	–	–	2
Z.Crawley (E/K)	2019	15	27	2	90	691	27.64	–	6	12
M.J.J.Critchley (De)	2019	14	26	3	109	1000	43.47	1	8	8
H.T.Crocombe (Sx)		9	17	2	46*	83	5.53	–	–	–
S.J.Croft (La)	2010	11	14	2	103*	330	27.50	1	1	8
B.C.Cullen (M)		4	5	–	27	55	11.00	–	–	–
† M.L.Cummins (K)		8	10	2	28*	108	13.50	–	–	1
† B.J.Curran (Nh)		7	10	–	36	148	14.80	–	–	6
† S.M.Curran (E)	–	3	5	1	32	74	18.50	–	–	1
S.W.Currie (H)		1	2	–	4	5	2.50	–	–	1
A.K.Dal (De)		8	13	2	106	333	30.27	1	1	6
J.H.Davey (Sm)	2021	12	16	7	75*	238	26.44	–	1	2
A.L.Davies (La)	2017	14	21	2	84	670	35.26	–	6	18/4
† J.L.B.Davies (M)		2	4	–	24	35	8.75	–	–	1
† S.M.Davies (Sm)	2017	13	22	2	87	634	31.70	–	5	37/1
W.S.Davis (Le)		6	7	3	42	54	13.50	–	–	3
L.A.Dawson (H)	2013	12	20	2	152*	449	24.94	1	1	17
J.M.de Caires (M)		2	4	–	17	28	7.00	–	–	1
C.de Grandhomme (H/NZ)		4	6	3	174*	208	69.33	1	–	3
M.de Lange (Sm)		10	14	–	75	297	21.21	–	2	4
† H.E.Dearden (Le)		3	6	–	62	126	21.00	–	1	1
J.L.Denly (K)	2008	9	14	–	63	246	17.57	–	1	–
† C.D.J.Dent (Gs)	2010	12	23	2	91*	560	26.66	–	5	5
S.R.Dickson (Du)		3	4	1	46	79	26.66	–	–	–
B.L.D'Oliveira (Wo)	2012	14	21	2	71	480	25.26	–	3	4
D.A.Douthwaite (Gm)		13	16	1	96	482	32.13	–	4	3
† J.L.du Plooy (De)		13	24	1	98	428	18.60	–	2	5
† B.M.Duckett (Nt)	2020	13	21	2	177*	705	37.10	1	4	15
H.G.Duke (Y)		9	13	1	54	197	16.41	–	2	31
† M.P.Dunn (Sy)		1	1	–	23	23	23.00	–	–	1
E.J.H.Eckersley (Du)		13	18	1	113*	520	30.58	1	3	28/1
S.S.Eskinazi (M)	2018	9	17	2	102	453	30.20	1	2	8
† H.A.Evans (Le)		4	6	2	12	29	7.25	–	–	–
L.J.Evans (Sy)		2	3	–	11	21	7.00	–	–	2
S.T.Evans (Le)		11	18	–	138	591	32.83	3	1	3
J.D.M.Evison (Nt)		4	6	–	58	121	20.16	–	1	–
T.C.Fell (Wo)	2013	12	19	–	69	324	17.05	–	2	9
A.W.Finch (Wo)	2019	3	4	1	31	37	12.33	–	–	–
H.Z.Finch (K)		1	2	–	115	139	69.50	1	–	–
S.T.Finn (M)	2009	2	4	1	13*	17	5.66	–	–	–
M.D.Fisher (Y)		5	7	2	17	55	11.00	–	–	1
L.J.Fletcher (Nt)	2014	13	17	5	51	140	11.66	–	1	1
B.T.Foakes (Sy)	2016	8	10	2	133	350	43.75	1	2	16/2
W.A.R.Fraine (Y)		3	6	–	12	35	5.83	–	–	1
J.K.Fuller (H)		2	4	–	21	34	8.50	–	–	–
† G.H.S.Garton (Sx)		7	11	–	97	247	22.45	–	1	4
† E.N.Gay (Nh)		9	17	–	101	391	23.00	1	1	5
B.B.A.Geddes (Sy)		1	2	–	15	19	9.50	–	–	–
N.N.Gilchrist (K)		9	8	1	13	52	7.42	–	–	2
S.Gill (I)	–	1	2	–	28	36	18.00	–	–	1
† B.A.Godleman (De)	2015	10	18	2	100*	530	33.12	1	3	5
L.P.Goldsworthy (Sm)		10	15	1	48	297	21.21	–	–	1
D.C.Goodman (Gs)	2021	4	5	3	9*	20	10.00	–	–	–
J.A.Gordon (K)		1	2	–	8	8	4.00	–	–	–

	Cap	M	I	NO	HS	Runs	Avge	100	50	Ct/St
H.O.M.Gouldstone (Nh)		4	8	2	67*	155	25.83	–	1	–
B.G.F.Green (Sm)		4	8	1	43	154	22.00	–	–	2
L.Gregory (Sm)	2015	9	10	2	107	389	48.62	1	3	7
G.T.Griffiths (Le)		5	6	3	16	44	14.66	–	–	–
† N.R.T.Gubbins (H/M)	2016	14	26	2	137*	769	32.04	2	5	7
B.D.Guest (De)		12	20	1	116	489	25.73	1	1	26/3
S.R.Hain (Wa)	2018	15	26	2	118	881	36.70	1	7	21
† T.J.Haines (Sx)	2021	13	25	–	156	1176	47.04	3	6	2
H.Hameed (CS/E/Nt)	2020	15	26	2	114*	944	39.33	3	6	11
Hamidullah Qadri (K)		1	2	1	30*	34	34.00	–	–	–
M.A.H.Hammond (Gs)	2013	9	17	2	94	547	36.46	–	4	11
P.S.P.Handscomb (M)		7	13	–	70	227	17.46	–	1	3
G.T.Hankins (Gs)	2016	5	7	1	37	120	20.00	–	–	6
† O.J.Hannon-Dalby (Wa)	2019	8	11	6	26	48	9.60	–	–	2
S.R.Harmer (Ex)	2018	14	16	4	82*	317	26.41	–	2	14
J.A.R.Harris (Gm/M)	2010/2015	5	8	1	26	90	12.85	–	–	2
† M.S.Harris (Le)		8	13	1	185	655	54.58	3	1	7
† T.W.Hartley (La)		3	4	1	25	61	20.33	–	–	2
J.A.Haynes (Wo)	2019	9	14	–	97	491	35.07	–	4	8
† T.M.Head (Sx)		6	11	1	49*	183	18.30	–	–	3
T.G.Helm (M)	2019	4	8	2	17	49	8.16	–	–	1
M.J.Henry (NZ)	–	1	1	–	12	12	12.00	–	–	–
R.F.Higgins (Gs)	2018	13	19	1	73	376	20.88	–	1	3
J.C.Hildreth (Sm)	2007	13	20	–	107	456	22.80	1	1	14
G.C.H.Hill (Y)		7	11	–	71	263	23.90	–	2	1
L.J.Hill (Le)	2021	14	22	1	145	944	44.95	3	5	3
† T.I.Hinley (Sx)		1	2	–	19	20	10.00	–	–	–
M.G.Hogan (Gm)	2013	13	14	6	54	113	14.12	–	1	2
† M.D.E.Holden (M)		10	19	1	52	325	18.05	–	1	6
C.K.Holder (Wa)		2	3	1	6	6	3.00	–	–	–
I.G.Holland (H)	2021	14	24	1	146*	766	33.30	2	4	8
† L.B.K.Hollman (M)		6	9	1	46	176	22.00	–	–	3
H.R.Hosein (De)		8	14	5	83*	371	41.22	–	4	11
H.F.Houillon (K)		1	2	–	9	9	4.50	–	–	3
F.J.Hudson-Prentice (De/Sx)		12	20	3	67	354	20.82	–	1	5
A.L.Hughes (De)	2017	5	9	1	25	84	10.50	–	–	1
S.F.Hunt (Sx)		6	10	4	7	12	2.00	–	–	–
B.A.Hutton (Nt)	2021	8	11	–	51	174	15.81	–	1	8
D.K.Ibrahim (Sx)		6	11	–	94	328	29.81	–	3	3
J.P.Inglis (Le)		2	3	–	52	128	42.66	–	1	4
† C.A.Ingram (Gm)	2017	1	2	–	27	34	17.00	–	–	–
W.G.Jacks (Sy)		6	5	1	60	146	36.50	–	2	4
† R.A.Jadeja (I)	–	6	11	–	75	317	28.81	–	3	1
L.W.James (CS/Nt)		13	19	1	91	585	32.50	–	5	1
K.A.Jamieson (NZ/Sy)		3	3	1	21	30	15.00	–	–	1
† K.K.Jennings (La)	2018	10	13	1	132	577	48.08	2	3	8
M.S.Johal (Wa)		1	1	–	19	19	19.00	–	–	–
M.A.Jones (Du)		8	13	1	81	337	28.08	–	2	2
R.P.Jones (La)		9	11	–	58	199	18.09	–	1	11
A.S.Joseph (Wo)	2021	6	8	–	61	148	18.50	–	1	–
R.I.Keogh (Nh)	2019	14	24	2	126	766	34.81	2	4	1
S.C.Kerrigan (Nh)		11	19	6	45*	224	17.23	–	–	3
L.P.J.Kimber (Le)		4	6	1	71	151	30.20	–	2	6
F.J.Klaassen (K)		2	4	1	5	8	2.66	–	–	–
D.Klein (Le)		3	4	–	12	12	3.00	–	–	–
T.Kohler-Cadmore (Y)	2019	11	18	–	89	353	19.61	–	1	21

	Cap	M	I	NO	HS	Runs	Avge	100	50	Ct/St
V.Kohli (I)	–	5	9	–	55	275	30.55	–	2	8
H.G.Kuhn (K)	2018	4	8	–	32	108	13.50	–	–	4
M.Labuschagne (Gm)	2019	6	9	2	77	228	32.57	–	2	1
T.C.Lace (Gs)	2020	14	26	4	118	573	26.04	1	3	9
D.J.Lamb (La)		11	14	1	125	365	28.07	1	2	5
M.J.Lamb (Wa)		14	24	5	67	565	29.73	–	3	5
† T.A.Lammonby (Sm)		13	22	2	100	392	19.60	1	2	7
† T.W.M.Latham (NZ)	–	3	6	1	36	127	25.40	–	–	7
G.I.D.Lavelle (La)		2	3	–	32	36	12.00	–	–	5
D.W.Lawrence (E/Ex)	2017	13	18	2	152*	746	46.62	1	5	8
J.Leach (Wo)	2012	13	19	5	84	377	26.92	–	1	2
† M.J.Leach (Sm)	2017	10	15	4	49	276	25.09	–	–	2
J.A.Leaning (K)	2021	13	21	5	127*	745	46.56	1	6	11
D.J.Leech (Y)		1	–	–	–	–	–	–	–	–
† A.Z.Lees (Du)		11	17	1	129	625	39.06	1	5	6
A.D.Lenham (Sx)		1	2	–	20	29	14.50	–	–	–
E.O.Leonard (Sm)		1	2	1	6	10	10.00	–	–	1
J.D.Libby (CS/Wo)	2020	15	25	5	180*	1104	55.20	4	4	8
D.J.Lincoln (K)		1	2	–	41	41	20.50	–	–	1
J.B.Lintott (Wa)		1	1	–	15	15	15.00	–	–	1
L.S.Livingstone (La)	2017	6	7	–	25	77	11.00	–	–	5
D.L.Lloyd (Gm)	2019	14	25	1	121	828	34.50	1	5	7
† J.E.G.Logan (K)		4	6	1	21	51	10.20	–	–	1
T.W.Loten (Y)		2	4	–	27	57	14.25	–	–	–
† A.Lyth (Y)	2010	14	22	1	153	819	39.00	3	3	25
B.R.McDermott (De)		2	4	–	25	49	12.25	–	–	1
J.P.McIlroy (Gm)		2	1	–	0	0	0.00	–	–	–
M.H.McKiernan (De)		1	1	–	23	23	23.00	–	–	1
L.D.McManus (H)	2021	11	14	2	91	320	26.66	–	2	28/1
W.L.Madsen (De)	2011	11	20	–	111	675	33.75	1	4	20
S.Mahmood (La)	2021	8	11	4	20	73	10.42	–	–	2
† D.J.Malan (E/Y)	2020	4	6	–	199	326	54.33	1	1	2
P.J.Malan (Wa)		6	10	1	141	339	37.66	1	1	–
S.C.Meaker (Sx)		6	9	1	30*	113	14.12	–	–	2
D.R.Melton (De)		5	8	3	15	39	7.80	–	–	2
B.W.M.Mike (Le)		13	19	1	74	495	27.50	–	4	2
C.N.Miles (CS/Wa)		13	18	4	30*	177	12.64	–	–	5
M.E.Milnes (K)	2021	8	14	4	78	244	24.40	–	1	2
D.J.Mitchell (M/NZ)		3	5	–	73	140	28.00	–	1	3
D.K.H.Mitchell (Wo)	2005	14	23	1	113	470	21.36	1	3	13
Mohammad Abbas (H)		10	14	7	6	28	4.00	–	–	2
Mohammed Shami (I)	–	4	7	2	56*	92	18.40	–	1	2
T.J.Moores (Nt)	2021	12	19	3	97	486	30.37	–	3	52/2
† D.T.Moriarty (Sy)		4	3	–	8	12	4.00	–	–	2
C.A.J.Morris (Wo)	2014	6	8	2	50	116	19.33	–	1	–
E.H.T.Moulton (De)		2	2	1	6*	9	9.00	–	–	–
S.J.Mullaney (Nt)	2013	14	22	–	117	657	29.86	1	3	6
† T.J.Murtagh (M)	2008	12	20	7	31	88	6.76	–	–	3
T.S.Muyeye (K)		4	6	2	89	142	35.50	–	1	–
† J.D.S.Neesham (Ex)		1	1	1	10*	10	–	–	–	–
M.G.Neser (Gm)	2021	5	3	1	24	58	29.00	–	–	3
† H.M.Nicholls (NZ)	–	3	4	–	61	112	28.00	–	1	2
† A.S.S.Nijjar (Ex)		1	1	–	2	2	2.00	–	–	–
S.A.Northeast (H/Nt/Y)	2019	12	18	2	118	474	29.62	1	3	4
L.C.Norwell (Wa)		13	18	5	30*	120	9.23	–	–	1
D.Olivier (Y)	2020	7	11	5	21	61	10.16	–	–	1

	Cap	M	I	NO	HS	Runs	Avge	100	50	Ct/St
F.S.Organ (H)		6	10	–	67	213	21.30	–	1	6
M.K.O'Riordan (K)		7	7	–	47	140	20.00	–	–	4
A.G.H.Orr (Sx)		7	14	–	119	548	39.14	1	4	1
C.Overton (E/Sm)	2016	10	14	1	74	280	21.53	–	2	12
J.Overton (Sy)		8	9	1	50	154	19.25	–	1	6
† R.R.Pant (I)	–	5	9	–	50	191	21.22	–	1	14/1
C.F.Parkinson (Le)		13	18	2	41	253	15.81	–	–	2
M.W.Parkinson (La)	2019	12	12	9	21*	63	21.00	–	–	1
† W.D.Parnell (Nh)		6	7	–	54	107	15.28	–	1	–
† A.R.Patel (I)	–	1	1	–	0	0	0.00	–	–	–
† A.Y.Patel (NZ)	–	1	1	–	20	20	20.00	–	–	–
R.K.Patel (Le)		5	7	–	44	143	20.42	–	–	4
† R.S.Patel (Sy)		6	10	–	62	250	25.00	–	2	3
D.Paterson (Nt)	2021	12	15	11	22	64	16.00	–	–	4
S.A.Patterson (Y)	2012	13	17	2	47*	191	12.73	–	–	3
† L.A.Patterson-White (CS/Nt)		15	21	3	101	571	31.72	1	3	4
D.A.Payne (Gs)	2011	10	12	3	34	102	11.33	–	–	6
D.Y.Pennington (Wo)	2018	10	14	4	56	156	15.60	–	1	1
M.S.Pepper (Ex)		6	7	–	92	204	29.14	–	2	3
G.D.Phillips (Gs)	2021	3	6	–	47	109	18.16	–	–	5
H.W.Podmore (K)	2019	5	6	1	37	107	21.40	–	–	–
O.J.D.Pope (E/Sy)	2018	12	19	3	274	1028	64.25	3	1	7
J.A.Porter (Ex)	2015	12	13	7	30	73	12.16	–	–	1
M.J.Potts (Du)		7	9	2	81	206	29.42	–	1	3
S.W.Poynter (Du)		6	8	2	52*	85	14.16	–	1	22
T.J.Prest (H)		2	1	–	18	18	18.00	–	–	1
O.J.Price (Gs)	2021	4	7	–	33	110	15.71	–	–	4
T.J.Price (Gs)	2020	6	9	4	71	177	35.40	–	1	1
† L.A.Procter (Nh)	2020	13	21	2	93	597	31.42	–	5	2
C.A.Pujara (I)	–	6	12	1	91	309	28.09	–	2	–
M.R.Quinn (K)		6	5	3	13*	32	16.00	–	–	–
A.M.Rahane (I)	–	5	9	–	61	173	19.22	–	1	2
K.L.Rahul (I)	–	5	9	–	129	416	46.22	2	1	5
† B.A.Raine (Du)		13	15	3	74	308	25.66	–	2	3
† D.M.W.Rawlins (Sx)		10	17	–	58	233	13.70	–	1	3
† L.M.Reece (De)	2019	9	17	–	63	231	13.58	–	1	3
S.J.Reingold (Gm)		1	2	–	9	13	6.50	–	–	1
M.L.Revis (Y)		1	2	–	34	34	17.00	–	–	–
† J.E.K.Rew (CS)	–	1	1	–	2	2	2.00	–	–	1/1
G.H.Rhodes (Le)		3	4	–	90	208	52.00	–	2	2
† W.M.H.Rhodes (CS/Wa)	2020	16	28	2	156	800	30.76	1	5	13
K.A.J.Roach (Sy)		5	3	1	8	13	6.50	–	–	–
O.E.Robinson (E/Sx)	2019	11	16	2	67	337	24.07	–	2	4
O.G.Robinson (K)		13	21	1	120	725	36.25	2	3	38/1
S.D.Robson (M)	2013	14	27	1	253	1047	40.26	3	2	16
G.H.Roderick (Wo)	2021	7	11	2	42*	167	18.55	–	–	1
T.S.Roland-Jones (M)	2012	6	11	2	46*	138	15.33	–	–	–
J.E.Root (E/Y)	2012	11	19	1	180*	952	52.88	4	2	12
† W.T.Root (Gm)	2021	11	18	2	110*	442	27.62	1	1	4
A.M.Rossington (Nh)	2019	11	16	1	94	537	35.80	–	4	24/2
C.Rushworth (Du)		13	13	6	31	91	13.00	–	–	3
† H.D.Rutherford (Gm)		4	7	–	71	260	37.14	–	2	–
J.S.Rymell (Ex)		3	3	–	14	23	7.66	–	–	2
A.Sakande (Le)		3	4	2	9	23	11.50	–	–	2
J.J.G.Sales (Nh)		3	6	2	53	112	28.00	–	1	1
M.E.T.Salisbury (Du)		4	5	–	41	75	15.00	–	–	–

	Cap	M	I	NO	HS	Runs	Avge	100	50	Ct/St
A.G.Salter (Gm)		10	11	4	90	221	31.57	–	1	3
B.W.Sanderson (Nh)	2018	13	17	3	20	72	5.14	–	–	2
† M.J.Santner (NZ)	–	1	1	–	0	0	0.00	–	–	–
J.P.Sarro (Sx)		3	6	3	7*	8	2.66	–	–	1
D.J.Schadendorf (Nt)		1	1	–	24	24	24.00	–	–	4
G.F.B.Scott (Gs)	2020	5	7	–	31	100	14.28	–	–	3
G.L.S.Scrimshaw (De)		3	5	3	5*	5	2.50	–	–	1
N.J.Selman (Gm)		5	10	–	69	121	12.10	–	1	3
I.Sharma (I)	–	3	6	2	16	39	9.75	–	–	1
R.G.Sharma (I)	–	6	11	1	127	441	44.10	1	2	6
J.Shaw (Gs)	2016	4	6	2	41*	105	26.25	–	–	1
D.P.Sibley (E/Wa)	2019	14	24	3	80	687	32.71	–	6	4
P.M.Siddle (Ex)	2021	6	9	2	20	70	10.00	–	–	–
R.N.Sidebottom (Wa)		2	2	–	1	1	0.50	–	–	–
J.A.Simpson (M)	2011	13	22	2	95*	535	26.75	–	3	50/3
J.Singh (K)		2	2	–	2	2	1.00	–	–	1
M.Siraj (I)	–	5	7	5	7*	17	8.50	–	–	2
B.T.Slater (Nt)	2021	14	24	3	114*	837	39.85	2	5	8
J.L.Smith (Sy)		12	17	2	138	656	43.73	3	1	15/1
R.A.J.Smith (Gm)		1	2	–	8	12	6.00	–	–	–
T.M.J.Smith (Gs)	2013	5	8	1	47	76	10.85	–	–	2
S.Snater (Ex)		9	8	2	48	99	16.50	–	–	1
I.S.Sodhi (Wo)	2021	1	1	–	13	13	13.00	–	–	–
T.G.Southee (NZ)	–	2	2	–	30	38	19.00	–	–	2
N.A.Sowter (M)		3	6	1	24*	46	9.20	–	–	3
B.Stanlake (De)		1	2	–	8	8	4.00	–	–	–
C.T.Steel (H/Sy)		3	6	–	28	74	12.33	–	–	1
D.I.Stevens (K)	2005	12	18	3	190	650	43.33	3	2	4
G.Stewart (K)		6	9	2	40	134	19.14	–	–	–
† B.A.Stokes (Du)		1	–	–	–	–	–	–	–	1
O.P.Stone (E/Wa)	2020	5	7	1	43	98	16.33	–	–	–
† M.D.Stoneman (M/Sy)	2018	14	22	–	174	827	37.59	3	4	2
H.J.Swindells (Le)		13	19	3	171*	693	43.31	2	3	27/1
J.A.Tattersall (Gs/Sy/Y)	2021	8	13	2	86*	267	24.27	–	2	23
C.Z.Taylor (Gm)		6	8	2	84	215	35.83	–	2	2
J.M.R.Taylor (Gs)	2010	3	5	–	40	133	26.60	–	–	1
J.P.A.Taylor (Sy)		1	1	–	19	19	19.00	–	–	–
L.R.P.L.Taylor (NZ)	–	3	6	2	80	185	46.25	–	1	4
M.D.Taylor (Gs)	2013	9	12	3	56	166	18.44	–	1	–
T.A.I.Taylor (Nh)		11	17	2	50	316	21.06	–	1	6
R.N.ten Doeschate (Ex)	2006	10	12	–	56	314	26.16	–	3	9
S.N.Thakur (I)	–	3	5	1	60	143	35.75	–	2	1
A.D.Thomason (Sx)		9	17	2	78*	379	25.26	–	3	16
† J.A.Thompson (Y)		13	20	–	57	411	20.55	–	1	4
A.T.Thomson (De)		4	6	–	18	65	10.83	–	–	1
C.O.Thurston (Nh)		6	10	–	48	142	14.20	–	–	3
J.C.Tongue (Wo)	2017	4	6	1	17	66	13.20	–	–	–
R.J.W.Topley (Sy)		7	9	2	10	31	4.42	–	–	–
† L.Trevaskis (Du)		3	4	2	77*	135	67.50	–	2	2
G.L.van Buuren (Gs)	2016	6	9	2	110*	354	50.57	1	4	3
T.van der Gugten (Gm)	2018	11	13	2	85*	194	17.63	–	1	5
R.E.van der Merwe (Sm)		6	8	–	88	241	30.12	–	2	4
† S.van Zyl (Sx)	2019	9	17	–	113	422	24.82	1	3	4
† R.S.Vasconcelos (Nh)	2021	14	24	1	185*	845	36.73	2	2	32/1
G.H.Vihari (I/Wa)		4	8	1	52	167	23.85	–	1	3
D.J.Vilas (La)	2018	15	18	1	189	584	34.35	1	2	20

	Cap	M	I	NO	HS	Runs	Avge	100	50	Ct/St
J.M.Vince (H)	2013	13	20	–	231	816	40.80	1	4	13
G.S.Virdi (Sy)		11	12	6	47	59	9.83	–	–	1
† N.Wagner (NZ)	–	3	4	1	25*	35	11.66	–	–	–
A.G.Wakely (Nh)	2012	1	1	–	4	4	4.00	–	–	1
† T.N.Walallawita (M)		4	6	3	20*	54	18.00	–	–	2
† P.I.Walter (Ex)		13	16	1	96	544	36.26	–	4	5
† H.D.Ward (Sx)		3	6	–	19	30	5.00	—	–	2
J.D.Warner (Gs)	2021	2	2	1	10*	20	20.00	–	–	1
† M.S.Washington Sundar (CS)	–	1	1	–	1	1	1.00	–	–	1
B.J.Watling (NZ)	–	2	3	1	15*	17	8.50	–	–	8
J.J.Weatherley (H)	2021	13	22	–	78	406	18.45	–	1	21
† W.J.Weighell (Gm)		4	5	–	21	52	10.40	–	–	2
B.J.J.Wells (Gs)	2021	1	1	–	40	40	40.00	–	–	2
† L.W.P.Wells (La)		13	18	2	103	613	38.31	1	3	18
M.H.Wessels (Wo)	2019	7	10	–	60	202	20.20	–	2	3
T.Westley (Ex)	2013	13	18	1	213	631	37.11	3	1	5
B.T.J.Wheal (H)	2021	13	16	6	46*	181	18.10	–	–	2
A.J.A.Wheater (Ex)	2020	14	16	–	87	434	27.12	–	2	23/4
† C.White (Nh)		4	7	5	15*	29	14.50	–	–	–
R.G.White (M)		14	26	4	120	765	34.77	2	4	19
† R.A.Whiteley (Wo)	2013	2	3	–	22	34	11.33	–	–	1
B.J.Wightman (K)		1	2	1	0*	0	0.00	–	–	–
† D.J.Willey (Y)	2016	6	8	4	41*	165	41.25	–	–	1
K.S.Williamson (NZ)	–	2	4	1	52*	115	38.33	–	1	–
C.R.Woakes (E/Wa)	2009	3	5	–	50	87	17.40	–	1	2
† L.Wood (La)		10	13	2	119	431	39.18	1	1	3
M.A.Wood (Du/E)		6	8	1	41	105	15.00	–	–	–
T.A.Wood (De)		7	13	–	31	129	9.92	–	–	6
D.J.Worrall (Gs)	2018	8	12	3	24	75	8.33	–	–	–
C.J.C.Wright (Le)	2021	12	16	2	87	257	18.35	–	1	2
U.T.Yadav (I)	–	2	3	–	25	47	15.66	–	–	1
† R.M.Yates (CS/Wa)		15	25	2	132*	907	39.43	5	2	21
W.A.Young (Du/NZ)		5	9	–	124	368	40.88	2	1	1
† Zafar Gohar (Gs)	2021	4	6	–	30	78	13.00	–	–	–
† S.A.Zaib (Nh)		13	22	1	135	576	27.42	1	3	4

BOWLING

See BATTING AND FIELDING section for details of matches and caps

	Cat	O	M	R	W	Avge	Best	5wI	10wM
Aavesh Khan (CS)	RM	9.5	2	41	0				
K.J.Abbott (H)	RFM	329.3	87	996	46	21.65	6-44	3	1
S.A.Abbott (Sy)	RMF	15	8	27	2	13.50	2- 5	–	–
T.B.Abell (Sm)	RM	168.3	44	558	13	42.92	3-63	–	–
C.N.Ackermann (Le)	OB	96	22	324	9	36.00	3-44	–	–
B.W.Aitchison (De)	RFM	275.4	50	792	34	23.29	6-28	1	–
K.L.Aldridge (Sm)	RM	22	2	101	0				
M.M.Ali (E)	OB	86	3	299	6	49.83	2-84	–	–
B.M.J.Allison (Ex)	RFM	36	7	94	1	94.00	1-67	–	–
J.M.Anderson (E/La)	RFM	287	90	659	29	22.72	7-19	2	–
M.K.Andersson (M)	RM	250.1	41	916	29	31.58	4-27	–	–
J.C.Archer (Sx)	RF	18	4	43	3	14.33	2-29	–	–
R.Ashwin (I/Sy)	OB	83	23	171	11	15.54	6-27	1	–
J.A.Atkins (Sx)	RMF	137.4	14	469	20	23.45	5-51	2	–
A.A.P.Atkinson (Sy)	RM	47	7	172	5	34.40	3-78	–	–
T.E.Bailey (La)	RMF	368	111	955	51	18.72	7-37	1	–
J.O.Baker (Wo)	SLA	144.2	30	408	12	34.00	3-49	–	–

	Cat	O	M	R	W	Avge	Best	5wI	10wM
A.Balbirnie (Gm)	OB	3	0	17	0				
G.P.Balderson (La)	RM	152.5	29	427	12	35.58	3- 21	–	–
J.T.Ball (Nt)	RFM	17.3	7	43	2	21.50	2- 43	–	–
E.R.Bamber (M)	RMF	407	111	1084	52	20.84	5- 41	1	–
K.H.D.Barker (H)	LMF	310	88	755	41	18.41	7- 46	3	–
E.G.Barnard (Wo)	RMF	368.1	83	1052	25	42.08	4- 43	–	–
E.Barnes (Le)	RFM	204.2	30	724	18	40.22	4- 61	–	–
W.A.T.Beer (Sx)	LB	29	6	70	3	23.33	2- 29	–	–
D.J.Bell-Drummond (K)	RMF	19	3	70	3	23.33	3- 47	–	–
G.K.Berg (Nh)	RMF	199.4	48	600	24	25.00	5- 18	1	–
D.M.Bess (Y)	OB	405.4	122	912	28	32.57	7- 43	2	–
J.M.Blatherwick (La)	RMF	66.1	14	236	9	26.22	4- 28	–	–
J.J.Bohannon (La)	RM	31.1	5	94	3	31.33	1- 11	–	–
S.G.Borthwick (Du)	LBG	130.5	22	455	12	37.91	4- 32	–	–
T.A.Boult (NZ)	LFM	75.2	14	205	11	18.63	4- 85	–	–
K.C.Brathwaite (Gs)	OB	4	0	16	0				
T.T.Bresnan (Wa)	RFM	175	59	453	13	34.84	3- 35	–	–
D.R.Briggs (Wa)	SLA	309	82	722	33	21.87	4- 36	–	–
S.C.J.Broad (E/Nt)	RFM	241.1	53	630	30	21.00	4- 37	–	–
H.C.Brook (Y)	RM	82.1	18	194	7	27.71	3- 15	–	–
E.A.Brookes (Wa)	RMF	7	2	22	0				
J.A.Brooks (Sm)	RFM	142	28	499	12	41.58	4- 77	–	–
N.L.Buck (Nh)	RMF	107.4	11	436	10	43.60	3- 65	–	–
J.J.Bumrah (I)	RFM	207.4	59	507	19	26.68	5- 64	1	–
R.J.Burns (E/Sy)	RM	7	1	22	0				
E.J.Byrom (Gm/Sm)	OB	16	0	64	2	32.00	2- 64	–	–
L.J.Carey (Gm)	RFM	54	9	179	4	44.75	3- 56	–	–
K.S.Carlson (Gm)	OB	14.3	4	43	1	43.00	1- 37	–	–
B.A.Carse (Du)	RF	203.2	26	724	34	21.29	5- 49	2	–
J.J.Carson (CS/Sx)	OB	489.4	68	1471	40	36.77	5- 85	1	–
Z.J.Chappell (Nt)	RFM	100	21	306	6	51.00	3- 64	–	–
B.G.Charlesworth (Gs)	RM/OB	7.2	0	37	0				
J.Clark (Sy)	RMF	276	36	904	32	28.25	6- 21	2	–
T.G.R.Clark (Sx)	RM	33	3	120	1	120.00	1- 37	–	–
R.Clarke (Sy)	RMF	197.5	45	582	16	36.37	3- 34	–	–
M.E.Claydon (Sx)	RMF	17	3	54	2	27.00	2- 51	–	–
B.O.Coad (Y)	RMF	287.1	79	766	35	21.88	4- 48	–	–
M.A.R.Cohen (De)	LFM	99.5	19	280	11	25.45	5- 43	1	–
J.M.Coles (Sx)	SLA	22	0	92	0				
S.Conners (De)	RM	225.5	44	750	26	28.84	5- 83	1	–
A.N.Cook (Ex)	OB	1	0	5	0				
S.J.Cook (Ex)	RFM	382.2	128	837	58	14.43	5- 20	3	1
C.B.Cooke (Gm)	RM	3	0	19	0				
J.M.Cooke (Gm)	RMF	11	0	51	0				
P.Coughlin (Du)	RM	88.4	22	279	12	23.25	5- 64	1	–
J.M.Cox (K)	RM	1	0	3	0				
M.S.Crane (H)	LB	195.5	39	587	23	25.52	5- 41	1	–
M.J.J.Critchley (De)	LB	343.3	42	1230	32	38.43	5- 67	1	–
H.T.Crocombe (Sx)	RMF	211	29	756	20	37.80	4- 92	–	–
S.J.Croft (La)	RMF	22	3	77	0				
B.C.Cullen (M)	RMF	109.2	19	393	10	39.30	3- 30	–	–
M.L.Cummins (K)	RF	162.2	19	622	6	103.66	2-100	–	–
S.M.Curran (E)	LMF	74	10	238	3	79.33	2- 27	–	–
S.W.Currie (H)	RMF	27.5	2	109	4	27.25	4-109	–	–
A.K.Dal (De)	RM	110	18	298	9	33.11	2- 17	–	–
J.H.Davey (Sm)	RMF	292.2	84	781	35	22.31	5- 30	2	–

	Cat	O	M	R	W	Avge	Best	5wI	10wM
W.S.Davis (Le)	RFM	157.4	32	416	15	27.73	5-66	1	–
L.A.Dawson (H)	SLA	257	55	624	18	34.66	5-45	1	–
J.M.de Caires (M)	RM	3	0	7	0				
C.de Grandhomme (H/NZ)	RMF	71	34	136	6	22.66	4-31	–	–
M.de Lange (Sm)	RF	231.5	49	685	20	34.25	4-55	–	–
H.E.Dearden (Le)	OB	0.5	0	8	0				
J.L.Denly (K)	LB	89.2	12	274	4	68.50	2-61	–	–
C.D.J.Dent (Gs)	SLA	3	0	18	0				
B.L.D'Oliveira (Wo)	LB	253.4	29	808	15	53.86	3-95	–	–
D.A.Douthwaite (Gm)	RMF	181.1	18	781	17	45.94	2-16	–	–
J.L.du Plooy (De)	SLA	8	1	21	0				
B.M.Duckett (Nt)	OB	3	0	17	0				
M.P.Dunn (Sy)	RFM	36	2	145	0				
E.J.H.Eckersley (Du)	OB	4	1	7	0				
H.A.Evans (Le)	RFM	79	8	297	4	74.25	2-50	–	–
J.D.M.Evison (Nt)	RM	82.1	23	249	14	17.78	5-21	1	–
A.W.Finch (Wo)	RMF	76	13	250	8	31.25	2-32	–	–
S.T.Finn (M)	RFM	68.2	4	266	12	22.16	5-77	1	–
M.D.Fisher (Y)	RFM	121	29	393	20	19.65	5-41	1	–
L.J.Fletcher (Nt)	RMF	420.5	135	984	66	14.90	7-37	4	1
J.K.Fuller (H)	RFM	17	4	37	3	12.33	2-22	–	–
G.H.S.Garton (Sx)	LF	134.5	11	559	13	43.00	4-69	–	–
E.N.Gay (Nh)	RM	5	0	22	1	22.00	1- 8	–	–
N.N.Gilchrist (K)	RFM	160.1	26	620	30	20.66	5-38	1	–
L.P.Goldsworthy (Sm)	SLA	24	8	45	0				
D.C.Goodman (Gs)	RM	104	25	252	5	50.40	2-19	–	–
B.G.F.Green (Sm)	RFM	40	11	93	1	93.00	1-29	–	–
L.Gregory (Sm)	RMF	209.3	60	645	21	30.71	5-68	1	–
G.T.Griffiths (Le)	RMF	92	8	388	7	55.42	3-93	–	–
N.R.T.Gubbins (H/M)	LB	1	0	2	0				
T.J.Haines (Sx)	RM	41	4	114	1	114.00	1-21	–	–
Hamidullah Qadri (K)	OB	17	2	44	1	44.00	1-20	–	–
M.A.H.Hammond (Gs)	OB	19	2	85	3	28.33	2-37	–	–
O.J.Hannon-Dalby (Wa)	RMF	258.5	73	698	24	29.08	5-76	1	–
S.R.Harmer (Ex)	OB	558.4	182	1233	53	23.26	9-80	3	2
J.A.R.Harris (Gm/M)	RFM	110.2	6	389	14	27.78	3-50	–	–
T.W.Hartley (La)	SLA	83	32	143	4	35.75	4-42	–	–
T.M.Head (Sx)	OB	27.4	4	109	1	109.00	1-23	–	–
T.G.Helm (M)	RMF	131.1	21	413	8	51.62	3-47	–	–
M.J.Henry (NZ)	RFM	38	9	114	6	19.00	3-36	–	–
R.F.Higgins (Gs)	RM	481	118	1143	51	22.41	5-46	2	–
G.C.H.Hill (Y)	RMF	48	12	128	7	18.28	2-12	–	–
L.J.Hill (Le)	RM	4	0	22	0				
T.I.Hinley (Sx)	SLA	6	0	35	0				
M.G.Hogan (Gm)	RFM	332.5	78	874	34	25.70	5-28	1	–
M.D.E.Holden (M)	OB	1	0	8	0				
C.K.Holder (Wa)	RFM	45	9	177	2	88.50	1-23	–	–
I.G.Holland (H)	RMF	147.1	35	433	6	72.16	3-19	–	–
L.B.K.Hollman (M)	LB	105.4	16	363	13	27.92	5-65	2	1
F.J.Hudson-Prentice (De/Sx)	RMF	240.2	52	752	26	28.92	5-68	1	–
A.L.Hughes (De)	RM	31	8	83	1	83.00	1- 9	–	–
S.F.Hunt (Sx)	LMF	127.5	18	487	13	37.46	3-47	–	–
B.A.Hutton (Nt)	RM	254	75	679	29	23.41	5-62	2	–
D.K.Ibrahim (Sx)	RM	67.4	11	236	3	78.66	2- 9	–	–
W.G.Jacks (Sy)	RM	64	9	216	4	54.00	1- 7	–	–
R.A.Jadeja (I)	SLA	153.2	33	372	8	46.50	2-36	–	–

	Cat	O	M	R	W	Avge	Best	5wI	10wM
L.W.James (CS/Nt)	RMF	160	33	478	16	29.87	4- 51	–	–
K.A.Jamieson (NZ/Sy)	RFM	93	39	184	10	18.40	5- 31	1	–
M.S.Johal (Wa)	RFM	18	5	59	4	14.75	3- 29	–	–
R.P.Jones (La)	LB	3	0	7	1	7.00	1- 4	–	–
A.S.Joseph (Wo)	RFM	158	21	574	15	38.26	2- 22	–	–
R.I.Keogh (Nh)	OB	126.4	15	462	5	92.40	2- 8	–	–
S.C.Kerrigan (Nh)	SLA	298.5	57	766	29	26.41	5- 39	2	–
L.P.J.Kimber (Le)	OB	3	1	15	0				
F.J.Klaassen (K)	LMF	42.5	3	172	3	57.33	2-110	–	–
D.Klein (Le)	LMF	53.5	5	254	4	63.50	2- 74	–	–
M.Labuschagne (Gm)	LB	32.2	3	127	2	63.50	2- 27	–	–
D.J.Lamb (La)	RMF	280.5	67	780	23	33.91	4- 60	–	–
M.J.Lamb (Wa)	RM	21	2	50	2	25.00	2- 38	–	–
T.A.Lammonby (Sm)	LM	77	13	287	4	71.75	1- 20	–	–
D.W.Lawrence (E/Ex)	LB	52.1	7	171	6	28.50	2- 28	–	–
J.Leach (Wo)	RMF	428	108	1141	38	30.02	5- 68	1	–
M.J.Leach (Sm)	SLA	241	77	562	18	31.22	6- 43	1	–
J.A.Leaning (K)	RMF	103.5	12	356	6	59.33	2-101	–	–
D.J.Leech (Y)	RMF	17	1	79	0				
A.D.Lenham (Sx)	LBG	13	0	71	1	71.00	1- 60	–	–
E.O.Leonard (Sm)	RMF	18	2	85	1	85.00	1- 68	–	–
J.D.Libby (CS/Wo)	OB	38.2	5	129	1	129.00	1- 45	–	–
J.B.Lintott (Wa)	SLA	39	2	103	0				
L.S.Livingstone (La)	LB	91	17	248	4	62.00	2- 34	–	–
D.L.Lloyd (Gm)	RM	170.3	24	558	21	26.57	4- 11	–	–
J.E.G.Logan (K)	SLA	47.1	11	119	8	14.87	3- 8	–	–
A.Lyth (Y)	RM	13	8	6	0				
J.P.McIlroy (Gm)	LFM	38	10	131	1	131.00	1- 12	–	–
M.H.McKiernan (De)	LB	4	0	16	0				
W.L.Madsen (De)	OB	43.5	8	130	4	32.50	2- 8	–	–
S.Mahmood (La)	RFM	233.1	52	669	28	23.89	5- 47	1	–
S.C.Meaker (Sx)	RFM	135.4	11	525	9	58.33	3- 22	–	–
D.R.Melton (De)	RFM	93	15	390	9	43.33	3- 57	–	–
B.W.M.Mike (Le)	RM	256	40	1002	23	43.56	4- 34	–	–
C.N.Miles (CS/Wa)	RMF	327.4	68	988	47	21.02	5- 28	3	–
M.E.Milnes (K)	RMF	205.3	42	687	32	21.46	6- 53	2	–
D.J.Mitchell (M/NZ)	RM	55	10	165	9	18.33	4- 42	–	–
D.K.H.Mitchell (Wo)	RM	93.5	15	291	4	72.75	2- 34	–	–
Mohammad Abbas (H)	RMF	309.5	113	651	41	15.87	6- 11	3	–
Mohammed Shami (I)	RFM	133.4	30	410	15	27.33	4- 76	–	–
D.T.Moriarty (Sy)	SLA	181.4	31	521	18	28.94	6- 60	1	–
C.A.J.Morris (Wo)	RMF	189.3	45	621	19	32.68	6- 52	1	–
E.H.T.Moulton (De)	RMF	40	8	159	3	53.00	2- 24	–	–
S.J.Mullaney (Nt)	RM	151.2	29	423	7	60.42	2- 37	–	–
T.J.Murtagh (M)	RMF	402.4	113	1079	58	18.60	5- 64	1	–
J.D.S.Neesham (Ex)	RM	4.1	0	15	2	7.50	2- 15	–	–
M.G.Neser (Gm)	RMF	127	29	386	23	16.78	5- 39	1	–
A.S.S.Nijjar (Ex)	SLA	13	5	21	0				
L.C.Norwell (Wa)	RMF	367	101	964	54	17.85	6- 57	2	–
D.Olivier (Y)	RF	175.1	26	610	18	33.88	4- 61	–	–
F.S.Organ (H)	OB	73	20	205	8	25.62	3- 22	–	–
M.K.O'Riordan (K)	OB	50	9	145	2	72.50	1- 14	–	–
C.Overton (E/Sm)	RMF	333	109	818	50	16.36	5- 25	4	–
J.Overton (Sy)	RFM	142.1	30	454	6	75.66	2- 36	–	–
C.F.Parkinson (Le)	SLA	479.4	122	1452	50	29.04	5- 45	3	1
M.W.Parkinson (La)	LB	352.5	90	818	40	20.45	7-126	1	–

	Cat	O	M	R	W	Avge	Best	5wI	10wM
W.D.Parnell (Nh)	LFM	114.4	26	427	18	23.72	5-64	2	1
A.R.Patel (I)	SLA	10.3	3	41	1	41.00	1-41	–	–
A.Y.Patel (NZ)	SLA	23	8	59	4	14.75	2-25	–	–
R.S.Patel (Sy)	RMF	23	5	80	0				
D.Paterson (Nt)	RFM	352.5	98	971	54	17.98	5-90	1	–
S.A.Patterson (Y)	RMF	364	111	815	32	25.46	4-26	–	–
L.A.Patterson-White (CS/Nt)	SLA	323	72	876	26	33.69	5-41	1	–
D.A.Payne (Gs)	LMF	258.2	59	719	34	21.14	6-56	2	1
D.Y.Pennington (Wo)	RMF	282.4	57	898	29	30.96	5-32	1	–
G.D.Phillips (Gs)	OB	40	3	159	4	39.75	2-67	–	–
H.W.Podmore (K)	RMF	114.3	16	419	12	34.91	4-77	–	–
J.A.Porter (Ex)	RFM	299.4	73	842	34	24.76	4-31	–	–
M.J.Potts (Du)	RM	204.3	51	613	23	26.65	4-32	–	–
T.J.Prest (H)	OB	1	0	5	0				
O.J.Price (Gs)	OB	33	5	100	0				
T.J.Price (Gs)	RM	128	37	368	15	24.53	4-72	–	–
L.A.Procter (Nh)	RM	115.5	29	352	13	27.07	5-42	1	–
M.R.Quinn (K)	RMF	149.3	34	413	18	22.94	4-54	–	–
B.A.Raine (Du)	RMF	406.1	128	968	43	22.51	5- 9	2	–
D.M.W.Rawlins (Sx)	SLA	171	17	573	4	143.25	2-12	–	–
L.M.Reece (De)	LM	183.3	46	555	12	46.25	2-25	–	–
S.J.Reingold (Gm)	OB	6	1	15	3	5.00	3-15	–	–
M.L.Revis (Y)	RM	9	2	19	2	9.50	2-19	–	–
G.H.Rhodes (Le)	OB	32	2	97	0				
W.M.H.Rhodes (CS/Wa)	RMF	190	53	523	26	20.11	5-23	1	–
K.A.J.Roach (Sy)	RF	134	28	452	22	20.54	8-40	2	1
O.E.Robinson (E/Sx)	RMF	415.2	107	1096	61	17.96	9-78	4	1
S.D.Robson (M)	LB	17	0	72	2	36.00	1- 8	–	–
T.S.Roland-Jones (M)	RFM	167.4	38	460	25	18.40	5-36	1	–
J.E.Root (E/Y)	OB	76.4	10	213	3	71.00	1-16	–	–
W.T.Root (Gm)	OB	13	0	64	0				
C.Rushworth (Du)	RMF	435.3	125	1073	59	18.18	6-49	3	–
H.D.Rutherford (Gm)	SLA	8	1	26	1	26.00	1-26	–	–
A.Sakande (Le)	RFM	89.2	14	309	7	44.14	3-66	–	–
J.J.G.Sales (Nh)	RM	40	9	154	3	51.33	2-61	–	–
M.E.T.Salisbury (Du)	RMF	142.4	38	440	16	27.50	4-74	–	–
A.G.Salter (Gm)	OB	218.5	41	687	15	45.80	4-18	–	–
B.W.Sanderson (Nh)	RMF	435.2	117	1155	43	26.86	5-28	3	1
M.J.Santner (NZ)	SLA	23	7	68	0				
J.P.Sarro (Sx)	RM	43	3	220	4	55.00	2-53	–	–
G.F.B.Scott (Gs)	RM	51	13	149	2	74.50	1-22	–	–
G.L.S.Scrimshaw (De)	RMF	35	6	154	3	51.33	2-40	–	–
I.Sharma (I)	RFM	87.2	18	243	8	30.37	3-48	–	–
J.Shaw (Gs)	RMF	86	10	333	9	37.00	4-48	–	–
P.M.Siddle (Ex)	RFM	176.2	37	488	20	24.40	6-38	1	–
R.N.Sidebottom (Wa)	RMF	46	9	113	0				
J.Singh (K)	RFM	40	5	140	7	20.00	4-51	–	–
M.Siraj (I)	RFM	142.5	24	466	16	29.12	4-32	–	–
B.T.Slater (Nt)	OB	2	0	8	0				
R.A.J.Smith (Gm)	RM	22	3	84	1	84.00	1-84	–	–
T.M.J.Smith (Gs)	SLA	104	8	303	4	75.75	1-21	–	–
S.Snater (Ex)	RM	168.5	42	511	31	16.48	7-98	2	–
I.S.Sodhi (Wo)	LBG	49.2	3	148	6	24.66	6-89	1	–
T.G.Southee (NZ)	RMF	83.1	19	192	12	16.00	6-43	1	–
N.A.Sowter (M)	LB	68	7	237	2	118.50	1-15	–	–
B.Stanlake (De)	RFM	17	2	91	2	45.50	2-91	–	–

	Cat	O	M	R	W	Avge	Best	5wI	10wM
C.T.Steel (H/Sy)	LB	24	1	120	1	120.00	1- 9	–	–
D.I.Stevens (K)	RM	284	93	725	39	18.58	5- 53	2	–
G.Stewart (K)	RMF	120	31	384	17	22.58	5- 23	1	–
B.A.Stokes (Du)	RFM	17	1	55	3	18.33	3- 55	–	–
O.P.Stone (E/Wa)	RF	149.3	25	492	16	30.75	4- 89	–	–
M.D.Stoneman (M/Sy)	OB	3	0	13	0				
C.Z.Taylor (Gm)	OB	146.2	16	484	5	96.80	2- 16	–	–
J.P.A.Taylor (Sy)	RM	15.1	5	44	2	22.00	2- 44	–	–
M.D.Taylor (Gs)	LMF	266.1	67	818	27	30.29	5- 40	1	–
T.A.I.Taylor (Nh)	RMF	263.2	63	783	29	27.00	5- 41	1	–
R.N.ten Doeschate (Ex)	RMF	9	0	35	1	35.00	1- 10	–	–
S.N.Thakur (I)	RFM	68	15	196	8	24.50	2- 22	–	–
A.D.Thomason (Sx)	RMF	3	0	30	0				
J.A.Thompson (Y)	RM	329.5	91	949	46	20.63	5- 52	1	–
A.T.Thomson (De)	OB	53.2	6	186	7	26.57	3- 71	–	–
J.C.Tongue (Wo)	RM	115.5	18	358	14	25.57	5- 39	1	–
R.J.W.Topley (Sy)	LFM	199.3	46	616	21	29.33	5- 66	1	–
L.Trevaskis (Du)	SLA	81.4	27	176	9	19.55	5- 78	1	–
G.L.van Buuren (Gs)	SLA	48.4	11	119	7	17.00	3- 28	–	–
T.van der Gugten (Gm)	RFM	274.3	54	823	27	30.48	4- 34	–	–
R.E.van der Merwe (Sm)	SLA	96.1	26	241	8	30.12	4- 54	–	–
S.van Zyl (Sx)	RM	11	2	22	1	22.00	1- 10	–	–
G.H.Vihari (I/Wa)	OB	1	0	11	0				
D.J.Vilas (La)	(WK)	1	0	6	0				
J.M.Vince (H)	RM	13	1	85	1	85.00	1- 55	–	–
G.S.Virdi (Sy)	OB	299.4	48	961	28	34.32	6-171	1	–
N.Wagner (NZ)	LMF	101	24	280	10	28.00	3- 18	–	–
T.N.Walallawita (M)	SLA	102.2	20	326	3	108.66	2- 84	–	–
P.I.Walter (Ex)	LMF	34	4	120	2	60.00	2- 18	–	–
H.D.Ward (Sx)	OB	1	0	2	0				
J.D.Warner (Gs)	RFM	37.3	7	118	4	29.50	2- 54	–	–
J.J.Weatherley (H)	OB	9	2	22	1	22.00	1- 22	–	–
W.J.Weighell (Gm)	RMF	80.1	9	359	7	51.28	2- 46	–	–
L.W.P.Wells (La)	LB	68	13	186	9	20.66	3- 8	–	–
T.Westley (Ex)	OB	10	1	12	0				
B.T.J.Wheal (H)	RMF	298.5	62	882	34	25.94	4- 59	–	–
C.White (Nh)	RFM	94	10	319	5	63.80	4- 40	–	–
R.A.Whiteley (Wo)	LM	10	1	33	1	33.00	1- 22	–	–
B.J.Wightman (K)	RM	12	4	23	0				
D.J.Willey (Y)	LMF	148.3	30	479	20	23.95	5- 61	1	–
K.S.Williamson (NZ)	OB	3	0	12	0				
C.R.Woakes (E/Wa)	RFM	119.3	37	343	19	18.05	4- 55	–	–
L.Wood (La)	LFM	205	32	660	18	36.66	3- 31	–	–
M.A.Wood (Du/E)	RF	181	36	580	21	27.61	3- 28	–	–
D.J.Worrall (Gs)	RFM	249.5	80	621	27	23.00	5- 54	2	–
C.J.C.Wright (Le)	RFM	351	74	1116	49	22.77	7- 53	4	–
U.T.Yadav (I)	RFM	55.1	12	163	9	18.11	3- 22	–	–
R.M.Yates (CS/Wa)	OB	51	9	118	3	39.33	2- 54	–	–
Zafar Gohar (Gs)	SLA	117.3	32	287	20	14.35	6- 43	3	1
S.A.Zaib (Nh)	SLA	43.1	6	139	3	46.33	2- 32	–	–

FIRST-CLASS CAREER RECORDS

Compiled by Philip Bailey

The following career records are for all players who appeared in first-class, county cricket and The Hundred during the 2021 season, and are complete to the end of that season. Some players who did not appear in 2021 but may do so in 2022 are included.

BATTING AND FIELDING

'1000' denotes instances of scoring 1000 runs in a season. Where these have been achieved outside the British Isles they are shown after a plus sign.

	M	*I*	*NO*	*HS*	*Runs*	*Avge*	*100*	*50*	*1000*	*Ct/St*
Aavesh Khan	27	27	7	64	292	14.60	–	1	–	5
Abbott, K.J.	125	169	33	97*	2575	18.93	–	10	–	19
Abbott, S.A.	64	91	9	102*	1893	23.08	1	10	–	37
Abell, T.B.	93	166	16	135	4952	33.01	8	28	–	66
Ackermann, C.N.	140	243	28	196*	8728	40.59	18	55	0+1	138
Agarwal, M.A.	69	119	6	304*	5167	45.72	11	27	0+1	40
Aitchison, B.W.	16	21	4	50	208	12.23	–	1	–	14
Aldridge, K.L.	1	–	–	–	–	–	–	–	–	0
Ali, M.M.	198	339	27	250	11334	36.32	20	69	2	119
Allen, F.H.	12	20	2	66	343	19.05	–	3	–	12
Allison, B.M.J.	3	4	–	52	69	17.25	–	1	–	1
Alsop, T.P.	63	105	6	150	2563	25.88	4	14	–	79
Amla, H.M.	251	418	34	311*	18803	48.96	55	90	0+2	188
Anderson, J.M.	267	342	141	81	1903	9.46	–	1	–	153
Andersson, M.K.	26	48	3	92	860	19.11	–	5	–	15
Archer, J.C.	43	63	10	81*	1201	22.66	–	6	–	21
Ashwin, R.	135	188	31	124	4597	29.28	7	22	–	52
Atkins, J.A.	5	9	5	10*	21	5.25	–	–	–	0
Atkinson, A.A.P.	4	8	1	41*	73	10.42	–	–	–	0
Azad, M.H.	41	66	7	152	2321	39.33	6	12	1	18
Azhar Ali	218	381	31	302*	13730	39.22	41	61	–	148
Bailey, T.E.	73	96	13	68	1505	18.13	–	7	–	15
Bairstow, J.M.	191	317	34	246	12029	42.50	24	64	3	487/24
Baker, J.O.	5	7	2	61*	84	16.80	–	1	–	4
Balbirnie, A.	33	48	3	205*	1353	30.06	2	8	–	31
Balderson, G.P.	11	16	3	77	367	28.23	–	3	–	0
Ball, J.T.	67	102	24	49*	1024	13.12	–	–	–	13
Ballance, G.S.	170	276	25	210	11876	47.31	41	55	4+1	122
Bamber, E.R.	26	44	11	27*	311	9.42	–	–	–	4
Bancroft, C.T.	114	207	16	228*	7216	37.78	17	29	–	145/1
Banton, T.	22	38	1	79	848	22.91	–	6	–	12
Barber, T.E.	5	6	4	3	5	2.50	–	–	–	0
Barker, K.H.D.	139	188	32	125	4397	28.18	6	20	–	37
Barnard, E.G.	78	114	19	128	2858	30.08	2	15	–	52
Barnes, E.	12	13	4	83*	263	29.22	–	2	–	4
Bartlett, G.A.	40	67	4	137	1711	27.15	5	5	–	10
Bates, S.D.	1	2	–	6	6	3.00	–	–	–	2/1
Batty, G.J.	261	389	68	133	7399	23.04	3	30	–	163
Bedingham, D.G.	50	83	9	257	3524	47.62	10	12	1	46
Beer, W.A.T.	28	36	8	97	797	28.46	–	4	–	6
Bell-Drummond, D.J.	127	218	18	206*	6416	32.08	11	32	1	49
Benjamin, C.G.	5	9	–	127	244	27.11	1	–	–	3
Berg, G.K.	142	211	26	130*	5227	28.25	2	28	–	72
Bess, D.M.	65	97	15	107	1874	22.85	1	8	–	26
Bethell, J.G.	1	2	–	15	23	11.50	–	–	–	1
Billings, S.W.	74	108	11	171	3327	34.29	6	15	–	173/11

	M	I	NO	HS	Runs	Avge	100	50	1000	Ct/St
Bird, J.M.	99	136	35	64	1257	12.44	–	3	–	48
Blake, A.J.	46	72	6	105*	1511	22.89	1	6	–	25
Blatherwick, J.M.	6	7	2	11	23	4.60	–	–	–	1
Blundell, T.A.	72	121	15	153	3856	36.37	10	16	–	155/6
Bohannon, J.J.	36	48	6	174	1862	44.33	3	11	–	17
Bopara, R.S.	221	357	40	229	12821	40.44	31	55	1	118
Borthwick, S.G.	182	305	25	216	9762	34.86	20	51	4	235
Boult, T.A.	108	128	52	61	1140	15.00	–	2	–	55
Bracey, J.R.	52	90	8	156	2819	34.37	6	14	–	88
Brathwaite, C.R.	39	64	9	109	1522	27.67	1	9	–	20
Brathwaite, K.C.	176	317	21	246	11173	37.74	24	57	–	111
Bresnan, T.T.	213	294	45	169*	7128	28.62	7	36	–	125
Briggs, D.R.	121	158	41	120*	2182	18.64	1	4	–	42
Broad, S.C.J.	239	337	56	169	5427	19.31	1	25	–	85
Brook, H.C.	47	76	2	124	2082	28.13	4	11	–	36
Brookes, E.A.	3	3	1	15*	21	10.50	–	–	–	0
Brooks, J.A.	139	175	62	109*	1874	16.58	1	5	–	32
Brown, B.C.	157	250	36	163	8649	40.41	22	44	2	434/21
Browne, N.L.J.	109	176	12	255	6197	37.78	16	28	3	79
Buck, N.L.	100	140	38	53	1475	14.46	–	3	–	18
Bulpitt, J.	1	–	–	–	–	–	–	–	–	0
Bumrah, J.J.	52	67	33	55*	310	9.11	–	1	–	15
Burgess, M.G.K.	53	77	4	146	2474	33.89	3	13	–	91/6
Burnham, J.T.A.	52	87	7	135	2045	25.56	2	11	–	17
Burns, R.J.	156	271	15	219*	10714	41.85	21	63	7	131
Buttleman, W.E.L.	1	1	–	0	0	0.00	–	–	–	3
Buttler, J.C.	118	191	15	152	5781	32.84	7	33	–	262/3
Byrom, E.J.	34	61	3	152	1585	27.32	3	5	–	17
Came, H.R.C.	8	11	1	45	140	14.00	–	–	–	2
Campbell, J.O.I.	3	4	2	2	2	1.00	–	–	–	0
Carey, L.J.	33	46	6	62*	631	15.77	–	3	–	5
Carlson, K.S.	48	83	6	191	2430	31.55	7	9	–	19
Carse, B.A.	33	41	10	77*	804	25.93	–	2	–	5
Carson, J.J.	19	32	4	87	445	15.89	–	3	–	5
Carter, M.	17	27	2	33	241	9.64	–	–	–	16
Carter, O.J.	6	12	1	51	235	21.36	–	1	–	14
Carver, K.	8	13	6	20	108	15.42	–	–	–	4
Chappell, Z.J.	26	39	7	96	659	20.59	–	2	–	5
Charlesworth, B.G.	18	27	2	77*	529	21.16	–	4	–	5
Chopra, V.	192	317	20	233*	10243	34.48	20	50	3	228
Christian, D.T.	83	141	17	131*	3783	30.50	5	16	–	90
Clark, G.	37	67	2	109	1626	25.01	1	10	–	25
Clark, J.	64	90	9	140	2100	25.92	1	12	–	9
Clark, T.G.R.	12	22	2	65	363	18.15	–	2	–	8
Clarke, J.M.	93	160	11	194	5609	37.64	18	23	1	44
Clarke, R.	267	403	49	214	11387	32.16	17	58	1	391
Claydon, M.E.	113	146	36	77	1710	15.54	–	4	–	11
Coad, B.O.	48	63	21	48	603	14.35	–	–	–	2
Cobb, J.J.	127	218	22	148*	5156	26.30	4	30	–	54
Cockbain, I.A.	57	97	7	151*	2684	29.82	5	15	–	36
Cohen, M.A.R.	22	28	15	30*	172	13.23	–	–	–	2
Coles, J.M.	3	6	1	36	93	18.60	–	–	–	0
Compton, B.G.	5	8	1	20	98	14.00	–	–	–	3
Conners, S.	17	22	6	39	179	11.18	–	–	–	1
Conway, D.P.	113	183	23	327*	7630	47.68	19	35	–	99
Cook, A.N.	324	568	42	294	24841	47.22	69	117	9+1	349
Cook, S.J.	47	48	17	37*	266	8.58	–	–	–	4
Cooke, C.B.	103	174	26	205*	5588	37.75	8	33	–	197/7

	M	I	NO	HS	Runs	Avge	100	50	1000	Ct/St
Cooke, J.M.	14	19	2	68	279	16.41	–	1	–	14
Cornall, T.R.	2	4	–	19	43	10.75	–	–	–	2
Coughlin, P.	46	71	8	90	1571	24.93	–	8	–	25
Cox, J.M.	20	33	3	238*	974	32.46	1	4	–	17
Cox, O.B.	135	217	29	124	5177	27.53	4	28	–	372/15
Cracknell, J.B.	1	2	–	13	20	10.00	–	–	–	2
Crane, M.S.	48	65	20	29	511	11.35	–	–	–	11
Crawley, Z.	65	112	3	267	3415	31.33	5	21	–	55
Critchley, M.J.J.	67	114	13	137*	3254	32.21	4	18	1	42
Crocombe, H.T.	13	25	6	46*	128	6.73	–	–	–	1
Croft, S.J.	191	289	29	156	8792	33.81	14	52	–	190
Cullen, B.C.	6	8	–	34	104	13.00	–	–	–	1
Cullen, T.N.	20	31	3	63	582	20.78	–	4	–	50/1
Cummins, M.L.	90	115	44	29*	542	7.63	–	–	–	32
Curran, B.J.	25	42	4	83*	1075	28.28	–	6	–	18
Curran, S.M.	74	114	14	96	2732	27.32	–	18	–	19
Curran, T.K.	59	81	11	60	1241	17.72	–	5	–	20
Currie, S.W.	2	4	–	38	43	10.75	–	–	–	3
Dal, A.K.	27	43	7	106	843	23.41	1	4	–	17
Dale, A.S.	2	4	1	6	7	2.33	–	–	–	0
Davey, J.H.	50	77	19	75*	1076	18.55	–	4	–	15
Davies, A.L.	94	143	8	147	4773	35.35	5	33	1	181/19
Davies, J.L.B.	3	5	–	24	48	9.60	–	–	–	1
Davies, S.M.	244	406	39	200*	14051	38.28	25	67	6	588/34
Davis, W.S.	32	43	15	42	336	12.00	–	–	–	6
Dawson, L.A.	164	267	29	169	7812	32.82	10	42	1	165
de Caires, J.M.	2	4	–	17	28	7.00	–	–	–	1
de Grandhomme, C.	116	187	26	174*	6007	37.31	13	35	–	108
de Lange, M.	95	128	17	113	1878	16.91	1	5	–	40
Dearden, H.E.	45	78	2	87	1629	21.43	–	8	–	29
Dell, J.J.	7	12	–	61	158	13.16	–	1	–	5
Denly, J.L.	221	380	25	227	12720	35.83	29	64	4	88
Dent, C.D.J.	159	286	25	268	9711	37.20	18	58	4	165
Dernbach, J.W.	113	139	47	56*	871	9.46	–	1	–	17
Dickson, S.R.	77	129	10	318	3912	32.87	10	15	–	63
D'Oliveira, B.L.	78	130	6	202*	3640	29.35	8	11	–	34
Douthwaite, D.A.	27	41	3	100*	1085	28.55	1	6	–	7
Drissell, G.S.	7	11	–	19	77	7.00	–	–	–	0
du Plessis, F.	150	250	26	199	8798	39.27	18	52	–	142
du Plooy, J.L.	71	115	13	181	4094	40.13	12	21	–	57
Duckett, B.M.	108	185	10	282*	6845	39.11	19	30	2	85/3
Duke, H.G.	9	13	1	54	197	16.41	–	2	–	31
Dunn, M.P.	43	50	22	31*	197	7.03	–	–	–	10
Eckersley, E.J.H.	139	241	19	158	7171	32.30	16	27	1	248/4
Eskinazi, S.S.	65	116	7	179	3478	31.90	7	14	–	60
Evans, H.A.	9	14	5	15	61	6.77	–	–	–	1
Evans, L.J.	73	125	6	213*	3495	29.36	6	18	–	58
Evans, S.T.	23	36	1	138	988	28.22	4	2	–	8
Evison, J.D.M.	6	10	–	58	247	24.70	–	1	–	2
Fell, T.C.	96	162	7	171	4468	28.82	6	19	1	73
Ferguson, L.H.	45	60	23	41	505	13.64	–	–	–	16
Finch, A.W.	14	19	7	31	127	10.58	–	–	–	1
Finch, H.Z.	54	91	6	135*	2305	27.11	4	13	–	68
Finn, S.T.	159	195	63	56	1283	9.71	–	2	–	49
Fisher, M.D.	20	26	5	47*	303	14.42	–	–	–	7
Fletcher, L.J.	130	191	33	92	2169	13.72	–	5	–	29
Foakes, B.T.	122	192	32	141*	6129	38.30	11	33	–	249/29
Fraine, W.A.R.	19	30	1	106	557	19.20	1	–	–	10

	M	I	NO	HS	Runs	Avge	100	50	1000	Ct/St
Fuller, J.K.	59	78	10	93	1334	19.61	–	6	–	23
Garrett, G.A.	3	4	2	24	32	16.00	–	–	–	0
Garton, G.H.S.	24	34	6	97	569	20.32	–	4	–	14
Gay, E.N.	14	23	1	101	512	23.27	1	2	–	10
Geddes, B.B.A.	1	2	–	15	19	9.50	–	–	–	0
Gilchrist, N.N.	10	10	1	25	90	10.00	–	–	–	2
Gill, S.	31	53	7	268	2684	58.34	7	14	–	19
Gleeson, R.J.	34	39	16	31	259	11.26	–	–	–	8
Glover, B.D.	10	15	6	12*	38	4.22	–	–	–	1
Godleman, B.A.	173	311	15	227	9559	32.29	22	44	2	105
Goldsworthy, L.P.	10	15	1	48	297	21.21	–	–	–	1
Goodman, D.C.	4	5	3	9*	20	10.00	–	–	–	0
Gordon, J.A.	1	2	–	8	8	4.00	–	–	–	0
Gouldstone, H.O.M.	5	8	2	67*	155	25.83	–	1	–	1
Green, B.G.F.	9	17	1	54	324	20.25	–	1	–	5
Gregory, L.	98	142	15	137	2958	23.29	3	11	–	56
Griffiths, G.T.	31	42	16	40	370	14.23	–	–	–	4
Gubbins, N.R.T.	91	163	4	201*	5303	33.35	10	32	1	36
Guest, B.D.	15	24	1	116	525	22.82	1	1	–	31/3
Hain, S.R.	95	151	14	208	4924	35.94	11	28	–	90
Haines, T.J.	34	60	1	156	2008	34.03	5	8	1	8
Hales, A.D.	107	182	6	236	6655	37.81	13	38	3	84
Hameed, H.	83	139	13	122	4123	32.72	8	24	1	54
Hamidullah Qadri	15	27	11	30*	126	7.87	–	–	–	6
Hammond, M.A.H.	36	63	5	123*	1561	26.91	2	9	–	34
Handscomb, P.S.P.	126	211	14	215	7238	36.74	15	42	–	194/4
Hankins, G.T.	38	60	3	116	1211	21.24	1	7	–	42
Hannon-Dalby, O.J.	83	102	37	40	497	7.64	–	–	–	10
Haris Rauf	3	2	2	9*	9	–	–	–	–	3
Harmer, S.R.	165	243	48	102*	4718	24.19	2	24	–	164
Harris, J.A.R.	153	224	52	87*	3952	22.97	–	18	–	44
Harris, M.S.	114	204	14	250*	7567	39.82	18	31	0+1	58
Harrison, C.G.	2	3	1	37*	65	32.50	–	–	–	1
Hartley, T.W.	7	8	4	25	96	24.00	–	–	–	4
Haynes, J.A.	19	30	2	97	895	31.96	–	6	–	10
Head, T.M.	121	219	13	223	8183	39.72	15	49	0+1	58
Helm, T.G.	34	49	10	52	608	15.58	–	1	–	10
Hendricks, B.E.	93	110	36	68	730	9.86	–	1	–	26
Henry, M.J.	74	95	16	81	1562	19.77	–	5	–	32
Higgins, R.F.	51	80	10	199	2162	30.88	5	7	–	15
Hildreth, J.C.	280	461	32	303*	17744	41.36	47	78	7	247
Hill, G.C.H.	9	13	1	71	296	24.66	–	2	–	1
Hill, L.J.	55	93	10	145	2403	28.95	4	10	–	99/3
Hinley, T.I.	1	2	–	19	20	10.00	–	–	–	0
Hogan, M.G.	172	239	95	57	2361	16.39	–	4	–	81
Holden, M.D.E.	53	97	5	153	2356	25.60	3	9	–	21
Holder, C.K.	23	33	14	34*	153	8.05	–	–	–	13
Holland, I.G.	45	72	7	146*	1752	26.95	3	9	–	21
Hollman, L.B.K.	6	9	1	46	176	22.00	–	–	–	3
Hooper, E.O.	1	1	–	20	20	20.00	–	–	–	0
Hose, A.J.	19	35	1	111	746	21.94	1	4	–	5
Hosein, H.R.	59	100	20	138*	2580	32.25	2	20	–	132/5
Houillon, H.F.	1	2	–	9	9	4.50	–	–	–	3
Howell, B.A.C.	86	136	13	163	3378	27.46	2	18	–	52
Hudson-Prentice, F.J.	27	45	7	99	925	24.34	–	4	–	7
Hughes, A.L.	78	136	12	142	3401	27.42	6	13	–	54
Hunt, S.F.	6	10	4	7	12	2.00	–	–	–	0
Hurt, L.J.	3	3	–	38	41	13.66	–	–	–	0

	M	I	NO	HS	Runs	Avge	100	50	1000	Ct/St
Hutton, B.A.	66	100	12	74	1554	17.65	–	5	–	43
Ibrahim, D.K.	6	11	–	94	328	29.81	–	3	–	3
Inglis, J.P.	44	73	9	153*	2205	34.45	3	12	–	145/4
Ingram, C.A.	112	197	17	190	6675	37.08	14	30	–	75
Jacks, W.G.	30	44	5	120	1142	29.28	1	9	–	32
Jadeja, R.A.	110	162	27	331	6201	45.93	10	33	–	90
James, L.W.	15	22	2	91	635	31.75	–	5	–	2
Jamieson, K.A.	37	47	9	67	803	21.13	–	5	–	7
Jennings, K.K.	148	254	17	221*	8078	34.08	20	31	1	121
Johal, M.S.	1	1	–	19	19	19.00	–	–	–	0
Jones, M.A.	13	21	1	82	443	22.15	–	3	–	4
Jones, R.P.	39	56	5	122	1374	26.94	2	6	–	38
Jordan, C.J.	114	159	23	166	3443	25.31	3	15	–	137
Joseph, A.S.	49	76	12	89	1024	16.00	–	5	–	18
Kelly, M.L.	32	42	9	89	551	16.69	–	1	–	13
Keogh, R.I.	97	159	10	221	4453	29.88	11	14	–	24/1
Kerrigan, S.C.	117	142	48	62*	1283	13.64	–	3	–	40
Khushi, F.I.N.	4	5	–	66	125	25.00	–	1	–	5
Kimber, L.P.J.	6	9	1	71	250	31.25	–	3	–	7
Klaassen, F.J.	5	8	3	14*	45	9.00	–	–	–	3
Klein, D.	71	100	19	94	1455	17.96	–	6	–	19
Kohler-Cadmore, T.	77	126	8	176	3812	32.30	9	16	1	108
Kohli, V.	128	210	17	254*	10014	51.88	34	35	0+1	127
Kuhn, H.G.	179	315	28	244*	11550	40.24	24	58	0+1	378/18
Labuschagne, M.	94	164	11	215	6999	45.74	18	38	1+2	85
Lace, T.C.	33	61	5	143	1730	30.89	4	7	–	22
Lakmal, R.A.S.	126	163	36	58*	1480	11.65	–	1	–	43
Lamb, D.J.	19	25	4	125	575	27.38	1	3	–	7
Lamb, M.J.	33	56	7	173	1356	27.67	1	7	–	11
Lammonby, T.A.	19	33	4	116	851	29.34	4	2	–	11
Latham, T.W.M.	126	216	14	264*	8668	42.91	20	48	–	163/1
Lavelle, G.I.D.	3	5	–	32	56	11.20	–	–	–	7
Lawrence, D.W.	92	145	16	161	4942	38.31	11	25	1	64
Leach, J.	106	157	22	114	3296	24.41	2	19	–	25
Leach, M.J.	106	149	37	92	1467	13.09	–	3	–	44
Leaning, J.A.	86	137	17	220*	3979	33.15	6	22	–	72
Leech, D.J.	3	2	1	1	1	1.00	–	–	–	0
Lees, A.Z.	126	215	14	275*	7075	35.19	17	35	2	87
Lenham, A.D.	1	2	–	20	29	14.50	–	–	–	0
Leonard, E.O.	1	2	1	6	10	10.00	–	–	–	1
Levi, R.E.	106	176	18	168	5722	36.21	10	32	–	89
Libby, J.D.	75	130	11	184	4176	35.09	10	18	1	29
Lilley, A.M.	16	20	5	63	444	29.60	–	2	–	5
Lincoln, D.J.	1	2	–	41	41	20.50	–	–	–	1
Linde, G.F.	58	85	9	148*	2287	30.09	4	10	–	33
Lintott, J.B.	1	1	–	15	15	15.00	–	–	–	1
Livingstone, L.S.	62	94	14	224	3069	38.36	7	15	–	74
Lloyd, D.L.	83	141	13	121	3767	29.42	5	16	–	41
Logan, J.E.G.	6	9	2	21	84	12.00	–	–	–	2
Loten, T.W.	5	7	–	58	126	18.00	–	1	–	0
Lyth, A.	195	326	16	251	11713	37.78	27	61	3	261
McDermott, B.R.	40	71	8	107*	2060	32.69	2	15	–	27
McIlroy, J.P.	2	1	–	0	0	0.00	–	–	–	0
McKerr, C.	14	15	4	29	133	12.09	–	–	–	2
McKiernan, M.H.	4	7	–	52	133	19.00	–	1	–	7
MacLeod, C.S.	28	41	6	84	904	25.82	–	5	–	20
McManus, L.D.	55	77	8	132*	1876	27.18	1	9	–	122/13
Madsen, W.L.	200	357	24	231*	12852	38.59	32	66	5	218

	M	I	NO	HS	Runs	Avge	100	50	1000	Ct/St
Mahmood, S.	24	29	11	34	227	12.61	–	–	–	3
Malan, D.J.	195	332	21	219	11887	38.22	27	61	3	202
Malan, P.J.	164	273	21	264	11294	44.81	35	46	0+2	109
Maxwell, G.J.	67	112	10	278	4061	39.81	7	23	–	55
Mayers, K.R.	40	69	5	210*	1971	30.79	3	14	–	23
Meaker, S.C.	98	132	26	94	1664	15.69	–	6	–	22
Melton, D.R.	11	15	6	15	51	5.66	–	–	–	3
Mike, B.W.M.	28	43	4	74	887	22.74	–	6	–	6
Miles, C.N.	89	125	21	62*	1624	15.61	–	5	–	24
Mills, T.S.	32	38	15	31*	260	11.30	–	–	–	9
Milne, A.F.	30	45	14	97	756	24.38	–	4	–	10
Milnes, M.E.	35	52	15	78	632	17.08	–	1	–	15
Mitchell, D.J.	81	129	17	170*	4278	38.19	10	23	–	88
Mitchell, D.K.H.	225	403	40	298	13920	38.34	39	55	6	301
Mohammad Abbas	128	180	66	40	733	6.42	–	–	–	35
Mohammad Nabi	35	57	4	117	1284	24.22	2	5	–	20
Mohammad Rizwan	97	147	24	224	5337	43.39	11	27	–	272/18
Mohammed Shami	78	106	32	56*	889	12.01	–	2	–	19
Montgomery, M.	4	6	1	50*	175	35.00	–	1	–	4
Moores, T.J.	51	85	4	106	1858	22.93	2	5	–	144/4
Morgan, E.J.G.	102	169	18	209*	5042	33.39	11	24	1	76/1
Moriarty, D.T.	6	6	–	8	13	2.16	–	–	–	2
Morley, J.P.	1	1	–	3	3	3.00	–	–	–	0
Morris, C.A.J.	69	91	49	53*	570	13.57	–	2	–	12
Moulton, E.H.T.	3	4	1	6*	9	3.00	–	–	–	0
Mousley, D.R.	3	5	–	71	152	30.40	–	1	–	1
Mujeeb Zadran	1	2	–	15	18	9.00	–	–	–	0
Mullaney, S.J.	157	263	9	179	8384	33.00	16	45	1	148
Munsey, H.G.	4	5	1	100*	224	56.00	1	1	–	1
Murtagh, T.J.	248	333	97	74*	4285	18.15	–	11	–	68
Muyeye, T.S.	4	6	2	89	142	35.50	–	1	–	0
Naseem Shah	18	21	7	12	56	4.00	–	–	–	2
Naveen-ul-Haq	10	13	1	34	93	7.75	–	–	–	5
Neesham, J.D.S.	66	111	10	147	3249	32.16	5	17	–	66
Neser, M.G.	67	92	12	121	2010	25.12	1	11	–	29
Nicholls, H.M.	91	147	11	174	5436	39.97	12	30	–	72
Nijjar, A.S.S.	14	16	5	53	239	21.72	–	1	–	3
Northeast, S.A.	182	306	23	191	10839	38.30	25	56	4	89
Norwell, L.C.	86	112	42	102	962	13.74	1	2	–	17
Olivier, D.	121	157	51	72	1324	12.49	–	3	–	34
Organ, F.S.	18	29	–	100	589	20.31	1	3	–	11
O'Riordan, M.K.	13	17	3	52*	377	26.92	–	1	–	5
Orr, A.G.H.	7	14	–	119	548	39.14	1	4	–	1
Overton, C.	105	154	19	138	2920	21.62	1	13	–	79
Overton, J.	77	108	22	120	1660	19.30	1	9	–	44
Pant, R.R.	49	78	6	308	3401	47.23	8	15	–	159/15
Parkinson, C.F.	41	60	10	75	888	17.76	–	1	–	6
Parkinson, M.W.	32	38	18	21*	153	7.65	–	–	–	7
Parnell, W.D.	81	108	11	111*	2609	26.89	2	16	–	23
Patel, A.R.	43	60	8	110*	1720	33.07	1	13	–	21
Patel, A.Y.	67	96	25	52	972	13.69	–	1	–	47
Patel, R.K.	12	17	–	44	313	18.41	–	–	–	10
Patel, R.S.	32	52	4	100*	1176	24.50	1	4	–	17
Patel, S.R.	231	376	20	257*	12692	35.65	26	64	4	140
Paterson, D.	115	143	42	59	1278	12.65	–	1	–	43
Patterson, S.A.	172	207	45	63*	2568	15.85	–	4	–	34
Patterson-White, L.A.	20	29	5	101	662	27.58	1	4	–	7
Pattinson, J.L.	76	97	21	89*	1659	21.82	–	5	–	23

	M	I	NO	HS	Runs	Avge	100	50	1000	Ct/St
Payne, D.A.	109	134	42	67*	1754	19.06	–	6	–	37
Pearce, S.J.	4	4	–	35	55	13.75	–	–	–	0
Pennington, D.Y.	25	40	9	56	309	9.96	–	1	–	6
Pepper, M.S.	9	13	–	92	265	20.38	–	2	–	9
Petersen, K.D.	99	166	16	225*	6063	40.42	16	26	0+1	71/4
Phillips, G.D.	40	68	4	138*	2440	38.12	6	14	–	35
Pillans, M.W.	42	59	5	56	730	13.51	–	1	–	20
Plom, J.H.	1	–	–	–	–	–	–	–	–	0
Podmore, H.W.	50	71	19	66*	959	18.44	–	3	–	12
Pollock, E.J.	5	7	1	52	184	30.66	–	1	–	1
Pope, O.J.D.	59	91	13	274	4153	53.24	12	13	2	62
Porter, J.A.	102	118	45	34	460	6.30	–	–	–	28
Potts, M.J.	18	25	6	81	382	20.10	–	2	–	5
Poynter, S.W.	47	73	4	170	1522	22.05	2	6	–	139/4
Poysden, J.E.	14	14	4	47	96	9.60	–	–	–	2
Prest, T.J.	2	1	–	18	18	18.00	–	–	–	1
Price, O.J.	4	7	–	33	110	15.71	–	–	–	4
Price, T.J.	7	11	4	71	177	25.28	–	1	–	1
Procter, L.A.	111	176	19	137	4905	31.24	4	27	–	26
Pujara, C.A.	218	359	38	352	16538	51.52	50	67	0+3	139/1
Qais Ahmad	12	17	2	46*	226	15.06	–	–	–	7
Quinn, M.R.	42	51	14	50	392	10.59	–	1	–	7
Rahane, A.M.	160	273	27	265*	11621	47.23	35	51	0+3	165
Rahmanullah Gurbaz	12	19	–	153	941	49.52	1	7	–	16/5
Rahul, K.L.	83	140	5	337	6218	46.05	16	30	0+2	89
Raine, B.A.	96	151	18	82	2897	21.78	–	12	–	19
Rampaul, R.	92	135	33	64*	1317	12.91	–	2	–	25
Rashid, A.U.	175	251	41	180	6822	32.48	10	37	–	79
Rashid Khan	9	11	1	52	231	23.10	–	2	–	0
Rawlins, D.M.W.	29	51	1	100	1127	22.54	1	7	–	8
Reece, L.M.	76	137	8	184	4036	31.28	7	23	–	36
Reingold, S.J.	3	5	–	22	42	8.40	–	–	–	1
Renshaw, M.T.	69	125	9	184	4248	36.62	12	12	–	58
Revis, M.L.	2	4	–	34	43	10.75	–	–	–	1
Rew, J.E.K.	1	1	–	2	2	2.00	–	–	–	1/1
Rhodes, G.H.	31	56	8	90	1164	24.25	–	7	–	16
Rhodes, W.M.H.	71	116	6	207	3897	35.42	7	19	–	46
Roach, K.A.J.	132	183	38	53	1930	13.31	–	3	–	38
Robinson, O.E.	69	101	18	110	1775	21.38	1	7	–	23
Robinson, O.G.	36	57	3	143	1708	31.62	4	7	–	115/1
Robson, S.D.	176	313	20	253	11012	37.58	26	42	3	168
Roderick, G.H.	107	174	23	171	5069	33.56	6	32	–	278/5
Roland-Jones, T.S.	120	170	32	103*	2962	21.46	1	11	–	33
Root, J.E.	174	304	26	254	13657	49.12	34	68	3	185
Root, W.T.	44	74	5	229	2193	31.78	6	5	–	12
Rossington, A.M.	91	145	14	138*	4636	35.38	7	32	–	199/13
Roy, J.J.	87	144	11	143	4850	36.46	9	23	1	75
Rushworth, C.	144	199	65	57	1605	11.97	–	1	–	31
Rutherford, H.D.	115	199	3	239	7090	36.17	15	37	0+1	73
Rymell, J.S.	3	3	–	14	23	7.66	–	–	–	2
Sakande, A.	21	27	11	33	174	10.87	–	–	–	8
Sales, J.J.G.	3	6	2	53	112	28.00	–	1	–	1
Salisbury, M.E.T.	38	61	11	41	454	9.08	–	–	–	4
Salt, P.D.	38	66	2	148	1967	30.73	4	10	–	33
Salter, A.G.	66	98	21	90	1850	24.02	–	9	–	31
Sanderson, B.W.	75	97	33	42	516	8.06	–	–	–	11
Santner, M.J.	54	81	5	126	2152	28.31	3	12	–	45
Sarro, J.P.	3	6	3	7*	8	2.66	–	–	–	1

	M	I	NO	HS	Runs	Avge	100	50	1000	Ct/St
Schadendorf, D.J.	1	1	–	24	24	24.00	–	–	–	4
Scott, G.F.B.	21	31	5	55	444	17.07	–	1	–	8
Scrimshaw, G.L.S.	3	5	3	5*	5	2.50	–	–	–	1
Scriven, T.A.R.	2	3	–	68	84	28.00	–	1	–	1
Selman, N.J.	61	113	6	150	2863	26.75	7	14	–	67
Shaheen Shah Afridi	25	33	6	25	153	5.66	–	–	–	2
Shan Masood	132	225	10	199	7440	34.60	15	36	0+1	79
Sharif, S.M.	9	12	4	60	229	28.62	–	1	–	5
Sharma, I.	148	187	66	66	1061	8.76	–	2	–	33
Sharma, R.G.	104	165	18	309*	8033	54.64	25	34	–	91
Shaw, J.	43	58	11	42	566	12.04	–	–	–	9
Short, D.J.M.	16	29	2	66	776	28.74	–	5	–	12
Shutt, J.W.	3	4	3	7*	7	7.00	–	–	–	2
Sibley, D.P.	100	170	16	244	5899	38.30	15	30	1	69
Siddle, P.M.	191	258	49	103*	3547	16.97	1	6	–	59
Sidebottom, R.N.	23	32	16	27*	101	6.31	–	–	–	5
Simpson, J.A.	173	276	41	167*	7465	31.76	7	42	–	536/28
Singh, J.	2	2	–	2	2	1.00	–	–	–	1
Siraj, M.	48	61	13	46	378	7.87	–	–	–	11
Sisodiya, P.	4	7	1	38	83	13.83	–	–	–	2
Slater, B.T.	102	185	10	172	5866	33.52	9	31	1	40
Smit, D.	137	208	37	156*	6077	35.53	9	33	0+1	362/22
Smith, J.L.	26	42	4	138	1395	36.71	4	4	–	28/3
Smith, R.A.J.	31	46	6	57*	693	17.32	–	2	–	4
Smith, T.M.J.	55	77	14	84	1422	22.57	–	4	–	17
Snater, S.	13	13	4	50*	185	20.55	–	1	–	2
Sodhi, I.S.	85	124	18	82*	2272	21.43	–	11	–	38
Southee, T.G.	119	159	16	156	2539	17.75	1	7	–	72
Sowter, N.A.	13	23	4	57*	292	15.36	–	2	–	12
Stanlake, B.	9	15	7	8	17	2.12	–	–	–	2
Steel, C.T.	43	76	2	224	2081	28.12	3	11	–	19
Steel, S.	2	4	–	39	48	12.00	–	–	–	1
Steketee, M.T.	45	60	12	53	721	15.02	–	2	–	18
Stevens, D.I.	320	500	33	237	16360	35.03	37	81	3	204
Stevenson, R.A.	7	7	1	51	124	20.66	–	1	–	1
Stewart, G.	27	41	6	103	805	23.00	1	4	–	3
Stirling, P.R.	70	110	5	146	2932	27.92	6	14	–	40
Stoinis, M.P.	61	105	7	170	3255	33.21	4	24	–	22
Stokes, B.A.	148	251	13	258	8424	35.39	18	43	–	123
Stone, O.P.	44	58	12	60	708	15.39	–	1	–	17
Stoneman, M.D.	208	361	8	197	12113	34.31	26	62	5	91
Swindells, H.J.	25	36	5	171*	1049	33.83	2	4	–	50/2
Tattersall, J.A.	35	54	6	135*	1540	32.08	1	10	–	87/4
Taylor, C.Z.	8	12	2	106	368	36.80	1	2	–	2
Taylor, J.M.R.	82	127	9	156	3433	29.09	7	9	–	41
Taylor, J.P.A.	6	8	3	22	64	12.80	–	–	–	1
Taylor, L.R.P.L.	188	316	27	290	12250	42.38	27	65	–	246
Taylor, M.D.	66	86	33	56	723	13.64	–	1	–	7
Taylor, T.A.I.	44	66	10	80	1137	20.30	–	5	–	14
ten Doeschate, R.N.	203	294	39	259*	11298	44.30	29	53	1	127
Thakur, S.N.	66	90	7	87	1444	17.39	–	9	–	19
Thomason, A.D.	16	31	2	90	619	21.34	–	4	–	18
Thompson, J.A.	20	29	1	98	681	24.32	–	3	–	6
Thomson, A.T.	18	24	–	46	381	15.87	–	–	–	6
Thurston, C.O.	19	28	–	126	735	26.25	2	2	–	7
Tongue, J.C.	39	52	10	41	459	10.92	–	–	–	4
Topley, R.J.W.	43	52	22	16	131	4.36	–	–	–	8
Trego, P.D.	223	332	38	154*	9644	32.80	15	54	1	90

	M	I	NO	HS	Runs	Avge	100	50	1000	Ct/St
Trevaskis, L.	14	23	3	7*	541	27.05	–	4	–	4
van Beek, L.V.	61	83	18	111*	1479	22.75	1	7	–	42
van Buuren, G.L.	96	149	23	235	5309	42.13	11	34	–	52
van der Gugten, T.	58	82	23	85*	944	16.00	–	4	–	16
van der Merwe, R.E.	77	122	16	205*	3482	32.84	6	21	–	61
van Meekeren, P.A.	8	14	3	34	106	9.63	–	–	–	2
van Vollenhoven, K.T.	1	1	–	23	23	23.00	–	–	–	0
van Zyl, S.	184	310	42	228	11554	43.11	28	53	1+1	103
Vasconcelos, R.S.	52	93	7	185*	3124	36.32	7	15	–	89/6
Vihari, G.H.	94	152	20	302*	7261	55.00	21	37	0+1	89/1
Vilas, D.J.	176	264	30	266	9703	41.46	22	44	1	455/20
Vince, J.M.	175	289	20	240	10508	39.06	26	40	2	150
Virdi, G.S.	39	48	24	47	210	8.75	–	–	–	7
Wade, M.S.	156	249	41	152	8492	40.82	17	51	0+1	434/21
Wagner, N.	184	241	53	70	3139	16.69	–	9	–	55
Waite, M.J.	8	11	1	42	160	16.00	–	–	–	1
Wakely, A.G.	148	236	16	123	6880	31.27	9	37	–	98
Walallawita, T.N.	9	12	5	20*	76	10.85	–	–	–	2
Waller, M.T.C.	9	10	1	28	91	10.11	–	–	–	5
Walter, P.I.	28	35	6	96	1050	36.20	–	5	–	7
Ward, H.D.	3	6	–	19	30	5.00	–	–	–	2
Warner, J.D.	5	5	3	13*	38	19.00	–	–	–	1
Washington Sundar, M.S.	17	24	2	159	798	36.27	1	5	–	8
Watling, B.J.	178	297	36	205	10034	38.44	18	59	–	450/10
Weatherley, J.J.	50	81	4	126*	1827	23.72	1	8	–	37
Weighell, W.J.	20	31	4	84	581	21.51	–	3	–	6
Welch, N.R.	5	7	–	83	179	25.57	–	1	–	1
Wells, B.J.J.	1	1	–	40	40	40.00	–	–	–	2
Wells, L.W.P.	154	255	18	258	8392	35.40	19	36	2	81
Wessels, M.H.	224	369	31	202*	11701	34.61	23	61	2	339/16
Westley, T.	199	328	23	254	10849	35.57	24	49	1	123
Wheal, B.T.J.	41	48	16	46*	362	11.31	–	–	–	13
Wheater, A.J.A.	158	227	28	204*	7098	35.66	12	39	–	275/21
White, C.	8	11	7	15*	38	9.50	–	–	–	0
White, G.G.	39	55	5	65	659	13.18	–	2	–	12
White, R.G.	33	54	5	120	1215	24.79	2	6	–	44/2
Whiteley, R.A.	89	145	13	130*	3577	27.09	3	19	–	60
Wiese, D.	124	194	20	208	5814	33.41	11	32	–	70
Wightman, B.J.	1	2	1	0*	0	0.00	–	–	–	0
Willey, D.J.	77	108	16	104*	2515	27.33	2	14	–	18
Williamson, K.S.	153	261	21	284*	12041	50.17	34	60	–	136
Woakes, C.R.	155	229	50	152*	6016	33.60	10	25	–	66
Wood, C.P.	43	62	6	105*	1326	23.67	1	6	–	14
Wood, L.	52	78	16	119	1694	27.32	2	6	–	17
Wood, M.A.	62	99	19	72*	1643	20.53	–	5	–	16
Wood, T.A.	11	19	–	31	202	10.63	–	–	–	9
Worrall, D.J.	58	89	35	50	707	13.09	–	1	–	14
Wright, C.J.C.	176	227	48	87	3288	18.36	–	13	–	31
Wright, L.J.	144	223	23	226*	7622	38.11	17	38	1	58
Yadav, U.T.	98	117	45	128*	1042	14.47	1	1	–	35
Yates, R.M.	32	53	3	141	1614	32.28	6	5	–	33
Young, W.A.	86	142	13	162	5506	42.68	12	30	–	45
Zafar Gohar	44	64	6	100*	1232	21.24	1	5	–	19
Zaib, S.A.	33	51	4	135	1106	23.53	1	6	–	9

BOWLING

'50wS' denotes instances of taking 50 or more wickets in a season. Where these have been achieved outside the British Isles they are shown after a plus sign.

	Runs	Wkts	Avge	Best	5wI	10wM	50wS
Aavesh Khan	2342	100	23.42	7- 24	4	1	–
Abbott, K.J.	10252	488	21.00	9- 40	33	5	3+1
Abbott, S.A.	5594	169	33.10	7- 45	4	–	–
Abell, T.B.	1566	53	29.54	4- 39	–	–	–
Ackermann, C.N.	3024	73	41.42	5- 69	1	–	–
Agarwal, M.A.	257	3	85.66	2- 18	–	–	–
Aitchison, B.W.	1003	40	25.07	6- 28	1	–	–
Aldridge, K.L.	101	0					
Ali, M.M.	14490	382	37.93	6- 29	12	2	–
Allen, F.H.	15	1	15.00	1- 15	–	–	–
Allison, B.M.J.	233	5	46.60	3-109	–	–	–
Alsop, T.P.	81	3	27.00	2- 59	–	–	–
Amla, H.M.	277	1	277.00	1- 10	–	–	–
Anderson, J.M.	25147	1018	24.70	7- 19	52	6	4
Andersson, M.K.	1405	55	25.54	4- 25	–	–	–
Archer, J.C.	4510	181	24.91	7- 67	8	1	1
Ashwin, R.	16699	655	25.49	7- 59	49	11	0+1
Atkins, J.A.	469	20	23.45	5- 51	2	–	–
Atkinson, A.A.P.	300	9	33.33	3- 78	–	–	–
Azad, M.H.	17	1	17.00	1- 15	–	–	–
Azhar Ali	2067	47	43.97	4- 34	–	–	–
Bailey, T.E.	6110	257	23.77	7- 37	10	2	2
Bairstow, J.M.	1	0					
Baker, J.O.	408	12	34.00	3- 49	–	–	–
Balbirnie, A.	262	13	20.15	4- 23	–	–	–
Balderson, G.P.	723	21	34.42	3- 21	–	–	–
Ball, J.T.	5813	203	28.63	6- 49	6	–	1
Ballance, G.S.	154	0					
Bamber, E.R.	2317	100	23.17	5- 41	2	–	1
Bancroft, C.T.	77	2	38.50	1- 10	–	–	–
Barber, T.E.	420	7	60.00	3- 42	–	–	–
Barker, K.H.D.	11079	445	24.89	7- 46	18	1	3
Barnard, E.G.	6528	230	28.38	6- 37	5	1	–
Barnes, E.	831	21	39.57	4- 61	–	–	–
Bartlett, G.A.	27	0					
Batty, G.J.	22356	682	32.78	8- 64	27	4	2
Bedingham, D.G.	18	0					
Beer, W.A.T.	1550	43	36.04	6- 29	2	1	–
Bell-Drummond, D.J.	333	13	25.61	3- 47	–	–	–
Berg, G.K.	9378	303	30.95	6- 56	6	–	–
Bess, D.M.	5264	174	30.25	7- 43	12	1	–
Billings, S.W.	4	0					
Bird, J.M.	10067	414	24.31	7- 18	18	5	0+2
Blake, A.J.	138	3	46.00	2- 9	–	–	–
Blatherwick, J.M.	428	11	38.90	4- 28	–	–	–
Blundell, T.A.	65	1	65.00	1- 15	–	–	–
Bohannon, J.J.	562	13	43.23	3- 46	–	–	–
Bopara, R.S.	9381	257	36.50	5- 49	3	–	–
Borthwick, S.G.	8556	220	38.89	6- 70	3	–	–
Boult, T.A.	10997	408	26.95	6- 30	16	1	–
Bracey, J.R.	35	0					
Brathwaite, C.R.	2098	88	23.84	7- 90	2	–	–
Brathwaite, K.C.	1623	34	47.73	6- 29	1	–	–
Bresnan, T.T.	17820	575	30.99	5- 28	9	–	–

	Runs	Wkts	Avge	Best	5wI	10wM	50wS
Briggs, D.R.	10112	303	33.37	6- 45	8	–	–
Broad, S.C.J.	22550	841	26.81	8- 15	30	4	–
Brook, H.C.	375	8	46.87	3- 15	–	–	–
Brookes, E.A.	76	0					
Brooks, J.A.	13384	487	27.48	6- 65	20	–	4
Brown, B.C.	109	1	109.00	1- 48	–	–	–
Browne, N.L.J.	175	0					
Buck, N.L.	9135	269	33.95	6- 34	8	–	–
Bulpitt, J.	32	0					
Bumrah, J.J.	4666	193	24.17	6- 27	12	–	–
Burgess, M.G.K.	14	0					
Burnham, J.T.A.	17	0					
Burns, R.J.	149	2	74.50	1- 18	–	–	–
Buttler, J.C.	11	0					
Byrom, E.J.	107	2	53.50	2- 64	–	–	–
Campbell, J.O.I.	261	1	261.00	1- 43	–	–	–
Carey, L.J.	3009	87	34.58	4- 54	–	–	–
Carlson, K.S.	338	7	48.28	5- 28	1	–	–
Carse, B.A.	2814	95	29.62	6- 26	5	–	–
Carson, J.J.	1811	55	32.92	5- 85	2	–	–
Carter, M.	1989	50	39.78	7- 56	2	1	–
Carver, K.	543	18	30.16	4-106	–	–	–
Chappell, Z.J.	2106	59	35.69	6- 44	1	–	–
Charlesworth, B.G.	271	8	33.87	3- 25	–	–	–
Chopra, V.	128	0					
Christian, D.T.	5679	163	34.84	5- 24	3	–	–
Clark, G.	58	2	29.00	1- 10	–	–	–
Clark, J.	4298	131	32.80	6- 21	4	–	–
Clark, T.G.R.	120	1	120.00	1- 37	–	–	–
Clarke, J.M.	22	0					
Clarke, R.	16296	534	30.51	7- 55	8	–	–
Claydon, M.E.	9943	312	31.86	6-104	9	–	2
Coad, B.O.	3896	192	20.29	6- 25	9	2	1
Cobb, J.J.	1607	18	89.27	2- 11	–	–	–
Cockbain, I.A.	44	1	44.00	1- 23	–	–	–
Cohen, M.A.R.	1777	68	26.13	5- 40	3	–	–
Coles, J.M.	127	3	42.33	2- 32	–	–	–
Conners, S.	1191	40	29.77	5- 83	1	–	–
Conway, D.P.	467	9	51.88	3- 36	–	–	–
Cook, A.N.	216	7	30.85	3- 13	–	–	–
Cook, S.J.	3298	162	20.35	7- 23	10	2	1
Cooke, C.B.	19	0					
Cooke, J.M.	359	3	119.66	1- 26	–	–	–
Coughlin, P.	3409	101	33.75	5- 49	3	1	–
Cox, J.M.	3	0					
Crane, M.S.	4921	119	41.35	5- 35	3	–	–
Crawley, Z.	33	0					
Critchley, M.J.J.	4908	114	43.05	6- 73	3	1	–
Crocombe, H.T.	1001	23	43.52	4- 92	–	–	–
Croft, S.J.	3057	72	42.45	6- 41	1	–	–
Cullen, B.C.	503	13	38.69	3- 30	–	–	–
Cummins, M.L.	6563	237	27.69	7- 45	10	1	–
Curran, S.M.	6001	200	30.00	7- 58	7	1	–
Curran, T.K.	5613	195	28.78	7- 20	7	1	1
Currie, S.W.	167	7	23.85	4-109	–	–	–
Dal, A.K.	574	20	28.70	3- 11	–	–	–
Dale, A.S.	73	4	18.25	3- 20	–	–	–
Davey, J.H.	3090	140	22.07	5- 21	4	–	–

	Runs	Wkts	Avge	Best	5wI	10wM	50wS
Davies, A.L.	6	0					
Davis, W.S.	2739	87	31.48	7-146	2	–	–
Dawson, L.A.	7844	223	35.17	7- 51	4	–	–
de Caires, J.M.	7	0					
de Grandhomme, C.	5609	186	30.15	6- 24	2	–	–
de Lange, M.	10071	334	30.15	7- 23	11	2	–
Dearden, H.E.	116	2	58.00	1- 0	–	–	–
Denly, J.L.	2984	72	41.44	4- 36	–	–	–
Dent, C.D.J.	831	9	92.33	2- 21	–	–	–
Dernbach, J.W.	10139	311	32.60	6- 47	10	–	1
Dickson, S.R.	53	2	26.50	1- 15	–	–	–
D'Oliveira, B.L.	3657	72	50.79	7- 92	2	–	–
Douthwaite, D.A.	2156	52	41.46	4- 48	–	–	–
Drissell, G.S.	504	8	63.00	4- 83	–	–	–
du Plessis, F.	1477	41	36.02	4- 39	–	–	–
du Plooy, J.L.	1239	25	49.56	3- 76	–	–	–
Duckett, B.M.	84	1	84.00	1- 21	–	–	–
Dunn, M.P.	4237	117	36.21	5- 43	4	–	–
Eckersley, E.J.H.	74	2	37.00	2- 29	–	–	–
Eskinazi, S.S.	4	0					
Evans, H.A.	666	14	47.57	3- 49	–	–	–
Evans, L.J.	270	2	135.00	1- 29	–	–	–
Evans, S.T.	46	0					
Evison, J.D.M.	356	18	19.77	5- 21	1	–	–
Fell, T.C.	17	0					
Ferguson, L.H.	3975	161	24.68	7- 34	11	1	–
Finch, A.W.	1147	28	40.96	4- 38	–	–	–
Finch, H.Z.	118	2	59.00	1- 9	–	–	–
Finn, S.T.	16247	563	28.85	9- 37	15	1	2
Fisher, M.D.	1650	61	27.04	5- 41	2	–	–
Fletcher, L.J.	10638	409	26.00	7- 37	10	1	1
Foakes, B.T.	6	0					
Fuller, J.K.	5294	162	32.67	6- 24	5	1	–
Garrett, G.A.	302	8	37.75	2- 53	–	–	–
Garton, G.H.S.	1890	53	35.66	5- 26	1	–	–
Gay, E.N.	22	1	22.00	1- 8	–	–	–
Gilchrist, N.N.	672	30	22.40	5- 38	1	–	–
Gill, S.	31	0					
Gleeson, R.J.	3053	143	21.34	6- 43	10	1	–
Glover, B.D.	827	24	34.45	4- 83	–	–	–
Godleman, B.A.	35	0					
Goldsworthy, L.P.	45	0					
Goodman, D.C.	252	5	50.40	2- 19	–	–	–
Green, B.G.F.	110	2	55.00	1- 8	–	–	–
Gregory, L.	7745	303	25.56	6- 32	15	2	1
Griffiths, G.T.	2324	67	34.68	6- 49	1	1	–
Gubbins, N.R.T.	56	0					
Hain, S.R.	31	0					
Haines, T.J.	480	10	48.00	1- 9	–	–	–
Hales, A.D.	173	3	57.66	2- 63	–	–	–
Hameed, H.	21	0					
Hamidullah Qadri	974	25	38.96	5- 60	1	–	–
Hammond, M.A.H.	453	5	90.60	2- 37	–	–	–
Handscomb, P.S.P.	79	0					
Hankins, G.T.	13	0					
Hannon-Dalby, O.J.	6805	224	30.37	6- 33	8	1	–
Haris Rauf	275	7	39.28	3- 73	–	–	–
Harmer, S.R.	18739	699	26.80	9- 80	40	9	4+1

	Runs	Wkts	Avge	Best	5wI	10wM	50wS
Harris, J.A.R.	14583	508	28.70	9-34	15	2	3
Harris, M.S.	64	0					
Harrison, C.G.	113	3	37.66	1-30	–	–	–
Hartley, T.W.	467	10	46.70	4-42	–	–	–
Head, T.M.	3365	49	68.67	3-42	–	–	–
Helm, T.G.	2772	87	31.86	5-36	3	–	–
Hendricks, B.E.	7718	325	23.74	7-29	19	2	0+1
Henry, M.J.	7906	314	25.17	7-42	15	3	1
Higgins, R.F.	3889	178	21.84	7-42	7	1	2
Hildreth, J.C.	492	6	82.00	2-39	–	–	–
Hill, G.C.H.	182	8	22.75	2-12	–	–	–
Hill, L.J.	28	0					
Hinley, T.I.	35	0					
Hogan, M.G.	15623	636	24.56	7-92	24	2	3
Holden, M.D.E.	460	5	92.00	2-59	–	–	–
Holder, C.K.	2229	83	26.85	6-47	5	1	–
Holland, I.G.	1926	63	30.57	6-60	1	–	–
Hollman, L.B.K.	363	13	27.92	5-65	2	1	–
Hooper, E.O.	65	1	65.00	1-65	–	–	–
Howell, B.A.C.	3222	96	33.56	5-57	1	–	–
Hudson-Prentice, F.J.	1373	47	29.21	5-68	1	–	–
Hughes, A.L.	1897	37	51.27	4-46	–	–	–
Hunt, S.F.	487	13	37.46	3-47	–	–	–
Hurt, L.J.	248	7	35.42	4-27	–	–	–
Hutton, B.A.	5860	222	26.39	8-57	11	2	–
Ibrahim, D.K.	236	3	78.66	2- 9	–	–	–
Ingram, C.A.	2133	50	42.66	4-16	–	–	–
Jacks, W.G.	320	4	80.00	1- 7	–	–	–
Jadeja, R.A.	10713	438	24.45	7-31	27	7	0+3
James, L.W.	601	20	30.05	4-51	–	–	–
Jamieson, K.A.	2891	138	20.94	8-74	11	2	–
Jennings, K.K.	988	30	32.93	3-37	–	–	–
Johal, M.S.	59	4	14.75	3-29	–	–	–
Jones, R.P.	49	2	24.50	1- 4	–	–	–
Jordan, C.J.	10730	335	32.02	7-43	10	–	1
Joseph, A.S.	4113	141	29.17	7-46	6	–	–
Kelly, M.L.	2840	101	28.11	6-67	5	–	–
Keogh, R.I.	4333	94	46.09	9-52	1	1	–
Kerrigan, S.C.	10699	354	30.22	9-51	15	3	2
Kimber, L.P.J.	101	2	50.50	1-34	–	–	–
Klaassen, F.J.	422	9	46.88	4-44	–	–	–
Klein, D.	6626	225	29.44	8-72	10	1	–
Kohli, V.	338	3	112.66	1-19	–	–	–
Kuhn, H.G.	12	0					
Labuschagne, M.	2786	62	44.93	3-45	–	–	–
Lakmal, R.A.S.	10927	343	31.85	6-68	9	–	–
Lamb, D.J.	1218	41	29.70	4-55	–	–	–
Lamb, M.J.	304	8	38.00	2-38	–	–	–
Lammonby, T.A.	325	6	54.16	1- 4	–	–	–
Latham, T.W.M.	18	1	18.00	1- 7	–	–	–
Lawrence, D.W.	567	15	37.80	2-28	–	–	–
Leach, J.	9756	368	26.51	6-73	14	1	3
Leach, M.J.	8978	339	26.48	8-85	22	3	3
Leaning, J.A.	813	14	58.07	2-20	–	–	–
Leech, D.J.	213	4	53.25	2-72	–	–	–
Lees, A.Z.	96	3	32.00	2-51	–	–	–
Lenham, A.D.	71	1	71.00	1-60	–	–	–
Leonard, E.O.	85	1	85.00	1-68	–	–	–

	Runs	Wkts	Avge	Best	5wI	10wM	50wS
Libby, J.D.	471	7	67.28	2- 45	–	–	–
Lilley, A.M.	1428	43	33.20	5- 23	2	–	–
Linde, G.F.	5081	211	24.08	7- 29	14	3	–
Lintott, J.B.	103	0					
Livingstone, L.S.	1552	43	36.09	6- 52	1	–	–
Lloyd, D.L.	3370	82	41.09	4- 11	–	–	–
Logan, J.E.G.	204	12	17.00	4- 22	–	–	–
Lyth, A.	1705	36	47.36	2- 9	–	–	–
McDermott, B.R.	75	0					
McIlroy, J.P.	131	1	131.00	1- 12	–	–	–
McKerr, C.	1054	38	27.73	5- 54	2	1	–
McKiernan, M.H.	64	2	32.00	2- 3	–	–	–
MacLeod, C.S.	444	16	27.75	4- 66	–	–	–
Madsen, W.L.	1842	37	49.78	3- 45	–	–	–
Mahmood, S.	1883	70	26.90	5- 47	1	–	–
Malan, D.J.	2455	61	40.24	5- 61	1	–	–
Malan, P.J.	487	20	24.35	5- 35	1	–	–
Maxwell, G.J.	3174	77	41.22	5- 40	1	–	–
Mayers, K.R.	1895	85	22.29	6- 29	3	–	–
Meaker, S.C.	9451	290	32.58	8- 52	11	2	1
Melton, D.R.	772	19	40.63	4- 22	–	–	–
Mike, B.W.M.	2315	63	36.74	5- 37	1	–	–
Miles, C.N.	8600	323	26.62	6- 63	17	1	3
Mills, T.S.	2008	55	36.50	4- 25	–	–	–
Milne, A.F.	2872	88	32.63	5- 47	2	–	–
Milnes, M.E.	3155	119	26.51	6- 53	4	–	1
Mitchell, D.J.	2664	89	29.93	5- 44	1	–	–
Mitchell, D.K.H.	1649	33	49.96	4- 49	–	–	–
Mohammad Abbas	10998	532	20.67	8- 46	38	11	1+2
Mohammad Nabi	2178	94	23.17	6- 33	3	–	–
Mohammad Rizwan	131	4	32.75	2- 10	–	–	–
Mohammed Shami	8025	298	26.92	7- 79	11	2	–
Morgan, E.J.G.	94	2	47.00	2- 24	–	–	–
Moriarty, D.T.	863	35	24.65	6- 60	4	1	–
Morley, J.P.	71	5	14.20	4- 62	–	–	–
Morris, C.A.J.	6400	216	29.62	7- 45	7	–	2
Moulton, E.H.T.	269	3	89.66	2- 24	–	–	–
Mousley, D.R.	37	0					
Mujeeb Zadran	75	1	75.00	1- 75	–	–	–
Mullaney, S.J.	4507	120	37.55	5- 32	1	–	–
Murtagh, T.J.	21915	899	24.37	7- 82	38	4	9
Naseem Shah	1450	54	26.85	6- 59	3	–	–
Naveen-ul-Haq	782	31	25.22	8- 35	1	–	–
Neesham, J.D.S.	3955	120	32.95	5- 65	2	–	–
Neser, M.G.	5600	226	24.77	6- 57	6	–	–
Nicholls, H.M.	24	0					
Nijjar, A.S.S.	806	19	42.42	2- 28	–	–	–
Northeast, S.A.	147	1	147.00	1- 60	–	–	–
Norwell, L.C.	8109	320	25.34	8- 43	13	3	3
Olivier, D.	11154	474	23.53	6- 37	24	4	0+3
Organ, F.S.	420	23	18.26	5- 25	1	–	–
O'Riordan, M.K.	433	10	43.30	3- 50	–	–	–
Overton, C.	8680	372	23.33	6- 24	13	–	1
Overton, J.	5773	185	31.20	6- 95	4	–	–
Pant, R.R.	9	1	9.00	1- 9	–	–	–
Parkinson, C.F.	3792	104	36.46	8-148	4	2	1
Parkinson, M.W.	2382	102	23.35	7-126	4	1	–
Parnell, W.D.	6969	238	29.28	7- 51	9	2	–

	Runs	Wkts	Avge	Best	5wI	10wM	50wS
Patel, A.R.	3996	162	24.66	7- 54	10	2	–
Patel, A.Y.	8012	248	32.30	6- 48	18	3	–
Patel, R.S.	853	15	56.86	6- 5	1	–	–
Patel, S.R.	13650	357	38.23	7- 68	5	1	–
Paterson, D.	9550	409	23.34	7- 20	14	1	1+2
Patterson, S.A.	12466	452	27.57	6- 40	8	–	2
Patterson-White, L.A.	1296	46	28.17	5- 41	2	–	–
Pattinson, J.L.	6799	302	22.51	6- 32	11	–	–
Payne, D.A.	9132	311	29.36	6- 26	6	1	–
Pearce, S.J.	164	1	164.00	1- 74	–	–	–
Pennington, D.Y.	2225	70	31.78	5- 32	1	–	–
Petersen, K.D.	323	3	107.66	3- 49	–	–	–
Phillips, G.D.	1085	26	41.73	4- 70	–	–	–
Pillans, M.W.	3710	131	28.32	6- 67	3	1	0+1
Podmore, H.W.	4175	161	25.93	6- 36	4	–	1
Porter, J.A.	9396	390	24.09	7- 41	13	2	5
Potts, M.J.	1422	42	33.85	4- 32	–	–	–
Poynter, S.W.	21	0					
Poysden, J.E.	1084	33	32.84	5- 29	2	–	–
Prest, T.J.	5	0					
Price, O.J.	100	0					
Price, T.J.	448	16	28.00	4- 72	–	–	–
Procter, L.A.	4301	121	35.54	7- 71	4	–	–
Pujara, C.A.	157	6	26.16	2- 4	–	–	–
Qais Ahmad	1395	68	20.51	7- 41	5	3	–
Quinn, M.R.	4128	141	29.27	7- 76	1	1	–
Rahane, A.M.	75	0					
Rahul, K.L.	83	0					
Raine, B.A.	8247	319	25.85	6- 27	10	–	3
Rampaul, R.	8160	274	29.78	7- 51	11	1	–
Rashid, A.U.	17949	512	35.05	7-107	20	1	2
Rashid Khan	1287	69	18.65	8- 74	8	3	–
Rawlins, D.M.W.	1391	18	77.27	3- 19	–	–	–
Reece, L.M.	3167	113	28.02	7- 20	4	–	1
Reingold, S.J.	271	6	45.16	3- 15	–	–	–
Renshaw, M.T.	180	2	90.00	1- 12	–	–	–
Revis, M.L.	19	2	9.50	2- 19	–	–	–
Rhodes, G.H.	728	6	121.33	2- 83	–	–	–
Rhodes, W.M.H.	2276	79	28.81	5- 17	2	–	–
Roach, K.A.J.	11092	432	25.67	8- 40	17	2	–
Robinson, O.E.	6541	311	21.03	9- 78	18	5	3
Robson, S.D.	277	8	34.62	2- 0	–	–	–
Roland-Jones, T.S.	10847	428	25.34	7- 52	20	4	2
Root, J.E.	2834	60	47.23	5- 8	1	–	–
Root, W.T.	240	8	30.00	3- 29	–	–	–
Rossington, A.M.	86	0					
Roy, J.J.	495	14	35.35	3- 9	–	–	–
Rushworth, C.	12707	569	22.33	9- 52	29	4	6
Rutherford, H.D.	107	1	107.00	1- 26	–	–	–
Sakande, A.	1734	47	36.89	5- 43	1	–	–
Sales, J.J.G.	154	3	51.33	2- 61	–	–	–
Salisbury, M.E.T.	3392	111	30.55	6- 37	1	–	–
Salt, P.D.	32	1	32.00	1- 32	–	–	–
Salter, A.G.	4817	101	47.69	4- 18	–	–	–
Sanderson, B.W.	5997	287	20.89	8- 73	16	3	3
Santner, M.J.	3981	84	47.39	4-111	–	–	–
Sarro, J.P.	220	4	55.00	2- 53	–	–	–
Scott, G.F.B.	545	10	54.50	2- 34	–	–	–

	Runs	Wkts	Avge	Best	5wI	10wM	50wS
Scrimshaw, G.L.S.	154	3	51.33	2- 40	–	–	–
Scriven, T.A.R.	79	3	26.33	2- 24	–	–	–
Selman, N.J.	36	1	36.00	1- 22	–	–	–
Shaheen Shah Afridi	2469	102	24.20	8- 39	4	1	–
Shan Masood	607	8	75.87	2- 52	–	–	–
Sharif, S.M.	654	18	36.33	4- 94	–	–	–
Sharma, I.	13588	481	28.24	7- 24	16	2	–
Sharma, R.G.	1154	24	48.08	4- 41	–	–	–
Shaw, J.	3818	106	36.01	5- 79	2	–	–
Short, D.J.M.	874	21	41.61	3- 78	–	–	–
Shutt, J.W.	104	2	52.00	2- 14	–	–	–
Sibley, D.P.	271	4	67.75	2-103	–	–	–
Siddle, P.M.	17564	655	26.81	8- 54	25	–	0+1
Sidebottom, R.N.	1810	59	30.67	6- 35	1	1	–
Simpson, J.A.	23	0					
Singh, J.	140	7	20.00	4- 51	–	–	–
Siraj, M.	4482	184	24.35	8- 59	5	2	–
Sisodiya, P.	369	15	24.60	4- 79	–	–	–
Slater, B.T.	121	0					
Smit, D.	3501	106	33.02	7- 27	3	–	–
Smith, R.A.J.	2413	69	34.97	5- 87	1	–	–
Smith, T.M.J.	4171	82	50.86	4- 35	–	–	–
Snater, S.	929	51	18.21	7- 98	5	–	–
Sodhi, I.S.	9253	270	34.27	7- 30	15	2	–
Southee, T.G.	12392	472	26.25	8- 27	22	1	–
Sowter, N.A.	1032	20	51.60	3- 42	–	–	–
Stanlake, B.	747	23	32.47	3- 50	–	–	–
Steel, C.T.	758	22	34.45	2- 7	–	–	–
Steel, S.	16	0					
Steketee, M.T.	4135	150	27.56	5- 19	2	–	–
Stevens, D.I.	14197	585	24.26	8- 75	31	2	4
Stevenson, R.A.	460	9	51.11	4- 70	–	–	–
Stewart, G.	1791	61	29.36	6- 22	2	–	–
Stirling, P.R.	1118	27	41.40	2- 21	–	–	–
Stoinis, M.P.	2686	66	40.69	4- 73	–	–	–
Stokes, B.A.	9919	338	29.34	7- 67	7	1	–
Stone, O.P.	3717	150	24.78	8- 80	6	1	–
Stoneman, M.D.	178	0					
Taylor, C.Z.	565	7	80.71	2- 16	–	–	–
Taylor, J.M.R.	3345	75	44.60	4- 16	–	–	–
Taylor, J.P.A.	366	13	28.15	3- 26	–	–	–
Taylor, L.R.P.L.	378	6	63.00	2- 4	–	–	–
Taylor, M.D.	5882	180	32.67	5- 15	6	–	1
Taylor, T.A.I.	3867	125	30.93	6- 47	4	1	–
ten Doeschate, R.N.	7242	214	33.84	6- 20	7	–	–
Thakur, S.N.	6233	221	28.20	6- 31	12	–	0+1
Thomason, A.D.	388	4	97.00	2-107	–	–	–
Thompson, J.A.	1300	66	19.69	5- 31	2	–	–
Thomson, A.T.	957	27	35.44	6-138	1	–	–
Thurston, C.O.	16	0					
Tongue, J.C.	3395	138	24.60	6- 97	6	–	–
Topley, R.J.W.	4098	154	26.61	6- 29	8	2	–
Trego, P.D.	14359	395	36.35	7- 84	5	1	1
Trevaskis, L.	712	16	44.50	5- 78	1	–	–
van Beek, L.V.	5004	155	32.28	6- 46	6	1	–
van Buuren, G.L.	2991	95	31.48	4- 12	–	–	–
van der Gugten, T.	5289	192	27.54	7- 42	10	1	1
van der Merwe, R.E.	4768	142	33.57	4- 22	–	–	–

	Runs	Wkts	Avge	Best	5wI	10wM	50wS
van Meekeren, P.A.	785	21	37.38	4- 60	–	–	–
van Vollenhoven, K.T.	37	1	37.00	1- 18	–	–	–
van Zyl, S.	2557	69	37.05	5- 32	1	–	–
Vasconcelos, R.S.	9	0					
Vihari, G.H.	1163	27	43.07	3- 17	–	–	–
Vilas, D.J.	9	0					
Vince, J.M.	1116	23	48.52	5- 41	1	–	–
Virdi, G.S.	3517	119	29.55	8- 61	5	1	–
Wade, M.S.	354	8	44.25	3- 13	–	–	–
Wagner, N.	20314	762	26.65	7- 39	36	2	0+2
Waite, M.J.	583	23	25.34	5- 16	1	–	–
Wakely, A.G.	426	6	71.00	2- 62	–	–	–
Walallawita, T.N.	571	9	63.44	3- 28	–	–	–
Waller, M.T.C.	493	10	49.30	3- 33	–	–	–
Walter, P.I.	713	15	47.53	3- 44	–	–	–
Ward, H.D.	2	0					
Warner, J.D.	282	9	31.33	3- 35	–	–	–
Washington Sundar, M.S.	1107	36	30.75	6- 87	2	1	–
Watling, B.J.	9	0					
Weatherley, J.J.	250	5	50.00	1- 2	–	–	–
Weighell, W.J.	1860	59	31.52	7- 32	2	–	–
Wells, L.W.P.	3358	78	43.05	5- 63	1	–	–
Wessels, M.H.	130	3	43.33	1- 10	–	–	–
Westley, T.	2705	59	45.84	4- 55	–	–	–
Wheal, B.T.J.	3165	95	33.31	6- 51	1	–	–
Wheater, A.J.A.	86	1	86.00	1- 86	–	–	–
White, C.	579	18	32.16	4- 35	–	–	–
White, G.G.	2730	65	42.00	6- 44	1	–	–
Whiteley, R.A.	2097	41	51.14	2- 6	–	–	–
Wiese, D.	9638	344	28.01	6- 58	10	1	–
Wightman, B.J.	23	0					
Willey, D.J.	5895	198	29.77	5- 29	6	1	–
Williamson, K.S.	3721	86	43.26	5- 75	1	–	–
Woakes, C.R.	13435	533	25.20	9- 36	21	4	3
Wood, C.P.	3174	105	30.22	5- 39	3	–	–
Wood, L.	3986	117	34.06	5- 40	3	–	–
Wood, M.A.	5442	200	27.21	6- 46	10	–	–
Worrall, D.J.	6069	222	27.33	7- 64	9	1	–
Wright, C.J.C.	16410	513	31.98	7- 53	17	–	2
Wright, L.J.	4862	120	40.51	5- 65	3	–	–
Yadav, U.T.	9127	321	28.43	7- 48	15	2	–
Yates, R.M.	155	3	51.66	2- 54	–	–	–
Young, W.A.	8	0					
Zafar Gohar	4560	164	27.80	7- 79	9	3	–
Zaib, S.A.	636	20	31.80	6-115	2	–	–

LIMITED-OVERS CAREER RECORDS

Compiled by Philip Bailey

The following career records, to the end of the 2021 season, include all players currently registered with first-class counties or teams in The Hundred. These records are restricted to performances in limited-overs matches of 'List A' status as defined by the Association of Cricket Statisticians and Historians now incorporated by ICC into their Classification of Cricket. The following matches qualify for List A status and are included in the figures that follow: Limited-Overs Internationals; Other International matches (e.g. Commonwealth Games, 'A' team internationals); Premier domestic limited-overs tournaments in Test status countries; Official tourist matches against the main first-class teams.

The following matches do NOT qualify for inclusion: World Cup warm-up games; Tourist matches against first-class teams outside the major domestic competitions (e.g. Universities, Minor Counties etc.); Festival, pre-season friendly games and Twenty20 Cup matches.

	M	*Runs*	*Avge*	*HS*	*100*	*50*	*Wkts*	*Avge*	*Best*	*Econ*
Abbott, K.J.	112	536	16.24	56	–	1	149	29.62	5-43	5.22
Abell, T.B.	25	636	31.80	106	1	1	2	13.00	2-19	4.33
Ackermann, C.N.	83	2260	36.45	152*	2	15	42	39.59	4-48	4.83
Ahmed, R.	7	89	44.50	40*	–	–	5	63.60	2-25	5.74
Aitchison, B.W.	6	31	15.50	19	–	–	2	102.50	2-51	6.94
Aldridge, K.L.	6	27	13.50	12	–	–	6	34.83	3-39	6.96
Ali, M.M.	229	5172	28.10	158	11	20	162	45.10	4-33	5.36
Allison, B.M.J.	8	4	4.00	3	–	–	7	50.14	2-33	6.13
Alsop, T.P.	54	1703	33.39	130*	4	9	–	–	–	35/5
Amla, H.M.	247	10019	44.72	159	30	52	0	–	–	10.50
Anderson, J.M.	261	378	9.00	28	–	–	358	28.57	5-23	4.82
Andersson, M.K.	4	133	133.00	44*	–	–	1	166.00	1-83	7.54
Archer, J.C.	31	219	18.25	45	–	–	51	26.76	5-42	4.98
Atkinson, A.A.P.	2	15	15.00	15	–	–	5	22.60	4-43	7.06
Azhar Ali	170	6278	47.20	132*	17	36	69	33.46	5-23	5.51
Bailey, T.E.	22	142	17.75	45	–	–	30	28.90	3-23	5.12
Bairstow, J.M.	157	5420	42.01	174	14	24	–	–	–	96/9
Baker, J.O.	7	84	28.00	25	–	–	7	39.00	2-53	6.02
Baker, S.	8	7	7.00	7*	–	–	10	33.00	3-46	6.03
Balderson, G.P.	6	46	23.00	19	–	–	5	27.20	3-25	5.03
Ball, J.T.	95	198	8.60	28	–	–	118	33.51	5-51	5.87
Ballance, G.S.	119	4540	47.78	156	8	27	–	–	–	–
Bamber, E.R.	6	37	12.33	21	–	–	10	29.70	3-41	6.02
Banton, J.	3	56	18.66	33	–	–	4	13.75	3-15	4.58
Banton, T.	24	658	29.90	112	2	4	–	–	–	16/1
Barker, K.H.D.	62	560	20.00	56	–	1	69	32.79	4-33	5.79
Barnard, E.G.	51	665	26.60	61	–	3	62	34.38	3-26	5.84
Barnes, E.	8	53	26.50	33*	–	–	9	38.44	2-34	5.78
Bartlett, G.A.	15	366	33.27	108	1	1	–	–	–	–
Bedingham, D.G.	28	796	33.16	104*	2	6	0	–	–	3.84
Beer, W.A.T.	66	535	16.21	75	–	1	62	40.00	3-27	5.13
Bell-Drummond, D.J.	89	3381	42.26	171*	6	22	5	24.20	2-22	4.68
Benjamin, C.G.	1	50	50.00	50	–	1	–	–	–	–
Benkenstein, L.M.	1	–	–	–	–	–	1	30.00	1-30	7.50
Berg, G.K.	103	1474	23.03	75	–	7	97	32.82	5-26	5.25
Bess, D.M.	19	119	8.50	24*	–	–	12	67.00	3-35	5.73
Bethell, J.G.	8	141	23.50	66	–	1	11	27.36	4-36	5.28
Billings, S.W.	100	3030	42.08	175	7	20	–	–	–	87/8

	M	Runs	Avge	HS	100	50	Wkts	Avge	Best	Econ
Bird, J.M.	39	170	14.16	28*	–	–	51	32.96	6-25	4.79
Blake, A.J.	106	2125	30.35	116	1	12	4	55.75	2-13	6.55
Blatherwick, J.M.	3	6	6.00	3*	–	–	1	72.00	1-55	9.00
Bohannon, J.J.	22	373	26.64	55*	–	2	1	208.00	1-33	8.32
Bopara, R.S.	323	9845	40.18	201*	15	60	248	29.02	5-63	5.33
Borthwick, S.G.	108	1610	24.02	87	–	10	79	40.45	5-38	5.92
Bracey, J.R.	14	648	49.84	113*	1	5	1	23.00	1-23	13/1
Brathwaite, C.R.	92	1350	20.14	113	2	4	103	28.77	5-27	5.16
Briggs, D.R.	107	402	12.56	37*	–	–	112	37.39	4-32	5.11
Broad, S.C.J.	151	620	11.92	45*	–	–	216	30.51	5-23	5.27
Brook, H.C.	15	343	31.18	103	1	1	0	–	–	6.33
Brookes, E.A.	8	107	21.40	63	–	1	7	29.57	3-15	6.75
Brooks, J.A.	38	49	4.90	10	–	–	40	34.10	3-30	4.85
Brown, B.C.	79	1354	27.08	105	1	9	–	–	–	68/12
Browne, N.L.J.	22	560	29.47	99	–	3	–	–	–	8/1
Buck, N.L.	61	141	7.83	21	–	–	69	38.14	4-39	6.24
Budinger, S.G.	8	165	20.62	71	–	1	–	–	–	–
Bulpitt, J.	3	–	–	–	–	–	2	41.00	2-33	5.12
Burgess, M.G.K.	27	638	26.58	73	–	4	–	–	–	20/3
Burns, R.J.	57	1722	35.14	95	–	12	–	–	–	–
Buttleman, W.E.L.	5	48	9.60	23	–	–	–	–	–	–
Buttler, J.C.	218	6037	43.43	150	11	36	–	–	–	231/37
Byrom, E.J.	7	49	9.80	18	–	–	–	–	–	–
Came, H.R.C.	7	141	23.50	57	–	1	–	–	–	–
Campbell, J.O.I.	5	–	–	–	–	–	6	37.66	3-58	6.45
Carey, L.J.	28	175	29.16	39	–	–	24	46.12	2-24	5.56
Carlson, K.S.	27	573	24.91	82	–	4	1	47.00	1-30	6.71
Carse, B.A.	10	45	22.50	31	–	–	16	22.43	5-61	5.45
Carter, M.	16	65	7.22	21*	–	–	23	27.17	4-40	5.34
Carter, O.J.	7	151	25.16	59	–	2	–	–	–	7/2
Carver, K.	20	70	70.00	35*	–	–	19	33.84	3- 5	5.31
Chakrapani, A.M.	2	22	11.00	18	–	–	–	–	–	–
Chappell, Z.J.	17	141	17.62	59*	–	1	17	45.00	3-45	6.27
Charlesworth, B.G.	7	274	45.66	99*	–	2	0	–	–	6.50
Christian, D.T.	120	2844	32.68	117	2	14	107	33.50	6-48	5.52
Clark, G.	41	1311	33.61	141*	4	3	4	12.50	3-18	5.55
Clark, J.	51	954	30.77	79*	–	5	34	45.17	4-34	6.34
Clark, T.G.R.	3	76	25.33	44	–	–	–	–	–	–
Clarke, J.M.	62	1846	34.18	139	4	9	–	–	–	22/2
Coad, B.O.	25	27	9.00	10	–	–	28	36.89	4-63	5.56
Cobb, J.J.	99	3330	38.27	146*	7	21	35	48.91	3-34	5.84
Cockbain, I.A.	68	1633	34.02	108*	2	10	–	–	–	–
Cohen, M.A.R.	4	16	16.00	16	–	–	3	53.33	1-17	5.00
Coles, J.M.	7	95	19.00	32	–	–	8	27.12	3-27	4.45
Compton, B.G.	1	71	71.00	71	–	1	–	–	–	–
Conners, S.	3	4	4.00	4	–	–	2	75.00	1-45	6.52
Cook, A.N.	178	6510	39.93	137	13	38	0	–	–	3.33
Cook, S.J.	12	9	4.50	6	–	–	11	41.54	3-37	4.71
Cooke, C.B.	88	2607	36.20	161	3	14	–	–	–	54/5
Cooke, J.M.	10	174	34.80	66*	–	1	20	14.30	5-61	4.55
Cornall, T.R.	2	30	–	23*	–	–	–	–	–	–
Coughlin, P.	27	177	12.64	22	–	–	18	50.83	3-36	5.61
Cox, J.M.	1	21	21.00	21	–	–	–	–	–	1/0
Cox, O.B.	74	1371	27.97	122*	1	5	–	–	–	80/9

	M	Runs	Avge	HS	100	50	Wkts	Avge	Best	Econ
Cracknell, J.B.	1	2	2.00	2	–	–	–	–	–	–
Crane, M.S.	39	112	28.00	28*	–	–	67	29.98	4-30	6.08
Crawley, Z.	26	840	36.52	120	1	5	0	–	–	8.50
Critchley, M.J.J.	43	685	27.40	64*	–	2	31	54.00	4-48	6.56
Crocombe, H.T.	4	16	8.00	9*	–	–	3	72.66	1-33	7.03
Croft, S.J.	164	4435	36.95	127	3	32	64	41.28	4-24	5.53
Cullen, T.N.	10	175	35.00	58*	–	1	–	–	–	18/1
Curran, B.J.	11	284	31.55	94	–	3	–	–	–	–
Curran, S.M.	60	721	22.53	95*	–	2	78	31.65	5-48	5.56
Curran, T.K.	86	739	21.11	47*	–	–	126	28.83	5-16	5.57
Currie, S.W.	5	17	8.50	8	–	–	6	22.00	3-58	7.13
Dal, A.K.	12	103	14.71	52	–	1	0	–	–	7.30
Davey, J.H.	91	1280	23.27	91	–	6	113	26.61	6-28	5.34
David, T.H.	15	709	78.77	140*	2	5	7	18.00	3-26	3.93
Davies, A.L.	49	1380	32.09	147	1	7	–	–	–	48/11
Davies, J.L.B.	5	164	32.80	70	–	2	–	–	–	–
Davies, S.M.	192	5914	35.62	127*	9	37	–	–	–	157/42
Davis, W.S.	8	47	23.50	15*	–	–	8	45.12	2-40	7.00
Dawson, L.A.	159	3499	33.00	113*	3	18	161	30.04	6-47	4.72
de Caires, J.M.	3	68	22.66	43	–	–	1	95.00	1-13	5.27
de Lange, M.	98	776	15.52	58*	–	2	170	26.03	5-49	5.54
Dell, J.J.	6	136	27.20	46	–	–	–	–	–	–
Denly, J.L.	159	4902	36.58	150*	8	26	47	25.51	4-35	5.11
Dent, C.D.J.	77	2136	32.36	151*	4	6	12	34.33	4-43	5.64
Dickson, S.R.	51	1285	31.34	103*	1	9	0	–	–	10.00
D'Oliveira, B.L.	72	1299	25.47	123	1	7	57	41.22	3- 8	5.25
Doneathy, L.	9	152	38.00	69*	–	2	8	37.50	4-36	6.61
Douthwaite, D.A.	4	99	49.50	52*	–	1	5	25.20	3-43	5.47
Drissell, G.S.	6	32	16.00	17*	–	–	2	58.00	1-21	5.80
du Plessis, F.	262	9483	46.94	185	25	57	54	37.59	4-47	5.44
du Plooy, J.L.	45	1865	58.28	155	5	10	11	35.36	3-19	5.84
Duckett, B.M.	73	2341	38.37	220*	3	16	–	–	–	38/3
Duke, H.G.	9	206	29.42	125	1	–	–	–	–	4/1
Dunn, M.P.	11	9	9.00	8*	–	–	13	34.23	2-32	6.05
Eckersley, E.J.H.	46	1091	29.48	108	1	5	–	–	–	28/1
Eskinazi, S.S.	21	697	38.72	130	2	1	–	–	–	–
Evans, L.J.	63	1735	37.71	134*	3	5	1	82.00	1-29	9.11
Evans, S.T.	2	20	20.00	20	–	–	–	–	–	–
Evison, J.D.M.	5	72	24.00	54	–	1	4	40.75	2-33	7.08
Fell, T.C.	52	1541	33.50	116*	1	13	–	–	–	–
Finch, A.W.	7	25	12.50	23*	–	–	6	37.00	2-54	6.00
Finn, S.T.	143	411	12.08	42*	–	–	199	29.27	5-33	5.14
Fisher, M.D.	34	228	28.50	36*	–	–	32	42.68	3-32	5.92
Fletcher, L.J.	79	505	20.20	53*	–	1	87	35.25	5-56	5.67
Foakes, B.T.	73	1941	37.32	92	–	18	–	–	–	86/11
Fraine, W.A.R.	13	254	28.22	69*	–	1	–	–	–	–
Fuller, J.K.	69	884	23.26	55*	–	2	79	33.03	6-35	5.92
Garrett, G.A.	4	8	4.00	7	–	–	5	27.00	3-50	5.00
Garton, G.H.S.	24	103	11.44	38	–	–	29	34.24	4-43	6.32
Gay, E.N.	8	189	37.80	84*	–	1	0	–	–	6.33
Geddes, B.B.A.	4	84	28.00	32	–	–	–	–	–	–
Gilchrist, N.N.	6	19	6.33	8	–	–	8	22.62	5-45	7.09
Gleeson, R.J.	21	53	6.62	13	–	–	28	29.14	5-47	5.82
Glover, B.D.	8	75	18.75	27	–	–	5	56.40	2-60	5.09

	M	Runs	Avge	HS	100	50	Wkts	Avge	Best	Econ
Godleman, B.A.	71	2687	44.04	137	7	12	–	–	–	–
Goldsworthy, L.P.	8	381	63.50	96	–	4	3	70.00	1-17	5.25
Gorvin, A.W.	4	12	–	12*	–	–	1	74.00	1-11	4.11
Greatwood, T.L.	1	7	–	7*	–	–	2	15.00	2-30	5.00
Green, B.G.F.	8	145	48.33	87	–	1	9	27.66	3-64	5.47
Gregory, L.	79	1323	24.96	105*	1	8	110	27.66	4-23	5.95
Griffiths, G.T.	26	39	9.75	15*	–	–	33	35.60	4-30	6.00
Gubbins, N.R.T.	63	2385	40.42	141	6	14	4	20.25	4-38	5.40
Guest, B.D.	9	211	26.37	74	–	1	–	–	–	4/2
Hain, S.R.	58	2810	59.78	161*	10	15	–	–	–	–
Haines, T.J.	7	252	36.00	123	1	–	–	–	–	–
Hales, A.D.	175	6260	38.40	187*	17	32	0	–	–	15.00
Hameed, H.	21	663	36.83	103	1	4	–	–	–	–
Hamidullah Qadri	8	107	53.50	42*	–	–	5	42.60	3-47	6.23
Hammond, M.A.H.	8	185	30.83	95	–	1	5	19.40	2-18	5.10
Handscomb, P.S.P.	118	3594	38.23	140	4	22	–	–	–	106/5
Hannon-Dalby, O.J.	43	91	15.16	21*	–	–	65	31.92	5-27	6.29
Haris Rauf	12	11	3.66	8	–	–	21	29.38	4-65	5.82
Harmer, S.R.	93	1136	21.43	44*	–	–	96	38.03	4-42	4.93
Harris, J.A.R.	70	458	13.87	117	1	–	95	31.04	4-38	5.84
Harris, M.S.	51	1488	31.00	127	1	8	–	–	–	–
Haynes, J.A.	8	395	49.37	153	1	2	–	–	–	–
Head, T.M.	106	3769	39.26	202	8	21	24	62.91	2- 9	6.01
Heldreich, F.J.	3	5	5.00	5	–	–	3	50.00	2-69	7.50
Helm, T.G.	40	206	12.87	30	–	–	56	31.10	5-33	5.75
Hendricks, B.E.	80	168	8.00	24	–	–	104	32.43	5-31	5.77
Henry, M.J.	130	636	12.72	48*	–	–	211	26.92	6-45	5.23
Higgins, R.F.	33	680	28.33	81*	–	3	24	35.20	4-50	5.54
Hildreth, J.C.	220	6087	36.01	159	8	29	6	30.83	2-26	7.40
Hill, G.C.H.	9	222	37.00	90*	–	2	10	24.90	3-47	5.29
Hill, L.J.	49	1168	27.80	118	3	4	–	–	–	27/2
Hogan, M.G.	79	187	18.70	27	–	–	118	27.27	5-44	4.87
Holden, M.D.E.	16	613	43.78	166	1	3	1	104.00	1-29	4.95
Holland, I.G.	28	465	22.14	75	–	3	25	35.72	4-12	5.42
Hollman, L.B.K.	4	28	9.33	14*	–	–	8	24.50	4-56	5.29
Hose, A.J.	29	761	33.08	101*	1	4	–	–	–	–
Howell, B.A.C.	86	2050	35.34	122	1	13	76	34.73	3-37	5.20
Hudson-Prentice, F.J.	10	328	54.66	93	–	3	6	56.50	3-37	6.62
Hughes, A.L.	71	894	21.80	96*	–	3	43	44.13	4-44	5.61
Hurt, L.J.	12	49	16.33	15*	–	–	15	30.73	3-55	5.91
Hutton, B.A.	23	245	24.50	46	–	–	22	43.68	3-72	6.03
Ibrahim, D.K.	7	59	11.80	46	–	–	5	39.40	2-54	5.62
Ingram, C.A.	186	7584	47.40	142	18	48	40	33.62	4-39	5.44
Jacks, W.G.	22	506	24.09	121	1	2	11	38.45	2-32	5.26
James, L.W.	7	40	10.00	16*	–	–	5	9.60	5-48	5.33
Jennings, K.K.	73	2404	41.44	139	4	17	11	60.90	2-19	5.82
Johal, M.S.	6	16	8.00	10*	–	–	7	32.57	2-35	5.47
Jones, M.A.	8	281	35.12	87	–	3	–	–	–	–
Jones, R.P.	20	425	32.69	72	–	3	2	61.00	1- 3	6.00
Jordan, C.J.	84	634	15.46	55	–	1	121	30.02	5-28	5.73
Kelly, M.L.	12	47	11.75	16	–	–	18	25.05	4-25	4.92
Keogh, R.I.	54	1432	32.54	134	2	12	11	94.18	2-26	5.42
Kerrigan, S.C.	39	35	2.91	10	–	–	34	43.91	4-48	5.30
Khushi, F.I.N.	5	234	46.80	109	1	1	–	–	–	–

	M	Runs	Avge	HS	100	50	Wkts	Avge	Best	Econ
Kimber, L.P.J.	8	197	32.83	85	–	2	–	–	–	–
Kimber, N.J.H.	3	16	16.00	16	–	–	2	43.50	2-57	7.25
King, S.I.M.	1	11	11.00	11	–	–	–	–	–	–
Klaassen, F.J.	22	63	7.87	13	–	–	32	25.28	3-23	4.52
Kohler-Cadmore, T.	56	1808	34.11	164	3	10	–	–	–	–
Labuschagne, M.	50	1791	38.10	135	2	15	8	65.75	3-46	6.26
Lace, T.C.	15	205	15.76	48	–	–	2	10.00	2-20	10.00
Lakmal, R.A.S.	170	467	9.93	38*	–	–	240	28.35	5-31	5.33
Lamb, D.J.	9	152	50.66	86*	–	1	14	29.00	5-30	5.58
Lamb, M.J.	11	421	46.77	119*	1	2	4	40.00	4-35	5.51
Lavelle, G.I.D.	7	100	25.00	52	–	1	–	–	–	6/1
Lawrence, D.W.	28	670	26.80	115	1	4	11	54.27	3-35	6.25
Leach, J.	45	708	29.50	88	–	2	49	40.08	4-30	5.97
Leach, M.J.	17	22	7.33	18	–	–	21	33.19	3- 7	4.79
Leaning, J.A.	54	1123	28.79	131*	2	5	10	32.70	5-22	5.68
Lees, A.Z.	63	2095	40.28	126*	4	16	–	–	–	–
Lenham, A.D.	7	47	15.66	16	–	–	8	40.12	4-59	6.05
Leonard, E.O.	4	1	–	1*	–	–	3	55.33	2-84	7.54
Libby, J.D.	14	356	29.66	76	–	3	0	–	–	3.25
Lilley, A.M.	27	262	16.37	46	–	–	19	37.63	4-30	5.54
Linde, G.F.	64	1173	24.95	93*	–	8	89	28.78	6-47	5.31
Livingstone, L.S.	58	1624	36.08	129	1	10	24	48.08	3-51	5.23
Lloyd, D.L.	46	942	24.78	92	–	5	17	43.58	5-53	5.96
Logan, J.E.G.	6	46	23.00	17*	–	–	3	69.00	2-45	6.27
Loten, T.W.	1	–	–	–	–	–	–	–	–	–
Luxton, W.A.	7	165	33.00	68	–	1	–	–	–	–
Lyth, A.	122	3765	35.18	144	5	18	6	62.16	2-27	6.21
McDermott, B.R.	25	1032	44.86	117	3	6	–	–	–	–
McKerr, C.	16	86	14.33	26*	–	–	26	27.69	4-64	6.19
McKiernan, M.H.	7	113	22.60	38	–	–	3	66.66	1-26	6.89
McManus, L.D.	37	563	23.45	50	–	1	–	–	–	27/8
Madsen, W.L.	105	3323	41.53	138	6	19	16	35.81	3-27	5.14
Mahmood, S.	34	137	17.12	45	–	–	64	24.14	6-37	5.56
Malan, D.J.	154	5269	41.48	185*	10	27	40	32.75	4-25	5.83
Marshall, C.R.	5	55	13.75	19	–	–	0	–	–	6.00
Maxwell, G.J.	188	5115	34.10	146	5	32	95	45.57	4-46	5.50
Middleton, F.S.	1	16	16.00	16	–	–	–	–	–	–
Mike, B.W.M.	10	159	19.87	41	–	–	10	37.60	3-34	7.54
Miles, C.N.	39	146	12.16	31*	–	–	46	37.67	4-29	6.35
Mills, T.S.	23	7	1.75	3*	–	–	22	35.77	3-23	5.97
Milne, A.F.	73	392	17.81	45	–	–	103	30.00	5-61	5.27
Milnes, M.E.	12	101	16.83	26	–	–	19	34.05	5-79	6.75
Mohammad Abbas	55	137	7.61	15*	–	–	75	29.21	4-31	4.88
Mohammad Rizwan	144	4558	46.98	141*	11	22	–	–	–	134/18
Montgomery, M.	12	421	52.62	104	1	1	0	–	–	5.81
Moores, T.J.	21	566	35.37	76	–	5	–	–	–	18/5
Morgan, E.J.G.	376	11559	38.91	161	22	67	0	–	–	7.00
Moriarty, D.T.	10	8	4.00	5	–	–	15	23.80	4-30	4.36
Morley, J.P.	7	6	6.00	6	–	–	9	24.88	2-22	4.00
Morris, C.A.J.	41	110	15.71	25*	–	–	44	37.38	4-33	5.94
Mousley, D.R.	4	166	41.50	61	–	2	1	53.00	1-31	5.88
Mujeeb Zadran	50	92	8.36	18*	–	–	78	22.94	5-50	3.95
Mullaney, S.J.	123	2611	35.28	124	2	19	100	34.58	4-29	5.21
Murtagh, T.J.	213	828	10.09	35*	–	–	277	29.64	5-21	5.00

	M	Runs	Avge	HS	100	50	Wkts	Avge	Best	Econ
Muyeye, T.S.	8	140	23.33	30	–	–	0	–	–	2.66
Naseem Shah	1	1	1.00	1	–	–	–	–	–	–
Naveen-ul-Haq	23	92	10.22	30	–	–	34	34.47	5-40	5.94
Neesham, J.D.S.	128	3083	34.25	120*	2	18	143	28.16	5-27	5.81
Neser, M.G.	57	685	22.83	122	1	1	67	34.50	4-41	5.24
Nijjar, A.S.S.	13	136	34.00	32*	–	–	13	42.92	2-26	5.15
Northeast, S.A.	106	2986	33.93	132	4	17	–	–	–	–
Norwell, L.C.	18	47	5.87	16	–	–	23	32.82	6-52	5.39
Olivier, D.	50	201	13.40	25*	–	–	64	28.70	4-34	5.33
Organ, F.S.	11	120	17.14	79	–	1	5	43.80	2-43	4.57
O'Riordan, M.K.	5	119	39.66	60	–	1	1	157.00	1-77	7.47
Orr, A.G.H.	5	144	28.80	108	1	–	–	–	–	–
Overton, C.	72	774	22.11	66*	–	2	94	31.34	5-18	5.30
Overton, J.	42	399	17.34	40*	–	–	57	30.54	4-42	6.28
Parkinson, C.F.	13	222	27.75	52*	–	1	4	147.25	1-34	6.40
Parkinson, M.W.	30	50	16.66	15*	–	–	47	28.04	5-51	5.23
Patel, R.K.	11	384	38.40	118	1	1	–	–	–	–
Patel, R.S.	13	443	49.22	131	2	1	4	33.25	2-65	6.13
Patel, S.R.	245	6270	35.22	136*	8	33	225	33.29	6-13	5.40
Paterson, D.	91	302	11.61	29	–	–	123	30.43	5-19	5.20
Patterson, S.A.	97	250	12.50	25*	–	–	122	28.88	6-32	5.13
Patterson-White, L.A.	8	51	8.50	27	–	–	13	14.46	5-19	5.37
Pattinson, J.L.	66	398	14.21	54	–	1	98	29.79	6-48	5.28
Payne, D.A.	66	171	17.10	36*	–	–	110	24.96	7-29	5.74
Pennington, D.Y.	3	7	7.00	4*	–	–	8	22.25	5-67	6.84
Pepper, M.S.	5	40	13.33	34	–	–	–	–	–	0/0
Petersen, K.D.	66	1780	32.96	134*	3	11	3	48.33	1-18	5.24
Plom, J.H.	5	11	11.00	9*	–	–	6	40.50	3-34	6.62
Podmore, H.W.	21	140	15.55	40	–	–	20	51.50	4-57	6.45
Pollock, E.J.	25	599	27.22	103*	1	2	–	–	–	–
Pope, O.J.D.	31	767	33.34	93*	–	5	–	–	–	–
Porter, J.A.	33	35	8.75	7*	–	–	35	35.91	4-29	5.04
Potts, M.J.	10	53	13.25	30	–	–	16	23.37	4-62	5.84
Prest, T.J.	7	108	15.42	41	–	–	2	19.50	2-28	4.87
Price, O.J.	2	43	21.50	24	–	–	1	30.00	1- 9	7.50
Price, T.J.	2	1	0.50	1	–	–	0	–	–	7.00
Procter, L.A.	48	820	32.80	97	–	5	26	41.92	3-29	5.74
Qais Ahmad	14	184	26.28	66	–	1	19	31.73	3-21	4.78
Quinn, M.R.	39	132	14.66	36	–	–	52	37.07	4-71	6.01
Rahmanullah Gurbaz	32	984	41.00	128	3	3	–	–	–	32/7
Raine, B.A.	29	402	21.15	83	–	1	30	40.63	3-31	5.68
Rampaul, R.	202	662	11.41	86*	–	1	302	24.94	5-48	4.90
Rashid, A.U.	229	1780	18.93	71	–	2	304	31.87	5-27	5.46
Rashid Khan	76	1029	20.58	60*	–	5	144	18.67	7-18	4.20
Rawlins, D.M.W.	11	285	25.90	53	–	2	3	89.66	1-27	5.38
Reece, L.M.	40	908	29.29	128	1	5	19	50.73	4-35	6.16
Reifer, N.M.J.	10	63	12.60	28	–	–	–	–	–	–
Reingold, S.J.	10	187	20.77	40	–	–	5	32.60	1-16	6.03
Renshaw, M.T.	36	1000	32.25	109	1	8	5	34.40	2-17	5.21
Revis, M.L.	9	186	31.00	58*	–	1	5	45.80	2-43	5.32
Rew, J.E.K.	2	26	13.00	20	–	–	–	–	–	0/0
Rhodes, G.H.	18	306	25.50	106	1	1	12	41.58	3-44	5.54
Rhodes, W.M.H.	39	773	23.42	69	–	3	21	36.04	3-40	5.78
Robinson, O.E.	14	122	17.42	30	–	–	14	40.57	3-31	5.91

	M	Runs	Avge	HS	100	50	Wkts	Avge	Best	Econ
Robinson, O.G.	16	287	23.91	75	–	1	–	–	–	8/0
Robson, S.D.	24	772	35.09	106	1	5	2	68.00	1-26	7.15
Roderick, G.H.	58	1262	30.04	104	2	8	–	–	–	56/6
Roland-Jones, T.S.	79	684	21.37	65	–	1	126	25.24	4-10	5.19
Root, J.E.	190	7322	48.81	133*	17	43	39	50.46	3-52	5.58
Root, W.T.	34	964	40.16	113*	2	5	6	51.66	2-36	6.36
Rossington, A.M.	49	1381	37.32	97	–	11	–	–	–	34/5
Roy, J.J.	193	6639	37.93	180	16	35	0	–	–	12.00
Rushworth, C.	80	188	11.75	38*	–	–	128	24.16	5-31	5.19
Rymell, J.S.	7	331	55.16	121	1	1	–	–	–	–
Sakande, A.	10	11	2.75	7*	–	–	9	55.44	2-53	6.94
Sales, J.J.G.	3	47	47.00	28	–	–	0	–	–	6.40
Salisbury, M.E.T.	17	10	10.00	5*	–	–	17	38.35	4-55	5.66
Salt, P.D.	19	598	33.22	137*	1	3	–	–	–	–
Salter, A.G.	43	413	21.73	51	–	1	26	50.73	3-37	5.09
Sanderson, B.W.	41	140	10.76	31	–	–	52	29.96	3-29	5.69
Sarro, J.P.	5	4	–	4*	–	–	4	47.25	2-41	7.26
Schadendorf, D.J.	8	95	23.75	44*	–	–	–	–	–	6/1
Scott, G.F.B.	19	432	39.27	66*	–	3	1	317.00	1-65	6.60
Scrimshaw, G.L.S.	3	13	–	13*	–	–	3	28.66	2-41	8.60
Scriven, T.A.R.	5	63	31.50	42	–	–	1	46.00	1- 6	6.00
Shaheen Shah Afridi	33	90	12.85	19*	–	–	58	27.00	6-35	5.58
Shan Masood	97	4540	57.46	182*	14	26	2	8.50	2- 0	4.25
Shaw, J.	7	2	1.00	2	–	–	8	41.75	4-36	5.85
Shutt, J.W.	5	2	–	1*	–	–	1	88.00	1-33	8.00
Sibley, D.P.	22	416	23.11	115	1	–	1	62.00	1-20	6.88
Siddle, P.M.	65	251	10.91	62	–	1	78	33.30	4-27	4.75
Sidebottom, R.N.	2	11	–	9*	–	–	2	48.50	1-41	5.82
Simpson, J.A.	96	1607	25.50	82*	–	8	–	–	–	90/19
Singh, F.	3	27	27.00	21	–	–	0	–	–	3.23
Slater, B.T.	44	2006	55.72	148*	5	13	–	–	–	–
Smit, D.	124	2160	31.76	109	1	11	45	38.06	4-39	116/11
Smith, J.L.	15	425	42.50	85	–	3	–	–	–	13/2
Smith, R.A.J.	18	71	8.87	14	–	–	18	32.83	4- 7	6.19
Smith, T.M.J.	91	575	23.95	65	–	2	77	39.88	4-26	5.26
Snater, S.	22	104	11.55	23*	–	–	27	31.22	5-60	5.36
Sowter, N.A.	19	134	14.88	31	–	–	36	25.77	6-62	5.52
Steel, C.T.	16	186	16.90	77	–	1	10	26.70	4-33	5.34
Steel, S.	8	227	32.42	68	–	2	1	53.00	1-38	5.88
Steketee, M.T.	34	294	21.00	30*	–	–	52	27.28	4-25	5.34
Stevens, D.I.	321	7692	29.24	147	7	46	162	32.64	6-25	4.80
Stewart, G.	12	104	13.00	44	–	–	11	32.90	3-17	4.81
Stirling, P.R.	225	7853	37.39	177	20	36	71	41.28	6-55	4.99
Stoinis, M.P.	95	2478	32.18	146*	4	14	71	37.14	4-43	5.86
Stokes, B.A.	171	4711	37.68	164	7	27	137	33.12	5-61	5.76
Stone, O.P.	30	122	24.40	24*	–	–	24	42.62	4-71	5.45
Stoneman, M.D.	91	3092	39.13	144*	7	18	1	8.00	1- 8	12.00
Sullivan, J.R.	3	6	6.00	6	–	–	5	15.80	4-11	5.64
Swindells, H.J.	10	222	31.71	75	–	2	–	–	–	10/2
Tattersall, J.A.	24	528	35.20	89	–	6	–	–	–	21/3
Taylor, C.Z.	3	53	17.66	36	–	–	3	30.33	1- 6	5.05
Taylor, J.M.R.	59	1357	35.71	75	–	12	29	36.17	4-38	5.22
Taylor, J.P.A.	2	6	–	6*	–	–	3	31.00	2-66	7.15
Taylor, M.D.	35	105	21.00	51*	–	1	27	52.03	3-39	5.43

	M	Runs	Avge	HS	100	50	Wkts	Avge	Best	Econ
Taylor, T.A.I.	19	387	55.28	98*	–	4	22	38.18	3-24	5.94
Thomas, G.W.	2	82	41.00	75	–	1	0	–	–	9.33
Thompson, J.A.	1	–	–	–	–	–	0	–	–	8.60
Thomson, A.T.	15	301	33.44	68*	–	2	18	30.83	3-27	5.38
Thurston, C.O.	8	153	30.60	53	–	1	–	–	–	–
Tongue, J.C.	13	76	19.00	34	–	–	14	42.85	2-35	6.80
Topley, R.J.W.	58	55	9.16	19	–	–	97	25.90	4-16	5.55
Trevaskis, L.	17	95	10.55	23	–	–	14	42.00	3-38	4.98
Turner, J.A.	6	11	–	6*	–	–	7	27.85	3-44	5.41
van Beek, L.V.	80	693	17.32	64*	–	3	94	31.89	6-18	5.52
van Buuren, G.L.	78	1656	29.57	119*	1	8	63	32.76	5-35	4.74
van der Gugten, T.	61	400	17.39	49	–	–	71	34.52	5-24	5.40
van der Merwe, R.E.	187	2901	26.86	165*	1	11	250	26.62	5-26	4.87
van Meekeren, P.A.	54	129	9.21	15*	–	–	60	27.26	3-22	4.84
van Vollenhoven, K.T.	2	21	10.50	20	–	–	0	–	–	6.42
Vasconcelos, R.S.	34	931	30.03	112	1	6	–	–	–	27/3
Vilas, D.J.	173	4919	36.98	166	9	24	–	–	–	174/29
Vince, J.M.	142	5063	40.50	190	10	24	3	54.00	1-18	5.58
Wade, M.S.	180	4675	32.69	155	9	20	–	–	–	191/20
Wagstaff, M.D.	5	74	18.50	36	–	–	–	–	–	–
Waite, M.J.	22	437	36.41	71	–	1	28	30.07	5-59	6.37
Walallawita, T.N.	6	69	13.80	29	–	–	4	71.75	2-54	5.21
Walker, R.I.	2	22	–	15*	–	–	1	74.00	1-53	5.55
Waller, M.T.C.	58	109	15.57	25*	–	–	45	37.68	3-37	5.65
Walter, P.I.	16	253	25.30	50	–	1	14	31.00	4-37	7.07
Ward, H.D.	2	24	12.00	20	–	–	–	–	–	–
Warner, J.D.	7	0	0.00	0	–	–	6	46.33	3-42	5.45
Weatherley, J.J.	27	664	28.86	105*	1	4	8	27.62	4-25	4.05
Weighell, W.J.	17	64	8.00	23	–	–	30	26.70	5-57	6.06
Welch, N.R.	6	134	22.33	52	–	1	–	–	–	–
Wells, B.J.J.	4	9	4.50	7	–	–	–	–	–	2/0
Wells, L.W.P.	33	390	15.60	66*	–	2	14	36.85	3-19	5.27
Westley, T.	98	3268	38.00	134	5	26	29	36.72	4-60	4.87
Wheal, B.T.J.	28	63	7.00	18*	–	–	44	26.22	4-38	5.24
Wheater, A.J.A.	89	1924	28.71	135	2	11	–	–	–	51/14
White, C.	7	20	10.00	10*	–	–	10	22.00	4-20	5.11
White, G.G.	89	558	15.08	41*	–	–	94	29.82	6-37	5.00
White, R.G.	15	239	23.90	55	–	1	–	–	–	19/3
Whiteley, R.A.	81	1660	27.66	131	1	10	14	40.21	4-58	6.66
Willey, D.J.	135	1859	25.46	167	3	7	157	30.71	5-30	5.67
Woakes, C.R.	188	2056	23.36	95*	–	6	233	32.37	6-45	5.46
Wood, C.P.	79	400	12.90	41	–	–	106	27.96	5-22	5.38
Wood, L.	4	73	73.00	52	–	1	5	25.00	2-36	5.95
Wood, M.A.	91	134	7.05	24	–	–	115	32.88	4-33	5.29
Wood, T.A.	9	235	33.57	109	1	–	3	31.00	1-13	5.47
Worrall, D.J.	39	96	10.66	18	–	–	48	36.79	5-62	5.33
Wright, C.J.C.	107	271	11.29	42	–	–	104	38.20	4-20	5.67
Wright, L.J.	211	5126	33.07	166	11	19	111	38.11	4-12	5.34
Yates, R.M.	8	348	43.50	103	1	3	2	60.50	1-27	5.11
Young, W.A.	63	2110	36.37	136	5	12	–	–	–	–
Zafar Gohar	60	501	13.54	53	–	1	89	27.41	5-56	4.86
Zaib, S.A.	18	205	17.08	43	–	–	8	36.75	3-37	5.76

TWENTY20 CAREER RECORDS

Compiled by Philip Bailey

The following career records, to the end of the 2021 season, include all players currently registered with first-class counties or teams in The Hundred. Performances in The Hundred are included.

	M	Runs	Avge	HS	100	50	Wkts	Avge	Best	Econ
Abbott, K.J.	153	324	13.33	30	–	–	157	28.36	5-14	8.24
Abell, T.B.	53	1277	34.51	101*	1	8	2	50.00	1-11	10.00
Ackermann, C.N.	135	3051	27.73	79*	–	16	68	28.10	7-18	7.22
Albert, T.E.	2	18	9.00	13	–	–	–	–	–	–
Ali, M.M.	197	4246	24.83	121*	2	22	128	26.53	5-34	7.59
Allison, B.M.J.	1	1	–	1*	–	–	1	32.00	1-32	10.66
Alsop, T.P.	42	793	22.65	85	–	3	–	–	–	15/3
Amla, H.M.	164	4563	30.83	104*	2	30	0	–	–	15.00
Anderson, J.M.	44	23	5.75	16	–	–	41	32.14	3-23	8.47
Andersson, M.K.	11	95	9.50	24	–	–	0	–	–	13.75
Archer, J.C.	121	551	17.21	36	–	–	153	22.52	4-18	7.65
Atkinson, A.A.P.	17	39	9.75	14	–	–	22	19.22	4-36	8.87
Azhar Ali	49	985	21.88	72	–	3	15	18.86	3-10	6.35
Bailey, T.E.	24	21	4.20	10	–	–	25	23.60	5-17	9.36
Bairstow, J.M.	160	3857	31.35	114	3	22	–	–	–	95/15
Ball, J.T.	93	53	8.83	18*	–	–	116	23.42	4-11	8.89
Ballance, G.S.	100	1807	23.16	79	–	7	–	–	–	–
Bamber, E.R.	5	3	–	3*	–	–	0	–	–	11.54
Banton, T.	62	1459	25.15	107*	2	9	–	–	–	32/6
Barker, K.H.D.	65	383	13.67	46	–	–	69	23.01	4-19	7.90
Barnard, E.G.	88	569	16.25	43*	–	–	52	38.32	3-29	8.91
Barnes, E.	5	7	7.00	7	–	–	2	57.50	2-27	11.50
Bartlett, G.A.	6	64	10.66	24	–	–	–	–	–	–
Bedingham, D.G.	46	895	21.82	73	–	6	–	–	–	11/1
Beer, W.A.T.	131	375	9.37	37	–	–	106	27.04	3-14	7.48
Bell-Drummond, D.J.	124	3562	31.24	112*	1	29	5	35.80	2-19	10.22
Benjamin, C.G.	11	183	45.75	60*	–	1	–	–	–	–
Berg, G.K.	94	1083	21.66	90	–	3	74	29.22	4-20	8.00
Bess, D.M.	17	41	8.20	24	–	–	16	26.06	3-17	7.44
Bethell, J.G.	3	12	6.00	7	–	–	0	–	–	10.16
Billings, S.W.	201	3807	23.64	95*	–	22	–	–	–	111/19
Bird, J.M.	72	75	8.33	14*	–	–	61	30.01	4-31	7.64
Blake, A.J.	141	1898	20.40	71*	–	9	1	96.00	1-17	7.38
Bohannon, J.J.	22	112	12.44	35	–	–	–	–	–	–
Bopara, R.S.	398	7744	27.26	105*	1	40	243	25.37	6-16	7.50
Borthwick, S.G.	106	650	17.56	62	–	1	74	25.20	4-18	8.06
Bracey, J.R.	30	425	18.47	64	–	1	–	–	–	9/10
Brathwaite, C.R.	223	2122	15.95	64*	–	4	199	26.91	4-15	8.16
Briggs, D.R.	201	189	10.50	35*	–	–	219	22.46	5-19	7.23
Broad, S.C.J.	85	152	7.60	18*	–	–	100	21.44	4-24	7.19
Brook, H.C.	43	1231	39.70	91*	–	4	1	26.00	1-13	13.00
Brooks, J.A.	65	76	15.20	33*	–	–	55	27.38	5-21	7.50
Brown, B.C.	82	840	15.00	68	–	1	–	–	–	41/7
Brown, P.R.	54	22	7.33	7*	–	–	66	24.09	4-21	9.04
Browne, N.L.J.	14	165	16.50	38	–	–	–	–	–	–
Buck, N.L.	66	96	12.00	26*	–	–	71	26.54	4-26	8.84
Budinger, S.G.	5	52	13.00	21	–	–	–	–	–	–
Burgess, M.G.K.	52	491	14.87	56	–	1	–	–	–	21/12

	M	Runs	Avge	HS	100	50	Wkts	Avge	Best	Econ
Burns, R.J.	63	725	16.47	56*	–	2	–	–	–	27/2
Buttleman, W.E.L.	9	158	19.75	56*	–	1	–	–	–	2/1
Buttler, J.C.	292	7066	31.68	124	1	49	–	–	–	159/33
Byrom, E.J.	18	269	17.93	54*	–	1	–	–	–	–
Came, H.R.C.	11	207	18.81	56	–	1	–	–	–	–
Campbell, J.O.I.	2	6	6.00	6	–	–	1	21.00	1-21	10.50
Carey, L.J.	9	7	7.00	5	–	–	4	52.25	1-15	9.08
Carlson, K.S.	34	480	16.55	58	–	1	0	–	–	6.00
Carse, B.A.	40	390	21.66	51	–	1	21	45.19	3-30	8.78
Carter, M.	45	110	12.22	23*	–	–	50	21.58	3-14	7.45
Carter, O.J.	2	0	–	0*	–	–	–	–	–	1/1
Carver, K.	10	2	2.00	2	–	–	8	26.00	3-40	9.45
Chappell, Z.J.	18	69	8.62	16	–	–	15	33.13	3-23	9.71
Christian, D.T.	363	5276	23.24	129	2	15	265	28.80	5-14	8.44
Clark, G.	71	1594	24.15	91*	–	9	0	–	–	15.23
Clark, J.	101	1013	22.02	60	–	1	58	30.60	4-22	9.04
Clarke, J.M.	93	2353	28.01	136	3	12	–	–	–	29/0
Coad, B.O.	12	14	4.66	7	–	–	13	24.84	3-40	8.93
Cobb, J.J.	167	3548	24.98	103	1	20	61	33.19	4-22	7.84
Cockbain, I.A.	135	3395	33.28	123	1	18	–	–	–	–
Cohen, M.A.R.	12	22	22.00	7*	–	–	9	32.11	2-17	8.58
Conners, S.	6	2	–	2*	–	–	3	40.00	2-38	10.00
Cook, A.N.	32	892	31.85	100*	1	5	–	–	–	–
Cook, S.J.	29	28	5.60	18	–	–	32	24.50	4-15	8.52
Cooke, C.B.	128	2022	22.71	72	–	6	–	–	–	79/11
Coughlin, P.	47	555	24.13	53	–	1	50	22.22	5-42	9.64
Cox, J.M.	29	500	33.33	64	–	3	–	–	–	19/4
Cox, O.B.	133	2060	27.83	61*	–	5	–	–	–	58/30
Cracknell, J.B.	18	459	25.50	77	–	3	–	–	–	–
Crane, M.S.	56	59	29.50	12*	–	–	64	22.07	3-15	7.27
Crawley, Z.	38	1096	32.23	108*	1	5	–	–	–	–
Crawshaw, H.M.	3	9	4.50	5	–	–	0	–	–	9.20
Critchley, M.J.J.	77	963	19.65	80*	–	2	59	26.77	4-36	7.70
Crocombe, H.T.	1	–	–	–	–	–	0	–	–	19.00
Croft, S.J.	209	4388	30.05	94*	–	24	78	28.17	3- 6	7.40
Cullen, B.C.	20	61	12.20	20*	–	–	30	17.70	4-32	9.28
Cullen, T.N.	1	5	5.00	5	–	–	–	–	–	1/0
Curran, B.J.	9	125	13.88	62	–	1	–	–	–	–
Curran, S.M.	109	1236	20.60	72*	–	6	103	28.21	4-11	8.62
Curran, T.K.	152	1112	19.85	62	–	3	177	25.19	4-22	8.85
Currie, S.W.	13	7	2.33	3	–	–	20	15.10	4-24	8.16
Dal, A.K.	21	159	15.90	35	–	–	0	–	–	8.00
Davey, J.H.	57	239	18.38	24	–	–	65	21.36	4-34	8.87
David, T.H.	63	1469	34.97	92*	–	7	5	53.20	1-18	8.96
Davies, A.L.	88	1901	27.15	94*	–	14	–	–	–	49/10
Davies, J.L.B.	4	48	12.00	23	–	–	–	–	–	–
Davies, S.M.	153	2850	20.95	99*	–	16	–	–	–	69/24
Davis, W.S.	21	6	2.00	4*	–	–	16	28.43	3-24	8.77
Dawson, L.A.	181	1983	19.44	82	–	5	129	27.52	5-17	7.27
de Caires, J.M.	1	14	14.00	14	–	–	–	–	–	–
de Kock, Q.	233	7044	34.19	126*	4	44	–	–	–	164/42
de Lange, M.	122	340	11.72	28*	–	–	141	24.21	5-20	8.58
Denly, J.L.	247	5771	26.11	127	4	31	45	24.11	4-19	7.77
Dent, C.D.J.	69	1337	23.87	87	–	7	5	33.60	1- 4	8.40
Dickson, S.R.	32	568	28.40	53	–	3	1	9.00	1- 9	9.00
D'Oliveira, B.L.	105	1456	24.67	69	–	8	50	34.92	4-26	7.65

	M	Runs	Avge	HS	100	50	Wkts	Avge	Best	Econ
Doneathy, L.	2	10	10.00	5*	–	–	1	19.00	1-19	9.50
Douthwaite, D.A.	29	346	16.47	53	–	1	20	26.80	3-28	8.83
du Plessis, F.	266	6845	30.97	120*	2	44	50	18.34	5-19	6.96
du Plooy, J.L.	67	1460	31.73	92	–	8	13	17.00	4-15	7.80
Duckett, B.M.	129	3057	30.26	96	–	19	–	–	–	58/2
Duke, H.G.	4	–	–	–	–	–	–	–	–	3/0
Dunn, M.P.	23	4	2.00	2	–	–	27	22.88	3- 8	9.15
Eckersley, E.J.H.	78	848	16.62	50*	–	1	–	–	–	25/7
Eskinazi, S.S.	50	1524	36.28	102*	1	12	–	–	–	–
Evans, L.J.	184	4334	33.85	108*	2	31	1	35.00	1- 5	9.54
Fell, T.C.	9	69	9.85	28	–	–	–	–	–	–
Finch, A.W.	5	3	–	3*	–	–	4	36.75	1-22	9.18
Finn, S.T.	130	78	9.75	11*	–	–	162	22.01	5-16	8.09
Fisher, M.D.	39	61	8.71	19	–	–	43	26.23	5-22	9.10
Fletcher, L.J.	93	155	6.73	27	–	–	102	25.34	5-43	8.31
Foakes, B.T.	77	856	21.40	75*	–	4	–	–	–	38/10
Fraine, W.A.R.	26	321	18.88	44*	–	–	–	–	–	–
Fuller, J.K.	112	1038	20.76	53*	–	2	97	25.29	6-28	8.94
Garrett, G.A.	2	–	–	–	–	–	1	39.00	1-19	9.75
Garton, G.H.S.	44	230	20.90	46	–	–	49	21.26	4-16	8.28
Gay, E.N.	1	15	15.00	15	–	–	–	–	–	–
Geddes, B.B.A.	6	44	7.33	28	–	–	–	–	–	–
Gleeson, R.J.	52	24	4.80	7*	–	–	50	26.92	3-12	8.00
Glover, B.D.	33	12	12.00	6*	–	–	39	19.89	4-12	7.89
Godleman, B.A.	96	1867	22.49	92	–	12	–	–	–	–
Goldsworthy, L.P.	15	210	21.00	48	–	–	14	22.28	3-14	7.42
Green, B.G.F.	18	165	20.62	43*	–	–	8	33.12	4-26	8.83
Gregory, L.	150	1871	21.02	76*	–	5	133	26.00	5-24	8.99
Griffiths, G.T.	60	56	18.66	12	–	–	53	27.49	4-24	8.81
Gubbins, N.R.T.	39	515	14.71	53	–	1	1	30.00	1-22	6.00
Guest, B.D.	16	173	28.83	34*	–	–	–	–	–	13/1
Hain, S.R.	81	2386	37.28	95	–	17	–	–	–	–
Hales, A.D.	314	8733	30.53	116*	5	53	0	–	–	14.00
Hamidullah Qadri	1	–	–	–	–	–	0	–	–	12.00
Hammond, M.A.H.	60	1181	23.15	63	–	3	0	–	–	8.50
Handscomb, P.S.P.	98	1526	23.47	103*	1	5	–	–	–	49/13
Hannon-Dalby, O.J.	60	53	10.60	14*	–	–	75	24.38	4-20	8.76
Haris Rauf	79	76	6.90	19	–	–	106	22.29	5-27	8.51
Harmer, S.R.	122	874	18.20	43	–	–	103	28.13	4-19	7.58
Harris, J.A.R.	58	164	10.93	18	–	–	48	33.20	4-23	9.28
Harris, M.S.	48	970	21.08	85	–	4	–	–	–	–
Harrison, C.G.	23	92	10.22	23	–	–	23	17.91	4-17	7.40
Hartley, T.W.	32	46	9.20	16*	–	–	25	28.96	4-16	6.98
Haynes, J.A.	9	171	19.00	41	–	–	–	–	–	–
Head, T.M.	93	2214	29.13	101*	1	9	22	27.09	3-16	8.49
Heldreich, F.J.	5	–	–	–	–	–	5	23.40	2-17	6.50
Helm, T.G.	57	120	12.00	28*	–	–	64	25.34	5-11	8.83
Hendricks, B.E.	83	33	4.71	12*	–	–	109	22.00	6-29	8.43
Henry, M.J.	90	383	12.76	42	–	–	88	29.35	4-43	8.71
Higgins, R.F.	87	1346	25.39	77*	–	4	62	24.11	5-13	8.91
Hildreth, J.C.	205	3900	24.52	107*	1	17	10	24.70	3-24	8.76
Hill, G.C.H.	10	57	9.50	19*	–	–	1	50.00	1- 9	7.69
Hill, L.J.	65	776	18.47	59	–	2	–	–	–	24/2
Hogan, M.G.	97	78	9.75	17*	–	–	105	24.42	5-17	7.82
Holden, M.D.E.	24	539	26.95	102*	1	2	0	–	–	12.00
Holland, I.G.	17	191	27.28	65	–	1	5	50.60	1-14	7.86

	M	Runs	Avge	HS	100	50	Wkts	Avge	Best	Econ
Hollman, L.B.K.	19	269	22.41	51	–	1	18	19.94	3-18	7.63
Hose, A.J.	65	1642	28.31	119	1	9	–	–	–	–
Howell, B.A.C.	144	1913	22.50	57	–	6	158	19.85	5-18	7.08
Hudson-Prentice, F.J.	27	244	15.25	41	–	–	28	24.89	3-36	9.29
Hughes, A.L.	89	869	17.03	43*	–	–	54	35.24	4-42	8.06
Hurt, L.J.	7	0	0.00	0	–	–	6	30.83	3-22	9.73
Hutton, B.A.	9	50	16.66	18*	–	–	5	51.00	2-28	8.89
Imran Tahir	334	284	9.16	23	–	–	420	19.77	5-23	6.96
Ingram, C.A.	300	7236	28.82	127*	4	43	38	32.81	4-32	7.88
Jacks, W.G.	64	1299	24.50	87	–	8	18	25.05	4-15	7.17
James, L.W.	4	8	4.00	7	–	–	–	–	–	–
Jennings, K.K.	70	1252	36.82	108	1	5	22	28.54	4-37	7.38
Jones, R.P.	21	238	39.66	61*	–	1	0	–	–	10.00
Jordan, C.J.	244	1231	14.83	45*	–	–	253	27.32	4- 6	8.56
Kelly, M.L.	21	61	15.25	23*	–	–	27	22.51	3-27	8.17
Keogh, R.I.	71	921	27.90	59*	–	4	16	27.43	3-30	8.28
Kerrigan, S.C.	24	9	–	4*	–	–	20	29.75	3-17	6.91
Khushi, F.I.N.	3	19	6.33	17	–	–	–	–	–	–
Kimber, L.P.J.	9	102	17.00	53	–	1	–	–	–	–
Klaassen, F.J.	65	56	6.22	13	–	–	71	26.35	4-17	8.80
Kohler-Cadmore, T.	95	2589	30.10	127	1	20	–	–	–	–
Labuschagne, M.	24	663	31.57	93*	–	4	20	21.00	3-13	9.13
Lakmal, R.A.S.	57	128	9.84	33	–	–	62	23.85	5-34	7.90
Lamb, D.J.	34	170	21.25	29*	–	–	28	27.46	3-23	8.26
Lamb, M.J.	10	168	24.00	39	–	–	0	–	–	9.00
Lammonby, T.A.	36	488	23.23	90	–	1	11	28.18	2-32	10.00
Lavelle, G.I.D.	2	18	9.00	12	–	–	–	–	–	0/0
Lawrence, D.W.	74	1575	27.15	86	–	9	26	22.30	3-21	7.73
Leach, J.	54	261	10.44	24	–	–	52	26.05	5-33	9.57
Leach, M.J.	2	–	–	–	–	–	5	12.00	3-28	7.50
Leaning, J.A.	77	1474	28.90	81*	–	6	8	21.00	3-15	7.63
Lees, A.Z.	56	1350	28.72	77*	–	8	–	–	–	–
Lenham, A.D.	11	7	7.00	5*	–	–	11	17.63	4-26	7.46
Libby, J.D.	42	1002	34.55	78*	–	5	1	77.00	1-11	8.55
Lilley, A.M.	108	1415	20.50	99*	–	3	49	32.06	3-26	7.50
Linde, G.F.	100	904	17.05	52*	–	2	105	22.93	4-19	7.31
Lintott, J.B.	38	85	9.44	41	–	–	44	20.84	4-20	7.03
Livingstone, L.S.	154	3992	29.79	103	2	23	57	21.17	4-17	7.97
Lloyd, D.L.	67	1407	23.84	97*	–	8	6	25.33	2-13	8.94
Logan, J.E.G.	2	–	–	–	–	–	2	9.00	1- 4	4.50
Lynn, C.A.	218	5928	31.36	113*	2	39	3	31.00	2-15	7.15
Lyth, A.	142	3265	25.11	161	1	20	25	26.16	5-31	7.66
McDermott, B.R.	78	1726	29.75	114	1	7	–	–	–	38/2
McKerr, C.	9	8	4.00	7*	–	–	5	43.40	2-23	9.23
McKiernan, M.H.	13	79	8.77	25	–	–	6	36.16	3- 9	7.23
McManus, L.D.	61	674	16.85	60*	–	2	–	–	–	27/15
Madsen, W.L.	125	3018	29.88	86*	–	20	19	33.94	2-20	7.86
Mahmood, S.	48	31	7.75	7*	–	–	59	21.67	4-14	8.56
Malan, D.J.	247	6659	32.32	117	5	40	23	31.39	2-10	7.64
Maxwell, G.J.	321	7187	27.74	145*	3	44	113	31.77	3-10	7.73
Melton, D.R.	4	–	–	–	–	–	4	31.00	2-37	9.53
Mike, B.W.M.	28	270	19.28	37	–	–	15	28.26	4-22	10.96
Miles, C.N.	27	42	8.40	11*	–	–	30	24.60	3-19	8.09
Mills, T.S.	142	109	6.81	27	–	–	156	24.22	4-22	7.77
Milne, A.F.	126	284	14.20	18*	–	–	146	22.99	5-11	7.65
Milnes, M.E.	29	24	6.00	13*	–	–	32	26.18	5-22	8.93

	M	Runs	Avge	HS	100	50	Wkts	Avge	Best	Econ
Mohammad Abbas	32	32	10.66	15*	–	–	26	37.34	3-22	8.59
Mohammad Amir	208	272	6.47	21*	–	–	235	23.08	6-17	7.17
Mohammad Rizwan	148	3282	38.61	104*	1	22	1	22.00	1-22	96/34
Montgomery, M.	2	30	–	30*	–	–	–	–	–	–
Moores, T.J.	90	1377	22.57	80*	–	6	–	–	–	49/15
Morgan, E.J.G.	347	7378	26.44	91	–	37	–	–	–	–
Moriarty, D.T.	26	15	–	9*	–	–	28	20.21	3-25	6.81
Morris, C.A.J.	26	8	4.00	3	–	–	28	28.21	3-21	9.49
Mousley, D.R.	9	189	27.00	58*	–	2	3	30.66	1- 3	7.66
Mujeeb Zadran	150	175	8.75	27	–	–	165	23.06	5-15	6.73
Mullaney, S.J.	158	1464	17.22	55	–	2	114	28.35	4-19	7.89
Munro, C.	311	7675	29.98	109*	4	45	31	32.48	4-15	9.21
Murtagh, T.J.	109	227	9.08	40*	–	–	113	25.61	6-24	8.16
Narine, S.P.	383	2767	14.95	79	–	9	425	20.72	5-19	6.04
Naseem Shah	23	19	6.33	7	–	–	16	40.43	2-17	8.18
Naveen-ul-Haq	76	154	9.62	20*	–	–	92	22.63	4-14	7.83
Neesham, J.D.S.	166	2237	23.30	59*	–	5	149	25.39	4-24	9.05
Neser, M.G.	75	420	14.00	40*	–	–	75	27.26	3-24	8.43
Nijjar, A.S.S.	25	75	10.71	27*	–	–	25	27.40	3-22	7.32
Northeast, S.A.	127	2966	28.51	114	1	20	–	–	–	–
Norwell, L.C.	26	5	5.00	2*	–	–	13	56.69	3-27	9.63
Olivier, D.	56	85	14.16	15*	–	–	66	23.77	4-28	8.62
Organ, F.S.	3	21	7.00	9	–	–	3	18.00	2-21	6.75
O'Riordan, M.K.	3	15	15.00	13*	–	–	3	18.33	2-24	5.50
Overton, C.	63	322	16.10	35*	–	–	58	30.39	3-17	8.90
Overton, J.	70	405	16.20	40*	–	–	59	30.42	5-47	9.48
Parkinson, C.F.	68	233	12.94	27*	–	–	73	23.75	4-20	7.61
Parkinson, M.W.	67	24	3.42	7*	–	–	103	17.36	4- 9	7.51
Patel, R.K.	14	175	15.90	35	–	–	–	–	–	–
Patel, R.S.	7	7	3.50	5*	–	–	0	–	–	10.28
Patel, S.R.	337	5766	25.85	90*	–	32	273	26.78	4- 5	7.28
Paterson, D.	94	157	8.72	24*	–	–	99	24.67	4-24	7.81
Patterson, S.A.	63	9	1.80	3*	–	–	61	29.68	4-30	8.42
Pattinson, J.L.	49	106	8.15	27*	–	–	58	25.06	5-33	8.41
Payne, D.A.	109	49	4.90	10	–	–	133	23.24	5-24	8.51
Pearce, S.J.	4	11	5.50	5	–	–	0	–	–	10.32
Pennington, D.Y.	36	35	8.75	10*	–	–	36	25.69	4- 9	9.00
Pepper, M.S.	22	362	24.13	55*	–	1	–	–	–	11/0
Petersen, K.D.	44	717	26.55	66*	–	3	0	–	–	17/1
Plom, J.H.	13	38	7.60	12	–	–	16	24.43	3-31	9.61
Podmore, H.W.	23	37	5.28	9	–	–	23	26.91	3-13	9.08
Pollock, E.J.	46	969	21.53	77	–	6	–	–	–	–
Pope, O.J.D.	41	904	30.13	60	–	2	–	–	–	–
Porter, J.A.	25	5	5.00	1*	–	–	19	33.47	4-20	9.06
Potts, M.J.	40	127	21.16	40*	–	–	49	22.46	3- 8	8.37
Prest, T.J.	7	135	22.50	59*	–	1	–	–	–	–
Procter, L.A.	37	240	14.11	25*	–	–	14	31.28	3-22	8.87
Qais Ahmad	87	405	13.50	50*	–	1	95	22.25	5-18	7.09
Quinn, M.R.	67	28	14.00	8*	–	–	72	26.70	4-20	8.81
Rahmanullah Gurbaz	48	1186	25.23	99	–	8	–	–	–	24/4
Raine, B.A.	84	1013	19.11	113	1	3	71	27.45	3- 7	8.94
Rampaul, R.	163	194	9.23	23*	–	–	211	21.05	5- 9	7.60
Rashid, A.U.	202	704	12.35	36*	–	–	232	22.23	4-19	7.45
Rashid Khan	284	1312	12.26	56*	–	1	392	17.62	5- 3	6.35
Rawlins, D.M.W.	55	989	23.00	69	–	4	15	33.86	3-21	7.58
Reece, L.M.	65	1441	25.28	97*	–	12	29	29.13	3-33	8.38

	M	Runs	Avge	HS	100	50	Wkts	Avge	Best	Econ
Renshaw, M.T.	38	756	22.90	90*	–	4	6	38.66	1- 2	8.00
Revis, M.L.	2	0	–	0*	–	–	–	–	–	–
Rhodes, G.H.	20	103	11.44	30*	–	–	10	16.40	4-13	8.63
Rhodes, W.M.H.	56	659	14.64	79	–	1	36	20.58	4-34	9.01
Robinson, O.E.	49	92	7.07	31	–	–	45	29.02	4-15	8.86
Robinson, O.G.	18	243	18.69	53	–	1	–	–	–	11/2
Robson, S.D.	7	128	25.60	60	–	1	–	–	–	–
Roderick, G.H.	41	213	13.31	32	–	–	–	–	–	20/1
Roland-Jones, T.S.	54	317	16.68	40	–	–	64	24.20	5-21	8.72
Root, J.E.	83	1994	32.16	92*	–	13	21	31.19	2- 7	8.41
Root, W.T.	38	460	20.90	41*	–	–	0	–	–	12.33
Rossington, A.M.	98	1824	20.96	85	–	10	–	–	–	45/18
Roy, J.J.	257	6719	28.23	122*	4	45	1	39.00	1-23	13.00
Rushworth, C.	85	20	3.33	5	–	–	78	27.19	3-14	7.84
Rymell, J.S.	1	21	21.00	21	–	–	–	–	–	–
Salisbury, M.E.T.	8	2	–	1*	–	–	10	25.60	2-19	8.93
Salt, P.D.	111	2465	24.89	78*	–	18	–	–	–	52/3
Salter, A.G.	85	347	13.34	39*	–	–	60	29.35	4-12	8.26
Sanderson, B.W.	53	57	9.50	12*	–	–	57	25.98	4-21	8.90
Scott, G.F.B.	34	352	22.00	38*	–	–	3	41.33	1-14	10.05
Scrimshaw, G.L.S.	14	5	5.00	3*	–	–	17	19.17	3-23	7.95
Scriven, T.A.R.	2	2	2.00	2	–	–	0	–	–	8.00
Shaheen Shah Afridi	90	87	5.43	14	–	–	118	21.97	6-19	7.78
Shamsi, T.	167	63	4.84	15*	–	–	187	22.49	4-10	7.18
Shan Masood	71	1582	23.61	103*	1	8	–	–	–	–
Shaw, J.	21	2	2.00	1*	–	–	17	28.88	3-32	8.76
Shutt, J.W.	11	0	0.00	0*	–	–	12	22.58	5-11	7.52
Sibley, D.P.	35	859	29.62	74*	–	7	5	67.60	2-33	8.89
Siddle, P.M.	73	48	5.33	11	–	–	78	23.24	5-16	7.32
Sidebottom, R.N.	1	3	3.00	3	–	–	1	37.00	1-37	9.25
Simpson, J.A.	137	2342	23.89	84*	–	9	–	–	–	69/28
Sisodiya, P.	19	14	14.00	6*	–	–	18	31.00	3-26	7.44
Slater, B.T.	15	305	21.78	57	–	1	–	–	–	–
Smeed, W.C.F.	25	645	29.31	82	–	3	–	–	–	–
Smit, D.	112	966	25.42	57	–	2	28	25.75	3-19	62/11
Smith, J.L.	25	393	30.23	60	–	3	–	–	–	10/0
Smith, R.A.J.	30	91	11.37	22*	–	–	24	30.54	4- 6	8.09
Smith, T.M.J.	150	306	18.00	36*	–	–	147	23.54	5-16	7.30
Snater, S.	28	61	8.71	16*	–	–	24	32.50	3-42	10.15
Sowter, N.A.	76	184	10.22	37*	–	–	73	26.53	4-23	7.96
Steel, C.T.	6	93	15.50	37	–	–	2	44.00	2-60	11.00
Steel, S.	33	713	25.46	70	–	4	16	27.56	3-20	6.75
Steketee, M.T.	53	95	5.27	15	–	–	66	24.77	4-33	8.90
Stevens, D.I.	225	4154	26.29	90	–	17	125	26.04	4-14	8.00
Stewart, G.	25	121	10.08	21*	–	–	18	37.11	3-33	9.23
Stirling, P.R.	254	6377	26.57	115*	2	43	74	27.52	4-10	7.34
Stoinis, M.P.	163	3507	31.88	147*	1	19	80	27.51	4-15	8.90
Stokes, B.A.	148	2865	24.91	107*	2	9	86	31.03	4-16	8.52
Stone, O.P.	51	66	9.42	22*	–	–	48	29.27	3-22	8.89
Stoneman, M.D.	77	1343	20.04	89*	–	8	–	–	–	–
Swindells, H.J.	23	376	20.88	63	–	3	–	–	–	6/0
Tattersall, J.A.	35	382	22.47	53*	–	1	–	–	–	23/6
Taylor, C.Z.	16	138	12.54	23	–	–	5	17.20	2- 9	7.81
Taylor, J.M.R.	103	1288	21.11	80	–	2	26	33.15	4-16	8.15
Taylor, J.P.A.	2	3	3.00	3	–	–	1	34.00	1- 6	17.00
Taylor, M.D.	42	34	6.80	9*	–	–	36	31.05	3-16	8.88

	M	Runs	Avge	HS	100	50	Wkts	Avge	Best	Econ
Taylor, T.A.I.	19	173	14.41	50*	–	1	15	31.93	3-33	9.51
Thompson, J.A.	41	453	20.59	74	–	3	34	27.52	4-44	9.26
Thomson, A.T.	19	88	14.66	28	–	–	14	29.71	4-35	8.15
Thurston, C.O.	12	109	12.11	41	–	–	–	–	–	–
Tongue, J.C.	7	3	–	2*	–	–	4	40.75	2-32	8.57
Topley, R.J.W.	92	22	4.40	5*	–	–	119	21.57	4-20	8.26
Trevaskis, L.	41	229	14.31	31*	–	–	34	26.52	4-16	7.32
van Beek, L.V.	110	341	9.47	29*	–	–	103	26.85	4-17	8.85
van Buuren, G.L.	71	780	22.94	64	–	4	47	24.87	5- 8	6.99
van der Gugten, T.	108	294	12.25	40*	–	–	122	21.58	5-21	8.06
van der Merwe, R.E.	256	2693	22.44	89*	–	10	242	24.76	5-32	7.18
van Meekeren, P.A.	71	77	5.13	18	–	–	64	27.37	4-11	7.73
Vasconcelos, R.S.	25	557	27.85	78*	–	2	–	–	–	13/2
Vilas, D.J.	185	3328	27.96	75*	–	12	–	–	–	100/29
Vince, J.M.	267	7146	30.53	107*	2	44	3	29.00	1- 5	6.69
Wade, M.S.	149	2943	26.27	130*	1	19	–	–	–	76/9
Wahab Riaz	291	1500	14.85	53	–	1	349	21.96	5- 8	7.39
Waite, M.J.	17	52	13.00	19*	–	–	11	31.36	2-17	8.96
Walallawita, T.N.	1	0	0.00	0	–	–	3	6.33	3-19	4.75
Walker, R.I.	9	3	1.00	2	–	–	13	19.00	3-15	8.27
Waller, M.T.C.	143	106	7.06	17	–	–	137	24.69	4-16	7.36
Walter, P.I.	61	581	18.74	76	–	1	29	31.79	3-24	9.12
Ward, H.D.	6	73	14.60	22	–	–	–	–	–	–
Weatherley, J.J.	33	712	24.55	71	–	3	0	–	–	9.00
Weighell, W.J.	34	197	14.07	51	–	1	25	36.08	3-28	9.75
Welch, N.R.	5	101	20.20	43	–	–	–	–	–	–
Wells, L.W.P.	12	66	7.33	30	–	–	3	40.66	1-15	7.54
Westley, T.	93	2341	30.01	109*	2	8	7	42.28	2-27	7.58
Wheal, B.T.J.	28	27	9.00	16	–	–	37	20.02	4-17	8.05
Wheater, A.J.A.	129	1736	19.28	78	–	4	–	–	–	52/28
White, G.G.	131	449	14.48	37*	–	–	107	27.09	5-22	8.10
White, R.G.	3	11	11.00	11*	–	–	–	–	–	1/0
Whiteley, R.A.	153	2585	25.59	91*	–	5	4	45.25	1-10	10.64
Willey, D.J.	203	2943	23.73	118	2	12	196	23.13	4- 7	7.90
Woakes, C.R.	119	845	24.85	57*	–	2	130	24.93	4-21	8.28
Wood, C.P.	146	397	10.72	27	–	–	152	26.77	5-32	8.23
Wood, L.	56	94	7.83	33*	–	–	46	27.56	4-20	8.25
Wood, M.A.	38	106	17.66	27*	–	–	46	23.63	4-25	8.14
Wood, T.A.	8	242	40.33	67	–	2	–	–	–	–
Worrall, D.J.	51	135	16.87	62*	–	1	39	36.17	4-23	8.17
Wright, C.J.C.	62	30	4.28	6*	–	–	53	34.60	4-24	9.00
Wright, L.J.	336	8369	29.46	153*	7	46	79	32.44	3-17	8.54
Yates, R.M.	9	144	16.00	37	–	–	1	66.00	1-13	8.25
Young, W.A.	80	1869	26.70	101	1	10	–	–	–	–
Zafar Gohar	56	238	15.86	32*	–	–	64	22.50	4-14	7.79
Zaib, S.A.	25	257	17.13	36	–	–	2	75.00	1-20	8.33

FIRST-CLASS CRICKET RECORDS

To the end of the 2021 season

TEAM RECORDS

HIGHEST INNINGS TOTALS

1107	Victoria v New South Wales	Melbourne	1926-27
1059	Victoria v Tasmania	Melbourne	1922-23
952-6d	Sri Lanka v India	Colombo	1997-98
951-7d	Sind v Baluchistan	Karachi	1973-74
944-6d	Hyderabad v Andhra	Secunderabad	1993-94
918	New South Wales v South Australia	Sydney	1900-01
912-8d	Holkar v Mysore	Indore	1945-46
910-6d	Railways v Dera Ismail Khan	Lahore	1964-65
903-7d	England v Australia	The Oval	1938
900-6d	Queensland v Victoria	Brisbane	2005-06
887	Yorkshire v Warwickshire	Birmingham	1896
863	Lancashire v Surrey	The Oval	1990
860-6d	Tamil Nadu v Goa	Panjim	1988-89
850-7d	Somerset v Middlesex	Taunton	2007

Excluding penalty runs in India, there have been 36 innings totals of 800 runs or more in first-class cricket. Tamil Nadu's total of 860-6d was boosted to 912 by 52 penalty runs.

HIGHEST SECOND INNINGS TOTAL

770	New South Wales v South Australia	Adelaide	1920-21

HIGHEST FOURTH INNINGS TOTAL

654-5	England (set 696 to win) v South Africa	Durban	1938-39

HIGHEST MATCH AGGREGATE

2376-37	Maharashtra v Bombay	Poona	1948-49

RECORD MARGIN OF VICTORY

Innings and 851 runs: Railways v Dera Ismail Khan	Lahore	1964-65

MOST RUNS IN A DAY

721	Australians v Essex	Southend	1948

MOST HUNDREDS IN AN INNINGS

6	Holkar v Mysore	Indore	1945-46

LOWEST INNINGS TOTALS

12	†Oxford University v MCC and Ground	Oxford	1877
12	Northamptonshire v Gloucestershire	Gloucester	1907
13	Auckland v Canterbury	Auckland	1877-78
13	Nottinghamshire v Yorkshire	Nottingham	1901
14	Surrey v Essex	Chelmsford	1983
15	MCC v Surrey	Lord's	1839
15	†Victoria v MCC	Melbourne	1903-04
15	†Northamptonshire v Yorkshire	Northampton	1908
15	Hampshire v Warwickshire	Birmingham	1922

† *Batted one man short*

There have been 29 instances of a team being dismissed for under 20.

LOWEST MATCH AGGREGATE BY ONE TEAM'

34 (16 and 18)	Border v Natal	East London	1959-60

LOWEST COMPLETED MATCH AGGREGATE BY BOTH TEAMS

105	MCC v Australians	Lord's	1878

FEWEST RUNS IN AN UNINTERRUPTED DAY'S PLAY

95	Australia (80) v Pakistan (15-2)	Karachi	1956-57

TIED MATCHES

Before 1949 a match was considered to be tied if the scores were level after the fourth innings, even if the side batting last had wickets in hand when play ended. Law 22 was amended in 1948 and since then a match has been tied only when the scores are level after the fourth innings has been completed. There have been 61 tied first-class matches, five of which would not have qualified under the current law. The most recent is:

Lancashire (99 & 170) v Somerset (192 & 77)	Taunton	2018

BATTING RECORDS

35,000 RUNS IN A CAREER

	Career	*I*	*NO*	*HS*	***Runs***	*Avge*	*100*
J.B.Hobbs	1905-34	1315	106	316*	**61237**	50.65	197
F.E.Woolley	1906-38	1532	85	305*	**58969**	40.75	145
E.H.Hendren	1907-38	1300	166	301*	**57611**	50.80	170
C.P.Mead	1905-36	1340	185	280*	**55061**	47.67	153
W.G.Grace	1865-1908	1493	105	344	**54896**	39.55	126
W.R.Hammond	1920-51	1005	104	336*	**50551**	56.10	167
H.Sutcliffe	1919-45	1088	123	313	**50138**	51.95	149
G.Boycott	1962-86	1014	162	261*	**48426**	56.83	151
T.W.Graveney	1948-71/72	1223	159	258	**47793**	44.91	122
G.A.Gooch	1973-2000	990	75	333	**44846**	49.01	128
T.W.Hayward	1893-1914	1138	96	315*	**43551**	41.79	104
D.L.Amiss	1960-87	1139	126	262*	**43423**	42.86	102
M.C.Cowdrey	1950-76	1130	134	307	**42719**	42.89	107
A.Sandham	1911-37/38	1000	79	325	**41284**	44.82	107
G.A.Hick	1983/84-2008	871	84	405*	**41112**	52.23	136
L.Hutton	1934-60	814	91	364	**40140**	55.51	129
M.J.K.Smith	1951-75	1091	139	204	**39832**	41.84	69
W.Rhodes	1898-1930	1528	237	267*	**39802**	30.83	58
J.H.Edrich	1956-78	979	104	310*	**39790**	45.47	103
R.E.S.Wyatt	1923-57	1141	157	232	**39405**	40.04	85
D.C.S.Compton	1936-64	839	88	300	**38942**	51.85	123
G.E.Tyldesley	1909-36	961	106	256*	**38874**	45.46	102
J.T.Tyldesley	1895-1923	994	62	295*	**37897**	40.60	86
K.W.R.Fletcher	1962-88	1167	170	228*	**37665**	37.77	63
C.G.Greenidge	1970-92	889	75	273*	**37354**	45.88	92
J.W.Hearne	1909-36	1025	116	285*	**37252**	40.98	96
L.E.G.Ames	1926-51	951	95	295	**37248**	43.51	102
D.Kenyon	1946-67	1159	59	259	**37002**	33.63	74
W.J.Edrich	1934-58	964	92	267*	**36965**	42.39	86
J.M.Parks	1949-76	1227	172	205*	**36673**	34.76	51
M.W.Gatting	1975-98	861	123	258	**36549**	49.52	94
D.Denton	1894-1920	1163	70	221	**36479**	33.37	69
G.H.Hirst	1891-1929	1215	151	341	**36323**	34.13	60
I.V.A.Richards	1971/72-93	796	63	322	**36212**	49.40	114
A.Jones	1957-83	1168	72	204*	**36049**	32.89	56
W.G.Quaife	1894-1928	1203	185	255*	**36012**	35.37	72
R.E.Marshall	1945/46-72	1053	59	228*	**35725**	35.94	68
M.R.Ramprakash	1987-2012	764	93	301*	**35659**	53.14	114
G.Gunn	1902-32	1061	82	220	**35208**	35.96	62

HIGHEST INDIVIDUAL INNINGS

501*	B.C.Lara	Warwickshire v Durham	Birmingham	1994
499	Hanif Mohammed	Karachi v Bahawalpur	Karachi	1958-59
452*	D.G.Bradman	New South Wales v Queensland	Sydney	1929-30
443*	B.B.Nimbalkar	Maharashtra v Kathiawar	Poona	1948-49
437	W.H.Ponsford	Victoria v Queensland	Melbourne	1927-28

429	W.H.Ponsford	Victoria v Tasmania	Melbourne	1922-23
428	Aftab Baloch	Sind v Baluchistan	Karachi	1973-74
424	A.C.MacLaren	Lancashire v Somerset	Taunton	1895
405*	G.A.Hick	Worcestershire v Somerset	Taunton	1988
400*	B.C.Lara	West Indies v England	St John's	2003-04
394	Naved Latif	Sargodha v Gujranwala	Gujranwala	2000-01
390	S.C.Cook	Lions v Warriors	East London	2009-10
385	B.Sutcliffe	Otago v Canterbury	Christchurch	1952-53
383	C.W.Gregory	New South Wales v Queensland	Brisbane	1906-07
380	M.L.Hayden	Australia v Zimbabwe	Perth	2003-04
377	S.V.Manjrekar	Bombay v Hyderabad	Bombay	1990-91
375	B.C.Lara	West Indies v England	St John's	1993-94
374	D.P.M.D.Jayawardena	Sri Lanka v South Africa	Colombo	2006
369	D.G.Bradman	South Australia v Tasmania	Adelaide	1935-36
366	N.H.Fairbrother	Lancashire v Surrey	The Oval	1990
366	M.V.Sridhar	Hyderabad v Andhra	Secunderabad	1993-94
365*	C.Hill	South Australia v NSW	Adelaide	1900-01
365*	G.St A.Sobers	West Indies v Pakistan	Kingston	1957-58
364	L.Hutton	England v Australia	The Oval	1938
359*	V.M.Merchant	Bombay v Maharashtra	Bombay	1943-44
359*	S.B.Gohel	Gujarat v Orissa	Jaipur	2016-17
359	R.B.Simpson	New South Wales v Queensland	Brisbane	1963-64
357*	R.Abel	Surrey v Somerset	The Oval	1899
357	D.G.Bradman	South Australia v Victoria	Melbourne	1935-36
356	B.A.Richards	South Australia v W Australia	Perth	1970-71
355*	G.R.Marsh	W Australia v S Australia	Perth	1989-90
355*	K.P.Pietersen	Surrey v Leicestershire	The Oval	2015
355	B.Sutcliffe	Otago v Auckland	Dunedin	1949-50
354*	L.D.Chandimal	Sri Lanka Army v Saracens	Katunayake	2020
353	V.V.S.Laxman	Hyderabad v Karnataka	Bangalore	1999-00
352	W.H.Ponsford	Victoria v New South Wales	Melbourne	1926-27
352	C.A.Pujara	Saurashtra v Karnataka	Rajkot	2012-13
351*	S.M.Gugale	Maharashtra v Delhi	Mumbai	2016-17
351	K.D.K.Vithanage	Tamil Union v SL Air	Katunayake	2014-15
350	Rashid Israr	Habib Bank v National Bank	Lahore	1976-77

There have been 230 triple hundreds in first-class cricket, W.V.Raman (313) and Arjan Kripal Singh (302*) for Tamil Nadu v Goa at Panjim in 1988-89 providing the only instance of two batsmen scoring 300 in the same innings.

MOST HUNDREDS IN SUCCESSIVE INNINGS

6	C.B.Fry	Sussex and Rest of England	1901
6	D.G.Bradman	South Australia and D.G.Bradman's XI	1938-39
6	M.J.Procter	Rhodesia	1970-71

TWO DOUBLE HUNDREDS IN A MATCH

244	202*	A.E.Fagg	Kent v Essex	Colchester	1938
201	231	A.K.Perera	Nondescripts v Sinhalese	Colombo (PSO)	2018-19

TRIPLE HUNDRED AND HUNDRED IN A MATCH

333	123	G.A.Gooch	England v India	Lord's	1990
319	105	K.C.Sangakkara	Sri Lanka v Bangladesh	Chittagong	2013-14

DOUBLE HUNDRED AND HUNDRED IN A MATCH MOST TIMES

4	Zaheer Abbas	Gloucestershire	1976-81

TWO HUNDREDS IN A MATCH MOST TIMES

8	Zaheer Abbas	Gloucestershire and PIA	1976-82
8	R.T.Ponting	Tasmania, Australia and Australians	1992-2006

MOST HUNDREDS IN A SEASON

18	D.C.S.Compton	1947	16	J.B.Hobbs	1925

100 HUNDREDS IN A CAREER

	Total Hundreds	Inns	100th Hundred Season	Inns
J.B.Hobbs	197	1315	1923	821
E.H.Hendren	170	1300	1928-29	740
W.R.Hammond	167	1005	1935	679
C.P.Mead	153	1340	1927	892
G.Boycott	151	1014	1977	645
H.Sutcliffe	149	1088	1932	700
F.E.Woolley	145	1532	1929	1031
G.A.Hick	136	871	1998	574
L.Hutton	129	814	1951	619
G.A.Gooch	128	990	1992-93	820
W.G.Grace	126	1493	1895	1113
D.C.S.Compton	123	839	1952	552
T.W.Graveney	122	1223	1964	940
D.G.Bradman	117	338	1947-48	295
I.V.A.Richards	114	796	1988-89	658
M.R.Ramprakash	114	764	2008	676
Zaheer Abbas	108	768	1982-83	658
A.Sandham	107	1000	1935	871
M.C.Cowdrey	107	1130	1973	1035
T.W.Hayward	104	1138	1913	1076
G.M.Turner	103	792	1982	779
J.H.Edrich	103	979	1977	945
L.E.G.Ames	102	951	1950	915
G.E.Tyldesley	102	961	1934	919
D.L.Amiss	102	1139	1986	1081

MOST 400s: 2 – B.C.Lara, W.H.Ponsford
MOST 300s or more: 6 – D.G.Bradman; 4 – W.R.Hammond, W.H.Ponsford
MOST 200s or more: 37 – D.G.Bradman; 36 – W.R.Hammond; 22 – E.H.Hendren

MOST RUNS IN A MONTH

1294 (avge 92.42)	L.Hutton	Yorkshire	June 1949

MOST RUNS IN A SEASON

Runs			I	NO	HS	Avge	100	Season
3816	D.C.S.Compton	Middlesex	50	8	246	90.85	18	1947
3539	W.J.Edrich	Middlesex	52	8	267*	80.43	12	1947
3518	T.W.Hayward	Surrey	61	8	219	66.37	13	1906

The feat of scoring 3000 runs in a season has been achieved 28 times, the most recent instance being by W.E.Alley (3019) in 1961. The highest aggregate in a season since 1969 is 2755 by S.J.Cook in 1991.

1000 RUNS IN A SEASON MOST TIMES

28 W.G.Grace (Gloucestershire), F.E.Woolley (Kent)

HIGHEST BATTING AVERAGE IN A SEASON

(Qualification: 12 innings)

Avge			I	NO	HS	Runs	100	Season
115.66	D.G.Bradman	Australians	26	5	278	2429	13	1938
106.50	K.C.Sangakkara	Surrey	16	2	200	1491	8	2017
104.66	D.R.Martyn	Australians	14	5	176*	942	5	2001
103.54	M.R.Ramprakash	Surrey	24	2	301*	2278	8	2006
102.53	G.Boycott	Yorkshire	20	5	175*	1538	6	1979
102.00	W.A.Johnston	Australians	17	16	28*	102	–	1953
101.70	G.A.Gooch	Essex	30	3	333	2746	12	1990
101.30	M.R.Ramprakash	Surrey	25	5	266*	2026	10	2007
100.12	G.Boycott	Yorkshire	30	5	233	2503	13	1971

FASTEST HUNDRED AGAINST AUTHENTIC BOWLING

35 min	P.G.H.Fender	Surrey v Northamptonshire	Northampton	1920

FASTEST DOUBLE HUNDRED

103 min	Shafiqullah Shinwari	Kabul v Boost	Asadabad	2017-18

FASTEST TRIPLE HUNDRED

181 min	D.C.S.Compton	MCC v NE Transvaal	Benoni	1948-49

MOST SIXES IN AN INNINGS

23	C.Munro	Central Districts v Auckland	Napier	2014-15

MOST SIXES IN A MATCH

24	Shafiqullah Shinwari	Kabul v Boost	Asadabad	2017-18

MOST SIXES IN A SEASON

80	I.T.Botham	Somerset and England		1985

MOST BOUNDARIES IN AN INNINGS

72	B.C.Lara	Warwickshire v Durham	Birmingham	1994

MOST RUNS OFF ONE OVER

36	G.St A.Sobers	Nottinghamshire v Glamorgan	Swansea	1968
36	R.J.Shastri	Bombay v Baroda	Bombay	1984-85

Both batsmen hit for six all six balls of overs bowled by M.A.Nash and Tilak Raj respectively.

MOST RUNS IN A DAY

390*	B.C.Lara	Warwickshire v Durham	Birmingham	1994

There have been 19 instances of a batsman scoring 300 or more runs in a day.

LONGEST INNINGS

1015 min	R.Nayyar (271)	Himachal Pradesh v Jammu & Kashmir	Chamba	1999-00

HIGHEST PARTNERSHIPS FOR EACH WICKET

First Wicket

561	Waheed Mirza/Mansoor Akhtar	Karachi W v Quetta	Karachi	1976-77
555	P.Holmes/H.Sutcliffe	Yorkshire v Essex	Leyton	1932
554	J.T.Brown/J.Tunnicliffe	Yorkshire v Derbys	Chesterfield	1898

Second Wicket

580	Rafatullah Mohmand/Aamer Sajjad	WAPDA v SSGC	Sheikhupura	2009-10
576	S.T.Jayasuriya/R.S.Mahanama	Sri Lanka v India	Colombo	1997-98
480	D.Elgar/R.R.Rossouw	Eagles v Titans	Centurion	2009-10
475	Zahir Alam/L.S.Rajput	Assam v Tripura	Gauhati	1991-92
465*	J.A.Jameson/R.B.Kanhai	Warwickshire v Glos	Birmingham	1974

Third Wicket

624	K.C.Sangakkara/D.P.M.D.Jayawardena	Sri Lanka v South Africa	Colombo	2006
594*	S.M.Gugale/A.R.Bawne	Maharashtra v Delhi	Mumbai	2016-17
539	S.D.Jogiyani/R.A.Jadeja	Saurashtra v Gujarat	Surat	2012-13
523	M.A.Carberry/N.D.McKenzie	Hampshire v Yorkshire	Southampton	2011

Fourth Wicket

577	V.S.Hazare/Gul Mahomed	Baroda v Holkar	Baroda	1946-47
574*	C.L.Walcott/F.M.M.Worrell	Barbados v Trinidad	Port-of-Spain	1945-46
502*	F.M.M.Worrell/J.D.C.Goddard	Barbados v Trinidad	Bridgetown	1943-44
470	A.I.Kallicharran/G.W.Humpage	Warwickshire v Lancs	Southport	1982

Fifth Wicket

520*	C.A.Pujara/R.A.Jadeja	Saurashtra v Orissa	Rajkot	2008-09
494	Marchall Ayub/Mehrab Hossain Jr	Central Zone v East Zone	Bogra	2012-13
479	Misbah-ul-Haq/Usman Arshad	Sui NGP v Lahore Shalimar	Lahore	2009-10
464*	M.E.Waugh/S.R.Waugh	NSW v W Australia	Perth	1990-91
428*	B.C.Williams/M.Marais	Border v Eastern Province	East London	2017-18
423	Mosaddek Hossain/Al-Amin	Barisal v Rangpur	Savar	2014-15
420	Mohd. Ashraful/Marshall Ayub	Dhaka v Chittagong	Chittagong	2006-07

410*	A.S.Chopra/S.Badrinath	India A v South Africa A	Delhi	2007-08
405	S.G.Barnes/D.G.Bradman	Australia v England	Sydney	1946-47
401	M.B.Loye/D.Ripley	Northants v Glamorgan	Northampton	1998
Sixth Wicket				
487*	G.A.Headley/C.C.Passailaigue	Jamaica v Tennyson's	Kingston	1931-32
428	W.W.Armstrong/M.A.Noble	Australians v Sussex	Hove	1902
417	W.P.Saha/L.R.Shukla	Bengal v Assam	Kolkata	2010-11
411	R.M.Poore/E.G.Wynyard	Hampshire v Somerset	Taunton	1899
Seventh Wicket				
460	Bhupinder Singh jr/P.Dharmani	Punjab v Delhi	Delhi	1994-95
399	A.N.Khare/A.J.Mandal	Chhattisgarh v Uttarakhand	Naya Raipur	2019-20
371	M.R.Marsh/S.M.Whiteman	Australia A v India A	Brisbane	2014
366*	J.M.Bairstow/T.T.Bresnan	Yorkshire v Durham	Chester-le-Street	2015
Eighth Wicket				
433	V.T.Trumper/A.Sims	Australians v C'bury	Christchurch	1913-14
392	A.Mishra/J.Yadav	Haryana v Karnataka	Hubli	2012-13
332	I.J.L.Trott/S.C.J.Broad	England v Pakistan	Lord's	2010
Ninth Wicket				
283	J.Chapman/A.Warren	Derbys v Warwicks	Blackwell	1910
268	J.B.Commins/N.Boje	SA 'A' v Mashonaland	Harare	1994-95
261	W.L.Madsen/T.Poynton	Derbys v Northants	Northampton	2012
251	J.W.H.T.Douglas/S.N.Hare	Essex v Derbyshire	Leyton	1921
Tenth Wicket				
307	A.F.Kippax/J.E.H.Hooker	NSW v Victoria	Melbourne	1928-29
249	C.T.Sarwate/S.N.Banerjee	Indians v Surrey	The Oval	1946
239	Aqil Arshad/Ali Raza	Lahore Whites v Hyderabad	Lahore	2004-05

BOWLING RECORDS
2000 WICKETS IN A CAREER

	Career	*Runs*	*Wkts*	*Avge*	*100w*
W.Rhodes	1898-1930	69993	**4187**	16.71	23
A.P.Freeman	1914-36	69577	**3776**	18.42	17
C.W.L.Parker	1903-35	63817	**3278**	19.46	16
J.T.Hearne	1888-1923	54352	**3061**	17.75	15
T.W.J.Goddard	1922-52	59116	**2979**	19.84	16
W.G.Grace	1865-1908	51545	**2876**	17.92	10
A.S.Kennedy	1907-36	61034	**2874**	21.23	15
D.Shackleton	1948-69	53303	**2857**	18.65	20
G.A.R.Lock	1946-70/71	54709	**2844**	19.23	14
F.J.Titmus	1949-82	63313	**2830**	22.37	16
M.W.Tate	1912-37	50571	**2784**	18.16	13+1
G.H.Hirst	1891-1929	51282	**2739**	18.72	15
C.Blythe	1899-1914	42136	**2506**	16.81	14
D.L.Underwood	1963-87	49993	**2465**	20.28	10
W.E.Astill	1906-39	57783	**2431**	23.76	9
J.C.White	1909-37	43759	**2356**	18.57	14
W.E.Hollies	1932-57	48656	**2323**	20.94	14
F.S.Trueman	1949-69	42154	**2304**	18.29	12
J.B.Statham	1950-68	36999	**2260**	16.37	13
R.T.D.Perks	1930-55	53771	**2233**	24.07	16
J.Briggs	1879-1900	35431	**2221**	15.95	12
D.J.Shepherd	1950-72	47302	**2218**	21.32	12
E.G.Dennett	1903-26	42571	**2147**	19.82	12
T.Richardson	1892-1905	38794	**2104**	18.43	10
T.E.Bailey	1945-67	48170	**2082**	23.13	9
R.Illingworth	1951-83	42023	**2072**	20.28	10
F.E.Woolley	1906-38	41066	**2068**	19.85	8

	Career	Runs	Wkts	Avge	100w
N.Gifford	1960-88	48731	**2068**	23.56	4
G.Geary	1912-38	41339	**2063**	20.03	11
D.V.P.Wright	1932-57	49307	**2056**	23.98	10
J.A.Newman	1906-30	51111	**2032**	25.15	9
A.Shaw	1864-97	24580	**2026**+1	12.12	9
S.Haigh	1895-1913	32091	**2012**	15.94	11

ALL TEN WICKETS IN AN INNINGS

This feat has been achieved 82 times in first-class matches (excluding 12-a-side fixtures).
Three Times: A.P.Freeman (1929, 1930, 1931)
Twice: V.E.Walker (1859, 1865); H.Verity (1931, 1932); J.C.Laker (1956)
Instances since 1945:

W.E.Hollies	Warwickshire v Notts	Birmingham	1946
J.M.Sims	East v West	Kingston on Thames	1948
J.K.R.Graveney	Gloucestershire v Derbyshire	Chesterfield	1949
T.E.Bailey	Essex v Lancashire	Clacton	1949
R.Berry	Lancashire v Worcestershire	Blackpool	1953
S.P.Gupte	President's XI v Combined XI	Bombay	1954-55
J.C.Laker	Surrey v Australians	The Oval	1956
K.Smales	Nottinghamshire v Glos	Stroud	1956
G.A.R.Lock	Surrey v Kent	Blackheath	1956
J.C.Laker	England v Australia	Manchester	1956
P.M.Chatterjee	Bengal v Assam	Jorhat	1956-57
J.D.Bannister	Warwicks v Combined Services	Birmingham (M & B)	1959
A.J.G.Pearson	Cambridge U v Leicestershire	Loughborough	1961
N.I.Thomson	Sussex v Warwickshire	Worthing	1964
P.J.Allan	Queensland v Victoria	Melbourne	1965-66
I.J.Brayshaw	Western Australia v Victoria	Perth	1967-68
Shahid Mahmood	Karachi Whites v Khairpur	Karachi	1969-70
E.E.Hemmings	International XI v W Indians	Kingston	1982-83
P.Sunderam	Rajasthan v Vidarbha	Jodhpur	1985-86
S.T.Jefferies	Western Province v OFS	Cape Town	1987-88
Imran Adil	Bahawalpur v Faisalabad	Faisalabad	1989-90
G.P.Wickremasinghe	Sinhalese v Kalutara	Colombo	1991-92
R.L.Johnson	Middlesex v Derbyshire	Derby	1994
Naeem Akhtar	Rawalpindi B v Peshawar	Peshawar	1995-96
A.Kumble	India v Pakistan	Delhi	1998-99
D.S.Mohanty	East Zone v South Zone	Agartala	2000-01
O.D.Gibson	Durham v Hampshire	Chester-le-Street	2007
M.W.Olivier	Warriors v Eagles	Bloemfontein	2007-08
Zulfiqar Babar	Multan v Islamabad	Multan	2009-10
P.M.Pushpakumara	Colombo v Saracens	Moratuwa	2018-19

MOST WICKETS IN A MATCH

19	J.C.Laker	England v Australia	Manchester	1956

MOST WICKETS IN A SEASON

Wkts		Season	Matches	Overs	Mdns	Runs	Avge
304	A.P.Freeman	1928	37	1976.1	423	5489	18.05
298	A.P.Freeman	1933	33	2039	651	4549	15.26

The feat of taking 250 wickets in a season has been achieved on 12 occasions, the last instance being by A.P.Freeman in 1933. 200 or more wickets in a season have been taken on 59 occasions, the last being by G.A.R.Lock (212 wickets, average 12.02) in 1957.

The highest aggregates of wickets taken in a season since the reduction of County Championship matches in 1969 are as follows:

Wkts		Season	Matches	Overs	Mdns	Runs	Avge
134	M.D.Marshall	1982	22	822	225	2108	15.73
131	L.R.Gibbs	1971	23	1024.1	295	2475	18.89
125	F.D.Stephenson	1988	22	819.1	196	2289	18.31
121	R.D.Jackman	1980	23	746.2	220	1864	15.40

Since 1969 there have been 50 instances of bowlers taking 100 wickets in a season.

MOST HAT-TRICKS IN A CAREER

7	D.V.P.Wright
6	T.W.J.Goddard, C.W.L.Parker
5	S.Haigh, V.W.C.Jupp, A.E.G.Rhodes, F.A.Tarrant

ALL-ROUND RECORDS
THE 'DOUBLE'

3000 runs and 100 wickets: J.H.Parks (1937)

2000 runs and 200 wickets: G.H.Hirst (1906)

2000 runs and 100 wickets: F.E.Woolley (4), J.W.Hearne (3), W.G.Grace (2), G.H.Hirst (2), W.Rhodes (2), T.E.Bailey, D.E.Davies, G.L.Jessop, V.W.C.Jupp, J.Langridge, F.A.Tarrant, C.L.Townsend, L.F.Townsend

1000 runs and 200 wickets: M.W.Tate (3), A.E.Trott (2), A.S.Kennedy

Most Doubles: 16 – W.Rhodes; 14 – G.H.Hirst; 10 – V.W.C.Jupp

Double in Debut Season: D.B.Close (1949) – aged 18, the youngest to achieve this feat.

The feat of scoring 1000 runs and taking 100 wickets in a season has been achieved on 305 occasions, R.J.Hadlee (1984) and F.D.Stephenson (1988) being the only players to complete the 'double' since the reduction of County Championship matches in 1969.

WICKET-KEEPING RECORDS
1000 DISMISSALS IN A CAREER

	Career	Dismissals	Ct	St
R.W.Taylor	1960-88	**1649**	1473	176
J.T.Murray	1952-75	**1527**	1270	257
H.Strudwick	1902-27	**1497**	1242	255
A.P.E.Knott	1964-85	**1344**	1211	133
R.C.Russell	1981-2004	**1320**	1192	128
F.H.Huish	1895-1914	**1310**	933	377
B.Taylor	1949-73	**1294**	1083	211
S.J.Rhodes	1981-2004	**1263**	1139	124
D.Hunter	1889-1909	**1253**	906	347
H.R.Butt	1890-1912	**1228**	953	275
J.H.Board	1891-1914/15	**1207**	852	355
H.Elliott	1920-47	**1206**	904	302
J.M.Parks	1949-76	**1181**	1088	93
R.Booth	1951-70	**1126**	948	178
L.E.G.Ames	1926-51	**1121**	703	418
C.M.W.Read	1997-2017	**1104**	1051	53
D.L.Bairstow	1970-90	**1099**	961	138
G.Duckworth	1923-47	**1096**	753	343
H.W.Stephenson	1948-64	**1082**	748	334
J.G.Binks	1955-75	**1071**	895	176
T.G.Evans	1939-69	**1066**	816	250
A.Long	1960-80	**1046**	922	124
G.O.Dawkes	1937-61	**1043**	895	148
R.W.Tolchard	1965-83	**1037**	912	125
W.L.Cornford	1921-47	**1017**	675	342

MOST DISMISSALS IN AN INNINGS

9	(8ct, 1st)	Tahir Rashid	Habib Bank v PACO	Gujranwala	1992-93
9	(7ct, 2st)	W.R.James	Matabeleland v Mashonaland CD	Bulawayo	1995-96
8	(8ct)	A.T.W.Grout	Queensland v W Australia	Brisbane	1959-60
8	(8ct)	D.E.East	Essex v Somerset	Taunton	1985
8	(8ct)	S.A.Marsh	Kent v Middlesex	Lord's	1991
8	(6ct, 2st)	T.J.Zoehrer	Australians v Surrey	The Oval	1993
8	(7ct, 1st)	D.S.Berry	Victoria v South Australia	Melbourne	1996-97
8	(7ct, 1st)	Y.S.S.Mendis	Bloomfield v Kurunegala Youth	Colombo	2000-01
8	(7ct, 1st)	S.Nath	Assam v Tripura (*on debut*)	Gauhati	2001-02
8	(8ct)	J.N.Batty	Surrey v Kent	The Oval	2004
8	(8ct)	Golam Mabud	Sylhet v Dhaka	Dhaka	2005-06
8	(8ct)	D.C.de Boorder	Otago v Wellington	Wellington	2009-10
8	(8ct)	R.S.Second	Free State v North West	Bloemfontein	2011-12
8	(8ct)	T.L.Tsolekile	South Africa A v Sri Lanka A	Durban	2012
8	(7ct, 1st)	M.A.R.S.Fernando	Chilaw Marians v Colts	Columbo (SSC)	2017-18

MOST DISMISSALS IN A MATCH

14	(11ct, 3st)	I.Khaleel	Hyderabad v Assam	Guwahati	2011-12
13	(11ct, 2st)	W.R.James	Matabeleland v Mashonaland CD	Bulawayo	1995-96
12	(8ct, 4st)	E.Pooley	Surrey v Sussex	The Oval	1868
12	(9ct, 3st)	D.Tallon	Queensland v NSW	Sydney	1938-39
12	(9ct, 3st)	H.B.Taber	NSW v South Australia	Adelaide	1968-69
12	(12ct)	P.D.McGlashan	Northern Districts v Central Districts	Whangarei	2009-10
12	(11ct, 1st)	T.L.Tsolekile	Lions v Dolphins	Johannesburg	2010-11
12	(12ct)	Kashif Mahmood	Lahore Shalimar v Abbottabad	Abbottabad	2010-11
12	(12ct)	R.S.Second	Free State v North West	Bloemfontein	2011-12

MOST DISMISSALS IN A SEASON

128	(79ct, 49st)	L.E.G.Ames	1929

FIELDING RECORDS

750 CATCHES IN A CAREER

1018	F.E.Woolley	1906-38	784	J.G.Langridge	1928-55
887	W.G.Grace	1865-1908	764	W.Rhodes	1898-1930
830	G.A.R.Lock	1946-70/71	758	C.A.Milton	1948-74
819	W.R.Hammond	1920-51	754	E.H.Hendren	1907-38
813	D.B.Close	1949-86			

MOST CATCHES IN AN INNINGS

7	M.J.Stewart	Surrey v Northamptonshire	Northampton	1957
7	A.S.Brown	Gloucestershire v Nottinghamshire	Nottingham	1966
7	R.Clarke	Warwickshire v Lancashire	Liverpool	2011

MOST CATCHES IN A MATCH

10	W.R.Hammond	Gloucestershire v Surrey	Cheltenham	1928
9	R.Clarke	Warwickshire v Lancashire	Liverpool	2011

MOST CATCHES IN A SEASON

78	W.R.Hammond	1928	77	M.J.Stewart	1957

ENGLAND LIMITED-OVERS INTERNATIONALS 2021

INDIA v ENGLAND

TWENTY20 INTERNATIONALS

Narendra Modi Stadium, Ahmedabad, 12 March. Toss: England. **ENGLAND** won by eight wickets. India 124-7 (20; S.S.Iyer 67, J.C.Archer 3-23). England 130-2 (15.3; J.J.Roy 49). Award: J.C.Archer.

Narendra Modi Stadium, Ahmedabad, 14 March. Toss: India. **INDIA** won by seven wickets. England 164-6 (20; J.J.Roy 46). India 166-3 (17.5; V.Kohli 73*, I.P.Kishan 56). Award: I.P.Kishan.

Narendra Modi Stadium, Ahmedabad, 16 March. Toss: England. **ENGLAND** won by eight wickets. India 156-6 (20; V.Kohli 77*, M.A.Wood 3-31). England 158-2 (18.2; J.C.Buttler 83*, J.M.Bairstow 40*). Award: J.C.Buttler.

Narendra Modi Stadium, Ahmedabad, 18 March. Toss: England. **INDIA** won by 8 runs. India 185-8 (20; S.A.Yadav 57, J.C.Archer 4-33). England 177-8 (20; B.A.Stokes 46, J.J.Roy 40, S.N.Thakur 3-42). Award: S.A.Yadav.

Narendra Modi Stadium, Ahmedabad, 20 March. Toss: England. **INDIA** won by 36 runs. India 224-2 (20; V.Kohli 80*, R.G.Sharma 64). England 188-8 (20; D.J.Malan 68, J.C.Buttler 52, S.N.Thakur 3-45). Award: B.Kumar. Series award: V.Kohli.

LIMITED-OVERS INTERNATIONALS

Maharashtra CA Stadium, Pune, 23 March. Toss: England. **INDIA** won by 66 runs. India 317-5 (50; S.Dhawan 98, K.L.Rahul 62*, K.H.Pandya 58*, V.Kohli 56, B.A.Stokes 3-34). England 251 (42.1; J.M.Bairstow 94, M.P.Krishna 4-54, S.N.Thakur 3-37). Award: S.Dhawan.

Maharashtra CA Stadium, Pune, 26 March. Toss: England. **ENGLAND** won by six wickets. India 336-6 (50; K.L.Rahul 108, R.R.Pant 77, V.Kohli 66). England 337-4 (43.3; J.M.Bairstow 124, B.A.Stokes 99, J.J.Roy 55). Award: J.M.Bairstow. England debut: L.S.Livingstone..

Maharashtra CA Stadium, Pune, 28 March. Toss: England. **INDIA** won by 7 runs. India 329 (48.2; R.R.Pant 78, S.Dhawan 67, H.H.Pandya 64, M.A.Wood 3-34). England 322-9 (50; S.M.Curran 95*, D.J.Malan 50, S.N.Thakur 4-67, B.Kumar 3-42). Award: S.M.Curran. Series award: J.M.Bairstow.

ENGLAND v SRI LANKA

TWENTY20 INTERNATIONALS

Sophia Gardens, Cardiff, 23 June. Toss: Sri Lanka. **ENGLAND** won by eight wickets. Sri Lanka 129-7 (20; M.D.Shanaka 50). England 130-2 (17.1; J.C.Buttler 68*). Award: J.C.Buttler.

Sophia Gardens, Cardiff, 24 June. Toss: Sri Lanka. **ENGLAND** won by five wickets. Sri Lanka 111-7 (20; B.K.G.Mendis 39). England 108-5 (16.1/18). Award: L.S.Livingstone.

The Rose Bowl, Southampton, 26 June. Toss: Sri Lanka. **ENGLAND** won by 89 runs. England 180-6 (20; D.J.Malan 76, J.M.Bairstow 51, P.V.D.Chameera 4-17). Sri Lanka 91 (18.5; D.J.Willey 3-27). Award: D.J.Malan. Series award: S.M.Curran.

LIMITED-OVERS INTERNATIONALS

Riverside Ground, Chester-le-Street, 29 June. Toss: England. **ENGLAND** won by five wickets. Sri Lanka 185 (42.3; M.D.K.J.Perera 73, P.W.H.de Silva 54, C.R.Woakes 4-18, D.J.Willey 3-44). England 189-5 (34.5; J.E.Root 79*, P.V.D.Chameera 3-50). Award: C.R.Woakes.

The Oval, London, 1 July. Toss: England. **ENGLAND** won by eight wickets. Sri Lanka 241-9 (50; D.M.de Silva 91, S.M.Curran 5-48, D.J.Willey 4-64). England 244-2 (43; E.J.G.Morgan 75*, J.E.Root 68*, J.J.Roy 60). Award: S.M.Curran.

County Ground, Bristol, 4 July. Toss: England. **NO RESULT**. Sri Lanka 166 (41.1; T.K.Curran 4-35). Series award: D.J.Willey.

ENGLAND v PAKISTAN

LIMITED-OVERS INTERNATIONALS

Sophia Gardens, Cardiff, 8 July. Toss: England. **ENGLAND** won by nine wickets. Pakistan 141 (35.2; Fakhar Zaman 47, S.Mahmood 4-42). England 142-1 (21.5; D.J.Malan 68*, Z.Crawley 58*). Award: S.Mahmood. England debuts: B.A.Carse, Z.Crawley, L.Gregory, P.D.Salt, J.A.Simpson.

Lord's, London, 10 July. Toss: Pakistan. **ENGLAND** won by 52 runs. England 247 (45.2/47; P.D.Salt 60, J.M.Vince 56, Hasan Ali 5-51). Pakistan 195 (41/47; Saud Shakil 56, L.Gregory 3-44). Award: L.Gregory.

Edgbaston, Birmingham, 13 July. Toss: England. **ENGLAND** won by three wickets. Pakistan 331-9 (50; Babar Azam 158, Mohammad Rizwan 74, Imam-ul-Haq 56, B.A.Carse 5-61, S.Mahmood 3-60). England 332-7 (48; J.M.Vince 102, L.Gregory 77, Haris Rauf 4-65). Award: J.M.Vince. Series award: S.Mahmood.

TWENTY20 INTERNATIONALS

Trent Bridge, Nottingham, 16 July. Toss: England. **PAKISTAN** won by 31 runs. Pakistan 232-6 (20; Babar Azam 85, Mohammad Rizwan 63). England 201 (19.2; L.S.Livingstone 103, Shaheen Shah Afridi 3-30, Shadab Khan 3-52). Award: Shaheen Shah Afridi.
L.S.Livingstone reached his fifty in 17 balls, the fastest by an England batter; his nine sixes were the most in an innings by an England batter.

Headingley, Leeds, 18 July. Toss: Pakistan. **ENGLAND** won by 45 runs. England 200 (19.5; J.C.Buttler 59, Mohammad Hosnain 3-51). Pakistan 155-9 (20; S.Mahmood 3-33). Award: M.M.Ali.

Old Trafford, Manchester, 20 July. Toss: Pakistan. **ENGLAND** won by three wickets. Pakistan 154-6 (20; Mohammad Rizwan 76*, A.U.Rashid 4-35). England 155-7 (19.4; J.J.Roy 64, Mohammad Hafeez 3-28). Award: J.J.Roy. Series award: L.S.Livingstone.

For England's results in the ICC Men's T20 World Cup, see pages 304-305.

ENGLAND RESULTS IN 2021

	P	W	L	T	NR
Limited Overs	9	6	2	–	1
Twenty20	17	11	6	–	–
Overall	26	17	8	–	1

200 RUNS IN LIMITED-OVERS INTERNATIONALS IN 2021

	P	I	NO	HS	Runs	Ave	100	50	S/Rate
J.M.Bairstow	6	5	–	124	291	58.20	1	1	121.75

9 WICKETS IN LIMITED-OVERS INTERNATIONALS IN 2021

Part1	P	O	M	Runs	W	Ave	Best	4wI	Econ
S.Mahmood	3	28.0	3	123	9	13.66	4-42	1	4.39
D.J.Willey	3	27.0	2	144	9	16.00	4-64	1	5.33

300 RUNS IN TWENTY20 INTERNATIONALS IN 2021

	P	I	NO	HS	Runs	Ave	100	50	S/Rate
J.C.Buttler	14	14	5	101*	589	65.44	1	5	143.30
J.J.Roy	15	15	1	64	426	30.42	–	2	146.89
D.J.Malan	17	16	2	76	384	27.42	–	2	116.01

15 WICKETS IN TWENTY20 INTERNATIONALS IN 2021

	P	O	M	Runs	W	Ave	Best	4wI	Econ
A.U.Rashid	16	58.2	1	409	23	17.78	4-2	2	7.01

ICC ODI Rankings (to 31 December)

	Played	Points	Rating
1. New Zealand	17	2054	121
2. England	**32**	**3793**	**119**
3. Australia	28	3244	116

ICC IT20 Rankings (to 31 December)

	Played	Points	Rating
1. England	**34**	**9354**	**275**
2. India	36	9627	267
3. Pakistan	46	12225	266

LIMITED-OVERS INTERNATIONALS CAREER RECORDS

These records, complete to 17 March 2022, include all players registered for county cricket and The Hundred for the 2022 season at the time of going to press, plus those who have appeared in LOI matches for ICC full member countries since 27 November 2020. Some players who may return to LOI action have also been listed, even if their most recent game was earlier than this date.

ENGLAND – BATTING AND FIELDING

	M	*I*	*NO*	*HS*	*Runs*	*Avge*	*100*	*50*	*Ct/St*
M.M.Ali	112	89	14	128	1877	25.02	3	5	36
J.M.Anderson	194	79	43	28	273	7.58	–	–	53
J.C.Archer	17	9	5	8*	27	6.75	–	–	5
J.M.Bairstow	89	81	8	141*	3498	47.91	11	14	45/3
J.T.Ball	18	6	2	28	38	9.50	–	–	5
G.S.Ballance	16	15	1	79	279	21.21	–	2	8
T.Banton	6	5	–	58	134	26.80	–	1	2
S.W.Billings	25	20	2	118	607	33.72	1	4	18
R.S.Bopara	120	109	21	101*	2695	30.62	1	14	35
S.G.Borthwick	2	2	–	15	18	9.00	–	–	–
D.R.Briggs	1	–	–	–	–	–	–	–	–
S.C.J.Broad	121	68	25	45*	529	12.30	–	–	27
J.C.Buttler	148	123	23	150	3872	38.72	9	20	181/32
B.A.Carse	3	2	1	31	43	43.00	–	–	–
A.N.Cook	92	92	4	137	3204	36.40	5	19	36
Z.Crawley	3	3	1	58*	97	48.50	–	1	4
S.M.Curran	11	7	2	95*	141	28.20	–	1	2
T.K.Curran	28	17	9	47*	303	37.87	–	–	5
S.M.Davies	8	8	–	87	244	30.50	–	1	8
L.A.Dawson	3	2	–	10	14	7.00	–	–	–
J.L.Denly	16	13	–	87	446	34.30	–	4	7
B.M.Duckett	3	3	–	63	123	41.00	–	2	–
S.T.Finn	69	30	13	35	136	8.00	–	–	15
B.T.Foakes	1	1	1	61*	61	–	–	–	2/1
L.Gregory	3	2	–	77	117	58.50	–	1	–
A.D.Hales	70	67	3	171	2419	37.79	6	14	27
C.J.Jordan	34	23	9	38*	170	12.14	–	–	19
L.S.Livingstone	3	3	1	36	72	36.00	–	–	1
S.Mahmood	7	2	–	12	20	10.00	–	–	1
D.J.Malan	6	6	2	68*	158	39.50	–	2	3
E.J.G.Morgan †	223	205	32	148	6957	40.21	13	42	78
C.Overton	4	2	1	18*	18	18.00	–	–	4
M.W.Parkinson	5	1	1	7*	7	–	–	–	1
S.R.Patel	36	22	7	70*	482	32.13	–	1	7
A.U.Rashid	112	50	14	69	663	18.41	–	1	35
T.S.Roland-Jones	1	1	1	37*	37	–	–	–	–
J.E.Root	152	142	23	133*	6109	51.33	16	35	77
J.J.Roy	98	93	2	180	3658	40.19	9	20	35
P.D.Salt	3	3	–	60	104	34.66	–	1	–
J.A.Simpson	3	2	–	17	20	10.00	–	–	9
B.A.Stokes	101	86	15	102*	2871	40.43	3	21	47
O.P.Stone	4	1	1	9*	9	–	–	–	–
R.J.W.Topley	13	6	5	6	8	8.00	–	–	4

	M	I	NO	HS	Runs	Avge	100	50	Ct/St
J.M.Vince	19	16	–	102	480	30.00	1	2	7
D.J.Willey	52	29	13	51	377	23.56	–	2	23
C.R.Woakes	106	72	21	95*	1315	25.78	–	5	46
M.A.Wood	57	19	11	14	72	9.00	–	–	12
L.J.Wright	50	39	4	52	707	20.20	–	2	18

ENGLAND – BOWLING

	O	M	R	W	Avge	Best	4wI	R/Over
M.M.Ali	842.4	10	4424	87	50.85	4-46	1	5.25
J.M.Anderson	1597.2	125	7861	269	29.22	5-23	13	4.92
J.C.Archer	151.5	12	720	30	24.00	3-27	–	4.74
J.T.Ball	157.5	5	980	21	46.66	5-51	1	6.20
R.S.Bopara	310	11	1523	40	38.07	4-38	1	4.91
S.G.Borthwick	9	0	72	0	–	–	–	8.00
D.R.Briggs	10	0	39	2	19.50	2-39	–	3.90
S.C.J.Broad	1018.1	56	5364	178	30.13	5-23	10	5.26
B.A.Carse	25	0	136	6	22.66	5-61	1	5.44
S.M.Curran	73.4	3	430	12	35.83	5-48	1	5.83
T.K.Curran	218	8	1290	34	37.94	5-35	3	5.91
L.A.Dawson	14	0	96	3	32.00	2-70	–	6.85
J.L.Denly	17	0	101	1	101.00	1-24	–	5.94
S.T.Finn	591.4	38	2996	102	29.37	5-33	6	5.06
L.Gregory	19	1	97	4	24.25	3-44	–	5.10
C.J.Jordan	269.4	5	1611	45	35.80	5-29	1	5.97
L.S.Livingstone	3	0	20	1	20.00	1-20	–	6.66
S.Mahmood	60.5	5	279	14	19.92	4-42	1	4.58
C.Overton	32.2	2	181	4	45.25	2-23	–	5.59
M.W.Parkinson	34.4	0	203	5	40.60	2-28	–	5.85
S.R.Patel	197.5	4	1091	24	45.45	5-41	1	5.51
A.U.Rashid	928.5	10	5251	159	33.02	5-27	9	5.65
T.S.Roland-Jones	7	2	34	1	34.00	1-34	–	4.85
J.E.Root	258.4	2	1491	26	57.34	3-52	–	5.76
B.A.Stokes	510.2	8	3078	74	41.59	5-61	2	6.03
O.P.Stone	16	0	97	1	97.00	1-23	–	6.06
R.J.W.Topley	103.3	7	557	20	27.85	4-50	1	5.38
J.M.Vince	7	0	38	1	38.00	1-18	–	5.42
D.J.Willey	384.1	23	2181	69	31.60	5-30	4	5.67
C.R.Woakes	836	49	4567	155	29.46	6-45	13	5.46
M.A.Wood	483.5	17	2642	69	38.28	4-33	2	5.46
L.J.Wright	173	2	884	15	58.93	2-34	–	5.10

† *E.J.G.Morgan has also made 23 appearances for Ireland (see below).*

AUSTRALIA – BATTING AND FIELDING

	M	I	NO	HS	Runs	Avge	100	50	Ct/St
A.C.Agar	15	13	3	46	236	23.60	–	–	7
W.A.Agar	2	2	–	41	50	25.00	–	–	–
A.T.Carey	45	40	7	106	1203	36.45	1	5	51/6
D.T.Christian	20	18	5	39	273	21.00	–	–	10
P.J.Cummins	69	44	15	36	285	9.82	–	–	16
A.J.Finch	132	128	3	153*	5232	41.85	17	29	63

AUSTRALIA – BATTING AND FIELDING (continued)

	M	I	NO	HS	Runs	Avge	100	50	Ct/St
C.D.Green	1	1	–	21	21	21.00	–	–	–
P.S.P.Handscomb	22	20	1	117	632	33.26	1	4	14
J.R.Hazlewood	56	19	16	11*	54	18.00	–	–	17
T.M.Head	42	39	2	128	1273	34.40	1	10	12
M.C.Henriques	16	15	2	22	117	9.00	–	–	6
M.Labuschagne	13	12	–	108	473	39.41	1	3	4
B.R.McDermott	2	2	–	28	28	14.00	–	–	–
M.R.Marsh	63	59	9	102*	1672	33.44	1	12	30
G.J.Maxwell	116	106	12	108	3230	34.36	2	22	72
R.P.Meredith	1	1	1	0*	0	–	–	–	–
M.G.Neser	2	2	–	6	8	4.00	–	–	–
J.L.Pattinson	15	8	4	13	42	10.50	–	–	3
J.R.Philippe	3	3	–	39	65	21.66	–	–	1
P.M.Siddle	20	6	3	10*	31	10.33	–	–	1
S.P.D.Smith	128	113	12	164	4378	43.34	11	25	70
M.A.Starc	99	56	21	52*	428	12.22	–	1	33
M.P.Stoinis	45	42	7	146*	1106	31.60	1	6	12
A.J.Turner	9	7	1	84*	192	32.00	–	1	4
M.S.Wade	97	83	12	100*	1867	26.29	1	11	108/9
D.A.Warner	128	126	6	179	5710	45.45	18	23	56
D.J.Worrall	3	1	1	6*	6	–	–	–	1
A.Zampa	64	29	8	36	176	8.38	–	–	12

AUSTRALIA – BOWLING

	O	M	R	W	Avge	Best	4wI	R/Over
A.C.Agar	129	4	694	14	49.57	2-31	–	5.37
W.A.Agar	11	1	39	0	–	–	–	3.54
D.T.Christian	121.1	4	595	20	29.75	5-31	1	4.91
P.J.Cummins	608.3	38	3195	111	28.78	5-70	6	5.25
A.J.Finch	47.2	0	259	4	64.75	1- 2	–	5.47
C.D.Green	4	0	27	0	–	–	–	6.75
J.R.Hazlewood	494.5	35	2333	93	25.08	6-52	4	4.71
T.M.Head	127.3	0	737	12	61.41	2-22	–	5.78
M.C.Henriques	67	1	347	8	43.37	3-32	–	5.17
M.Labuschagne	4	0	36	0	–	–	–	9.00
M.R.Marsh	330.5	8	1829	50	36.58	5-33	2	5.52
G.J.Maxwell	473.2	9	2683	51	52.60	4-46	2	5.66
R.P.Meredith	5	0	36	0	–	–	–	7.20
M.G.Neser	16.4	1	120	2	60.00	2-46	–	7.20
J.L.Pattinson	121.1	6	681	16	42.56	4-51	1	5.62
P.M.Siddle	150.1	10	743	17	43.70	3-55	–	4.94
S.P.D.Smith	179.2	1	971	28	34.67	3-16	–	5.41
M.A.Starc	849.5	42	4379	195	22.45	6-28	19	5.15
M.P.Stoinis	246	2	1506	33	45.63	3-16	–	6.12
A.J.Turner	14	1	60	2	30.00	1-23	–	4.28
D.A.Warner	1	0	8	0	–	–	–	8.00
D.J.Worrall	26.2	0	171	1	171.00	1-43	–	6.49
A.Zampa	563.4	8	3115	97	32.11	4-43	3	5.52

SOUTH AFRICA – BATTING AND FIELDING

	M	I	NO	HS	Runs	Avge	100	50	Ct/St
K.J.Abbott	28	13	4	23	76	8.44	–	–	7
H.M.Amla	181	178	14	159	8113	49.46	27	39	87
T.Bavuma	16	15	2	113	652	50.15	2	2	15
Q.de Kock	127	127	6	178	5584	46.14	17	27	173/11
M.de Lange	4	–	–	–	–	–	–	–	–
F.du Plessis	143	136	20	185	5507	47.47	12	35	81
D.M.Dupavillon	2	1	–	17	17	17.00	–	–	–
M.Z.Hamza	1	1	–	56	56	56.00	–	1	–
B.E.Hendricks	8	3	1	3	6	3.00	–	–	2
R.R.Hendricks	24	24	2	102	565	25.68	1	3	15
C.A.Ingram	31	29	3	124	843	32.42	3	3	12
M.Jansen	1	–	–	–	–	–	–	–	–
H.Klaasen	24	23	4	123*	613	32.26	1	3	26/5
G.F.Linde	2	2	1	18	27	27.00	–	–	3
S.S.B.Magala	3	1	–	0	0	0.00	–	–	2
K.A.Maharaj	18	9	2	19	102	14.57	–	–	1
J.N.Malan	14	13	2	177*	759	69.00	3	3	8
A.K.Markram	37	34	2	96	899	28.09	–	3	18
D.A.Miller	140	120	36	139	3408	40.57	5	16	63
P.W.A.Mulder	12	10	4	19*	81	13.50	–	–	5
L.T.Ngidi	32	10	7	19*	47	15.66	–	–	8
A.A.Nortje	12	3	1	10	19	9.50	–	–	2
D.Olivier	2	–	–	–	–	–	–	–	–
W.D.Parnell	66	39	14	56	518	20.72	–	1	12
D.Paterson	4	–	–	–	–	–	–	–	2
A.L.Phehlukwayo	71	44	15	69*	735	25.34	–	2	16
D.Pretorius	23	11	1	50	155	15.50	–	1	7
K.Rabada	82	33	15	31*	310	17.22	–	–	26
T.Shamsi	33	5	4	9*	9	9.00	–	–	6
L.L.Sipamla	5	2	2	10*	14	–	–	–	1
J.T.Smuts	6	5	1	84	180	45.00	–	1	3
H.E.van der Dussen	32	26	9	129*	1267	74.52	2	10	13
R.E.van der Merwe †	13	7	3	12	39	9.75	–	–	3
K.Verreynne	9	7	–	95	283	40.42	–	3	8
L.B.Williams	1	–	–	–	–	–	–	–	–
K.Zondo	6	6	1	54	146	29.20	–	1	1

SOUTH AFRICA – BOWLING

	O	M	R	W	Avge	Best	4wI	R/Over
K.J.Abbott	217.1	13	1051	34	30.91	4-21	1	4.83
M.de Lange	34.5	1	198	10	19.80	4-46	1	5.68
F.du Plessis	32	0	189	2	94.50	1- 8	–	5.90
D.M.Dupavillon	11	0	51	1	51.00	1-21	–	4.63
B.E.Hendricks	46	1	249	5	49.80	3-59	–	5.41
R.R.Hendricks	7	0	47	1	47.00	1-13	–	6.71
C.A.Ingram	1	0	17	0	–	–	–	17.00
M.Jansen	9	0	49	0	–	–	–	5.44
H.Klaasen	3	0	19	0	–	–	–	6.33
G.F.Linde	15	1	72	3	24.00	2-32	–	4.80
S.S.B.Magala	18	0	133	2	66.50	1-64	–	7.38
K.A.Maharaj	158.1	3	735	22	33.40	3-25	–	4.64
A.K.Markram	67	0	355	9	39.44	2-18	–	5.29

SOUTH AFRICA – BOWLING (continued)

	O	*M*	*R*	*W*	*Avge*	*Best*	*4wI*	*R/Over*
P.W.A.Mulder	59	0	341	10	34.10	2-59	–	5.77
L.T.Ngidi	260	16	1461	59	24.76	6-58	3	5.61
A.A.Nortje	102.5	2	567	22	25.77	4-51	1	5.51
D.Olivier	19	0	124	3	41.33	2-73	–	6.52
W.D.Parnell	486.1	20	2743	94	29.18	5-48	5	5.64
D.Paterson	34.5	1	217	4	54.25	3-44	–	6.22
A.L.Phehlukwayo	465.1	16	2664	86	30.97	4-22	3	5.72
D.Pretorius	179.4	9	867	31	27.96	3- 5	–	4.82
K.Rabada	701.4	47	3522	126	27.95	6-16	7	5.01
T.Shamsi	278.1	6	1471	44	33.43	5-49	2	5.28
L.L.Sipamla	30.2	1	172	2	86.00	1-40	–	5.67
J.T.Smuts	30	1	164	4	41.00	2-42	–	5.46
R.E.van der Merwe	117.3	2	561	17	33.00	3-27	–	4.77
L.B.Williams	8	0	62	1	62.00	1-62	–	7.75

† *R.E.van der Merwe has also made 2 appearances for Netherlands (see below).*

WEST INDIES – BATTING AND FIELDING

	M	*I*	*NO*	*HS*	*Runs*	*Avge*	*100*	*50*	*Ct/St*
F.A.Allen	20	16	3	51	200	15.38	–	1	10
S.W.Ambris	16	15	2	148	473	36.38	1	2	2
N.E.Bonner	3	3	–	31	51	17.00	–	–	–
C.R.Brathwaite	44	37	3	101	559	16.44	1	1	11
D.M.Bravo	122	117	14	124	3109	30.18	4	18	35
S.S.J.Brooks	6	6	–	93	193	32.16	–	1	3
R.L.Chase	33	26	3	94	553	24.04	–	2	13
S.S.Cottrell	38	19	11	17	88	11.00	–	–	19
J.Da Silva	2	2	–	9	14	7.00	–	–	1/1
J.P.Greaves	3	3	–	12	29	9.66	–	–	–
J.N.Hamilton	1	1	–	5	5	5.00	–	–	–
K.J.Harding	1	1	1	1*	1	–	–	–	–
S.O.Hetmyer	47	44	3	139	1447	35.29	5	4	19
C.K.Holder	1	1	1	0*	0	–	–	–	–
J.O.Holder	127	103	21	99*	2019	24.62	–	11	60
S.D.Hope	89	84	10	170	3738	50.51	10	20	98/10
A.J.Hosein	14	10	2	34	89	11.12	–	–	5
A.S.Joseph	43	25	10	29*	249	16.60	–	–	15
B.A.King	7	7	–	39	142	20.28	–	–	3
E.Lewis	57	54	4	176*	1847	36.94	4	10	20
A.M.McCarthy	2	2	–	12	15	7.50	–	–	–
K.R.Mayers	3	3	–	40	51	17.00	–	–	–
J.N.Mohammed	36	31	2	91*	630	21.72	–	4	4
S.P.Narine	65	45	12	36	363	11.00	–	–	14
K.Y.Ottley	2	2	–	24	25	12.50	–	–	1
A.Phillip	1	–	–	–	–	–	–	–	–
K.A.Pollard	123	113	9	119	2706	26.01	3	13	64
N.Pooran	37	34	6	118	1121	40.03	1	8	12/2
R.Powell	37	34	3	101	786	25.35	1	2	14
R.A.Reifer	5	4	–	27	36	9.00	–	–	–
K.A.J.Roach	95	60	36	34	308	12.83	–	–	22
R.Shepherd	10	6	–	50	80	13.33	–	–	4
O.F.Smith	5	5	1	46	144	36.00	–	–	1
H.R.Walsh †	13	7	2	46*	112	22.40	–	–	2

WEST INDIES – BOWLING

	O	M	R	W	Avge	Best	4wI	R/Over
F.A.Allen	111	0	627	7	89.57	2-40	–	5.64
N.E.Bonner	2.5	0	15	0	–	–	–	5.29
C.R.Brathwaite	304.1	11	1766	43	41.06	5-27	3	5.80
R.L.Chase	168.5	3	812	19	42.73	3-30	–	4.80
S.S.Cottrell	287	11	1685	52	32.40	5-46	3	5.87
K.J.Harding	10	0	88	0	–	–	–	8.80
C.K.Holder	3	0	26	0	–	–	–	8.66
J.O.Holder	977.1	54	5412	146	37.06	5-27	7	5.53
A.J.Hosein	124.2	3	553	22	25.13	3-26	–	4.44
A.S.Joseph	364.2	15	1971	70	28.15	5-56	5	5.40
A.M.McCarthy	2	0	10	0	–	–	–	5.00
K.R.Mayers	9	0	49	1	49.00	1-34	–	5.44
J.N.Mohammed	73.2	2	340	8	42.50	3-47	–	4.63
S.P.Narine	590	35	2435	92	26.46	6-27	6	4.12
A.Phillip	6	0	43	0	–	–	–	7.16
K.A.Pollard	379.1	4	2161	55	39.29	3-27	–	5.69
N.Pooran	0.3	0	6	0	–	–	–	12.00
R.Powell	40.5	0	243	3	81.00	1- 7	–	5.95
R.A.Reifer	23.5	0	133	5	26.60	2-23	–	5.58
K.A.J.Roach	763.1	53	3885	125	31.08	6-27	6	5.09
R.Shepherd	66.1	3	331	8	41.37	3-50	–	5.00
O.F.Smith	24.1	0	122	6	20.33	2-26	–	5.04
H.R.Walsh	98.4	0	493	21	23.47	5-39	2	4.99

† *H.R.Walsh has also made 1 appearance for the USA v PNG, scoring 27 and taking 0-9.*

NEW ZEALAND – BATTING AND FIELDING

	M	I	NO	HS	Runs	Avge	100	50	Ct/St
T.A.Boult	93	40	23	21*	159	9.35	–	–	34
D.P.Conway	3	3	–	126	225	75.00	1	1	3
M.J.Guptill	186	183	19	237*	6927	42.23	16	37	93
M.J.Henry	55	21	7	48*	211	15.07	–	–	17
K.A.Jamieson	5	1	1	25*	25	–	–	–	2
T.W.M.Latham	102	94	11	137	2824	34.02	5	16	85/8
D.J.Mitchell	3	2	2	100*	112	–	1	–	–
J.D.S.Neesham	66	56	10	97*	1320	28.69	–	6	24
H.M.Nicholls	52	50	11	124*	1409	36.12	1	11	21
M.J.Santner	75	57	23	67	927	27.26	–	2	30
T.G.Southee	143	86	32	55	679	12.57	–	1	39
L.R.P.L.Taylor	233	217	39	181*	8581	48.20	21	51	139
K.S.Williamson	151	144	14	148	6173	47.48	13	39	60
W.A.Young	2	2	1	11*	12	12.00	–	–	1

NEW ZEALAND – BOWLING

	O	M	R	W	Avge	Best	4wI	R/Over
T.A.Boult	852.5	59	4261	169	25.21	7-34	13	4.99
M.J.Guptill	18.1	0	98	4	24.50	2- 6	–	5.39
M.J.Henry	479.3	33	2538	98	25.89	5-30	10	5.29
K.A.Jamieson	46	4	186	5	37.20	2-42	–	4.04
D.J.Mitchell	5	0	33	0	–	–	–	6.60
J.D.S.Neesham	352.3	6	2139	68	31.45	5-27	4	6.06

NEW ZEALAND – BOWLING (continued)

	O	*M*	*R*	*W*	*Avge*	*Best*	*4wI*	*R/Over*
M.J.Santner	564.1	12	2742	75	36.56	5-50	1	4.86
T.G.Southee	1199.1	74	6558	190	34.51	7-33	7	5.46
L.R.P.L.Taylor	7	0	35	0	–	–	–	5.00
K.S.Williamson	244.3	2	1310	37	35.40	4-22	1	5.35

INDIA – BATTING AND FIELDING

	M	*I*	*NO*	*HS*	*Runs*	*Avge*	*100*	*50*	*Ct/St*
M.A.Agarwal	5	5	–	32	86	17.20	–	–	2
R.Ashwin	113	63	20	65	707	16.44	–	1	30
J.J.Bumrah	70	19	12	14*	45	6.42	–	–	17
Y.S.Chahal	61	12	5	18*	66	9.42	–	–	16
D.L.Chahar	7	5	2	69*	179	59.66	–	2	1
R.D.Chahar	1	1	–	13	13	13.00	–	–	–
S.Dhawan	149	146	8	143	6284	45.53	17	35	71
S.Gill	3	3	–	33	49	16.33	–	–	–
K.Gowtham	1	1	–	2	2	2.00	–	–	1
D.J.Hooda	2	2	1	29	55	55.00	–	–	1
S.S.Iyer	26	24	1	103	947	41.17	1	9	10
V.R.Iyer	2	2	–	22	24	12.00	–	–	–
R.A.Jadeja	168	113	39	87	2411	32.58	–	13	60
I.P.Kishan	3	3	–	59	88	29.33	–	1	2
V.Kohli	260	251	39	183	12311	58.07	43	64	137
P.M.Krishna	7	4	3	2*	2	2.00	–	–	–
Kuldeep Yadav	66	22	12	19	123	12.30	–	–	9
B.Kumar	121	55	16	53*	552	14.15	–	1	29
Mohammed Shami	79	38	17	25	161	7.66	–	–	28
T.Natarajan	2	1	1	0*	0	–	–	–	–
M.K.Pandey	29	24	7	104*	566	33.29	1	2	10
H.H.Pandya	63	46	7	92*	1286	32.97	–	7	24
R.R.Pant	24	22	–	85	715	32.50	–	5	19/1
K.L.Rahul	42	41	6	112	1634	46.68	5	10	238/2
N.Rana	1	1	–	7	7	7.00	–	–	–
N.A.Saini	8	5	3	45	107	53.50	–	–	3
C.Sakariya	1	1	1	0*	0	–	–	–	2
S.V.Samson	1	1	–	46	46	46.00	–	–	1
R.G.Sharma	230	223	32	264	9283	48.60	29	44	82
P.P.Shaw	6	6	–	49	189	31.50	–	–	2
M.Siraj	4	2	–	4	7	3.50	–	–	–
S.N.Thakur	19	11	5	50*	205	34.16	–	1	4
M.S.Washington Sundar	4	2	–	33	57	28.50	–	–	2
J.Yadav	2	2	1	2	3	3.00	–	–	1
S.A.Yadav	7	7	2	64	267	53.40	–	2	6

INDIA – BOWLING

	O	*M*	*R*	*W*	*Avge*	*Best*	*4wI*	*R/Over*
M.A.Agarwal	1	0	10	0	–	–	–	10.00
R.Ashwin	1023.3	36	5058	151	33.49	4-25	1	4.94
J.J.Bumrah	617.1	39	2873	113	25.42	5-27	6	4.65
Y.S.Chahal	551	14	2854	104	27.44	6-42	5	5.17
D.L.Chahar	52	4	313	10	31.30	2-37	–	6.01

INDIA – BOWLING (continued)

	O	M	R	W	Avge	Best	4wI	R/Over
R.D.Chahar	10	0	54	3	18.00	3-54	–	5.40
K.Gowtham	8	0	49	1	49.00	1-49	–	6.12
D.J.Hooda	4	0	24	1	24.00	1-24	–	6.00
S.S.Iyer	5.1	0	37	0	–	–	–	7.16
V.R.Iyer	5	0	28	0	–	–	–	5.60
R.A.Jadeja	1426.1	50	7024	188	37.36	5-36	8	4.92
V.Kohli	106.5	1	665	4	166.25	1-15	–	6.22
P.M.Krishna	62.1	5	301	18	16.72	4-12	2	4.84
Kuldeep Yadav	588	13	3084	109	28.29	6-25	5	5.24
B.Kumar	974.3	68	4951	141	35.11	5-42	5	5.08
Mohammed Shami	674	39	3793	148	25.62	5-69	10	5.62
T.Natarajan	20	1	143	3	47.66	2-70	–	7.15
H.H.Pandya	421.4	5	2364	57	41.47	3-31	–	5.60
N.Rana	3	0	10	0	–	–	–	3.33
N.A.Saini	70	0	481	6	80.16	2-58	–	6.87
C.Sakariya	8	0	34	2	17.00	2-34	–	4.25
R.G.Sharma	98.5	2	515	8	64.37	2-27	–	5.21
M.Siraj	36	4	169	5	33.80	3-29	–	4.69
S.N.Thakur	151.3	4	1004	25	40.16	4-52	2	6.62
M.S.Washington Sundar	28	1	140	5	28.00	3-30	–	5.00
J.Yadav	14	0	61	1	61.00	1- 8	–	4.35

PAKISTAN – BATTING AND FIELDING

	M	I	NO	HS	Runs	Avge	100	50	Ct/St
Asif Ali	20	16	1	52	382	25.46	–	3	6
Azhar Ali	53	53	3	102	1845	36.90	3	12	8
Babar Azam	83	81	11	158	3985	56.92	14	17	39
Danish Aziz	2	2	–	9	12	6.00	–	–	–
Faheem Ashraf	31	22	3	28	218	11.47	–	–	8
Fakhar Zaman	53	53	4	210*	2325	47.44	6	13	23
Haris Rauf	8	4	3	1*	2	2.00	–	–	3
Hasan Ali	57	33	10	59	353	15.34	–	2	12
Imam-ul-Haq	46	46	5	151	2023	49.34	7	10	8
Mohammad Abbas	3	–	–	–	–	–	–	–	–
Mohammad Hasnain	8	4	2	28	43	21.50	–	–	2
Mohammad Nawaz	16	13	3	53	203	20.30	–	–	5
Mohammad Rizwan	41	37	7	115	864	28.80	2	4	37/1
Sarfraz Ahmed	117	91	22	105	2315	33.55	2	11	119/24
Saud Shakeel	3	3	1	56	64	32.00	–	1	–
Shadab Khan	48	27	9	54	434	24.11	–	3	11
Shaheen Shah Afridi	28	15	9	19*	87	14.50	–	–	4
Shan Masood	5	5	–	50	111	22.20	–	1	1
Sohaib Maqsood	29	28	2	89*	781	30.03	–	5	10
Usman Qadir	1	–	–	–	–	–	–	–	1
Zafar Gohar	1	1	–	15	15	15.00	–	–	–

PAKISTAN – BOWLING

	O	M	R	W	Avge	Best	4wI	R/Over
Asif Ali	0.5	0	9	0	–	–	–	10.80
Azhar Ali	43	0	260	4	65.00	2-26	–	6.04

PAKISTAN – BOWLING (continued)

	O	M	R	W	Avge	Best	4wI	R/Over
Danish Aziz	5	0	27	0	–	–	–	5.40
Faheem Ashraf	207.2	8	1060	23	46.08	5-22	1	5.11
Fakhar Zaman	22.3	0	111	1	111.00	1-19	–	4.93
Haris Rauf	68	2	406	14	29.00	4-65	1	5.97
Hasan Ali	457	14	2610	89	29.32	5-34	5	5.71
Mohammad Abbas	27	0	153	1	153.00	1-44	–	5.66
Mohammad Hasnain	71	5	455	12	37.91	5-26	1	6.40
Mohammad Nawaz	123.2	2	641	20	32.05	4-42	1	5.19
Sarfraz Ahmed	2	0	15	0	–	–	–	7.50
Saud Shakeel	7.5	0	37	1	37.00	1-14	–	4.72
Shadab Khan	388	8	1988	62	32.06	4-28	3	5.12
Shaheen Shah Afridi	236.3	11	1305	53	24.62	6-35	6	5.51
Sohaib Maqsood	9	0	42	1	42.00	1-16	–	4.66
Usman Qadir	9	0	48	1	48.00	1-48	–	5.33
Zafar Gohar	10	0	54	2	27.00	2-54	–	5.40

SRI LANKA – BATTING AND FIELDING

	M	I	NO	HS	Runs	Avge	100	50	Ct/St
K.I.C.Asalanka	11	11	–	77	472	42.90	–	5	1
K.N.A.Bandara	5	5	1	55*	141	35.25	–	2	3
P.V.D.Chameera	39	28	10	29	217	12.05	–	–	7
L.D.Chandimal	153	139	21	111	3801	32.21	4	24	61/8
D.M.de Silva	56	53	8	91	1199	26.64	–	7	27
P.W.H.de Silva	29	27	4	80*	546	23.73	–	3	8
D.P.D.N.Dickwella	53	50	1	116	1578	32.20	2	9	41/9
A.M.Fernando	4	2	1	1*	1	1.00	–	–	–
A.N.P.R.Fernando	49	25	17	7	35	4.37	–	–	7
B.O.P.Fernando	8	8	–	49	148	18.50	–	–	1
K.B.U.Fernando	4	3	–	17	26	8.66	–	–	1
W.I.A.Fernando	26	26	–	127	964	37.07	3	5	9
C.D.Gunasekara	1	–	–	–	–	–	–	–	–
M.D.Gunathilleke	44	43	1	133	1520	36.19	2	10	13
P.A.K.P.Jayawickrama	5	3	2	4	7	7.00	–	–	–
C.Karunaratne	13	12	5	44*	269	38.42	–	–	3
F.D.M.Karunaratne	34	30	2	97	767	27.39	–	6	11
R.A.S.Lakmal	86	48	22	26	244	9.38	–	–	20
P.A.D.Lakshan	1	1	–	2	2	2.00	–	–	–
A.D.Mathews	218	188	48	139*	5835	41.67	3	40	53
B.K.G.Mendis	82	80	3	119	2297	29.83	2	17	42/3
P.H.K.D.Mendis	7	7	1	57	127	21.16	–	1	2
M.D.K.J.Perera	107	102	5	135	3071	31.65	6	15	47/3
M.K.P.A.D.Perera	39	30	6	50*	291	12.12	–	1	14
N.L.T.C.Perera	166	133	16	140	2338	19.98	1	10	62
P.B.B.Rajapaksa	5	5	–	65	89	17.80	–	1	–
C.A.K.Rajitha	10	4	3	1*	1	1.00	–	–	1
M.B.Ranasinghe	6	6	–	36	140	23.33	–	–	5/1
P.A.D.L.R.Sandakan	31	19	7	16*	64	5.33	–	–	8
M.D.Shanaka	37	34	3	102	842	27.16	1	3	6
P.N.Silva	12	12	–	75	232	19.33	–	2	3
M.M.Theekshana	4	3	3	10*	15	–	–	–	1
I.Udana	21	18	4	78	237	16.92	–	1	6

	M	I	NO	HS	Runs	Avge	100	50	Ct/St
J.D.F.Vandersay	15	9	2	25	78	11.14	–	–	3
R.T.M.Wanigamuni	4	4	2	26	50	25.00	–	–	1

SRI LANKA – BOWLING

	O	M	R	W	Avge	Best	4wI	R/Over
K.I.C.Asalanka	9	0	57	1	57.00	1- 3	–	6.33
K.N.A.Bandara	1	0	8	0	–	–	–	8.00
P.V.D.Chameera	269.3	12	1449	41	35.34	5-16	1	5.37
D.M.de Silva	224.2	1	1162	28	41.50	3-32	–	5.17
P.W.H.de Silva	218.1	10	1099	29	37.89	3-15	–	5.03
A.M.Fernando	20	0	138	0	–	–	–	6.90
A.N.P.R.Fernando	390.5	20	2339	63	37.12	4-31	2	5.98
B.O.P.Fernando	2	0	16	0	–	–	–	8.00
K.B.U.Fernando	25.2	0	136	2	68.00	1-33	–	5.36
C.D.Gunasekara	1	0	8	0	–	–	–	8.00
M.D.Gunathilleke	67	1	371	8	46.37	3-48	–	5.53
P.A.K.P.Jayawickrama	33	0	177	5	35.40	3-59	–	5.36
C.Karunaratne	59	2	313	11	28.45	3-69	–	5.30
F.D.M.Karunaratne	2.4	0	18	0	–	–	–	6.75
R.A.S.Lakmal	646.5	36	3534	109	32.42	4-13	3	5.46
P.A.D.Lakshan	2	0	12	0	–	–	–	6.00
A.D.Mathews	865.1	54	4003	120	33.35	6-20	3	4.62
B.K.G.Mendis	3.2	0	28	0	–	–	–	8.40
P.H.K.D.Mendis	25	0	151	2	75.50	1-32	–	6.04
M.K.P.A.D.Perera	322.3	5	1661	56	29.66	6-29	4	5.15
N.L.T.C.Perera	983.2	28	5740	175	32.80	6-44	9	5.83
C.A.K.Rajitha	66	0	432	10	43.20	2-17	–	6.54
P.A.D.L.R.Sandakan	248	3	1539	27	57.00	4-52	1	6.20
M.D.Shanaka	76	0	438	12	36.50	5-43	1	5.76
M.M.Theekshana	36	1	136	6	22.66	4-37	1	3.77
I.Udana	151.3	2	950	18	52.77	3-82	–	6.27
J.D.F.Vandersay	104.3	4	585	20	29.25	4-10	1	5.59
R.T.M.Wanigamuni	12	0	74	4	18.50	2-26	–	6.16

A.N.P.R.Fernando is also known as N.Pradeep; M.K.P.A.D.Perera is also known as A.Dananjaya; M.B.Ranasinghe is also known as M.Bhanuka; P.N.Silva is also known as P.Nissanka; R.T.M.Wanigamuni is also known as W.R.T.Mendis.

ZIMBABWE – BATTING AND FIELDING

	M	I	NO	HS	Runs	Avge	100	50	Ct/St
R.P.Burl	24	21	3	59	351	19.50	–	2	10
R.W.Chakabva	50	46	2	84	937	21.29	–	4	45/5
T.L.Chatara	76	50	24	23	181	6.96	–	–	7
C.R.Ervine	102	98	11	130*	2837	32.60	3	18	48
L.M.Jongwe	28	24	4	46	276	13.80	–	–	10
T.Kaitano	3	3	–	42	87	29.00	–	–	–
T.S.Kamunhukamwe	7	7	–	51	94	13.42	–	1	1
W.N.Madhevere	14	13	–	56	351	27.00	–	3	3
T.H.Maruma	22	18	1	35	196	11.52	–	–	12
T.Marumani	3	3	–	13	21	7.00	–	–	1
W.P.Masakadza	23	14	2	15	67	5.58	–	–	7

	M	I	NO	HS	Runs	Avge	100	50	Ct/St
B.Muzarabani	30	24	8	17	45	2.81	–	–	10
D.N.Myers	4	4	–	34	93	23.25	–	–	2
R.Ngarava	20	13	5	10*	35	4.37	–	–	3
M.Shumba	2	1	–	9	9	9.00	–	–	1
Sikandar Raza	111	106	16	141	3086	34.28	3	19	46
B.R.M.Taylor	205	203	15	145*	6684	35.55	11	39	133/29
D.T.Tiripano	36	27	8	55*	344	18.10	–	1	4
S.C.Williams	142	137	19	129*	4149	35.16	5	32	53

ZIMBABWE – BOWLING

	O	M	R	W	Avge	Best	4wI	R/Over
R.P.Burl	54.2	2	329	8	41.12	4-32	1	6.05
T.L.Chatara	622.5	48	3205	100	32.05	4-33	1	5.14
L.M.Jongwe	187.5	11	1039	33	31.48	5- 6	1	5.53
W.N.Madhevere	69.2	0	370	7	52.85	2-45	–	5.33
T.H.Maruma	37.3	1	230	4	57.50	2-50	–	6.13
W.P.Masakadza	184.1	8	913	25	36.52	4-21	1	4.95
B.Muzarabani	240.2	13	1264	39	32.41	5-49	3	5.25
R.Ngarava	154.5	7	898	23	39.04	3-52	–	5.79
Sikandar Raza	558.2	21	2727	63	43.28	3-21	–	4.88
B.R.M.Taylor	66	0	406	9	45.11	3-54	–	6.15
D.T.Tiripano	240.2	12	1398	35	39.94	5-63	1	5.81
S.C.Williams	738	32	3617	76	47.59	4-43	1	4.90

BANGLADESH – BATTING AND FIELDING

	M	I	NO	HS	Runs	Avge	100	50	Ct/St
Afif Hossain	10	10	4	93*	257	42.83	–	1	5
Hasan Mahmud	3	1	–	1	1	1.00	–	–	–
Liton Das	50	50	3	176	1558	33.14	5	4	34/3
Mahedi Hasan	3	3	–	14	24	8.00	–	–	–
Mahmudullah	203	177	47	128*	4512	34.70	3	25	71
Mehedi Hasan	55	34	5	81*	513	17.68	–	2	20
Mithun Ali	34	30	4	73*	714	27.46	–	6	7
Mohammad Naim	2	1	–	1	1	1.00	–	–	2
Mohammad Saifuddin	29	19	9	51*	362	36.20	–	2	4
Mosaddek Hossain	40	34	10	52*	620	25.83	–	3	16
Mushfiqur Rahim	230	216	36	144	6677	37.09	8	41	194/49
Mustafizur Rahman	71	32	20	18*	80	6.66	–	–	13
Nazmul Hossain	8	8	–	29	93	11.62	–	–	2
Nurul Hasan	3	3	1	45*	113	56.50	–	–	2/1
Rubel Hossain	104	53	24	17	144	4.96	–	–	20
Shakib Al Hasan	218	206	29	134*	6660	37.62	9	49	52
Shoriful Islam	7	4	1	8	15	5.00	–	–	–
Soumya Sarkar	61	58	3	127*	1768	32.14	2	11	34
Tamim Iqbal	222	220	9	158	7697	36.47	14	51	62
Taskin Ahmed	45	21	6	14	61	4.06	–	–	9
Yasir Ali	3	2	–	1	1	0.50	–	–	1

BANGLADESH – BOWLING

	O	M	R	W	Avge	Best	4wI	R/Over
Afif Hossain	5.1	0	31	2	15.50	1- 0	–	6.00
Hasan Mahmud	19.2	1	131	5	26.20	3-28	–	6.77
Mahedi Hasan	23	1	105	2	52.50	2-42	–	4.56
Mahmudullah	702.5	14	3624	80	45.30	3- 4	–	5.15
Mehedi Hasan	461.2	20	2039	58	35.15	4-25	3	4.41
Mithun Ali	2	0	12	0	–	–	–	6.00
Mohammad Saifuddin	213.5	7	1279	41	31.19	4-41	1	5.98
Mosaddek Hossain	159	1	842	14	60.14	3-13	–	5.29
Mustafizur Rahman	581	26	3012	131	22.99	6-43	8	5.18
Nazmul Hossain	1	0	4	0	–	–	–	4.00
Rubel Hossain	779.4	29	4427	129	34.31	6-26	8	5.67
Shakib Al Hasan	1862.5	89	8290	282	29.39	5-29	12	4.45
Shoriful Islam	53	2	274	10	27.40	4-46	1	5.16
Soumya Sarkar	66.4	0	389	11	35.36	3-56	–	5.83
Tamim Iqbal	1	0	13	0	–	–	–	13.00
Taskin Ahmed	344.5	11	1938	59	32.84	5-28	4	5.62
Yasir Ali	1	0	2	0	–	–	–	2.00

IRELAND – BATTING AND FIELDING

	M	I	NO	HS	Runs	Avge	100	50	Ct/St
M.R.Adair	24	19	7	32	226	18.83	–	–	10
A.Balbirnie	85	82	5	145*	2533	32.89	7	13	27
C.Campher	13	11	1	68	388	38.80	–	4	2
G.J.Delany	12	12	4	22	137	17.12	–	–	4
G.H.Dockrell	99	68	24	62*	772	17.54	–	2	39
S.C.Getkate	4	2	1	16*	23	23.00	–	–	1
J.B.Little	19	8	2	9*	25	4.16	–	–	1
A.R.McBrine	65	42	11	79	573	18.48	–	2	25
B.J.McCarthy	38	26	6	18	162	8.10	–	–	11
J.A.McCollum	10	10	–	73	188	18.80	–	2	2
E.J.G.Morgan †	23	23	2	115	744	35.42	1	5	9
T.J.Murtagh	58	36	12	23*	188	7.83	–	–	16
K.J.O'Brien	153	141	18	142	3619	29.42	2	18	67
W.T.S.Porterfield	148	145	3	139	4343	30.58	11	20	68
N.A.Rock	3	2	–	5	7	3.50	–	–	2
Simi Singh	33	28	4	100*	547	22.79	1	1	13
P.R.Stirling	136	133	3	177	5047	38.82	12	26	52
H.T.Tector	20	20	4	79	670	41.87	–	7	10
L.J.Tucker	26	21	1	83	401	20.05	–	2	36/1
C.A.Young	33	19	9	12*	76	7.60	–	–	8

IRELAND – BOWLING

	O	M	R	W	Avge	Best	4wI	R/Over
M.R.Adair	171.5	9	1051	23	45.69	4-19	2	6.11
A.Balbirnie	10	0	68	2	34.00	1-26	–	6.80
C.Campher	64.3	3	362	10	36.20	2-31	–	5.61
G.J.Delany	22	0	148	3	49.33	1-10	–	6.72
G.H.Dockrell	730.2	31	3487	93	37.49	4-24	4	4.77
S.C.Getkate	32	2	145	7	20.71	2-30	–	4.53
J.B.Little	156.5	9	867	30	28.90	4-39	2	5.52

IRELAND – BOWLING (continued)

	O	M	R	W	Avge	Best	4wI	R/Over
A.R.McBrine	520.5	34	2276	74	30.75	5-29	3	4.36
B.J.McCarthy	315	11	1819	61	29.81	5-46	3	5.77
T.J.Murtagh	503.2	45	2290	74	30.94	5-21	5	4.54
K.J.O'Brien	716	309	3726	114	32.68	4-13	5	5.20
Simi Singh	235	19	908	37	24.54	5-10	1	3.86
P.R.Stirling	406.5	8	1942	43	45.16	6-55	2	4.77
H.T.Tector	8	0	52	1	52.00	1-52	–	6.50
C.A.Young	261.3	12	1400	56	25.00	5-46	2	5.35

† *E.J.G.Morgan has also made 223 appearances for England (see above).*

AFGHANISTAN – BATTING AND FIELDING

	M	I	NO	HS	Runs	Avge	100	50	Ct/St
Asghar Stanikzai	114	108	10	101	2424	24.73	1	12	24
Azmatullah Omarzai	4	3	1	15*	26	13.00	–	–	1
Fareed Ahmad	8	3	3	6*	7	–	–	–	2
Fazalhaq Farooqi	4	2	1	0*	0	0.00	–	–	1
Gulbadin Naib	72	61	8	82*	1114	21.01	–	5	22
Hashmatullah Shahidi	47	47	6	97*	1344	32.78	–	12	11
Ibrahim Zadran	2	2	–	19	21	10.50	–	–	1
Javed Ahmadi	47	44	–	81	1049	23.84	–	7	11
Mohammad Nabi	130	116	12	116	2869	27.58	1	15	56
Mujeeb Zadran	49	25	12	18*	96	7.38	–	–	8
Najibullah Zadran	76	70	11	104*	1837	31.13	1	14	38
Naveen-ul-Haq	7	5	4	10*	21	21.00	–	–	2
Qais Ahmad	1	–	–	–	–	–	–	–	–
Rahmanullah Gurbaz	9	9	1	127	428	53.50	3	–	6/2
Rahmat Shah	82	78	3	114	2753	36.70	5	18	19
Rashid Khan	80	63	10	60*	1069	20.16	–	5	25
Riaz Hassan	3	3	–	50	86	28.66	–	1	–
Shahidullah	1	1	–	1	1	1.00	–	–	1
Sharafuddin Ashraf	19	11	4	21	66	9.42	–	–	5
Usman Ghani	17	17	–	118	435	25.58	1	2	3
Yamin Ahmadzai	7	3	1	5	8	4.00	–	–	3

AFGHANISTAN – BOWLING

	O	M	R	W	Avge	Best	4wI	R/Over
Asghar Stanikzai	23.1	1	91	3	30.33	1- 1	–	3.92
Azmatullah Omarzai	23	0	113	2	56.50	1-23	–	4.91
Fareed Ahmad	49	1	251	10	25.10	3-65	–	5.12
Fazalhaq Farooqi	33.5	3	176	7	25.14	4-54	1	5.20
Gulbadin Naib	406.3	11	2197	61	36.01	6-43	3	5.40
Hashmatullah Shahidi	3	0	25	0	–	–	–	8.33
Javed Ahmadi	75.2	0	363	9	40.33	4-37	1	4.81
Mohammad Nabi	1040.3	40	4459	134	33.27	4-30	3	4.28
Mujeeb Zadran	443.3	30	1761	78	22.57	5-50	4	3.97
Najibullah Zadran	5	0	30	0	–	–	–	6.00
Naveen-ul-Haq	61.3	1	356	14	25.42	4-42	1	5.78
Qais Ahmad	7.4	0	32	3	10.66	3-32	–	4.17
Rahmat Shah	88.2	2	514	14	36.71	5-32	1	5.81
Rashid Khan	679	28	2821	151	18.68	7-18	9	4.15

AFGHANISTAN – BOWLING (continued)

	O	*M*	*R*	*W*	*Avge*	*Best*	*4wI*	*R/Over*
Shahidullah	3	0	16	0	–	–	–	5.33
Sharafuddin Ashraf	141.2	4	605	13	46.53	3-29	–	4.28
Usman Ghani	6.2	0	34	1	34.00	1-21	–	5.36
Yamin Ahmadzai	50.4	4	258	5	51.60	2-34	–	5.09

ASSOCIATES – BATTING AND FIELDING

	M	*I*	*NO*	*HS*	*Runs*	*Avge*	*100*	*50*	*Ct/St*
C.N.Ackermann (Neth)	4	3	–	81	96	32.00	–	1	1
J.H.Davey (Scot)	31	28	6	64	497	22.59	–	2	10
B.D.Glover (Neth)	6	4	3	18	21	21.00	–	–	2
I.G.Holland (USA)	8	8	–	75	244	30.50	–	2	3
M.A.Jones (Scot)	8	8	–	87	281	35.12	–	3	3
F.J.Klaassen (Neth)	10	7	1	13	41	6.83	–	–	3
S.Lamichhane (Nepal)	16	11	2	28	105	11.66	–	–	2
R.A.J.Smith (Scot)	2	1	–	10	10	10.00	–	–	–
S.Snater (Neth)	2	2	–	12	12	6.00	–	–	3
T.van der Gugten (Neth)	8	4	–	49	54	13.50	–	–	–
R.E.van der Merwe (Neth)	16	8	3	57	96	19.20	–	1	6
P.A.van Meekeren (Neth)	7	5	4	15*	36	36.00	–	–	1
B.T.J.Wheal (Scot)	13	7	3	14	16	4.00	–	–	3

ASSOCIATES – BOWLING

	O	*M*	*R*	*W*	*Avge*	*Best*	*4wI*	*R/Over*
C.N.Ackermann	19	0	81	2	40.50	1-10	–	4.26
J.H.Davey	216.5	18	1082	49	22.08	6-28	3	4.99
B.D.Glover	55	2	298	8	37.25	3-43	–	5.41
I.G.Holland	45.5	2	209	7	29.85	3-11	–	4.56
F.J.Klaassen	96	10	351	20	17.55	3-23	–	3.65
S.Lamichhane	131	13	508	41	12.39	6-11	6	3.87
R.A.J.Smith	15	0	97	1	97.00	1-34	–	6.46
S.Snater	11.5	1	63	1	63.00	1-41	–	5.32
T.van der Gugten	54	7	195	12	16.25	5-24	1	3.61
R.E.van der Merwe	137.3	2	685	19	36.05	3-27	–	4.98
P.A.van Meekeren	49	5	218	7	31.14	2-28	–	4.44
B.T.J.Wheal	114.3	9	508	23	22.08	3-34	–	4.43

LIMITED OVERS INTERNATIONALS RESULTS

1970-71 to 17 March 2022

This chart excludes all matches involving multinational teams.

	Opponents	*Matches*	*Won*													*Tied*	*NR*
			E	*A*	*SA*	*WI*	*NZ*	*I*	*P*	*SL*	*Z*	*B*	*Ire*	*Afg*	*Ass*		
England	Australia	152	63	84	–	–	–	–	–	–	–	–	–	–	–	2	3
	South Africa	63	28	–	30	–	–	–	–	–	–	–	–	–	–	1	4
	West Indies	102	52	–	–	44	–	–	–	–	–	–	–	–	–	–	6
	New Zealand	91	41	–	–	–	43	–	–	–	–	–	–	–	–	3	4
	India	103	43	–	–	–	–	55	–	–	–	–	–	–	–	2	3
	Pakistan	91	56	–	–	–	–	–	32	–	–	–	–	–	–	–	3
	Sri Lanka	78	38	–	–	–	–	–	–	36	–	–	–	–	–	1	3
	Zimbabwe	30	21	–	–	–	–	–	–	–	8	–	–	–	–	–	1
	Bangladesh	21	17	–	–	–	–	–	–	–	–	4	–	–	–	–	–
	Ireland	13	10	–	–	–	–	–	–	–	–	–	2	–	–	–	1
	Afghanistan	2	2	–	–	–	–	–	–	–	–	–	–	0	–	–	–
	Associates	15	13	–	–	–	–	–	–	–	–	–	–	–	1	–	1
Australia	South Africa	103	–	48	51	–	–	–	–	–	–	–	–	–	–	3	1
	West Indies	143	–	76	–	61	–	–	–	–	–	–	–	–	–	3	3
	New Zealand	138	–	92	–	–	39	–	–	–	–	–	–	–	–	–	7
	India	143	–	80	–	–	–	53	–	–	–	–	–	–	–	–	10
	Pakistan	104	–	68	–	–	–	–	32	–	–	–	–	–	–	1	3
	Sri Lanka	97	–	61	–	–	–	–	–	32	–	–	–	–	–	–	4
	Zimbabwe	30	–	27	–	–	–	–	–	–	2	–	–	–	–	–	1
	Bangladesh	21	–	19	–	–	–	–	–	–	–	1	–	–	–	–	1
	Ireland	5	–	4	–	–	–	–	–	–	–	–	0	–	–	–	1
	Afghanistan	3	–	3	–	–	–	–	–	–	–	–	–	0	–	–	–
	Associates	16	–	16	–	–	–	–	–	–	–	–	–	–	0	–	–
S Africa	West Indies	62	–	–	44	15	–	–	–	–	–	–	–	–	–	1	2
	New Zealand	71	–	–	41	–	25	–	–	–	–	–	–	–	–	–	5
	India	87	–	–	49	–	–	35	–	–	–	–	–	–	–	–	3
	Pakistan	82	–	–	51	–	–	–	30	–	–	–	–	–	–	–	1
	Sri Lanka	80	–	–	45	–	–	–	–	33	–	–	–	–	–	1	1
	Zimbabwe	41	–	–	38	–	–	–	–	–	2	–	–	–	–	–	1
	Bangladesh	21	–	–	17	–	–	–	–	–	–	4	–	–	–	–	–
	Ireland	8	–	–	6	–	–	–	–	–	–	–	1	–	–	–	1
	Afghanistan	1	–	–	1	–	–	–	–	–	–	–	–	0	–	–	–
	Associates	19	–	–	18	–	–	–	–	–	–	–	–	–	0	–	1
W Indies	New Zealand	65	–	–	–	30	28	–	–	–	–	–	–	–	–	–	7
	India	136	–	–	–	63	–	67	–	–	–	–	–	–	–	2	4
	Pakistan	134	–	–	–	71	–	–	60	–	–	–	–	–	–	3	–
	Sri Lanka	63	–	–	–	31	–	–	–	29	–	–	–	–	–	–	3
	Zimbabwe	48	–	–	–	36	–	–	–	–	10	–	–	–	–	1	1
	Bangladesh	41	–	–	–	21	–	–	–	–	–	18	–	–	–	–	2
	Ireland	15	–	–	–	11	–	–	–	–	–	–	3	–	–	–	1
	Afghanistan	9	–	–	–	5	–	–	–	–	–	–	–	3	–	–	1
	Associates	19	–	–	–	18	–	–	–	–	–	–	–	–	1	–	–
N Zealand	India	110	–	–	–	–	49	55	–	–	–	–	–	–	–	1	5
	Pakistan	107	–	–	–	–	48	–	55	–	–	–	–	–	–	1	3
	Sri Lanka	99	–	–	–	–	49	–	–	41	–	–	–	–	–	1	8
	Zimbabwe	38	–	–	–	–	27	–	–	–	9	–	–	–	–	1	1
	Bangladesh	38	–	–	–	–	28	–	–	–	–	10	–	–	–	–	–
	Ireland	4	–	–	–	–	4	–	–	–	–	–	0	–	–	–	–
	Afghanistan	2	–	–	–	–	2	–	–	–	–	–	–	0	–	–	–
	Associates	12	–	–	–	–	12	–	–	–	–	–	–	–	0	–	–
India	Pakistan	132	–	–	–	–	–	55	73	–	–	–	–	–	–	–	4
	Sri Lanka	162	–	–	–	–	–	93	–	57	–	–	–	–	–	1	11
	Zimbabwe	63	–	–	–	–	–	51	–	–	10	–	–	–	–	2	–
	Bangladesh	36	–	–	–	–	–	30	–	–	–	5	–	–	–	–	1

	Opponents	*Matches*	*Won*													*Tied*	*NR*
			E	*A*	*SA*	*WI*	*NZ*	*I*	*P*	*SL*	*Z*	*B*	*Ire*	*Afg*	*Ass*		
	Ireland	3	–	–	–	–	–	3	–	–	–	–	0	–	–	–	–
	Afghanistan	3	–	–	–	–	–	2	–	–	–	–	–	0	–	1	–
	Associates	24	–	–	–	–	–	22	–	–	–	–	–	–	2	–	–
Pakistan	Sri Lanka	155	–	–	–	–	–	–	92	58	–	–	–	–	–	1	4
	Zimbabwe	62	–	–	–	–	–	–	54	–	4	–	–	–	–	2	2
	Bangladesh	37	–	–	–	–	–	–	32	–	–	5	–	–	–	–	–
	Ireland	7	–	–	–	–	–	–	5	–	–	–	1	–	–	1	–
	Afghanistan	4	–	–	–	–	–	–	4	–	–	–	–	0	–	–	–
	Associates	21	–	–	–	–	–	–	21	–	–	–	–	–	0	–	–
Sri Lanka	Zimbabwe	60	–	–	–	–	–	–	–	46	12	–	–	–	–	–	2
	Bangladesh	51	–	–	–	–	–	–	–	40	–	9	–	–	–	–	2
	Ireland	4	–	–	–	–	–	–	–	4	–	–	0	–	–	–	2
	Afghanistan	4	–	–	–	–	–	–	–	3	–	–	–	1	–	–	–
	Associates	17	–	–	–	–	–	–	–	16	–	–	–	–	1	–	–
Zimbabwe	Bangladesh	78	–	–	–	–	–	–	–	–	28	50	–	–	–	–	–
	Ireland	16	–	–	–	–	–	–	–	–	7	–	7	–	–	1	1
	Afghanistan	25	–	–	–	–	–	–	–	–	10	–	–	15	–	–	–
	Associates	50	–	–	–	–	–	–	–	–	38	–	–	–	9	1	2
Bangladesh	Ireland	10	–	–	–	–	–	–	–	–	–	7	2	–	–	–	1
	Afghanistan	11	–	–	–	–	–	–	–	–	–	7	–	4	–	–	–
	Associates	26	–	–	–	–	–	–	–	–	–	18	–	–	8	–	–
Ireland	Afghanistan	30	–	–	–	–	–	–	–	–	–	–	13	16	–	–	1
	Associates	61	–	–	–	–	–	–	–	–	–	–	45	–	12	2	2
Afghanistan	Associates	41	–	–	–	–	–	–	–	–	–	–	–	27	13	–	1
Associates	Associates	180	–	–	–	–	–	–	–	–	–	–	–	–	174	–	6
		4349	384	578	391	406	354	521	490	395	140	138	74	66	221	39	153

MERIT TABLE OF ALL L-O INTERNATIONALS

	Matches	*Won*	*Lost*	*Tied*	*No Result*	*% Won (exc NR)*
South Africa	638	391	221	6	20	63.26
Australia	955	578	334	9	34	62.75
India	1002	521	431	9	41	54.21
Pakistan	936	490	417	9	20	53.49
England	761	384	339	9	29	52.45
West Indies	837	406	391	10	30	50.30
Afghanistan	135	66	65	1	3	50.00
New Zealand	775	354	374	7	40	48.16
Sri Lanka	870	395	432	5	38	47.47
Ireland	176	74	89	3	10	44.57
Bangladesh	391	138	246	–	7	35.93
Zimbabwe	541	140	381	8	12	26.46
Associate Members (v Full*)	321	47	264	3	7	14.96

* Results of games between two Associate Members and those involving multi-national sides are excluded from this list; Associate Members have participated in 501 LOIs, 180 LOIs being between Associate Members.

TEAM RECORDS

HIGHEST TOTALS

† Batting Second

481-6	(50 overs)	England v Australia	Nottingham	2018
444-3	(50 overs)	England v Pakistan	Nottingham	2016

443-9	(50 overs)	Sri Lanka v Netherlands	Amstelveen	2006
439-2	(50 overs)	South Africa v West Indies	Johannesburg	2014-15
438-9†	(49.5 overs)	South Africa v Australia	Johannesburg	2005-06
438-4	(50 overs)	South Africa v India	Mumbai	2015-16
434-4	(50 overs)	Australia v South Africa	Johannesburg	2005-06
418-5	(50 overs)	South Africa v Zimbabwe	Potchefstroom	2006-07
418-5	(50 overs)	India v West Indies	Indore	2011-12
418-6	(50 overs)	England v West Indies	St George's	2018-19
417-6	(50 overs)	Australia v Afghanistan	Perth	2014-15
414-7	(50 overs)	India v Sri Lanka	Rajkot	2009-10
413-5	(50 overs)	India v Bermuda	Port of Spain	2006-07
411-8†	(50 overs)	Sri Lanka v India	Rajkot	2009-10
411-4	(50 overs)	South Africa v Ireland	Canberra	2014-15
408-5	(50 overs)	South Africa v West Indies	Sydney	2014-15
408-9	(50 overs)	England v New Zealand	Birmingham	2015
404-5	(50 overs)	India v Sri Lanka	Kolkata	2014-15
402-2	(50 overs)	New Zealand v Ireland	Aberdeen	2008
401-3	(50 overs)	India v South Africa	Gwalior	2009-10
399-6	(50 overs)	South Africa v Zimbabwe	Benoni	2010-11
399-9	(50 overs)	England v South Africa	Bloemfontein	2015-16
399-1	(50 overs)	Pakistan v Zimbabwe	Bulawayo	2018
398-5	(50 overs)	Sri Lanka v Kenya	Kandy	1995-96
398-5	(50 overs)	New Zealand v England	The Oval	2015
397-5	(44 overs)	New Zealand v Zimbabwe	Bulawayo	2005
397-6	(50 overs)	England v Afghanistan	Manchester	2019
393-6	(50 overs)	New Zealand v West Indies	Wellington	2014-15
392-6	(50 overs)	South Africa v Pakistan	Pretoria	2006-07
392-4	(50 overs)	India v New Zealand	Christchurch	2008-09
392-4	(50 overs)	India v Sri Lanka	Mohali	2017-18
391-4	(50 overs)	England v Bangladesh	Nottingham	2005
389	(48 overs)	West Indies v England	St George's	2018-19
389-4	(50 overs)	Australia v India	Sydney	2020-21
387-5	(50 overs)	India v England	Rajkot	2008-09
387-5	(50 overs)	India v West Indies	Visakhapatnam	2019-20
386-6	(50 overs)	England v Bangladesh	Cardiff	2019
385-7	(50 overs)	Pakistan v Bangladesh	Dambulla	2010
384-6	(50 overs)	South Africa v Sri Lanka	Centurion	2016-17
383-6	(50 overs)	India v Australia	Bangalore	2013-14
381-6	(50 overs)	India v England	Cuttack	2016-17
381-3	(50 overs)	West Indies v Ireland	Dublin	2019
381-5	(50 overs)	Australia v Bangladesh	Nottingham	2019
378-5	(50 overs)	Australia v New Zealand	Canberra	2016-17
377-6	(50 overs)	Australia v South Africa	Basseterre	2006-07
377-8	(50 overs)	Sri Lanka v Ireland	Dublin	2016
377-5	(50 overs)	India v West Indies	Mumbai (BS)	2018-19
376-2	(50 overs)	India v New Zealand	Hyderabad, India	1999-00
376-9	(50 overs)	Australia v Sri Lanka	Sydney	2014-15
375-3	(50 overs)	Pakistan v Zimbabwe	Lahore	2015
375-5	(50 overs)	India v Sri Lanka	Colombo (RPS)	2017

The highest score for Zimbabwe is 351-7 (v Kenya, Mombasa, 2008-09), for Afghanistan is 338 (v Ire, Greater Noida, 2016-17), for Bangladesh is 333-8 (v A, Nottingham, 2019) and for Ireland is 331-8 (v Z, Hobart, 2014-15) and 331-6 (v Scotland, Dubai, 2017-18).

HIGHEST MATCH AGGREGATES

872-13	(99.5 overs)	South Africa v Australia	Johannesburg	2005-06
825-15	(100 overs)	India v Sri Lanka	Rajkot	2009-10
807-16	(98 overs)	West Indies v England	St George's	2018-19

LARGEST RUNS MARGINS OF VICTORY

290 runs	New Zealand beat Ireland	Aberdeen	2008
275 runs	Australia beat Afghanistan	Perth	2014-15
272 runs	South Africa beat Zimbabwe	Benoni	2010-11
258 runs	South Africa beat Sri Lanka	Paarl	2011-12
257 runs	India beat Bermuda	Port of Spain	2006-07
257 runs	South Africa beat West Indies	Sydney	2014-15
256 runs	Australia beat Namibia	Potchefstroom	2002-03
256 runs	India beat Hong Kong	Karachi	2008
255 runs	Pakistan beat Ireland	Dublin	2016
245 runs	Sri Lanka beat India	Sharjah	2000-01
244 runs	Pakistan beat Zimbabwe	Bulawayo	2018
243 runs	Sri Lanka beat Bermuda	Port of Spain	2006-07
242 runs	England beat Australia	Nottingham	2018
234 runs	Sri Lanka beat Pakistan	Lahore	2008-09
233 runs	Pakistan beat Bangladesh	Dhaka	1999-00
232 runs	Australia beat Sri Lanka	Adelaide	1984-85
231 runs	South Africa beat Netherlands	Mohali	2010-11
229 runs	Australia beat Netherlands	Basseterre	2006-07
226 runs	Ireland beat UAE	Harare	2017-18
224 runs	Australia beat Pakistan	Nairobi	2002
224 runs	India beat West Indies	Mumbai (BS)	2018-19
221 runs	South Africa beat Netherlands	Basseterre	2006-07

LOWEST TOTALS (Excluding reduced innings)

35	(18.0 overs)	Zimbabwe v Sri Lanka	Harare	2003-04
35	(12.0 overs)	USA v Nepal	Kirtipur	2019-20
36	(18.4 overs)	Canada v Sri Lanka	Paarl	2002-03
38	(15.4 overs)	Zimbabwe v Sri Lanka	Colombo (SSC)	2001-02
43	(19.5 overs)	Pakistan v West Indies	Cape Town	1992-93
43	(20.1 overs)	Sri Lanka v South Africa	Paarl	2011-12
44	(24.5 overs)	Zimbabwe v Bangladesh	Chittagong	2009-10
45	(40.3 overs)	Canada v England	Manchester	1979
45	(14.0 overs)	Namibia v Australia	Potchefstroom	2002-03
54	(26.3 overs)	India v Sri Lanka	Sharjah	2000-01
54	(23.2 overs)	West Indies v South Africa	Cape Town	2003-04
54	(13.5 overs)	Zimbabwe v Afghanistan	Harare	2016-17
55	(28.3 overs)	Sri Lanka v West Indies	Sharjah	1986-87
58	(18.5 overs)	Bangladesh v West Indies	Dhaka	2010-11
58	(17.4 overs)	Bangladesh v India	Dhaka	2014
58	(16.1 overs)	Afghanistan v Zimbabwe	Sharjah	2015-16
61	(22.0 overs)	West Indies v Bangladesh	Chittagong	2011-12
63	(25.5 overs)	India v Australia	Sydney	1980-81
63	(18.3 overs)	Afghanistan v Scotland	Abu Dhabi	2014-15
64	(35.5 overs)	New Zealand v Pakistan	Sharjah	1985-86
65	(24.0 overs)	USA v Australia	Southampton	2004
65	(24.3 overs)	Zimbabwe v India	Harare	2005
67	(31.0 overs)	Zimbabwe v Sri Lanka	Harare	2008-09
67	(24.4 overs)	Canada v Netherlands	King City	2013
67	(24.0 overs)	Sri Lanka v England	Manchester	2014
67	(25.1 overs)	Zimbabwe v Pakistan	Bulawayo	2018
68	(31.3 overs)	Scotland v West Indies	Leicester	1999
69	(28.0 overs)	South Africa v Australia	Sydney	1993-94
69	(22.5 overs)	Zimbabwe v Kenya	Harare	2005-06
69	(23.5 overs)	Kenya v New Zealand	Chennai	2010-11
70	(25.2 overs)	Australia v England	Birmingham	1977

70	(26.3 overs)	Australia v New Zealand	Adelaide	1985-86
70	(23.5 overs)	West Indies v Australia	Perth	2012-13
70	(24.4 overs)	Bangladesh v West Indies	St George's	2014
70	(24.4 overs)	Zimbabwe v Sri Lanka	Pallekele	2021-22

The lowest for England is 86 (v A, Manchester, 2001) and for Ireland is 77 (v SL, St George's, 2007).

LOWEST MATCH AGGREGATES

71-12	(17.2 overs)	USA (35) v Nepal (36-2)	Kirtipur	2019-20
73-11	(23.2 overs)	Canada (36) v Sri Lanka (37-1)	Paarl	2002-03
75-11	(27.2 overs)	Zimbabwe (35) v Sri Lanka (40-1)	Harare	2003-04
7811	(20.0 overs)	Zimbabwe (38) v Sri Lanka (40-1)	Colombo (SSC)	2001-02

BATTING RECORDS
6000 RUNS IN A CAREER

		LOI	*I*	*NO*	*HS*	***Runs***	*Avge*	*100*	*50*
S.R.Tendulkar	I	463	452	41	200*	**18426**	44.83	49	96
K.C.Sangakkara	SL/Asia/ICC	404	380	41	169	**14234**	41.98	25	93
R.T.Ponting	A/ICC	375	365	39	164	**13704**	42.03	30	82
S.T.Jayasuriya	SL/Asia	445	433	18	189	**13430**	32.36	28	68
D.P.M.D.Jayawardena	SL/Asia	448	418	39	144	**12650**	33.37	19	77
V.Kohli	I	260	251	39	183	**12311**	58.07	43	64
Inzamam-ul-Haq	P/Asia	378	350	53	137*	**11739**	39.52	10	83
J.H.Kallis	SA/Afr/ICC	328	314	53	139	**11579**	44.36	17	86
S.C.Ganguly	I/Asia	311	300	23	183	**11363**	41.02	22	72
R.S.Dravid	I/Asia/ICC	344	318	40	153	**10889**	39.16	12	83
M.S.Dhoni	I/Asia	350	297	84	183*	**10773**	50.57	10	73
C.H.Gayle	WI/ICC	301	294	17	215	**10480**	37.83	25	54
B.C.Lara	WI/ICC	299	289	32	169	**10405**	40.48	19	63
T.M.Dilshan	SL	330	303	41	161*	**10290**	39.27	22	47
Mohammad Yousuf	P/Asia	288	272	40	141*	**9720**	41.71	15	64
A.C.Gilchrist	A/ICC	287	279	11	172	**9619**	35.89	16	55
A.B.de Villiers	SA/Afr	228	218	39	176	**9577**	53.50	25	53
M.Azharuddin	I	334	308	54	153*	**9378**	36.92	7	58
P.A.de Silva	SL	308	296	30	145	**9284**	34.90	11	64
R.G.Sharma	I	230	223	32	264	**9283**	48.60	29	44
Saeed Anwar	P	247	244	19	194	**8824**	39.21	20	43
S.Chanderpaul	WI	268	251	40	150	**8778**	41.60	11	59
Yuvraj Singh	I/Asia	304	278	40	150	**8701**	36.55	14	52
D.L.Haynes	WI	238	237	28	152*	**8648**	41.37	17	57
L.R.P.L.Taylor	NZ	233	217	39	181*	**8581**	48.20	21	51
M.S.Atapattu	SL	268	259	32	132*	**8529**	37.57	11	59
M.E.Waugh	A	244	236	20	173	**8500**	39.35	18	50
V.Sehwag	I/Asia/ICC	251	245	9	219	**8273**	35.05	15	38
H.M.Amla	SA	181	178	14	159	**8113**	49.46	27	39
H.H.Gibbs	SA	248	240	16	175	**8094**	36.13	21	37
Shahid Afridi	P/Asia/ICC	398	369	27	124	**8064**	23.57	6	39
S.P.Fleming	NZ/ICC	280	269	21	134*	**8037**	32.40	8	49
M.J.Clarke	A	245	223	44	130	**7981**	44.58	8	58
E.J.G.Morgan	E/Ire	246	228	34	148	**7701**	39.69	14	47
Tamim Iqbal	B	222	220	9	158	**7697**	36.47	14	51
S.R.Waugh	A	325	288	58	120*	**7569**	32.90	3	45
Shoaib Malik	P	287	258	40	143	**7534**	34.55	9	44
A.Ranatunga	SL	269	255	47	131*	**7456**	35.84	4	49
Javed Miandad	P	233	218	41	119*	**7381**	41.70	8	50
Younus Khan	P	265	255	23	144	**7249**	31.24	7	48

Salim Malik	P	283	256	38	102	**7170**	32.88	5	47
N.J.Astle	NZ	223	217	14	145*	**7090**	34.92	16	41
G.C.Smith	SA/Afr	197	194	10	141	**6989**	37.98	10	47
W.U.Tharanga	SL/Asia	235	223	17	174*	**6951**	33.74	15	37
M.J.Guptill	NZ	186	183	19	237*	**6927**	42.23	16	37
M.G.Bevan	A	232	196	67	108*	**6912**	53.58	6	46
G.Kirsten	SA	185	185	19	188*	**6798**	40.95	13	45
A.Flower	Z	213	208	16	145	**6786**	35.34	4	55
I.V.A.Richards	WI	187	167	24	189*	**6721**	47.00	11	45
B.R.M.Taylor	Z	205	203	15	145*	**6684**	35.55	11	39
Mushfiqur Rahim	B	230	216	36	144	**6677**	37.09	8	41
Shakib Al Hasan	B	218	206	29	134*	**6660**	37.62	9	49
Mohammad Hafeez	P	218	216	15	140*	**6614**	32.90	11	38
G.W.Flower	Z	221	214	18	142*	**6571**	33.52	6	40
Ijaz Ahmed	P	250	232	29	139*	**6564**	32.33	10	37
A.R.Border	A	273	252	39	127*	**6524**	30.62	3	39
S.Dhawan	I	149	146	8	143	**6284**	45.53	17	35
R.B.Richardson	WI	224	217	30	122	**6248**	33.41	5	44
K.S.Williamson	NZ	151	144	14	148	**6173**	47.48	13	39
M.L.Hayden	A/ICC	161	155	15	181*	**6133**	43.80	10	36
J.E.Root	E	152	142	23	133*	**6109**	51.33	16	35
B.B.McCullum	NZ	260	228	28	166	**6083**	30.41	5	32
D.M.Jones	A	164	161	25	145	**6068**	44.61	7	46

The most runs for Ireland is 5047 by P.R.Stirling (133 innings) and for Afghanistan 2869 by Mohammad Nabi (116 innings).

HIGHEST INDIVIDUAL INNINGS

264	R.G.Sharma	India v Sri Lanka	Kolkata	2014-15
237*	M.J.Guptill	New Zealand v West Indies	Wellington	2014-15
219	V.Sehwag	India v West Indies	Indore	2011-12
215	C.H.Gayle	West Indies v Zimbabwe	Canberra	2014-15
210*	Fakhar Zaman	Pakistan v Zimbabwe	Bulawayo	2018
209	R.G.Sharma	India v Australia	Bangalore	2013-14
208*	R.G.Sharma	India v Sri Lanka	Mohali	2017-18
200*	S.R.Tendulkar	India v South Africa	Gwalior	2009-10
194*	C.K.Coventry	Zimbabwe v Bangladesh	Bulawayo	2009
194	Saeed Anwar	Pakistan v India	Madras	1996-97
193	Fakhar Zaman	Pakistan v South Africa	Johannesburg	2020-21
189*	I.V.A.Richards	West Indies v England	Manchester	1984
189*	M.J.Guptill	New Zealand v England	Southampton	2013
189	S.T.Jayasuriya	Sri Lanka v India	Sharjah	2000-01
188*	G.Kirsten	South Africa v UAE	Rawalpindi	1995-96
186*	S.R.Tendulkar	India v New Zealand	Hyderabad	1999-00
185*	S.R.Watson	Australia v Bangladesh	Dhaka	2010-11
185	F.du Plessis	South Africa v Sri Lanka	Cape Town	2016-17
183*	M.S.Dhoni	India v Sri Lanka	Jaipur	2005-06
183	S.C.Ganguly	India v Sri Lanka	Taunton	1999
183	V.Kohli	India v Pakistan	Dhaka	2011-12
181*	M.L.Hayden	Australia v New Zealand	Hamilton	2006-07
181*	L.R.P.L.Taylor	New Zealand v England	Dunedin	2017-18
181	I.V.A.Richards	West Indies v Sri Lanka	Karachi	1987-88
180*	M.J.Guptill	New Zealand v South Africa	Hamilton	2016-17
180	J.J.Roy	England v Australia	Melbourne	2017-18
179	D.A.Warner	Australia v Pakistan	Adelaide	2016-17
179	J.D.Campbell	West Indies v Ireland	Dublin	2019
178*	H.Masakadza	Zimbabwe v Kenya	Harare	2009-10

178	D.A.Warner	Australia v Afghanistan	Perth	2014-15
178	Q.de Kock	South Africa v Australia	Centurion	2016-17
177*	J.N.Malan	South Africa v Ireland	Dublin	2021
177	P.R.Stirling	Ireland v Canada	Toronto	2010
176*	E.Lewis	West Indies v England	The Oval	2017
176	A.B.de Villiers	South Africa v Bangladesh	Paarl	2017-18
176	Liton Das	Bangladesh v Zimbabwe	Sylhet	2019-20
175*	Kapil Dev	India v Zimbabwe	Tunbridge Wells	1983
175	H.H.Gibbs	South Africa v Australia	Johannesburg	2005-06
175	S.R.Tendulkar	India v Australia	Hyderabad, India	2009-10
175	V.Sehwag	India v Bangladesh	Dhaka	2010-11
175	C.S.MacLeod	Scotland v Canada	Christchurch	2013-14
174*	W.U.Tharanga	Sri Lanka v India	Kingston	2013
173*	J.S.Malhotra	USA v PNG	Al Amerat	2021
173	M.E.Waugh	Australia v West Indies	Melbourne	2000-01
173	D.A.Warner	Australia v South Africa	Cape Town	2016-17
172*	C.B.Wishart	Zimbabwe v Namibia	Harare	2002-03
172	A.C.Gilchrist	Australia v Zimbabwe	Hobart	2003-04
172	L.Vincent	New Zealand v Zimbabwe	Bulawayo	2005
171*	G.M.Turner	New Zealand v East Africa	Birmingham	1975
171*	R.G.Sharma	India v Australia	Perth	2015-16
171	A.D.Hales	England v Pakistan	Nottingham	2016
170*	L.Ronchi	New Zealand v Sri Lanka	Dunedin	2014-15
170	S.D.Hope	West Indies v Ireland	Dublin	2019

The highest for Afghanistan is 131* by Mohammad Shahzad (v Z, Sharjah, 2015-16).

HUNDRED ON DEBUT

D.L.Amiss	103	England v Australia	Manchester	1972
D.L.Haynes	148	West Indies v Australia	St John's	1977-78
A.Flower	115*	Zimbabwe v Sri Lanka	New Plymouth	1991-92
Salim Elahi	102*	Pakistan v Sri Lanka	Gujranwala	1995-96
M.J.Guptill	122*	New Zealand v West Indies	Auckland	2008-09
C.A.Ingram	124	South Africa v Zimbabwe	Bloemfontein	2010-11
R.J.Nicol	108*	New Zealand v Zimbabwe	Harare	2011-12
P.J.Hughes	112	Australia v Sri Lanka	Melbourne	2012-13
M.J.Lumb	106	England v West Indies	North Sound	2013-14
M.S.Chapman	124*	Hong Kong v UAE	Dubai	2015-16
K.L.Rahul	100*	India v Zimbabwe	Harare	2016
T.Bavuma	113	South Africa v Ireland	Benoni	2016-17
Imam-ul-Haq	100	Pakistan v Sri Lanka	Abu Dhabi	2017-18
R.R.Hendricks	102	South Africa v Sri Lanka	Pallekele	2018
Abid Ali	112	Pakistan v Australia	Dubai, DSC	2018-19
Rahmanullah Gurbaz	127	Afghanistan v Ireland	Abu Dhabi	2020-21

Shahid Afridi scored 102 for P v SL, Nairobi, 1996-97, in his second match having not batted in his first.

Fastest 100	31 balls	A.B.de Villiers (149)	SA v WI	Johannesburg	2014-15
Fastest 50	16 balls	A.B.de Villiers (149)	SA v WI	Johannesburg	2014-15

16 HUNDREDS

		Inns	***100***	*E*	*A*	*SA*	*WI*	*NZ*	*I*	*P*	*SL*	*Z*	*B*	*Ire*	*Afg*	*Ass*
S.R.Tendulkar	I	452	**49**	2	9	5	4	5	–	5	8	5	1	–	–	5
V.Kohli	I	251	**43**	3	8	4	9	5	–	2	8	1	3	–	–	–
R.T.Ponting	A	365	**30***	5	–	2	2	6	6	1	4	1	1	–	–	1
R.G.Sharma	I	223	**29**	2	8	3	3	1	–	2	6	1	3	–	–	–
S.T.Jayasuriya	SL	433	**28**	4	2	–	1	5	7	3	–	1	4	–	–	1

H.M.Amla	SA	178	**27**	2	1	–	5	2	2	3	5	3	2	1	–	1
A.B.de Villiers	SA	218	**25**	2	1	–	5	1	6	3	2	3	1	–	–	1
C.H.Gayle	WI	294	**25**	4	–	3	–	2	4	3	1	3	1	–	–	4
K.C.Sangakkara	SL	380	**25**	4	2	2	–	2	6	2	–	–	5	–	–	2
S.C.Ganguly	I	300	**22**	1	1	3	–	3	–	2	4	3	1	–	–	4
T.M.Dilshan	SL	303	**22**	2	1	2	–	3	4	2	–	2	4	–	–	2
L.R.P.L.Taylor	NZ	217	**21**	5	2	1	1	–	3	3	2	2	2	–	–	–
H.H.Gibbs	SA	240	**21**	2	3	–	5	2	2	2	1	2	1	–	–	1
Saeed Anwar	P	244	**20**	–	1	–	2	4	4	–	7	2	–	–	–	–
B.C.Lara	WI	289	**19**	1	3	3	–	2	–	5	2	1	1	–	–	1
D.P.M.D.Jayawardena	SL	418	**19***	5	–	–	1	3	4	2	–	–	1	–	1	1
D.A.Warner	A	126	**18**	1	–	4	–	2	3	3	3	–	1	–	1	–
M.E.Waugh	A	236	**18**	1	–	2	3	3	3	1	1	3	–	–	–	1
Q.de Kock	SA	127	**17**	3	2	–	–	–	6	1	3	–	1	1	–	–
A.J.Finch	A	128	**17**	7	–	2	–	–	4	2	1	–	–	–	–	1
S.Dhawan	I	146	**17**	–	4	3	2	–	–	1	4	1	–	1	–	1
D.L.Haynes	WI	237	**17**	2	6		–	2	2	4	1		–	–	–	–
J.H.Kallis	SA	314	**17**	1	1	–	4	3	2	1	3	1	–	–	–	1
J.E.Root	E	142	**16**	–	–	2	4	3	3	1	2	–	1	–	–	–
M.J.Guptill	NZ	183	**16**	2	1	2	2	–	1	1	2	2	3	–	–	–
N.J.Astle	NZ	217	**16**	2	1	1	1	–	5	2	–	3	–	–	–	1
A.C.Gilchrist	A	279	**16***	2	–	2	–	2	1	1	6	1	–	–	–	–

* = Includes hundred scored against multi-national side.

The most for Zimbabwe is 11 by B.R.M.Taylor (203 innings), for Bangladesh 14 by Tamim Iqbal (220), for Ireland 12 by P.R.Stirling (133), and for Afghanistan 6 by Mohammad Shahzad (84).

HIGHEST PARTNERSHIP FOR EACH WICKET

1st	365	J.D.Campbell/S.D.Hope	West Indies v Ireland	Dublin	2019
2nd	372	C.H.Gayle/M.N.Samuels	West Indies v Zimbabwe	Canberra	2014-15
3rd	258	D.M.Bravo/D.Ramdin	West Indies v Bangladesh	Basseterre	2014
4th	275*	M.Azharuddin/A.Jadeja	India v Zimbabwe	Cuttack	1997-98
5th	256*	D.A.Miller/J.P.Duminy	South Africa v Zimbabwe	Hamilton	2014-15
6th	267*	G.D.Elliott/L.Ronchi	New Zealand v Sri Lanka	Dunedin	2014-15
7th	177	J.C.Buttler/A.U.Rashid	England v New Zealand	Birmingham	2015
8th	138*	J.M.Kemp/A.J.Hall	South Africa v India	Cape Town	2006-07
9th	132	A.D.Mathews/S.L.Malinga	Sri Lanka v Australia	Melbourne	2010-11
10th	106*	I.V.A.Richards/M.A.Holding	West Indies v England	Manchester	1984

BOWLING RECORDS
200 WICKETS IN A CAREER

		LOI	*Balls*	*R*	*W*	*Avge*	*Best*	*5w*	*R/Over*
M.Muralitharan	SL/Asia/ICC	350	18811	12326	**534**	23.08	7-30	10	3.93
Wasim Akram	P	356	18186	11812	**502**	23.52	5-15	6	3.89
Waqar Younis	P	262	12698	9919	**416**	23.84	7-36	13	4.68
W.P.J.U.C.Vaas	SL/Asia	322	15775	11014	**400**	27.53	8-19	4	4.18
Shahid Afridi	P/Asia/ICC	398	17620	13632	**395**	34.51	7-12	9	4.62
S.M.Pollock	SA/Afr/ICC	303	15712	9631	**393**	24.50	6-35	5	3.67
G.D.McGrath	A/ICC	250	12970	8391	**381**	22.02	7-15	7	3.88
B.Lee	A	221	11185	8877	**380**	23.36	5-22	9	4.76
S.L.Malinga	SL	226	10936	9760	**338**	28.87	6-38	8	5.35
A.Kumble	I/Asia	271	14496	10412	**337**	30.89	6-12	2	4.30
S.T.Jayasuriya	SL	445	14874	11871	**323**	36.75	6-29	4	4.78
J.Srinath	I	229	11935	8847	**315**	28.08	5-23	3	4.44
D.L.Vettori	NZ/ICC	295	14060	9674	**305**	31.71	5- 7	2	4.12
S.K.Warne	A/ICC	194	10642	7541	**293**	25.73	5-33	1	4.25

		LOI	Balls	R	W	Avge	Best	5w	R/Over
Saqlain Mushtaq	P	169	8770	6275	**288**	21.78	5-20	6	4.29
A.B.Agarkar	I	191	9484	8021	**288**	27.85	6-42	2	5.07
Shakib Al Hasan	B	218	11177	8290	**282**	29.39	5-29	3	4.45
Z.Khan	I/Asia	200	10097	8301	**282**	29.43	5-42	1	4.93
J.H.Kallis	SA/Afr/ICC	328	10750	8680	**273**	31.79	5-30	2	4.84
A.A.Donald	SA	164	8561	5926	**272**	21.78	6-23	2	4.15
Mashrafe Mortaza	B/Asia	220	10922	8893	**270**	32.93	6-26	1	4.88
J.M.Anderson	E	194	9584	7861	**269**	29.22	5-23	2	4.92
Abdul Razzaq	P/Asia	265	10941	8564	**269**	31.83	6-35	3	4.69
Harbhajan Singh	I/Asia	236	12479	8973	**269**	33.35	5-31	3	4.31
M.Ntini	SA/ICC	173	8687	6559	**266**	24.65	6-22	4	4.53
Kapil Dev	I	225	11202	6945	**253**	27.45	5-43	1	3.72
Shoaib Akhtar	P/Asia/ICC	163	7764	6169	**247**	24.97	6-16	4	4.76
K.D.Mills	NZ	170	8230	6485	**240**	27.02	5-25	1	4.72
M.G.Johnson	A	153	7489	6038	**239**	25.26	6-31	3	4.83
H.H.Streak	Z/Afr	189	9468	7129	**239**	29.82	5-32	1	4.51
D.Gough	E/ICC	159	8470	6209	**235**	26.42	5-44	2	4.39
C.A.Walsh	WI	205	10822	6918	**227**	30.47	5- 1	1	3.83
C.E.L.Ambrose	WI	176	9353	5429	**225**	24.12	5-17	4	3.48
Abdur Razzak	B	153	7965	6065	**207**	29.29	5-29	4	4.56
C.J.McDermott	A	138	7460	5018	**203**	24.71	5-44	1	4.03
C.Z.Harris	NZ	250	10667	7613	**203**	37.50	5-42	1	4.28
C.L.Cairns	NZ/ICC	215	8168	6594	**201**	32.80	5-42	1	4.84

The most wickets for Ireland is 114 by K.J.O'Brien (153 matches) and for Afghanistan 151 by Rashid Khan (80).

BEST FIGURES IN AN INNINGS

8-19	W.P.J.U.C.Vaas	Sri Lanka v Zimbabwe	Colombo (SSC)	2001-02
7-12	Shahid Afridi	Pakistan v West Indies	Providence	2013
7-15	G.D.McGrath	Australia v Namibia	Potchefstroom	2002-03
7-18	Rashid Khan	Afghanistan v West Indies	Gros Islet	2017
7-20	A.J.Bichel	Australia v England	Port Elizabeth	2002-03
7-30	M.Muralitharan	Sri Lanka v India	Sharjah	2000-01
7-33	T.G.Southee	New Zealand v England	Wellington	2014-15
7-34	T.A.Boult	New Zealand v West Indies	Christchurch	2017-18
7-36	Waqar Younis	Pakistan v England	Leeds	2001
7-37	Aqib Javed	Pakistan v India	Sharjah	1991-92
7-45	Imran Tahir	South Africa v West Indies	Basseterre	2016
7-51	W.W.Davis	West Indies v Australia	Leeds	1983
6- 4	S.T.R.Binny	India v Bangladesh	Dhaka	2014
6-11	S.Lamichhane	Nepal v PNG	Al Amerat	2021
6-12	A.Kumble	India v West Indies	Calcutta	1993-94
6-13	B.A.W.Mendis	Sri Lanka v India	Karachi	2008
6-14	G.J.Gilmour	Australia v England	Leeds	1975
6-14	Imran Khan	Pakistan v India	Sharjah	1984-85
6-14	M.F.Maharoof	Sri Lanka v West Indies	Mumbai	2006-07
6-15	C.E.H.Croft	West Indies v England	Kingstown	1980-81
6-16	Shoaib Akhtar	Pakistan v New Zealand	Karachi	2001-02
6-16	K.Rabada	South Africa v Bangladesh	Dhaka	2015
6-16	S.Lamichhane	Nepal v USA	Kirtipur	2019-20
6-18	Azhar Mahmood	Pakistan v West Indies	Sharjah	1999-00
6-19	H.K.Olonga	Zimbabwe v England	Cape Town	1999-00
6-19	S.E.Bond	New Zealand v Zimbabwe	Harare	2005
6-20	B.C.Strang	Zimbabwe v Bangladesh	Nairobi	1997-98
6-20	A.D.Mathews	Sri Lanka v India	Colombo (RPS)	2009-10

6-22	F.H.Edwards	West Indies v Zimbabwe	Harare	2003-04
6-22	M.Ntini	South Africa v Australia	Cape Town	2005-06
6-23	A.A.Donald	South Africa v Kenya	Nairobi	1996-97
6-23	A.Nehra	India v England	Durban	2002-03
6-23	S.E.Bond	New Zealand v Australia	Port Elizabeth	2002-03
6-24	Imran Tahir	South Africa v Zimbabwe	Bloemfontein	2018-19
6-25	S.B.Styris	New Zealand v West Indies	Port of Spain	2002
6-25	W.P.J.U.C.Vaas	Sri Lanka v Bangladesh	Pietermaritzburg	2002-03
6-25	Kuldeep Yadav	India v England	Nottingham	2018
6-26	Waqar Younis	Pakistan v Sri Lanka	Sharjah	1989-90
6-26	Mashrafe Mortaza	Bangladesh v Kenya	Nairobi	2006
6-26	Rubel Hossain	Bangladesh v New Zealand	Dhaka	2013-14
6-26	Yasir Shah	Pakistan v Zimbabwe	Harare	2015-16
6-27	Naved-ul-Hasan	Pakistan v India	Jamshedpur	2004-05
6-27	C.R.D.Fernando	Sri Lanka v England	Colombo (RPS)	2007-08
6-27	M.Kartik	India v Australia	Mumbai	2007-08
6-27	K.A.J.Roach	West Indies v Netherlands	Delhi	2010-11
6-27	S.P.Narine	West Indies v South Africa	Providence	2016
6-28	H.K.Olonga	Zimbabwe v Kenya	Bulawayo	2002-03
6-28	J.H.Davey	Scotland v Afghanistan	Abu Dhabi	2014-15
6-28	M.A.Starc	Australia v New Zealand	Auckland	2014-15
6-29	B.P.Patterson	West Indies v India	Nagpur	1987-88
6-29	S.T.Jayasuriya	Sri Lanka v England	Moratuwa	1992-93
6-29	B.A.W.Mendis	Sri Lanka v Zimbabwe	Harare	2008-09
6-29	M.K.P.A.D.Perera	Sri Lanka v South Africa	Colombo (RPS)	2018
6-30	Waqar Younis	Pakistan v New Zealand	Auckland	1993-94
6-31	P.D.Collingwood	England v Bangladesh	Nottingham	2005
6-31	M.G.Johnson	Australia v Sri Lanka	Pallekele	2011
6-33	T.A.Boult	New Zealand v Australia	Hamilton	2016-17
6-34	Zahoor Khan	UAE v Ireland	Dubai (ICCA)	2016-17
6-35	S.M.Pollock	South Africa v West Indies	East London	1998-99
6-35	Abdul Razzaq	Pakistan v Bangladesh	Dhaka	2001-02
6-35	Shaheen Shah Afridi	Pakistan v Bangladesh	Lord's	2019

The best figures for Ireland are 6-55 by P.R.Stirling (v Afg, Greater Noida, 2016-17).

HAT-TRICKS

Jalaluddin	Pakistan v Australia	Hyderabad	1982-83
B.A.Reid	Australia v New Zealand	Sydney	1985-86
C.Sharma	India v New Zealand	Nagpur	1987-88
Wasim Akram	Pakistan v West Indies	Sharjah	1989-90
Wasim Akram	Pakistan v Australia	Sharjah	1989-90
Kapil Dev	India v Sri Lanka	Calcutta	1990-91
Aqib Javed	Pakistan v India	Sharjah	1991-92
D.K.Morrison	New Zealand v India	Napier	1993-94
Waqar Younis	Pakistan v New Zealand	East London	1994-95
Saqlain Mushtaq	Pakistan v Zimbabwe	Peshawar	1996-97
E.A.Brandes	Zimbabwe v England	Harare	1996-97
A.M.Stuart	Australia v Pakistan	Melbourne	1996-97
Saqlain Mushtaq	Pakistan v Zimbabwe	The Oval	1999
W.P.J.U.C.Vaas	Sri Lanka v Zimbabwe	Colombo (SSC)	2001-02
Mohammad Sami	Pakistan v West Indies	Sharjah	2001-02
W.P.J.U.C.Vaas[1]	Sri Lanka v Bangladesh	Pietermaritzburg	2002-03
B.Lee	Australia v Kenya	Durban	2002-03
J.M.Anderson	England v Pakistan	The Oval	2003
S.J.Harmison	England v India	Nottingham	2004
C.K.Langeveldt	South Africa v West Indies	Bridgetown	2004-05

Shahadat Hossain	Bangladesh v Zimbabwe	Harare	2006
J.E.Taylor	West Indies v Australia	Mumbai	2006-07
S.E.Bond	New Zealand v Australia	Hobart	2006-07
S.L.Malinga[2]	Sri Lanka v South Africa	Providence	2006-07
A.Flintoff	England v West Indies	St Lucia	2008-09
M.F.Maharoof	Sri Lanka v India	Dambulla	2010
Abdur Razzak	Bangladesh v Zimbabwe	Dhaka	2010-11
K.A.J.Roach	West Indies v Netherlands	Delhi	2010-11
S.L.Malinga	Sri Lanka v Kenya	Colombo (RPS)	2010-11
S.L.Malinga	Sri Lanka v Australia	Colombo (RPS)	2011
D.T.Christian	Australia v Sri Lanka	Melbourne	2011-12
N.L.T.C.Perera	Sri Lanka v Pakistan	Colombo (RPS)	2012
C.J.McKay	Australia v England	Cardiff	2013
Rubel Hossain	Bangladesh v New Zealand	Dhaka	2013-14
P.Utseya	Zimbabwe v South Africa	Harare	2014
Taijul Islam	Bangladesh v Zimbabwe	Dhaka	2014-15
S.T.Finn	England v Australia	Melbourne	2014-15
J.P.Duminy	South Africa v Sri Lanka	Sydney	2014-15
K.Rabada	South Africa v Bangladesh	Mirpur	2015
J.P.Faulkner	Australia v Sri Lanka	Colombo (RPS)	2016
Taskin Ahmed	Bangladesh v Sri Lanka	Dambulla	2016-17
P.W.H.de Silva	Sri Lanka v Zimbabwe	Galle	2017
Kuldeep Yadav	India v Australia	Kolkata	2017-18
D.S.K.Madushanka	Sri Lanka v Bangladesh	Dhaka	2017-18
Imran Tahir	South Africa v Zimbabwe	Bloemfontein	2018-19
T.A.Boult	New Zealand v Pakistan	Abu Dhabi	2018-19
Mohammed Shami	India v Afghanistan	Southampton	2019
T.A.Boult	New Zealand v Australia	Lord's	2019
Kuldeep Yadav	India v West Indies	Visakhapatnam	2019-20

[1] The first three balls of the match. Took four wickets in opening over (W W W 4 wide W 0).
[2] Four wickets in four balls.

WICKET-KEEPING RECORDS
150 DISMISSALS IN A CAREER

Total			*LOI*	*Ct*	*St*
482†‡	K.C.Sangakkara	Sri Lanka/Asia/ICC	360	384	98
472‡	A.C.Gilchrist	Australia/ICC	287	417	55
444	M.S.Dhoni	India/Asia	350	321	123
424	M.V.Boucher	South Africa/Africa	295	402	22
287‡	Moin Khan	Pakistan	219	214	73
242†‡	B.B.McCullum	New Zealand	185	227	15
241	Mushfiqur Rahim	Bangladesh	230	192	49
233	I.A.Healy	Australia	168	194	39
220‡	Rashid Latif	Pakistan	166	182	38
213	J.C.Buttler	England	148	181	32
206‡	R.S.Kaluwitharana	Sri Lanka	187	131	75
204‡	P.J.L.Dujon	West Indies	169	183	21
189	R.D.Jacobs	West Indies	147	160	29
188	D.Ramdin	West Indies	139	181	7
187	Kamran Akmal	Pakistan	154	156	31
184	Q.de Kock	South Africa	127	173	11
181	B.J.Haddin	Australia	126	170	11
165	D.J.Richardson	South Africa	122	148	17
165†‡	A.Flower	Zimbabwe	213	133	32
163†‡	A.J.Stewart	England	170	148	15
154‡	N.R.Mongia	India	140	110	44

† *Excluding catches taken in the field.* ‡ *Excluding matches when not wicket-keeper.*
The most for Ireland is 96 by N.J.O'Brien (103 matches) and for Afghanistan 88 by Mohammad Shahzad (84).

SIX DISMISSALS IN AN INNINGS

6	(6ct)	A.C.Gilchrist	Australia v South Africa	Cape Town	1999-00
6	(6ct)	A.J.Stewart	England v Zimbabwe	Manchester	2000
6	(5ct/1st)	R.D.Jacobs	West Indies v Sri Lanka	Colombo (RPS)	2001-02
6	(5ct/1st)	A.C.Gilchrist	Australia v England	Sydney	2002-03
6	(6ct)	A.C.Gilchrist	Australia v Namibia	Potchefstroom	2002-03
6	(6ct)	A.C.Gilchrist	Australia v Sri Lanka	Colombo (RPS)	2003-04
6	(6ct)	M.V.Boucher	South Africa v Pakistan	Cape Town	2006-07
6	(5ct/1st)	M.S.Dhoni	India v England	Leeds	2007
6	(6ct)	A.C.Gilchrist	Australia v India	Baroda	2007-08
6	(5ct/1st)	A.C.Gilchrist	Australia v India	Sydney	2007-08
6	(6ct)	M.J.Prior	England v South Africa	Nottingham	2008
6	(6ct)	J.C.Buttler	England v South Africa	The Oval	2013
6	(6ct)	M.H.Cross	Scotland v Canada	Christchurch	2013-14
6	(5ct/1st)	Q.de Kock	South Africa v New Zealand	Mt Maunganui	2014-15
6	(6ct)	Sarfraz Ahmed	Pakistan v South Africa	Auckland	2014-15

FIELDING RECORDS
100 CATCHES IN A CAREER

Total			*LOI*	*Total*			*LOI*
218	D.P.M.D.Jayawardena	Sri Lanka/Asia	448	120	B.C.Lara	West Indies/ICC	299
160	R.T.Ponting	Australia/ICC	375	118	T.M.Dilshan	Sri Lanka	330
156	M.Azharuddin	India	334	113	Inzamam-ul-Haq	Pakistan/Asia	378
140	S.R.Tendulkar	India	463	111	S.R.Waugh	Australia	325
139	L.R.P.L.Taylor	New Zealand	233	109	R.S.Mahanama	Sri Lanka	213
137	V.Kohli	India	260	108	P.D.Collingwood	England	197
133	S.P.Fleming	New Zealand/ICC	280	108	M.E.Waugh	Australia	244
131	J.H.Kallis	South Africa/Africa/ICC	328	108	H.H.Gibbs	South Africa	248
130	Younus Khan	Pakistan	265	108	S.M.Pollock	South Africa/Africa/ICC	303
130	M.Muralitharan	Sri Lanka/Asia/ICC	350	106	M.J.Clarke	Australia	245
127	A.R.Border	Australia	273	105	M.E.K.Hussey	Australia	185
127	Shahid Afridi	Pakistan/Asia/ICC	398	105	G.C.Smith	South Africa/Africa	197
124	C.H.Gayle	West Indies/ICC	301	105	J.N.Rhodes	South Africa	245
124	R.S.Dravid	India/Asia/ICC	344	102	S.K.Raina	India	226
123	S.T.Jayasuriya	Sri Lanka/Asia	445	100	I.V.A.Richards	West Indies	187
120	C.L.Hooper	West Indies	227	100	S.C.Ganguly	India/Asia	311

The most for Zimbabwe is 86 by G.W.Flower (221), for Bangladesh 71 by Mahmudullah (203), for Ireland 68 by W.T.S.Porterfield (148), and for Afghanistan 56 by Mohammad Nabi (130).

FIVE CATCHES IN AN INNINGS

5	J.N.Rhodes	South Africa v West Indies	Bombay (BS)	1993-94

APPEARANCE RECORDS
250 MATCHES

463	S.R.Tendulkar	India	356	Wasim Akram	Pakistan
448	D.P.M.D.Jayawardena	Sri Lanka/Asia	350	M.S.Dhoni	India/Asia
445	S.T.Jayasuriya	Sri Lanka/Asia	350	M.Muralitharan	Sri Lanka/Asia/ICC
404	K.C.Sangakkara	Sri Lanka/Asia/ICC	344	R.S.Dravid	India/Asia/ICC
398	Shahid Afridi	Pakistan/Asia/ICC	334	M.Azharuddin	India
378	Inzamam-ul-Haq	Pakistan/Asia	330	T.M.Dilshan	Sri Lanka
375	R.T.Ponting	Australia/ICC	328	J.H.Kallis	South Africa/Africa/ICC

325	S.R.Waugh	Australia	273	A.R.Border	Australia
322	W.P.J.U.C.Vaas	Sri Lanka/Asia	271	A.Kumble	India/Asia
311	S.C.Ganguly	India/Asia	269	A.Ranatunga	Sri Lanka
308	P.A.de Silva	Sri Lanka	268	M.S.Atapattu	Sri Lanka
304	Yuvraj Singh	India/Asia	268	S.Chanderpaul	West Indies
303	S.M.Pollock	South Africa/Africa/ICC	265	Abdul Razzaq	Pakistan/Asia
301	C.H.Gayle	West Indies/ICC	265	Younus Khan	Pakistan
299	B.C.Lara	West Indies/ICC	262	Waqar Younis	Pakistan
295	M.V.Boucher	South Africa/Africa	260	B.B.McCullum	New Zealand
295	D.L.Vettori	New Zealand/ICC	260	V.Kohli	India
288	Mohammad Yousuf	Pakistan/Asia	251	V.Sehwag	India/Asia/ICC
287	A.C.Gilchrist	Australia/ICC	250	C.Z.Harris	New Zealand
287	Shoaib Malik	Pakistan	250	Ijaz Ahmed	Pakistan
283	Salim Malik	Pakistan	250	G.D.McGrath	Australia/ICC
280	S.P.Fleming	New Zealand/ICC			

The most for England is 223 by E.J.G.Morgan, for Zimbabwe 221 by G.W.Flower, for Bangladesh 230 by Mushfiqur Rahim, for Ireland 153 by K.J.O'Brien, and for Afghanistan 130 by Mohammad Nabi.
The most consecutive appearances is 185 by S.R.Tendulkar for India (Apr 1990-Apr 1998).

100 MATCHES AS CAPTAIN

			W	*L*	*T*	*NR*	*% Won (exc NR)*
230	R.T.Ponting	Australia/ICC	165	51	2	12	75.68
218	S.P.Fleming	New Zealand	98	106	1	13	47.80
200	M.S.Dhoni	India	110	74	5	11	58.20
193	A.Ranatunga	Sri Lanka	89	95	1	8	48.10
178	A.R.Border	Australia	107	67	1	3	61.14
174	M.Azharuddin	India	90	76	2	6	53.57
150	G.C.Smith	South Africa/Africa	92	51	1	6	63.88
147	S.C.Ganguly	India/Asia	76	66	–	5	53.52
139	Imran Khan	Pakistan	75	59	1	4	55.55
138	W.J.Cronje	South Africa	99	35	1	3	73.33
129	D.P.M.D.Jayawardena	Sri Lanka	71	49	1	8	58.67
125	B.C.Lara	West Indies	59	59	–	7	50.42
124	E.J.G.Morgan	England	74	40	2	8	63.79
118	S.T.Jayasuriya	Sri Lanka	66	47	2	3	57.39
113	W.T.S.Porterfield	Ireland	50	55	2	6	46.72
109	Wasim Akram	Pakistan	66	41	2	–	60.55
106	A.D.Mathews	Sri Lanka	49	51	1	5	48.51
106	S.R.Waugh	Australia	67	35	3	1	63.80
105	I.V.A.Richards	West Indies	67	36	–	2	65.04
103	A.B.de Villers	South Africa	59	39	1	4	59.59

The most for Zimbabwe is 86 by A.D.R.Campbell, for Bangladesh 88 by Mashrafe Mortaza, and for Afghanistan 59 by Asghar Afghan.

150 LOI UMPIRING APPEARANCES

211	Alim Dar	Pakistan	16.02.2000	to	03.11.2020
209	R.E.Koertzen	South Africa	09.12.1992	to	09.06.2010
200	B.F.Bowden	New Zealand	23.03.1995	to	06.02.2016
181	S.A.Bucknor	West Indies	18.03.1989	to	29.03.2009
174	D.J.Harper	Australia	14.01.1994	to	19.03.2011
174	S.J.A.Taufel	Australia	13.01.1999	to	02.09.2012
172	D.R.Shepherd	England	09.06.1983	to	12.07.2005
154	R.B.Tiffin	Zimbabwe	25.10.1992	to	22.07.2018

ICC MEN'S T20 WORLD CUP 2021-22

The seventh ICC Men's T20 World Cup was held in Oman and the UAE between 17 October and 14 November.

GROUP ONE

	Team	*P*	*W*	*L*	*T*	*NR*	*Pts*	*Net RR*
1	England	5	4	1	–	–	8	+2.46
2	Australia	5	4	1	–	–	8	+1.21
3	South Africa	5	4	1	–	–	8	+0.73
4	Sri Lanka	5	2	3	–	–	4	–0.26
5	West Indies	5	1	4	–	–	2	–1.64
6	Bangladesh	5	–	5	–	–	0	–2.38

GROUP TWO

	Team	*P*	*W*	*L*	*T*	*NR*	*Pts*	*Net RR*
1	Pakistan	5	5	–	–	–	10	+1.58
2	New Zealand	5	4	1	–	–	8	+1.16
3	India	5	3	2	–	–	6	+1.74
4	Afghanistan	5	2	3	–	–	4	+1.05
5	Namibia	5	1	4	–	–	2	–1.89
6	Scotland	5	–	5	–	–	0	–3.54

England's Group Stage games:

Dubai International Cricket Stadium, 23 October. Toss: England. **ENGLAND** won by six wickets. West Indies 55 (14.2; A.U.Rashid 4-2). England 56-4 (8.2). Award: M.M.Ali.

Zayed Cricket Stadium, Abu Dhabi, 27 October. Toss: Bangladesh. **ENGLAND** won by eight wickets. Bangladesh 124-9 (20; T.S.Mills 3-27). England 126-2 (14.1; J.J.Roy 61). Award: J.J.Roy.

Dubai International Cricket Stadium, 30 October. Toss: England. **ENGLAND** won by eight wickets. Australia 125 (20; A.J.Finch 44, C.J.Jordan 3-17). England 126-2 (11.4; J.C.Buttler 71*). Award: C.J.Jordan.

Sharjah Cricket Stadium, 1 November. Toss: Sri Lanka. **ENGLAND** won by 26 runs. England 163-4 (20; J.C.Buttler 101*, E.J.G.Morgan 40, P.W.H.de Silva 3-21). Sri Lanka 137 (19). Award: J.C.Buttler.

Sharjah Cricket Stadium, 6 November. Toss: England. **SOUTH AFRICA** won by 10 runs. South Africa 189-2 (20; H.E.van der Dussen 94*, A.K.Markram 52*). England 179-8 (20; M.M.Ali 37, K.Rabada 3-48). Award: H.E.van der Dussen.

Semi-finals

Zayed Cricket Stadium, Abu Dhabi, 10 November. Toss: New Zealand. **NEW ZEALAND** won by five wickets. England 166-4 (20; M.M.Ali 51*, D.J.Malan 41). New Zealand 167-5 (19; D.J.Mitchell 72*, D.P.Conway 46). Award: D.J.Mitchell.

Dubai International Cricket Stadium, 11 November. Toss: Australia. **AUSTRALIA** won by five wickets. Pakistan 176-4 (20; Mohammad Rizwan 67, Fakhar Zaman 55*). Australia 177-5 (19; D.A.Warner 49, M.S.Wade 41*, M.P.Stoinis 40*, Shadab Khan 4-26). Award: M.S.Wade.

FINAL

Dubai International Cricket Stadium, 14 November. Toss: Australia. **AUSTRALIA** won by eight wickets. New Zealand 172-4 (20; K.S.Williamson 85, J.R.Hazlewood 3-16). Australia 173-2 (18.5; M.R.Marsh 77*, D.A.Warner 53). Award: M.R.Marsh. Series award: D.A.Warner.

Statistical Highlights in ICC Men's T20 World Cup 2021-22

Highest total	210-2	India v Afghanistan		Abu Dhabi
Biggest victory (runs)	130	Afghanistan v Scotland		Sharjah
Biggest victory (wkts)	10	Oman beat PNG		Al Amerat
	10	Pakistan beat India		Dubai
Biggest victory (balls)	82	Australia beat Bangladesh		Dubai
Most runs	303 (ave 60.60)	Babar Azam (Pakistan)		
Highest innings	101*	J.C.Buttler	England v Sri Lanka	Sharjah
Most sixes (inns)	7	M.J.Guptill	New Zealand v Scotland	Dubai
Highest partnership	152	Moh'd Rizwan/Babar Azam	Pakistan v India	Dubai
Most wickets	16 (ave 9.75)	P.W.H.de Silva (Sri Lanka)		
Best bowling	5-19	A.Zampa	Australia v Bangladesh	Dubai
Most expensive	4-0-60-0	M.A.Starc	Australia v New Zealand	Dubai
Most w/k dismissals	9	M.S.Wade (Australia)		
Most w/k dismissals (inns)	4	M.H.Cross	Scotland v PNG	Al Amerat
Most catches	8	C.S.MacLeod (Scotland)		
	8	S.P.D.Smith (Australia)		

PREVIOUS WINNERS

Season	*Hosts*	*Winners*
2007-08	South Africa	India
2009	England	Pakistan
2010	West Indies	England
2012-13	Sri Lanka	West Indies
2013-14	Bangladesh	Sri Lanka
2015-16	India	West Indies

ENGLAND TWENTY20 INTERNATIONALS CAREER RECORDS

These records, complete to 7 April 2022, include all players registered for county cricket for the 2022 season at the time of going to press.

BATTING AND FIELDING

	M	*I*	*NO*	*HS*	*Runs*	*Avge*	*100*	*50*	*Ct/St*
M.M.Ali	49	44	10	72*	637	18.73	–	4	13
J.M.Anderson	19	4	3	1*	1	1.00	–	–	3
J.C.Archer	12	2	1	18*	19	19.00	–	–	4
J.M.Bairstow	63	57	12	86*	1190	26.44	–	7	44/1
J.T.Ball	2	–	–	–	–	–	–	–	1
T.Banton	14	14	–	73	327	23.35	–	2	9
S.W.Billings†	36	32	5	87	474	17.55	–	2	17/2
R.S.Bopara	38	35	10	65*	711	28.44	–	3	7
S.G.Borthwick	1	1	–	14	14	14.00	–	–	1
D.R.Briggs	7	1	1	0*	0	–	–	–	1
S.C.J.Broad	56	26	10	18*	118	7.37	–	–	21
H.C.Brook	1	1	–	10	10	10.00	–	–	–
P.R.Brown	4	1	1	4*	4	–	–	–	2
J.C.Buttler	88	80	18	101*	2140	34.51	1	15	39/10
A.N.Cook	4	4	–	26	61	15.25	–	–	1
M.S.Crane	2	–	–	–	–	–	–	–	–
S.M.Curran	16	10	5	24	91	18.20	–	–	–
T.K.Curran	30	13	7	14*	64	10.66	–	–	8
S.M.Davies	5	5	–	33	102	20.40	–	–	2/1
L.A.Dawson	8	4	1	10	23	7.66	–	–	2
J.L.Denly	13	12	2	30	125	12.50	–	–	4
B.M.Duckett	1	1	–	9	9	9.00	–	–	–
S.T.Finn	21	3	3	8*	14	–	–	–	6
B.T.Foakes	1	–	–	–	–	–	–	–	1
G.H.S.Garton	1	1	–	2	2	2.00	–	–	–
L.Gregory	9	7	1	15	45	7.50	–	–	–
A.D.Hales	60	60	7	116*	1664	31.01	1	8	32
C.J.Jordan	75	43	19	36	358	14.91	–	–	40
L.S.Livingstone	17	13	1	103	285	23.75	1	–	8
S.Mahmood	12	7	4	7*	22	7.33	–	–	2
D.J.Malan	36	35	5	103*	1239	41.30	1	11	14
T.S.Mills†	11	3	2	1*	1	1.00	–	–	1
E.J.G.Morgan	115	107	21	91	2458	28.58	–	14	46
M.W.Parkinson	4	2	–	5	5	2.50	–	–	–
S.D.Parry	5	1	–	1	1	1.00	–	–	2
S.R.Patel	18	14	2	67	189	15.75	–	1	3
A.U.Rashid	73	26	14	22	85	7.08	–	–	17
J.E.Root	32	30	5	90*	893	35.72	–	5	18
J.J.Roy	58	58	1	78	1446	25.36	–	8	15
P.D.Salt	3	3	–	57	60	20.00	–	1	2
B.A.Stokes	34	28	6	47*	442	20.09	–	–	15
R.J.W.Topley	10	3	3	2*	2	–	–	–	1
J.M.Vince	17	17	–	59	463	27.23	–	2	7
D.J.Willey	32	21	8	29*	182	14.00	–	–	15
C.R.Woakes	16	8	4	37	98	24.50	–	–	5
M.A.Wood	19	3	3	5*	11	–	–	–	–
L.J.Wright	51	45	5	99*	759	18.97	–	4	14

BOWLING

	O	M	R	W	Avge	Best	4wI	R/Over
M.M.Ali	108.1	1	854	33	25.87	3-24	–	7.89
J.M.Anderson	70.2	1	552	18	30.66	3-23	–	7.84
J.C.Archer	47	0	371	14	26.50	4-33	1	7.89
J.T.Ball	7	0	83	2	41.50	1-39	–	11.85
R.S.Bopara	53.4	1	387	16	24.18	4-10	1	7.21
S.G.Borthwick	4	0	15	1	15.00	1-15	–	3.75
D.R.Briggs	18	0	199	5	39.80	2-25	–	11.05
S.C.J.Broad	195.3	2	1491	65	22.93	4-24	1	7.62
P.R.Brown	13	0	128	3	42.66	1-29	–	9.84
M.S.Crane	8	0	62	1	62.00	1-38	–	7.75
S.M.Curran	46	0	365	16	22.81	3-28	–	7.93
T.K.Curran	98	1	907	29	31.27	4-36	1	9.25
L.A.Dawson	25	0	177	5	35.40	3-27	–	7.08
J.L.Denly	12	0	93	7	13.28	4-19	1	7.75
S.T.Finn	80	0	583	27	21.59	3-16	–	7.28
G.H.S.Garton	4	0	57	1	57.00	1-57	–	14.25
L.Gregory	13	0	117	2	58.50	1-10	–	9.00
C.J.Jordan	259.5	2	2250	80	28.12	4- 6	2	8.65
L.S.Livingstone	33	0	235	12	19.58	2-15	–	7.12
S.Mahmood	38	0	398	7	56.85	3-33	–	10.47
D.J.Malan	2	0	27	1	27.00	1-27	–	13.50
T.S.Mills	41.4	1	339	11	30.81	3-27	–	8.13
M.W.Parkinson	14	0	133	6	22.16	4-47	1	9.50
S.D.Parry	16	0	138	3	46.00	2-33	–	8.62
S.R.Patel	42	0	321	7	45.85	2- 6	–	7.64
A.U.Rashid	253.2	3	1840	81	22.71	4- 2	2	7.26
J.E.Root	14	0	139	6	23.16	2- 9	–	9.92
B.A.Stokes	81.4	1	717	19	37.73	3-26	–	8.77
R.J.W.Topley	33.1	0	285	8	35.62	3-24	–	8.59
D.J.Willey	106.5	0	854	38	22.47	4- 7	1	7.99
C.R.Woakes	54.3	1	427	15	28.64	2-23	–	7.83
M.A.Wood	71.3	1	621	26	23.88	3- 9	–	8.68
L.J.Wright	55	0	465	18	25.83	2-24	–	8.45

† S.W.Billings and T.S.Mills also played one game for an ICC World XI v West Indies at Lord's in 2018.

INTERNATIONAL TWENTY20 RECORDS

From 1 January 2019, the ICC granted official IT20 status to all 20-over matches between its 105 members. As a result, there has been a vast increase in the number of games played, many featuring very minor nations. In the records that follow, except for the first-ranked record, only those IT20s featuring a nation that has also played a full LOI are listed.

MATCH RESULTS

2004-05 to 16 March 2022

	Opponents	*Matches*	*Won*													*Tied*	*NR*
			E	*A*	*SA*	*WI*	*NZ*	*I*	*P*	*SL*	*Z*	*B*	*Ire*	*Afg*	*Ass*		
England	Australia	20	9	10	–	–	–	–	–	–	–	–	–	–	–	–	1
	South Africa	22	11	–	10	–	–	–	–	–	–	–	–	–	–	–	1
	West Indies	24	10	–	–	14	–	–	–	–	–	–	–	–	–	–	–
	New Zealand	22	12	–	–	–	8	–	–	–	–	–	–	–	–	1	1
	India	19	9	–	–	–	–	10	–	–	–	–	–	–	–	–	–
	Pakistan	21	13	–	–	–	–	–	6	–	–	–	–	–	–	1	1
	Sri Lanka	13	9	–	–	–	–	–	–	4	–	–	–	–	–	–	–
	Zimbabwe	1	1	–	–	–	–	–	–	–	0	–	–	–	–	–	–
	Bangladesh	1	1	–	–	–	–	–	–	–	–	0	–	–	–	–	–
	Ireland	1	0	–	–	–	–	–	–	–	–	–	0	–	–	–	1
	Afghanistan	2	2	–	–	–	–	–	–	–	–	–	–	0	–	–	–
	Associates	2	0	–	–	–	–	–	–	–	–	–	–	–	2	–	–
Australia	South Africa	22	–	14	8	–	–	–	–	–	–	–	–	–	–	–	–
	West Indies	17	–	7	–	10	–	–	–	–	–	–	–	–	–	–	–
	New Zealand	15	–	10	–	–	4	–	–	–	–	–	–	–	–	1	–
	India	23	–	9	–	–	–	13	–	–	–	–	–	–	–	–	1
	Pakistan	24	–	10	–	–	–	–	12	–	–	–	–	–	–	1	1
	Sri Lanka	22	–	12	–	–	–	–	–	9	–	–	–	–	–	1	–
	Zimbabwe	3	–	2	–	–	–	–	–	–	1	–	–	–	–	–	–
	Bangladesh	10	–	6	–	–	–	–	–	–	–	4	–	–	–	–	–
	Ireland	1	–	1	–	–	–	–	–	–	–	–	0	–	–	–	–
	Afghanistan	0	–	0	–	–	–	–	–	–	–	–	–	0	–	–	–
	Associates	1	–	1	–	–	–	–	–	–	–	–	–	–	0	–	–
S Africa	West Indies	16	–	–	10	6	–	–	–	–	–	–	–	–	–	–	–
	New Zealand	15	–	–	11	–	4	–	–	–	–	–	–	–	–	–	–
	India	15	–	–	6	–	–	9	–	–	–	–	–	–	–	–	–
	Pakistan	21	–	–	10	–	–	–	11	–	–	–	–	–	–	–	–
	Sri Lanka	17	–	–	11	–	–	–	–	5	–	–	–	–	–	1	–
	Zimbabwe	5	–	–	5	–	–	–	–	–	0	–	–	–	–	–	–
	Bangladesh	7	–	–	7	–	–	–	–	–	–	0	–	–	–	–	–
	Ireland	3	–	–	3	–	–	–	–	–	–	–	0	–	–	–	–
	Afghanistan	2	–	–	2	–	–	–	–	–	–	–	–	0	–	–	–
	Associates	2	–	–	2	–	–	–	–	–	–	–	–	–	0	–	–
W Indies	New Zealand	16	–	–	–	3	8	–	–	–	–	–	–	–	–	3	2
	India	20	–	–	–	6	–	13	–	–	–	–	–	–	–	–	1
	Pakistan	21	–	–	–	3	–	–	15	–	–	–	–	–	–	–	3
	Sri Lanka	15	–	–	–	7	–	–	–	8	–	–	–	–	–	–	–
	Zimbabwe	3	–	–	–	2	–	–	–	–	1	–	–	–	–	–	–
	Bangladesh	13	–	–	–	7	–	–	–	–	–	5	–	–	–	–	1
	Ireland	7	–	–	–	3	–	–	–	–	–	–	2	–	–	–	2
	Afghanistan	7	–	–	–	4	–	–	–	–	–	–	–	3	–	–	–
	Associates	0	–	–	–	0	–	–	–	–	–	–	–	–	0	–	–
N Zealand	India	20	–	–	–	–	9	9	–	–	–	–	–	–	–	2	–
	Pakistan	25	–	–	–	–	10	–	15	–	–	–	–	–	–	–	–
	Sri Lanka	19	–	–	–	–	10	–	–	7	–	–	–	–	–	1	1
	Zimbabwe	6	–	–	–	–	6	–	–	–	0	–	–	–	–	–	–
	Bangladesh	15	–	–	–	–	12	–	–	–	–	3	–	–	–	–	–
	Ireland	1	–	–	–	–	1	–	–	–	–	–	0	–	–	–	–
	Afghanistan	1	–	–	–	–	1	–	–	–	–	–	–	0	–	–	–
	Associates	5	–	–	–	–	5	–	–	–	–	–	–	–	0	–	–

	Opponents	Matches	Won E	A	SA	WI	NZ	I	P	SL	Z	B	Ire	Afg	Ass	Tied	NR
India	Pakistan	9	–	–	–	–	–	6	2	–	–	–	–	–	–	1	–
	Sri Lanka	25	–	–	–	–	–	17	–	7	–	–	–	–	–	–	1
	Zimbabwe	7	–	–	–	–	–	5	–	–	2	–	–	–	–	–	–
	Bangladesh	11	–	–	–	–	–	10	–	–	–	1	–	–	–	–	–
	Ireland	3	–	–	–	–	–	3	–	–	–	–	0	–	–	–	–
	Afghanistan	3	–	–	–	–	–	3	–	–	–	–	–	0	–	–	–
	Associates	4	–	–	–	–	–	3	–	–	–	–	–	–	0	–	1
Pakistan	Sri Lanka	21	–	–	–	–	–	–	13	8	–	–	–	–	–	–	–
	Zimbabwe	17	–	–	–	–	–	–	16	–	1	–	–	–	–	–	–
	Bangladesh	15	–	–	–	–	–	–	13	–	–	2	–	–	–	–	
	Ireland	1	–	–	–	–	–	–	1	–	–	–	0	–	–	–	–
	Afghanistan	2	–	–	–	–	–	–	2	–	–	–	–	0	–	–	–
	Associates	9	–	–	–	–	–	–	9	–	–	–	–	–	0	–	–
Sri Lanka	Zimbabwe	3	–	–	–	–	–	–	–	3	0	–	–	–	–	–	–
	Bangladesh	12	–	–	–	–	–	–	–	8	–	4	–	–	–	–	–
	Ireland	2	–	–	–	–	–	–	–	2	–	–	0	–	–	–	–
	Afghanistan	1	–	–	–	–	–	–	1	–	–	–	0	–	–	–	
	Associates	6	–	–	–	–	–	–	–	6	–	–	–	–	0	–	–
Zimbabwe	Bangladesh	16	–	–	–	–	–	–	–	–	5	11	–	–	–	–	–
	Ireland	8	–	–	–	–	–	–	–	–	3	–	5	–	–	–	–
	Afghanistan	12	–	–	–	–	–	–	–	–	1	–	–	11	–	–	–
	Associates	15	–	–	–	–	–	–	–	–	10	–	–	–	3	2	–
Bangladesh	Ireland	5	–	–	–	–	–	–	–	–	–	3	1	–	–	–	1
	Afghanistan	8	–	–	–	–	–	–	–	–	–	3	–	5	–	–	–
	Associates	12	–	–	–	–	–	–	–	–	–	8	–	–	4	–	–
Ireland	Afghanistan	18	–	–	–	–	–	–	–	–	–	–	3	14	–	1	–
	Associates	72	–	–	–	–	–	–	–	–	–	–	41	–	27	1	3
Afghanistan	Associates	35	–	–	–	–	–	–	–	–	–	–	–	28	7	–	–
Associates	Associates	558	–	–	–	–	–	–	–	–	–	–	–	–	543	3	12
		1493	77	82	85	65	78	101	115	68	24	44	52	61	586	20	35

MATCH RESULTS SUMMARY

	Matches	Won	Lost	Tied	NR	% Won (ex NR)
Afghanistan	91	61	29	1	0	67.03
India	159	101	51	3	4	65.16
Pakistan	186	115	63	3	5	63.53
South Africa	147	85	60	1	1	58.21
England	148	77	64	2	5	53.84
Australia	158	82	70	3	3	52.90
New Zealand	160	78	70	8	4	50.00
Ireland	122	52	61	2	7	45.21
Sri Lanka	156	68	83	3	2	44.15
West Indies	159	65	82	3	9	43.33
Bangladesh	125	44	79	0	2	35.77
Associates (v Full)	163	43	113	3	4	27.04
Zimbabwe	96	24	70	2	0	25.00

Results of games between two Associate Members and Pakistan's three IT20s v a World XI in 2017 (W2, L1) and West Indies' IT20 v an ICC World XI in 2018 (W1) are excluded from these figures.

INTERNATIONAL TWENTY20 RECORDS

(To 16 March 2022)

TEAM RECORDS

HIGHEST INNINGS TOTALS

† Batting Second

278-3	Afghanistan v Ireland	Dehradun	2018-19
263-3	Australia v Sri Lanka	Pallekele	2016
260-6	Sri Lanka v Kenya	Johannesburg	2007-08
260-5	India v Sri Lanka	Indore	2017-18
252-3	Scotland v Netherlands	Dublin	2019
248-6	Australia v England	Southampton	2013
245-6	West Indies v India	Lauderhill	2016
245-5†	Australia v New Zealand	Auckland	2017-18
245-1	Canada v Panama	Coolidge	2021-22
244-4†	India v West Indies	Lauderhill	2016
243-5	New Zealand v West Indies	Mt Maunganui	2017-18
243-6	New Zealand v Australia	Auckland	2017-18
241-6	South Africa v England	Centurion	2009-10
241-3	England v New Zealand	Napier	2019-20
240-3	Namibia v Botswana	Windhoek	2019
240-3	India v West Indies	Mumbai	2019-20
238-3	New Zealand v West Indies	Mt Maunganui	2020-21
238-3	Nepal v Netherlands	Kirtipur	2021
236-6†	West Indies v South Africa	Johannesburg	2014-15
236-3	Nepal v Bhutan	Kirtipur	2019-20
234-3	Canada v Belize	Coolidge	2021-22
233-8	Afghanistan v Ireland	Greater Noida	2016-17
233-2	Australia v Sri Lanka	Adelaide	2019-20
232-6	Pakistan v England	Nottingham	2021
231-7	South Africa v West Indies	Johannesburg	2014-15
230-8†	England v South Africa	Mumbai	2015-16
229-4	South Africa v England	Mumbai	2015-16
229-2	Australia v Zimbabwe	Harare	2018
226-5†	England v South Africa	Centurion	2019-20
225-7	Ireland v Afghanistan	Abu Dhabi	2013-14

The highest total for Zimbabwe is 200-2 (v New Zealand, Hamilton, 2011-12) and for Bangladesh is 215-5 (v Sri Lanka, Colombo (RPS), 2017-18).

LOWEST COMPLETED INNINGS TOTALS

† Batting Second

21†	(8.3)	Turkey v Czech Republic	Ilfov County	2019
36	(15.2)	Philippines v Oman	Al Amerat	2021-22
37†	(17.2)	Panama v Canada	Coolidge	2021-22
39	(10.3)	Netherlands v Sri Lanka	Chittagong	2013-14
44	(10.0)	Netherlands v Sri Lanka	Sharjah	2021-22
45†	(11.5)	West Indies v England	Basseterre	2018-19
46	(12.1)	Botswana v Namibia	Kampala	2019
53	(14.3)	Nepal v Ireland	Belfast	2015
55	(14.2)	West Indies v England	Dubai (DSC)	2021-22
56†	(18.4)	Kenya v Afghanistan	Sharjah	2013-14
60†	(15.3)	New Zealand v Sri Lanka	Chittagong	2013-14
60†	(13.4)	West Indies v Pakistan	Karachi	2017-18
60	(16.5)	New Zealand v Bangladesh	Mirpur	2021
60†	(10.2)	Scotland v Afghanistan	Sharjah	2021-22
61-8		Iran v UAE	Al Amerat	2019-20
62†	(13.4)	Australia v Bangladesh	Mirpur	2021
64	(11.0)	Nepal v Oman	Al Amerat	2019-20

66-9		Cayman Islands v USA	Sandys Parish	2019
66-9		Nigeria v Ireland	Abu Dhabi	2019-20
66		Thailand v Nepal	Bangkok	2019-20
67	(17.2)	Kenya v Ireland	Belfast	2008
68†	(16.4)	Ireland v West Indies	Providence	2009-10
68-8		Cayman Islands v USA	Hamilton, Ber	2019
68†	(15.2)	Bahamas v Canada	North Sound	2021-22
69†	(17.0)	Hong Kong v Nepal	Chittagong	2013-14
69†	(17.4)	Nepal v Netherlands	Amstelveen	2015
70		Bermuda v Canada	Belfast	2008
70†	(15.4)	Bangladesh v New Zealand	Kolkata	2015-16
70†	(12.3)	Ireland v India	Dublin	2018

The lowest total for England is 80 (v India, Colombo (RPS), 2012-13.

LARGEST RUNS MARGIN OF VICTORY

257 runs	Czech Republic beat Turkey	Ilfov County	2019
208 runs	Canada beat Panama	Coolidge	2021-22
172 runs	Sri Lanka beat Kenya	Johannesburg	2007
145 runs	Canada beat Belize	Coolidge	2021-22
143 runs	Pakistan beat West Indies	Karachi	2017-18
143 runs	India beat Ireland	Dublin	2018
142 runs	Nepal beat Netherlands	Kirtipur	2021
141 runs	Nepal beat Bhutan	Kirtipur	2019-20
137 runs	England beat West Indies	Basseterre	2018-19

There have been 31 victories by ten wickets, with Austria beating Turkey by a record margin of 104 balls remaining (Ilfov County, 2019).

BATTING RECORDS – 1700 RUNS IN A CAREER

Runs			*M*	*I*	*NO*	*HS*	*Avge*	*50*	*R/100B*
3313	R.G.Sharma	I	125	117	15	118	32.48	30	139.5
3299	M.J.Guptill	NZ	112	108	7	105	32.66	22	136.7
3296	V.Kohli	I	97	89	25	94*	51.50	30	137.6
2776	P.R.Stirling	Ire	102	101	8	115*	29.84	21	134.6
2686	A.J.Finch	A	88	88	10	172	34.43	17	145.4
2620	Babar Azam	P	73	68	10	122	45.17	26	129.1
2554	D.A.Warner	A	88	88	10	100*	32.74	22	140.4
2514	Mohammad Hafeez	P	119	108	13	99*	26.46	14	122.0
2458	E.J.G.Morgan	E	115	107	21	91	28.58	14	136.1
2435	Shoaib Malik	P/ICC	124	111	33	75	31.21	9	125.6
2140	B.B.McCullum	NZ	71	70	10	123	35.66	15	136.2
2140	J.C.Buttler	E	88	80	18	101*	34.51	16	141.1
2021	K.S.Williamson	NZ	74	72	10	95	32.59	14	123.9
2015	Mohammad Shahzad	Afg	70	70	3	118*	30.07	13	133.6
2002	Mahmudullah	B	115	107	23	64*	23.83	6	118.2
1982	G.J.Maxwell	A	84	77	13	145*	30.96	12	154.0
1973	K.J.O'Brien	Ire	110	103	10	124	21.21	6	130.9
1934	J.P.Duminy	SA	81	75	25	96*	38.68	11	126.2
1909	L.R.P.L.Taylor	NZ	102	94	21	63	26.15	7	122.3
1908	Shakib Al Hasan	B	96	95	10	84	22.44	9	119.7
1899	C.H.Gayle	WI	79	75	7	117	27.92	16	137.5
1889	T.M.Dilshan	SL	80	79	12	104*	28.19	14	120.5
1831	K.L.Rahul	I	56	52	7	110*	40.68	18	142.4
1827	Q.de Kock	SA	61	61	7	79*	33.83	11	135.0
1786	D.A.Miller	SA/Wd	95	83	27	101*	31.89	5	140.6
1759	S.Dhawan	I	68	66	3	92	27.92	11	126.3
1758	Tamim Iqbal	B/Wd	78	78	5	103*	24.08	8	116.9
1724	C.Munro	NZ	65	62	7	109*	31.34	14	156.4

HIGHEST INDIVIDUAL INNINGS

Score	*Balls*				
172	76	A.J.Finch	A v Z	Harare	2018
162*	62	Hazratullah Zazai	Afg v Ire	Dehradun	2018-19
156	63	A.J.Finch	A v E	Southampton	2013
145*	65	G.J.Maxwell	A v SL	Pallekele	2016
133*	73	M.P.O'Dowd	Neth v Malay	Kirtipur	2021
127*	56	H.G.Munsey	Scot v Neth	Dublin	2019
125*	62	E.Lewis	WI v I	Kingston	2017
124*	71	S.R.Watson	A v I	Sydney	2015-16
124	62	K.J.O'Brien	Ire v HK	Al Amerat	2019-20
123	58	B.B.McCullum	NZ v B	Pallekele	2012-13
122	60	Babar Hayat	HK v Oman	Fatullah	2015-16
122	59	Babar Azam	P v SA	Centurion	2021
119	56	F.du Plessis	SA v WI	Johannesburg	2014-15
118*	67	Mohammad Shahzad	Afg v Z	Sharjah	2015-16
118	43	R.G.Sharma	I v SL	Indore	2017-18
117*	51	R.E.Levi	SA v NZ	Hamilton	2011-12
117*	68	Shaiman Anwar	UAE v PNG	Abu Dhabi	2017
117	57	C.H.Gayle	WI v SA	Johannesburg	2007-08
116*	56	B.B.McCullum	NZ v A	Christchurch	2009-10
116*	64	A.D.Hales	E v SL	Chittagong	2013-14
115*	75	P.R.Stirling	Ire v Z	Bready	2021
114*	70	M.N.van Wyk	SA v WI	Durban	2014-15
113*	55	G.J.Maxwell	A v I	Bengalaru	2018-19
112	66	Muhammad Waseem	UAE v Ire	Al Amerat	2021-22
111*	62	Ahmed Shehzad	P v B	Dhaka	2013-14
111*	61	R.G.Sharma	I v WI	Lucknow	2018-19
110*	51	K.L.Rahul	I v WI	Lauderhill	2016
109*	58	C.Munro	NZ v I	Rajkot	2017-18
108*	66	M.Spoors	Can v Phil	Al Amerat	2021-22
108	51	G.D.Phillips	NZ v WI	Mt Maunganui	2020-21
107*	60	T.P.Ura	PNG v Phil	Port Moresby	2018-19
107*	62	Muhammad Waseem	UAE v Ire	Dubai	2021-22
107*	62	R.Pathan	Can v Pan	Coolidge	2021-22
107	55	G.Malla	Nep v Bhut	Kirtipur	2019-20
107	53	R.Powell	WI v E	Bridgetown	2021-22
106*	52	P.Khadka	Nep v Sing	Singapore	2019-20
106	66	R.G.Sharma	I v SA	Dharamsala	2015-16
105	54	M.J.Guptill	NZ v A	Auckland	2017-18

The highest score for Sri Lanka is 104* by T.M.Dilshan (v A, Pallekele, 2011), for Zimbabwe 94 by S.F.Mire (v P, Harare, 2018) and for Bangladesh 103* by Tamim Iqbal (v Oman, Dharamsala, 2015-16).

MOST SIXES IN AN INNINGS

16	Hazratullah Zazai (162*)	Afg v Ire	Dehradun	2018-19
14	A.J.Finch (156)	A v E	Southampton	2013
14	H.G.Munsey (127*)	Scot v Neth	Dublin	2019
13	R.E.Levi (117*)	SA v NZ	Hamilton	2011-12
12	E.Lewis (125*)	WI v I	Kingston	2017

HIGHEST PARTNERSHIP FOR EACH WICKET

1st	236	Hazratullah Zazai/Usmann Ghani	Afg v Ire	Dehradun	2018-19
2nd	167*	J.C.Buttler/D.J.Malan	E v SA	Cape Town	2020-21
3rd	184	D.P.Conway/G.D.Phillips	NZ v WI	Mt Maunganui	2020-21
4th	166*	B.Arora/V.P.Thamotharam	Malta v Gib	Albergaria	2021
5th	119*	Shoaib Malik/Misbah-ul-Haq	P v A	Johannesburg	2007-08
6th	101*	C.L.White/M.E.K.Hussey	A v SL	Bridgetown	2009-10

7th	92	M.P.Stoinis/D.R.Sams	A v NZ	Dunedin	2020-21
8th	80	P.L.Mommsen/S.M.Sharif	Scot v Neth	Edinburgh	2015
9th	132*	Saber Zakhil/Saqlain Ali	Belg v Austria	Waterloo	2021
10th	62*	K.B.Ahir/N.Ahir	Pan v Arg	North Sound	2021-22

BOWLING RECORDS
60 WICKETS IN A CAREER

Wkts			*Matches*	*Overs*	*Mdns*	*Runs*	*Avge*	*Best*	*R/Over*
119	Shakib Al Hasan	B	96	354.3	3	2366	19.88	5-20	6.67
111	T.G.Southee	NZ	92	332.5	2	2729	24.58	5-18	8.19
107	S.L.Malinga	SL	84	299.5	1	2225	20.79	5- 6	7.42
105	Rashid Khan	Afg/IC	58	219.2	1	1357	12.92	5- 3	6.18
98	Shahid Afridi	P/Wd	99	361.2	4	2396	24.44	4-11	6.63
87	Mustafizur Rahman	B	63	225.4	6	1710	19.65	5-22	7.57
85	Umar Gul	P	60	200.3	2	1443	16.97	5- 6	7.19
85	Saeed Ajmal	P	64	238.2	2	1516	17.83	4-19	6.36
83	I.S.Sodhi	NZ	66	226.3	–	1824	21.97	4-28	8.05
81	A.U.Rashid	E	73	253.2	3	1840	22.71	4- 2	7.26
80	C.J.Jordan	E	75	259.5	2	2250	28.12	4- 6	8.65
78	D.J.Bravo	WI	91	250.5	–	2036	26.10	4-19	8.11
76	G.H.Dockrell	Ire	93	230.2	1	1642	21.60	4-20	7.12
74	Mohammad Nabi	Afg	88	287.4	5	2074	28.02	4-10	7.20
73	Shadab Khan	P	64	223.3	3	1591	21.79	4-14	7.11
70	A.Zampa	A	61	217.5	1	1478	21.11	5-19	6.78
68	Y.S.Chahal	I	54	210.3	1	1723	25.33	6-25	8.18
67	J.J.Bumrah	I	57	204.5	8	1333	19.89	3-11	6.50
66	B.A.W.Mendis	SL	39	147.3	5	952	14.42	6- 8	6.45
66	M.J.Santner	NZ	62	208.2	1	1515	22.95	4-11	7.27
66	K.M.D.N.Kulasekara	SL	58	205.1	6	1530	23.18	4-31	7.45
65	S.C.J.Broad	E	56	195.3	2	1491	22.93	4-24	7.62
64	D.W.Steyn	SA	47	169.1	3	1175	18.35	4- 9	6.94
63	Imran Tahir	SA/Wd	38	140.5	–	948	15.04	5-23	6.73
63	Bilal Khan	Oman	46	162.1	6	1040	16.50	4-19	6.41
62	S.Lamichhane	Nep/Wd	34	126.5	3	802	12.93	4-20	6.32
62	T.A.Boult	NZ	44	165.3	1	1345	21.69	4-34	8.12
61	R.Ashwin	I	51	191.0	2	1298	21.27	4- 8	6.79
61	Mohammad Hafeez	P	119	210.1	3	1388	22.75	4-10	6.60
61	S.M.Sharif	Scot	53	181.1	–	1470	24.09	4-24	8.11
60	Rohan Mustafa	UAE	54	173.2	3	1178	19.63	4-18	6.79
60	Hasan Ali	P	48	163.1	5	1359	22.65	4-18	8.32
60	M.A.Starc	A	50	189.0	1	1432	23.86	3-11	7.57

The most wickets for Zimbabwe is 35 by A.G.Cremer (29 matches).

BEST FIGURES IN AN INNINGS

6- 5	P.Aho	Nig v S Leone	Lagos	2021-22
6- 7	D.L.Chahar	I v B	Nagpur	2019-20
6- 8	B.A.W.Mendis	SL v Z	Hambantota	2012-13
6-16	B.A.W.Mendis	SL v A	Pallekele	2011
6-24	J.N.Frylinck	Nam v UAE	Dubai	2021-22
6-25	Y.S.Chahal	I v E	Bangalore	2016-17
6-30	A.C.Agar	A v NZ	Wellington	2020-21
5- 3	H.M.R.K.B.Herath	SL v NZ	Chittagong	2013-14
5- 3	Rashid Khan	Afg v Ire	Greater Noida	2016-17
5- 4	Khizar Hayat	Malay v HK	Kuala Lumpur	2019-20
5- 6	Umar Gul	P v NZ	The Oval	2009
5- 6	Umar Gul	P v SA	Centurion	2012-13
5- 6	S.L.Malinga	SL v NZ	Pallekele	2019
5- 9	C.Viljoen	Nam v Bots	Kampala	2019

5-11	Karim Janat	Afg v WI	Lucknow	2019-20
5-12	Vraj Patel	Ken v Nig	Kigali	2021-22
5-13	Elias Sunny	B v Ire	Belfast	2012
5-13	Samiullah Shenwari	Afg v Ken	Sharjah	2013-14
5-14	Imad Wasim	P v WI	Dubai	2016-17
5-15	K.M.A.Paul	WI v B	Dhaka	2018-19
5-15	D.Ravu	PNG v Vanu	Apia	2019
5-15	Aamir Kaleem	Oman v Nep	Al Amerat	2019-20
5-16	Haroon Arshad	HK v Nep	Bangkok	2019-20
5-16	D.Heyliger	Can v Arg	North Sound	2021-22
5-17	N.Vanua	PNG v Vanu	Apia	2019
5-17	D.Pretorius	SA v P	Lahore	2020-21
5-18	T.G.Southee	NZ v P	Auckland	2010-11
5-18	A.C.Douglas	Ber v Cay Is	Sandys Parish	2019

The best figures for England are 4-2 by A.U.Rashid (v WI, Dubai, 2021-22), for Zimbabwe 4-18 by L.M.Jongwe (v P, Harare, 2021), and for Ireland 4-11 by A.R.Cusack (v WI, Kingston, 2013-14).

HAT-TRICKS (excluding minor nations)

B.Lee	Australia v Bangladesh	Melbourne	2007-08
J.D.P.Oram	New Zealand v Sri Lanka	Colombo (RPS)	2009
T.G.Southee	New Zealand v Pakistan	Auckland	2010-11
N.L.T.C.Perera	Sri Lanka v India	Ranchi	2015-16
S.L.Malinga	Sri Lanka v Bangladesh	Colombo (RPS)	2016-17
Faheem Ashraf	Pakistan v Sri Lanka	Abu Dhabi	2017-18
Rashid Khan†	Afghanistan v Ireland	Dehradun	2018-19
S.L.Malinga†	Sri Lanka v New Zealand	Pallekele	2019
Mohammad Hasnain	Pakistan v Sri Lanka	Lahore	2019-20
Khawar Ali	Oman v Netherlands	Al Amerat	2019-20
N.Vanua	PNG v Bermuda	Dubai	2019-20
D.L.Chahar	India v Bangladesh	Nagpur	2019-20
A.C.Agar	Australia v South Africa	Johannesburg	2019-20
M.K.P.A.D.Perera	Sri Lanka v West Indies	Antigua	2020-21
N.T.Ellis	Australia v Bangladesh	Dhaka	2021
E.Otieno	Kenya v Uganda	Entebbe	2021
C.Campher	Ireland v Netherlands	Abu Dhabi	2021-22
P.W.H.de Silva	Sri Lanka v South Africa	Sharjah	2021-22
K.Rabada	South Africa v England	Sharjah	2021-22
J.O.Holder	West Indies v England	Bridgetown	2021-22

† Four wickets in four balls.

WICKET-KEEPING RECORDS – 34 DISMISSALS IN A CAREER

Dis			*Matches*	*Ct*	*St*
91	M.S.Dhoni	India	98	57	34
64	Q.de Kock	South Africa	61	49	15
63	D.Ramdin	West Indies	71	43	20
61	Mushfiqur Rahim	Bangladesh	100	32	29
60	Kamran Akmal	Pakistan	58	28	32
58	Mohammad Shahzad	Afghanistan	70	30	28
47	J.C.Buttler	England	88	37	10
46	Sarfraz Ahmed	Pakistan	61	36	10
45	M.H.Cross	Scotland	56	31	14
45	K.C.Sangakkara	Sri Lanka	56	25	20
42	M.S.Wade	Australia	60	38	4

MOST DISMISSALS IN AN INNINGS

5 (3 ct, 2 st)	Mohammad Shahzad	Afghanistan v Oman	Abu Dhabi	2015-16
5 (5 ct)	M.S.Dhoni	India v England	Bristol	2018
5 (2 ct, 3 st)	I.A.Karim	Kenya v Ghana	Kampala	2019

5 (5 ct)	K.Doriga	PNG v Vanuatu	Apia	2019
5 (5 ct)	I.A.Karim	Kenya v Uganda	Kigali	2021-22

FIELDING RECORDS – 40 CATCHES IN A CAREER

Total			*Matches*	*Total*			*Matches*
69	D.A.Miller	South Africa/Wd	95	45	G.H.Dockrell	Ireland	93
64	M.J.Guptill	New Zealand	112	44†	A.B.de Villiers	South Africa	78
50	Shoaib Malik	Pakistan/ICC	124	44	D.J.Bravo	West Indies	91
50	R.G.Sharma	India	125	43	V.Kohli	India	97
49	Mohammad Nabi	Afghanistan	88	43	Mahmudullah	Bangladesh	115
47	D.A.Warner	Australia	88	42	S.K.Raina	India	78
47	T.G.Southee	New Zealand	92	42	K.A.Pollard	West Indies	101
46	L.R.P.L.Taylor	New Zealand	102	40	C.J.Jordan	England	75
46	E.J.G.Morgan	England	115	40	K.J.O'Brien	Ireland	110

† *Excluding catches taken as a wicket-keeper.*

MOST CATCHES IN AN INNINGS

4	D.J.G.Sammy	West Indies v Ireland	Providence	2009-10
4	P.W.Borren	Netherlands v Bangladesh	The Hague	2012
4	C.J.Anderson	New Zealand v South Africa	Port Elizabeth	2012-13
4	L.D.Chandimal	Sri Lanka v Bangladesh	Chittagong	2013-14
4	A.M.Rahane	India v England	Birmingham	2014
4	Babar Hayat	Hong Kong v Afghanistan	Dhaka	2015-16
4	D.A.Miller	South Africa v Pakistan	Cape Town	2018-19
4	L.Siaka	PNG v Vanuatu	Apia	2019
4	C.S.MacLeod	Scotland v Ireland	Dublin	2019
4	T.H.David	Singapore v Scotland	Dubai	2019-20
4	C.de Grandhomme	New Zealand v England	Wellington	2019-20
4	P.Sarraf	Nepal v Malaysia	Bangkok	2019-20
4	M.G.Erasmus	Namibia v UAE	Dubai	2021-22

APPEARANCE RECORDS – 85 APPEARANCES

125	R.G.Sharma	India	98	M.S.Dhoni	India
124	Shoaib Malik	Pakistan/ICC	97	V.Kohli	India
119	Mohammad Hafeez	Pakistan	96	Shakib Al Hasan	Bangladesh
115	Mahmudullah	Bangladesh	95	D.A.Miller	South Africa/World
115	E.J.G.Morgan	England	93	G.H.Dockrell	Ireland
112	M.J.Guptill	New Zealand	92	T.G.Southee	New Zealand
110	K.J.O'Brien	Ireland	91	D.J.Bravo	West Indies
102	P.R.Stirling	Ireland	88	J.C.Buttler	England
102	L.R.P.L.Taylor	New Zealand	88	A.J.Finch	Australia
101	K.A.Pollard	West Indies	88	Mohammad Nabi	Afghanistan
100	Mushfiqur Rahim	Bangladesh	88	D.A.Warner	Australia
99	Shahid Afridi	Pakistan/ICC			

The most appearances for Sri Lanka is 84 by S.L.Malinga, and for Zimbabwe 66 by H.Masakadza.

50 MATCHES AS CAPTAIN

			W	*L*	*T*	*NR*	*%age wins*
72	M.S.Dhoni	India	41	28	1	2	58.57
72	E.J.G.Morgan	England	42	27	2	1	59.15
61	A.J.Finch	Australia	32	26	1	2	54.23
56	W.T.S.Porterfield	Ireland	26	26	–	4	50.00
56	K.S.Williamson	New Zealand	28	26	1	1	50.90
52	Asghar Stanikzai	Afghanistan	42	9	1	–	80.76
50	V.Kohli	India	30	16	2	2	62.50

INDIAN PREMIER LEAGUE 2021

The 14th IPL tournament was held in India and the UAE between 9 April and 15 October.

	Team	*P*	*W*	*L*	*T*	*NR*	*Pts*	*Net RR*
1	Delhi Capitals (2)	14	10	4	–	–	20	+0.48
2	Chennai Super Kings (7)	14	9	5	–	–	18	+0.45
3	Royal Challengers Bangalore (4)	14	9	5	–	–	18	–0.14
4	Kolkata Knight Riders (5)	14	7	7	–	–	14	+0.58
5	Mumbai Indians (1)	14	7	7	–	–	14	+0.11
6	Punjab Kings (6)	14	6	8	–	–	12	–0.00
7	Rajasthan Royals (8)	14	5	9	–	–	10	–0.99
8	Sunrisers Hyderabad (3)	14	3	11	–	–	6	–0.54

1st Qualifying Match: At Dubai International Cricket Stadium, 10 October (floodlit). Toss: Chennai Super Kings. **CHENNAI SUPER KINGS** won by four wickets. Delhi Capitals 172-5 (20; P.P.Shaw 60, R.R.Pant 51*. Chennai Super Kings 173-6 (19.4; R.D.Gaikwad 70, R.V.Uthappa 63, T.K.Curran 3-29). Award: R.D.Gaikwad.

Eliminator: At Sharjah Cricket Stadium, 11 October (floodlit). Toss: Royal Challengers Bangalore. **KOLKATA KNIGHT RIDERS** won by four wickets. Royal Challengers Bangalore 138-7 (20; V.Kohli 39, S.P.Narine 4-21). Kolkata Knight Riders 139-6 (19.4). Award: S.P.Narine.

2nd Qualifying Match: At Sharjah Cricket Stadium, 13 October (floodlit). Toss: Kolkata Knight Riders. **KOLKATA KNIGHT RIDERS** won by three wickets. Delhi Capitals 135-5 (20; S.Dhawan 36, S.S.Iyer 30*). Kolkata Knight Riders 136-7 (19.5; V.R.Iyer 55, S.Gill 46). Award: V.R.Iyer.

FINAL: At Dubai International Cricket Stadium, 15 October (floodlit). Toss: Kolkata Knight Riders. **CHENNAI SUPER KINGS** won by 27 runs. Chennai Super Kings 192-3 (20; F.du Plessis 86). Kolkata Knight Riders 165-9 (20; S.Gill 51, V.R.Iyer 50, S.N.Thakur 3-38). Award: F.du Plessis. Series award: H.V.Patel (RCB).

IPL winners:				
	2008	Rajasthan Royals	2009	Deccan Chargers
	2010	Chennai Super Kings	2011	Chennai Super Kings
	2012	Kolkata Knight Riders	2013	Mumbai Indians
	2014	Kolkata Knight Riders	2015	Mumbai Indians
	2016	Sunrisers Hyderabad	2017	Mumbai Indians
	2018	Chennai Super Kings	2019	Mumbai Indians
	2020	Mumbai Indians		

TEAM RECORDS

HIGHEST TOTALS

263-5 (20)	Bangalore v Pune	Bangalore	2013
248-3 (20)	Bangalore v Gujarat	Bangalore	2016

LOWEST TOTALS

49 (9.4)	Bangalore v Kolkata	Kolkata	2017
58 (15.1)	Rajasthan v Bangalore	Cape Town	2009

LARGEST MARGINS OF VICTORY

146 runs	Mumbai (212-3) beat Delhi (66)	Delhi	2017
87 balls	Mumbai (68-2) beat Kolkata (67)	Mumbai	2008

There have been 15 victories in IPL history by ten wickets.

BATTING RECORDS

MOST RUNS IN IPL

6283	V.Kohli	Bangalore	2008-21
5784	S.Dhawan	Deccan, Delhi, Mumbai, Hyderabad	2008-21

800 RUNS IN A SEASON

Runs			*Year*	*M*	*I*	*NO*	*HS*	*Ave*	*100*	*50*	*6s*	*4s*	*R/100B*
973	V.Kohli	Bangalore	2016	16	16	4	113	81.08	4	7	38	83	152.0
848	D.A.Warner	Hyderabad	2016	17	17	3	93*	60.57	–	9	31	88	151.4

HIGHEST SCORES

Runs	*Balls*				
175*	66	C.H.Gayle	Bangalore v Pune	Bangalore	2013
158*	73	B.B.McCullum	Kolkata v Bangalore	Bangalore	2008
133*	59	A.B.de Villiers	Bangalore v Mumbai	Mumbai	2015
132*	69	K.L.Rahul	Punjab v Bangalore	Dubai (DSC)	2020

K.P.Pietersen 103* (Delhi v Deccan at Delhi, 2012), B.A.Stokes 103* (Pune v Gujarat at Pune, 2017) and 107* (Rajasthan v Mumbai at Abu Dhabi, 2020), J.M.Bairstow 114 (Hyderabad v Bangalore at Hyderabad, 2019) and J.C.Buttler (Rajasthan v Hyderabad at Delhi, 2021) are the only England-qualified centurions in the IPL.

FASTEST HUNDRED

30 balls	C.H.Gayle (175*)	Bangalore v Pune	Bangalore	2013

MOST SIXES IN AN INNINGS

17	C.H.Gayle	Bangalore v Pune	Bangalore	2013

HIGHEST STRIKE RATE IN A SEASON (Qualification: 100 runs or more)

R/100B	*Runs*	*Balls*			
204.81	510	249	A.D.Russell	Kolkata	2019

HIGHEST STRIKE RATE IN AN INNINGS (Qualification: 30 runs, 350+ strike rate)

R/100B	*Runs*	*Balls*				
422.2	38*	9	C.H.Morris	Delhi v Pune	Pune	2017
387.5	31	8	A.B.de Villiers	Bangalore v Pune	Bangalore	2013
372.7	41	11	A.B.de Villiers	Bangalore v Mumbai	Bangalore	2015
369.2	48*	13	A.D.Russell	Kolkata v Bangalore	Bangalore	2019
350.0	35	10	C.H.Gayle	Bangalore v Hyderabad	Hyderabad	2015
350.0	35*	10	S.N.Khan	Bangalore v Hyderabad	Bangalore	2016

BOWLING RECORDS

MOST WICKETS IN IPL

170	S.L.Malinga	Mumbai	2009-19
167	D.J.Bravo	Chennai, Gujarat, Mumbai	2008-21

28 WICKETS IN A SEASON

Wkts			*Year*	*P*	*O*	*M*	*Runs*	*Avge*	*Best*	*4w*	*R/Over*
32	H.V.Patel	Bangalore	2021	15	56.2	–	459	14.34	5-27	2	8.14
32	D.J.Bravo	Chennai	2013	18	62.3	–	497	15.53	4-42	1	7.95
30	K.Rabada	Delhi	2020	17	65.4	1	548	18.26	4-24	2	8.34
28	S.L.Malinga	Mumbai	2011	16	63.0	2	375	13.39	5-13	1	5.95
28	J.P.Faulkner	Rajasthan	2013	16	63.1	2	427	15.25	5-16	2	6.75

BEST BOWLING FIGURES IN AN INNINGS

6-12	A.S.Joseph	Mumbai v Hyderabad	Hyderabad	2019
6-14	Sohail Tanvir	Rajasthan v Chennai	Jaipur	2008
6-19	A.Zampa	Pune v Hyderabad	Visakhapatnam	2016
5-5	A.Kumble	Bangalore v Rajasthan	Cape Town	2009

A.D.Mascarenhas 5-25 (Punjab v Pune at Mohali, 2012) is the only England-qualified bowler to take five wickets in an innings in the IPL.

MOST ECONOMICAL BOWLING ANALYSIS

O	*M*	*R*	*W*				
4	1	6	0	F.H.Edwards	Deccan v Kolkata	Cape Town	2009
4	1	6	1	A.Nehra	Delhi v Punjab	Bloemfontein	2009
4	1	6	1	Y.S.Chahal	Bangalore v Chennai	Chennai	2019

MOST EXPENSIVE BOWLING ANALYSIS

O	*M*	*R*	*W*				
4	0	70	0	Basil Thampi	Hyderabad v Bangalore	Bangalore	2018
4	0	66	0	I.Sharma	Hyderabad v Chennai	Hyderabad	2013
4	0	66	0	Mujeeb Zadran	Punjab v Hyderabad	Hyderabad	2019

BIG BASH 2021-22

The eleventh Big Bash tournament was held in Australia between 5 December and 28 January.

	Team	P	W	L	T	NR	Pts	Net RR
1	Perth Scorchers (2)	14	11	3	–	–	40	+0.92
2	Sydney Sixers (1)	14	9	4	–	1	35	+1.02
3	Sydney Thunder (3)	14	9	5	–	–	35	+0.72
4	Adelaide Strikers (5)	14	6	8	–	–	28	+0.23
5	Hobart Hurricanes (6)	14	7	7	–	–	27	–0.33
6	Melbourne Stars (7)	14	7	7	–	–	26	–0.22
7	Brisbane Heat (4)	14	3	11	–	–	16	–0.91
8	Melbourne Renegades (8)	14	3	10	–	1	16	–1.47

Knockout: At Melbourne Cricket Ground, 23 January. Toss: Adelaide Strikers. **ADELAIDE STRIKERS** won by 6 runs. Adelaide Strikers 184-6 (20; I.A.Cockbain 65). Sydney Thunder 178-6 (20; J.J.S.Sangha 61, Al.Ross 56). Award: I.A.Cockbain.

Challenger: At Sydney Cricket Ground, 26 January. Toss: Sydney Sixers. **SYDNEY SIXERS** won by four wickets. Adelaide Strikers 167-4 (20; J.W.Wells 62*, S.A.Abbott 3-27). Sydney Sixers 170-6 (20; H.Kerr 98*). Award: H.Kerr.

FINAL: At Docklands Stadium, Melbourne, 28 January. Toss: Sydney Sixers. **PERTH SCORCHERS** won by 79 runs. Perth Scorchers 171-6 (20; L.J.Evans 76*, A.J.Turner 54). Sydney Sixers 92 (16.2; D.P.Hughes 42, A.J.Tye 3-15). Award: L.J.Evans. Series award: B.R.McDermott (Hobart Hurricanes).

Big Bash winners:				
	2011-12	Sydney Sixers	2012-13	Brisbane Heat
	2013-14	Perth Scorchers	2014-15	Perth Scorchers
	2015-16	Sydney Thunder	2016-17	Perth Scorchers
	2017-18	Adelaide Strikers	2018-19	Melbourne Renegades
	2019-20	Sydney Sixers	2020-21	Sydney Sixers

TEAM RECORDS

HIGHEST TOTALS

273-2 (20)	Stars v Hurricanes	Melbourne	2021-22
232-5 (20)	Thunder v Sixers	Adelaide	2020-21

LOWEST TOTALS

57 (12.4)	Renegades v Stars	Melbourne (Dock)	2014-15
60 (10.4)	Renegades v Sixers	Hobart	2020-21

LARGEST MARGINS OF VICTORY

152 runs	Sixers (213-4) v Stars (61)	Sydney	2021-22
10 wickets	Scorchers (171-0) v Renegades (170-4)	Melbourne (Dock)	2015-16
10 wickets	Strikers (154-5) v Hurricanes (158-0)	Adelaide	2018-19
10 wickets	Stars (156-8) v Heat (158-0)	Brisbane	2018-19
10 wickets	Heat (100) v Strikers (104-0)	Adelaide	2019-20

BATTING RECORDS

MOST RUNS IN BIG BASH

3005 (av 34.54)	C.A.Lynn	Heat	2011-22
2817 (av 34.77)	A.J.Finch	Renegades	2011-22

MOST RUNS IN A SEASON

Runs			*Year*	*M*	*I*	*NO*	*HS*	*Ave*	*100*	*50*	*6s*	*4s*	*R/100B*
705	M.P.Stoinis	Stars	2019-20	17	17	4	147*	54.23	1	6	28	62	136.6

HIGHEST SCORES

Score	*Balls*				
154*	64	G.J.Maxwell	Stars v Hurricanes	Melbourne	2021-22
147*	79	M.P.Stoinis	Stars v Sixers	Melbourne	2019-20
130*	61	M.S.Wade	Hurricanes v Strikers	Adelaide	2019-20

FASTEST HUNDRED

39 balls	C.J.Simmons (102)	Scorchers v Strikers	Perth	2013-14

MOST SIXES IN AN INNINGS

11	C.H.Gayle (100*)	Thunder v Strikers	Sydney (SA)	2011-12
11	C.J.Simmons (112)	Scorchers v Sixers	Sydney	2013-14
11	C.A.Lynn (98*)	Heat v Scorchers	Perth	2016-17
11	C.A.Lynn (94)	Heat v Sixers	Sydney	2019-20

HIGHEST STRIKE RATE IN AN INNINGS (Qualification: 25 runs, 325+ strike rate)

R/100B	*Score*	*Balls*				
377.7	34	9	D.T.Christian	Heat v Hurricanes	Hobart	2014-15
333.3	30*	9	T.H.David	Hurricanes v Renegades	Melbourne (Dk)	2021-22
329.4	56	17	C.H.Gayle	Renegades v Strikers	Melbourne (Dk)	2015-16
327.2	36*	11	B.J.Rohrer	Renegades v Heat	Melbourne (Dk)	2013-14

HIGHEST PARTNERSHIPS

207	M.P.Stoinis/H.W.R.Cartwright	Stars v Sixers	Melbourne	2019-20
203	M.S.Wade/D.J.M.Short	Hurricanes v Strikers	Adelaide	2019-20

BOWLING RECORDS
MOST WICKETS IN BIG BASH

125	S.A.Abbott	Sixers, Thunder	2011-22
118	A.J.Tye	Scorchers, Thunder	2014-22

MOST WICKETS IN A SEASON

Wkts			*Year*	*P*	*O*	*M*	*Runs*	*Avge*	*Best*	*4w*	*R/Over*
30	D.R.Sams	Thunder	2019-20	17	58.5	2	461	15.36	4-34	1	7.83
30	P.M.Siddle	Strikers	2021-22	17	63.5	–	532	17.73	5-23	2	8.33

BEST BOWLING FIGURES IN AN INNINGS

6-7	S.L.Malinga	Stars v Scorchers	Perth	2012-13
6-11	I.S.Sodhi	Strikers v Thunder	Sydney (Show)	2016-17
6-17	Rashid Khan	Strikers v Heat	Brisbane	2021-22

MOST ECONOMICAL BOWLING ANALYSIS

O	*M*	*R*	*W*				
4	2	3	3	M.G.Johnson	Scorchers v Stars	Perth	2016-17
4	0	6	1	A.F.Milne	Thunder v Strikers	Adelaide	2020-21

MOST EXPENSIVE BOWLING ANALYSIS

O	*M*	*R*	*W*				
4	0	70	2	L.Guthrie	Heat v Stars	Brisbane	2021-22
4	0	63	0	K.W.Richardson	Renegades v Hurricanes	Melbourne (Dk)	2021-22
4	0	61	0	B.J.Dwarshuis	Sixers v Stars	Melbourne	2019-20

WICKET-KEEPING RECORDS
MOST DISMISSALS IN BIG BASH

60	J.J.Peirson	Heat	2014-22

MOST DISMISSALS IN A SERIES

17	J.R.Philippe	Sixers	2021-22

MOST DISMISSALS IN AN INNINGS

5 (5ct)	T.I.F.Triffitt	Scorchers v Renegades	Perth	2012-13
5 (4ct, 1st)	J.J.Peirson	Heat v Strikers	Brisbane	2019-20

THE MEN'S HUNDRED 2021

In 2021, the Hundred was launched, featuring eight franchise sides in matches of 100 balls per side and incorporating various innovations to the playing rules. The second- and third-placed sides played off for a place in the final, held at Lord's.

	P	*W*	*L*	*T*	*NR*	*Pts*	*Net RR*
1. Birmingham Phoenix	8	6	2	–	–	12	+1.08
2. Southern Brave	8	5	2	–	1	11	+0.03
3. Trent Rockets	8	5	3	–	–	10	+0.03
4. Oval Invincibles	8	4	3	–	1	9	+0.12
5. Northern Superchargers	8	3	4	–	1	7	+0.51
6. Manchester Originals	8	2	4	–	2	6	–0.36
7. Welsh Fire	8	3	5	–	–	6	–0.82
8. London Spirit	8	1	6	–	1	3	–0.64

Eliminator: At The Oval, London, 20 August. Toss: Southern Brave. **SOUTHERN BRAVE** won by seven wickets. Trent Rockets 96 (91 balls; T.S.Mills 3-8, G.H.S.Garton 3-18). Southern Brave 97-3 (68 balls; J.M.Vince 45*, P.R.Stirling 31). Award: G.H.S.Garton.

LEADING AGGREGATES AND RECORDS 2021

BATTING (225 runs)	*M*	*I*	*NO*	*HS*	*Runs*	*Avge*	*100*	*50*	*R/100b*	*Sixes*
L.S.Livingstone (Phoenix)	9	9	3	92*	348	58.00	–	3	178.4	27
B.M.Duckett (Fire)	8	8	–	65	232	29.00	–	2	137.2	3
J.M.Vince (Brave)	10	9	1	60	229	28.62	–	2	129.3	6
M.M.Ali (Phoenix)	7	7	–	59	225	32.14	–	1	148.0	15

BOWLING (12 wkts)	*Balls*	*R*	*W*	*Avge*	*BB*	*4w*	*R/100b*
A.F.Milne (Phoenix)	135	129	12	10.75	3-15	–	95.5
M.de Lange (Rockets)	119	157	12	13.08	5-20	1	131.9
A.U.Rashid (Superchargers)	135	173	12	14.41	3-13	–	128.1
Rashid Khan (Rockets)	170	231	12	19.25	3-16	–	135.8

Highest total	200-5	Superchargers v Originals		Leeds
Biggest win (runs)	93	Phoenix (184-5) beat Fire (91)		Birmingham
Biggest win (balls)	32	Brave (97-3) beat Rockets (96)		The Oval
Highest innings	92*	L.S.Livingstone	Phoenix v Superchargers	Leeds
Most sixes	27	L.S.Livingstone (Phoenix)		
Most sixes (inns)	10	L.S.Livingstone	Phoenix v Superchargers	Leeds
Highest partnership	124*	D.J.M.Short/D.J.Malan	Rockets v Brave	Nottingham
Best bowling	5-20	M.de Lange	Rockets v Brave	Nottingham
Most economical	20b-6-2	Mujeeb Zadran	Superchargers v Spirit	Lord's
Most expensive	15b-51-2	S.T.Finn	Originals v Superchargers	Leeds
Most w/k dismissals	12	Q.de Kock (Brave)		
Most w/k dismissals (inns)	4	Q.de Kock	Brave v Rockets	The Oval
Most catches	7	A.L.Davies (Brave)		

2021 THE HUNDRED FINAL
SOUTHERN BRAVE v BIRMINGHAM PHOENIX

At Lord's, London, on 21 August (floodlit).

Result: **SOUTHERN BRAVE** won by 32 runs.

Toss: Birmingham Phoenix. Award: P.R.Stirling.

	SOUTHERN BRAVE		*Runs*	*Balls*	*4/6*	*Fall*
†	Q.de Kock	c Pennington b Milne	7	7	–/1	1- 15
	P.R.Stirling	c Benjamin b Howell	61	36	2/6	3- 85
	J.M.Vince	b Imran Tahir	4	8	–	2- 35
*	A.L.Davies	c Imran Tahir b Milne	27	20	1/1	5-145
	T.H.David	c Bedingham b Livingstone	15	6	–/2	4-103
	R.A.Whiteley	not out	44	19	4/4	
	C.J.Jordan	not out	5	4	–	
	G.H.S.Garton					
	C.Overton				–	
	T.S.Mills					
	J.B.Lintott					
	Extras	(LB 5)	5			
	Total	**(5 wkts; 100 balls)**	**168**			

	BIRMINGHAM PHOENIX		*Runs*	*Balls*	*4/6*	*Fall*
	D.G.Bedingham	c David b Garton	0	2	–	1- 0
	W.C.F.Smeed	c Davies b Overton	2	6	–	2-14
*	M.M.Ali	c Overton b Lintott	36	30	1/3	2- 3
	L.S.Livingstone	run out	46	19	4/4	5-97
	M.A.H.Hammond	c Garton b Mills	3	4	–	4-83
†	C.G.Benjamin	not out	23	25	1/1	
	B.A.C.Howell	not out	20	14	3	
	A.F.Milne					
	D.Y.Pennington					
	P.R.Brown					
	Imran Tahir					
	Extras	(LB 2, W 4)	6			
	Total	**(5 wkts; 100 balls)**	**136**			

PHOENIX	*B*	*0*	*R*	*W*	BRAVE	*B*	*0*	*R*	*W*
Milne	20	14	8	2	Garton	20	12	27	1
Pennington	10	4	29	0	Overton	20	8	26	1
Imran Tahir	20	3	33	1	Mills	20	11	13	1
Howell	20	6	34	1	Lintott	20	6	30	1
Brown	15	2	36	0	Jordan	20	5	38	0
Livingstone	10	3	18	1					
Ali	5	1	5	0					

Umpires: M.J.Saggers and A.G.Wharf

IRELAND INTERNATIONALS

The following players have played for Ireland in any format of international cricket since 1 November 2020. Details correct to 7 April 2022.

ADAIR, Mark Richard (Sullivan Upper S, Holywood), b Belfast 27 Mar 1996. 6'2". RHB, RFM. Warwickshire 2015-16. Northern Knights debut 2018. Ireland Wolves 2018-19 to 2020-21. **Tests**: 1 (2019); HS 8 and BB 3-32 v E (Lord's) 2019. **LOI**: 24 (2019 to 2021-22); HS 32 v E (Dublin) 2019; BB 4-19 v Afg (Belfast) 2019. **IT20**: 39 (2019 to 2021-22); HS 38 v Z (Bready) 2019; BB 4-23 v Z (Bready) 2021. HS 91 Northern v Leinster (Dublin, Sandymount) 2018. BB 3-22 IW v Bangladesh EP (Chittagong) 2021-22. LO HS 45 IW v Bangladesh EP (Mirpur) 2020-21. LO BB 4-19 (*see LOI*). T20 HS 38. T20 BB 4-14.

BALBIRNIE, Andrew (St Andrew's C, Dublin; UWIC), b Dublin 28 Dec 1990. 6'2". RHB, OB. Cardiff MCCU 2012-13. Ireland debut 2012. Middlesex 2012-15. Leinster Lightning debut 2017. Ireland Wolves 2017-18. Glamorgan 2021. **Tests**: 3 (2018 to 2019); HS 82 v Afg (Dehradun) 2018-19. **LOI**: 85 (2010 to 2021-22, 21 as captain); HS 145* v Afg (Dehradun) 2018-19; BB 1-26 v Afg (Dubai, DSC) 2014-15. **IT20**: 67 (2015 to 2021-22, 30 as captain); HS 83 v Neth (Al Amerat) 2018-19. HS 205* Ire v Neth (Dublin) 2017. BB 4-23 Lein v NW (Bready) 2017. LO HS 160* Ire W v Bangladesh A (Dublin, CA) 2018. LO BB 1-26 (*see LOI*). T20 HS 99*.

CAMPHER, Curtis (St Stithians C), b Johannesburg, South Africa 20 Apr 1999. RHB, RM. Ireland Wolves debut 2020-21. Leinster Lightning 2020 (not f-c). **LOI**: 13 (2020 to 2021-22); HS 68 v E (Southampton); BB 2-31 v UAE (Abu Dhabi) 2020-21. **IT20**: 12 (2021 to 2021-22); HS 40 v UAE (Al Amerat) 2021-22; BB 4-25 v USA (Lauderhill) 2021-22. HS 39 v Bangladesh EP (Chittagong) 2020-21. LO HS 68 (*see LOI*). LO BB 4-46 Lein v NW (Bready) 2020. T20 HS 62*. T20 BB 4-25.

DELANY, Gareth James, b Dublin 28 Apr 1997. Cousin of D.C.A.Delany. RHB, LBG. Leinster Lightning 2017-19. Ireland Wolves 2018-19 to 2020-21. Leicestershire 2020 (T20 only). Munster Reds 2021 (not f-c). **LOI**: 12 (2019-20 to 2021-22); HS 22 v E (Southampton) 2020; BB 1-10 v UAE (Abu Dhabi) 2020-21. **IT20**: 37 (2019 to 2021-22); HS 89* v Oman (Abu Dhabi, TO) 2019-20; BB 2-21 v Afg (Greater Noida) 2019-20. HS 22 Ire W v Sri Lanka A (Colombo, SSC) 2018-19. BB 3-48 Leinster v Northern (Belfast) 2017. LO HS 67 Leinster v NW (Dublin, OL) 2018. LO BB 3-47 Leinster v NW (Bready) 2019. T20 HS 89*. T20 BB 3-8.

DOCKRELL, George Henry (Gonzaga C, Dublin), b Dublin 22 Jul 1992. 6'3". RHB, SLA. Ireland 2010 to date. Somerset 2011-14. Sussex 2015. Leinster Lightning debut 2017. Ireland Wolves 2017-18. **Tests**: 1 (2018-19); HS 39 and BB 2-63 v Afg (Dehradun) 2018-19. **LOI**: 99 (2009-10 to 2021-22); HS 62* v Afg (Sharjah) 2017-18; BB 4-24 v Scot (Belfast) 2013. **IT20**: 93 (2009-10 to 2021-22); HS 34* v Afg (Dehradun) 2018-19; BB 4-20 v Neth (Dubai) 2009-10. HS 92 Leinster v NW (Bready) 2018. BB 6-27 Sm v Middx (Taunton) 2012. LO HS 100* Leinster v Northern (Dublin, SP) 2021. LO BB 5-21 Leinster v Northern (Dublin, V) 2018. T20 HS 55*. T20 BB 4-20.

GETKATE, Shane Charles, b Durban, South Africa 2 Oct 1991. Grandson of R.S.Getkate (Natal 1936-37). RHB, RMF. Northern Knights 2017-19. Ireland Wolves 2017-18. North West Warriors 2021 (not f-c). **LOI**: 4 (2019 to 2021); HS 16* v Z (Bready) 2019; BB 2-30 v Z (Belfast) 2019. **IT20**: 30 (2018-19 to 2021-22); HS 30 v UAE (Al Amerat) 2021-22; BB 3-20 v Z (Dublin) 2021. HS 70 Northern v Leinster (Comber) 2018. BB 4-62 Northern v Leinster (Dublin, CA) 2017. LO HS 86 Ire W v Sri Lanka A (Colombo, SSC) 2018-19. LO BB 5-44 Northern v Leinster (Downpatrick) 2017. T20 HS 49. T20 BB 5-8.

LITTLE, Joshua Brian (St Andrew's C), b Dublin 1 Nov 1999. RHB, LFM. Leinster Lightning debut 2018. Ireland Wolves 2018-19. **LOI**: 19 (2019 to 2021-22); HS 9* v Neth (Utrecht) 2021; BB 4-39 v Neth (Utrecht) 2021 – separate matches. **IT20**: 34 (2016 to 2021-22); HS 15* v SA (Dublin) 2021; BB 4-23 v SL (Abu Dhabi) 2021-22. HS 27 Leinster v NW (Bready) 2018. BB 3-95 Leinster v Northern (Dublin) 2018. LO HS 22 Leinster v Munster (Dublin, SP) 2021. LO BB 4-39 (*see LOI*). T20 HS 27*. T20 BB 4-23.

McBRINE, Andrew Robert, b Londonderry 30 Apr 1993. Son of A.McBrine (Ireland 1985-92), nephew of J.McBrine (Ireland 1986). LHB, OB. Ireland debut 2013. North-West Warriors debut 2017. Ireland Wolves 2017-18. **Tests**: 2 (2018-19 to 2019); HS 11 v E (Lord's) 2019; BB 2-77 v Afg (Dehradun) 2018-19. **LOI**: 65 (2014 to 2021-22); HS 79 v SL (Dublin) 2016; BB 5-29 v Afg (Abu Dhabi) 2020-21. **IT20**: 26 (2013-14 to 2021-22); HS 36 v Oman (Al Amerat) 2021-22; BB 2-7 v PNG (Townsville) 2015-16. HS 77 NW v Northern (Comber) 2018. BB 4-35 NW v Northern (Bready) 2018. LO HS 89 Ire W v Bangladesh A (Dublin, CA) 2018. LO BB 5-29 (*see LOI*). T20 HS 52*. T20 BB 3-19.

McCARTHY, Barry John (St Michael's C, Dublin; University C, Dublin), b Dublin 13 Sep 1992. 5'11". RHB, RMF. Durham 2015-18. Leinster Lightning debut 2019. **LOI**: 38 (2016 to 2021); HS 18 v Afg (Belfast) 2019; BB 5-46 v Afg (Sharjah) 2017-18. **IT20**: 19 (2016-17 to 2021-22); HS 30* v SA (Dublin) 2021; BB 4-30 v USA (Lauderhill) 2021-22. HS 51* Du v Hants (Chester-le-St) 2016. BB 6-63 Du v Kent (Canterbury) 2017. LO HS 43 Du v Leics (Leicester) 2018 (RLC). LO BB 6-39 Leinster v Munster (Dublin, SP) 2021. T20 HS 30*. T20 BB 4-30.

McCLINTOCK, William T., b Londonderry 1 Jan 1997. Twin brother of G.S.McClintock (North West Warriors 2017). RHB, RM. North West Warriors debut 2017 (white ball only). **IT20**: 5 (2021 to 2021-22); HS 15* v Z (Bready) 2021. LO HS 72* NW v Northern (Belfast) 2021. T20 HS 54.

McCOLLUM, James Alexander (Methodist C, Belfast; Durham U), b Craigavon 1 Aug 1995. RHB, RM. Durham MCCU 2017. Northern Knights debut 2017. Ireland Wolves 2018-19 to 2020-21. **Tests**: 2 (2018-19 to 2019); HS 39 v Afg (Dehradun) 2018-19. **LOI**: 10 (2018-19 to 2020-21); HS 73 v Z (Belfast) 2019. HS 119* Northern v Leinster (Belfast) 2017. BB 5-32 Northern v NW (Bready) 2018. LO HS 102 Ire W v Sri Lanka A (Colombo, RPS) 2018-19. LO BB 1-14 Northern v NW (Eglinton) 2018. T20 HS 79*.

O'BRIEN, Kevin Joseph (Marian C, Dublin; Tallaght I of Tech), b Dublin 4 Mar 1984. RHB, RM. Son of B.A.O'Brien (Ireland 1966-81) and younger brother of N.J.O'Brien (Kent, Northamptonshire, Leicestershire, North-West and Ireland 2004-18). Ireland debut 2006-07. Nottinghamshire 2009. Surrey 2014. Leicestershire 2015-16 (l-o and T20 only). Leinster Lightning debut 2017. Gloucestershire 2011 (T20 only). Somerset 2012 (T20 only). **Tests**: 3 (2018 to 2019); HS 118 v P (Dublin) 2018 – on debut and Ire record; BB –. **LOI**: 153 (2006 to 2021, 4 as captain); HS 142 v Kenya (Nairobi) 2006-07; BB 4-13 v Neth (Amstelveen) 2013. **IT20**: 110 (2008 to 2021-22, 4 as captain); HS 124 v Hong Kong (Al Amerat) 2019-20 – Ire record; BB 4-45 v Afg (Greater Noida) 2016-17. HS 171* Ire v Kenya (Nairobi) 2008-09. BB 5-39 Ire v Canada (Toronto) 2010. LO HS 142 (*see LOI*). LO BB 4-13 (*see LOI*). T20 HS 124. T20 BB 4-22.

PORTERFIELD, William Thomas Stuart (Strabane GS; Leeds Met U), b Londonderry 6 Sep 1984. 5'11". LHB, OB. Ireland 2006-07 to date. Gloucestershire 2008-10; cap 2008. Warwickshire 2011-17; cap 2014. North West Warriors debut 2018. MCC 2007. **Tests**: 3 (2018 to 2019, 3 as captain); HS 32 v P (Dublin) 2018. **LOI**: 148 (2006 to 2021-22, 113 as captain); HS 139 v UAE (Dubai, ICCA) 2017-18. **IT20**: 61 (2008 to 2018, 56 as captain); HS 72 v UAE (Abu Dhabi) 2015-16. HS 207 NW v Leinster (Bready) 2018. BB 1-29 Ire v Jamaica (Spanish Town) 2009-10. LO HS 139 (*see LOI*). T20 HS 127*.

ROCK, Neil Alan, b Dublin 24 Sep 2000. LHB, WK. Northern Knights debut 2018. Ireland Wolves 2018-19. Munster Reds 2020 (T20 only). **LOI**: 3 (2021-22); HS 5 v WI (Kingston) 2021-22. **IT20**: 13 (2021 to 2021-22); HS 22 v Z (Bready) 2021. HS 85 Ire W v Sri Lanka A (Hambantota) 2018-19. LO HS 78 Ire W v Sri Lanka A (Colombo, RPS) 2018-19. T20 HS 58*.

SINGH, Simranjit ('**Simi**'), b Bathlana, Punjab, India 4 Feb 1987. RHB, OB. Leinster Lightning debut 2017. Ireland debut 2017. Ireland Wolves 2017-18. **LOI**: 33 (2017 to 2021); HS 100* v SA (Dublin) 2021; BB 5-10 v UAE (Abu Dhabi) 2020-21. **IT20**: 47 (2018 to 2021-22); HS 57* v Neth (Rotterdam) 2018; BB 3-9 v Oman (Al Amerat) 2021-22. HS 121 Ire W v Bangladesh A (Sylhet) 2017-18. BB 5-38 Leinster v Northern (Dublin) 2019. LO HS 121* Leinster v Northern (Dublin, V) 2018. LO BB 5-10 (*see LOI*). T20 HS 109. T20 BB 3-9.

STIRLING, Paul Robert (Belfast HS), b Belfast, N Ireland 3 Sep 1990. Father Brian Stirling was an international rugby referee. 5'10". RHB, OB. Ireland 2007-08 to date. Middlesex 2013-19; cap 2016. Northamptonshire 2020 (T20 only). Northern Knights debut 2020 (white-ball only). **Tests**: 3 (2018 to 2019); HS 36 v E (Lord's) 2019; BB –. **LOI**: 136 (2008 to 2021-22); HS 177 v Canada (Toronto) 2010 – Ire record; BB 6-55 v Afg (Greater Noida) 2016-17 – Ire record. **IT20**: 102 (2009 to 2021-22); HS 115* v Z (Bready) 2021; BB 3-21 v B (Belfast) 2012. HS 146 Ire v UAE (Dublin) 2015. CC HS 138 and BB 2-21 M v Glamorgan (Radlett) 2019. LO HS 177 (*see LOI*). LO BB 6-55 (*see LOI*). T20 HS 115*. T20 BB 4-10.

TECTOR, Harry Tom, b Dublin 6 Nov 1999. Younger brother of J.B.Tector (Leinster 2017 to date). RHB, OB. Northern Knights debut 2018. Ireland Wolves 2018-19 to 2020-21. **LOI**: 20 (2020 to 2021-22); HS 79 v SA (Dublin) 2021; BB 1-52 v Afg (Abu Dhabi) 2020-21. **IT20**: 32 (2019 to 2021-22); HS 60 v Neth (Dublin) 2019. HS 146 Northern v Leinster (Dublin) 2019. BB 4-70 Northern v NW (Bready) 2018. LO HS 103 Ire W v Sri Lanka A (Colombo, SSC) 2018-19. LO BB 5-36 Northern v NW (La Manga) 2019. T20 HS 91. T20 BB 4-21.

TUCKER, Lorcan John, b Dublin 10 Sep 1996. RHB, WK. Leinster Lightning debut 2017. Ireland Wolves 2018-19 to 2020-21. **LOI**: 26 (2019 to 2021-22); HS 83 v Afg (Abu Dhabi) 2020-21. **IT20**: 30 (2016 to 2021-22); HS 84 v USA (Lauderhill) 2021-22. HS 80 Ire W v Sri Lanka A (Hambantota) 2018-19. LO HS 109 Ire W v Sri Lanka A (Hambantota) 2018-19. T20 HS 84.

WHITE, Benjamin Charlie, b Dublin 29 Aug 1998. RHB, LB. Northern Knights debut 2021 (white ball only). **IT20**: 9 (2021 to 2021-22); HS 2* v SA (Belfast) 2021 and 2* v USA (Lauderhill) 2021-22; BB 2-23 v Z (Bready) 2021. LO HS 12 Northern v NW (Belfast) 2021. LO BB 3-16 Ire W v Netherlands A (Oak Hill) 2021. T20 HS 12*. T20 BB 5-13.

YOUNG, Craig Alexander (Strabane HS; North West IHE, Belfast), b Londonderry 4 Apr 1990. RHB, RM. Ireland debut 2013. North-West Warriors debut 2017. Ireland Wolves 2018-19. **LOI**: 33 (2014 to 2021-22); HS 12* v Afg (Abu Dhabi) 2020-21; BB 5-46 v Scot (Dublin) 2014. **IT20**: 48 (2015 to 2021-22); HS 22 v SA (Belfast) 2021; BB 4-13 v Nigeria (Abu Dhabi) 2019-20. HS 23 and BB 5-37 NW v Northern (Eglinton) 2017. LO HS 30 Ire W v Netherlands A (Oak Hill) 2021. LO BB 5-46 (*see LOI*). T20 HS 22. T20 BB 5-15.

ENGLAND WOMEN INTERNATIONALS

The following players have played for England since 1 July 2020 and are still available for selection. Details correct to 4 March 2022.

BEAUMONT, Tamsin ('**Tammy**') Tilley, b Dover, Kent 11 Mar 1991. RHB, WK. MBE 2018. Kent 2007-19. Diamonds 2007-12. Sapphires 2008. Emeralds 2011-13. Surrey Stars 2016-17. Adelaide Strikers 2016-17 to 2017-18. Southern Vipers 2018-19. Melbourne Renegades 2019-20. Lightning 2020 to date. Sydney Thunder 2020-21. London Spirit 2021. *Wisden* 2018. **Tests**: 6 (2013 to 2021-22); HS 70 v A (Sydney) 2017-18. **LOI**: 85 (2009-10 to 2021-22); HS 168* v P (Taunton) 2016. **IT20**: 99 (2009-10 to 2021-22); HS 116 v SA (Taunton) 2018.

BOUCHIER, Maia Emily (Dragon S; Rugby S; Oxford Brookes U), b Kensington, London 5 Dec 1998. RHB, RM. Middlesex 2014-18. Auckland 2017-18. Southern Vipers 2018 to date. Hampshire 2019. Southern Brave 2021. Melbourne Stars 2021-22. **IT20**: 3 (2021 to 2021-22); HS 25 v NZ (Hove) 2021.

BRUNT, Katherine Helen, b Barnsley, Yorks 2 Jul 1985. RHB, RMF. Yorkshire 2004-19. Sapphires 2006-08. Diamonds 2011-12. Perth Scorchers 2015-16 to 2017-18. Yorkshire Diamonds 2016-18. Northern Diamonds 2020 to date. Melbourne Stars 2020-21. Trent Rockets 2021. **Tests**: 14 (2004 to 2021-22); HS 52 v A (Worcester) 2005; BB 6-69 v A (Worcester) 2009. **LOI**: 131 (2004-05 to 2021-22); HS 72* v SA (Worcester) 2018; BB 5-18 v A (Wormsley) 2011. **IT20**: 96 (2005 to 2021-22); HS 42* v SA (Taunton) 2018; BB 3-6 v NZ (Lord's) 2009.

CROSS, Kathryn ('**Kate**') Laura, b Manchester, Lancs 3 Oct 1991. RHB, RMF. Lancashire 2005-19. Sapphires 2007-08. Emeralds 2012. W Australia 2017-18 to 2018-19. Brisbane Heat 2015-16. Lancashire Thunder 2016-19. Perth Scorchers 2018-19. Thunder 2020 to date. Manchester Originals 2021. **Tests**: 5 (2013-14 to 2021-22); HS 11 v A (Canberra) 2021-22; BB 3-29 v I (Wormsley) 2014. **LOI**: 37 (2013-14 to 2021-22); HS 29 v NZ (Leicester) 2021; BB 5-24 v NZ (Lincoln) 2014-15. **IT20**: 13 (2013-14 to 2019-20); HS 0*; BB 2-18 v I (Guwahati) 2018-19.

DAVIES, Freya Ruth, b Chichester, Sussex 27 Oct 1995. RHB, RMF. Sussex 2012-19. Western Storm 2016-19. South East Stars 2020 to date. London Spirit 2021. **LOI**: 6 (2019-20 to 2021-22); HS 2 v NZ (Dunedin) 2020-21; BB 2-46 v NZ (Derby) 2021. **IT20**: 17 (2018-19 to 2021-22); HS 1* v NZ (Wellington) 2020-21; BB 4-23 v NZ (Wellington) 2020-21 – separate matches.

DEAN, Charlotte Ellen (Portsmouth GS), b Burton-upon-Trent, Staffs 22 Dec 2000. Daughter of S.J.Dean (Staffordshire and Warwickshire 1986-2002 – List-A only). RHB, OB. Hampshire 2016-19. Southern Vipers 2017 to date. London Spirit 2021. **Tests**: 1 (2021-22); HS 9 and BB 2-24 v A (Canberra) 2021-22. **LOI**: 7 (2021 to 2021-22); HS 18* v A (Melbourne) 2021-22; BB 4-36 v NZ (Worcester) 2021. **IT20**: 1 (2021-22); did not bat or bowl.

DUNKLEY, Sophia Ivy Rose, b Lambeth, Surrey 16 Jul 1998. RHB, LB. Middlesex 2013-19. Surrey Stars 2016-18. Lancashire Thunder 2019. South East Stars 2020 to date. Southern Brave 2021. **Tests**: 2 (2021 to 2021-22); HS 74* v I (Bristol) 2021; BB –. **LOI**: 10 (2021 to 2021-22); HS 73* v I (Taunton) 2021. **IT20**: 23 (2018-19 to 2021-22); HS 35 v WI (Gros Islet) 2018-19; BB 1-6 v SL (Colombo, PSS) 2018-19.

ECCLESTONE, Sophie (Helsby HS), b Chester 6 May 1999. 5'11". RHB, SLA. Cheshire 2013-14. Lancashire 2015-19. Lancashire Thunder 2016-19. Thunder 2020 to date. Manchester Originals 2021. **Tests**: 4 (2017-18 to 2021-22); HS 34 v A (Canberra) 2021-22; BB 4-88 v I (Bristol) 2021. **LOI**: 38 (2016-17 to 2021-22); HS 32* v A (Melbourne) 2021-22; BB 4-14 v I (Nagpur) 2017-18. **IT20**: 50 (2016 to 2021-22); HS 17* v A (Hove) 2019; BB 4-18 v NZ (Taunton) 2018.

ELWISS, Georgia Amanda, b Wolverhampton, Staffs 31 May 1991. RHB, RMF. Staffordshire 2004-10. Sapphires 2006-12. Diamonds 2008. Australia CT 2009-10 to 2010-11. Emeralds 2011. Sussex 2011-19. Rubies 2013. Loughborough Lightning 2016-19. Melbourne Stars 2017-18 to 2018-19. Southern Vipers 2021. Birmingham Phoenix 2021. **Tests**: 4 (2015 to 2021); HS 46 v A (Canterbury) 2015; BB 1-40 v A (Sydney) 2017-18. **LOI**: 36 (2011-12 to 2018-19); HS 77 v P (Taunton) 2016; BB 3-17 v I (Wormsley) 2012. **IT20**: 14 (2011-12 to 2019); HS 18 v SA (Paarl) 2015-16; BB 2-9 v P (Chennai) 2015-16.

FARRANT, Natasha ('**Tash**') Eleni (Sevenoaks S), b Athens, Greece 29 May 1996. LHB, LMF. Kent 2012-19. Sapphires 2013. W Australia 2016-17. Southern Vipers 2016-19. South East Stars 2020 to date. Oval Invincibles 2021. **LOI**: 6 (2013-14 to 2021-22); HS 22 v NZ (Worcester) 2021; BB 2-31 v NZ (Christchurch) 2020-21. **IT20**: 18 (2013 to 2021); HS 3* v A (Mumbai, BS) 2017-18; BB 2-15 v P (Loughborough) 2013.

GLENN, Sarah, b Derby 27 Feb 1999. RHB, LB. Derbyshire 2013-18. Worcestershire 2019. Loughborough Lightning 2017-19. Central Sparks 2020 to date. Perth Scorchers 2020-21. Trent Rockets 2021. **LOI**: 9 (2019-20 to 2021); HS 11 v NZ (Dunedin) 2020-21; BB 4-18 v P (Kuala Lumpur) 2019-20. **IT20**: 26 (2019-20 to 2021-22); HS 26 v WI (Derby) 2020; BB 3-15 v P (Canberra) 2019-20.

JONES, Amy Ellen, b Solihull, Warwicks 13 Jun 1993. RHB, WK. Warwickshire 2008-19. Diamonds 2011. Emeralds 2012. Rubies 2013. W Australia 2017-18. Loughborough Lightning 2016-19. Sydney Sixers 2016-17 to 2017-18. Perth Scorchers 2018-19 to 2020-21. Central Sparks 2020 to date. Birmingham Phoenix 2021. **Tests**: 3 (2019 to 2021-22); HS 64 v A (Taunton) 2019. **LOI**: 58 (2012-13 to 2021-22); HS 94 v I (Nagpur) 2017-18. **IT20**: 65 (2013 to 2021-22); HS 89 v P (Kuala Lumpur) 2019-20.

KNIGHT, Heather Clare, b Rochdale, Lancs 26 Dec 1990. RHB, OB. OBE 2018. Devon 2008-09. Emeralds 2008-13. Berkshire 2010-19. Sapphires 2011-12. Tasmania 2014-15 to 2015-16. Hobart Hurricanes 2015-16 to 2019-20. Western Storm 2016 to date. Sydney Thunder 2020-21. London Spirit 2021. *Wisden* 2017. **Tests**: 9 (2010-11 to 2021-22, 4 as captain); HS 168* v A (Canberra) 2021-22; BB 2-25 v A (Taunton) 2019. **LOI**: 115 (2009-10 to 2021-22, 60 as captain); HS 106 v P (Leicester) 2017; BB 5-26 v P (Leicester) 2016. **IT20**: 87 (2010-11 to 2021-22, 54 as captain); HS 108* v Thai (Canberra) 2019-20; BB 3-9 v I (North Sound) 2018-19.

LAMB, Emma Louise, b Preston, Lancs 16 Dec 1997. Sister of D.J.Lamb (*see LANCASHIRE*). RHB, RM. Lancashire 2012-19. Thunder 2020 to date. Manchester Originals 2021. **LOI**: 1 (2021-22); HS 0. **IT20**: 1 (2021); HS 0*.

SCIVER, Natalie Ruth (Epsom C), b Tokyo, Japan 20 Aug 1992. RHB, RM. Surrey 2010-19. Rubies 2011. Emeralds 2012-13. Melbourne Stars 2015-16 to 2020-21. Surrey Stars 2016-19. Perth Scorchers 2017-18 to 2019-20. Northern Diamonds 2020 to date. Trent Rockets 2021. *Wisden* 2017. **Tests**: 7 (2013-14 to 2021-22); HS 88 v A (Taunton) 2019; BB 3-41 v A (Canberra) 2021-22. **LOI**: 80 (2013 to 2021-22); HS 137 v P (Leicester) 2017; BB 3-3 v WI (Bristol) 2017. **IT20**: 91 (2013 to 2021-22, 1 as captain); HS 82 v WI (Derby) 2020. BB 4-15 v A (Cardiff) 2015.

SHRUBSOLE, Anya, b Bath, Somerset 7 Dec 1991. RHB, RMF. MBE 2018. Somerset 2004-18. Rubies 2006-12. Emeralds 2006-13. Berkshire 2019. Western Storm 2016 to date. Perth Scorchers 2016-17. Southern Brave 2021. *Wisden* 2017. **Tests**: 8 (2013 to 2021-22); HS 47 v I (Bristol) 2021; BB 4-51 v A (Perth) 2013-14. **LOI**: 78 (2008 to 2021-22, 1 as captain); HS 32* v WI (Worcester) 2019; BB 6-46 v I (Lord's) 2017, in World Cup final. **IT20**: 79 (2008 to 2020); HS 29 v WI (Gros Islet) 2018-19; BB 5-11 v NZ (Wellington) 2011-12.

VILLIERS, Mady Kate, b Havering, Essex 26 Aug 1998. RHB, OB. Essex 2013-19. Surrey Stars 2018-19. Sunrisers 2020 to date. Oval Invincibles 2021. **IT20**: 17 (2019 to 2021); HS 9* v NZ (Hove) 2021; BB 3-10 v NZ (Wellington) 2020-21.

WINFIELD-HILL, Lauren, b York 16 Aug 1990. RHB, WK. Yorkshire 2007-19. Diamonds 2011. Sapphires 2012. Rubies 2013. Brisbane Heat 2015-16 to 2016-17. Yorkshire Diamonds 2016-19. Hobart Hurricanes 2017-18. Adelaide Strikers 2019-20. Northern Diamonds 2020 to date. Northern Superchargers 2021. **Tests**: 5 (2014 to 2021-2); HS 35 v I (Wormsley) 2014 and 35 v I (Bristol) 2021. **LOI**: 53 (2013 to 2021-22); HS 123 v P (Worcester) 2016. **IT20**: 40 (2013 to 2019-20); HS 74 v SA (Birmingham) 2014 and 74 v P (Bristol) 2016.

WYATT, Danielle ('**Danni**') Nicole, b Stoke-on-Trent, Staffs 22 Apr 1991. RHB, OB/RM. Staffordshire 2005-12. Emeralds 2006-08. Sapphires 2011-13. Victoria 2011-12 to 2015-16. Nottinghamshire 2013-15. Sussex 2016-19. Melbourne Renegades 2015-16 to 2019-20. Lancashire Thunder 2016. Southern Vipers 2017 to date. Southern Brave 2021. **LOI**: 84 (2009-10 to 2021-22); HS 110 v P (Kuala Lumpur) 2019-20; BB 3-7 v SA (Cuttack) 2012-13. **IT20**: 124 (2009-10 to 2021-22); HS 124 v I (Mumbai, BS) 2017-18; BB 4-11 v SA (Basseterre) 2010.

WOMEN'S TEST CRICKET RECORDS

1934-35 to 7 April 2022
RESULTS SUMMARY

	Opponents	*Tests*	*Won by*										*Drawn*
			E	*A*	*NZ*	*SA*	*WI*	*I*	*P*	*SL*	*Ire*	*H*	
England	Australia	51	9	12	–	–	–	–	–	–	–	–	30
	New Zealand	23	6	–	0	–	–	–	–	–	–	–	17
	South Africa	6	2	–	–	0	–	–	–	–	–	–	4
	West Indies	3	2	–	–	–	0	–	–	–	–	–	1
	India	14	1	–	–	–	–	2	–	–	–	–	11
Australia	New Zealand	13	–	4	1	–	–	–	–	–	–	–	8
	West Indies	2	–	0	–	–	0	–	–	–	–	–	2
	India	10	–	4	–	–	–	0	–	–	–	–	6
New Zealand	South Africa	3	–	–	1	0	–	–	–	–	–	–	2
	India	6	–	–	0	–	–	0	–	–	–	–	6
South Africa	India	2	–	–	–	0	–	2	–	–	–	–	–
	Netherlands	1	–	–	–	1	–	–	–	–	–	0	–
West Indies	India	6	–	–	–	–	1	1	–	–	–	–	4
	Pakistan	1	–	–	–	–	0	–	0	–	–	–	1
Pakistan	Sri Lanka	1	–	–	–	–	–	–	0	1	–	–	–
	Ireland	1	–	–	–	–	–	–	0	–	1	–	–
		143	20	20	2	1	1	5	0	1	1	0	92

	Tests	*Won*	*Lost*	*Drawn*	*Toss Won*
England	97	20	14	63	57
Australia	76	20	10	46	27
New Zealand	45	2	10	33	21
South Africa	12	1	5	6	6
West Indies	12	1	3	8	6†
India	38	5	6	27	18†
Pakistan	3	–	2	1	1
Sri Lanka	1	1	–	–	1
Ireland	1	1	–	–	–
Netherlands	1	–	1	–	1

† *Results of tosses in five of the six India v West Indies Tests in 1976-77 are not known*

TEAM RECORDS
HIGHEST INNINGS TOTALS

569-6d	Australia v England	Guildford	1998
525	Australia v India	Ahmedabad	1983-84
517-8	New Zealand v England	Scarborough	1996
503-5d	England v New Zealand	Christchurch	1934-35
497	England v South Africa	Shenley	2003
467	India v England	Taunton	2002
455	England v South Africa	Taunton	2003
448-9d	Australia v England	Sydney	2017-18
440	West Indies v Pakistan	Karachi	2003-04
427-4d	Australia v England	Worcester	1998
426-7d	Pakistan v West Indies	Karachi	2003-04
426-9d	India v England	Blackpool	1986
420-8d	Australia v England	Taunton	2019
414	England v New Zealand	Scarborough	1996
414	England v Australia	Guildford	1998
404-9d	India v South Africa	Paarl	2001-02

403-8d	New Zealand v India	Nelson	1994-95
400-6d	India v South Africa	Mysore	2014-15

The highest totals for countries not included above are:

316	South Africa v England	Shenley	2003
193-3d	Ireland v Pakistan	Dublin	2000
108	Netherlands v South Africa	Rotterdam	2007

LOWEST INNINGS TOTALS

35	England v Australia	Melbourne	1957-58
38	Australia v England	Melbourne	1957-58
44	New Zealand v England	Christchurch	1934-35
47	Australia v England	Brisbane	1934-35
50	Netherlands v South Africa	Rotterdam	2007
53	Pakistan v Ireland	Dublin	2000

The lowest innings totals for countries not included above are:

65	India v West Indies	Jammu	1976-77
67	West Indies v England	Canterbury	1979
89	South Africa v New Zealand	Durban	1971-72

BATTING RECORDS
1000 RUNS IN TESTS

		Career	*M*	*I*	*NO*	*HS*	*Avge*	*100*	*50*
1935	J.A.Brittin (E)	1979-98	27	44	5	167	49.61	5	11
1676	C.M.Edwards (E)	1996-2015	23	43	5	117	44.10	4	9
1594	R.Heyhoe-Flint (E)	1960-79	22	38	3	179	45.54	3	10
1301	D.A.Hockley (NZ)	1979-96	19	29	4	126*	52.04	4	7
1164	C.A.Hodges (E)	1984-92	18	31	2	158*	40.13	2	6
1110	S.Agarwal (I)	1984-95	13	23	1	190	50.45	4	4
1078	E.Bakewell (E)	1968-79	12	22	4	124	59.88	4	7
1030	S.C.Taylor (E)	1999-2009	15	27	2	177	41.20	4	2
1007	M.E.Maclagan (E)	1934-51	14	25	1	119	41.95	2	6
1002	K.L.Rolton (A)	1995-2009	14	22	4	209*	55.66	2	5

HIGHEST INDIVIDUAL INNINGS

242	Kiran Baluch	P v WI	Karachi	2003-04
214	M.Raj	I v E	Taunton	2002
213*	E.A.Perry	A v E	Sydney	2017-18
209*	K.L.Rolton	A v E	Leeds	2001
204	K.E.Flavell	NZ v E	Scarborough	1996
204‡	M.A.J.Goszko	A v E	Shenley	2001
200	J.Broadbent	A v E	Guildford	1998
193	D.A.Annetts	A v E	Collingham	1987
192	M.D.T.Kamini	I v SA	Mysore	2014-15
190	S.Agarwal	I v E	Worcester	1986
189	E.A.Snowball	E v NZ	Christchurch	1934-35
179	R.Heyhoe-Flint	E v A	The Oval	1976
177	S.C.Taylor	E v SA	Shenley	2003
176*	K.L.Rolton	A v E	Worcester	1998
168*	H.C.Knight	E v A	Canberra	2021-22
167	J.A.Brittin	E v A	Harrogate	1998
161*	E.C.Drumm	E v A	Christchurch	1994-95
160	B.A.Daniels	E v NZ	Scarborough	1996
158*	C.A.Hodges	E v NZ	Canterbury	1984
157	H.C.Knight	E v A	Wormsley	2013
155*	P.F.McKelvey	NZ v E	Wellington	1968-69

‡ *On debut*

FIVE HUNDREDS

		M	I	E	A	NZ	SA	WI	Ind	P	SL	Ire
				Opponents								
5	J.A.Brittin (E)	27	44	–	3	1	–	–	1	–	–	–

HIGHEST PARTNERSHIP FOR EACH WICKET

1st	241	Kiran Baluch/Sajjida Shah	P v WI	Karachi	2003-04
2nd	275	M.D.T.Kamini/P.G.Raut	I v SA	Mysore	2014-15
3rd	309	L.A.Reeler/D.A.Annetts	A v E	Collingham	1987
4th	253	K.L.Rolton/L.C.Broadfoot	A v E	Leeds	2001
5th	138	J.Logtenberg/C.van der Westhuizen	SA v E	Shenley	2003
6th	229	J.M.Fields/R.L.Haynes	A v E	Worcester	2009
7th	157	M.Raj/J.Goswami	I v E	Taunton	2002
8th	181	S.J.Griffiths/D.L.Wilson	A v NZ	Auckland	1989-90
9th	107	B.Botha/M.Payne	SA v NZ	Cape Town	1971-72
10th	119	S.Nitschke/C.R.Smith	A v E	Hove	2005

BOWLING RECORDS
50 WICKETS IN TESTS

Wkts		*Career*	*M*	*Balls*	*Runs*	*Avge*	*Best*	*5wI*	*10wM*
77	M.B.Duggan (E)	1949-63	17	3734	1039	13.49	7- 6	5	–
68	E.R.Wilson (A)	1948-58	11	2885	803	11.80	7- 7	4	2
63	D.F.Edulji (I)	1976-91	20	5098†	1624	25.77	6- 64	1	–
60	M.E.Maclagan (E)	1934-51	14	3432	935	15.58	7- 10	3	–
60	C.L.Fitzpatrick (A)	1991-2006	13	3603	1147	19.11	5- 29	2	–
60	S.Kulkarni (I)	1976-91	19	3320†	1647	27.45	6- 99	5	–
57	R.H.Thompson (A)	1972-85	16	4304	1040	18.24	5- 33	1	–
55	J.Lord (NZ)	1966-79	15	3108	1049	19.07	6-119	4	1
51	K.H.Brunt (E)	2004-22	14	2611	1098	21.52	6- 69	3	–
50	E.Bakewell (E)	1968-79	12	2697	831	16.62	7- 61	3	1

TEN WICKETS IN A TEST

13-226	Shaiza Khan	P v WI	Karachi	2003-04
11- 16	E.R.Wilson	A v E	Melbourne	1957-58
11- 63	J.M.Greenwood	E v WI	Canterbury	1979
11-107	L.C.Pearson	E v A	Sydney	2002-03
10- 65	E.R.Wilson	A v NZ	Wellington	1947-48
10- 75	E.Bakewell	E v WI	Birmingham	1979
10- 78	J.Goswami	I v E	Taunton	2006
10-107	K.Price	A v I	Lucknow	1983-84
10-118	D.A.Gordon	A v E	Melbourne	1968-69
10-137	J.Lord	NZ v A	Melbourne	1978-79

SEVEN WICKETS IN AN INNINGS

8-53	N.David	I v E	Jamshedpur	1995-96
7- 6	M.B.Duggan	E v A	Melbourne	1957-58
7- 7	E.R.Wilson	A v E	Melbourne	1957-58
7-10	M.E.Maclagan	E v A	Brisbane	1934-35
7-18	A.Palmer	A v E	Brisbane	1934-35
7-24	L.Johnston	A v NZ	Melbourne	1971-72
7-34	G.E.McConway	E v I	Worcester	1986
7-41	J.A.Burley	NZ v E	The Oval	1966
7-51	L.C.Pearson	E v A	Sydney	2002-03
7-59	Shaiza Khan	P v WI	Karachi	2003-04
7-61	E.Bakewell	E v WI	Birmingham	1979

HAT-TRICKS

E.R.Wilson	Australia v England	Melbourne	1957-58
Shaiza Khan	Pakistan v West Indies	Karachi	2003-04
R.M.Farrell	Australia v England	Sydney	2010-11

WICKET-KEEPING AND FIELDING RECORDS
25 DISMISSALS IN TESTS

Total			*Tests*	*Ct*	*St*	
58	C.Matthews	Australia	20	46	12	1984-95
43	J.Smit	England	21	39	4	1992-2006
36	S.A.Hodges	England	11	19	17	1969-79
28	B.A.Brentnall	New Zealand	10	16	12	1966-72

EIGHT DISMISSALS IN A TEST

9 (8ct, 1st)	C.Matthews	A v I	Adelaide	1990-91
8 (6ct, 2st)	L.Nye	E v NZ	New Plymouth	1991-92

SIX DISMISSALS IN AN INNINGS

8 (6ct, 2st)	L.Nye	E v NZ	New Plymouth	1991-92
6 (2ct, 4st)	B.A.Brentnall	NZ v SA	Johannesburg	1971-72
6 (6ct)	A.E.Jones	E v A	Canberra	2021-22

20 CATCHES IN THE FIELD IN TESTS

Total			*Tests*	
25	C.A.Hodges	England	18	1984-92
21	S.Shah	India	20	1976-91
20	L.A.Fullston	Australia	12	1984-87

APPEARANCE RECORDS
25 TEST MATCH APPEARANCES

27	J.A.Brittin	England	1979-98

12 MATCHES AS CAPTAIN

			Won	*Lost*	*Drawn*	
14	P.F.McKelvey	New Zealand	2	3	9	1966-79
12	R.Heyhoe-Flint	England	2	–	10	1966-76
12	S.Rangaswamy	India	1	2	9	1976-84

England Results Since April 2021

At County Ground, Bristol, 16-19 June. Toss: England. Result: **MATCH DRAWN**. England 396-9d (H.C.Knight 95, S.I.R.Dunkley 74*, T.T.Beaumont 66, S.Rana 4-131). India 231 (S.Verma 96, S.S.Mandhana 78, S.Ecclestone 4-88) and 344-8 (S.Rana 80*, S.Verma 63, D.B.Sharma 54, S.Ecclestone 4-118). England debut: S.I.R.Dunkley. Award: S.Verma.

At Manuka Oval, Canberra, 27-30 January. Toss: England. Result: **MATCH DRAWN**. Australia 337-9d (M.M.Lanning 93, R.L.Haynes 86, A.K.Gardner 56, T.M.McGrath 52, K.H.Brunt 5-60) and 216-7d (B.L.Mooney 63). England 297 (H.C.Knight 168*) and 245-9 (N.R.Sciver 58). England debut: C.E.Dean. Award: H.C.Knight.

WOMEN'S LIMITED-OVERS RECORDS

1973 to 3 March 2022

RESULTS SUMMARY

	Matches	Won	Lost	Tied	No Result	% Won (exc NR)
Australia	341	269	64	2	6	80.29
England	362	212	137	2	11	60.39
India	288	155	128	1	4	54.57
South Africa	213	110	89	5	9	53.92
New Zealand	357	176	173	2	6	50.14
West Indies	195	87	99	3	6	46.03
Sri Lanka	167	56	106	–	5	34.56
Trinidad & Tobago	6	2	4	–	–	33.33
Bangladesh	42	13	27	–	2	32.50
Pakistan	178	51	123	1	3	29.14
Ireland	153	42	105	–	6	28.57
Jamaica	5	1	4	–	–	20.00
Netherlands	101	19	81	–	1	19.00
Denmark	33	6	27	–	–	18.18
International XI	18	3	14	–	1	17.64
Young England	6	1	5	–	–	16.66
Scotland	8	1	7	–	–	12.50
Zimbabwe	8	1	7	–	–	12.50
Japan	5	–	5	–	–	0.00

TEAM RECORDS – HIGHEST INNINGS TOTALS

491-4	(50 overs)	New Zealand v Ireland	Dublin	2018
455-5	(50 overs)	New Zealand v Pakistan	Christchurch	1996-97
440-3	(50 overs)	New Zealand v Ireland	Dublin	2018
418	(49.5 overs)	New Zealand v Ireland	Dublin	2018
412-3	(50 overs)	Australia v Denmark	Mumbai	1997-98
397-4	(50 overs)	Australia v Pakistan	Melbourne	1996-97
378-5	(50 overs)	England v Pakistan	Worcester	2016

LARGEST RUNS MARGIN OF VICTORY

408 runs	New Zealand beat Pakistan	Christchurch	1996-97
374 runs	Australia beat Pakistan	Melbourne	1996-97

LOWEST INNINGS TOTALS

22	(23.4 overs)	Netherlands v West Indies	Deventer	2008
23	(24.1 overs)	Pakistan v Australia	Melbourne	1996-97
24	(21.3 overs)	Scotland v England	Reading	2001

BATTING RECORDS – 2900 RUNS IN A CAREER

Runs		Career	M	I	NO	HS	Avge	100	50
7623	M.Raj (I)	1999-2022	225	204	57	125*	51.85	7	62
5992	C.M.Edwards (E)	1997-2016	191	180	23	173*	38.16	9	46
5147	S.R.Taylor (WI)	2008-2022	137	133	20	171	45.54	7	36
4844	B.J.Clark (A)	1991-2005	118	114	12	229*	47.49	5	30
4814	K.L.Rolton (A)	1995-2009	141	132	32	154*	48.14	8	33
4790	S.W.Bates (NZ)	2006-2022	135	129	12	168	40.94	11	27
4464	A.E.Satterthwaite (NZ)	2007-2022	138	132	17	137*	38.81	7	26
4101	S.C.Taylor (E)	1998-2011	126	120	18	156*	40.20	8	23
4069	M.M.Lanning (A)	2011-2022	91	91	14	152*	52.84	14	17
4064	D.A.Hockley (NZ)	1982-2000	118	115	18	117	41.89	4	34
4056	S.J.Taylor (E)	2006-2019	126	119	13	147	38.26	7	20
3599	M.du Preez (SA)	2007-2022	146	133	25	116*	33.32	2	17
3528	D.J.S.Dottin (WI)	2008-2022	135	128	13	150*	30.67	3	21
3492	A.J.Blackwell (A)	2003-2017	144	124	27	114	36.00	3	25
3250	H.C.Knight (E)	2010-2022	115	110	23	106	37.35	2	22
3234	L.Lee (SA)	2013-2021	93	92	8	132*	38.50	3	23
3206	E.A.Perry (A)	2007-2022	121	97	33	112*	50.09	2	28
2949	T.T.Beaumont (E)	2009-2022	85	77	9	168*	43.36	8	14

Runs		Career	M	I	NO	HS	Avge	100	50
2919	H.M.Tiffen (NZ)	1999-2009	117	111	16	100	30.72	1	18
2918	S.F.M.Devine (NZ)	2006-2022	121	108	11	145	30.08	5	13

HIGHEST INDIVIDUAL INNINGS

232*	A.C.Kerr	New Zealand v Ireland	Dublin	2018
229*	B.J.Clark	Australia v Denmark	Mumbai	1997-98
188	D.B.Sharma	India v Ireland	Potchefstroom	2017
178*	A.C.Jayangani	Sri Lanka v Australia	Bristol	2017
173*	C.M.Edwards	England v Ireland	Pune	1997-98
171*	H.Kaur	India v Australia	Derby	2017
171	S.R.Taylor	West Indies v Sri Lanka	Mumbai	2012-13
168*	T.T.Beaumont	England v Pakistan	Taunton	2016
168	S.W.Bates	New Zealand v Pakistan	Sydney	2008-09
157	R.H.Priest	New Zealand v Sri Lanka	Lincoln	2015-16
156*	L.M.Keightley	Australia v Pakistan	Melbourne	1996-97
156*	S.C.Taylor	England v India	Lord's	2006
154*	K.L.Rolton	Australia v Sri Lanka	Christchurch	2000-01
153*	J.Logtenberg	South Africa v Netherlands	Deventer	2007
152*	M.M.Lanning	Australia v Sri Lanka	Bristol	2017
151	K.L.Rolton	Australia v Ireland	Dublin	2005
151	S.W.Bates	New Zealand v Ireland	Dublin	2018
150*	D.J.S.Dottin	West Indies v South Africa	Johannesburg	2021-22

HIGHEST PARTNERSHIP FOR EACH WICKET

1st	320	D.B.Sharma/P.G.Raut	India v Ireland	Potchefstroom	2017
2nd	295	A.C.Kerr/L.M.Kasperek	New Zealand v Ireland	Dublin	2018
3rd	244	K.L.Rolton/L.C.Sthalekar	Australia v Ireland	Dublin	2005
4th	224*	J.Logtenberg/M.du Preez	South Africa v Netherlands	Deventer	2007
5th	188*	S.C.Taylor/J.Cassar	England v Sri Lanka	Lincoln	2000-01
6th	142	S.Luus/C.L.Tryon	South Africa v Ireland	Dublin	2016
7th	104*	S.J.Tsukigawa/N.J.Browne	New Zealand v England	Chennai	2006-07
8th	88	N.N.D.de Silva/O.U.Ranasinghe	Sri Lanka v England	Hambantota	2018-19
9th	73	L.R.F.Askew/I.T.Guha	England v New Zealand	Chennai	2006-07
10th	76	A.J.Blackwell/K.M.Beams	Australia v India	Derby	2017

BOWLING RECORDS – 100 WICKETS IN A CAREER

		LOI	Balls	Runs	W	Avge	Best	4w	R/Over
J.Goswami (I)	2002-2022	195	9549	5327	**245**	21.74	6-31	9	3.34
C.L.Fitzpatrick (A)	1993-2007	109	6017	3023	**180**	16.79	5-14	11	3.01
A.Mohammed (WI)	2003-2022	136	6074	3551	**174**	20.40	7-14	13	3.50
S.Ismail (SA)	2007-2022	114	5554	3394	**164**	20.69	6-10	7	3.66
K.H.Brunt (E)	2005-2022	131	6410	3759	**163**	23.06	5-18	8	3.51
E.A.Perry (A)	2007-2022	121	5350	3873	**156**	24.82	7-22	4	4.34
Sana Mir (P)	2005-2019	120	5942	3665	**151**	24.27	5-32	8	3.70
S.R.Taylor (WI)	2008-2022	137	5513	3191	**148**	21.56	4-17	5	3.47
L.C.Sthalekar (A)	2001-2013	125	5964	3646	**146**	24.97	5-35	2	3.66
N.David (I)	1995-2008	97	4892	2305	**141**	16.34	5-20	6	2.82
D.van Niekerk (SA)	2009-2021	107	4578	2642	**138**	19.14	5-17	8	3.46
J.L.Gunn (E)	2004-2019	144	5906	3822	**136**	28.10	5-22	6	3.88
M.Kapp (SA)	2009-2021	118	5229	3200	**134**	23.88	4-14	4	3.67
L.A.Marsh (E)	2006-2019	103	5328	3463	**129**	26.84	5-15	4	3.89
H.A.S.D.Siriwardene (SL)	2003-2019	118	5449	3577	**124**	28.84	4-11	6	3.93
J.L.Jonassen (A)	2012-2022	77	3549	2332	**118**	19.76	5-27	8	3.94
S.Luus (SA)	2012-2022	92	2991	2211	**108**	20.47	6-36	8	4.43
M.Schutt (A)	2012-2022	68	3227	2247	**103**	21.81	4-18	5	4.17
C.E.Taylor (E)	1988-2005	105	5140	2443	**102**	23.95	4-13	2	2.85
I.T.Guha (E)	2001-2011	83	3767	2345	**101**	23.21	5-14	4	3.73
N.Al Khadeer (I)	2002-2012	78	4036	2402	**100**	24.02	5-14	5	3.57

SIX OR MORE WICKETS IN AN INNINGS

7 -4	Sajjida Shah	Pakistan v Japan	Amsterdam	2003
7 -8	J.M.Chamberlain	England v Denmark	Haarlem	1991
7-14	A.Mohammed	West Indies v Pakistan	Dhaka	2011-12

7-22	E.A.Perry	Australia v England	Canterbury	2019
7-24	S.Nitschke	Australia v England	Kidderminster	2005
6-10	J.Lord	New Zealand v India	Auckland	1981-82
6-10	M.Maben	India v Sri Lanka	Kandy	2003-04
6-10	S.Ismail	South Africa v Netherlands	Savar	2011-12
6-20	G.L.Page	New Zealand v Trinidad & T	St Albans	1973
6-20	D.B.Sharma	India v Sri Lanka	Ranchi	2015-16
6-20	Khadija Tul Kubra	Bangladesh v Pakistan	Cox's Bazar	2018-19
6-31	J.Goswami	India v New Zealand	Southgate	2011
6-32	B.H.McNeill	New Zealand v England	Lincoln, NZ	2007-08
6-36	S.Luus	South Africa v Ireland	Dublin	2016
6-45	S.Luus	South Africa v New Zealand	Hamilton	2019-20
6-46	A.Shrubsole	England v India	Lord's	2017
6-46	L.M.Kasperek	New Zealand v Australia	Mt Maunganui	2020-21

WICKET-KEEPING AND FIELDING RECORDS – 100 DISMISSALS IN A CAREER

Total			*LOI*	*Ct*	*St*
165	T.Chetty	South Africa	120	116	49
136	S.J.Taylor	England	126	85	51
133	R.J.Rolls	New Zealand	104	89	44
114	J.Smit	England	109	69	45
102	M.R.Aguillera	West Indies	112	76	26

SIX DISMISSALS IN AN INNINGS

6	(4ct, 2st)	S.L.Illingworth	New Zealand v Australia	Beckenham	1993
6	(1ct, 5st)	V.Kalpana	India v Denmark	Slough	1993
6	(2ct, 4st)	Batool Fatima	Pakistan v West Indies	Karachi	2003-04
6	(4ct, 2st)	Batool Fatima	Pakistan v Sri Lanka	Colombo (PSS)	2011

50 CATCHES IN THE FIELD IN A CAREER

Total			*LOI*	*Career*
75	S.W.Bates	New Zealand	135	2006-2022
66	J.Goswami	India	195	2002-2022
62	S.R.Taylor	West Indies	137	2008-2022
61	M.Raj	India	225	1999-2022
56	D.van Niekerk	South Africa	107	2009-2021
55	A.E.Satterthwaite	New Zealand	138	2007-2022
55	A.J.Blackwell	Australia	144	2003-2017
52	L.S.Greenway	England	126	2003-2016
52	C.M.Edwards	England	191	1997-2016

FOUR CATCHES IN THE FIELD IN AN INNINGS

4	Z.J.Goss	Australia v New Zealand	Adelaide	1995-96
4	J.L.Gunn	England v New Zealand	Lincoln, NZ	2014-15
4	Nahida Khan	Pakistan v Sri Lanka	Dambulla	2017-18
4	A.C.Kerr	New Zealand v India	Queenstown	2021-22

APPEARANCE RECORDS – 140 APPEARANCES

225	M.Raj	India	1999-2022
195	J.Goswami	India	2002-2022
191	C.M.Edwards	England	1997-2016
146	M.du Preez	South Africa	2007-2022
144	A.J.Blackwell	Australia	2003-2017
144	J.L.Gunn	England	2004-2019
141	K.L.Rolton	Australia	1995-2009

100 CONSECUTIVE APPEARANCES

109	M.Raj	India	17.04.2004 to 07.02.2013
101	M.du Preez	South Africa	08.03.2009 to 05.02.2018

100 MATCHES AS CAPTAIN

			Won	*Lost*	*No Result*	
148	M.Raj	India	86	59	3	2004-2022
117	C.M.Edwards	England	72	38	7	2005-2016
101	B.J.Clark	Australia	83	17	1	1994-2005

WOMEN'S INTERNATIONAL TWENTY20 RECORDS

2004 to 7 April 2022

As for the men's IT20 records, in the section that follows, except for the first-ranked record and the highest partnerships, only those games featuring a nation that has also played a full LOI are listed.

MATCH RESULTS SUMMARY

	Matches	*Won*	*Lost*	*Tied*	*NR*	*Win %*
Zimbabwe	24	22	2	–	–	91.66
England	157	111	41	3	2	71.61
Australia	149	97	46	3	3	66.43
New Zealand	137	78	55	2	2	57.77
West Indies	141	74	59	5	3	53.62
India	133	69	61	–	3	53.07
South Africa	120	54	63	–	3	46.15
Pakistan	123	48	70	3	2	39.66
Bangladesh	79	30	49	–	–	37.97
Ireland	82	28	53	–	1	34.56
Sri Lanka	104	28	72	–	4	28.00

WOMEN'S INTERNATIONAL TWENTY20 RECORDS

TEAM RECORDS – HIGHEST INNINGS TOTALS † Batting Second

314-2	Uganda v Mali	Rwanda	2019
255-2	Bangladesh v Maldives	Pokhara	2019-20
250-3	England v South Africa	Taunton	2018
226-3	Australia v England	Chelmsford	2019
226-2	Australia v Sri Lanka	Sydney (NS)	2019-20
217-4	Australia v Sri Lanka	Sydney (NS)	2019-20
216-1	New Zealand v South Africa	Taunton	2018
213-4	Ireland v Netherlands	Deventer	2019
209-4	Australia v England	Mumbai (BS)	2017-18
205-1	South Africa v Netherlands	Potchefstroom	2010-11
205-3	Zimbabwe v Mozambique	Gaborone	2021
204-2	England v Sri Lanka	Colombo (PSS)	2018-19
199-3†	England v India	Mumbai (BS)	2017-18

LOWEST COMPLETED INNINGS TOTALS † Batting Second

6†	(12.1)	Maldives v Bangladesh	Pokhara	2019-20
6	(9.0)	Mali v Rwanda	Rwanda	2019
17	(9.2)	Eswatini v Zimbabwe	Gaborone	2021
24	(16.1)	France v Ireland	Cartagena	2021
27†	(13.4)	Malaysia v India	Kuala Lumpur	2018
30†	(18.4)	Malaysia v Pakistan	Kuala Lumpur	2018
30†	(12.5)	Bangladesh v Pakistan	Cox's Bazar	2018-19

The lowest score for England is 87 (v Australia, Hove, 2015).

BATTING RECORDS – 2000 RUNS IN A CAREER

Runs			*M*	*I*	*NO*	*HS*	*Avge*	*50*	*R/100B*
3380	S.W.Bates	NZ	126	123	9	124*	29.64	22	110.1
3121	S.R.Taylor	WI	111	109	22	90	35.87	21	101.0†
3007	M.M.Lanning	A	115	109	24	133*	36.22	16	115.7
2681	D.J.S.Dottin	WI	124	122	20	112*	26.28	14	123.7†
2605	C.M.Edwards	E	95	93	14	92*	32.97	12	106.9
2592	S.F.M.Devine	NZ	102	99	12	105	29.79	16	123.7
2364	M.Raj	I	89	84	21	97*	37.52	17	96.3†
2319	H.Kaur	I	121	109	21	103	26.35	7	103.0†
2225	Bismah Maroof	P	108	102	21	70*	27.46	11	92.8
2177	S.J.Taylor	E	90	87	12	77	29.02	16	110.6

Runs			M	I	NO	HS	Avge	50	R/100B
2136	A.J.Healy	A	123	106	17	148*	24.00	13	129.6

† No information on balls faced for games at Roseau on 22 and 23 February 2012.

HIGHEST INDIVIDUAL INNINGS

Score	Balls				
148*	61	A.J.Healy	A v SL	Sydney (NS)	2019-20
133*	63	M.M.Lanning	A v E	Chelmsford	2019
126	65	M.M.Lanning	A v Ire	Sylhet	2013-14
124*	66	S.W.Bates	NZ v SA	Taunton	2018
124	64	D.N.Wyatt	E v I	Mumbai (BS)	2017-18
117*	70	B.L.Mooney	A v E	Canberra	2017-18
116*	71	S.A.Fritz	SA v Neth	Potchefstroom	2010-11
116	52	T.T.Beaumont	E v SA	Taunton	2018

HIGHEST PARTNERSHIP FOR EACH WICKET

1st	182	S.W.Bates/S.F.M.Devine	NZ v SA	Taunton	2018
2nd	162*	H.K.Matthews/C.N.Nation	WI v Ire	Dublin	2019
3rd	236*	Nigar Sultana/Fargana Hoque	B v Mald	Pokhara	2019-20
4th	147*	K.L.Rolton/K.A.Blackwell	A v E	Taunton	2005
5th	119*	M.M.Lanning/R.L.Haynes	A v NZ	Sydney	2018-19
6th	84	M.A.A.Sanjeewani/N.N.D.de Silva	SL v P	Colombo (SSC)	2017-18
7th	75*	Salma Khatun/Ritu Moni	B v Ken	Kuala Lumpur	2021-22
8th	42*	M.McColl/S.Haggo	Scot v Ire	Belfast	2021
9th	33*	D.Hazell/H.L.Colvin	E v WI	Bridgetown	2013-14
10th	37*	P.Vastrakar/R.S.Gayakwad	I v A	Carrara	2021-22

BOWLING RECORDS – 90 WICKETS IN A CAREER

Wkts			Matches	Overs	Mdns	Runs	Avge	Best	R/Over
125	A.Mohammed	WI	117	395.3	6	2206	17.64	5-10	5.57
115	E.A.Perry	A	126	380.5	6	2237	19.45	4-12	5.87
110	S.Ismail	SA	98	343.5	14	1990	18.09	5-12	5.78
103	Nida Dar	P	108	347.2	8	1871	18.16	5-21	5.38
102	A.Shrubsole	E	79	266.2	10	1587	15.55	5-11	5.95
98	Poonam Yadav	I	72	260.0	5	1495	15.25	4- 9	5.75
98	S.R.Taylor	WI	111	289.3	4	1639	16.72	4-12	5.66
98	S.F.M.Devine	NZ	102	273.0	6	1733	17.68	4-22	6.34
98	K.H.Brunt	E	96	340.5	15	1888	19.26	3- 6	5.53
96	M.Schutt	A	75	248.3	6	1510	15.72	4-18	6.07

BEST FIGURES IN AN INNINGS

7- 3	F.Overdijk	Neth v Fra	Cartagena	2021
6-11	E.Mbofana	Z v Eswatini	Gaborone	2021
6-17	A.E.Satterthwaite	NZ v E	Taunton	2007
5- 5	D.J.S.Dottin	WI v B	Providence	2018-19
5- 6	L.Phiri	Z v Bot	Gaborone	2021
5- 8	S.Luus	SA v Ire	Chennai	2015-16
5-10	A.Mohammed	WI v SA	Cape Town	2009-10
5-10	M.Strano	A v NZ	Geelong	2016-17
5-11	A.Shrubsole	E v NZ	Wellington	2011-12
5-11	J.Goswami	I v A	Visakhapatnam	2011-12
5-12	A.Mohammed	WI v NZ	Bridgetown	2013-14
5-12	W.Liengprasert	Thai v SL	Kuala Lumpur	2018
5-12	J.L.Jonassen	A v I	Melbourne (JO)	2019-20
5-12	S.Ismail	SA v P	Durban	2020-21
5-12	Nahida Akter	B v Ken	Kuala Lumpur	2021-22

HAT-TRICKS

Asmavia Iqbal	Pakistan v England	Loughborough	2012
Ekta Bisht	Sri Lanka v India	Colombo (NCC)	2012-13

M.Kapp	South Africa v Bangladesh	Potchefstroom	2013-14
N.R.Sciver	England v New Zealand	Bridgetown	2013-14
Sana Mir	Pakistan v Sri Lanka	Sharjah	2014-15
A.M.Peterson	New Zealand v Australia	Geelong	2016-17
M.Schutt	Australia v India	Mumbai (BS)	2017-18
Fahima Khatun	Bangladesh v UAE	Utrecht	2018
A.Mohammed	West Indies v South Africa	Tarouba	2018-19
A.Shrubsole	England v South Africa	Gros Islet	2018-19
O.Kamchomphu	Thailand v Ireland	Deventer	2019
S.R.Taylor	West Indies v Pakistan	North Sound	2021

WICKET-KEEPING RECORDS – 50 DISMISSALS IN A CAREER

Dis			*Matches*	*Ct*	*St*
96	A.J.Healy	Australia	123	44	52
74	S.J.Taylor	England	90	23	51
72	R.H.Priest	New Zealand	75	41	31
70	M.R.Aguilleira	West Indies	95	36	34
67	T.Bhatia	India	50	23	44
66	T.Chetty	South Africa	79	39	27
51	K.J.Martin	New Zealand	95	27	24
50	Batool Fatima	Pakistan	45	11	39

FIVE DISMISSALS IN AN INNINGS

5 (1ct, 4st)	Kycia A.Knight	West Indies v Sri Lanka	Colombo (RPS)	2012-13
5 (1ct, 4st)	Batool Fatima	Pakistan v Ireland	Dublin	2013
5 (1ct, 4st)	Batool Fatima	Pakistan v Ireland	Dublin	2013
5 (3ct, 2st)	B.Bezuidenhout	New Zealand v Ireland	Dublin	2018
5 (1ct, 4st)	S.J.Bryce	Scotland v Netherlands	Arbroath	2019

FIELDING RECORDS – 35 CATCHES IN A CAREER

Total			*Matches*
68	S.W.Bates	New Zealand	126
58	J.L.Gunn	England	104
54	L.S.Greenway	England	85
47	H.Kaur	India	121
45	N.R.Sciver	England	91
41	M.M.Lanning	Australia	115
38	V.Krishnamurthy	India	76
37	E.A.Perry	Australia	126
36	A.E.Satterthwaite	New Zealand	111
35	S.F.M.Devine	New Zealand	102

FOUR CATCHES IN AN INNINGS

4	L.S.Greenway	England v New Zealand	Chelmsford	2010
4	V.Krishnamurthy	India v Australia	Providence	2018-19
4	R.M.A.M.Avery	Brazil v Canada	Naucalpan	2021-22

APPEARANCE RECORDS – 110 APPEARANCES

126	S.W.Bates	New Zealand
126	E.A.Perry	Australia
124	D.J.S.Dottin	West Indies
124	D.N.Wyatt	England
123	A.J.Healy	Australia
121	H.Kaur	India
117	A.Mohammed	West Indies
115	M.M.Lanning	Australia
111	A.E.Satterthwaite	New Zealand
111	S.R.Taylor	West Indies

65 MATCHES AS CAPTAIN

			W	*L*	*T*	*NR*	*%age wins*
93	C.M.Edwards	England	68	23	1	1	73.91
83	M.M.Lanning	Australia	61	18	1	3	76.25
73	M.R.Aguilleira	West Indies	39	29	3	2	54.92
66	H.Kaur	India	39	24	–	3	61.90
65	Sana Mir	Pakistan	26	36	2	1	40.62
65	Salma Khatun	Bangladesh	27	38	–	–	41.53

THE WOMEN'S HUNDRED 2021

In 2021, the Women's Hundred was launched, featuring eight franchise sides in matches of 100 balls per side, with all games played alongside the men's version. The second- and third-placed sides played off for a place in the final, held at Lord's.

	P	*W*	*L*	*T*	*NR*	*Pts*	*Net RR*
1. Southern Brave	8	7	1	–	–	14	+1.05
2. Oval Invincibles	8	4	3	–	1	9	+0.01
3. Birmingham Phoenix	8	4	4	–	–	8	+0.18
4. London Spirit	8	4	4	–	–	8	+0.04
5. Manchester Originals	8	3	4	–	1	7	+0.01
6. Northern Superchargers	8	3	4	–	1	7	–0.04
7. Trent Rockets	8	3	4	–	1	7	–0.29
8. Welsh Fire	8	2	6	–	–	4	–1.01

Eliminator: At The Oval, London, 20 August. Toss: Birmingham Phoenix. **OVAL INVINCIBLES** won by 20 runs. Oval Invincibles 114-7 (100 balls; M.Kapp 37). Birmingham Phoenix 94 (94 balls; A.E.Jones 35, N.E.Farrant 4-10, M.Kapp 3-21). Award: N.E.Farrant.

FINAL: At Lord's, 21 August. Toss: Southern Brave. **OVAL INVINCIBLES** won by 48 runs. Oval Invincibles 121-6 (100 balls). Southern Brave 73 (98 balls; M.Kapp 4-9). Award: M.Kapp. Series award: D.van Niekerk (Invincibles).

LEADING AGGREGATES AND RECORDS 2021

BATTING (225 runs)	*M*	*I*	*NO*	*HS*	*Runs*	*Avge*	*100*	*50*	*R/100b*	*Sixes*
D.van Niekerk (Invincibles)	10	9	3	67*	259	43.16	–	2	105.7	2
J.I.Rodrigues (Superchargers)	7	7	1	92*	249	41.50	–	3	150.9	1
S.I.R.Dunkley (Brave)	9	9	3	58*	244	40.66	–	2	141.8	3
E.Jones (Phoenix)	9	9	1	64	233	29.12	–	2	118.2	3

BOWLING (14 wkts)	*Balls*	*R*	*W*	*Avge*	*BB*	*4w*	*R/100b*
N.E.Tarrant (Invincibles)	179	185	18	10.27	4-10	1	103.3
S.J.Johnson (Rockets)	134	154	15	10.26	4-15	1	114.9
K.L.Gordon (Phoenix)	170	212	14	14.13	3-14	–	124.7
A.Wellington (Brave)	175	161	14	11.50	4-12	2	92.0

Highest total	166-3	Brave v Fire		Southampton
Biggest win (runs)	48	Invincibles (121-6) beat Brave (73)		Lord's
Biggest win (balls)	42	Spirit (96-3) beat Fire (95-9)		Cardiff
Highest innings	92*	J.I.Rodrigues	Superchargers v Fire	Leeds
Most sixes	7	S.J.Johnson (Rockets)		
Highest partnership	131*	Shafali Verma/E.Jones	Phoenix v Fire	Birmingham
Best bowling	4-9	M.Kapp	Invincibles v Brave	Lord's
Most economical	20b-9-2	A.Capsey	Invincibles v Superchargers	Leeds
Most expensive	20b-39-1	S.Glenn	Rockets v Superchargers	Nottingham
	20b-39-1	D.R.Gibson	Spirit v Rockets	Lord's
Most w/k dismissals	11	S.J.Bryce (Invincibles)		
Most catches	6	M.E.Boucher (Brave), A.Capsey (Invincibles), G.J.Gibbs (Invincibles), D.R.Gibson (Spirit)		
Most catches (inns)	3	K.L.George	Fire v Invincibles	The Oval

PRINCIPAL WOMEN'S FIXTURES 2022

F	Floodlit match
100	The Hundred
TM	LV= Insurance Test Match
IT20	Vitality International Twenty20
RHF	Rachael Heyhoe Flint Trophy (50 overs)
CEC	Charlotte Edwards Cup (Twenty20)
LOI	Royal London Limited-Overs International

Sat 14 May

CEC	Loughborough	Lightning v Diamonds
CEC	Hove	Vipers v Thunder
CEC	Chelmsford	Sunrisers v SE Stars
CEC	Cardiff	Storm v Sparks

Wed 18 May

CEC	Guildford	SE Stars v Sparks
CEC	Southampton	Vipers v Lightning
CEC	Chelmsford	Sunrisers v Storm
CEC	Sale	Thunder v Diamonds

Sat 21 May

CEC	Birmingham	Sparks v Sunrisers
CEC	tbc	Diamonds v Vipers
CEC	Leicester	Lightning v Thunder
CEC	Beckenham	SE Stars v Storm

Sun 29 May

CEC	Birmingham	Sparks v SE Stars
CEC	Nottingham	Lightning v Vipers
CEC	Leeds	Diamonds v Thunder
CEC	Taunton	Storm v Sunrisers

Wed 1 June

CEC	Chester-le-St	Diamonds v Lightning
CEC	Northampton	Sunrisers v Sparks
CEC[F]	Manchester	Thunder v Vipers
CEC	Bristol	Storm v SE Stars

Fri 3 June

CEC	Manchester	Thunder v Lightning

Sat 4 June

CEC	Worcester	Sparks v Storm
CEC	Southampton	Vipers v Diamonds

Sun 5 June

CEC	Guildford	SE Stars v Sunrisers

Sat 11 June

CEC	Northampton	Semi-final and FINAL

Mon 27 – Thu 30 June

TM	**Taunton**	**ENGLAND v SOUTH AFRICA**

Sat 2 July

RHF	tbc	Sparks v Vipers
RHF	Loughborough	Lightning v Storm
RHF	Beckenham	SE Stars v Sunrisers

Sun 3 July

RHF	Sale	Thunder v Diamonds

Sat 9 July

RHF	Loughborough	Lightning v Thunder
RHF	Leeds	Diamonds v Sunrisers
RHF	Hove	Vipers v Stars
RHF	Bristol	Storm v Sparks

Mon 11 July

LOI	**Northampton**	**England v South Africa**

Fri 15 July

LOI	**Bristol**	**England v South Africa**

Sat 16 July

RHF	Worcester	Sparks v Diamonds
RHF	Derby	Lightning v Vipers
RHF	Chelmsford	Sunrisers v Storm
RHF	Southport	Thunder v SE Stars

Mon 18 July

LOI	**Leicester**	**England v South Africa**

Thu 21 July

IT20[F]	**Chelmsford**	**England v South Africa**

Sat 23 July

IT20	**Worcester**	**England v South Africa**
RHF	Chester-le-St	Diamonds v Lightning
RHF	Southampton	Vipers v Sunrisers
RHF	Manchester	Thunder v Sparks
RHF	Cheltenham	Storm v SE Stars

Mon 25 July

IT20[F]	**Derby**	**England v South Africa**

Thu 11 August

100[F]	The Oval	Invincibles v Superchargers

Fri 12 August

100	Southampton	Brave v Spirit

Sat 13 August
100 Manchester Originals v Rockets
100 Cardiff Fire v Phoenix

Sun 14 August
100 Leeds Superchargers v Spirit
100 The Oval Invincibles v Brave

Mon 15 August
100 Birmingham Phoenix v Rockets

Tue 16 August
100 Manchester Originals v Fire

Wed 17 August
100 Nottingham Rockets v Invincibles

Thu 18 August
100 Southampton Brave v Originals

Fri 19 August
100 Birmingham Phoenix v Superchargers

Sat 20 August
100 Nottingham Rockets v Spirit

Sun 21 August
100 Leeds Superchargers v Originals

Mon 22 August
100 Cardiff Fire v Brave

Tue 23 August
100 The Oval Invincibles v Phoenix

Wed 24 August
100 Lord's Spirit v Fire

Thu 25 August
100 Southampton Brave v Rockets

Fri 26 August
100 Cardiff Fire v Superchargers

Sat 27 August
100 Lord's Spirit v Invincibles

Sun 28 August
100 Birmingham Phoenix v Originals

Mon 29 August
100 Nottingham Rockets v Fire

Tue 30 August
100 Lord's Spirit v Phoenix

Wed 31 August
100 Manchester Originals v Invincibles
100 Leeds Superchargers v Brave

Fri 2 September
100 Southampton Eliminator

Sat 3 September
100 Lord's FINAL

Fri 9 September
RHF Worcester Sparks v Lightning
RHF Beckenham SE Stars v Diamonds
RHF Hove Vipers v Storm
RHF Northampton Sunrisers v Thunder

Sat 10 September
IT20[F] Chester-le-St England v India

Sun 11 September
RHF Beckenham SE Stars v Sparks
RHF Southampton Vipers v Thunder
RHF Chelmsford Sunrisers v Lightning
RHF Taunton Storm v Diamonds

Tue 13 September
IT20[F] Derby England v India

Thu 15 September
IT20[F] Bristol England v India

Sat 17 September
RHF Worcester Sparks v Sunrisers
RHF Leicester Lightning v SE Stars
RHF Leeds Diamonds v Vipers
RHF Manchester Thunder v Storm

Sun 18 September
LOI Hove England v India

Wed 21 September
LOI[F] Canterbury England v India
RHF tbc Play-off

Sat 24 September
LOI Lord's England v India

Sun 25 September
RHF Lord's FINAL

NATIONAL COUNTIES FIXTURES 2022

Sun 17 April	**TWENTY20 COMPETITION**
Oxton	Cheshire v Shropshire (1)
Porthill Park	Staffordshire v Northumberland (1)
Bashley	Dorset v Wiltshire (2)
Brockhampton	Herefordshire v Cornwall (2)
Wisbech	Cambridgeshire v Suffolk (3)
Grantham	Lincolnshire v Hertfordshire (3)
Falkland	Berkshire v Oxfordshire (4)
Bangor	Wales NC v Bedfordshire (4)

Sun 24 April	**TWENTY20 COMPETITION**
S.Northumberland	Northumberland v Cumbria (1)
Whitchurch	Shropshire v Staffordshire (1)
Werrington	Cornwall v Devon (2)
South Wilts	Wiltshire v Herefordshire (2)
Haileybury School	Hertfordshire v Norfolk (3)
Ipswich School	Suffolk v Lincolnshire (3)
Dunstable Town	Bedfordshire v Buckinghamshire (4)
Wormsley	Oxfordshire v Wales NC (4)

Sun 1 May	**TWENTY20 COMPETITION**
Netherfield	Cumbria v Shropshire (1)
Leek	Staffordshire v Cheshire (1)
Exmouth	Devon v Wiltshire (2)
Colwall	Herefordshire v Dorset (2)
Grantham	Lincolnshire v Cambridgeshire (3)
Manor Park	Norfolk v Suffolk (3)
High Wycombe	Buckinghamshire v Oxfordshire (4)
Newport	Wales NC v Berkshire (4)

Mon 2 May	**TWENTY20 COMPETITION**
Toft	Cheshire v Cumbria (1)
Whitchurch	Shropshire v Northumberland (1)
North Perrott	Dorset v Devon (2)
South Wilts	Wiltshire v Cornwall (2)
Wisbech	Cambridgeshire v Norfolk (3)
Copdock & OI	Suffolk v Hertfordshire (3)
Wargrave	Berkshire v Buckinghamshire (4)
Wormsley	Oxfordshire v Bedfordshire (4)

Sun 8 May	**TWENTY20 COMPETITION**
Carlisle	Cumbria v Staffordshire (1)
S.Northumberland	Northumberland v Cheshire (1)
Wadebridge	Cornwall v Dorset (2)
North Devon	Devon v Herefordshire (2)
Welwyn Garden City	Hertfordshire v Cambridgeshire (3)
Manor Park	Norfolk v Lincolnshire (3)
Ampthill Town	Bedfordshire v Berkshire (4)
High Wycombe	Buckinghamshire v Wales NC (4)

Sun 22 May	**TWENTY20 COMPETITION**
Tring Park	Finals Day (23 May Reserve Day)

Sun 29 May	**NCCA TROPHY**
Eastnor	Herefordshire v Oxfordshire (1)
Scunthorpe	Lincolnshire v Cumbria (1)
Bedford School	Bedfordshire v Hertfordshire (2)
Henley	Berkshire v Devon (2)
Exning	Cambridgeshire v Cheshire (3)
Mildenhall	Suffolk v Norfolk (3)
Port Talbot	Wales NC v Buckinghamshire (4)

Marlborough College	Wiltshire v Dorset (4)
Sun 5 June	**NCCA TROPHY**
Cockermouth	Cumbria v Herefordshire (1)
Allendale	Northumberland v Lincolnshire (1)
Truro	Cornwall v Berkshire (2)
Exeter	Devon v Bedfordshire (2)
Manor Park	Norfolk v Cambridgeshire (3)
Oswestry	Shropshire v Suffolk (3)
High Wycombe	Buckinghamshire v Wiltshire (4)
Himley	Staffordshire v Wales NC (4)
Sun 12 June	**NCCA TROPHY**
Brockhampton	Herefordshire v Northumberland (1)
Banbury	Oxfordshire v Cumbria (1)
Southill Park	Bedfordshire v Cornwall (2)
Hertford	Hertfordshire v Devon (2)
Exning	Cambridgeshire v Shropshire (3)
Chester Boughton	Cheshire v Norfolk (3)
Dorchester	Dorset v Buckinghamshire (4)
Warminster	Wiltshire v Staffordshire (4)
Sun 19 June	**NCCA TROPHY**
Bracebridge Heath	Lincolnshire v Herefordshire (1)
Jesmond	Northumberland v Oxfordshire (1)
Wargrave	Berkshire v Bedfordshire (2)
Redruth	Cornwall v Hertfordshire (2)
Wem	Shropshire v Cheshire (3)
Sudbury	Suffolk v Cambridgeshire (3)
Dartmouth, West Brom	Staffordshire v Dorset (4)
Llandysul	Wales NC v Wiltshire (4)
Sun 26 June	**NCCA TROPHY**
Keswick	Cumbria v Northumberland (1)
Aston Rowant	Oxfordshire v Lincolnshire (1)
Sidmouth	Devon v Cornwall (2)
North Mymms	Hertfordshire v Berkshire (2)
Didsbury	Cheshire v Suffolk (3)
Manor Park	Norfolk v Shropshire (3)
Gerrards Cross	Buckinghamshire v Staffordshire (4)
Wimborne	Dorset v Wales NC (4)
Sun 3 – Tue 5 July	**CHAMPIONSHIP**
Dunstable Town	Bedfordshire v Staffordshire (E1)
Bury St Edmunds	Suffolk v Lincolnshire (E1)
March	Cambridgeshire v Hertfordshire (E2)
Tynemouth	Northumberland v Cumbria (E2)
Alderley Edge	Cheshire v Oxfordshire (W1)
Eastnor	Herefordshire v Dorset (W1)
Abergavenny	Wales NC v Devon (W2)
Corsham	Wiltshire v Shropshire (W2)
Sun 10 – Tue 12 July	**CHAMPIONSHIP**
Cleethorpes	Lincolnshire v Staffordshire (E1)
Woolpit	Suffolk v Norfolk (E1)
Barrow	Cumbria v Cambridgeshire (E2)
Bishop's Stortford	Hertfordshire v Buckinghamshire (E2)
Wimborne	Dorset v Berkshire (W1)
Thame	Oxfordshire v Herefordshire (W1)
Sandford	Devon v Cornwall (W2)
Oswestry	Shropshire v Wales NC (W2)
Sun 17 July	**NCCA TROPHY**
	Quarter-finals Day

Sun 24 – Tue 26 July	**CHAMPIONSHIP**
Grantham	Lincolnshire v Bedfordshire (E1)
Longton	Staffordshire v Norfolk (E1)
Chesham	Buckinghamshire v Cumbria (E2)
Peterborough	Cambridgeshire v Northumberland (E2)
Finchampstead	Berkshire v Oxfordshire (W1)
Brockhampton	Herefordshire v Cheshire (W1)
St Austell	Cornwall v Shropshire (W2)
Usk	Wales NC v Wiltshire (W2)
Sun 31 July	**SHOWCASE GAMES**
Tbc	Bedfordshire v Northamptonshire
Tbc	Berkshire v Middlesex
High Wycombe	Buckinghamshire v Surrey
Saffron Walden	Cambridgeshire v Essex
Chester Boughton	Cheshire v Warwickshire
Truro	Cornwall v Somerset
Sedbergh School	Cumbria v Lancashire
Tbc	Dorset v Hampshire
Eastnor	Herefordshire v Worcestershire
Grantham	Lincolnshire v Durham
Manor Park	Norfolk v Nottinghamshire
S.Northumberland	Northumberland v Yorkshire
Tbc	Oxfordshire v Sussex
Tbc	Shropshire v Derbyshire
Tbc	Staffordshire v Leicestershire
Woolpit	Suffolk v Kent
Cardiff	Wales NC v Glamorgan
Tbc	Wiltshire v Gloucestershire
Tue 2 August	**SHOWCASE GAMES**
Bovey Tracey	Devon v Somerset
Tbc	Hertfordshire v Middlesex
Sun 7 August	**NCCA TROPHY**
	Semi-finals Day (Reserve day 8 August)
Sun 14 – Tue 16 August	**CHAMPIONSHIP**
Manor Park	Norfolk v Bedfordshire (E1)
Checkley	Staffordshire v Suffolk (E1)
Furness	Cumbria v Hertfordshire (E2)
Jesmond	Northumberland v Buckinghamshire (E2)
Nantwich	Cheshire v Berkshire (W1)
Banbury	Oxfordshire v Dorset (W1)
Bridgnorth	Shropshire v Devon (W2)
South Wilts	Wiltshire v Cornwall (W2)
Sun 21 – Tue 23 August	**CHAMPIONSHIP**
Flitwick	Bedfordshire v Suffolk (E1)
Manor Park	Norfolk v Lincolnshire (E1)
Tring Park	Buckinghamshire v Cambridgeshire (E2)
Hertford	Hertfordshire v Northumberland (E2)
Falkland	Berkshire v Herefordshire (W1)
Wimborne	Dorset v Cheshire (W1)
Truro	Cornwall v Wales NC (W2)
Sidmouth	Devon v Wiltshire (W2)
Sun 28 August	**NCCA TROPHY**
Wormsley	Trophy Final Day (Reserve day 29 August)
Sun 4 – Wed 7 September	**CHAMPIONSHIP**
Dartmouth, West Brom	Final

SECOND XI CHAMPIONSHIP FIXTURES 2022

FOUR-DAY MATCHES

APRIL

Date	Venue	Match
Mon 11	Southampton	Hampshire v Durham
	Blackstone	Sussex v Kent
	Birm EFSG	Warwicks v Glamorgan
	Kidderminster	Worcs v Glos
	Bradford PA	Yorkshire v Northants
Tue 12	Kibworth	Leics v Lancashire
	Radlett	Middlesex v Essex
Mon 18	Belper Mead	Derbyshire v Leics
	Bristol	Glos v Sussex
	Polo Farm, Cant	Kent v Northants
	Southport	Lancashire v Notts
	Taunton Vale	Somerset v Middlesex
Tue 19	Southampton	Hampshire v Surrey
Mon 25	Newport	Glamorgan v Lancashire
	Beckenham	Kent v Essex
	Kibworth	Leics v Northants
	Taunton Vale	Somerset v Notts
	Birm EFSG	Warwicks v Glos
Tue 26	Guildford	Surrey v Durham

MAY

Date	Venue	Match
Mon 2	Repton S	Derbyshire v Durham
	Rockhampton	Glos v Somerset
	Northampton	Northants v Worcs
	Notts SC	Notts v Leics
	tbc	Yorkshire v Lancashire
Tue 3	Radlett	Middlesex v Hampshire
Sun 8	tbc	Yorkshire v Kent
Mon 9	Newport	Glamorgan v Worcs
	Crosby	Lancashire v Middlesex
	Notts SC	Notts v Derbyshire
	New Malden	Surrey v Essex

JUNE

Date	Venue	Match
Mon 13	Abergavenny	Glamorgan v Somerset
	Rockhampton	Glos v Surrey
	Chester BH	Lancashire v Warwicks
	Barnt Green	Worcs v Leics
Mon 20	Richmondshire	Durham v Yorkshire
	Billericay	Essex v Sussex
	Southampton	Hampshire v Kent
	Radlett	Middlesex v Surrey
	Notts SC	Notts v Lancashire
Mon 27	Richmondshire	Durham v Kent
	Southampton	Hampshire v Essex
	Sale	Lancashire v Derbyshire
	Milton Keynes	Northants v Glamorgan
	Notts SC	Notts v Yorkshire
	Birm EFSG	Warwicks v Worcs

JULY

Date	Venue	Match
Mon 4	Rockhampton	Glos v Glamorgan
	Crosby	Lancashire v Durham
	Uppingham S	Leics v Notts
	Taunton Vale	Somerset v Northants
	New Malden	Surrey v Sussex
	tbc	Yorkshire v Essex
Tue 5	Radlett	Middlesex v Kent
Mon 11	Chesterfield	Derbyshire v Yorkshire
	Colchester	Essex v Glos
	Tonbridge S	Kent v Warwicks
	Notts SC	Notts v Worcs
	Taunton Vale	Somerset v Hampshire
	Horsham	Sussex v Middlesex
Mon 18	Billericay	Essex v Lancashire
	Bristol CC	Glos v Northants
	Southampton	Hampshire v Glamorgan
	Notts SC	Notts v Warwicks
	New Malden	Surrey v Kent
	Stourport	Worcs v Somerset
	tbc	Yorkshire v Leics

AUGUST

Date	Venue	Match
Mon 22	Belper Mead	Derbyshire v Notts
	Panteg	Glamorgan v Glos
	tbc	Kent v Leics
Mon 29	Chester-le-St	Durham v Notts
	Rockhampton	Glos v Worcs
	Loughborough	Leics v Glamorgan
	Northampton	Northants v Warwicks
Tue 30	Preston Nom	Sussex v Hampshire

SEPTEMBER

Date	Venue	Match
Mon 5	Denby	Derbyshire v Middlesex
	Newport	Glamorgan v Sussex
	Folkestone	Kent v Hampshire
	Notts SC	Notts v Northants
	Guildford	Surrey v Somerset
	Birm EFSG	Warwicks v Essex
	Kidderminster	Worcs v Lancashire
Tue 6	S.Northumb	Durham v Leics
Mon 12	Southampton	Hampshire v Worcs
	Polo Farm, Cant	Kent v Glos
	Blackpool	Lancashire v Yorkshire
	Notts SC	Notts v Durham
	Taunton Vale	Somerset v Warwicks
	Blackstone	Sussex v Northants
Tue 13	Billericay	Essex v Middlesex

SECOND XI TWENTY20 CUP FIXTURES 2022

Date	Venue	Match
MAY		
Mon 16	tbc	Durham v Yorkshire (x 2)
	Kibworth	Leics v Lancashire (x 2)
	Worksop Coll	Notts v Derbyshire
	Taunton Vale	Somerset v Worcs
	New Malden	Surrey v Essex
	Birm EFSG	Warwicks v Glamorgan
Tue 17	Derby	Derbyshire v Leics
	Polo Farm, Cant	Kent v Middlesex
	Northampton	Northants v Glos (x 2)
	Preston Nom	Sussex v Surrey
	Worcester	Worcs v Glamorgan
Wed 18	Chester-le-St	Durham v Notts (x 2)
	Southend	Essex v Middlesex
	Cardiff	Glamorgan v Somerset
	Southampton	Hampshire v Sussex
	Birm EFSG	Warwicks v Glos
Thu 19	Derby	Derbyshire v Lancashire
	Southampton	Hampshire v Essex (x 2)
	Taunton Vale	Somerset v Northants (x 2)
	Barnt Green	Worcs v Warwicks
Fri 20	Sudbrook	Glamorgan v Worcs
	Beckenham	Kent v Sussex (x 2)
	Leicester	Leics v Durham (x 2)
	Taunton Vale	Somerset v Glos
Mon 23	Chelmsford	Essex v Kent (x 2)
	Bristol	Glos v Glamorgan
	Southampton	Hampshire v Middlesex
	Leicester	Leics v Derbyshire
	The Oval	Surrey v Sussex
	tbc	Yorkshire v Lancashire
Tue 24	Derby	Derbyshire v Notts
	Newport	Glamorgan v Glos
	The Oval	Surrey v Middlesex
	Horsham	Sussex v Hampshire
	Birm EFSG	Warwicks v Northants (x 2)
	Worcester	Worcs v Somerset
Wed 25	Beckenham	Kent v Hampshire (x 2)
	Horsham	Sussex v Middlesex
	Birm EFSG	Warwicks v Somerset
	tbc	Yorkshire v Leics
Thu 26	Southampton	Hampshire v Surrey
	Worksop Coll	Notts v Lancashire (x 2)
Fri 27	Chesterfield	Derbyshire v Yorkshire (x 2)
	Northwood	Middlesex v Essex
	New Malden	Surrey v Kent
Sun 29	Beckenham	Kent v Surrey
Mon 30	Blackpool	Lancashire v Derbyshire
	Leicester	Leics v Yorkshire
	Northwood	Middlesex v Sussex
	Taunton Vale	Somerset v Glamorgan
	New Malden	Surrey v Hampshire
	Birm EFSG	Warwicks v Worcs
Tue 31	Southend	Essex v Sussex
	Newport	Glamorgan v Northants (x 2)
	Cheltenham C	Glos v Worcs (x 2)
	Leicester	Leics v Notts
	Northwood	Middlesex v Kent
JUNE		
Wed 1	tbc	Derbyshire v Durham (x 2)
	Southend	Essex v Surrey
	Cheltenham C	Glos v Warwicks
	Blackpool	Lancashire v Yorkshire
	Grantham	Notts v Leics
Thu 2	Newport	Glamorgan v Warwicks
	Cheltenham C	Glos v Somerset
	Northwood	Middlesex v Surrey
	Northampton	Northants v Worcs (x 2)
	Hove	Sussex v Essex
Fri 3	Westhoughton	Lancashire v Durham (x 2)
	Northwood	Middlesex v Hampshire
	Taunton Vale	Somerset v Warwicks
	Leeds, Weet	Yorkshire v Notts (x 2)
Thu 9	Arundel	Semi-finals and FINAL

THE HUNDRED FIXTURES 2022

Wed 3 August
100[F] Southampton Brave v Fire

Thu 4 August
100[F] The Oval Invincibles v Spirit

Fri 5 August
100[F] Manchester Originals v Superchargers

Sat 6 August
100 Nottingham Rockets v Phoenix

Sun 7 August
100 Cardiff Fire v Invincibles

Mon 8 August
100[F] Lord's Spirit v Originals

Tue 9 August
100[F] Leeds Superchargers v Rockets

Wed 10 August
100[F] Birmingham Phoenix v Brave

Thu 11 August
100 The Oval Invincibles v Superchargers

Fri 12 August
100[F] Southampton Brave v Spirit

Sat 13 August
100 Manchester Originals v Rockets
100[F] Cardiff Fire v Phoenix

Sun 14 August
100 Leeds Superchargers v Spirit
100[F] The Oval Invincibles v Brave

Mon 15 August
100[F] Birmingham Phoenix v Rockets

Tue 16 August
100[F] Manchester Originals v Fire

Wed 17 August
100[F] Nottingham Rockets v Invincibles

Thu 18 August
100[F] Southampton Brave v Originals

Fri 19 August
100[F] Birmingham Phoenix v Superchargers

Sat 20 August
100[F] Nottingham Rockets v Spirit

Sun 21 August
100[F] Leeds Superchargers v Originals

Mon 22 August
100[F] Cardiff Fire v Brave

Tue 23 August
100[F] The Oval Invincibles v Phoenix

Wed 24 August
100[F] Lord's Spirit v Fire

Thu 25 August
100[F] Southampton Brave v Rockets

Fri 26 August
100[F] Cardiff Fire v Superchargers

Sat 27 August
100[F] Lord's Spirit v Invincibles

Sun 28 August
100[F] Birmingham Phoenix v Originals

Mon 29 August
100[F] Nottingham Rockets v Fire

Tue 30 August
100[F] Lord's Spirit v Phoenix

Wed 31 August
100[F] Manchester Originals v Invincibles
100 Leeds Superchargers v Brave

Fri 2 September
100[F] Southampton Eliminator

Sat 3 September
100[F] Lord's FINAL

PRINCIPAL FIXTURES 2022

CC1	LV= Insurance County Championship Division 1
CC2	LV= Insurance County Championship Division 2
F	Floodlit
FCF	First-Class Friendly
LOI	Royal London Limited-Overs International
50L	Royal London One-Day Cup
[50o]	Limited-overs Friendly
T20	Vitality Blast
[T20]	Friendly Twenty20 Match
IT20	Vitality Twenty20 International
TM	Test Match

Thu 7 – Sun 10 April

CC1	Chelmsford	Essex v Kent
CC1	Southampton	Hampshire v Somerset
CC1	Northampton	Northants v Glos
CC1	Birmingham	Warwicks v Surrey
CC2	Cardiff	Glamorgan v Durham
CC2	Leicester	Leics v Worcs
CC2	Lord's	Middlesex v Derbys
CC2	Hove	Sussex v Notts

Thu 14 – Sun 17 April

CC1	Bristol	Glos v Yorkshire
CC1	Canterbury	Kent v Lancashire
CC1	Taunton	Somerset v Essex
CC1	The Oval	Surrey v Hampshire
CC2	Derby	Derbyshire v Sussex
CC2	Chester-le-St	Durham v Leics
CC2	Nottingham	Notts v Glamorgan

Thu 21 – Sun 24 April

CC1	Canterbury	Kent v Hampshire
CC1	Manchester	Lancashire v Glos
CC1	Northampton	Northants v Yorkshire
CC1	The Oval	Surrey v Somerset
CC1	Birmingham	Warwicks v Essex
CC2	Chester-le-St	Durham v Notts
CC2	Cardiff	Glamorgan v Middlesex
CC2	Leicester	Leics v Derbyshire
CC2	Worcester	Worcs v Sussex

Thu 28 April – Sun 1 May

CC1	Chelmsford	Essex v Northants
CC1	Bristol	Glos v Surrey
CC1	Southampton	Hampshire v Lancashire
CC1	Taunton	Somerset v Warwicks
CC1	Leeds	Yorkshire v Kent
CC2	Derby	Derbyshire v Glamorgan
CC2	Lord's	Middlesex v Leics
CC2	Nottingham	Notts v Worcs
CC2	Hove	Sussex v Durham

Thu 5 – Sun 8 May

CC1	Chelmsford	Essex v Yorkshire
CC1	Southampton	Hampshire v Glos
CC1	Manchester	Lancashire v Warwicks
CC1	The Oval	Surrey v Northants
CC2	Cardiff	Glamorgan v Leics
CC2	Hove	Sussex v Middlesex
CC2	Worcester	Worcs v Durham

Fri 6 – Mon 9 May

FCF	Canterbury	Kent v Sri Lanka Dev

Thu 12 – Sun 15 May

CC1	Bristol	Glos v Somerset
CC1	Beckenham	Kent v Surrey
CC1	Birmingham	Warwicks v Northants
CC1	Leeds	Yorkshire v Lancashire
CC2	Derby	Derbyshire v Worcs
CC2	Chester-le-St	Durham v Glamorgan
CC2	Leicester	Leics v Sussex
CC2	Lord's	Middlesex v Notts

Fri 13 – Mon 16 May

FCF	Southampton	Hampshire v Sri Lanka Dev

Thu 19 – Sun 22 May

CC1	Manchester	Lancashire v Essex
CC1	Northampton	Northants v Kent
CC1	Taunton	Somerset v Hampshire
CC1	Leeds	Yorkshire v Warwicks
CC2	Lord's	Middlesex v Durham
CC2	Nottingham	Notts v Derbyshire
CC2	Worcester	Worcs v Leics

Fri 20 – Mon 23 May

FCF	Guildford	Surrey v Sri Lanka Dev
FCF	Hove	Sussex v New Zealanders

Wed 25 May

T20F	Canterbury	Kent v Somerset
T20F	Leeds	Yorkshire v Worcs
[T20]F	The Oval	Surrey v Sri Lanka Dev

Thu 26 – Sun 29 May

FCF	Chelmsford	County Select v New Zealanders

Thu 26 May

T20F	Leicester	Leics v Durham

T20	Radlett	Middlesex v Glos
T20^F	Hove	Sussex v Glamorgan
T20^F	Birmingham	Warwicks v Northants

Fri 27 May

T20^F	Derby	Derbyshire v Warwicks
T20^F	Bristol	Glos v Sussex
T20^F	Southampton	Hampshire v Middlesex
T20^F	Canterbury	Kent v Essex
T20^F	Manchester	Lancashire v Yorkshire
T20^F	Northampton	Northants v Durham
T20^F	Nottingham	Notts v Worcs
T20^F	The Oval	Surrey v Glamorgan
[T20]^F	Taunton	Somerset v Sri Lanka Dev

Sat 28 May

T20^F	Leicester	Leics v Derbyshire

Sun 29 May

T20	Manchester	Lancashire v Worcs
T20	Radlett	Middlesex v Glamorgan
T20	Nottingham	Notts v Northants
T20	Taunton	Somerset v Essex
T20	Hove	Sussex v Kent
T20	Birmingham	Warwicks v Durham
T20	Leeds	Yorkshire v Leics
[T20]	Bristol	Glos v Sri Lanka Dev XI

Mon 30 May

T20^F	Southampton	Hampshire v Somerset

Tue 31 May

T20^F	Chelmsford	Essex v Hampshire
T20^F	Nottingham	Notts v Lancashire
T20^F	The Oval	Surrey v Glos
T20^F	Leeds	Yorkshire v Derbyshire

Wed 1 June

T20^F	Chester-le-St	Durham v Worcs
T20^F	Bristol	Glos v Kent
T20	Manchester	Lancashire v Derbyshire
T20^F	Northampton	Northants v Leics
T20^F	Taunton	Somerset v Sussex

Thu 2 – Mon 6 June

TM1	**Lord's**	**ENGLAND v NEW ZEALAND**

Thu 2 June

T20^F	Cardiff	Glamorgan v Essex
T20^F	The Oval	Surrey v Hampshire
T20^F	Birmingham	Warwicks v Leics

Fri 3 June

T20^F	Derby	Derbyshire v Notts
T20^F	Bristol	Glos v Essex
T20^F	Canterbury	Kent v Surrey
T20^F	Manchester	Lancashire v Northants
T20^F	Taunton	Somerset v Glamorgan
T20^F	Hove	Sussex v Middlesex
T20	Worcester	Worcs v Warwicks
T20^F	Leeds	Yorkshire v Durham

Sat 4 June

T20^F	Southampton	Hampshire v Sussex

Sun 5 June

T20	Chester-le-St	Durham v Northants
T20	Cardiff	Glamorgan v Surrey
T20	Canterbury	Kent v Middlesex
T20	Birmingham	Warwicks v Notts
T20	Worcester	Worcs v Leics

Mon 6 June

T20^F	Leeds	Yorkshire v Notts

Tue 7 June

T20^F	Chelmsford	Essex v Kent
T20^F	Cardiff	Glamorgan v Glos
T20^F	Leicester	Leics v Lancashire
T20	Radlett	Middlesex v Hampshire
T20^F	Northampton	Northants v Derbyshire

Wed 8 June

T20^F	Chester-le-St	Durham v Warwicks
T20^F	The Oval	Surrey v Sussex
T20^F	Leeds	Yorkshire v Lancashire

Thu 9 June

T20^F	Derby	Derbyshire v Leics
T20^F	Bristol	Glos v Somerset
T20^F	Southampton	Hampshire v Essex
T20^F	Lord's	Middlesex v Surrey
T20^F	Northampton	Northants v Worcs

Fri 10 – Tue 14 June

TM2	**Nottingham**	**ENGLAND v NEW ZEALAND**

Fri 10 June

T20^F	Chester-le-St	Durham v Lancashire
T20^F	Chelmsford	Essex v Middlesex
T20^F	Cardiff	Glamorgan v Hampshire
T20^F	Leicester	Leics v Notts
T20^F	Taunton	Somerset v Kent
T20^F	Hove	Sussex v Glos
T20^F	Birmingham	Warwicks v Yorkshire
T20	Worcester	Worcs v Derbyshire

Sun 12 – Wed 15 June

CC1	Southampton	Hampshire v Yorkshire
CC1	Canterbury	Kent v Glos
CC1	Taunton	Somerset v Surrey
CC1	Birmingham	Warwicks v Lancashire
CC2	Chesterfield	Derbyshire v Middlesex
CC2	Chester-le-St	Durham v Worcs
CC2	Cardiff	Glamorgan v Sussex
CC2	Leicester	Leics v Notts

Fri 17 June
LOI Amstelveen Netherlands v England
T20[F] Chester-le-St Durham v Yorkshire
T20[F] Chelmsford Essex v Sussex
T20[F] Southampton Hampshire v Kent
T20[F] Leicester Leics v Worcs
T20[F] Northampton Northants v Lancashire
T20[F] Nottingham Notts v Warwicks
T20[F] Taunton Somerset v Glos
T20[F] The Oval Surrey v Middlesex

Sat 18 June
T20 Chesterfield Derbyshire v Yorkshire
T20[F] Bristol Glos v Glamorgan
T20 Worcester Worcs v Northants

Sun 19 June
LOI Amstelveen Netherlands v England
T20 Chester-le-St Durham v Leics
T20 Chelmsford Essex v Somerset
T20 Cardiff Glamorgan v Sussex
T20 Southampton Hampshire v Surrey
T20 Blackpool Lancashire v Notts
T20 Lord's Middlesex v Kent
T20 Birmingham Warwicks v Derbyshire

Tue 21 June
T20[F] Derby Derbyshire v Northants
T20[F] Cardiff Glamorgan v Middlesex
T20[F] Canterbury Kent v Glos
T20[F] Nottingham Notts v Leics
T20[F] The Oval Surrey v Somerset

Wed 22 June
LOI Amstelveen Netherlands v England
T20[F] Northampton Northants v Warwicks

Thu 23 – Mon 27 June
TM3 Leeds ENGLAND v NEW ZEALAND

Thu 23 June
T20 Blackpool Lancashire v Durham
T20[F] Lord's Middlesex v Essex
T20[F] Nottingham Notts v Derbyshire
T20[F] Taunton Somerset v Hampshire
T20[F] Hove Sussex v Surrey
T20 Worcester Worcs v Yorkshire

Fri 24 – Mon 27 June
FCF Leicester Leics v Indians

Fri 24 June
T20[F] Derby Derbyshire v Lancashire
T20[F] Chester-le-St Durham v Notts
T20[F] Chelmsford Essex v Surrey
T20[F] Cardiff Glamorgan v Somerset
T20[F] Bristol Glos v Hampshire
T20[F] Canterbury Kent v Sussex
T20[F] Northampton Northants v Yorkshire
T20[F] Birmingham Warwicks v Worcs

Sun 26 – Wed 29 June
CC1 Chelmsford Essex v Hampshire
CC1 Bristol Glos v Lancashire
CC1 Northampton Northants v Warwicks
CC1 The Oval Surrey v Kent
CC2 Nottingham Notts v Middlesex
CC2 Hove Sussex v Derbyshire
CC2 Worcester Worcs v Glamorgan

Fri 1 – Tue 5 July
TM Birmingham ENGLAND v INDIA

Fri 1 July
T20[F] Southampton Hampshire v Glos
T20[F] Leicester Leics v Northants
T20[F] Lord's Middlesex v Somerset
T20[F] Nottingham Notts v Durham
T20[F] The Oval Surrey v Kent
T20[F] Hove Sussex v Essex
T20 Worcester Worcs v Lancashire
T20[F] Leeds Yorkshire v Warwicks

Sat 2 July
T20[F] Chelmsford Essex v Glamorgan

Sun 3 July
T20[F] Chester-le-St Durham v Derbyshire
T20[F] Bristol Glos v Middlesex
T20[F] Canterbury Kent v Glamorgan
T20[F] Manchester Lancashire v Warwicks
T20[F] Leicester Leics v Yorkshire
T20[F] Taunton Somerset v Surrey
T20[F] Hove Sussex v Hampshire
T20 Worcester Worcs v Notts

Wed 6 July
T20[F] tbc Quarter-final 1

Thu 7 July
IT20[F] Southampton England v India

Fri 8 July
T20[F] tbc Quarter-finals 2 & 3

Sat 9 July
IT20 Birmingham England v India
T20[F] tbc Quarter-final 4

Sun 10 July
IT20 Nottingham England v India

Mon 11 – Thu 14 July
CC1 Chelmsford Essex v Glos
CC1 Southampton Hampshire v Warwicks
CC1 Canterbury Kent v Northants
CC1 Southport Lancashire v Somerset

CC1 Scarborough Yorkshire v Surrey
CC2 Chester-le-St Durham v Derbyshire
CC2 Cardiff Glamorgan v Notts
CC2 Northwood Middlesex v Worcs
CC2 Hove Sussex v Leics

Tue 12 July
LOI[F] The Oval England v India
[50o] Taunton Eng Lions v South Africans

Thu 14 July
LOI[F] Lord's England v India
[50o] Worcester Eng Lions v South Africans

Sat 16 July
T20[F] Birmingham Semi-finals and FINAL

Sun 17 July
LOI Manchester England v India

Tue 19 – Fri 22 July
CC1 Cheltenham Glos v Hampshire
CC1 Northampton Northants v Lancashire
CC1 Taunton Somerset v Yorkshire
CC1 The Oval Surrey v Essex
CC1 Birmingham Warwicks v Kent
CC2 Derby Derbyshire v Notts
CC2 Lord's Middlesex v Sussex

Tue 19 July
LOI[F] Chester-le-St England v South Africa

Wed 20 – Sat 23 July
CC2 Leicester Leics v Glamorgan

Fri 22 July
LOI[F] Manchester England v South Africa

Sun 24 July
LOI Leeds England v South Africa

Mon 25 – Thu 28 July
CC1 Chelmsford Essex v Somerset
CC1 Cheltenham Glos v Northants
CC1 Manchester Lancashire v Kent
CC1 The Oval Surrey v Warwicks
CC1 Scarborough Yorkshire v Hampshire
CC2 Chester-le-St Durham v Middlesex
CC2 Worcester Worcs v Derbyshire

Tue 26 – Fri 29 July
CC2 Nottingham Notts v Sussex

Wed 27 July
IT20[F] Bristol England v South Africa

Thu 28 July
IT20[F] Bristol England v South Africa

Sun 31 July
IT20 Southampton England v South Africa

Tue 2 August
50L Derby Derbyshire v Glamorgan
50L Cheltenham Glos v Warwicks
50L Sedbergh Lancashire v Essex
50L Nottingham Notts v Sussex
50L Guildford Surrey v Leics
50L Worcester Worcs v Kent
50L York Yorkshire v Northants

Thu 4 August
50L Gosforth Durham v Surrey
50L Cardiff Glamorgan v Kent
50L Radlett Middlesex v Leics
50L Taunton Somerset v Notts
50L York Yorkshire v Lancashire

Fri 5 August
50L[F] Chelmsford Essex v Derbyshire
50L Southampton Hampshire v Worcs
50L Hove Sussex v Glos

Sun 7 August
50L Chester-le-St Durham v Middlesex
50L Bristol Glos v Somerset
50L Beckenham Kent v Hampshire
50L Manchester Lancashire v Derbyshire
50L Northampton Northants v Essex
50L The Oval Surrey v Warwicks
50L Hove Sussex v Leics
50L Scarborough Yorkshire v Worcs

Tue 9 – Fri 12 August
FCF Canterbury County Select v South Africans

Tue 9 August
50L Newclose, IoW Hampshire v Northants

Wed 10 August
50L Cardiff Glamorgan v Yorkshire
50L Bristol Glos v Notts
50L[F] Manchester Lancashire v Worcs
50L Radlett Middlesex v Surrey
50L Taunton Somerset v Durham

Thu 11 August
50L[F] Chelmsford Essex v Kent

Fri 12 August
50L Derby Derbyshire v Hampshire
50L Chester-le-St Durham v Glos
50L Leicester Leics v Somerset
50L Northampton Northants v Glamorgan
50L Grantham Notts v Middlesex
50L Birmingham Warwicks v Sussex

Sun 14 August

50L	Chelmsford	Essex v Glamorgan
50L	Southampton	Hampshire v Lancashire
50L	Canterbury	Kent v Northants
50L	Leicester	Leics v Warwicks
50L	Grantham	Notts v Durham
50L	Taunton	Somerset v Middlesex
50L	Hove	Sussex v Surrey
50L	Worcester	Worcs v Derbyshire

Wed 17 – Sun 21 August

TM1	**Lord's**	**ENGLAND v SOUTH AFRICA**

Wed 17 August

50L	Derby	Derbyshire v Kent
50L	Chester-le-St	Durham v Sussex
50L	Chelmsford	Essex v Yorkshire
50L	Neath	Glamorgan v Lancashire
50L	Bristol	Glos v Leics
50L	Northampton	Northants v Leics
50L	The Oval	Surrey v Somerset
50L	Birmingham	Warwicks v Notts

Fri 19 August

50L	Neath	Glamorgan v Hampshire
50L	Canterbury	Kent v Yorkshire
50L	Blackpool	Lancashire v Northants
50L	Radlett	Middlesex v Warwicks
50L[F]	Taunton	Somerset v Sussex
50L	The Oval	Surrey v Glos
50L	Worcester	Worcs v Essex

Sat 20 August

50L	Leicester	Leics v Notts

Sun 21 August

50L	Chesterfield	Derbyshire v Yorkshire
50L	Southampton	Hampshire v Essex
50L	Radlett	Middlesex v Glos
50L	Birmingham	Warwicks v Durham

Tue 23 August

50L	Canterbury	Kent v Lancashire
50L	Leicester	Leics v Durham
50L	Northampton	Northants v Derbyshire
50L	Welbeck	Notts v Surrey
50L	Hove	Sussex v Middlesex
50L	Birmingham	Warwicks v Somerset
50L	Worcester	Worcs v Glamorgan
50L	Scarborough	Yorkshire v Hampshire

Thu 25 – Mon 29 August

TM2	**Manchester**	**ENGLAND v SOUTH AFRICA**

Fri 26 August

50L[F]	tbc	Quarter-finals 1 & 2

Tue 30 August

50L[F]	tbc	Semi-finals 1 & 2

Mon 5 – Thu 8 September

CC1	Southampton	Hampshire v Northants
CC1	Canterbury	Kent v Essex
CC1	Manchester	Lancashire v Yorkshire
CC1	Taunton	Somerset v Glos
CC2	Derby	Derbyshire v Durham
CC2	Cardiff	Glamorgan v Worcs
CC2	Nottingham	Notts v Leics

Thu 8 – Mon 12 September

TM3	**The Oval**	**ENGLAND v SOUTH AFRICA**

Mon 12 – Thu 15 September

CC1	Northampton	Northants v Surrey
CC1	Birmingham	Warwicks v Somerset
CC1	Leeds	Yorkshire v Essex
CC2	Leicester	Leics v Durham
CC2	Lord's	Middlesex v Glamorgan
CC2	Hove	Sussex v Worcs

Sat 17 September

50L	Nottingham	FINAL

Tue 20 – Fri 23 September

CC1	Chelmsford	Essex v Lancashire
CC1	Bristol	Glos v Warwicks
CC1	Southampton	Hampshire v Kent
CC1	Taunton	Somerset v Northants
CC1	The Oval	Surrey v Yorkshire
CC2	Chester-le-St	Durham v Sussex
CC2	Cardiff	Glamorgan v Derbyshire
CC2	Leicester	Leics v Middlesex
CC2	Worcester	Worcs v Notts

Mon 26 – Thu 29 September

CC1	Canterbury	Kent v Somerset
CC1	Manchester	Lancashire v Surrey
CC1	Northampton	Northants v Essex
CC1	Birmingham	Warwicks v Hampshire
CC1	Leeds	Yorkshire v Glos
CC2	Derby	Derbyshire v Leics
CC2	Nottingham	Notts v Durham
CC2	Hove	Sussex v Glamorgan
CC2	Worcester	Worcs v Middlesex

First published in 2022

by HEADLINE PUBLISHING GROUP

Front cover photograph © Adil Rashid (Yorkshire and England)/ Harry Trump/Getty Images

Back cover photograph © Heather Knight (England)/ LUKAS COCH/EPA-EFE/Shutterstock

1

Cataloguing in Publication Data is available from the British Library

ISBN: 978 1 4722 9086 1

Typeset in Times by
Letterpart Limited, Caterham on the Hill, Surrey

Printed and bound in Great Britain by
Clays Ltd, Elcograf S.p.A.

Headline's policy is to use papers that are natural, renewable and recyclable products and made from wood grown in sustainable forests. The logging and manufacturing processes are expected to conform to the environmental regulations of the country of origin.

HEADLINE PUBLISHING GROUP

An Hachette UK Company
Carmelite House
50 Victoria Embankment
London EC4Y ODZ

www.headline.co.uk
www.hachette.co.uk